FRIENDS, FOES, and FURS

Rupert's Land Record Society Series
Jennifer S.H. Brown, Editor

FRIENDS, FOES, and FURS

George Nelson's Lake Winnipeg Journals, 1804–1822

Edited by

HARRY W. DUCKWORTH

McGill-Queen's University Press
Montreal & Kingston • London • Chicago

ISBN 978-0-7735-5874-8 (cloth)
ISBN 978-0-2280-0000-6 (ePDF)
ISBN 978-0-2280-0001-3 (ePUB)

Legal deposit fourth quarter 2019
Bibliothèque nationale du Québec

Printed in Canada on acid-free paper that is 100% ancient forest free
(100% post-consumer recycled), processed chlorine free

Funded by the   Financé par le
Government   gouvernement
of Canada   du Canada

Canada Council   Conseil des arts
for the Arts   du Canada

We acknowledge the support of the Canada Council for the Arts.
Nous remercions le Conseil des arts du Canada de son soutien.

Library and Archives Canada Cataloguing in Publication

Title: Friends, foes, and furs : George Nelson's Lake Winnipeg journals, 1804–1822 /
edited by Harry W. Duckworth.
Other titles: Journals. Selections | George Nelson's Lake Winnipeg journals, 1804–1822
Names: Nelson, George, 1786–1859, author. | Duckworth, Harry W., editor.
Series: Rupert's Land Record Society series ; 15.
Description: Series statement: Rupert's Land Record Society series ; 15 | Includes
bibliographical references and index.
Identifiers: Canadiana (print) 20190171006 | Canadiana (ebook) 20190171022
| ISBN 9780773558748 (hardcover) | ISBN 9780228000006 (ePDF) | ISBN
9780228000013 (ePUB)
Subjects: LCSH: Nelson, George, 1786–1859—Diaries. | LCSH: North West Company.
| LCSH: Fur traders—Manitoba—Diaries. | LCSH: Fur traders—Manitoba—History
19th century. | LCSH: Fur trade—Manitoba—History—19th century. | LCSH: Winnipeg,
Lake (Man.)—History—19th century.
Classification: LCC FC3212.3 .N45 2019 | DDC 971.27/01—dc23

This book was typeset in 10.5/13 Sabon.

Contents

MAPS

Preface

George Nelson was the eldest son of an English-speaking family at William Henry (now Sorel), Lower Canada. He entered the fur trade as a clerk in 1802 at the age of fifteen, and served for most of the next twenty-one years in different parts of the Canadian Northwest. He married an Ojibwe, whom he brought home to William Henry in 1816. After another few years in the fur trade, he retired to William Henry, where he and his wife and children lived a rather precarious existence, sometimes dependent on the grudging generosity of Nelson's more successful brothers. Nelson died in 1859, at the age of seventy-three; his wife and most of his children had died long before him, leaving no descendants. To an outside observer he would have seemed an unexceptional man. Little seemed to distinguish him from dozens of others who had toiled for years in the fur trade, retired with little to show for it, and spent the rest of their lives on the edge of penury.

But George Nelson left the world a remarkable legacy. He loved to write, and he produced a series of lively, detailed, perceptive, and deeply personal journals of his life in the Northwest. These journals – daily records, written as the events occurred – were later supplemented, after his retirement, by two attempts at memoirs of his fur trade career. Though these were never finished, and what survive today are only portions of what he did write, they contain vivid anecdotes of his experiences, and they fill in gaps or give a context to episodes that the journals themselves leave mysterious or incomplete.

Almost all of the George Nelson papers are now at the Toronto Reference Library. Few fur trade historians ever noticed the Nelson Papers, and they remained largely unknown until Sylvia Van Kirk came upon them in the 1970s while doing her doctoral research at the

University of London, and immediately realized their importance. Van Kirk also uncovered one more Nelson journal, held at the Archives of Ontario. It was probably originally part of the main Nelson collection, and had become separated by chance.

Some thirty years ago, Van Kirk conceived a plan to publish the largest group of George Nelson's journals, those he kept on or around Lake Winnipeg. Grant support was obtained for the project, and much effort was put into making exact transcripts, developing interpretations of the contents, and following up the many insights that the texts provide. A number of articles resulted from her work, although the plan to publish the actual journals could not be carried through. I learned of the journals through my friendship with Jennifer S.H. Brown, who had co-edited another part of Nelson's writings (Brown and Brightman 1988), and was discovering their immense value for our understanding of the ethnohistory of the region. Brown encouraged me to revive the plan to edit the Lake Winnipeg journals, as they are such rich sources for a part of the fur trader's Northwest that is poorly documented elsewhere.

I owe both Sylvia and Jennifer a great debt for all their preparatory work, and for the generosity with which they have shared their transcripts, research materials, analysis, and expertise with me. The present volume would not have been possible without their contributions and their encouragement. An extra debt is due to Jennifer Brown, as general editor of the Rupert's Land Record Society documentary series, for inviting me to prepare the Lake Winnipeg journals for publication as part of that series. She has also given me much good advice about particular points, drawing on her masterful knowledge of the history and cultural practices of First Nations people, and of their relations with the fur trade.

Nancy McElwee, whom I have never met, transcribed George Nelson's journals with exemplary care and accuracy, under a grant to Sylvia Van Kirk from the Social Sciences and Humanities Research Council of Canada, some thirty-five years ago. These transcripts, which Sylvia passed on to me in WordPerfect format, were converted to Microsoft Word documents and have been used here.

It is a pleasure to thank Shirlee Anne Smith, Judith Hudson Beattie, and Maureen Dolyniuk, the three successive Keepers of the Hudson's Bay Company Archives since the transfer of that magnificent collection to Winnipeg in 1974, for help, encouragement, and learned advice during the development of this and other fur trade projects. My friend Warren Baker has my thanks for generously providing me with copies of many documents now in private hands, and for his knowledge and advice. Anne Lindsay has shared her research into First Nations individuals and several other important topics. David Malaher has drawn the maps for this book and supplied information from David Thompson's little-known map of 1825, and has been a stimulating sounding board on various matters. My wife, Mary Lynn, has listened patiently as I wondered how best to manage Nelson's sprawling materials. She has often provided useful insights, and she has been an unfailing source of encouragement and support.

I am grateful for the encouraging assistance of Finn Purcell, Kathleen Fraser, and Lisa Aitken, of the editorial and production staff at McGill-Queen's University Press, and for the timely and perceptive advice of my copy editor, Gillian Scobie.

Publication of this book has been greatly aided by the financial support of a number of organizations and individuals. For their generous contributions, I am most grateful to the North West Company; the St Andrew's Society of Winnipeg; and the 78th Fraser Highlanders, Fort Garry Garrison; and to the following persons: Jennifer S.H. Brown, Edward Kennedy, Bob Darling, Anne Monk, James G. Oborne, James Skinner, and Bob Vandewater. Jim Oborne has my special thanks for his heroic efforts in raising these funds.

In discussing the first inhabitants of North America and their descendants, authors have used various terms in referring to these peoples. In Canada, the favoured term at present is "Indigenous people," or sometimes "First Nations." In the United States, "Native Americans" is in frequent use. In George Nelson's time, "Indian" was the common term in English, and this is what he uses throughout his writings.

Although Nelson's tone in reporting his encounters with Indigenous people is generally respectful, sometimes he used terms that we now recognize as offensive, such as "superstition" to describe religious or spiritual practices. Nelson was describing what he saw and heard from a standpoint outside Indigenous society, and did not fully understand what a source of guidance and reassurance those practices were to those who had grown up within that society.

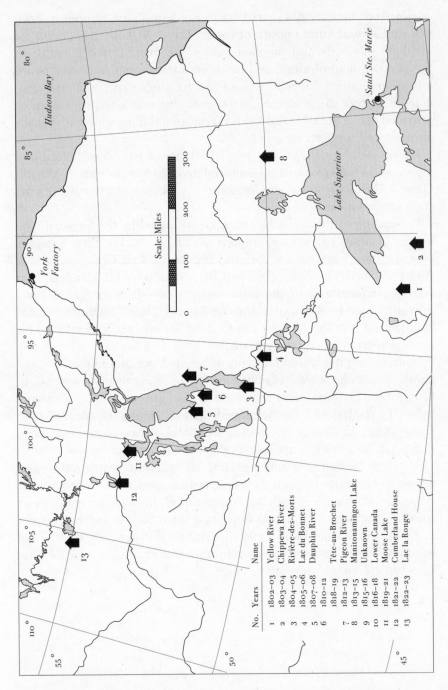

Map 1 George Nelson's wintering places during his years in the Northwest,
1802–1823.

Introduction

George Nelson was still three months short of his sixteenth birthday when he joined the XY Company (XYC), a Montreal-based fur trading enterprise, in the spring of 1802. The contract between George Nelson and Alexander Mackenzie & Co., Montreal agents of the XYC, was signed on 13 March 1802 in the offices of the notary Henri Crebassa at Sorel. Nelson agreed to winter as a *commis* (clerk) for five years "dans les frontières du Nord Ouest." William Nelson, George's father, also signed the contract, probably because George was so young.[1]

Although completely unfamiliar with the life that he was about to enter, young George knew how to read and write, and he was willing to winter in the Northwest, so the XYC would have been glad to enlist him to help with the record-keeping functions of their fur trade. Almost before he knew it, Nelson was sitting in one of the large Montreal canoes, surrounded by packs of trade goods, hearty voyageurs, and a few other clerks, all of them strangers to him. Amid waves of homesickness, he endured the long voyage to Grand Portage at the far end of Lake Superior. There, he was assigned to an outfit that would establish a new trading post in the interior of the Folle Avoine district, south of Lake Superior, in what is now northern Wisconsin.

In 1802, the XYC was deep in a struggle with the major fur trading company in Montreal, the North West Company (NWC), and the rivalry was being carried to every part of the country where the Nor'Westers operated. Nelson spent two years in the Folle Avoine district, learning the rudiments of the trade, and taking in the exotic flavours of the new world around him. Among other things, he formed an attachment with the daughter of one of the Indigenous leaders in the district. We know nothing else about her. His bosses had given Nelson strict instructions not to get involved with a woman. In 1804 he was shifted to a new district, Lake Winnipeg, probably in part as a penalty for his behaviour, and the woman was passed on to another man.[2]

In this somewhat inauspicious manner, George Nelson began his fur trade career. The conflict between the XYC and the NWC was bitter, and it taught its employees, particularly its ambitious young men, to deal with problems in a confrontational way. There were at least two outright murders of traders by their opponents during this turbulent time, and probably much more bloodshed than we can now know, for what happened in the Northwest stayed in the Northwest. During the winter of Nelson's first season on Lake Winnipeg, 1804–05, news reached all the fur traders in the Northwest that the two companies had agreed to merge, and he found himself an employee of the new, expanded NWC. Apart from two years in Canada (1816–18), he would remain in the fur trade till 1823, two years after the NWC merged with its archrivals, the Hudson's Bay Company (HBC). In 1813, as the enmity between the NWC and the HBC intensified, Nelson was transferred from Lake Winnipeg to the hinterland of the ancient post of The Pic, back of the north shore of Lake Superior, where he encountered bitter opposition from the HBC traders. Disgusted with the experience, and seeing no prospect of advancement within his own company, he retired to Lower Canada in 1816. He had saved what money he could, but in 1818 he signed a two-year contract to return as a clerk to the Northwest, doubtless in the hope of earning more. After one more season on Lake Winnipeg, he spent two at Moose Lake on the lower Saskatchewan River.[3] Following the merger of the NWC and the HBC in 1821, Nelson continued in the service of the combined company, with one season at Cumberland House and another at Lac La Ronge. In 1823, his last contract came to an end and he returned to Canada for good.

In the early fall of 1808, at Fort Alexander, Nelson took a new wife, under the informal arrangements then usual in the fur country.[4] This time it was with the full support, indeed the urging, of Duncan Cameron, the *bourgeois*,* or NWC partner in charge of the Lake Winnipeg department. In his *Reminiscences* (Part 5, 207), Nelson explained that she was "a young woman, a cousin of Mr. Cameron's wife that Duncan Cameron [*sic*], living with the family. She was an orphan, about 20 years of age, & in whom C. took great interest, he wanted to provide for her, & pitched upon me!" Cameron had raised the subject with Nelson in the spring of 1808, but Nelson was not interested in forming what he then considered an improper connection. The pressure continued, however, and the match was duly concluded, Cameron giving the couple a ball at Fort Alexander. The occasion must have been one of the three dances that Nelson mentions in his journal on 3 September 1808, in connection with another marriage, that of the clerk Seraphin Lamar. According to his account in the *Reminiscences*, Nelson felt at the time that he had been weak to have agreed to the union, and deplored the fact that many such relationships had ended in the woman and children being abandoned "to linger in want and wretchedness."[5]

This would not be the case with Nelson and his wife, whom Nelson called Mary Ann. He tells us two important things about her. First, she was a cousin of Cameron's wife, and she was an orphan. Second, while stationed in 1813 at Manitounamingan, near the present Longlac, Ontario, Nelson met two Ojibwe from the Nipigon country, brothers of Mary Ann, who brought the news that both her parents had been murdered, in separate incidents. We have further information from the register of the Anglican parish of Christ Church, William Henry (Sorel), where Nelson's wife and their children were baptized, and where they were eventually married. Two entries say that Mary Ann was "of the Loon Tribe of Indians, inhabiting the Shores of Lake Winnipic." All this information points to her being an Indigenous person, whose father (from whom Ojibwe clan designation was inherited) was of the Loon clan or totem. There would have been difficulties with such a marriage in 1808, however, for the NWC partners' meeting of 1806 had resolved that "no Man whatever, either Partner, Clerk, or Engagé, belonging to the Concern shall henceforth take or suffer to be taken ... any woman or maid from any of the tribes of Indians ... to live with him after the fashion of the North West." Where a violation occurred, the partner in charge was liable to a fine of £100, but an exception was made when the relationship was with "the Daughter of a white Man" (Wallace 1934, 211). One of the entries from the Christ Church, William Henry register, which records the baptism of three of Nelson's children on 17 April 1819, is signed with an X, and labelled "Mary Ann Peruse the Mother her Mark."[6] Perusse is a Quebec surname. This entry raises the possibility that Mary Ann's father was a Canadian;[7] such a relationship would have been within the company's regulations. Louis Periffle dit Perusse or Peruze, an engagé,[*8] was working for the NWC in Nipigon in 1805 and 1812, in the Lake Winnipeg department in 1809–10, and in English River in 1813–18 (see his entry in Appendix B). Perhaps he was Mary Ann's father, and her mother was an Ojibwe from Nipigon country. One might further suggest that Mary Ann's parents' relationship ended when their daughter was small, and her mother then married an Ojibwe of the Loon clan, from whom Mary Ann inherited her clan membership.

Duncan Cameron, Nelson's bourgeois, who had been in the Nipigon country for many years before he took over at Lake Winnipeg, would almost certainly have had a wife from among the Ojibwe. He may also have had a hand in finding a wife for his clerk in Nipigon, John Dougald Cameron. In October of 1810, Nelson heard that the voyageur Perusse had been seen passing Pigeon Point "with Mr Dougald Cameron's woman & family who is now travelling as fast as the weather & fear of starvation will allow (them) in quest of her husband who probably winters at Loon lake near Nepigon." This reference may offer a further glimpse of Mary Ann's extended family.

Though doubtful at first, Nelson eventually accepted that his union with Mary Ann was a lasting relationship. They were to have eight children, four born in the Northwest and four in Lower Canada. After they left the fur country in 1816, Nelson settled Mary Ann and their children at William Henry, where his parents and most of his family still lived. When he returned to the North again in 1818, Mary Ann was pregnant, but Nelson would not see his fifth child for another five years. Three more children were born after his return to Lower Canada in 1823. He and Mary Ann were finally married in church by John Jackson, the Anglican rector of Christ Church, William Henry, on 16 January 1825. The delay may suggest a reluctance, on Nelson's part, to submit to the expectations of Anglican propriety. Nelson's father and sisters were present at the wedding, and also his friend and fellow clerk from the fur trade days, John Crebassa. Mary Ann died in November 1831, and was buried at William Henry. Her husband survived her by twenty-eight years.

George Nelson was a competent fur trader who understood his responsibilities, lived temperately, and had his employers' interests at heart. Always in good health, he was capable of great physical exertion, was a strong winter traveller, and a canoeman when necessary. Besides his accounting and journal writing, he had other skills, such as net-making and sled-making, which were important at a small post with few men. He seems to have got along well with his Ojibwe and Swampy Cree customers and his voyageurs alike. Yet, like most other clerks, he never progressed to a partnership in the NWC. Nelson had no relative or other sponsor among the company's partners to push him forward, at a time when almost every new partner, after the merger of the NWC and XYC in 1804, had a brother, uncle, or father to speak for him. The fact that Nelson served in relatively unimportant districts, where no improvement of the trade was possible, also gave him little chance to impress his superiors. Moreover, it cannot have been an advantage to him that in 1807 he was sent to establish a post at Dauphin River, on the edge of the neighbouring NWC department of Fort Dauphin. John McDonald "le Borgne" (the One-Eyed), the partner in charge at Fort Dauphin, deeply resented what he saw as an intrusion by the Lake Winnipeg department, and though Nelson did his best to avoid conflict, that issue must have stirred negative feelings whenever his name was mentioned at the partners' meetings.

A clear indication that the NWC partners had no thought of advancing George Nelson to a partnership, in spite of his competence, is that he was never sent to the Fort William partners' meetings, but was kept in the country during the summer.

Nelson's life after 1823 must also have been a disappointment to him. After his retirement to Lower Canada, he involved himself in ill-judged business projects that left him in near-poverty, and increasingly dependent on grudging handouts from his more successful brothers. He died in 1859, at the age of seventy-three. His wife and most of his children were long dead, and he was a boarder in a house where he could not even be sure that the children would not spill ink on his papers.

GEORGE NELSON'S WRITINGS

The bulk of Nelson's writings at the Toronto Reference Library (Baldwin Collection of Canadiana, Fonds S13) consists of seventeen daily journals or diaries, which he kept at various places in the fur country between 1803 and 1822. Some journals cover a full trading season or more, and some only a few weeks. Besides the journals, the library holds two memoirs of Nelson's time in the fur trade, written in Lower Canada after his retirement; and six letters to his parents and sister in Lower Canada, all dated at Lake Winnipeg in 1811–12. There is also a long treatise on Indigenous myths and stories, a collection of Nelson's observations on Cree and Ojibwe spiritual practices.[9] Finally, there are miscellaneous writings, some of them mere scraps. The longest of these is Nelson's account of events during the Rebellion of 1837 in Lower Canada, particularly those in which his brother Wolfred Nelson played a part.

One more of Nelson's daily journals, covering most of the trading season of 1818–19, is held by the Archives of Ontario, Accession no. 4245. This was located by the late Hugh P. MacMillan, and acquired for the Archives from a private owner (MacMillan 2009, 145–6).

Presumably it had been separated from the main Nelson collection by chance, but it clearly belongs to the same series: the paper is similar to that used for the others, the handwriting is the same, and the last entry is immediately continued by the first entry in Nelson's "Journal B," part of the larger collection.

The fur trade journals that Nelson kept between 1803 and 1822 are not in bound books, but are constructed from folio-sized sheets of good-quality laid paper, about 32 cm high by 40 cm wide, which were cut and folded and assembled into books. For some journals, the full sheet was folded to make 32 cm x 20 cm pages. For others, the half-sheets were cut apart, then folded again to make four 20 cm x 16 cm pages. In some cases the folded sheets are nested to form a single gathering, held together by thread loosely stitched along the spine. Other journals are just stacks of sheets, either folded or flat. One journal (Lac du Bonnet, 1805–06) is a loose stack of pages that ends in mid-sentence, showing that one or more pages have been lost. Another (Dauphin River, 1808–10) is missing one full sheet, and thus several days of entries, from the middle of the book.[10]

All these journals are written in what appears to be the same hand as the family letters, that is, by George Nelson himself. Some pages are watermarked with portions of a large design, consisting of a seated Britannia, with spear or sceptre in one hand and a sprig of three leaves in the other. Her figure is enclosed in a double oval, about 10 cm x 7 cm, surmounted by a crown. One page of the 1822 journal also has the watermark "RADWAY/1818," and one page of the 1818–19 journal has "RADWAY/1816." The numbers must be the years in which the papers were made, and the manufacturer was probably Joshua Carby Radway, who operated a well-known paper mill at Quenington, Gloucestershire, for about forty years, ending with his death in 1840.[11] Radway's paper was likely the standard issue for the NWC in the period when Nelson's journals were written. The fact that at least some of the journals are dated only a few years after the paper was manufactured is a strong indication that the journals as we have them are either originals or contemporary copies that Nelson made himself.

The other Nelson documents that are relevant to his fur trade career are the two memoirs, written after he had left the North. Sylvia Van Kirk refers to the first of these as the *Sorel Journal*, a title that will be used here. It begins in 1825 as a journal of local occurrences, with occasional entries over the next eleven years. The nature of the document then changes, and the *Sorel Journal* becomes a memoir of the early years of Nelson's fur trade career. This includes the only account that survives of his first years on Lake Winnipeg. Portions of this account are printed in this book.

The second memoir is what Van Kirk has called the *Reminiscences*. This was another try at what Nelson had begun in the latter part of the *Sorel Journal*, but it is much better organized, with a proper introduction and a continuous narrative. It is a clean copy with numbered pages, but only three large fragments of it survive in the Nelson Fonds. The sections that we have are "no. 1" (pages 1–48), covering the first two seasons of Nelson's career in the fur country, from his enlistment with the XY Company in May 1802 to a point partway through the season of 1803–04; "no. 5" (pages 185–229), covering June 1807 to October 1809, part of his time on Lake Winnipeg; and "no. 7" (pages 278–92), covering another part of the Lake Winnipeg years, March to June 1812. The numbered parts are not chapters as such, but half-quires of 24 sheets (48 pages). At the end of the surviving part of no. 5, Nelson wrote, "The Children where I am now lodging (Labbés) so blotted the three following pages I must begin the next half quire) Maska 7" february 1851."[12] This gives us a date when Nelson was working on the *Reminiscences*, though, as this is a fair copy, he had probably been writing it for some time before that.

The three parts of the *Reminiscences* are closely written on a distinctive thin, grey-coloured paper, each page about 26 cm high x 20 cm wide. There are no erasures or insertions, so we have what appears to be a fair copy. If we take the page numbers on the surviving parts as a guide, the missing Parts 2, 3 and 4 must have totalled 137 pages, short of the 144 available in three half-quires. The missing Part 6 must have been a complete half-quire of 48 pages. Parts 2, 3, 4, and 6 must have existed once, for the surviving parts have occasional cross-references to pages that are now missing.[13] It is possible that there were parts of the *Reminiscences* beyond no. 7, but only fifteen pages of no. 7 are written upon (the rest of the half-quire being blank), and these consist of a disconnected series of anecdotes. Nelson's enthusiasm for an orderly account may have been fading, and he may never have carried the *Reminiscences* beyond the year 1812.

Several parts of the *Reminiscences* are printed in this volume, again to fill gaps left by the journals themselves. Each of the two longest passages has a good story to tell. The first recounts the explosion of a keg of powder in September 1807, which fatally injured Nelson's interpreter and left Nelson with serious burns. The second tells about the emergency winter journey that Nelson and a fellow clerk made to take over a post whose master had lost control of his situation. Both passages show what Nelson's pen could do, and give insight into his character. It is clear that he had an excellent visual memory, and that his relationship to his fellow creatures was warm and empathetic.

How the Nelson Fonds came to the Toronto Reference Library is a mystery. Grace Lee Nute, the Minnesota Historical Society's great author and curator of manuscripts, did know of them, and had probably discovered them during her comprehensive survey of fur trade materials relating to early Minnesota. She and Richard Bardon (1947) published parts covering Nelson's first season in the fur trade. According to Sylvia Van Kirk (personal communication), in the 1970s the Baldwin Room librarians had no definite information as to how the Nelson papers had come into their care. There was some vague memory that the documents had been associated with a wrapper or envelope from a manuscript dealer, who may have sent them on approval for possible purchase, but further details had been lost. Hugh P. MacMillan had somehow learned that "the complete set of Nelson's North West Company diaries, except for those of the winter of 1818–19, were donated by some unknown person in Calgary."[14]

Among the unanswered questions about the Nelson papers is the exact status of the journals themselves. They appear to be the originals, with the small misspellings, insertions, and crossings out that one would expect. As already noted, they are in Nelson's own hand, and the watermark evidence indicates that they were written as the events happened, or soon after. They could be official records kept on instructions from the NWC, or they could be Nelson's private journals. In only one place does Nelson indicate that there was more than one version of his daily record. This is in his journal for 1818–19, where the entry of 28 February 1819 concludes with the phrase "see Diary." Thus, in that season Nelson may have been keeping one version for company use, and another for himself. Whether this was the pattern throughout his fur trade career, we have no way of knowing. In light of the poor survival rate of NWC journals, and evidence that the company did not have a consistent policy for preserving them (see page xxii, below), we may assume that the Nelson journals we have were those he brought with him when he left the fur country.

Some portions of the Nelson Fonds have already appeared in print. A full edition of the portion of his *Reminiscences* covering Nelson's first winter in the Northwest, 1802–03, and his earliest surviving journal, covering 1803–04, have already been published by Laura Peers and Theresa Schenck, as part of the Rupert's Land Record Society's documentary series. They supplemented these texts with some passages from the *Sorel Journal* (Peers and Schenck 2002). Some of this was the material that Bardon and Nute had published earlier (1947). During those two seasons, Nelson was at the XYC's Folle Avoine post, now in northern Wisconsin. Also in print is Nelson's long letter addressed to his father, dated 1823, a remarkable memoir on the religious beliefs of the Cree and Ojibwe, drawn from his own observations. Brown and Brightman (1988) published this under the title *The Orders of the Dreamed*.

The documents printed in the present volume cover 1804–11, most of the second phase of Nelson's career, around Lake Winnipeg. The journals are presented in full, and are supplemented here and there where other Nelson writings exist to fill in gaps (see below). Also included are Nelson's journals for 1818–19, when he returned to Lake Winnipeg for one more season. Finally, this volume includes what Van Kirk refers to as the "Canoe Journal." In this journal, Nelson gave a detailed record of the old canoe route from Cumberland House to Fort William, written as he supervised a small brigade taking provisions out to Fort William. Students of the old canoe routes should find Nelson's Canoe Journal a welcome addition to the store of information available.

Parts of George Nelson's fur trade writings that remain unpublished include four fragments of journals that he kept in the Pic district, around the present Longlac, Ontario, between 1813 and 1815; a journal begun at Moose Lake (now northern Manitoba) in April 1821, and continued as he travelled to his summer rendezvous at Cumberland House; and a list of comings and goings at Cumberland House in 1820. Nelson was increasingly concerned that his writings would fall into the hands of the opposition company, the HBC, and he began to use his own cipher, first for key words (in the last Pic journal) and then for entire passages. Some twenty-one pages of the Moose Lake journal of 1821 are in this cipher. Sylvia Van Kirk has deciphered the code, which is a simple substitution code; her list of the symbols is included in the Nelson Fonds at the Toronto Reference Library. None of the documents printed in this volume made any use of this cipher.

FUR TRADE JOURNALS

All historians of the Canadian West know the importance of the post journals kept by the servants of the Hudson's Bay Company. This remarkable archive, which often includes continuous series of journals or diaries kept at certain posts over scores of years, is an inexhaustible mine of information about all aspects of the history of the West. A number of HBC post journals have been published in their entirety in the volumes of the Hudson's Bay Record Society. The post journals were an essential part of the HBC's business management, kept for the information of the company's governor and committee, located far away in London. The journals had to be carefully completed every year, fair-copied for ease in reading, sent home on the fall ships, and perused by the company's secretary, who drew important details to the committee's attention. The information in these journals, plus the financial accounts, letters, and reports written by the chief officers at the York, Churchill, Albany, and Moose forts, allowed the HBC Committee to make its detailed business decisions from year to year. By archiving the journals, the company could always look back for trends, and check whether its instructions were having effect.

The NWC (and the XYC, while it existed) had some kind of policy for the keeping of post journals, but the survival rate of such documents was very low. Unlike the HBC, neither company would have felt the same need for regular journal keeping, and central archiving. Both the NWC and the XYC had wintering partners at their major posts, who could report in person to the rest of the partnership at the annual summer meetings, answer questions, argue policy, and negotiate changes on the spot. Though journal keeping was still part of a businesslike enterprise, the NWC does not seem to have had a good system for archiving them. In the short term, journals probably remained at the posts where they were written, for the guidance of other traders. At Fort Qu'Appelle in the late winter of 1793–94, for instance, the clerk in charge, John Macdonell, used the records left by his predecessor of the previous season, Robert Grant, to judge the success of his trade.[15] In the longer term, what happened to the journals probably depended on individual officers. In a letter to Roderick McKenzie in 1814, the NWC clerk Willard Ferdinand Wentzel wrote:

> all the old journals and account books, &c. of Athabaska, of which you had taken so much care while you managed the affairs of the Department, have all been taken to Lac la Pluie during the reign of Mr. Arch: Normand McLeod and left there, for what purpose it is not easy to tell, but when I was on my way to Canada two years ago, I saw them laying scattered here and there in the garret of the Athabaska House mingled with the old useless agrès*[16] of canoes, some upon the beams, others among the old sails, old kettles, sponges, &c., &c.:

pages of different books and journals strewed all over the apartment. I acquainted Mr. McLeod and Mr. Kenneth McKenzie and was desired by the latter to mention the circumstance to you.[17]

The Athabasca House was a special depot at Lac la Pluie (Rainy Lake post, the precursor of Fort Frances), reserved for the use of the Athabasca canoe brigades, whose eastward journeys ended at that point. Perhaps Archibald Norman McLeod, the NWC partner then in charge at Athabasca, had intended to send the Athabasca journals to Fort William, or even Montreal, but never completed the task.[18]

A number of journals from the NWC, and a very few from the XYC, do survive. The largest group was collected by Roderick McKenzie, an NWC partner and one of its agents at Montreal. McKenzie evidently had thoughts of writing a history of the Northwest trade, a considerable expansion of the account that had appeared as an introduction to his cousin Alexander Mackenzie's *Voyages from Montreal* (Mackenzie 1801). As early as 1806, Roderick sent a circular letter to the NWC partners, asking for information about the Indigenous people with whom they traded, a scheme modelled on the *Statistical Account of Scotland*.[19] This request generated some original material (Peter Grant's account of the Rainy Lake Ojibwe is the best example), but it also seems to have brought in a large number of post journals, probably from partners who did not wish to ignore the request, but wanted to avoid extra work. More material may have come in during the following years. McKenzie's collection of these manuscripts passed into the hands of his granddaughter's husband, the lawyer and politician Louis-Rodrigue Masson, who studied them carefully and printed two extensive selections in 1889–90 under the title *Les bourgeois de la Compagnie du Nord-Ouest*.[20] Some of the journals in Masson's hands were sold at auction with the rest of his extensive library in April 1904, after his death. McGill University acquired most of those. The Masson family retained a few NWC documents. We know that yet others existed because they were printed by Senator Masson in 1889–90, but their present whereabouts are unknown.[21]

Another portion of the Masson collection of fur trade journals found its way to the Dominion of Canada Archives (now Library and Archives Canada [LAC]). The old Finding Aid to the Masson collection at LAC states that those papers were bought at the Masson auction in 1904. They cannot be recognized in the catalogue of that sale, however (I have examined a copy of the sale catalogue, kindly shown me by Warren Baker), and so it is unlikely that they were offered at that time. Douglas

Brymner, the first Dominion Archivist, had correspondence with Senator Masson, so some arrangement may have been made between them for the private transfer of the papers that the Dominion archives obtained, either before or after Masson's death.

A second important group of NWC journals survives as copies among the transcripts known as the Selkirk Papers. The originals, along with many private letters between NWC clerks and partners, and other NWC business documents, were formerly held at St Mary's Isle, the Scottish home of Thomas Douglas, Earl of Selkirk, but were destroyed in a fire at that house in 1940. Selkirk must have seized these documents in the course of his Upper Country expedition of 1816–17, when he captured and occupied Fort William and later made his way via Lac la Pluie to Red River. Selkirk was looking for evidence that the NWC had an organized conspiracy against his Red River Colony, and it is clear that the journals were examined closely, and extracts made, probably to be used as evidence in court. Though the documents themselves are gone, careful copies were made of all those then thought to be relevant to Canada, as a part of the program initiated by Brymner. The bound volumes of these transcripts, known as the Selkirk Papers, are held at LAC, and there are microfilm copies at several repositories.

All but one of the NWC journals in the Selkirk group come from the Athabasca district and farther north, and the last one comes from Eagle Lake, a post dependent on Lac la Pluie. It seems likely that Selkirk found all these journals in the disorderly stash, in the garrets of the Athabasca depot at Lac la Pluie, that Wentzel described in 1814.

A special case of NWC journals is the collection of David Thompson's survey books, now in the Archives of Ontario, which constitute an almost complete daily record of the explorer's professional life from shortly after he arrived in Rupert's Land until his latest years in the field. He spent the years 1797–1812 in the service of the NWC. Thompson was constantly on the move during those years, so his journals are not records kept for long periods at particular posts. Although he made frequent references to fur trade matters and personalities, most entries, when Thompson was making a careful record of territory that was new to him, are dominated by the minutiae of his surveying measurements. Some of the most journal-like portions, during the period Thompson was exploring the Columbia Basin, have been printed by Belyea (1994) as *The Columbia Journals*.

An unknown number of NWC journals are still in private hands, and examples emerge from time to time. The most remarkable of these was one kept on birchbark by an NWC clerk, Jean Steinbruck, at a post near the present Hay River, Northwest Territories, in 1802–03 (Duckworth 1999). Given its provenance, it is appropriate that it is now held at the Prince of Wales Northern Heritage Centre in Yellowknife.

Many of the surviving NWC journals in public collections have been published in one form or another.[22] Most cover only a single season, usually beginning in September (when the canoes arrived at the post), and running either until February (when the winter express* departed) or May (when the trading season was over, and the canoes were leaving for Grand Portage or Fort William). The George Nelson journals kept at Lake Winnipeg are practically unique among NWC documents because they include an almost unbroken series covering about three and a half years. Each journal follows the previous one without a break, and as Nelson spent all his summers either at his own post or elsewhere on Lake Winnipeg, there is no interruption, in contrast to the journal of Alexander Henry the younger, for instance, which is broken by his absences at Fort William meetings. With Nelson, we get to see the rhythm of post life throughout the year.

George Nelson's last Lake Winnipeg journal, kept at Tête-au-Brochet in 1818–19, has the additional interest of appearing to be the only NWC post journal to survive from the last turbulent years of the rivalry with the HBC. Though his own post was quiet, with no HBC men breathing fire at his door, Nelson was constantly aware of the possibilities for violence, and the danger that his men would be seized on some pretext while on their essential winter journeys. In this journal, we can also sense the fading of his earlier optimism, and an emerging impatience and sadness that weighed on him, as things were not going well. Many Nor'westers must have had feelings like this, and such a climate, apart from the business difficulties the NWC was suffering, must have been important in pushing them towards the merger with the HBC in 1821.

NELSON AS A JOURNALIST

A special quality of George Nelson's journals is his personal outlook, which clearly shows a greater respect for the people around him than one finds in most NWC journals. Although he sometimes indulged in sarcasm, he was almost never offensive in tone, in contrast to someone like James McKenzie, for instance, whose journal at Fort Chipewyan, kept in 1799–1800, drips with contempt for Indigenous people and voyageurs alike.[23] Nelson took a genuine, sympathetic interest in his customers, in the voyageurs whom he directed, in his fellow clerks, and in the "free-men" or independent traders – retirees or castoffs from the fur com-panies – who did not want to leave the Northwest, and were trying to scratch a living in a difficult environment. For his superiors, the NWC partners who ruled his department, he shows nothing but respect and his *Reminiscences*, written so long after, evince a lingering sense of regard.

Nelson liked all these people, and he often supplied details of their lives that most of the journal keepers never bothered to record.[24] Sprinkled among the records of the daily grind of fishing, summer and winter travelling, and trading for furs and provisions, are many glimpses of the personal lives of Indigenous people and voyageurs. Some are sen-sational, like the tale of the man who murdered his brother in a drinking bout, and then was shot himself; or the woman who dealt with her hus-band's brutality by stripping naked and running into the snow. Others are smaller, more poignant moments, like the Ojibwe leader Ayagon's admission that his little boy would cry if his father got drunk; or the young William Pritchard, ten years old, who earnestly joined the search for the voyageur Welles, probably his stepfather.

Daily journals, with their limited format and their necessary concentra-tion on routine, are rarely an opportunity for literary creativity. Nelson's are no exception, though in his last Lake Winnipeg journals, in 1818–19, he did allow himself some personal remarks. When he was writing only for himself, as in the *Sorel Journal* and the *Reminiscences*, and also in the series of long letters to his family in 1811–12, he expressed himself at greater length. His style is generally coherent and clear, and often peppered with classical references, aphorisms, or other quotations, which indicate a sound education and wide reading. Given that he had grown up in a small town in Lower Canada, at a time when the general level of literacy was not high, one must give credit to his father, the schoolmaster William Nelson, for having equipped his son as well as he did. The faults in Nelson's writing are poor organization, and a tendency (particularly in the *Sorel Journal*) to be overwhelmed by his awareness of the frailties of human nature, an emotional engagement that carried him away from his story. But when he focused and had a good story to tell he is always worth reading.

One feature of Nelson's writing is his matter-of-fact acceptance of a larger reality – not a full-fledged spiritualism, but an acceptance that information could come in supernatural ways. Most surviving fur trade documents are hard-headed and pragmatic in tone, as befits their business purpose. Their authors, proud of their veneer of intellec-tual Enlightenment, would have been embarrassed to admit that they believed in dreams, visions, or ghosts. Yet the people of the fur trade, in Nelson's time, moved in a world where those things were part of life. Scottish Highlanders, Canadian voyageurs, and Indigenous people all knew about ghosts and apparitions. Especially in a country where so much could go wrong so quickly, this atavistic part of belief was continually present. Nelson reports paranormal events and superstitious insights without scoffing at them, and his writings are full of warnings that had come to his voyageurs in dreams, or to his Indigenous acquaintances as visions, or as signs or omens from the natural world.[25]

THE MANAGEMENT OF THE
LAKE WINNIPEG FUR TRADE

The Lake Winnipeg department, or the Post of Lac Ouinipique, as the NWC called it, was a region that most fur traders travelled through, not one where they wintered. This can be sensed even from the very sketchy evidence for the *ancien régime* period, when La Vérendrye, his sons, and their successors settled their long-term trading posts on the Assiniboine River, at Fort Dauphin, and on the Saskatchewan. These pre-Conquest posts were the first to be re-established after the Conquest. The traders on the Saskatchewan pushed up their own river through the 1770s, '80s, and '90s, developing what they called the Fort des Prairies department. More important for the future, they made their way into the Churchill River basin in 1776, and later opened up what was known as the English River department. Following Peter Pond's pioneering expedition to Athabasca in 1778–79, that rich fur-bearing country became, first, a valuable appendage to English River, and then the most important fur district of all. To get to all these regions, the canoes from Grand Portage had to pass through Lake Winnipeg, but they were always going as fast as they could, giving little thought to the lake as a place where one might winter and acquire furs.

The canoemen did not like Lake Winnipeg. It was usually windy – often too windy to proceed, sometimes for days at a time. Taking canoes across the long traverses between points and islands was a tricky and sometimes dangerous business. Eric W. Morse, writing about Lake Winnipeg from a canoeist's point of view, said "This is probably the worst lake in Canada for small craft." Morse quoted a long passage from Alexander Henry's journal of his passage through the Lake in 1808 to illustrate the difficulties. On the inward trips that year, upwards of thirty pieces of goods were thrown overboard by various brigades while crossing the lake, to lighten the loads while struggling with strong winds.[26]

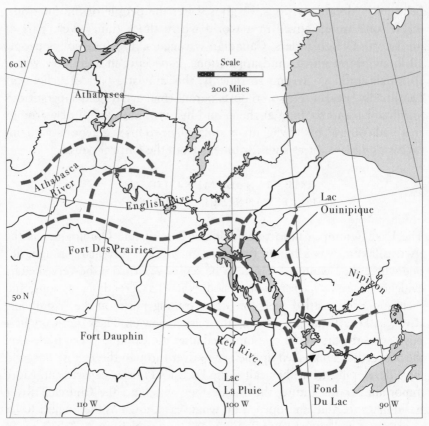

Map 2 The North West Company's trading districts, c. 1810.

Nelson's Lake Winnipeg journals give detailed accounts of eight of his canoe voyages through the south basin, between Fort Alexander and Dauphin River. In every one, the dominant topic is the wind – whether it was ahead (so that paddling was hard) or behind (so that they could carry sail), or so strong that the canoes were forced ashore or were kept in camp. On calm days, if Nelson was compelled to wait for someone else, one can sense his frustration at losing a good travel day. Nelson's canoes were smaller than those used by the long distance brigades, and they were not always in good repair, so he had to be more careful in windy conditions. But even for the long distance brigades, good travelling conditions through Lake Winnipeg were so precious that the canoemen, when they had the chance, would sometimes keep going day and night. In August 1794, the Athabasca and Saskatchewan inward brigades, stimulated by the rivalry between them, paddled about half the length of Lake Winnipeg in a continuous stretch of forty-eight hours, during which one steersman fell asleep and tumbled into the water. The other canoes kept going, ignoring his plight, but his own canoe came back and, with difficulty, rescued him. Neither brigade wanted to cease paddling before the other did. Both having proved their mettle, they finally agreed to stop and camp together (Morton 1929, 11–12).

The changing seasons, of course, decided how one travelled on and around Lake Winnipeg. In the winter months, from December to March, rivers and lakes were frozen solid and covered with snow, and long journeys on snowshoes, usually with dogs to pull sleighs laden with fish or supplies from post to post, were routine. Care was always taken to send at least two men on a trip in case of accidents. The main danger was in open country, or on a lake, when sudden squalls of drifting snow could make it impossible to see the track. Nelson's journals describe many winter journeys, sometimes under bad conditions.

One such description, of Nelson's winter trip from the Tête-au-Brochet post to Fort Alexander and back, in February 1819, gives an idea of travel times. On the way to Fort Alexander, Nelson and his companions were out 2½ days, travelling 16 leagues on each of the first 2 days, and 8 on the third. On the first day they travelled for about 8½ hours; on the second, about 9¾ hours (minus a stop of 1¾ hours for lunch); and on the third, about 5½ hours. The average rate of travel was thus about 1.7 leagues* or about 5 miles per hour. Less detail is provided for the return journey, but again the travellers were out about three days. On his return from visiting John Crebassa at Grand Rapids in March 1819, in very cold weather with few stops, Nelson travelled for most of three days, probably a total of about 33 hours "at the rate of a good trot"; he estimated the distance as nearly 200 miles, which, if accurate, means a rate of 6 miles per hour.[27]

Travel was avoided during the beginning and end of the winter, unless absolutely necessary, because of the danger of falling through the forming or melting ice. The canoeing season usually began in May, when the rivers were open, though the date of ice breakup on Lake Winnipeg itself was quite variable. In the spring of 1810, an unusual spell of hot weather cleared the ice out of the area around the Narrows so early that Nelson was able to make a canoe voyage from Dauphin River as far as the mouth of Broken River (now Rice River) and back between 3 and 11 April, though later it turned cold and ice formed again. In 1808, more typically, the lake ice kept him at his post until 26 May, and in 1809, having been delayed awaiting another trader who himself had trouble with ice, he did not set off for Fort Alexander until 1 June.

The fur trade around Lake Winnipeg was not negligible. There was a population of Indigenous hunters, small and highly migratory,[28] and there were beaver and other furs, particularly martens for them to trap and trade if they cared to do so. Several rivers, draining the western edges of the Canadian Shield, fall into Lake Winnipeg on the east, and these gave canoe access to good beaver country in what is now northwestern Ontario. This region was known as Rivière des Trembles, named for the Aspen or Poplar River, a principal canoe river on that side of the Lake. On the west side of Lake Winnipeg, the poorly drained lands of the Manitoba Interlake also had furs to offer, while the southwest shore was the edge of the great buffalo plains. As the NWC began to consolidate its position throughout the West in the 1780s and early '90s, it paid more attention to the fur trade around the lake, though the traders were careful not to commit too many resources to it.

The first known arrangement that the NWC made for the Lake Winnipeg district was in place by 1789, when Angus Shaw mentioned that "Lesieur and Simon Fraser have taken the post of Riviere des Trembles and Portage de l'Ile. They are in partnership. I wish them much joy of their bargain."[29] Rivière des Trembles, as already stated, was shorthand for the fur country to the east of the north basin of Lake Winnipeg, while Portage de l'Île, a trading post on the Winnipeg River near where the English River system drains in, represented the southern part of the same country. The word "partnership" is significant in this description, for it implies that in 1789 the Lake Winnipeg region was not being operated within the NWC itself, like the richer districts farther west and north, but was being treated as an independent enterprise. The partners were Toussaint Lesieur, an experienced North West trader with a reputation for success, and Simon Fraser, probably one of Simon McTavish's protégés.[30] In 1790, it was reported that Lesieur and Fraser had obtained thirty packs of furs, the first measure we have of what the Lake Winnipeg district could produce. One year later came the news, "Messrs. LeSieur and Fraser have continued their agreement with the Company for five years longer, with this advantage, they are to be allowed £200 per annum when their profits may not come up to that sum" (Lamb 1970, 442, 448). The profit guarantee suggests that the yields from around Lake Winnipeg had been disappointing; but at least the agreement would have settled the fur trade of the district until the end of the 1795–96 season.

In 1791, Toussaint Lesieur went down to Montreal "for his health," but he was back the next year, when he built a new post near the mouth of the Winnipeg River. This quickly became a key provisioning depot for the NWC canoes.[31] The post was originally known simply as Bas de la Rivière Ouinipique. The Hudson's Bay Company traders, briefly and rather innocently, knew it as "Pointe au Foutre," a vulgarity that was probably picked up from some Canadian voyageur.[32] During George Nelson's time, the depot would become known as Fort Alexander. Lesieur wintered at Bas de la Rivière in 1793–94 and 1794–95, but not in either of the next two seasons.[33] According to a report that reached HBC traders at Cat Lake in the spring of 1795, "frazer that is Trader at yunipick [Lake Winnipeg] had 100 packs of furs and all his goods was don sun [soon] in the spring."[34] The agreement with Lesieur and Fraser was to run out in the following year. In the fall of 1794, Joseph Frobisher, one of the NWC's agents, was anticipating that Lesieur would expect a partnership in the company, but Lesieur's interest was bought out by a document signed at Montreal early in 1796, ending his association with the fur trade.[35] Meanwhile, Simon Fraser, the other half of the Lake Winnipeg enterprise, had been made a partner in the NWC, doubtless because of his better connections within the company.

During the winter of 1795–96, Simon McTavish, no longer attending the annual NWC partners' meetings at Grand Portage but still making the key decisions at Montreal, took several steps to extend the company's control over the North West fur trade. The vast region around the upper Great Lakes in which most of the Montreal fur traders operated was about to shrink dramatically. Although the Treaty of Paris, which brought the American War of Independence to an end in 1783, had attempted to define the boundary between British dominions and the new United States far into the Prairies, it was not until 1796, following clarifications provided in Jay's Treaty, that the Americans actually took control of their part of the Great Lakes Basin. Detroit and Michilimackinac, the great depots of the fur trade southwest and west of the lakes, were both on the American side of the line, and it was agreed that their British garrisons would withdraw from both posts in the summer of 1796. Montreal merchants interested in the so-called Southwest trade, supplied from those two posts and extending into the Mississippi and Ohio valleys, would now have to compete with Americans, and would have to satisfy the requirements of American rather than British authorities. Most of the Montrealers would not try to do this. Now they would be casting their eyes upon the fur countries that remained within the British lines.

Simon McTavish realized that a turbulent period was about to begin in the Northwest trade, and he took steps to prepare for it. First, on behalf of the NWC he purchased the interests of various Montreal merchants who had controlled the fur trade of the upper Ottawa (known as the Temiskaming post) and the hinterland of Lake Superior. These regions closer to Montreal, which seem to have been known as the *Petit Nord*, were not particularly profitable, but once under direct NWC control they would act as a buffer, making it harder for rivals to penetrate into the *Grand Nord*, the true Northwest. Second, McTavish bought out the Montreal interests in certain small fur trade "adventures" that had already reached the Northwest, and were starting to disrupt the NWC's operations there. Third, he brought under direct NWC control two regions of the Northwest trade that had been operated in partnership with semi-independent traders: the Fond du Lac district west and south of Lake Superior, and the Lake Winnipeg district. So in 1796, Lake Winnipeg became a regular department of the NWC, under the command of a wintering partner.

The importance of the Post of Lac Ouinipique to the NWC was not the fur trade itself. As already noted, furs were to be had all around the lake, but the main responsibility for the NWC partner taking charge of the department was the provisioning post at Bas de la Rivière. All the goods that the NWC brought into the Northwest, and all the furs they took out, went past this point. Some of the canoe brigades went a very long way. The Athabasca brigade, in particular, made the annual trip beyond Portage la Loche into the Mackenzie River watershed, where the best furs came from. Pemmican,* prepared from the meat of bison hunted at posts on the upper Assiniboine (what was called the Upper Red River department), was brought down to Bas de la Rivière, where it was warehoused and issued to the canoes as they passed by. The availability of pemmican at Bas de la Rivière was so important that the NWC was willing to fight hard to protect it, as Miles Macdonell, governor of Lord Selkirk's Red River Colony, discovered to his cost when he tried to prevent the export of all foodstuffs from Assiniboia in 1814. The Bas de la Rivière post was rebuilt at least twice after Lesieur's original establishment in 1792 – first by the NWC partner William McKay, who in 1806 or 1807 dug up a graveyard to do it,[36] and again in 1808 by his brother Alexander McKay. The post was manned summer and winter, and some agricultural activity was pursued to ensure a food supply.

Surrounded as Lac Ouinipique was by other NWC departments, care had to be taken to avoid competition with the neighbours, and to define boundaries of influence. The overlaps were with the Lower Red River department (whose wintering partner usually lived at Pembina, well up Red River) and the Fort Dauphin department (whose wintering partner apparently lived at Fort Dauphin). The problem was that the company's system of fixed posts did not mesh well with the practices of the Indigenous hunters, who covered great distances in the course of the year, and were happy to take credit at two different posts if they could. The most notorious confusion may have occurred in 1798–99, when the NWC partners in charge of Fort Dauphin (Archibald Norman McLeod), Lower Red River (John Sayer), and Lake Winnipeg (William McKay) each sent a trader to Fisher River on the west shore of the lake, where they spent the season competing with each other (Lamb 1970, 480, 485). Competition between the Lake Winnipeg and Fort Dauphin departments, on their common but ill-defined boundary, continued to be an irritant for years.

NELSON'S BOURGEOIS ON LAKE WINNIPEG

In the Northwest fur trade, *bourgeois* was the usual term for the head of a fur district, though the engagés* at even a modest post might use it for the man in charge there. In the case of the NWC, a department was usually supervised by one or more wintering partners. The first wintering partner in charge of the Post of Lac Ouinipique, when it was brought into the NWC proper in 1796, was William McKay, fresh from signing the NWC Agreement as a new partner at Grand Portage.[37] His was an interesting career, characterized by an impulsive personality – he did not hesitate to use violence when he thought it useful to do so. During one of his early seasons in the Northwest, McKay had summarily hanged a Cree hunter, one of two suspected murderers of a company trader, and he fed on the reputation so acquired to keep control of his Indigenous customers for years after this. In spite of this rough and ready approach, George Nelson admired McKay's skill at anticipating problems among his men, encouraging the obedient, but using threats or ridicule to control the troublemakers. Once he was assigned to Lake Winnipeg, McKay remained there for ten seasons, taking one year of leave in 1804–05, but then returning until his retirement in 1807.

One of the most important duties of a NWC partner, through almost the whole history of the company, was to deal with interlopers, opposition traders who were trying to break down the trade monopoly that the company regarded as essential for its profitability. On Lake Winnipeg, William McKay had two oppositions to deal with – first the HBC traders from Fort Albany, and then the XYC. The HBC's Albany traders, who got their goods from the inland depot of Osnaburgh House in the Nipigon country, had started to invade Lake Winnipeg during the years of the Lesieur-Fraser partnership. In the fall of 1794, the HBC's John Best, chasing Duncan Cameron, his company's rival in the Nipigon country, made an arduous journey with trade goods from Red Lake, over the watershed and down the Bloodvein River, where he found himself on Lake Winnipeg, and founded what he called the Blood River post.[38] Best probably had only a vague understanding of where he was, and retracing his road back to Red Lake would have been difficult, but in the spring one of the rival traders showed him the way to the mouth of the Winnipeg River. Best and his fellow HBC servants now realized that they could supply the whole area from the HBC's inland depot at Osnaburgh House by way of Lac Seul, the English River, and the Winnipeg River route. This knowledge enabled the Albany-based HBC men to establish a trade in the southern part of the Lake Winnipeg district over the next few years, and even to build a permanent post far up the Assiniboine River, at Brandon House.

William McKay may not have realized at first that the HBC traders had to be taken seriously. The concern was not so much that furs would be lost, but that around Bas de la Rivière, with all the canoe traffic passing through, it was important that the NWC appear strong and in control. During the first years of his rule, McKay chose to winter at Cross Lake, at the very northern end of the district, near where he had spent his first trading seasons as a clerk. There, he knew his opponents, the other group of HBC traders who were outfitted from York Factory. McKay left outfits in 1796–97 at Bas de la Rivière and Pigeon River, on the east shore of the north basin of the Lake, while the HBC men from Albany had a post at Bas de la Rivière and another farther north in the lake, probably on a site near the present Gray Point on Black Island.[39] In 1797 and later, the HBC operations were led by an energetic young trader, Thomas Vincent, while McKay left the Bas de la Rivière post in the hands of an experienced man, Gabriel Atina Laviolette. Laviolette had grown up in more gentlemanly times and may not have been used to the confrontational style that was now thought necessary. By January 1799, Laviolette was reporting that he had seen none of the Indigenous hunters to whom he had given debt in the fall, and he himself was "in want of Provisions and discouraged."[40] For the next two seasons, between 1799 and 1801, William McKay took over at Bas de la Rivière himself, and the tactics he used to overwhelm his HBC rivals, threats, multiple posts, and superior numbers, effectively ended HBC opposition for the time being.

The second opposition that William McKay had to deal with was the XYC, a coalition of Montreal traders who had lost their fur trade business when Detroit and Michilimackinac were handed over to the Americans, and were seeking new opportunities in the Northwest. The XYC, the company for whom George Nelson first worked, was everywhere in the Northwest after 1800, though not particularly strong on Lake Winnipeg. They had only a few wintering partners, who were needed elsewhere, so XYC operations on Lake Winnipeg were directed by a clerk. In 1803–04 their man in charge was Charles Grignon, whose drunken habits were blamed for "numerous disasters" that befell the XYC operations during that season, the year before George Nelson arrived on the lake.[41] Grignon was replaced by Alexander Campbell, about whom little is known, except that the NWC took him over after the coalition, and that, like his predecessor, he was a heavy drinker. Campbell remained in the department, and in the summer of 1808 Duncan Cameron, the partner now in charge, proposed to "court martial" him for his drunkenness, but George Nelson, with his characteristic sense of fairness, denounced the proceedings, and Campbell was given a second chance. Placed in charge of a difficult post near Little Grand Rapids (Big Fall in HBC usage) in 1808–09, Campbell completely lost control of the situation, and had to be replaced in mid-season; Nelson's vivid account of this episode is printed in this volume. Campbell was released from the service in 1809, and sent down to Montreal. John Ogilvy, one of the old XYC partners, found some employment for Campbell there, but Nelson heard that he had continued to drink to excess, and died a few years later.[42]

William McKay, who had been prevailed upon for the two previous seasons to postpone taking the leave to which he was entitled, was permitted to go on leave to Canada in 1804–05. For that season, another partner, Alexander Fraser, took charge of the Lake Winnipeg department.[43] Simon McTavish, whose resentment of the XYC was highly personal and who was unwilling to make any accommodation with them, died in Montreal in July. With that barrier lifted, the Montreal agents of the NWC and XYC hammered out an agreement to amalgamate, and this was signed in November 1804. Special efforts were then made to get the news to the Northwest as quickly as possible, to avoid the economic waste and violence that had become routine there. Pierre Belleau, a recently retired NWC clerk, took a circular letter announcing the merger, signed by representatives of both companies, as far as the west end of Lake Superior. Belleau got there at some point in December, and copies of the circular letter were soon moving across what is now Minnesota on their way into the Northwest. George Nelson, wintering near the mouth of the Red River on

Lake Winnipeg, received his copy from a fellow XYC clerk, John Crebassa, who was trading at Pembina. Nelson would have been responsible for forwarding the news to the rest of his company's Lake Winnipeg operations. Other couriers took the news farther west and north. It did not reach Athabasca until early May 1805.[44]

As the season came to an end, the Lake Winnipeg traders of both sides came together at Bas de la Rivière, and letters passed back and forth, discussing how to proceed. Nelson, as a representative of the XYC interests, was sent to the NWC fort on behalf of his bourgeois, Campbell, and chose this moment for a badly timed show of bravado, refusing an order from the NWC partner, William McKay. Nelson, perhaps wrongly, later felt that he had missed an opportunity to advance his career by his behaviour on this occasion.

One of Nelson's mentors on Lake Winnipeg, whom he remembered fondly, was Charles Oakes Ermatinger. Ermatinger, son of a minor fur merchant of Montreal, was about ten years older than Nelson. Like Nelson, he had entered the fur trade as a clerk for the XYC, and in 1805, following the union with the NWC, he was put in charge of the Bas de la Rivière fort. He began the cultivation of potatoes there, and also brought two horses to the post from Red River, later used for ploughing the garden. Nelson credited Ermatinger with having introduced him to the pleasures of reading, by lending him books from his own library. Ermatinger had been promised a partnership in the NWC, to commence in 1808, but he left the company in 1807, and soon established himself as an independent trader at Sault Ste Marie (Momryk 1987). It is tempting to suggest that Ermatinger's son George, born on Lake Winnipeg in 1806, was named for George Nelson.

Most of the first season after the amalgamation, 1805–06, is covered by the earliest of George Nelson's Lake Winnipeg journals. William McKay, back from his leave in Montreal, continued in charge of the department. He found himself with too many men. Everyone had been busy enough as long as the opposition between the NWC and XYC continued, but now there were far more men than were needed. All contracts would be honoured, but once they ran out, only those men who had most impressed the company would be kept on.[45] To make use of all his men as well as possible, McKay greatly expanded his operations, establishing no fewer than six posts around the lake, plus three more in Winnipeg River. McKay himself wintered at Cross Lake in 1805–06, and his own journal of this season survives.[46] Of his clerks, George Venables was at Pike River, and John McPhail was at Lac la Folle Avoine, both on the east side of the north basin of Lake Winnipeg. François Richard was at Pigeon River farther south, and Alexander Campbell was at Broken River in the south basin.[47] Alexander Ferguson had an outfit at Tête-au-Brochet on the west side of the Lake, north of the Narrows.[48] In Winnipeg River, there was the depot at Bas de la Rivière, with Charles Oakes Ermatinger in charge. George Nelson was assigned to a new post at Lac du Bonnet, a day's walk up Winnipeg River from Bas de la Rivière, as writer to a veteran but illiterate trader named Louis Périgny. Nelson's journal of this season is printed in this volume. On his way in from Fort William, in the fall, McKay had established two more posts farther up Winnipeg River, with two old traders, Dominique Ducharme and Louis Ménéclier, in charge.[49]

At the end of the season, the conclusion of many mens' contracts allowed a severe reduction in manpower. Périgny's service with the NWC ended in 1806, though after a visit to Canada, he returned to the Northwest as a free trader. Venables, whose behaviour at Pike River had been "scandalous," also disappeared after 1806. George Nelson was kept on strength, along with three other clerks, Alexander Ferguson, John McPhail, and John Crebassa.

Nelson spent the summer of 1806 at Bas de la Rivière, and for the ensuing winter he was in charge of a post at Rivière-aux-Morts or Dead River (now Netley Creek), near the southwest corner of Lake Winnipeg. One Desfonds was appointed his interpreter. We have no day-to-day journal of this season, but the *Sorel Journal* describes some incidents, which are printed in this volume. The trading season went well in general, and Nelson passed the summer of 1807 again at Bas de la Rivière.

Elsewhere in the department, the HBC traders from Albany Fort, with their forward base at Osnaburgh House, were working their way back into the Lake Winnipeg country, not by way of Winnipeg River this time, but by much more remote canoe routes that brought them into the headwaters of the Berens and Poplar Rivers. These efforts were part of the HBC's response to the NWC's great expansion of their Nipigon department, directed by Duncan Cameron, a trader of long experience there. Cameron, as a NWC partner, had to take care not to infringe upon the Lake Winnipeg department's best fur grounds to the east of Lake Winnipeg, but the HBC had no such restriction.[50] As early as 1800–01, the HBC trader David Sanderson had brought an outfit through the maze of lakes and rivers that run northwest from Osnaburgh House, crossed the height of land into the headwaters of the Berens River, and built a post at what he called Sandy Narrows.

The next year he moved downstream to Great Fall (now Little Grand Rapids), which became a permanent HBC post. Sanderson established further outposts in the next few years.

William McKay was slow to respond to the challenge from the HBC, contenting himself with a post at the mouth of Pigeon River on Lake Winnipeg, so David Sanderson enjoyed a trade free of opposition for three seasons. As late as 1803–04 he had no rival post close by. In the following season, however, both the NWC and the XYC sent outfits up to oppose the HBC at Great Fall, and Sanderson found himself contending with both Alexander Campbell, the XYC's senior clerk in the district, and Alexander Macdonell for the NWC. Hereafter, the NWC's Lake Winnipeg bourgeois was careful to send at least one trader to oppose the HBC in this part of the fur country. During the season of 1806–07, the NWC's Alexander Macdonell was again at Great Fall, playing the bully. Twice during the winter he forced his way into the HBC's house and seized furs, provisions, and a canoe, wounding one of the HBC servants in the arm with a sword (Lytwyn 1986, 104, 107–8, 116). Aggressive tactics like these may have impressed Macdonell's superiors, but they were not without their hazards. Two years later, Alexander Macdonell's brother Æneas, a NWC clerk at Eagle Lake, tried the same methods with an HBC opposition, and was shot dead (Williams 1975, 95).

The fall of 1807 brought the news that William McKay was not coming back from the partners' meeting at Fort William, but had retired and gone down to Canada. Command of the Post of Lac Ouinipique was now given to two NWC partners, Duncan Cameron, from Nipigon, and William McKay's brother Alexander. Alexander McKay had a certain celebrity, as the clerk who had accompanied Alexander Mackenzie on his famous journey to the Pacific in 1793. He seems to have been a competent but not particularly talented man, who might not have got a partnership in the NWC without connections. Nelson, who rarely spoke ill of anyone, said of Alexander McKay, "nobody liked him." His main contribution in the Lake Winnipeg department was the rebuilding of the post at Bas de la Rivière, which was renamed Fort Alexander in 1808. At the end of this season he, too, retired from the Northwest fur trade.[51]

Duncan Cameron, who now assumed sole command of the Lake Winnipeg department, was a much more formidable character than Alexander McKay.[52] He had first come up from Canada in the mid-1780s, as a clerk for Gabriel Cotté, the Montreal trader who at that time had a de facto monopoly of the trade into the Nipigon country. Cameron was determined and resourceful, and soon changed the rather leisurely atmosphere of the Nipigon trade.[53] In or about 1794, Cameron and a partner, St Germain, made an agreement with Cotté that allowed them to share in the profits. Cameron himself spent the winter of 1794–95 at Montreal, probably to finalize these new arrangements, but he already knew what he was going to do next. Upon his return to the Upper Country, in the fall of 1795, he carried his trade far beyond Red Lake (Ontario), hitherto the farthest west he had wintered. Descending the Bloodvein River to Lake Winnipeg (where his men had already established a post), he crossed the lake, passed up the Dauphin River, and wintered at Partridge Crop, on the west shore of Lake St Martin in the Interlake region of present-day Manitoba. An advance party had already built a post for him there the previous summer.[54] By this unexpected and rather extravagant adventure, Cameron now placed himself right under the noses of the NWC. He may have been trying to provoke some settlement or takeover that would bring him into the NWC. Cotté, his Montreal supplier, died that winter. That event would have disrupted Cameron and St Germain's supply chain in the next season had they remained independent, but they were indeed taken over by the NWC in 1796, as part of Simon McTavish's absorption of the fur trade around Lake Superior already described.

Cameron spent the next eleven years in charge of the Nipigon district for the NWC, first as a highly paid clerk, then as a partner. The years passed in an endless struggle with the HBC traders based at Osnaburgh House. The district had a bad reputation among the voyageurs – a complex and confusing geography, uncertain food supplies that could mean starvation for traders and Indigenous people alike, and a small population of Ojibwe hunters who ranged widely across the region and were adept at playing the rival traders off against one another. To do well in such a country, year after year, Cameron had to tolerate the hunger and the drudgery, and he must also have had the temperament to enjoy the game-playing aspects of the struggle, its moves and counter-moves. The annual yield of furs from Nipigon was not large, but those furs were rich and thick, among the finest to reach the London market. After 1796, access to NWC resources allowed Cameron to expand much farther north, opening up new posts in the headwaters of the Severn River (Lytwyn 1986, Chapters 5–8).

One reason why Cameron may have been chosen to take over the NWC's interests on Lake Winnipeg, after William McKay's retirement in 1807, was that the Ojibwe around the lake were connected by family with his Indigenous customers in the Nipigon department. The HBC traders on and around the lake, moreover, were mostly his old opponents from

Osnaburgh House. Cameron was well acquainted with some of these men, and he had been trying to outwit them for years. His approach on Lake Winnipeg was ambitious. Responding to a request from an Ojibwe leader, Ayagon, he established a new post at the mouth of Dauphin River on the west side of Lake Winnipeg, and young George Nelson was put in charge of it. Cameron may have had a particular interest in pushing in this direction, having once wintered himself at Partridge Crop, even farther west, in his pre-NWC days. The siting of the new post recognized that the Ojibwe bands were gradually moving westwards too. But the move put the Post of Lac Ouinipique into conflict with the next NWC department to the west, Fort Dauphin, under the management of the partner, John McDonald, "le Borgne." The two departments rubbed together constantly at this sore place, irritation being fed by the fact that some hunters were taking credit both from Lake Winnipeg's Dauphin River post and from the Fort Dauphin outpost at Partridge Crop. It was George Nelson who had to manage this situation, doing his best to minimize the double dipping of those Ojibwe hunters, but he had been put at a distinct disadvantage if he hoped that his name would be mentioned favourably at the Fort William partners' meetings.

Once he had his first season at Lake Winnipeg under his belt, Duncan Cameron had to make his operations as efficient as possible. The department was not producing enough furs to justify the trade goods and manpower hitherto assigned to it. The economy of his department was fully discussed at the Fort William meeting in 1809. It is most unusual for the surviving minutes to report the decision in such detail. The minutes noted that ten canoes and ten posts had operated on Lake Winnipeg in the previous season, of which five posts had yielded only 32½ packs among them. Cameron was instructed to cut operations back to only five posts, and the partners, no doubt also trying to prevent overlapping with the Fort Dauphin department, spelled out where those posts should be: Skabitchiwine (Escabitchewan, near present-day Ear Falls, Ontario); Bas de la Rivière; Rivière Cassé (Broken River) and Rivière au Tourte (Pigeon River), both on the east side of Lake Winnipeg; and Les Dalles (on the upper part of Winnipeg River).[55] For the 1809-10 season, the number of canoes for Lake Winnipeg was reduced from ten to eight, and for 1810-11 it would be further cut to five.[56]

Cameron established six posts in 1809-10, rather than five, and he had his own ideas as to where he would locate them. Three posts, at Fort Alexander, Broken River, and Pigeon River, were part of the partners' design for the department. Cameron, however, ignored the instruction to place the remaining two at points along Winnipeg River, which would have shifted the centre of gravity of the department to the east. Instead, he sent an outfit to Grand Rapids (now Little Grand Rapids), well inland to the east of the lake, to oppose his old rivals, the HBC traders, and another to Rivière-des-Morts, at the southwest corner of the lake, where there was a danger of competition with the Lower Red River department. A sixth outfit he sent again with George Nelson to Dauphin River, ensuring that the irritating overlap with John McDonald's Fort Dauphin department would continue. Perhaps because Cameron had come into the NWC as a mature man, rather than working his way up through the company system from a young age, he was not completely dedicated to the wishes of the Fort William partners' meetings.

Duncan Cameron was a colourful character. Nelson describes him as "about, if not over 50 years of age. a Small, but very active man" (Nelson, *Reminiscences*, 190). When Nelson first met him, he was actually only about forty-three years of age, though the years in Nipigon may have told on him. But he still had an eye for a pretty face, as a letter from Dr John McLoughlin to John Dougald Cameron, one of Duncan's clansmen and protégés, shows:

> I have often thought of our friend your namesake [Duncan Cameron] and how he and the Colony came on … I suppose that old Ram of a namesake of yours has had you now and then with him courting the Scottish Lasses – write him for I cannot myself his letter is full that he must leave me Nancy you know he asked her to sleep with him before us. I am sure he will be always the same – write him I write you to write him that Demouchelles Grand daughter alias Madame Fournear was Brought to Bed of a fine Boy in December she says – The Childs father is an O-gi-ma an [and] she calls him Sha-ga-nash-ens tell him he will pay the hundred pound.[57]

Here, "namesake" means someone with the same surname as John Dougald Cameron, the addressee of the letter. As Duncan Cameron had taken over the NWC's command at Red River the previous fall, where he was dealing with Lord Selkirk's Red River Colony, the "old Ram of a namesake" must be Duncan Cameron. Though some details in this letter are obscure, it is clear enough what McLoughlin was writing about. "Nancy" was apparently an eligible Indigenous or Métis woman whom Cameron had made a lunge at, but he left Lac la Pluie without success. In

Madam Fournear's identification of her baby's father, *O-gi-ma* is Ojibwe for chief or boss, and could mean *bourgeois*; and *Shah-ga-nash-ens* in Ojibwe means "little white man." The reference to the "hundred pound" refers to the fine of £100 that had been specified at the partners' meeting in 1806 for those traders who had disobeyed a directive to marry only the daughters of white men.[58]

In the spring of 1810, Duncan Cameron was letting it be known that he intended to leave the country for good,[59] but he evidently changed his mind, for he continued in charge of the Post of Lac Ouinipique. When he came to the lake in 1807 he had a wife from among the Ojibwe of Nipigon,[60] but in 1810 he took a new wife, the daughter of the Lake Winnipeg interpreter, Joseph Lorrin.[61] It may have been the novelty of this new relationship, with a woman probably at least twenty-five years younger than him, that persuaded him not to leave the Northwest after all. In 1811, he was transferred to Lac la Pluie (Rainy Lake), the important eastern depot for the Athabasca canoes, remaining in charge of that post for three years. In 1814 he was assigned to Red River, and a letter that he wrote from there soon after his arrival confirms that, whatever philandering he had been up to in the meantime, Lorrin's daughter was still with him.

At Red River, Duncan Cameron would be responsible for implementing the NWC's policy of hostility towards the Red River Colony, the new settlement that the Earl of Selkirk had recently established near the Forks of the Red and the Assiniboine. It was an important assignment, with complex implications that reached far beyond the fur country and the fur trade. The NWC was gradually realizing that the colony, and in particular the attempts of its governor, Miles Macdonell, to block the production of pemmican for the canoe brigades, could prove a mortal blow to its operations. Cameron conducted a multi-pronged campaign against the colonists, with the aim of driving them from the country. Using a combination of threats, persuasion, and outright violence, he was on the very brink of success when the majority of the settlers decided to leave Red River in the summer of 1815, accepting the offer of a passage in NWC canoes down to Upper Canada. Just as Cameron's victory seemed absolute, the remnant of the colony, reinforced by a fresh contingent of settlers from Scotland, and encouraged by the leadership of a former NWC clerk, Colin Robertson, came back to the Forks. Robertson succeeded in arresting Cameron and taking him prisoner to York Factory, whence he was sent on to England. Removed from the scene in this way, Cameron did not have to preside over the last bloody incident of the NWC campaign, the affair at Seven Oaks.[62] He made his way back to Canada, rode out the legal battles in the aftermath of the events at Red River, and retired to Glengarry, Upper Canada, where he finally married yet another woman, this time in a church (Brown 1988).

Duncan Cameron's successor in charge of Lake Winnipeg, in 1811, was John Dougald Cameron, a friend and frequent correspondent, and, like him, a veteran of the Nipigon trade. John Dougald was not yet a partner in the NWC, but he had been promised that he would become one in 1814.[63] George Nelson was still on Lake Winnipeg in 1811–13, and so would have come under John Dougald's management; but Nelson's journals for those years do not survive, and apart from one long anecdote there is no relevant material in the *Sorel Journal* or the *Reminiscences*, either. Nelson was transferred to the Pic district on Lake Superior for the 1813–14 season, and would not return to Lake Winnipeg for five years.

In 1813–14, the complement of the Lake Winnipeg department consisted of one bourgeois (John Dougald Cameron, not yet a partner), two clerks, one interpreter, one guide, and sixteen engagés. Only two or three posts could have been occupied with this number of men. The mood of the partners' meeting of 1814 was for still further retrenchment, and for the 1814–15 season, the Lake Winnipeg department lost its guide and two of its engagés (Wallace 1934, 283, 286). Information about which posts were actually occupied has not been found. The only sources for the NWC's activities in these and the next two seasons are reports from the HBC servants in the region, which themselves are incomplete.[64] A further reorganization took place in 1815. According to the NWC's Grand Ledger of men's accounts, a number of the Lake Winnipeg voyageurs, and also its most experienced clerk still remaining in the district, John Crebassa, were formally transferred to the books of the Red River department, and the Post of Lac Ouinipique is not mentioned at all. Crebassa himself, however, is known to have been stationed at Bas de la Rivière in 1816–17, so the apparent transfers probably just mean that the Post of Lac Ouinipique was operated as part of the Red River department for two seasons, a further part of the retrenchment process.[65]

In 1817 or 1818, however, the NWC, scrambling to keep up with an increasingly aggressive HBC, decided that it had to reinvigorate the Post of Lac Ouinipique. It is doubtful that the yield of furs had improved, but the great lake was now of even more strategic importance. Both companies were using it as a crucial transportation route – the NWC for the Saskatchewan, English River, and Athabasca, as usual, and the HBC to supply the growing agricultural colony at Red River. Maintaining a presence on the lake, and some authority, was essential, and a new proprietor, Duncan McDougall, was brought in to take charge.[66]

McDougall's career had been a varied one. He had hired with the NWC "as clerk in the North-West trade" in the spring of 1801.[67] After some time with them, during which he had led an incursion into the HBC's home territories on James Bay, he quit the company, and obtained employment with John Jacob Astor's Pacific Fur Company where he helped to establish the main post at the mouth of the Columbia River – a step with far-reaching political significance, as it would be the basis of the American claim, ultimately successful, to the Oregon Territory. When the Astorians were confronted by a large NWC force that came to the Columbia in early 1813 (part of the company's contribution to the War of 1812–14), McDougall did not try to defend Astor's post, but negotiated its sale to the Nor'Westers. He then rejoined the NWC, and, perhaps in recognition of his help in this episode, the NWC made McDougall a partner. The Astorians, understandably, considered that he had betrayed them. He remained on the West Coast for the next season, then came east, and took over the Post of Lac Ouinipique in the fall of 1817. Next season, he was joined by the two most experienced Lake Winnipeg clerks, John Crebassa and George Nelson; Nelson had just returned from Canada. McDougall himself was based at Fort Alexander, Crebassa re-established the (Little) Grand Rapids post, in the East Winnipeg district, and Nelson returned to his former post at Tête-au-Brochet.

McDougall's second season was brief. He died at Fort Alexander on 25 October 1818; the nature of his illness is unknown. Nelson, though he had known McDougall for only a few months, showed his usual good will towards his superiors by praising McDougall's "generous, open, & truly candid & honest behaviour," and called him a friend. When the news of McDougall's death reached John McBean, the NWC partner in charge at Red River, McBean sent an experienced clerk, Charles Hesse, to take over at Lake Winnipeg for the rest of the season. Very little information has been discovered about the operations of the department for the two final seasons of the NWC, 1819–20 and 1820–21. The great ledger accounts show that it continued to run independently, but which partner was in charge remains unknown.[68]

NELSON'S LAKE WINNIPEG

When Nelson first established the post at Dauphin River in the fall of 1807, three leading Ojibwe hunters, all connected by marriage, formed the core of his trading community.[69] Most prominent was Ayagon, the man at whose invitation the post was established; the other two senior men were known to the traders as Mouffle d'Orignal and Cul-Fessé. Mouffle d'Orignal, whom Nelson usually called Old Muffle, was the eldest of the group, the head of a hunting family that included five sons, three of whom were known as The Martin, The Sourd, and The Bird; while a daughter was the wife of Jean-Baptiste Larocque, one of Nelson's voyageurs. One of Ayagon's wives (he had five in all) was another of Mouffle d'Orignal's daughters, and another wife was a daughter of Cul-Fessé. A second son-in-law of Cul-Fessé, La Bezette, was less influential, but he was one of Nelson's best hunters of furs. The women and children of these hunters' families go almost unmentioned in the Journals, but the total number of individuals in this band must have been twenty or thirty at least. The Ayagon/Mouffle d'Orignal band broke up into smaller groups, usually with two or three hunters and their families, during the winter, but they all kept track of one another's movements. Each time one hunting party came into the post, Nelson would get news of what success the others were having. Relations among the Ayagon/Mouffle d'Orignal group were not always completely peaceful: it must have been a strain on everyone when in the fall of 1809 Ayagon's brother eloped with La Bezette's youngest wife.

The hunting area of the Ayagon/Mouffle d'Orignal group was large. It ranged westward from the Dauphin River post upriver as far as Lake St Martin (the location of an island where Cul-Fessé's family made sugar from tree sap in the spring), and beyond that to the north end of Lake Manitoba. To the east, the band hunted through the multi-bayed peninsula that lies between present-day Sturgeon Bay and Jack Head (Tête-au-Brochet in NWC usage). Northwards, their territory extended far into the Warpath River system. Southwards, it reached through the Mantagao River basin to the southern margins of the forest, where Ayagon, at least, occasionally hunted buffalo. In summer, members of these families went across Lake Winnipeg, as far east as the mouth of the Bloodvein River, a place of rendezvous for Canadian traders and Indigenous people alike.

By Nelson's second season at Dauphin River, 1808–09, it was clear that this one hunting group was not producing enough furs to make the post viable. Two brothers, sons of an Ojibwe named Bras Court, were persuaded to attach themselves to the post. Bras Court himself was based at Lac la Pluie, much farther east, but his family hunted over a wide territory, as far west as the western edge of the Fort Dauphin department.

All these hunters and their families were part of an Ojibwe population that was gradually moving west. The NWC partners were well aware of this slow migration, and it was causing them problems. At Dauphin River, as we have seen, Nelson was in the middle of the territorial wrangle between his own Post of Lac Ouinipique and the NWC's Fort Dauphin department, to the west, over which was entitled to trade on the west side of the Lake. The Ojibwe bands had no reason to respect the fur traders' theoretical boundaries, and they dealt with the nearest post whenever they could. Sometimes they took goods on credit from more than one post at the start of the winter season, thus incurring debts beyond what they could repay. They knew that the traders were trying to avoid competing with each other, and they might take steps to mislead them. In February 1810, for instance, the Ojibwe hunter Cou-Fort, who had been trading at the Fort Dauphin post of Partridge Crop, managed to sell some meat to Nelson's interpreter John Inkster, by claiming that it had been killed by old Cul-Fessé, whom Nelson would consider one of his hunters. Nelson found out the ruse, and was not pleased. He had already accepted the loss of Cou-Fort's winter hunt to Fort Dauphin during the previous season.

John McDonald "le Borgne," the partner in charge of Fort Dauphin, finally won this struggle at the partners' Fort William meeting in 1810, and Nelson was required to move his post further east, to Tête-au-Brochet, though still on the west side of the lake. The Ayagon/Mouffle d'Orignal band continued to trade with him there, in 1810–11 at least, but by 1818–19, when Nelson was keeping his last journal at this post, they were not mentioned. Some may have died in the interim, but by 1819–20, Ayagon, much admired as a hunter, was taking his trade to the Fort Dauphin department.

The other group of Indigenous people who frequented Nelson's posts on Lake Winnipeg were what he calls Mashkiegons* (people of the muskeg), commonly known today as Swampies or Swampy Cree. This group had previously traded at the Pigeon River post, on the east side of the lake, and after some preliminary contacts they shifted their winter hunt to Dauphin River in the season of 1809–10.

This was a much larger group than the one comprising Ayagon and his relations. Its leaders were Le Ventre (The Belly), and his brother Le

Gendre (the Son-in-Law), so-called because his wife was a daughter of the Lake Winnipeg interpreter, Joseph Lorrin. Others included Cul-Levé; Nez Corbin, his twin sons Kiewaykoabow and Nécowatch, and his other sons Le Beson and Tabashish; Petites Couilles; Moose Eyes (also called Les Yeux de Male); Old Morpion (also known as Weaga) and his sons; the Old Brochet and Young Brochet, presumably father and son; and Kieshkieman. Judging by Nelson's comments, the best fur hunter among them was probably Nez Corbin. As new arrivals, this group was still working out what its hunting territory would be, and during the 1809–10 season, they overlapped much of the territory of the Ayagon/ Mouffle d'Orignal group, ranging as far south as Mantagao River, as far west as Lake Manitoba, and as far north as The Détour (Long Point), well up the west shore of the north basin of Lake Winnipeg. They also spent time on the east side of Lake Winnipeg, and occasionally visited the HBC opposition farther east.

Nelson did not report any friction between the Ojibwe and the Mashkiegons, because of their overlapping territories, but the region was large, and they would not have encountered one another very often during the winter. According to Peter Fidler, writing of the Ojibwe trading in the HBC's Manitoba district in 1820, "The Indians do not appear to hold any exclusive right, to any particular part to hunt in but range wherever their fancy or inclination leads them." Maple-sugar-making places, on the other hand, and gardens, provided they were kept up, were respected as the exclusive property of particular families.⁷⁰

The Mashkiegons were different in character from the Ojibwe, Nelson found – good-natured and obliging, and fond of joking, whereas the Ojibwe were restrained and formal. The Ojibwe regarded the Mashkiegons with condescension, if not contempt, as they "had never faced an enemy."⁷¹ At first, Nelson regarded the Mashkiegons as better hunters, no doubt because they seemed more willing to do what he wished.

Nelson stayed at Dauphin River for three seasons, making continual improvements to the post. He kept a garden in which he raised successful crops of potatoes. When he was required to move to Tête-au-Brochet, in the summer of 1810, it galled him to know that his Dauphin River potatoes were being dug up and eaten by an Indigenous band that had settled on the site for the rest of the summer.

Nelson's new site at Tête-au-Brochet, near the mouth of the present-day Jackhead River, had been occupied by fur trade posts, though not continuously, since the 1790s at least. It was about 35 miles due east of the

Dauphin River post by land, but the large bulk of two northward jutting peninsulas meant that for canoe travellers on the lake it was at least two good days' paddle in calm weather. The NWC partners apparently had accepted that this site was far enough away from Partridge Crop to avoid conflicts with the Fort Dauphin department. Nelson nonetheless found himself still trading with the same Indigenous people as at Dauphin River, though he felt that the new situation did not suit them as well as the old one had. Soon he had his post well arranged, and even managed to send parties back to Dauphin River to get the rest of the potatoes from his garden, and later to spear more whitefish at the rapids there. There was no spear fishing at Tête-au-Brochet, but there were fish in the river, and a *puise* or fish trap was built to collect them.

Nelson had not been well treated when the Dauphin River post was closed in 1810. He had learned the news of the partners' decision from others, not from his own bourgeois, Duncan Cameron, who was slow to return to the department, likely embarrassed by his loss of territory. For the move to the new trading site, Nelson was given but a single voyageur, and an old leaky canoe, to help him transfer his own family and baggage. He himself, he says, did most of the paddling (his wife must have helped) while the voyageur steered the canoe, a loss of face for a clerk, which many men would have found intolerable. He had a right to resent his treatment, and his experiences in the coming season would not make him feel any better. His 1810–11 journal at Tête-au-Brochet has no outright complaints, but he made some uncharacteristically cranky, even nasty remarks about his voyageurs and hunters, and expressed none of the optimism that he had shown in earlier seasons. He vacillated between two extreme views as to why his post was doing so poorly. Sometimes he believed that the hunters were trying their best in a poor country. At other times he felt that things were not really so bad for them, but that they were stubbornly refusing to hunt for furs because they resented the abandonment of the post at Dauphin River. There was probably truth in both opinions.

Nelson's journal at Tête-au-Brochet ends abruptly on 1 May 1811. His next surviving journal (not printed in this volume) does not begin until 2 August 1813, when he had just moved to a completely different part of the fur country, the Pic department, north of Lake Superior. For his two seasons on Lake Winnipeg before the move, only scattered information is available. In 1811–12 he was again at Tête-au-Brochet, but in 1812–13 he was assigned to the old post of Pigeon River, on the east side of the lake.[72] The move may have been a further requirement by the Fort William partners' meeting, to benefit the Fort

Dauphin department at the expense of Lake Winnipeg. Nelson would have known that provisioning the Pigeon River post was difficult, for during two seasons at Dauphin River he had been responsible for sending sleigh loads of whitefish to Pigeon River. The Mashkiegons would probably have continued to trade with him at Pigeon River, for this was their old hunting ground. But it may have been this move that caused the Ayagon/Mouffle d'Orignal group to break with Nelson, and transfer their hunts to Fort Dauphin.

Following his three years in the Pic department, and two years in Canada, Nelson returned to Lake Winnipeg in 1818 for one more season, and again we have a journal.[73] The local hunters were happy to see him back, for their trading opportunities had been slim since he had left. Some were Mashkiegons with whom he had traded before his departure in 1813, but as already noted, the Ayagon/Mouffle d'Orignal band was no longer on the scene. There were some new figures. Whereas Joseph Lorrin's son-in-law, the Mashkiegon Le Gendre, had been prominent in 1807–11, by 1818 Le Gendre was old enough to have a married daughter, and her husband, L'Assiniboine, now became one of Nelson's regular customers. The best hunter now was a new figure, Nez d'Argent, who hunted in the Fisher Bay area along with Frisé, probably the "young Frisé" whom Nelson knew from his previous years at the post. By the end of the season, Nez d'Argent alone had traded about 180 *plus** worth of furs, partly in moose meat, but mostly in furs – two or three times as many furs as a typical hunter would produce. The other new Mashkiegon was Red Breast or Estomac Rouge, along with his wives and at least three young and troublesome sons.

In his Manitoba District Report in 1820, Peter Fidler has an excellent description of the Tête-au-Brochet band:

There are a small Band of Indians – Eastard [Eastward] Crees who generally reside on the Borders of Lake Winnipic about The Jack head [Tête-au-Brochet], and the Fisher rivers which fall into that Lake. Mr Cribbasa [John Crebassa] the NW Clerk generally winters with them with four Men and a small quantity of Goods – sometimes these Indians winter on the East side of the Lake about Berens & Pidgeon rivers – none of the NW remain in their House during the Summer – this small band of wandering Inds may mount to Eight or ten able hunters with a proportional number of women & Children – about 4 years since we had people there, but they made little Trade – and since our people has not wintered with them.[74]

Nelson found other changes in the country. The Red River Colony, with its concentrated population of farming families from the British Isles, plus the European mercenaries whom Lord Selkirk had brought up in 1817, was no longer under threat, and was starting to thrive. Nelson never got to visit Red River after the colony was established, but he was well aware of it, if only because of the epidemics that he believed originated there. Measles, whooping cough, and scarlet fever were all present among the colonists, and soon spread out to an Indigenous population with none of the herd immunity needed to limit the danger.[75] And Nelson was now mentioning Métis individuals, whom he calls *brûlés**: the generation of children of Canadian men and Indigenous women was growing up. Although there had been people of mixed race in the West for generations, the population was now much larger, and it was developing its own sense of identity. Nelson, with the same open-hearted attitude that he had for everyone else, respected the Métis, and his sense of justice was offended by the prejudice that the NWC partners had already developed against this new generation.[76] By the early 1830s, George Simpson's remarks on "halfbreed" clerks in his "Character Book" show that the prejudice had become entrenched in the management of the amalgamated company.[77]

Nelson's last Tête-au-Brochet journal also shows modest technological advances at his post, slight improvements over the conditions when he had been there before 1813. Now he took his fall outfit and his spring furs over windy Lake Winnipeg in a boat large enough to hold twenty-nine persons plus dogs, rather than in the more dangerous canoes. In his outfit he had panes of glass for his windows, and when recording his progress on his journeys he had the use of a watch.

In the spring of 1819, Nelson was ordered to Cumberland House, in the Fort des Prairies department, to take over that post for the summer. For the winter, he was assigned to Moose Lake, outfitted from Cumberland House, and his life on Lake Winnipeg came to an end.[78]

NELSON'S VOYAGEURS

As already mentioned, the merger of the NWC and the XYC in 1804–05 left the Post of Lac Ouinipique with about eighty voyageurs, each with at least one year's contract remaining, far more than were required to maintain the provisions depot at Bas de la Rivière and operate the fur trade in that only modestly productive department. As elsewhere in the NWC's operations, many clerks and voyageurs were not hired again after their contracts expired, and the Post of Lac Ouinipique was greatly scaled back over the next few years. By the season of 1808–09, when Nelson gives a list, there were twenty voyageurs and interpreters in the department, at four posts on or back of the lake, besides an unknown number at Fort Alexander itself.[79] This list is especially informative, as it mentions not only the men, but also their wives and children, if they had them, so that we have an idea of the full population at each post.

In an earlier study of a complement of voyageurs, those who staffed the NWC's English River (Churchill River) department, and its rapidly expanding offshoot, Athabasca, in 1785–86, it was noted that about half of that group formed a kind of fur trade elite. These were men who would carry great responsibility for the further growth of the company's fur trade down the Mackenzie, up the Peace River, and over the Rocky Mountains over the next twenty-five years (Duckworth 1990, xxxv–xxxvii). The voyageurs working on Lake Winnipeg in Nelson's time were nothing like that. They did not have the same opportunities – their district was fully developed, and the animals were disappearing. The main purpose of the Post of Lac Ouinipique was to preserve the provisions depot at the bottom of Winnipeg River and to maintain the dignity and respect of the NWC in the neighbourhood. Nevertheless, the voyageurs on Lake Winnipeg were still *des hommes du nord*, men who had taken the step of going so far into the Northwest from Montreal that they could not return in the same season. Once through the first winter, many of them remained in the Upper Country for years, some of them for good. Individuals managed to find meaningful lives – some had wives and children, some eventually took them back to Canada, while others settled around the Forks of the Red and the Assiniboine, or else tried to make a hunter and trapper's life as a so-called "freeman" in the woods and on the lakes of Rupert's Land.

One aspect of the NWC winterers' lives was the inexorable accumulation of debt. Some contemporary commentators remarked on this, claiming that the voyageurs were deliberately kept in debt as a form of bondage. It certainly was a truck system, with an effectively compulsory company store – in Nelson's time, the companies were the only sources of European goods in the fur country, whether they were articles of adornment like beads or items of necessity like ammunition. The companies calculated their transportation costs, marked their goods up accordingly, and probably did not care whether a winterer with a wage of 350 livres per year (about £29 Halifax currency) could actually afford to buy what he needed to court a woman, or maintain a wife and their children. A very few voyageurs managed to hunt or trap well enough, once their modest winter duties were done, to build up small credits in the NWC's account books. In this their wives were probably more important than the voyageurs themselves, for voyageurs' wives prepared food, did their share of trapping, made clothing, dressed skins for moccasins, and cut hide for babiche for netting snowshoes.

But all but the most penurious voyageurs accumulated debts. In the post-coalition list for Lake Winnipeg in 1805, wages, debts, and credits are listed for seventy-four of the men. The ratio of net debts (total debts minus total credits) to total wages for this group is 1.26, that is, the total debt owed by this group of voyageurs in 1805 was 26 percent higher than the wages they would earn in that year. Some individuals' debt exceeded four years' wages. In some cases a heavily indebted man had his entire debt excused in return for a special service or for signing a long contract; but there must have been many men who felt unable to retire, or considered deserting to the HBC to escape the debt.[80]

The third group of individuals with whom Nelson had dealings on Lake Winnipeg was that of the freemen. A freeman was not employed by the fur trade companies on contract, but was still in the fur country, living off the land. Most of these men had been born in Canada, and had been fur trade employees at some point, but had been laid off because they were no longer needed, and, now, with Indigenous wives and mixed-race children, had decided not to return to their former lives in Canada. That staying in the fur country was a deliberate decision is shown in a few cases where a man went down to Lower Canada with his family, but later returned to the Upper Country.[81] The extensive layoffs of superfluous men, following the amalgamation of the NWC with the XYC in 1805, were probably a major source of these freemen. Their children, coming of age in the next decade of the century, would have been an important component of the emerging Métis nation.

The freeman who figures most prominently in the Nelson Journals was Charles Racette. Nelson first mentioned him at Dauphin River, where he and his family intended to winter, in the fall of 1807. There were frequent encounters after that. Racette's complicated career can be traced back to the 1780s.[82] He had a son named George, born at Lake Winnipeg about 1809, and it is tempting to guess that the boy's name, almost unheard of in the francophone population of Canada at the time, was given in honour of George Nelson. Nelson was always conscious of how thin the Racette family's resources seemed to be, and worried that they would starve to death. But Racette was living a life that was modelled mostly on the Ojibwe trading culture. He and his family trapped and traded furs, made nets that they could sell, and did other things to keep themselves in ammunition and the European goods they wanted, or even provisions if necessary. A freeman like Racette, true to this lifestyle, never settled down for long in one place. In the spring, when food was scarce and hunting difficult, a family like this kept near enough to the trading posts to be able to deal with emergencies.

There were a number of freemen and their families in the Red and Assiniboine River valleys by February 1814, when the HBC clerk and surveyor, Peter Fidler, attempted a census. He counted 42 households at Red River, 8 at Fort Qu'Appelle, and 10 at Swan River, for a total of 55 men, 45 women, and 128 children. Many of the families counted at Red River may have already been settled around the Forks of the Red and Assiniboine, on farms laid out as river lots, on the model used in Lower Canada.[83] Fidler's Census did not extend to the Métis community at Pembina, or to other freemen, such as Charles Racette, of whom he did not have detailed personal knowledge. How many there were cannot be stated with confidence, but Nelson encountered a few at different places around Lake Winnipeg from time to time. Their numbers were probably gradually increasing; Nelson met three different freemen, Lemire, Martin, and Montreuil, all "old" in his eyes, between Grand Rapids and Lac Bourbon in September 1819.

CHOICE OF MATERIALS PRINTED, AND EDITORIAL METHOD

George Nelson's writings are worthy of a wide audience not just for their factual content – though that is considerable and in some respects unique in Canadian fur trade literature – but also because of his empathy with those he met, and because of the intensely personal way in which he wrote. He is an appealing writer, but for an editor his work presents challenges. Working with Nelson's material for a long time it is all too easy to get caught up in his feelings, and sense the material pulling towards another book, in which Nelson's spiritual journey would be the central theme. What is needed is a solid framework, and that is what the Lake Winnipeg journals provide.

The decision taken here is to print the Lake Winnipeg journals in their entirety, and to fit some portions of Nelson's other writings into this structure, where they add new information about his fur trade activities. Passages from the *Sorel Journal* and the *Reminiscences* have therefore been used, but only when they fill in gaps left by the journals themselves. Nelson's seven long letters to his family in 1811–12, although they are almost his only surviving writings from that season, have not been printed; one short passage describing agriculture at Fort Alexander is the exception. Most of their contents do not concern the fur trade, but rather express the writer's general musings on life and his place in it. Nelson's journals kept in the Pic department during parts of the years 1813, 1815, and 1816 are also not printed here, coming as they do from a different part of the fur country. For the same reason, the journal written in Nelson's cipher in 1821, from Moose Lake and Cumberland House, has not been included here.

Last, there is the "Canoe Journal" of 1822. Only a part of it concerns Lake Winnipeg, but that entire journal has been printed, in light of its general interest as an original account of the old canoe route between Cumberland House and Fort William, just as it was passing from highway to byway, a sort of US Route 66 of its day.

As with most handwritten fur trade documents of this period, Nelson's journals are easy to read, with few illegible words or phrases, but they are full of spelling errors, idiosyncratic punctuation, inconsistent capitalization, and words or phrases omitted, duplicated, crossed out, or interlined. The *Reminiscences* are much cleaner, though they still have some of these features. The texts printed here have been edited to place insertions in the main text, and remove omissions, when it is clear what Nelson intended to write. The misspellings and punctuation have been retained, as they help to give the flavour of the documents. Among the words that Nelson consistently misspelled are "ammonition," "eaquel," "extreemely," "intirely," "knews" [news], "pikeral" [pickerel], "pritty" (a favourite adverb), "seperate," and "slay" [sleigh]. The daily entries in Nelson's journals are short, but the passages printed here from his longer writings sometimes contain very long paragraphs. In editing these passages I have introduced some new paragraphs: following the editorial method used by Moreau (2009), in his edition of David Thompson's writings. These new paragraphs are marked with the symbol ¶. Missing words, if needed for understanding the text, have been supplied in square brackets. Unusual words that may be unfamiliar to some readers, and some subjects (dogs, boats) that seem to require a special note, are marked with an asterisk*, showing that a definition is given in the glossary (Appendix A). Here, I follow Warkentin (2012, 2014) in her recent edition of Radisson's writings.

The journals mention many individuals – the Indigenous people with whom Nelson dealt, the voyageurs under his command, the clerks and partners of the NWC, a few freemen, and an occasional HBC servant whom he met or heard of. Notes on the Indigenous people appear in Appendix B; the voyageurs in Appendix C; and NWC clerks and partners, and the free-men, in Appendix D. Gathering information for Appendix B about the Indigenous people in Nelson's writings has been difficult, not only because few traders were as careful as Nelson in naming and describing them, but because the names used in the journals are usually nicknames conferred by the traders at particular posts and at particular times. Thus, though some of these individuals may be mentioned in other journals, the names used there may be different. Further research is still needed.

There is little published information about individual voyageurs, but many of them served in the NWC during the period 1811–21, for which a Grand Ledger of mens' accounts is preserved (HBCA, F.4/32). This account book has been used in Appendix C, with other sources as available, to provide an outline of the career of each Lake Winnipeg voyageur. For many of the NWC clerks and partners, there is much published information, and appropriate references are given in Appendix D where available.

Nelson's journals use many place names; in many cases these are the earliest recorded examples. Some remain on the modern map, but many do not. Some are remnants of the old culture of the NWC voyageurs that has passed away, and some are adaptations of original Cree or Ojibwe names. All of Nelson's place names are listed in Appendix E, and have been located where possible on the modern map. Of partic-ular interest are the traders' names for landmarks along the canoe and snowshoe routes between Nelson's posts at Rivière-aux-Morts, Lac du Bonnet, Dauphin River and Tête-au-Brochet, and the other posts around Lake Winnipeg. In a few cases the identification remains uncertain, even though recourse has been had to many other documents and early maps. The results are shown on the series of maps.

Throughout the text, the abbreviations HBC, NWC, and XYC mean Hudson's Bay Company, North West Company, and XY Company, respectively.

NOTES

1 The original contract is illustrated by Peers and Schenck 2002, 6–7.
2 For Nelson's writings on his experiences in the Folle Avoine district, see Peers and Schenck 2002.
3 For details of Nelson's account with the NWC, see his entry in Appendix D. His contract with the NWC to return to the Northwest, dated 8 May 1818, is Beek Repertoire, ANQ-M, Document No. 2321.

4 For marriage in the fur trade "after the custom of the country," which evolved out of Indigenous marriage practices, see Van Kirk 1980, 28–52.

5 Jennifer Brown (2017a) gives a full discussion of the nature and legality of the so-called country marriages, centring her study on George Nelson's two marriages and his attitudes to them.

6 Entries in parish register of Christ Church (Anglican), William Henry or Sorel, accessed as images from the Drouin Collection of Quebec church registers, at ancestry.com.

7 The fur traders used "Canadian" to mean men from the French-speaking community of Lower Canada (present-day Quebec). Most NWC voyageurs were Canadians in Nelson's time, though Métis were also hired, as that part of the Northwest population grew.

8 Words marked with an asterisk are defined in the glossary, Appendix A.

9 This document has been edited by Brown and Brightman 1988, under the title "The Orders of the Dreamed."

10 For physical descriptions of particular journals, see the introductory paragraphs to each journal in the main text.

11 For Radway, see www.the-kirbys.org.uk/gen/Places/Quenington/ QueningtonPapermill.html, accessed 1 October 2018; and references cited there. Some pages of the earliest of Nelson's journals, kept in the Folle Avoine department in 1803–04, also show the Britannia watermark. As Nelson was working for the XY Company in that season, it appears that the NWC was not the only fur trader using Radway's paper in Nelson's time.

12 Although Nelson says that the following three pages were badly blotted, they are blank and unblotted in the copy of Part 5 that we have, so some additional recopying has taken place.

13 The fact that the three known parts of the *Reminiscences* are all on the same distinctive grey paper, 26 cm x 20 cm, in gatherings of 24 sheets (48 pages), should make the missing parts easier to recognize, if they still exist somewhere.

14 MacMillan 2009, 146. Apart from the manuscripts themselves, the Nelson Fonds at the Toronto Reference Library include duplicate typed copies of a few of the items. A pencil note on the first page of one of the 1819 Journals, that which Nelson entitled "Journal B," reads "typed copy of this diary made July 1933." Whether all the copies were made at the same time is unknown (they are not dated), but the pencil note suggests that the Nelson papers were being evaluated for possible publication in 1933. This was the time when W. Stewart Wallace, Librarian at the University of Toronto, was assembling his *Documents Relating to the North West Company* for the Champlain Society (1934), and it is possible that he had

the transcripts made, but none of the material was used or referred to in that publication.

15 John Macdonell's Journal, Assiniboine and Fort Qu'Appelle [McGill University, MFTP #0007], entries of 11 January, 5 February 1794.

16 Words marked with asterisks are explained in the glossary, in Appendix A, pages 347ff.

17 Wentzel to McKenzie, 28 February 1814, in Masson 1960, 1:110–11.

18 Wallace 1934, 480-1, has a biographical note on Archibald Norman McLeod.

19 A copy of this circular is in the Masson Collection at McGill, MFTP #0001.

20 The edition used for this volume is Masson 1960.

21 Among the most important Masson manuscripts now missing are the NWC Agreements of 1802 and 1804. Wallace (1934), 108n, 143n, reprinted these in 1934 from Masson's edition of 1889–90, stating that he had been unable to discover where the originals were. They have not re-emerged since.

22 Major collections of journals were edited by Masson 1960 (greatly abridged); Gates 1965; and Keith 2001. Individual journals were edited by Birk 1989 (John Sayer's Snake River Post journal of 1803–04); Gough 1988 and 1992 (Alexander Henry's journal at Pembina, on the Saskatchewan, and at the Columbia, 1799–1814 – the earlier edition by Coues [1965], which is heavily annotated, is still useful); Hickerson 1959 (Charles Chaboillez's Pembina journal of 1797–98); Douglas 1929 (Edward Umfreville's exploration of a route from Lake Nipigon to the Winnipeg River in 1784); Duckworth 1990 (Cuthbert Grant's journal at Athabasca in spring 1786); and Morton 1929 (Duncan McGillivray's Saskatchewan River journal of 1794–95). McGill University Libraries, Rare Books and Special Collections, has provided an excellent web edition of the journals in its possession, with transcripts, at the website http://digital.library.mcgill.ca/nwc/.

23 For this journal, see the extracts printed by Masson 1960, 2:371–99, and the full set of scans and transcript at the McGill University website.

24 For Nelson's attitudes to the environment in which he found himself in the Northwest, see Van Kirk 1988.

25 Another fur trader who wrote about superstitious experiences in a matter-of-fact way was the NWC partner John McDonald of Garth; see his "Reminiscences" (written for his own purposes), for instance his story of James King's daughter's premonition of her father's death (Masson 1960, 2:25–6).

26 Morse 1979, 90; Alexander Henry, from Vermillion Fort (on the Saskatchewan) to Duncan Cameron, 1 February 1809 (Selkirk Papers, 8835–9).

27 Data from Nelson Journal 1818–19, entries of 15 February and 18 March
   1819. The voyageur's league was generally supposed to be 3 miles (about 5
   kilometres), though David Thompson, who had a professional interest in
   accurate distances, considered it to be less (Moreau 2009, 172).

28 For descriptions of the Indigenous people with whom Nelson traded, see
   Brown 1985a; and Peers 1994, 79–88. John Tanner, the American who was
   kidnapped as a boy from his parents' homestead on the Ohio River, and
   spent about twenty-five years with a band of Ottawas in what is now
   southern Manitoba and northwest Ontario, gives a vivid account of their
   nomadic life and movements with the seasons (James 1956).

29 Angus Shaw to Roderick McKenzie, 16 December 1789, in Masson 1960,
   1:32.

30 For Lesieur, see Duckworth 1990, 156–8. For his partner Simon Fraser
   (not the well-known explorer of Fraser River), see Wallace's classic article,
   "Simon Fraser of Ste Anne's" (Wallace 1954, 44–54).

31 Lamb 1970, 448; John Macdonell journal, in Gates 1965, 107.

32 Macdonnell in 1793 said that "point au F—e" was the men's name for the
   site of the old French fort, near the foot of the last rapid and on the opposite side of the river from the NWC fort (Gates 1965, 107). Nelson, Journal
   1807–08, under date 20 August 1808, mentions Point-aû-Foutre [sic] as an
   upstream landmark, visible from the NWC fort.

33 HBCA, B.166/a/1, entries of 11 November 1793, 2 February 1794;
   B.166/a/2, entries of 24 June, 19 August 1794; B.4/a/1, entry of 28
   September 1795; B.236/a/1, entries of 9 September 1796, 23 January 1797.
   The "Canadian" master at Bas de la Rivière in 1795–96, "Guiet"
   [Goyette?], who had been in charge of a post at Portage de l'Île the previ-
   ous season (HBCA, B.166/a/3), must have been a clerk working for Fraser
   & Lesieur.

34 HBCA, B.30/a/6, entry of 28 May 1795.

35 HBCA, F.3/1, fo. 204; Beek Repertoire, ANQ-M, 14 January 1796.

36 See pages 40–1.

37 The DCB biography of William McKay (Allen 1987) contains little information about McKay's life as a fur trader. It is mainly concerned with his
   activities during the War of 1812. A biographical note in Appendix D in
   this volume seeks to fill in the gaps.

38 HBCA, B.254/a/1.

39 See Edward Clouston's journal at "Lake Winnipeg," HBCA, B.236/a/1.
   Clouston gives no precise information about his post, except that it was
   north of Bas de la Rivière, and about 100 miles from Pigeon River. In
   1808, Peter Fidler noted the site of a post just north of Buffalo Head (the

present Gray Point) and wrote "8 years ago Mr. Clouston from Albany wintered here" (HBCA, E.3/3, fo. 60). This must actually have been Clouston's post of 1796–97.

40 The HBC journal kept by Thomas Vincent at Bas de la Rivière in 1797–98 gives the name of the "Canadian" master as "Monsieur Le,Valett" (HBCA, B.4/a/2), that is, Gabriel Atina Laviolette. Laviolette was again in charge at Bas de la Rivière in 1798–99 (Lamb 1970, 480).

41 Nelson, *Reminiscences*, 209. Charles Grignon is presumably the man of this name who was born at Mackinac in 1779, and eventually settled at Green Bay, Wisconsin, where he died in 1846. That he spent time in the service of the XYC seems to be new information.

42 Nelson, *Reminiscences*, 204–7, 210–18, 227. John Ogilvy was one of the original partners of the XYC (Campbell 1985).

43 An anecdote in Nelson's *Sorel Journal*, printed in this volume (pages 6–7), provides the only clear evidence that it was Fraser who was in charge of the NWC's Lake Winnipeg operations during William McKay's absence in 1804–05.

44 Birk (1989) provides a map to show how the news of the NWC-XYC merger made its way beyond the Fond du Lac district. Alexander Henry, who was trading at Pembina on Red River, received the news on 1 January (Gough 1988, 167). His XYC opponent there, John Crebassa (Coues 1965, 259), who initially did not believe the news, would have contributed jointly with Henry to the express snowshoe men who took the message north to Lake Winnipeg and west to Upper Red River. According to the HBC's Peter Fidler, who wintered at Nottingham House near Fort Chipewyan in 1804–05, news of the merger reached that place on 6 May 1805 (HBCA, B.39/a/5ᵇ, fo. 51d).

45 A list of manpower in most parts of the Northwest following the merger, compiled in 1805, has four clerks and eighty engagés (voyageurs) in Lake Winnipeg, of whom fifteen, apparently, were XYC men (McGill University Libraries, Rare Books and Special Collections Division, MS 472, MSS 2357.31).

46 This journal, which runs from 13 September 1805 to 14 June 1806 and is unsigned, is part of the Masson Collection at LAC, MG 19 C1, vol. 9. Various researchers have realized that the author must be William McKay. Lindsay and Brown 2010, Appendix D, provide a full transcript of this journal.

47 Broken River or Rivière Cassé, frequently mentioned in Nelson's journals, is now called Rice River: see Appendix E.

48 Nelson recorded the clerks and the arrangements for the six posts around the lake in his journal under the date 3 January 1806. McKay's own

journal confirms that Venables was at Pike River, and places McPhail at Poplar River; thus, McPhail's post of Lac la Folle Avoine (Wild Rice Lake) must have been somewhere up Poplar River.

49 For all of these clerks, see Appendix D.

50 See Lytwyn 1986, 103–11, for a detailed account of the activities of the Albany-based HBC traders in this period, drawn from their own journals. The HBC traders at York Factory were much slower than the Albany men to send outfits to Lake Winnipeg. Finally, in 1807, Donald Sutherland, from York Factory, established a post near the mouth of Big Black River, on the east shore of the north basin of the Lake, where he stayed four seasons; while Alexander Kennedy, also from York, built one on Drunken Lake (now Wrong Lake), well up the Poplar River, where he came into contact with the Albany traders. See Sutherland's map in his Berens River district report (HBCA, oB.16/e/2, fos. 3d–4).

51 For the rest of Alexander McKay's career, which took him to the Pacific Northwest, see Morrison 1983a.

52 For a biography, see Brown 1988.

53 Cameron is a prominent figure in the journals kept by the HBC traders at Osnaburgh House and the posts dependent on it, and much of our knowledge of his career before 1807, when he left Nipigon country, comes from those journals. Lytwyn 1986, 60–3, 67, is an excellent source for Cameron's years in Nipigon.

54 Cameron's activities in 1795–96 may be traced in the journals of the HBC trader John Best, who wintered at the mouth of Bloodvein River in 1794–95, and at the mouth of the Dauphin River, on the west shore of Lake Winnipeg in 1795–96 (HBCA, B.254/a/1, B.51/a/1). See also Duckworth 1983.

55 Minutes of Fort William partners' meeting, 24 July 1809 (Wallace 1934, 257). Lytwyn 1986, 121, states that Cameron planned the retrenchment of his department, but the Fort William minutes do not state this. The fact that he did not implement the plans exactly as the partners specified suggests that they were imposed on him.

56 Nelson Journals, 2 September 1809; Wallace 1934, 265.

57 McLoughlin at Lac la Pluie, 15 February 1815, to [John] Dougald Cameron Esq. at Fort Alexander (Selkirk Papers, 8616–19).

58 I am indebted to Jennifer Brown for identifying and explaining the Ojibwe words *O-gi-ma* and *Shag-ga-nash-ens*. For the £100 fine, see Wallace 1934, 211, 262.

59 Nelson journal, 7 April 1810. The very brief minutes of the Fort William meeting of 1810 do not mention any negotiations with Cameron, who was assigned to Lake Winnipeg as usual (Wallace 1934, 264–5).

60 The name of Cameron's wife during his years in Nipigon may have been
    Charlotte (see Ranald Cameron to John Cameron, 10 July 1801, Selkirk
    Papers, vol. 29, 8879–80). Why her relationship with Duncan Cameron
    ended is unknown. Perhaps she died. It would have been unusual for
    Cameron to have two wives à la façon du pays at the same time.

61 For Lorrin and his children, see Appendix D.

62 The story of the early years of the Red River Colony, and the Nor'Westers'
    tactics in trying to eliminate it, has been told many times. Two classic
    accounts are Morton 1973, 537–600; and Rich 1959, 317–32; a recent
    telling is Bumsted 2003.

63 For his biography, see Van Kirk 1985. There are copies of many letters
    between Duncan Cameron and John Dougald Cameron in the Selkirk
    Papers. Also in the collection is a letter to John Dougald Cameron from
    William McGillivray, Fort William 20 July 1811, in which McGillivray
    gives instructions for the conduct of the Lake Winnipeg department, noting
    that it had lost "upwards of £800 Currency" the previous year. This letter
    contains the promise that Cameron would be made a partner in 1814
    (Selkirk Papers, 9168–9).

64 The NWC operated a post at Tête-au-Brochet in 1814–15, besides the depot
    at Fort Alexander (Lytwyn 1986, 141).

65 For cases of the apparent transfer of Lake Winnipeg men, or at least their
    accounts, to the Red River department in 1816–17, and then back, see the
    entries for Antoine Lambert, Louis Potvin, and Jean-Baptiste Welles in
    Appendix C; and the entry for John Crebassa, in Appendix D.

66 For his biography, see Brown 1983.

67 Beek Repertoire, ANQ-M, Document No. 1559: Duncan McDougall hired
    on 29 May 1801 as a clerk in the Northwest trade.

68 John Crebassa, the NWC's most experienced clerk on Lake Winnipeg, oper-
    ated the post at Tête-au-Brochet in 1819–20 (HBCA, B.51/e/1, fo. 17v).

69 For the individual Indigenous people mentioned in the Nelson Journals, see
    Appendix B; and for a general account of the Ojibwe of the Manitoba
    Interlake region, based in large part on Nelson's writings, see Peers 1994,
    79–85.

70 HBCA, B.51/e/1, fo. 17v.

71 Nelson, *Reminiscences*, 228. This revealing remark shows the importance
    of warlike deeds as a source of respect or prestige among men in Ojibwe
    society.

72 In his journal entry for 15 December 1818, Nelson mentioned that he had
    once had a post at Pigeon River. He did not give the dates, but the only
    season unaccounted for is 1812–13. The baptismal record for Nelson's

daughter Anne, recorded in the Anglican register of Christ Church, William Henry, on 17 April 1819, states that she was "born on the eighteenth of March One thousand eight hundred & thirteen at Pigeon River on Lake Winnipic." This confirms Nelson's whereabouts in 1812–13.

73 George Nelson, of William Henry, signed a contract with the NWC at Montreal on 8 May 1818, to serve for two years as a clerk "in the Dependancies of the North West," before the notary John Gerbrand Beek. His salary was to be £125, and he received an advance of £110, which, no doubt, was left with his family towards their maintenance during his absence.

74 HBCA, B.51/e/1, fo. 17v.

75 Hackett 2002, 136ff., points out that the frequency of epidemics in this part of the fur country greatly increased after 1819, with simultaneous epidemics of measles and whooping cough in 1819–20. He presents evidence that the diseases came into the region by way of Lake Superior and the east, and also perhaps overland from the Mississippi. Measles, he believed, came in with the NWC brigades of 1819, though they managed to convince some Indigenous people that it was the HBC who had brought it in. Nelson's opinion that the Red River Colony was responsible was perhaps a version of this story.

76 This is illustrated by Nelson's reaction to the company's decision not to leave the command of Fort Alexander in the hands of the apprentice clerk, Roderick McKenzie, who, as Nelson noted, "is a brulée & appeared to me to be a fine young man, & his men say the same," after the death of the bourgeois Duncan McDougall [journal entry of 7 December 1818]. In fact, there were other reasons for replacing McKenzie – he was inexperienced compared with Charles Hesse, who was sent to take over, and he had been conducting an affair with the wife of an absent voyageur – but Nelson's suspicions about the growing institutional prejudice towards the Métis were correct.

77 Printed in Williams 1975, 151–236. Glyndwr Williams, the editor, points out Simpson's attitude to "halfbreeds" on page 163, and the text itself gives several examples.

78 For the last four years of Nelson's career in the Northwest, and in particular his final season at Lac la Ronge, see Brown and Brightman 1988, 14–20.

79 For notes on all voyageurs mentioned in the Nelson Journals, see Appendix C.

80 A number of voyageurs retired from the trade, still carrying considerable debt. According to some accounts in HBCA, F.4/32, such a man signed a

"note of hand" (an IOU) to acknowledge the debt. It was probably just a formality, and I know of no evidence that the NWC ever pursued a man to collect this debt, once he was back in Canada.

81 Examples include Louis Périgny (who returned to the Northwest as a free buffalo hunter) and Louis Ménéclier (whose children were baptized in Canada before he settled at Sault Ste Marie): see notes on these two men in Appendix D.

82 See entry for this man in Appendix D.

83 HBCA, B.235/a/3, fo. 29d. Fidler's census is one of the earliest written documents that gives any detail about the important Métis communities in southern Manitoba and Saskatchewan. It is generally believed that some Métis families were settled around the Forks of the Red before the establishment of Lord Selkirk's colony in 1812, but documentation is scarce.

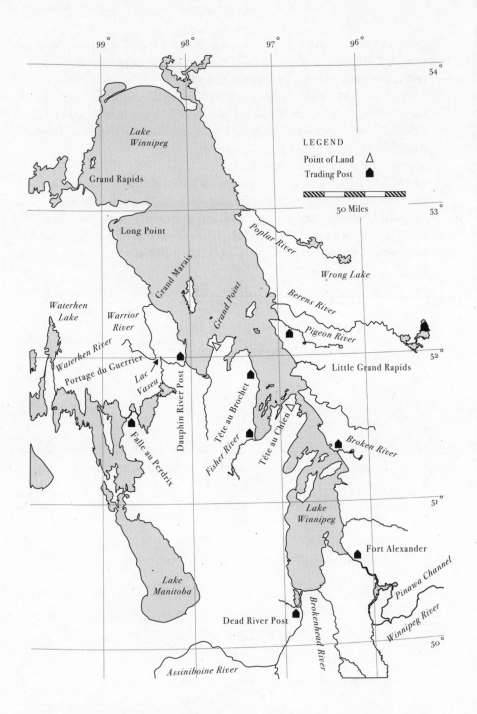

Map 3 George Nelson's Lake Winnipeg, 1804–1819.

The Lake Winnipeg
Journals

Journal.

The Commencement of this journal will be very incorrect; because the explosion, or rather that accident which unfortunately happened at Tête-au Chien had so stupefied me, as well as a very sore hand that I had, intirely prevented me keeping any exact account of our march, or voyage till a little after our arrival at rivière Dauphine;— however I recollect our encampment.

After our departure from Tête-au Chien with Mr. Ducan Cameron, and Mr. Alexr. McDonell (the day and date I do not recollect;) but being two invalids each in our own canoe we encamped in the Isle à Bërië early enough to have time to gather Vine for our burns: We were here detained one day by the wind; after-which we proceeded to the Tête-au-brochet where we remained for five or six days Constantly wind bound; at last we set off again but were soon obliged to put in near the Point à la Framboise on account of the wind & rain: after having passed another day here on account of the very high wind

First page of George Nelson's 1807 journal, kept at Dauphin River. For the text of this journal see page 61.

I

Extract from *Sorel Journal*, 1804–1805

George Nelson came to Lake Winnipeg in the season of 1804–05, still working for the XYC, but we have no actual journal from him until the next season, after the amalgamation with the NWC. The earlier of the two memoirs of his fur trade career, however, the so-called *Sorel Journal*,[1] has an excellent narrative account of his experiences in 1804–05, and that passage is the first document presented here. The *Sorel Journal* consists of eighty numbered pages, in two gatherings of forty pages each. The first was created by folding large sheets in half and nesting them to form a booklet; each page is 30 cm high x 20 cm wide. The second gathering is a stack of twenty flat sheets, 32 cm high x 21 cm wide. All pages are covered with writing on both sides. The pages in the gatherings have not been fastened together, but all leaves are present. Page 80 ends in mid-sentence, however, so the document must have continued beyond this, though no additional part has been found.

The *Sorel Journal* begins as a diary with an entry dated at Sorel (also known as William Henry), Lower Canada, where Nelson was living, on 1 December 1825. It is not a daily journal, but records local events that Nelson found significant, or items relevant to his rather unsuccessful business ventures. The entries frequently deviate into recollections of other incidents, or even into general musings on human nature. Details about Nelson's fur trade life occasionally appear. There is a description of his departure from Montreal for the Upper Country in 1802, triggered by his realization, on 3 May 1836, that this was the thirty-fourth anniversary of that event. There is also an account of his departure from Grand Portage for his first wintering season, again entered under its

---

1 Brown and Brightman (1988) cite this as "unpublished Reminiscences, 1825ff."

thirty-fourth anniversary, 13 September 1836. The exactness with which he identified these anniversaries surely indicates that he had written records to consult, although their whereabouts are unknown.

Writing the entry of 13 September 1836 finally stimulated Nelson to begin the story of his fur trade career in earnest. From this point, the *Sorel Journal* is largely a memoir of that phase of his life. This first attempt is poorly organized, and is interrupted from time to time by recollections of episodes from other years. Following the account of the first season, the *Sorel Journal* has a few more diary entries before Nelson returns to an account of his second fur-trading year. This format continues through that season, in considerable detail, and then goes on to his first season at Lake Winnipeg. Peers and Schenck (2002) published some passages from the *Sorel Journal* to flesh out Nelson's Folle Avoine journal of 1803–04.

The *Sorel Journal* carries on with its narrative till the start of the season of 1809–10, when, as already stated, it stops abruptly in mid-sentence.

Nelson's first season in Lake Winnipeg, 1804–05, was his third working for the XYC. The bitter competition with the NWC was continuing. Nelson was spared the worst of it: he was sent to operate a post a few miles up the Red River, where his NWC opponent, Louis Dorion, was a peaceful man and provoked no confrontations. Nelson had constant trouble, however, with an Indigenous man known as Red Bird's son-in-law, who made attempts to kill him over some grievance that Nelson did not understand. In defending himself against this man, Nelson was helped by young John Sayer, son of a NWC partner and an Ojibwe woman.

John Sayer also accompanied Nelson on a sight-seeing trip up the Red River, beyond the Forks. This gave Nelson his first and perhaps only opportunity to view the huge open space, almost completely flat and with a vast sky above it, that is the Canadian prairie. The *Sorel Journal* catches very well the experience that all the early travellers had, starting with Henry Kelsey, upon first seeing this remarkable sight. The rivers on which the canoes travelled were lined with trees and dense underbrush, screening what was beyond. It was a complete surprise when a traveller landed, pushed up the bank through the woods, and found himself staring at an open country stretching to the horizon. This section of the *Sorel Journal* is a good illustration of Nelson's occasional bursts of literary fluency and flights of fancy.

At this point in the *Sorel Journal*, Nelson proceeds to give an extended account of two linked episodes from before his time, which we know about from several other sources. His information was second-hand, but he had it from voyageurs who had been in the fur country when these events took place, and he recounts their stories in vivid language.

The first episode was an attempt made by the Indigenous people along the Assiniboine, in the spring of 1779, to overrun the fur post at Fort des Trembles.

Like the account in Alexander Mackenzie's *Voyages from Montreal*, Nelson describes the attack on Fort des Trembles as part of what was suspected to be a coordinated plan to drive the fur traders from the Northwest. The threat only ended with the smallpox epidemic that appeared soon after.[2] The Fort des Trembles attack, one of very few outright attacks on a fur trade post, was well remembered by the traders, though the names of those involved vary somewhat in the different accounts. All the accounts we have are second hand. The two traders whom Nelson names were Booty Graves and James Tute.[3] Peter Fidler, in his journal of his survey of the Assiniboine River in May 1808, gives a somewhat different account. According to him, "Messrs Bruice and Capt Tute" defended Fort des Trembles from the attack by the Assiniboines, and both later died in the smallpox epidemic.[4] The NWC clerk John Macdonell, who kept a journal of his trip up the Assiniboine in 1793, also tells the story, but says that the traders who were attacked at Fort des Trembles were Bruce and Boyer. He does not mention that either died of smallpox (Masson 1960, 1:270). For what it's worth, Bruce, Graves, and Tute all disappear from the fur trade records after 1781, the year in which smallpox tightened its grip on the Northwest. Charles Boyer survived, for he was still trading for the NWC at Athabasca in 1786, and at Lac la Pluie in the 1790s (Duckworth 1990, 138–9).

Following his account of the unsuccessful attack on Fort des Trembles, Nelson moves on to the dreadful smallpox epidemic that decimated the Indigenous population of the Prairies in 1781–83.[5] His vivid description has not yet been used by historians.

---

2 Mackenzie 1801, xiii–xiv, dates the attack to 1780, but the near-simultaneous attack of the posts on the Saskatchewan was in April 1779, as is shown by the contemporary account in Philip Turnor's journal of that season (Tyrrell 1934, 224ff.).

3 For Booty Graves, a wintering partner of Peter Pond, George McBeath, and their associates in the Northwest between 1775 and 1781 at least, see Chapin 2014, index. James Tute, an officer in Rogers' Rangers during the French and Indian War, accompanied Jonathan Carver on his explorations of 1767–68 (Parker 1976, 13–15), and then entered the Northwest fur trade (Chapin 2014, index).

4 HBCA, E.3/3, fo. 64d. "Bruice" is the fur trader William Bruce, another associate of Peter Pond; for him see Chapin 2014, index.

5 For a detailed account of the epidemic, with an emphasis on its progress in what is now northwest Ontario, see Hackett 2002, 93–118.

The section now quoted from Nelson's *Sorel Journal* begins with his arrival on Lake Winnipeg in the late summer of 1804, and follows him through the ensuing season.

... After a long & tedious route [by canoe from Grand Portage], we reached Lake Winnipick. We found a small establishment the Cº had there, in good order. Mʳ Alexʳ Campbell who was the Chief Clerk, sent Angus Bethune⁶ to the S. Side of the Lake, he himself went far into the interior on the East Side, & I was despatched to the entrance of Red River, where the indians of this place, with whom it was intended I should winter, had proposed hunting that year. What a good fortune this was! I had to remain a few days after their departure to await the arrival of Mʳ Jno: MᶜDonald⁷ with his people for the upper part of the Red Rivers. They came in due time. Here it is where I first became acquainted with Mʳ Jno: Crebassa.⁸

At this place, Bas de la Riviere Ouinipique, & entrance into that Sea [Lake Winnipeg], in the autumn of 1800, our people had set their nets about 1½ mile in the lake. The N.W. [NWC people] went one night, took their only Canoe, carried it some distance up the river, filled it with Stones & sank it. A Day or two after they went & took up the nets & carried them off, leaving our people to die or fly the place. I suppress a great many of these recitals and I have mentioned these few to shew to what extremes interest & ambition will lead men, who, in another state would shudder at such crimes. Why is this so? – are men then indeed all alike, "time & circumstances making the only difference"?

Whilst here awaiting the Red River canoes, the N.W. people, under Mʳ Alexʳ Fraser⁹ passed on their way to <u>their</u> winter quarters in this immense Lake, but the wind being high, they were obliged to put up in a small river, about a Mile from our place. I paid them a visit. They

---

6 See entry for him in Appendix D.

7 John McDonald "le Borgne" (the one-eyed), a partner with the XYC, and later with the NWC, who would have given Nelson his final instructions for the season. See Appendix D.

8 For John Crebassa see Appendix D. The section of the *Sorel Journal* omitted here consists of anecdotes told by Nelson about other people at other times. The general theme is the violence of the competition between the NWC and the XYC.

9 Alexander Fraser, partner in the NWC since about 1801 (Wallace 1934, 443–4). William McKay, the partner usually in charge of the Lake Winnipeg department for the NWC, was on leave in 1804–05 (Wallace 1934, 209), so Fraser would have been in charge for this one year.

seemed as if they could do without us, but M͏ʳ Fraser was a Gentleman. The wind falling in the night, they hurried off. The next day we returned & found a quantity of things, Blankets, knives, &c. &c. – I do not remember if we kept or returned them.

One of their Guides, Jos: Durocher, who afterwards wintered several years with me, and several other of the men, told me they were starving, at that time, hence their precipitate departure to take advantage of the calm. They did not proceed much above 30 miles when the wind rising again obliged them to put up. Being very short of provisions they went about gathering <u>mushrooms</u>! which they cooked & eat heartily. The wind fell again & off they went also, but one steered one way; one, another; some hoisted sail to go against the wind, singing, crying or laughing as their spirits were inclined. "What can be the meaning of all this? – those who were just now upbraiding the extravagancies of the others are now become much themselves!" – At last they found they were poisoned![10] They hasted to shore, & the Doctor who was with them, mixed up a quantity of powder (Gun Powder) in a Kettle full of warm water, poured it down their throats, made them <u>restitute</u>. This was something like my affair this last Spring.[11]

After a few days, every thing being ready, I set off too for my winter quarters in the Entrance of red river. This was the "land of milk & honey." But tho' I did not go so high up as the Cows & hives, yet I lived well. We took our precautions early, husbanded our fish & other provisions. On our way we killed plenty of game. We had to go about 12 or 15 miles up to build, a place more central. M͏ʳ Louis Dorion was my oponent, a quiet & decent elderly man; and we passed the winter without any broils.[12] We had however a dust in the fall with the indians, whom, in this place, I thought were worse than those I had ever seen. One of them, from mere wantonness, & without any provocation that I could assign, would assuredly have stabbed me in the back had not young Jno:

10 Wilson Brown (personal communication) suggested that the hallucinogenic mushrooms were likely the widely distributed *Amanita muscaria*.

11 The mention of a doctor may suggest that the NWC had medical expertise available in the Northwest, but it is not known who this was. Nelson's reference to "my affair this last Spring" is obscure.

12 For Dorion, see Appendix D. Alexander Henry, the younger, summarizing the trade of Red River for 1804–05, lists L. Dorion and Geo. Nelson at "Dead River," with a total yield of 16 packs between them (Coues 1965, vol. 1, 259). Dead River, or Rivière-aux-Morts, is the present Netley Creek, but Nelson's description of his post, 12 or 15 miles up Red River, suggests that he was farther south than that.

Sayre[13] perceived it & stopped him. I had many scuffles with this fellow
for some years after this. At this time, I let him pass with a warning of
what he should meet with if he dared return. A day or two after this they
were drinking upon the opposite side of the river, they took a fancy to
fire at us with ball. We heard their shots, and also the balls whiz by us;
but we supposed they were trying their Guns they had lately bought. At
last, some of the balls passing nearer than was conveniend for us, Sayre
crossed /59/ over in the midst of their balls, for they now aimed at him.
He was a young man, and a half breed. He gave them chace, beat some
of the most obstreprous & took their arms from them. They were then
quiet; but we, we had frequent squabbles with them.

Jollie, an old winterer, one of my men, went to see Mauricette, an old
acquaintance of his wintering in a Small river 6 or 7 miles below. The
Red-Bird's son in law, (& brothers) the dog who was for stabbing me,
happened to be there at the time. He got drunk; abused Jollie shame-
fully; being in opposition time, and one of their indians, Mauricette did
not like to exert his authority for fear of losing him, & without this he
would not be quiet. Taking his knife at last he made a blow at Jollie,
who, seizing an axe handle laid him senseless on the floor. Here was
an uproar, but Jollie was a man very difficult to intimidate. The indian
recovered; & with his brothers swore vengeance against us. Whether
it was really true, or merely to intimidate us, they gave out that they
would certainly revenge. We kept upon our guard. I beleive it was in
January, the three brothers came to the N.W. fort. They got some rum.*
They stoppd at our house, only 60 yards off, & at last asked lodgings.
I allowed them to remain, but warned them of the consequences if they
should attempt to injure us; and that they should not drink. We kept up
our guard, slept but turn about. They continued increasing more drunk,
tho' we could not observe how they became so; for tho' they went out
often, yet they remained but a short out & returned; we could observe
no liquor. I at last fell asleep. I awoke in the night and found my men
quite Jolly & the indians thoughtful & quiet. I was afraid they had
got into the shop & taken of my rum. "How comes this about?" They
replied that being at a loss to account for the indians becoming more &
more drunk Jollie, at last found they had hid a small Keg of rum near
the house where they helped themselves every time they went out! "as
they do design us mischief, I was resolved to be square with them, so I
helped myself to a dram, & told the others - they followed my example.

13 See Appendix D.

We drank as much as we thought was good for us, & after that p ..... d [pissed] their Keg full! now let them go & drink"!!!- I was alarmed a little, but for the life of me I could not help laughing. The indians after this behaved very well, & went away in the morning with their half rum & half ..... [piss] – They did not molest us for the remainder of the winter; but I had frequent squabbles in after years with this dog. A tragi-comic story with this fellow I will relate in its place.[14]

In the autumn I went frequently a hunting to the entrance of the river where there was an astonishing quantity of ducks & geese,* swans & Cranes. Sayre & I took an excursion in the early part of the fall to the Forks, where the Church now is, & beyond.[15] I was delighted with the beauty of the place. The wonderful calm & stillness of the country contributed not a little, to my ideas of beauty. The leaves were yet mostly upon the trees and cast a most delightful shade upon the water & in the low Points. This was greatly increased, in my opinion, by the naked banks in the bottom of the bends of the river, where the <u>plains</u> commence. It was a contrast. We met nothing worth /60/ mentioning on our way up. We passed by some few old houses, the first settlements ever made by the white[s] in these parts about 30 years before.[16] With these old buildings were connected Stories worthy of the Pen of Gibbon. I have now but a confused recollection of some of them related to me by the Persons who acted their Parts, & who, being men yet in the flower of their age, plainly told that the first arrival of the white there, could not be very remote, & their reports given at various periods agreeing so well in all particulars seemed also to attest the truth.[17]

¶Here, the Country being as it were an Elysium, the natives <u>very</u> numerous, independant & warlike, with every thing, they, in their Simple state, could wish or desire to render them happy in the fullest sense

---

14 This anecdote, if it is among Nelson's surviving writings, has not been identified.

15 The famous Forks of the Red and the Assiniboine, where Lord Selkirk's colony was established in the years after 1812. There was no church at Red River in 1804, so Nelson must mean the Catholic mission church, established in 1817, the first building for Christian worship in western Canada.

16 By "old houses" and "settlements" Nelson means abandoned fur trade posts, dating from the 1760s and '70s. Other early travellers passing up the Red and Assiniboine Rivers also noted these sites, and the names of those who occupied them. See John Macdonell's journal of 1793 (Gates 1965, 109–12); and Donald Mackay's Brandon House journal, also in 1793 (HBCA, B.22/a/1, 18 & 23 September 1793).

17 The name of Edward Gibbon, the eloquent historian of the decline and fall of the Roman Empire, would have been familiar to all English contemporaries when Nelson wrote. The reference does not necessarily mean that Nelson had read Gibbon himself.

of the word, they could not but view with distrust the arrival of such
a people as we, among them – their contrary, or counter part, or very
oppisites indeed, in every sense. This, it seems from their mythological
tales, had been foretold them. The old among them beleived, & were
sure of the truth & certainty of the Prophecy, & dreaded the fulfillment
of it: the young, too gay, haughty & independant heeded not. Trusting to
their numbers & their warlike dispositions, they despised a few weake
& scattered individuals, whose very food depended upon their charity
as it were, & whom they were sure of destroying when they pleased.
The numerous serious & frightful obstructions in the way to their lands,
from the narrow tortuous rivers in one place & the dreadful cataracts
& falls of water agitated almost to fury in numerous other parts: these
were so many causes to insure them as it were, of their independence.
Therefore they hesitated not tasting of the forbidden, being resolved
when, so disposed, to turn out the intruders! alas! what an error! The
old, harranged & bewailed the destruction of their race & Country – the
young went heedlessly on with the course of the times.

¶At last they resolved upon a decisive blow, to exterminate every
white in their extensive Country, and the skirmishes began accordingly.
A few old women, in whose tender & affectionate breast (for women
are lovely still all the world over) still lurked compassion, for the mothers of those destined to be the sacrifice they gave private intimation
of the secret decisions of their people. Among the number of Traders
there, were two military officers, Messrs: Graves & Tutt.[18] They forti-
fied themselves in the best manner they could, resolved to sell their lives
at the highest price. Several assaults took place, in which, though things
remained in Statu-quo as it were, the poor natives were still the losers.
All that disappointment, cunning, rage, despair & treachery could suggest, was determined upon, & a grand coup-de-main was to be given in
the spring. Division of counsel entered in their assemblies & delibera-
tions, and debauchery & drunkenness among the white.

¶Their fate, it seems however, had been decided in a higher tribunal,
where the motives are inscrutable to man! The small Pox declared
among them – thousands fell victims to this dreadful disease. Despair
seized them – they fled in every direction, abandoning or slaying, with
an arrow or two, or by any other means their nearest and dearest
relatives in the utmost consternation & despair. They concluded this

18 For different accounts of the attack on Fort des Trembles, and the traders involved, see
the Introduction to this journal, on page 5.

at first to have been introduced purposely by the white, with their magical powers, as they thought. But when they saw some of the leading men among them, Graves & Tutt, fall, they concluded it to be the will of the Supreme Being, though many thought it to be the workings & machinations of the inferior, but malignant Spirits that have an ill will to man, & who so artfully lead him to his ruin, & finally to his destruction, with his eyes open to the danger, yet going on, not well knowing wherefore, but merely from the impulse! The poor Creatures became so /61/ thinned, & of course humbled; & resumed their natural hospitality, even to those they could look upon in no other view than intruders. They very frequently cast this reproach in my teeth. Richard, Durocher & Lorrain,[19] who, in different & distant places, were passing that winter in camp with the indians, related to me stories sickening to the heart. Every other passion had given way to despair; & when they saw one of the relatives, a wife or a Child (& their affection to their children is passed into a Proverb) with the face red, from exertion or other cause; or pale, conceived them to be seized by this dreadful disease, they would utter the well known exclamations of tec-waye! haie! haie![20] Seize an arrow & drive it through the heart of the supposed diseased! and well it was, if the impulse of their despair stopped here.

¶Durocher who was then with some indians in Fort des Prairies,[21] told me that after 3 or 4 different indians with whom he was then living, dying one after the other, he was at last taken up by another who had 2 wives & I beleive three children. They had removed from the main camp. Seeing one of his wives, a fine, kind hearted young woman, with her face red from the exertion in collecting & carrying home a load of wood, observed her face through one of the holes of the lodge, to be red, he concluded she had the fever & shot an arrow through her heart! She gave a shrieke & expired. He done the same to his other wife & children after kissing the little ones, who did not even raise their heads,

19 François Richard, senior; Joseph Durocher; and Joseph Lorrin. All three were experienced men in the Lake Winnipeg department while Nelson was there, and they were probably Nelson's sources of the anecdotes about the previous twenty or thirty years of the Northwest fur trade. For notes on them see Appendix C (Durocher) and D (Lorrin and Richard).
20 Raymond De Mallie has identified the phrase as Lakota or Dakota (Sioux), and renders it T?ewáye! Hayé! Hayé!, to be translated as "I cause myself to die. So be it" (email to Jennifer Brown, 11 October 2011). Brown comments that it is remarkable that Nelson wrote down this Sioux phrase as accurately as he did, at third hand, for Nelson had little contact with Lakota speakers, and knew little or nothing of the language.
21 Not a specific post, but the Canadian traders' term for the whole of the Saskatchewan River valley.

or in any wise attempt to avert their fate! This was done so suddenly that poor Durocher, who was then a young man "had hardly time to stare." He wanted to fly, but the poor creature told him : "dont be afraid Frenchman! I have taken you into my lodge & I will not hurt you; but do not despise me nor my family after we are all dead! I see that we also are marked out as victims! Why should I allow them to linger & suffer under that loathesome distemper?" Inspite of the remonstrances of D. who became then re-assured, the poor creature bruised a flint into a very coarse powder & drank it down! He then eat tobacco, & drank a strong decoction of it, to produce vomiting, hoping by the exertions of heaving to die the sooner. Retarding beyond the time he expected, he, if I remember right, thrust his knife up to the handle, under his left breast, into the heart; never uttered a groan, & hardly a sigh!

¶I had then a retentive memory, & had stored up as I thought many of these melancholly acts of despair. I have too confused a notion of them now to relate more. Yet I may remark that the ravages of this disease carried off near nineteen twentieths. Camps of 50 or 80 tents were swept clean off save 2 or 3, & never, even out of 200 tents did more than 25 or 30 Persons at most survive. But these acts of their despair, probably carried off more than the disease itself.

¶There seems something very contradictory, & absolutely irreconciliable in this report, i.e. that they should attempt to destroy the body of the White, & yet show so much kindness to a few scattered individuals. The following is the reason. The Body of their nation had decided to drive off or extirpate the white; still, there were many individuals among them; nay indeed, I may be perhaps justified in saying, all of them, had compassion on the white when they saw them scattered individually & solitary through their country. In such cases, man is always humble & submissive: his solitary & helpless position reduces him to what he should always be, & he never will be happy, nor can be so, otherwise. He then behaves with decency. The indians on the other hand are naturally charitable & compassionate, whatever our writers may please to say to the contrary. But to return to our hunting excursion:

/62/ We proceeded leisurely on, hardly meeting one duck here. Early in the afternoon of the 2ᵈ day we entered the North branch of Red River;[22] called Riviere des Assiniboans up which we proceeded perhaps

---

22 Nelson's geography is twisted around severely, so that he refers to the country north of Lake Winnipeg as east of it; and here, describes the Assiniboine River as the North branch, whereas it really comes from the west.

a mile, & hauled our Canoe up in the <u>thick</u>, <u>dense</u> branches of that river, on the East Side. What trouble we had to extricate ourselves from this place; for the soil being rich in the extreme, the brush & vines of every description grew as thick as they could stand. After a few minutes toil, on rising the 2^d bank of the river, we emerged instantaneously into an immense large open Plain! "My eyes were not big enough. My understanding, my senses, all my faculties as it were, were arrested – I was lost in amazement and admiration! The people often told me that in those plains there was [not] a single shrub of any kind to be seen, only a short grass, & islands of wood in some few places – it was so indeed. Young & thoughtless, careless & indifferent as I was to every thing at this period of my life, but the numerous beauties of nature I found on my extensive routes, yet I could not help reflecting a little, but my ideas were quite confused, my senses only acted.

¶A vast plain open, as far as the eye could extend, & to the North, far beyond the limits of that organ – the woods which skirted these two rivers meandering in beautiful irregular curves, or few Islands of beautiful woods, & a small mountain with 2 or 3 other small risings, like islands in a large Lake, an even surface, & beautiful carpeting of Grass – a silent, still, dead Calm, & a beautiful day, all these beauties so absorbed all my thoughts, that even my senses were lost in extasy. I stood rivited to my place. I could exclaim o beautiful, beautiful! what art can ever come up to nature? My companion laughed at my <u>foolishness</u>.

¶It was natural that I should enquire how this became so? A confused mumble of ancient history occurred to my mind. Carthage, Palmyra, Assyria, Babylon – those Countries of Asia once so strongly inhabited, now exhibit a picture, if travellers say true, not unlike this place, where scarcely even a solitary individual is found running over that wild & barren extent: now & the indeed, a few families perhaps & wild Arabs passing with their herds, perhaps too ignorant of the causes of their present state of their country: here also, occasionally a family of indians passing, following the herds of Buffaloe, or deer, wild, free & independent as themselves; intent upon nothing but a bare sufficiency of food & raiment, light & simple as themselves, enjoying – fully enjoying their state; they live easy, contented & happy! "But how come this so?" was perpetually recurring to my mind. In Asia, there are monuments, ruins, history to guide & lead us in our enquiries: here, there is nothing we can discover – indeed, our time being employed in the pursuits of trade & [illegible], but above all our ignorance, our complete want of information, & very limited education, conferred

[by] reading, writing & the first four rules of arithmetic, absolutely preclude us being able to ascertain anything of the causes. Still I felt a strong impression that this beautiful country had been once inhabited, but the vices & the crimes of men of [illegible] had at last destroyed the whole race, leaving not one solitary trace of their having ever existed: Perhaps beyond the flood! Such thoughts were perpetually occurring to my mind, & impressed me with melancholly. At last I moved off.

We went in the direction of the mountain.²³ Having travelled about half a mile, my companion whose mind was taken up with the chase, pointed out to me 2 or 3 large objects, as Bulls. This was another wonder to me – their immense size – we got within about ⅓ of a mile & they flew off.

We took another direction, & soon espied a very large herd of Buffalo grazing quietly on towards us. We got within 4 or 500 hundred [*sic*] yards, but they also flew off. We were in too great haste. We fired several shots but to no effect, save that of hurrying them the more, & rousing a number /63/ of Wolves, badgers, foxes & Kitts [coyotes], a small animal partaking of the fox & dog, & who set up a beautiful medley of howling & yelping. I was here, again, much astonished; up to that moment, I did not see one single object of any kind, that could denote the existence of a living animal, yet the moment we had fired, up sprang these fellows. Sayre, who had been frequently in the plains told me they kept bed generally in badger or Fox holes, or otherwise, & always kept near the Buffaloe, "you may run over the plains, said he, & not see an animal before 2 or 3 Shots in quick succession, & you'll both see them stand. They think you are shooting deer or Buffaloe."

We returned after this to our Canoe, & went home. I was highly gratified with my excursion, tho' it left an impression of melancholy, Assyria, Palmyra, &c &c bearing hard on my mind. Eight years after this, in the autumn of 1812, Capt: Miles McDonell of upper Canada, & agent for Lord Selkirk came in to Red River with [illegible] persons, to begin a Colony! What a field here for speculative reflection, if I may be allowed the expression.

23 The "small mountain" mentioned a few lines earlier. As he was on the north side of the Assiniboine, Nelson probably meant the slight rise of Stony Mountain, about 15 miles northwest of the Forks, a feature worth noting only because the rest of the country is so flat. In September 1803, while encamped at the Forks of the Red and Assiniboine, Alexander Henry, junior, "sent a hunter to Petite Montagne de Roche, who returned with the meat of four cows." This reference shows that the French equivalent of the modern name Stony Mountain was in use as early as this (Coues 1965, 224).

In the Course of the winter I received from my friend Crebassa a
Copy of a circular letter from the agents in Montreal, announcing
the union of the two Companies & the death of the Great McTavish,
a man who came to Canada poor as poverty, it is said. To procure a
lively-hood, he purchased Deer Skins & muskrats, which selling to
advantage, he increased rapidly, joined with the late Mr Jos: Frobisher,
& for the sake of harmony of Sound! got Mr Frobisher to consent that
the Concern should go by the name of McTavish, Frobisher & Co.,
instead of Frobisher McT. & Co. as it was at first. So that even harmony contributed to raise a man.[24]

¶Our opposition therefore ceased. We pursued however each our
own business, but there was no more of that acrimony & villany, that
gave way to deceit & fraud, for the remainder of the Season, & in
the spring we joined stocks. I had a visit from Bethune in the Winter,
who was a days journey from me. I also went to see him, and in the
Spring, Mr. Campbell,[25] the Chief Clerk, joined us at the mouth of Red
River. Mr. Jno McDonald[26] also, with his people, who wintered near
the Source of this river, joined us. I was many days, say 37 or 38 at
the mouth of the river, when the N.W. people joined us, we had great
amusement for several days. The Chief of which was playing at Cold
[?].[27] I here saw one Bourasat, a Scioux indian, taken under the protection of a Mr Bourasat[28] of Mackinac, whose name he took, run for
a race, many could pass him but in a streak of 8 or 10, or 15 miles,
none could come near him. Tall & thin, he ran like a Deer, & seemed
to increase in speed as he increased his distance. The Canadians too ran
uncommonly well.

24 Nelson never met Simon McTavish, the guiding genius of the North West Company, so all
his knowledge and opinion came from others. Nelson's tone is consistent with other indications that McTavish was not well liked, that he pushed himself forward, and that his success
was resented. The firm of McTavish, Frobisher & Co. was formed in 1787 at the suggestion
of Simon McTavish; the surviving correspondence at that time does not suggest that the name
first selected was "Frobisher, McT. & Co." (Wallace 1934, 75–7).
25 Alexander Campbell was the xyc's chief clerk in Lake Winnipeg, the few xyc partners
being deployed to more important departments. See Introduction for more information about
him.
26 John McDonald, "le Borgne," xyc partner, who had been in charge of Upper Red River in
this season, as Nelson mentioned in his account of the start of the season.
27 Unidentified.
28 Probably René Bourassa Laronde (1718–1792), member of a well-known family of
fur traders before and after the Conquest, but the only one who lived permanently at
Michilimackinac.

I was happy to find that my conduct of this winter was approved [illegible word].

I shall relate here how I was cured of the Propensity of Gambling. That passion was just begginning to <u>Sprout</u> in me. We would beguile our long winter evenings by playing at Cards, a Game called "La Marche." It was played by five, sometimes by three. Pack had 50 markers. I lost with some, & gained with others; upon balancing, I had something over. Pay day came. Sha… who owed me, payed in rubbish; those to whom I was indebted, <u>insisted</u> upon good stuff. I saw I could not avoid without a serious quarrel, which would end either in having my property pillaged from me, or blood shed in its defence, I preferred paying, accompanying it with remarks sentable to their conduct. I found then [?] & have had too many occasions to see that remark verified since that, men measure their character with their purse, or rather that the Purse is the measure of the honor of most men, 49 perhaps out of 50. I took a disgust to each meanness, & unto this day do I despise & pity those who can have so little regard for themselves. Is it impossible to us to be honest even? Surely there are enough of the other passions to debase & degrade our nature without this one too!

/64/ I cannot now recall any striking or particular occurrence besides those already re[told] in this winters residence. There are many trifling things indeed, some of which I must silence for decency. I had plenty of provisions, & we enjoyed peace & comfort beyond any of my two former years; but our conduct in the latter part was not what it should have been.

On our arrival at Bas de la riviere, several letters passed between the Head men of the two parties, & I was sent to the N.W. on the part of our Bourgeois.*[29] I had a fine opportunity here of making my <u>way</u>, but I had imbibed those principles of exclusiveness which are so carefully & so successfully dissiminated among the inferior Clerks & men. I thought it was manly to reply impertinantly to a civil order, because it emanated from one of our former oponents; & consequently got into some trouble, through which I worked my way however with more credit than I deserved.

I was left to pass the Summer here. A Person of the name of Perigny[30] assumed the <u>mastery</u>; because we were left both masters, but I did not chuse to wrangle, & I prefered being without charge to enjoy my liberty.

29 Nelson's bourgeois at this point was Alexander Campbell, the XYC's senior clerk at Lake Winnipeg.

30 Louis Périgny (see Appendix D) was in charge of a small post on Lac du Bonnet, with Nelson as his writer, in 1805–06; see Nelson's journal of the season, below.

Provisions were very scarce. The people of the establishment were allowed none; & being left to our own resources, which with the means afforded us, i.e. nets & lines, being very scanty, & fish* very scarce, tied down besides to a small circuit, all these things together gave me another edition of the winter 1804. We frequently would gather up the fish we found dead, floating after storms upon the water. Some of these were so far decomposed that we could hardly take them in the Canoe. Still we cooked them, and eat such parts as were not too rotten. Thus passed I another Summer.

I had an instance here of that selfishness, which is called nationality. I was the only English person there, & a Protestant. Fortunately I was not readily cowed by such folks. The would take any opportunity of humiliating me [and] insult[ing] me on account of my creed. They bore me a hearty hatred for those two qualifications. I was too young & unread to answer them by arguments; but I did so in a more effectual way. With considerable difficulty I obtained an old net. Being broken, it required mending [but] he would not allow me thread. I had to mend pieces of the old one. The mending of a net was considered a great art there, & in those times those who could do it, received something extra. Of course this also was magnified, hence they would not allow me thread. I immediately got into [difficulty?], by discovering that the meshes were all at right angles. I then asked for thread again, was refused, I robbed some first, because I was afraid of the censure of the Partners; but after that I helped myself "nolens-volens," as boys say at school. By showing, when I found them combined to humble & insult me, an insulting contempt for them, they came about again & treated me much better. But I was too generous to keep a supremacy over them and despise them longer when [?] they kept up their degrading remarks. Several months after this Perigny had no one able to mend his nets, he asked me – I did, & told him that if I were to do right, & serve him as he deserved, I should not, & in a pompous insulting manner added "I despise such conduct & those who can do so." The Hudsons Bay people passed our place on their way from Albany Factory to red River,[31] as they were always well stocked in Civilized Provisions, I bartered a Jacket & some other articles of Clothing for flour, & those dogs were base enough to mess with me.

---

31 For the first twenty years after the HBC established Brandon House on the upper Assiniboine in 1793, the post was supplied by a brigade of boats originating at Osnaburgh House on the upper Albany River. In the fall of 1805 this brigade was commanded by the HBC servant, Thomas Miller (HBCA, B.22/a/13, fo. 8v).

Sometime in September Mr Wm McKay, one of the Partners arrived with 12 or 13 Canoes, in charge of this Departement. He <u>asked</u> me if I had any objections to winter with Perigny. We went a little up river Winnipic, /65/ a short days journey from this Fort, where Mr. Chs. O. Ermatinger was left in charge. We selected a place in <u>Lac du Bonet</u> to build.

The *Sorel Journal* continues with Nelson's winter at the Lac du Bonnet post, where he shared command with Périgny. The account, as usual, is disorganized, with various extraneous anecdotes inserted as they came to Nelson's mind. In the midst of it all he writes "I have now been writing a whole week at this reminiscence with only two days interval" (*Sorel Journal*, page 65).

For 1805–06 we have Nelson's journal, written at first-hand. It is presented here.

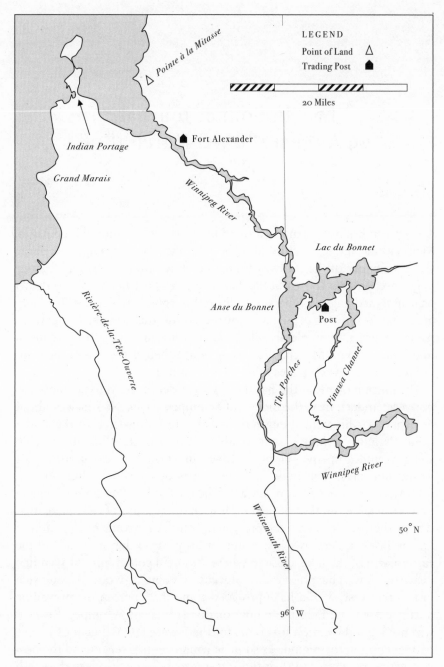

Map 4 Lac du Bonnet and the lower Winnipeg River.

2

Lac du Bonnet Journal, 29 August 1805–8 March 1806

The Lac du Bonnet journal is a small book of twelve unnumbered pages, each 33 cm high x 21 cm wide. The first and last four pages are large sheets of paper of the Radway type, folded in half, and the middle four pages are on two loose sheets. The pages are not fastened together. I have assigned page numbers for editorial purposes, which are in square brackets, to show that they are not present on the original manuscript. All the pages are completely filled with writing, and the last one ends in mid-sentence on 8 March, about two months before the end of the trading season, so several pages must have been lost.

The journal opens at the Bas de la Rivière depot (soon to be known as Fort Alexander), near the mouth of Winnipeg River. Nelson was about to depart for his winter quarters, as écrivain,* or writer, to the trader Louis Périgny. Périgny was to establish a new post at Lac du Bonnet, some 25 miles up the Winnipeg River. In normal times, another post would not have been built so close to Bas de la Rivière, but William McKay, the NWC partner in charge of the Post of Lac Ouinipique, had an unusually large number of men on his hands, because of the amalgamation of the NWC and XYC the previous winter. After some exploration of Lac du Bonnet, Périgny chose a site for his post on the south side of the eastern arm of the lake, close to where the small community of Wendigo Beach is now. The present-day Stevenson Point, a wooded peninsula just to the west, would have provided some shelter from the prevailing northwest winds. Like the whole of this stretch of Winnipeg River, it was not a good location for trade, for there were few Indigenous people permanently in the region. As soon as winter set in, Nelson and the post voyageurs spent most of their time on snowshoe expeditions to the south and east, looking for Indigenous hunting bands with whom they could trade. Because of pages missing from the end of the journal, what Nelson wrote about the spring trade, an important part of the season, is lost.

The 1805–06 season at Lac du Bonnet was not very profitable, and the bourgeois in charge of the Post of Lac Ouinipique probably did not intend to send an outfit there again. In the fall of 1807, however, the experienced HBC servant Thomas Miller, part of the Albany Factory establishment, did build a post on Lac du Bonnet, and the NWC's partners Alexander Mackay and Duncan Cameron sent their clerk, John Crebassa, to build alongside. The NWC people did their best to ruin Miller's trade, stealing his fishing nets, telling false stories about "Indian threats," stealing furs that Indigenous people owed the HBC for credit given, and at one point holding Miller captive. He was not released until he agreed to give no more liquor to his Indigenous customers, and to hand over a keg of liquor and a bale of cloth as a pledge for keeping the promise. Miller's journal of the season is in HBCA, B.103/a/1. He traded with Indigenous people from as far away as Rivière-aux-Morts near the mouth of Red River (he calls it "Nettley Creek," his spelling of the modern name), but he gives few names of the men he dealt with. None of those he mentions are recognizable among those with whom Périgny and Nelson traded in 1805–06.

/[1]/Journal for 1805. Thursday 29th August. William M[c]Kay Esq[r] having arrived the 26th of this Month from Kamanehtiequiä[1] with thirteen canoes but left two in River Ouinipique in Charge of Messrs Dominque Ducharme & Meniclier with a part of a Canoe load he left in River Blanche[2] where he had the misfortune of loosing two of his men in the /first/ rapids of that dangerous river (by the names of Sansfasson, & St Denis besides little Fran[s] Dunord in the first rapids from the New fort.)[3] and another part at L'Ense du Bonet in care of Alexis Bercier sent M[r] Perignie as master, myself, his Ecrivin* or writer

1 Kaministiquia, the NWC's great depot on Lake Superior since the move from Grand Portage in 1803. The partners named it Fort William, after William McGillivray, in 1807.
2 The Nor'westers' name for the turbulent lower part of the Winnipeg River. Ducharme himself wintered somewhere on the river itself, where Nelson visited him in March. Ménéclier's post was probably at some distance back from the river, and Ducharme lost touch with him. For Dominique Ducharme and Louis Ménéclier see Appendix D.
3 François Dunord evidently had died in an accident earlier in the trip, soon after McKay's brigade had set off from the "New Fort" on Lake Superior.

& five men by the names of Fertin, Lonquetin (or Gerome), Pinault, J
Bpt Welles, & Sam Welles a Negro we encamped in beautiful & early
enough in the day above the Terre Blanche to set two small nets.

Friday 30th. We embarked pritty early this morning & about noon we
arrived at L'Ense du Bonet where we found Bercier with the Goods.[4]
We emcamp here. At Sun set we put out our Nets. In those we took up
this morning there were but three small fish.[5]

Satur 31st. The wind blows very hard so much so that Perignie does
not think proper to send the men off to that cache Mr McKay made
above this. In our nets we take but one white fish* & a small sturgeon. About Noon to-day we seen the brigade pass that was for Fort
Dauphine and its dependencies[6] only one of them Stopped here. We
take a new net out of the bales & set it.

Sund 1st September. We visit our nets this morning & take but 3
Pikeral.* About Noon two indians La Grosse Tête, & L'Orignialle
Noire arrive from the Pin-a-wa where the rest of their friends are busy
in making of Oats* or wild rise [wild rice*]. Perignier gives each of
them each a small bit of tobacco & a little rum. At night Peri[gny] sets
off with Lonquetin & these indians a saining [seining].* About 10 P.M.
they arrive without anything.

Monday 2nd September. We set off pritty early this morning & having
proceeded about two leagues* we encamp at the mouth of the Pinawa
exactly opposite to L'Isle Du Windigo.* Before we arrived here we were
overtaken by La Cendre the Court-Oreille[7] from the Bottom of the

4 The goods that William Mackay had left with Bercier, to be used for the establishment of
Périgny's Lac du Bonnet post. L'Anse du Bonnet was the little bay at the northwest corner of
Lac du Bonnet, where the Winnipeg River exits the lake.
5 A good fishery was one of the main considerations in siting a new post, for the traders
were expected to find their own food once they reached their wintering quarters. Meat (especially moose) was gratefully eaten when it could be shot, or traded from Indigenous hunters,
but fish was the staple food, day after day.
6 The NWC's Fort Dauphin department comprised the present west central part of Manitoba,
running as far west and south as Riding Mountain, and including Lake Dauphin, Lake
Winnipegosis, Swan Lake, Red Deer Lake, and the northern part of Lake Manitoba. The
name goes back to the French period.
7 The Courtes Oreilles ("short ears"), or Odaawaa (Ottawas), are a branch of the
Anishinaabe, originally from the Sault Ste Marie region, who had been settling around the
west end of Lake Superior and beyond, gradually displacing the Sioux, since the mid-eigh-
teenth century. La Cendre and his band would have been among the various Ojibwe people
moving farther westwards in search of better hunting territories. This branch of the Ojibwe
(or Chippewa, as the name is used in the United States) is now represented by the people of
the Lac Courte Oreilles Indian Reservation in northwest Wisconsin.

river who told us of having orders from Mr Ermatinger to get as many indians as he could to go to that Place.[8] Near Sun set four indians, The Duck, Old Englishman, The Trout, and Cayen le Noire arrive from the Pinawa with 7 fens [fawns*], or small bags of oats for which they had one large Keg of mixed & were bid to return with more.

Tues 3^d. This morning a number of indians come here with 13 bags more of this rise [wild rice], with four Beavers, & two Bear skins for which they had rum also. Two otters also but were refused by Perignie from the Nepisingues.[9]

Wednes 4 Thurs 5th. Peri. finishes trading the best part of the [sic] which amount only to 45 bags, 4 Beavers &c &c & some other few things not worth mentioning.

/[2]/ Friday, 6th. After Sun rise this morning Perig. sends off all the men with Bercier in the large Canoe to Guide to the place where these Goods are hid. And before this time Red Stomach arrived from hunting in some of the bays, & made particular mention of one where he thought there was plenty of Sturgeon* as the water in that place was very muddy. We all went out a Saining & we take 9, five of which we keep & the other 4 the indian keeps himself. In his hunting trip of Yesterday he did [not] kill any thing.

Sepr Satur 7 September. It rains all day. Nothing new.

Sund 8th. The men from the Cache arrive with all the things; but they had a great deal of trouble to find the whole of what was there hid. Cayen le Noire & the Old Englishman arrive also from Saining: they give Peri. six sturgeons.

Mond. 9th. Perignie gives a 2½ pt blanket to the Duck's brother upon debt.[10] And he gives ½ Keg of mixed rum* among the whole of

---

8 Having been left in charge at the Bas de la Rivière post, Ermatinger was trying to draw in as many Indigenous traders as possible, in a region with little permanent population. Thus he was in conflict with Périgny's post at Lac du Bonnet. Both Ermatinger and Périgny, in this year of excess staff, were hoping to impress the NWC management with a good trading season.

9 Périgny may have refused the otters because they were summer furs, not suitable for the trade. The traditional lands of the Nipissings, linguistically related to the Ojibwe, are around Lake Nipissing, far to the east of Lake Superior, so this band was a long way from home. When Nelson visited the band in December, they had only two hunters; the Red Stomach, probably an Ojibwe, was with them for part of the season. As with the Courtes Oreilles just mentioned, the presence of Nipissings on the Winnipeg River illustrates how complex the hunting population of the Lake Winnipeg department was in this transitional period.

10 Trade goods were issued to the Indigenous customers for three reasons: in debt or credit (usually in the fall, as an advance on the furs to be brought in later in the season); in trade (in

the indians rather as an incentive to trade the remainder of their oats [wild rice] than any present gain he has from it.

Tues. 10th. Peri. gives debt to several of the indians, and last night he traded some more oats. The Trout after this sets off for the little white river, as does the Duck & several other indians besides Old Englishman. Bercier also as being a free man sets off for Bottom of the river. According to Perignie desire I give him a letter for M[r] Ermatinger.[11]

Wedneseday 11th. The rest of the indians take all up Credit what few things they may want for their winter. The Nepisingues return 2 Quarts of Powder & 40[lbs] of Shot being so much more than their due. Perignie traded some oats last night.

Thurs. 12th. We get one sturgeon from the Court'oreilles. Welles and Lonquetin are sent by Peri. round the east bay to look for two small canoes that we may set off soon to build. At sun set they arrive with them but both are very bad. A little before dusk La Grosse Tête arrives with the meat of a moose deer and a little bears meat for which he gives them 6. quarts of mixed rum.

Frid 13th. Perignie was out a looking for some proper place to build but found none to his fancy. We take many white fish & one in particular, weighing nine pound it was rather more than as large again as the commonality of them.

Satur. 14th. After sun rise this morning the Ducks brother arrived with the Knews [news] of his Nephew's death. It was occasioned by a horn full of powder that the children had taken to play with (while their parent were soliciting of Perignier for rum on the 3[d] of this month) this the Duck's child happening to find his father's Powder horn put the small end of it into the fire to see what sort of a report it might make, misfortunately the large end was towards its face when it blew up & burnt the poor infant very [much] all over the body. He brought 2 Sturgeon, & a Goose to get rum to cry for his nephew /[3]/ but Pérignie gave him only 4 quarts of mixed. Some time after this the two Nepisinques arrive with 2 Sturgeons, 2 Geese, & 7 Stock ducks; they get 3 quarts of rum. At Sun set the Duck comes himself escorted

---

payment on the spot for furs brought in); and as gifts, sometimes described as "for nothing." The last was part of maintaining the ceremonial relationship between hunter and trader, which was neglected at the trader's peril. Nelson and other fur trade journalists are careful to state the purpose of any goods they issued to their customers.

11 Bercier's contract must have come to an end, and the letter would have been asking Ermatinger what was to be done with him.

by a band of indians all in mourning : they bring six bags of oats, for which Perignie gives them ½ Keg of mixed rum.

Sunday 15th. Perignie trades from the Nepisinques two bags of oats for rum.

Mond. 16. and Tues 17th. Two men arrive from Bottom of the River this evening. They are sent by Mr Ermatinger for oats.

Wednes 18th. After the seperation of the oats 60 small bags in number these men set off with 30 of them & a letter. Not long after this Grosse-Tête & Griffes D'ourxes bring in a good deal of meat. They get rum for this & set off immediately. A high wind prevails all day.

Thursday 19th. At last, and with great difficulty we set off to build in the bottom of a bay on the South side of this lake between the Pinawa & the usual rout of the Canoes by river blanche.[12] The distance not being above one league we, therefore, soon encamped. Not long after this the Trout arrived from river blanche, from whom we got some meat; and afterwards twelve Sturgeons were brought us by Old Englishman & Cayen le Noire. Rum was given for all this.

Frid. 20th. The indians return each to his home in a very high wind. By orders from Pérignie the men begin to build our house which is 34 feet long & 18 wide.

Satur 21st. As Grosse-Tête sets off for bottom of river I give him a letter for Mr Ermatinger by Peri. desire.

Sund 22nd Septr. The men work these two day at the house, Peri. trades 8 Phiols of rum for near two bags of oats or rise.

Mond 23d. About 3 P.M., the duck & his brother arrive with some bear's & moose meat besides 2 black bear skins. One keg of mixed rum was given them. The men are employed cutting wood for the roof of the house.

Tues. 24th. The men put the covering on the house. Peri. gets two small & one large beaver from the indians.

Wednes. 25th. Early this morning Cayen le Noire was brought here in a Canoe & very sick. Perignie gives him a little medicine but has not had the desired effect for about 4 O'Clock P.M. They come back with this indian who died about an hour before. As far as I can judge his death was occasioned by the cold, which he got about 4th or fifth of this month as both these nights were very cold & each night he came from his lodge quite naked & drunk & upset several times, since which time

12 The location must have been near the modern community of Wendigo Beach, or in one of the bays just to the west of it.

especially he complained of having a sore throat & stomach, which increased, & very rapidly untill his death.

Thurs. 26th He was buried by his brother L'orignialle Noire & both their women & children at a few acres* below the house. The only ceremony was their usual harangue & a small bunch of hair from the crown of his head wrapped up in bark & to be kept in his family as a Commemorative of his being once existant. Part of his medicine bag & several other things were put with him.

/[4]/ Friday 27th September. This deceased indians women, Welles (J Bp.) & I go today for hay to cover our houses with. The Red Stomach's women arrive with half rotten meat, but is refused by Peri.

Satur. 28th. It rained all last night.

Sund. 29th. Monday 30th. Yesterday the men work at Perignie's Chimney.

October) Tues. 1st October, 1805th. The old Englishman gives Perignie three Geese. The day before Yesterday Red-Stomach came here to vindicate the lost Character of his women for bringing us rotten meat. He soon makes up again & takes for 86 skins more upon debt. Blows & rains.

Wednes 2nd. Old English & L'orignialle Noire bring here 21 Sturgeon, & Perignie gives them as may pints of rum.

Thurs 3[d]. The Old Englishman takes a few articles more upon debt & set off.

Frid. 4th. As the men want shoes & have no leather Perignie sell half a Moose Skin to each man.

Satur 5th. L'orinialle Noire or black Moose came to inform Peri. to send for a moose that he had killed a few hours ago.

Sund. 6th. All the men were sent for the meat & I through my own desire went also. We were soon returned to the lake but the wind blowing to high we could not recross it 'till near sun set. During the bad weather of last weeke it snowed & there is yet some upon the Ground.

Mond. 7th Tues 8th. The shop is finished today & all the Goods, Liquor, &c, oats, peltries & other things are put into it & shut up. The Key in P. own hands as he is master.

Wednes 9th. Perignie finishes his room & will soon Creep into it.

Thurs 10th. The house is at last finished; & Peri. gives each of the men one Pint of reduced rum as a regàle.

Frid. Satur 12. 'Tis now some time past since I began to make a Net, and the men are yet a drinking.

Tues 15th. Perignie sends Pinault & Fertin to make the fall fishery at the mouth of a small river in that deep bay, east of the Lake.[13]

Wednes. 16th. I finish the Net of 60 fathoms long it took up 3.[lbs] of thread. It snows all this afternoon.

Thurs 17th. Snows all day. Being out a hunting I kill ten Ducks.

Frid. 18th. It snows again all day.

Satur 19th. Perignie & I go to this small river where the fishermen are. We take with us a Leather lodge & the new Net. The people here seem to make but very little progress in fishing, as they have but very few here. Near night we return home & take back one of the old Nets which we set at l'isle du Windigo. It blows very hard all day.

Mond 21st. Yesterday bad weather but to-day 'tis very fine. Perignie and I set off again to go where the fishermen are, but were soon obliged to return home again for Black Moose & Old Englishmen whom we meet with 1 Bear Skin, dressed skins, other Peltries, with meat, Geese & Ducks all which they give to Perignie.

Tues 22nd. As it blows too very hard we must remain quiet at home.

/[5]/ Wedneseday 23[d] October 1805. After breakefast this morning Perignie & I set off to where the fisherman are. He takes them home with us as they might be better employed there. On our return we sained & took only 6 Sturgeons. 13 Pike* & two suckers* we take in the Net that we set the other day. As soon as we had done saining Peri. sends the men back to their old station as he thought that they might yet take a few fish.

Thurs. 24th. It was very cold all night in so much that it freezes quite across to the first islands exactly an half league from here. It snows all day.

Frid. 25th. Bad weather.

Satur 26th October. After Breakefast I went out a hunting & lost myself. The reason that I lost myself to day was, that after having followed a bear's track some distance I left it to go in a manner straight home, but having walked about two hours in one Continual swamp without arriving at the place I expected I returned back upon my road & having arrived upon the bear's track I wanted to straighten my road by cutting through to a small crick or rivulet where I had been this morning. I fell upon Perignie's track who had been this way also & had likewise lost himself as well as I did, at first I took it be my own but afterwards finding that I had not been in this direction, I visited the

---

13 Likely the present Bird River, which falls into the easternmost bay of Lac du Bonnet.

track more particularly & found my mistake though I thought it was some of the indians', which made me follow it the longer as I expected to arrive soon at their huts & sleep there. I soon found my mistake again from whence I concluded that it could be none else but our own people had lost themselves. Wherefore I resolved to go straight through at all hazards; but, this, was not yet done 'till I had fallen five different times in different parts of my former tracks & having gone so often in each as to make it almost a beaten road. I undertook again to go straight but in another direction when I fell again upon the Bear's track & followed it to the Pinawa & at last about 9 O'Clock at night I arrived at the house.

Sund 27ᵗʰ. Early this morning Perigni sends Longuetin to Carry a Cod-line* & some oats to the fishermen.

Mond. 28ᵗʰ. Perignie set off this morning upon the bear's track in hopes of Killing him but returned very late & without success. Firtin & Pinault arrive from fishing, but had not seen the least mark or sign of Longuetin.

Tues 29ᵗʰ. I made 5 martin traps to-day. Fine weather. Nothing new.

Wednese 30ᵗʰ. Perignie goes a saining with three of the men at a certain place in the Lake where it is not yet frozen over. The weather is very mild, but Cloudy.

Thurs 31ˢᵗ. All hands arrive, but have only 3 Sturgeon. Very fine weather.

November) Satur 2ⁿᵈ. Fertin & Longuetin are sent to fish while Pinault in employed in making slays [sleighs] for the Company. The weather is stormy & snowy all day.

Mond 4ᵗʰ. I mended a net to day & with the help of Peri & Welles I set it under the ice. Longuetin & Fertin arrive, but have not taken any thing.

/[6]/ November, Tues. 5ᵗʰ. The men are sent back again. In the Net that I set yesterday this morning we only take two fish.

Wednes. 6ᵗʰ. Perignie sets off to go to Red Stomach & the Népisingues, he JBpt Welles & me with him. We dragged a Canoe upon the ice & afterwards, P. & W. embarked in it while I walked on foot a long the beach, for the canoe had only its stern because the bow was broken off. At night we encamped at the foot of Porches[14] near rather in his road.

14 The Porches or Parches, apparently a long stretch of rapids at the foot of the Rivière Blanche section of the Winnipeg River, was at the south end of Lac du Bonnet. Here, Nelson left the main river, heading west or southwest across a mixture of forest and swamp, to find the Nipissing camp. His account of the second visit to the Nipissings, in December, mentions the Rivière de la Tête Ouverte (Brokenhead River), which shows the direction taken.

Thurs 7th. We set off at Day light & after having made 8 encampments we arrived at night at the lodges.[15] We missed our road to day
but were lucky enough to find it soon again. The men were not yet
arrived from hunting.

Frid. 8th. The indians were very troublesome all night & more so this
morning when they found that we were agoing to return home with yet
one bottle of HWines [high wines*]. Nevertheless we set off at about
8 A.M. with near 50 skins & a good deal of meat. We were obliged to
encamp long before we wished in very bad, snowy, weather.

Satur. 9th. Pritty early in the morning we fell upon the Grand river
where we took a Canoe belonging to the Nepisingues but were too
heavily loaded to remain all three in the Canoe; therefore, as soon as
we had crossed the river I debarked & walked again on foot along
the beach while P. & W. were breaking the ice to get through. When I
found this I took an ax to make an encampment in hopes of P's coming
to sleep with me.

Sund. 10th. I found it very cold all night having slept alone & nothing
but my old capot to cover me & a few pine bushes under me, with a
small beaver's tail to eat. However I returned from where I debarked
yesterday in hopes of finding Peri as I did neither hear nor see him pass
last night. About 1½ leagues from above my encampment I found them
both just ready to set off. We each took our loads & this afternoon we
arrive at the house. During our absence three men had been to black
moose's lodge for meat, as he came for them.

Monday, 11th. Pérignie sends the men with their slays for fish, where
Pinault & Fertin have made that sham fall fishing.

Tues 12th. The men go for the remainder of the fish, which they bring
with ease.

Wednes. 13th Thurs. 14th. Dark & dull weather with snow &
rain, nevertheless Perignie sets off for Black Mooses lodge & four
men with him, while the Negro[16] & I by his orders go towards the

15 The fact that Nelson passed eight campsites in one day shows that the Indigenous hunters
moved but a short distance in a day, while a determined winter traveller would go much
farther. From Nelson's accounts of his many winter trips on and around Lake Winnipeg, a
few years later than this, it is clear that he was capable of travelling 40 miles a day. Now, with
Périgny (an older man) with him, and with difficulties following the track, he would not have
gone so fast, so the Nipissing camps were probably about a league (3 miles) apart. Distances
that Nelson gives in the journal entries for 7 and 13 December confirm that this hunting
band's encampments were slightly more than a league apart.
16 Samuel Welles.

Lake-du-Limon in hopes of finding the Griffes D'ourxes, Grosse-Tête &c, and their families as well as Mr Meniclier[17] whom we think to be there also. We walked hard all in this bad weather & late at night we encamp about one league above the sixth Portage[18] without any signs or hopes of soon seeing any one, except a small poplar tree that was thrown upon the ice as a mark of their having been there.

Frid. 15th. Having nothing to eat, the weather cold & snowy, the ice entirely broken up on the river, & lastly now [no] snow shoes to facilitate our walking in deep snow over rocky mountains & deep wet swamps I think fit to return home, but not 'till we had endeavoured / [7]/ to continue our route along the beach in dangerous swamps & the Negro nearly drowning himself in them. From the appearance of the Country I think that we returned from about a league or a little more below the Lake. Had we taken even provisions enough for one meal we should have continued, though neither of us had the least knowledge of the Country we were to travel through: we only went upon conjecture. After the Negro & I had sunk several times in the river we encamped at night upon a high hill the only place where there was wood & only a small duck for supper.

November Satur. 16th. It has been so very cold last night that this morning we were able to walk upon good strong ice where at sun set Yesterday we might with as much case have gone in Canoe clear of all ice. The weather was so Cold (as I have just observed) that we were obliged continually to run to keep ourselves a little warm. At about 10 a.m. we overtook our people (Perignie excepted who passed last night) at our encampment of last fall at l'isle du Windigo; they were as badly off as we, only that they always had wherewith to eat plentifuly; soon after this we arrive at home.

Sund 17. Mond. 18th. Very fine weather these two days. According to Perignie's & my own desire I go to Black Mooses lodge with an ice Cutter, two files & some other small things. I arrive here early & as the men were out a hunting I remain also. But [sic].

Tues 19th. At the breake of day I set off & before noon arrive at the house.

17 One of the traders who had been left to winter at a place in the Rivière Blanche: see entry of 29 August. Lake-du-Limon has not been identified, but was probably east of Lac du Bonnet.

18 These must have been in the part of Winnipeg River known as the Rivière Blanche, which was full of rapids requiring repeated portages, so the travellers were walking up the river in the direction of the modern town of Pinawa.

Wednes 20. Thurs 21st. As the men's dogs* runaway yesterday, Welles goes after them to day to Black Moose's & Old Englishman's lodge they being together. Dull weather.

Frid. 22nd. The black Moose arrives to day before the Dutchman (Welles) he came in a straight line through the woods. He brings nothing & comes for nothing.

Satur. 23^d. The indian returns home. Yesterday we set a fresh Net.

Sund. 24th. We take four fish in the Net. & I mend another one that is much broken

Tues 26th [*sic*]. Very bad, Storm'y, & snow'y weather. Nothing new.

Tues 26th. About noon Le Comté one of Mr Ducharme's men arrives with two letters of the Knews of that place. One of these letters is for Perignie & the other for Meniclier. Mr Ducharme seems to make out pritty well in the Pack way &c.[19]

Wednes. 27th. Thurs 28th. Bad & snowy weather these two days.

Frid. 29th. Yet bad weather, nevertheless Le Compte returns home. We take 1 fish.

Satur. 30th. Fine weather only by Spells; but continually a hard wind.

Decr Sunday 1st December 1805. Perignie sends two men to put a Net opposite to the house between the two Islands. Bad weather this afternoon.

Mond 2nd. Fine weather. In the Net 3 Pike, & the men set another at the Point brulé.

Tues 3^d. In the net that was set last Sunday we take nothing.

Wednes. 4th. Fine weather. As our snow shoes are made Peri. sends Welles; Sam Welles the Negro, Firtin & myself to red stomach's & the Nepisingues' lodge: Firtin is to remain with them & the others are to come back. Perignie also comes with us as far as the Parches [Porches] about 6 Leagues from home when we seperate : he goes with Longuetin to the Trout's lodge /[8]/ some where in the little White River, and I go up the same road we went last November. All hands being tired we encamp at the first Campment in the woods; about one league from the river.

December Thurs 5th. As Welles has no snow shoes we put up at the end of 5 encampment[s] from where we set off this morning, & yet two upon this side of where P. W. & I found the indians.

---

19 Ducharme's post was well up Winnipeg River, perhaps at Portage de l'Île, or perhaps at a place called the Grand Equierre.

Frid. 6th. We encamp again at the end of five other Campments after having missed our road several times & lost ourselves as often for the roads appear but very little & in some place not.

Satur. 7th. About 8 A.M. we fell upon a fresh road & Camp upon the borders of a small Lake rather a beaver dam; here the indians had killed several beaver as we seen from the vestiges and from whence they rose camp about six days before. As upon this dam the indians seperated, it was hard for me to tell which was the right road as Perignie did not much wish that the Nepisingues should be with the Red Stomach : however, I take the one to the right hand as it was the newest. And two encampments from this we fell upon the River-de-la Tête-ouverte that empties its waters in Lake Winipick about three leagues to the South of Red River.[20] We continued our road & pritty soon arrived at the Nepisingues lodge; the men were both out a hunting & did not arrive 'till night. I got their peltries & as much meat as I chused to take as they had Killed three days since three large Moose. We are here at the end of 16 long encampments from the River & from there about 6 leagues to the house : However, I take it that we are about 24 or 25 leagues from home & nothing to Guide us back but a small indian path that the least shower of snow may fill so as with great difficulty to be seen; & often obliged to go by guess.

Mond 9th. We remained here Yesterday but set off early this morning & encamped from where the Red Stomach had set off this morning. As we were obliged to return to where the roads seperate from each other we there hang up all our things. And, [sic]

Tues. 10th. Early this morning we arrive at his lodge. I only find his women here as since last Sunday he is after a bear's track. At night he arrives with a little meat that he brings from the Népisingues; for he stopped there on his return home. Unless this little meat [had arrived] his Children & we, would have gone without eating as they have done since yesterday.

Wednes. 11th. What few Peltries he gives me & I set off leaving Firtin with him. At the forks[21] we take our loads & encamp a little beyond where we put [up] the 6th, now six day ago.

20 Nelson had his directions twisted: the mouth of Brokenhead River is east of the mouth of Red River, not south.
21 The major Fork of the Brokenhead River is where the tributary now called Hazel Creek comes in from the right, southeast of the modern town of Beausejour.

Thurs 12. We passed a very uncomfortable night always snowing as it does 'till noon to day Nevertheless we travel as usual.

Frid 13th From here to the river 6 Campments (about 8 leagues) & from there six leagues 'till home, for which reason at the breake of day I set off (having only my blanket my Gun & a two Gallon Keg) leaving the men to come on by **Degrees**. After walking very hard I arrive late at night at the house & pritty tired much more so than I would have been had I not drank so much water when I got upon the river. I find Perignie & Pinault ready to set off tommorrow for another Quarter.

/[9]/ December. Saturday 14th. Early this morning Perignie & Pinault set off to go upon the same little river that Sam (the Negro) & I had been upon in hopes of finding those same indians that we were in search of. Near dusk Sam, & Welles arrive. Our fishing is but one Pike.

Sund. 15 Mond. 16th. Nothing new yesterday. But to Peri. & Pi. arrive having travelled near three days over high rocky mountains & deep swamps without having the least success.

Tues. 17th. To the inexpressable joy of Perinie La Grosse-Tête arrives this evening from the upper part of river a l'ourx where he is encamped with all those indians (Griffes D'ouxxes [sic] & Frisé with their families) whom he took to be lost for this year.[22]

Wednes. 18th. About 10 O'Clock, A. M. Perignie sets off for these lodges with Sam, Longuetin & myself. The roads being very bad we encamp (about half way to their tents) at the foot of a Steep rock & a wet swamp.

Thurs. 19th. About noon we arrive, give them their liquor, & take their Peltries & other things; & pass the night very uncomfortably, continually quarreling, sometimes fighting, & more often walking about for what? I dont know. Among the different Peltries that we received from the indians there were several beaver four in particular that were remarkable from their size. The two largest were the size of the small avolas[23] & the other two were the common size of rats. I take this to be owing to their food & situation, the former was of the common swamp pine & small Alder bushes, & the latter was in a swamp whose waters (though precious little) were enough to poison almost any thing. Had I not seen the Beavers lodge myself I hardly should have beleived

22 Rivière d'Ours is the present Masqua River, so these hunters were wintering to the northeast of the Lac du Bonnet post.

23 Perhaps voles. Evidently these beaver were unusually small.

it; though the indians told me of it. The indians also give these same reasons for the smallness of this Beaver.

Frid. 20th. We return home & all pritty well loaded, with Peltries, meats &c. A little boy follows us to get some things upon debt from Peri.

Satur 21st. We arrive at home about noon.

December Sund 22nd. Bad weather. The indian returns home. We take three fish in our net.

Mond. 23^d. Pinault & Welles are sent to Black Moose's lodge for meat, if there be any.

Tues 24th. Pinault arrives with a little meat; but Welles remains 'till they kill more.

Wednes 25th December. This being Christmass day it is kept as such.

Thurs. 26th. Perignie sends Longuetin & Sam with me to the Trout's lodge in small white river. As the weather is bad & snowy we are obliged [to camp] at the foot of the Parches.

Frid. 27th. It snowed all last night & to-day. Yet we are obliged to travel.

Satur. 28th. About 4 O'Clock, P.M. I walking before as custom I find a small stick directing towards the woods but several other in different directions. I take the one towards the woods though the road was every where full of snow & appeared but very little. The reason why I took this road was not because I thought it to be the right one but as we were very short of Provisons (for Peri always takes good care not to overload us with this article), I thought if we happened to find no one we would have the shorter distance to go without eating. However, we were happily disappointed by arriving at his lodge, more by Guess than fair play; for the country we travelled through was a naked swamp & the roads full of hard drifted Snow that we might easily have walked upon it with out Snow shoes.

/[10]/ December, Sunday, 29th. We return home in very cold, bad, & stormy weather, loaded with two bags of Pounded meat, 3 pieces of dry meat, & a little tallow besides a few Peltries.

Mond 30th. By far the coldest day we have yet had. We stopped to make a fire that I might dry my shoes & socks, having sunk in the river. Nevertheless we put up in the Parches.

Tues 31st. At Sun set we arrive at home & find only Peri. as the others were at the lodges.

1806 (New Year's.) Wedneseday 1st January. Very bad & stormy weather yet the men arrive.

Thurs 2ⁿᵈ. Nothing new.

Frid. 3ᵈ. Agreeable to my own ardent desire I set off for the Bottom of the river with Longuetin. Perignie comes with us as far as the Portage du Bonet chiefly to Guide us through. At Sun set below the Portage of Les eaux qui remuent we meet one Fortier, & Péron both from Tête-aû-Brochet in Lake Winipick, where Mʳ Ferguson winters, with the express* letters from Mʳ McKay at Cross lake to the eastwards of this lake (Winipick) but at the N end. The Number of Posts in this lake are first Mʳ McKay at Cross Lake, Messrs. Venables at Pike river, McPhall at Lake la folle (avoine) eastwards of Lake W., Richard at Pigeon river, Ferguson at Pike head, & Campbell at Broken river, in all, six Posts & appear to make out pritty well.²⁴ I talked with the men some time & took them back to Bottom of the river where we arrive about 10 P.M.

Satur. 4ᵗʰ. Sund 5ᵗʰ. We remain here, but prepare for tomorrow.

January

Mond. 6ᵗʰ. We return home. Loaded with Potatoes²⁵ & arrive late at night.

Wednese 8. Perignie sends Sam, & Welles to Mʳ Ducharmes with the express.*

Thurs. 9ᵗʰ. Nothing new, only that we take two fish in the Net & lines.

Frid, Satur, & Sund. 12. Nothing new all this time. We take but one pike.

Mond 13. Tues 14ᵗʰ. 'Tis very cold. Only 1 Pike again.

January

Wednes 15ᵗʰ. This afternoon our men arrive with two others from Mʳ Ducharme namely, Le Comte & Vandalle bearing letters for Mʳ Meniclier from whom Mʳ Ducharme has had no knews as yet & is very uneasy. The Knews from Mʳ D.'s. are not altogether very pleasant; indans almost continually dying & as if a contagious sickness prevailed in that quarter his only child now about 1 year old is very bad with it.²⁶

---

24 This is valuable as an explicit statement of all the posts that William McKay had established on and near Lake Winnipeg in this season, in addition to the four along Winnipeg River. The total in the department, ten, was several more than would be operated in future years, but as already explained, McKay had an unusually large number of men under his command at this time. For all these clerks, see Appendix D.

25 Thus, potatoes had been grown at Bas de la Rivière in the summer of 1805.

26 Hackett (2002, 133) identifies this illness as whooping cough, the first appearance of this European disease in the Northwest.

Thurs 16ᵗʰ. Pinault is sent by Peri. to the bottom of river with Mʳ D's letters; & Le Comte & th'other are gone to Griffes D'ourxes lodge in hopes of getting some one to Guide them to Meniclier's.

Frid. 17. Peri, sends Longuetin & myself to G. D'ourxes's lodge but find gone to Guide the men. Frise & Grosse Tête are only here to whom I give the rum &c. I get but little here.

Satur 18ᵗʰ. We return home loaded with 20 Skins in different Peltries.

Sund 19ᵗʰ. L'orignialle Noire arrives. We take but one fish in our net & lines.

Mond 20ᵗʰ. Longuetin being sick Peri. sends Pinault & Sam with me to the Red Stomack's lodge. Peri. himself comes with Welles & us as far as Black moose's lodge at the foot of the Parches for meat. We leave Peri here & about 1 league further we encamp being late & having bad weather.

/[11]/ January 1806 Tues. 21ˢᵗ. Having walked very hard we encamp about ½ league from where Perignie, Welles, & I returned last fall.

Wednes. 22ⁿᵈ. We encamp about one league short of where we left Firtin last December.

Thurs. 23ᵈ. Though we lost the road several times we performed a Great day's journey.

Frid. 24ᵗʰ. Having put up (almost in a fresh 'indian' Camp) last night we expected to soon find the indians, & in walking over the second indian Campment we met Firtin who was looking after some martin traps.[27] To look at this man behind he had the appearance of a man but to look at him in the face all was lost for though his beard was long the grease, dirt, ashes & other filth that was in it almost prevent our seeing his eyes or distinguishing his nose & hardly his mouth. Having gone two Campments further we arrive at the lodges just as the indians were pitching off. At night the men arrive : they killed a moose, but brought none home. I gave them the rum as usual but did not trade.

Satur. 25ᵗʰ. I send Sam & Fertin to get meat upon that moose that was killed yesterday & the old Nepisingue & I went to look after a moose that was killed rather shot by the Red Stomach yesterday; we found it, dressed it, & left it.

Mond. 27ᵗʰ. We went & encamped upon say near the moose that we had dressed the 25ᵗʰ.

Tues. 28ᵗʰ. The red stomach kills a very large Moose towards the small white river wher[e] our road is to pass, being much shorter than the way we came which is 16 long & very long Encampments longer

27 Firtin had been left with the Red Stomach on 11 December.

than from where we returned last Decr. According to our own reckoning it is near 50 leagues from here to the house; for supposing the roads to be hard & good it is as much as can be done to do it in four days then we would have to run more often than walk.

Wednes 29. Thurs 30th. We encamp again towards the small white river.

Frid. 31st. The indian hunt as usual & I send the men for meat that the Nepisinge killed yesterday.

February, Satur. 1st. The distance being now not very long to go upon the small white river I set off Guided by the red Stomach & a little before sun set we got upon the river, but I returned with the indian to meet the men who are behind at dusk we meet them & Encamp but the indian return to his lodge.

Sund 2nd. We set off early & about 1 league from where we returned yesterday we arrived at the upper end of the Parches or the big river blanche. At the foot of the Parches about 3 leagues from the head we were obliged to put up very early as the dogs give up.

Mond. 3^d. About noon we overtake Mr Perignie at the opposite islands who had been at Griffes D'ourxes' lodge who encamped about one league from here a few days since.

Tues 4th. Peri. gives rum to the indians in payment for a good deal of meat he got from them.

Thurs 6th. We take 3 fish in the Nets but none in the lines. Pinault & I go to Griffes D's. lodge from whence we get 2 Shaved skins. At night the Frisé arrived with some bear's meat that G. D'ourxes has just now killed. He gets rum for the meat & skin.

Frid. 7th. Take 3 fish in the Net. Very bad weather.

Satur, Sund & Mond. 10th. Bad weather these two days past. Firtin is sent to live some time with B. Moose & Sam is sent also for meat if there be any.

/[12]/ February, Tues. 11th. We take but one small fish. G. D. & th'other indians raise camp towards L'Ense du Bonet [Anse du Bonnet] where they intend to go or raise camp through the woods 'till they reach B. Moose's lodge.

Wednes. 12th. Mr Perignie takes the Dutchman (Welles) with him & goes in search of Grosse-Tête whom he expects to be some where below the Portage du Bonet. Sam arrives with a rib piece & a brisket of moose meat. The Nets give us two fish.

Sund 16th. All this time nothing new has happened only that we take two small fish last Frid.

Mond. 17th. Peri. arrives with La Grosse-Tête but leaves Welles at the lodge.

Wednes. 19th. Mr Peri sends the other three men to this indians lodge for meat, & I go by gues[s] to Griffes D'ourxes lodge. Though I set off late & loose my [way] intirely so as to go quite in another direction I arrive a little after noon at the lodge; & a few minutes before sun set two boys having left B. Moose's lodge since morning Nevertheless I set off & after dusk I arrive there.

Thurs 20th. Early this morning I set off to go home Guided by Old Englishman & Blackmoose who go to the house for People to return to their lodges for meat having a Great deal. Longuetin, Welles, & Sam arrive before me all heavily loaded with meat so much so that Sam whose slay broke in a portage was obliged to leave a thigh & a rib piece. Pinault remains there.

Friday 21st. Mr Peri sets off with the men & the indians to their lodges for meat & other things. & I go for the meat that was left yesterday by Sam but found that a wolf had taken away the rib piece & a part of the thigh I brought the rest home.

Satur 22nd. P. & the men arrive with much meat & two bear skins. Fine weather.

Wednes 26th. The weather is amazing warm today, so much so, that four more like this would melt all the Snow upon the Ground; though there is upwards of 3½ feet thick.

Thurs 27th. Peri & Welles go on a visit to the bottom of the river.

Frid 28th. Longuetin takes 2 Pike in his lines – a miracle.

March. Sund 2nd. The Black moose with all his family arrive as does Perignie in a bad humour. Nevertheless he gives them to drink.

Mond 3d. Black Moose goes with his wife to Grosse Tête's lodge on a visit, & at the same time to have a drunken frolick of it. Pinault arrives from there with a little meat.

Tues 4th. Pinault & Welles return to the lodge for more meat.

Wednes 5th. Before Sun rise this morning I set off for Mr Ducharme's with Sam & Longuetin. About 11 O'Clock P.M. we encamp in Perinie's house of last year at the Barier, but [not] 'till after we were all three of us nearly drowning in falls it's being too dark to discover our road straight.

Thurs. 6th. Just at Sun set we arrive at Mr Ducharmes[28] but find him

---

28 Nelson does not give enough information to locate Ducharme's house, but from the time he took to get there, travelling along the Winnipeg River, the post must have been either at Portage de l'Île or somewhere below it, on the northernmost bend of the river, just west of the present Ontario border.

alone as Cournoyer's wife arrived almost as soon as we having left the Poivre's lodge for fear of being taken as a wife by Poivre's young son.

Frid 7. About 10 A.M. M^r La Croix arrives here on a visit also from his house at six days journey from here, he has Lambert with him.

Satur 8. M^r D's. men arrive with meat from the ducks lodge M^r D's. wife & her brother having arrived last night debauched & run away with Cournoyer's wife; but him on his arrival being informed of this Pursued her & her Paramour.[29] Every one was anxious of Going also, but for the want of

The rest of this journal is missing.

---

29 The story of Cournoyer's wife is given in the *Sorel Journal*, 72 (not printed here). It ended with a confrontation with levelled guns, after which Cournoyer and his companion got their wives back and returned with them to Ducharme's post.

3

Extract from *Sorel Journal*, 1806–1807

No daily journal survives for the season of 1806–07, but the *Sorel Journal* memoir again supplies the gap. Again Nelson passed the summer inland. He gives us a somewhat macabre anecdote of a NWC engagé whom William McKay employed to clear away an old graveyard at Bas de la Rivière, to make way for the rebuilt post. In the fall Nelson was sent to trade at Rivière-aux-Morts, now Netley Creek, a few miles below the place where he had last wintered for the XYC in 1804–05. In the spring, an ice jam caused the Red River to back up, as it still does today, and the traders had to withdraw to tents on higher ground. Once again, Nelson had trouble with an Indigenous man, who believed that by some magic the traders had caused the deaths of his children. There was a drunken "frolic" started up by the HBC trader, Thomas Miller, when most of Nelson's men had been sent away to take provisions to the Pembina post, far up Red River. Nelson tells a lively, extended story of his difficulties during the "frolic," but all ended well. He passed the summer of 1807 again at Bas de la Rivière. Although he does not mention it, his five-year contract with the XYC would have run out in March 1807, but evidently he had given satisfaction, and he was rehired.

The passage from the *Sorel Journal* now to be quoted begins with the conclusion of the trading season of 1805–06.

Our returns in this wintering ground had been good. But we had many squabbles with the indians. Did it not savour of vanity I could relate a few that would show much of the indian character, & my own indiscretion. Mr. McKay was well pleased with us all. My stock of delicacies this winter was about half a bag (50 lbs) of flour – 15 or 20 of Sugar, a couple of lbs. of tea & half a pint of Salt! But at this time I preferred fish or meat broth to tea by a great deal, & it is surely much more nourishing, & consequently better adapted to a man who usually walks much, since this exercise creates so much thirst. I have frequently drank upwards of a gallon of this liquor in an evening after a hard days walk.

Nothing extraordinary occurred during the course of this Summer (1806) – Mr McKay again returned in the autumn & took charge of this place, & sent Mr Ermatinger to Thunder Lake in the upper part of Poplar River, a hard country indeed. It required the utmost prudence, foresight & oeconomy that [?] to lay up a stock of provisions, that is out of the question, but to procure enough for mere subsistence. He managed so well however that he had a tolerable good winter of it.

The others were sent each to different quarters, & myself to Riviere aux Morts, the first small river we find on the right hand going up Red River. So called from a terrible slaughter of the Sauteuxs, by a large party of Siouxs, perhaps some sixty years or so before my time. Here, again, from my improvidence, & the culpable negligence of my men, I was hard pushed for a time for provisions, but at last all went on well....[1]

The Company had decided upon building a new fort at bas de la Riviere, & selected an old grave yard for the purpose, being the most eligible site, Mr McKay in the course of the autumn got the most of these graves levelled. Indians, Romans & Protestants, of all ages & sexes had been here consigned to their mother earth.[2] Among the men here employed, was one Alexis Bercier, or Mercier of St Lawrence Suburbs, Montreal, a very superstitious & humourous fellow. Every one employed in this business felt a sort of horror, or repugnance at least in thus disturbing the remains of the deceased. Bercier not; because he thought them all to be indians or Protestants! – Cursing and swearing, & making very light of so sacred an idea, he would ask those around him "who is buried here"? They would always answer, an indian or a P., he would then go on levelling the mound making the most singular, & sometimes most laughable remarks. Sometimes, whilst

---

1 Paragraph omitted, expressing Nelson's pleasure at realizing that telling his story in an orderly way is a good idea.
2 Native burial grounds were often sited close to trading posts (Willmott and Brownlee 2010, 51), but this one evidently was used for voyageurs as well. Levelling the burial ground must have caused great offence, but it was a typical act for the impatient, peremptory William McKay.

going on in this foolish manner, some one would say "stop, Beercier, let me look & consider. I believe it is such a one naming a Catholic" – he would then often turn pale & I have seen him trembling, shake like a leaf at the thought of this so religious intrusion. «mon pouvre ami pardonne moi je croyais que c'était un Sauvage ou un Protestant.»[3] The reason was, "a <u>Catholic</u> will rise in the night and ill treat me for disturbing him, but a Protestant or indian, <u>having no souls</u>, when they die, all is done – they cannot return; for they have no Soul."!!! And of this he was firmly convinced; "because out of the pale of our Church, there is no Salvation…[4]

Mr. McKay gave me some <u>good</u> men, active & wise fit for the trade; but like all others men, the Inhabitants from the Orkeny Islands per-haps alone excepted they required a much more muscular arm than I possessed or could wield.[5] My Interpreter was of the first, a Canadian of a respectable family but he forgot himself, & drank whenever occa-sion offered.

In the Spring of that year (1807) on account of the ice, we had to leave our houses & made ourselves tents on the border of Red River. Mr McKay desired me to send to Pimbinat [Pembina] River, near 200 miles perhaps, above. Having had several unpleasant occurrences with several of the Indians during the winter, & that they were now begin-ning to gather for their spring treat, I spoke to Miller,[6] an Orkney man, & clerk for the Hudson's Bay Co. here, either to give out the liquor now or await till my men had returned, for I apprehended very unpleasant work. He promised! My men were hardly 3 hours off before he gave out Rum! – How was I to do? Exposed in open tents, my furs & goods upon a Stage or scaffolding, my interpreter worth a host when sober,

---

3 That is, "my poor friend, pardon me, I thought it was a savage or a Protestant."

4 Passage omitted, in which Nelson describes some instances of Catholic prejudice towards Protestants among his neighbours in Lower Canada in 1831.

5 Nelson had no first-hand experience with Orkneymen, who were the backbone of the HBC's workforce and had a reputation for stubbornness and independence. Here he is admit-ting that good discipline among his own men would have required his establishing a physical dominance.

6 Thomas Miller, an HBC servant, first hired in 1787. He remained in the Company's service, working inland on the Albany Fort establishment, until 1809 when he returned to Britain. Although always described as a labourer in the records, he was entrusted with greater responsibilities, keeping post journals at Brandon House in 1798 (after the death of James Sutherland, the master there), at Lac du Bonnet in 1807–08, and at Henley House, Albany River, in 1808–09. He was recommended as a faithful servant, who deserved higher wages than he received. See HBCA, Biographical Sheet.

& as bad as a host of enemies when drunk, & it was very seldom he
could refrain from drinking with the indians. I had to gather up the
little nerve I might possess, & be on my guard & watch on Desfond
(the name of my Interp.). Shortly after the frolick began, & it was a
frolick with a vengeance, a terrible quarrel occurred between Miller &
some Court oreilles upon some provocation one of these latter fired a
ball through their tent, & sent off all the poor Orkneys a scampering
for dear life. I was sent for to pacify them. About now Mr Desfond
I perceived to be groggy. I then gave all up, but a man in liquor is an
Emperor – an Alexander. At last he got quarreling with an indian of
all others he should have avoided but it was "because, I cant drive into
that brute's head the <u>true</u> course of the death of his child," which was a
source of serious & grievous complaint, for they taxed us with it. There
were several large holes about us made as cellars to hide things in, but
at this time they were full of water, & all the dirt about was thrown in
them. There was in particular one large one, over a part of which /75/
of which had fallen the head of a large Elm, & in the branches of this
the Children would play, & like children would finish by <u>stealing</u> [?]
so that that hole in particular was a dirty one. The indian came back
again, the quarrel renewed. I pacified them, & thus were they going on
taunting & insulting each other; each one advancing or retreating as he
happened to have the advantage. Desfond at last, thinking it time, gave
his adversary a blow in the breast & sent him on his back in this large
hole! It was impossible to refrain from laughing, to see the poor fellow
come out of that place wet & full of dirt as he was. But he was in a
terrible rage. In the afternoon, that same fellow whose Pate Jollie nearly
broke two years before must have a quarrel with me & to show his
contempt of me endeavoured to stab one of our dogs with a large bone
made like a Chissel, & which they use to dress the skins. At night he
came again with his wife & renewed the quarrel. I had no relish at this
time for wrangling, for I apprehended something very bad: there was no
avoiding however, he seized me, using the most insulting language, by
the crotch, & raising his wifes Petticoats, pushed me as if he wanted to
thrust me under – "there dog! Is best place for thee, & if thou see'st the
day dawn tomorrow it shall be because my wife will have sheltered thee
under her Petticoat"! This was too elegant a Compliment to let pass
unthanked. I <u>replied</u> pretty near in the same words & Manner, shewing
him a place under the Pillows where before dawn "thou certainly shalt
cry to be hid." He setoff in a rage with his wife saying "presently thou
shalt pay for thy temerity, & for the deaths of our children."

¶He had been so frequently obstreprous that I thought he might at last put his threats into execution, as he could never have a more favorable opportunity. I made off too behind him towards their lodges where the others were performing all the parts & varieties of an indian drunken frolick. I made as much haste as I could consistent with caution & the extreme darkness of the night, intending to hide behind one of the large trees to be better able to judge what to do, i.e. whether to run off, hide, or brave out the storm – walking on smartly thinking on what might be the issue I came <u>bump</u> up against an indian standing so close to a large tree as if he had been glued to it. It was one of the Court'oreilles – he was evidently waiting for some female friend – but we each separated to different places. I heard my friend running still with his wife, for he too had the good fortune to fall into some of those fine clean holes, which was far from relenting his <u>love</u> for me. On entering the lodge he called out in an imperative manner, "Is there a man here? if there is let him take his arms & follow me." The words were hardly out of his mouth, when another indian, a stout sour dog who was quarreling with his wife, accepted this challenge, as it appeared addressed to him, seized his gun immediately, & fired at my <u>friend</u> before the poor devil could reach his gun, but fortunately some of those men raised the gun & the shot struck in the bark of the lodge which took fire!

Here was a <u>bedlam</u>. Lord, what a noise! Really I thought the ground quaked under me. Some extinguishing the fire, others appeared to be urging or setting it on, in other quarters, cries, shrieks, moans, reproaches, running, fighting, guns firing & the balls & shot whiz-zing round me, some in pursuit one way, others in another, calling, responding, challenging, vaunting. It seemed as if they wanted to try who would or could be, the most extravagant & make the most noise. I remained still behind my tree, for I knew no more where to steer to, putting my head now & then to one side to see what was going on, & I was hardly 50 yards from the place. This beautiful harmonium lasted about 15 minutes; and as almost always occurs in these extravagant ebullitions of the passions it died away gradually to a dead still silence /76/ a yell & a shot in various directions & at various distances. It still remained a few minutes to ascertain if I could safely move off.

¶Groping my way in the dark through the woods to my lodge I observed a light in Desfonds tent. I stole up silently & heard a great alter-cation in an under tone, complaining & lamenting, signs, exclamations & excirations. I entered to ascertain. I found them all drunk, my interpreter with the rest, & all around a woman full of blood – her face so disfigured with it & dirt that it was sometime before I could recognize her, & two women holding her head! "what is the matter now." "See! Said the two women, raising their hands, exposing thereby a dreadful gash the poor woman had rec^d from her husband, & which cut her forehead quite across!" They chewed astringent barks & roots, & raising up that thick skin again, applied this saliva, to dry it & stop the blood, & they bound the head very tight with a strip of Cloth. Her husband was that Sour dog who responded with his guns to the challenge of <u>my</u> friend (the <u>Red Birds</u> Son in law) when he entered so determinedly. It seems he was jealous of his wife, & was scolding her in consequence, & beating her as well as he could, for she durst sometimes make head he seized his knife immediately after firing & thus wounded her. They lost sight of each other immediately, she flew for protection, & he, either in pursuit of her or others, with his gun. While they were binding up her wound, we saw the husband standing in the door – he seemed to be effected & surprised.

¶I made my way to <u>my</u> tent, all was quiet, for I resided alone, & then went to the tent of my men where Battau Paul's wife lay with her twin daughters, children. Every thing quiet. Shortly after I went to examine the stage & see if the furs were right. I was passing water, & thinking on this fine concert. It struck me suddenly that I did not hear the water fall on the ground, & looking to see what might intervene .. lo! ... so far such a pen as Sterne! I was all the time [blank] upon a woman![7] I seized her I know not how, & dragged her into the tent, to see who she was, for she did not utter a word – it was my friends wife! She had fled here for protection, & begged it of me, I abused her heartily, & accused her of laying a trap for me to be as an apology for her husbands killing me at a future period she spoke, but I was too much surprised & agitated to <u>understand</u>. I returned again to finish.

¶I had just done, being under my stage, & looking up to see if all was right, I espied a man hardly 3 feet from me! I flew upon him too like a tiger, & leapt with him into my lodge, who should it be but my <u>friend</u>! I was then sure it was a trap laid for me, & was some time before I could get the idea out of my mind. Poor creature! He got such a scaring when the other fellow fired upon him that he ran off without any <u>explanation</u>, & lost all fancy for the time of injuring me. I actually made a place for him under /the pillows of the bed! And also for his wife! – Thousands of

7 Nelson apparently believed that the author Lawrence Sterne, the celebrated humourist, would have done better justice to his tale of accidently urinating on a poor woman who was hiding from her husband in the dark.

times have I thought of this business! There is intirely a Spirit guiding &
directing the affairs of men. This fellow, who hardly half an hour before
wanted to throw me under his wifes Petticoats for protection, abusing
me with the most opprobrious epithets, which by the bye I was by no
means slack in returning; that he should be obliged to crave protection
from me! How vain our vauntings. How childish how degrading a sensible, or a brave man, so very careful never, not merely to /not/ boast of
what he is able to do, but is reserved in relating what he has done. I must
confess that I never boasted, & I have had my wise days too, but I either
sneaked off, swallowed an insult, or performed my part with more fear
than became a man, & with all the dread of apprehension. But man is
man still, thoughtless, vain & weake.

The rest of the night passed quietly off & I went to sleep in my tent
alone as usual. Poor Miller this man had the Fever during the whole
frolick. I was obliged for he begged it of me, to pass some time in his
tent. /77/ The Cause of this trouble was that they had lost some of their
children, & believed those superstitions & the tricks of opposition,
those deaths were laid upon us – we "had used sorcery," said they.

Taking this winter (1806–7) as a whole, I had no reason to complain.
Sometimes a difficult or troublesome passage occurred, but it was of
short duration, & more owing to my own weakness than the character
or manner of the times. My great fault always was, & I see now, always
will be, that I took men to be what they should be, & not what they
were & are. With this erroneous and guilty idea I have been always so
strongly impressed, that notwithstanding I well saw & understood the
folly & sometimes the guilt of this false lenity, yet surely reason will,
& must shew them how wrong they are. But men are men still; fear or
interest will always make men do more than reason.

I travelled but little this year. In the early part of the winter I had
been with two of my men to the indians. We got two large slay loads
of provisions, & some furs. The day we returned being snowy & rainy,
of course the old snow wet & heavy, we had to encamp on the way,
at some old tents, & where we could not get any thing but a very
few dry branches to light our fire, the largest wood being hardly the
thickness of a man's thigh, & of that nasty wet Poplar called by the
french "Liard" – our clothes, shoes, socks & blankets all wet, & only
a wretched smoky little fire, we passed a most uncomfortable night.
Towards day it cleared up & the cold was severe. We pushed off before
day, the wind high & weather cold had dried the snow which drifted
smartly & completely filled & obliterated our road in the many lawns

or small plains we had to traverse. We had a singular concert of Kett's musick, a small animal between a dog & fox, partaking of both species.

/78/ A few days after Christmas I sent one of my men to pass a few days with the indians to collect meat i.e. to bring it in to the lodges as the hunters might kill it. He returned on New Year's eve (1806) with about one pound & a half! & made up such a long & pitiful story of his troubles, & dangers. I was much annoyed with this, & especially seeing the Hudsons bay people coming home well loaded with meat that he had brought in to the lodges. The day after N Years the 2ᵈ Jany (1807) I posted off with 3 slays & my interpreter. I had no difficulty in getting meat. I returned about 2 a.m. a fine clear & calm night, the moon at full, I was trudging along smartly to get home if possible by sun rise. I was thinking of the many wonderful stories of ghost, the man-wolf (Loup-garrouse) [*loup garou*, the werewolf] &c. &c. that so many people had seen, & been pursued by. Thinking also the like might possibly happen to me, for I was not, & could not be more exempt than others – I thought on a sudden to see my road barred, but at a distance before me! I kept on anxious look out, & continued at the same gait. Indeed my road was barred! There were beings of some kind or other laying wait for me! – I could not possibly conjecture who or what it or they might be.

¶For a time I thought of striking off to one side through the lawns & come again upon the road beyond, to avoid the dreadful beings which I was sure must be spirits, & of the malignant sort too! But my pride mastered my fear, & my track next day would tell I was a Coward. I prepared my pistles [pistols] & knife & held my Gun ready cocked in my hands to fire upon the least appearance of danger. Advancing a few steps further I hailed in french, no answer! in English, nothing! in Indian! A dead silence still! I bawled out again, giving warning I would fire, if anything attempted to molest me! upon this I heard a hoarse, croaking voice, pronounce "Ouah!" "oah!" who are you? – it was a party of my indians going to find their friends, those I had just left. My man had left them the 27ᵗʰ Decr at 2 days journey beyond my house & they were pitching off still further, & were not to be in before the end of Feby or beginning of March. I might well be at a loss. Most of those Ghosts & hobgoblins were of a sort with this story, I am sure.

I passed the Summer again at Bas de la Riviere. There were several of us, & as Red River had furnished abundance of Provisions we passed a very pleasant time. Nothing extraordinary that I remember, occurred…

❋

4

Extract from *Reminiscences*, Fall 1807

Nelson's next daily journal commences in the fall of 1807, at his new post at Dauphin River, close to where the river falls into Sturgeon Bay on the west side of the north basin of Lake Winnipeg. The journal begins late. For the first six weeks of the season Nelson was unable to write, as he was recovering from bad burns that he had suffered when a keg of gunpowder exploded during the trip inward. Nelson left two accounts of this episode, one in the *Sorel Journal* and one in Part 5 of the *Reminiscences*. I have chosen the latter account for printing here. The account in the *Reminiscences* starts at page 190 of his manuscript.

/190/ 1807 Septr

About the 10th of Se[pte]mber, at the usual period, <u>our</u> canoes arrived. Great changes had taken place. M^r W^m McKay, to my great regret, had retired from the Country. Mr Ermatinger who I have reason to remember with Kindness & respect, had also "gone to Montreal," an equivalent, in our vocabulary, to disgrace, which he certainly for many reasons did not deserve.[1]

This year, our Bourgeois were Mr Duncan Cameron, for a long course of years a trader in the Nepigon, about, if not over 50 years of age, a small, but very active man. Also Mr Alex^r. McKay, brother to my bourgeoi[s] of last year, about 30, & rather spare. He had accompanied Sir

---

1 It is unlikely that Charles Oakes Ermatinger had retired to Montreal in disgrace. He was in line for an NWC partnership, to commence with Outfit 1808, and it must have been his own choice to leave the company. See biographical note in Appendix D.

Alexander McKenzie when he went to the arctic Sea. He was rather of a curious temper, almost the antipodes of his brother. No one liked him.

It took us Several days to make all our arrangements for the winter. We at last set off, leaving Mr McK. in charge of this place & Mr Cameron accompanied us as far as Tête au chièn, where we were to Separate, I, to go to River Dauphine on the S. side of the Lake, & himself to a place name Drunken Lake, very near where Ermatinger had wintered the last year, & Campbell & McDonell in other places. A very serious accident befell us here, which I shall relate.

Explosion of a Keg of Powder.

We arrived at Tête au chien on the 12th Septr. I remember from its being the 48th anniversary of Wolfe's preparations for taking Quebec (which he did the next day). We had with us a Keg of damaged powder, in which there was still about 50 lbs. to be distributed equally between us. Mr Cameron sent one of the men to bring it up from the baggage to the camp for distribution; but being a great talker, he was so engaged telling his stories that night came on & it was put off to the next morning.[2]

The next morning, tho' clear, was very chilly, the wind blowing furiously from the N.W. This was sufficient cause to put off 'till <u>after</u> breakfast which the cook was preparing over a large blazing fire, & almost every Soul of us around. I was seated on one of his trunks at the door of his tent, smoking my pipe. But fortunately for me, being tired of that position, I seated myself on the /191/ ground, leaning my head on my left hand, my elbow resting on the trunk. I well saw a ricketty Keg, which I was told contained Sugar, at the other end of this same trunk, only 33 or 34 inches long, & therefore did not mind it. Poor old Richard, one of our Interpretors, was returning from lighting his pipe at the fire, when a Small coal fell on the bottom. I saw two Small flashes & then the whole went off! I had drawn my head a little to one side, but was Stunned with the report. I heard cries of "à l'eau, à l'eau – to the water, to the water." I had to pull open my eyes, for I found them as I thought, seared. Every thing was yellow before me. À l'eau again was cried, I knew not what for, the whole was so instantaneous, but rose & ran, & tripping, I was falling my whole length in the fire, when fortunately Laroque & Leblanc being there at the very moment, caught

2 In his 1818–19 journal, entry of 26 September, Nelson states that this incident took place on the south side of Isle á Beriau, one of the islands just NW of the Narrows of Lake Winnipeg.

me in their arms & ran with me to the Lake. I plunged in, & was not a little Surprised & annoyed at the two men, who, every time I attempted to rise, again forced me under & were rubbing me from head to foot. [in margin: "A terrible accident"] This, however was soon done, & we walked leisurely back, the men very kindly stripping me. I was shivering with cold, & finding them rather too long in unbottoning my vest, I attempted two or three times to tear it off, but finding my hands Smarting very much I looked to see the cause!. . . . ! to my horror & astonishment I saw all the Skin off my left hand, curled up between the fingers & the right hand almost as bad, a part of the little finger only excepted. Oh my God! what is the meaning of this?- How has this happened to me?" – This was the first I knew of my sad condition. On looking more carefully, I saw the Shirt stripp'd off my left arm entirely, & from the elbow, down, of my right arm. Of my trowsers, only the waist band & part of the seat, hanging in rags, with all the Skin from half of my right thigh to the ankle, litterally torn off! & the blood oozing in a hundred places. Both the out & inside of my left leg from the knee down to the ankle, stripped, & streaked black, brown & of a sooty yellow. also, almost the whole of my crotch besides several large large patches in my Sides, belly, neck, arm-pits &c. &c. I was lost in /192/ amasement, horror & fear!- "My God! what is the meaning of all this? How has this happened to me?" ... I was shivering with cold from head to foot, my teeth rattling in my head as if they [would] break.

   While the men were still busily employed in stripping the remnants of the sheds [shreds] of clothing hanging upon me, in which they were necessarily very Slow to give me the least possible pain being so lacerated & excoriated, I turned my head towards Mr Cameron's tent where I heard crying, weeping, lamentations &c. – – I saw...! Oh God! a tall black man, shining like a nigger, – a large frizzly head, blood shot eyes, a thick yellow Smoke issuing from his nostrils & mouth, and his tongue red as fire! [in margin: "A guilty conscience the consequence of Superstition"] "My God! my God! have mercy upon me! – this is certainly the devil come for me for my numerous Sins!!!" – I shook before, but it was vastly worse now, I shook with such violence as if my limbs wanted to throw themselves off & leave a heart whose corrupt desires they had been forced to administer to. I asked the men "who is that? is it not the evil one who is come for some of us – for me? – O Lord! what a terrible, what a frightful being!" They said "no; it is poor old Richard, who was thrown (some 10, or 15 feet) over a tuft of willows, & entirely stripped of every particle of clothing except the waist band

of his trowsers, & his Shoes. Those are his 2 Sons on each side exam-
ining & assisting him." I looked again; but whether it was owing to
the fright from the first view, or if it were really so, the figure appeared
precisely the same! It was only after I heard him speak to his wife &
children that I was <u>forced</u> to belive it was <u>him</u>.

At long last they got us ready & laid us in our blankets! and well
covered that I with considerable difficulty regained a little warmth; for
the wind was very high & easily penetrated thro' our thin tents.

A Sufficient number of men were sent to the woods for small larch-
pine (Epinette rouge) to make a Salve, others for Swamp-tea for a wash
&c. &c. – all hands were busy. [in margin: "Our Salves & remedies"]
But what quantities of plaister did it require to cover poor Richard,
from head to foot, for except the Soles of his feet, there was not half a
Square inch but was burnt; & myself, in so many places? Late in the
/193/ afternoon all was ready; & what with old shirts, old trowsers,
petticoats & bale cloths a sufficiency of rags were collected, filled with
this salve & applied to the wounds after washing them with the Swamp
tea, to moisten the parts & clean them. I found much ease after this, for
so many raw parts coming in contact with the blankets was often very
painful. But the Smart usual from burns I felt not in the least, probably
because most of the skin (where burnt) was all off & the general pain,
in so many places, absorbed, as it were, or rather was too great for the
other to be felt. My feelings may be conceived when I state that, when
they came to apply the plasters, they had to cut away with Scissors &
razors the loose Skin which was adhering by the narrow strip <u>between</u>
the fingers, particularly of the left hand - the nails all black & yellow.

It is a Somewhat singular circumstance that not one of the <u>common</u>
men was hurt, only those who held situations. [in margin: "A singular incidence explained"] Mr Cameron himself had his face merely
scorched, McDonell a few inches on his forehead, but not enough to
raise a blister; old Durocher the Guide a patch of about the size of his
hand, in the forehead also, it was supposed to be from a lump of powder, for it was rather a severe wound & threw him over on his back
rather violently. Even the cook, he was sitting on his hams frying cakes
for breakfast, received a blow in the forehand, from my calumet (Pipe)
as he thought, which toppled him over on one side, & his frying pan
on the other. Leblanc was the only one of the men who was struck, &
thrown over, but had no other injury. We attributed it to the high wind,
blowing with such violence that, altho' we were in a small low flatt,
well screened by the rocks & willows still drove the sparks & Smoke

so that they all kept to the windward, only Poor old Richard, sitting
on a bale of goods, about 12 or 13 feet distant from the Keg, but
immediately to the leeward and was thrown with the bale on which he
was sitting, completely over a tuft of willows. I was by far the nearest,
there being only the length of the trunk, 32, or 33 ins. long between me
& the Keg. Most fortunately, hardly a minute before the explosion I
removed & sat flat on the Ground!

Some indians came to see us & comfort us. I was most /194/ forcibly
struck with their sound rational remarks, equally far from those pite-
ous whining soothings & superstitious follies & nonsense so common
with us. Their conversation (for by this time I could converse freely with
them) [in margin: "Visits from the Indians"] was extremely gratifying,
pleasing & comfortable, because so rational, moral & philosophical.

One of them recommended a slight purging & vomiting. "You are
in no danger of dying, but you will suffer a long time, because the
smoke of the Sulphur & other matter of which powder is made, has
been violently forced into your Stomach [in margin: "their recommen-
dations & reasoning"]. It is a sort of poison, because it is unnatural:
in your stomach, it will affect your blood & retard its functions – a
gentle vomit will throw all that dirty stuff out – the organs being then
in their natural state will operate freely &c. and you will heal in half
a moon, whereas otherwise you will be perhaps two moons before
you completely recover.- Old Richard is very ill; he will die because
he is poisoned: if he could be induced to take several gentle vomits, he
would recover too; but he must die. You, white people, have a great
contempt for us indians because our ways are different from yours;–
that is wrong; for you yourselves have not all the same thoughts."

The next day I went to my breakfast but Mr Cameron told me not
to come any more. Indeed it was with difficulty I got there so many
plasters hanging about me, & would certainly not have gone but
for the unjust & ungenerous hints he & M^{c}D. let fall; that I was not
much hurt, altho the least of my 20 patches was by far worse than the
scorched forehead of M^{c}D. I was not pained, but I pitied them both
when I heard Mr C. extolling M^{c}D's <u>fortitude</u>! The vices of our friends
& those we love are only foibles, or at most only the sudden ebullitions
of an otherwise excellent heart, & the least notable thing they do is
invariably magnified into an heroic act. Such is man! Poor people, I
thought, why is it your prejudices so blind you to truth & equity!

But I had began to Swell, as the indians had told me. My left eye was
completely closed & the right so nearly so that I could only see such

objects as were immediately opposite to it. My face, and all my limbs,
in short my whole body became stiff as if incased in a thick crust of
something very hard. The 2ᵈ day they had to feed me – I could hardly
move a limb, so stiff was I could not close the right thumb on my hand.
I was completely helpless, after the first twenty four hours, but still I was
strong, and /195/ strong, & extremely averse of being assisted to do anything I could by any possibility do myself. I therefore got my numerous
plaisters stiched one to the other & wrapped a blanket round my waist.
This was too heavy, & out of compassion they procured me a petticoat,
which after a few hours I was also forced to put off.

A day or two after, the weather becoming calm, we had to separate;
for the advanced state of the year, in those latitudes & former bitter
experience were warnings to us of the urgent necessity of availing
ourselves of every favorable occurrence to better & improve our least
advantage. I was sent to River 'Dauphine, a beautiful river, the outlet of
a long string of fine & large lakes & rivers on the margin of the plains.
It is situated on the West shore of the lake, & north end of a very deep
bay that of itself would form a respectable lake. Richard, who was
intended to be my interpreter, had to be carried to his canoe & I to
mine, where couches were prepared for us. Mʳ Cameron & McDonell
continued on the North shore to their respective destinations. The
wind had quite subsided and we paddled along to the creek of Tête au
Brochet, where we encamped in a beautiful natural meadow.³

A long succession of Stormy & rainy weather detained us here about
2 weeks. There was abundance of fish & no want of game, i.e. ducks,
Geese &c, and the people fared well; as for Richard & myself our
appetites were very variable; and we had, on the 3ᵈ day, to be fed like
children, or people without limbs: we became so stiff & swelled we
could not even turn in our beds with several persons to assist us. Our
plasters were removed once a day, but very often sprinkled to prevent
their drying, which, in spite of all their attention would be the case
in one place or other, when the bark would dry, rub & excoriate that
particular place & cause much pain & always a fresh wound.

The weather again taking another turn, with good hopes of its continuing several days, we re-embarked, & at evening encamped in the
Sᵗ Martin islands (this place is considered half the lake) on a beautiful

---

3 From the Narrows the main canoe route to the Northwest, which Nelson's party followed,
made a long traverse across the wide mouth of the present Fisher Bay, and on the western
shore soon reached Tête-au-Brochet.

clean low sandy beach. We were again carried a-shore. The weather was delightful & our tents were not put up. The men here had a long game of <u>romps</u>. O! how I longed to be of the party; but all I could do was to turn my head a little more freely than usual.

/196/ The next morning we were off early & about mid-day, in the traverse* were greeted with a very strong odour of Cucumbers, a certain indication of abundance of the famed "White fish."

We soon entered the river, about 300 feet broad gliding placidly its silvery waters between too high banks. We were happy to find several of our indians here with abundance of fresh & Smoked white fish, which they freely gave us.

We at once landed on the left (S.E.) bank 2, or 300 yards from the lake. The goods were carried up; & while this was being done by the men Fr⁵ Richard (the old man's Son) put out a 20 fathom net, which so soon as he had dropped the <u>sink</u> at the further end, "overhauled" it for fear of its being tangled in some parts, & already found 7 or 8 fine white fish in it. We were in extacy that our lot for this whole winter, should be cast in a place where there was such abundance. Our joy had no bounds. It is not easy to imagine the grateful swelling of the heart & thankful feelings of men, who for so many years had been so stinted & hard pinched when they find themselves with a certainty of abundance for a long, cold, severe & dreary winter. But this feeling did not last long – it was too pure, too heavenly, to remain – tho' we were certainly not reprobates.

Here we were to winter, and a suitable spot was selected to plant our tents so as not to incommode the building of our houses. Every thing was devised the best we could; and we made the usual present of liquor to our indians who enjoyed it peaceably & quietly in the same way as a few friends with us would do at an evening party with a neighbor.

After the frolick was over, we gave out credits; for I could by this time, tho' with very great difficulty make use of two of my fingers, to write. The indians quietly dispersed to their respective hunting grounds. I found here A-ya-gon, he who so strongly recommended to me, purging. He showed himself truly delighted at my recovery. Old Racette (vid P.183–4)⁴ also was here & had already built his little house immediately opposite to us on the N.W. bank of the river.

Richard dies

We were so far advanced with our buildings that we hoped to enter into them about the latter end of October; but the /197/ very

4 These pages were on a part of the *Reminiscences* manuscript that is now missing.

frequent interruptions necessary to our attendance greatly retarded us. I could rise & set [sit] alone, but required help to regain my couch. Frs (Richard) who was our chief Surgeon, had at last, about the 20th succeed with Scissors & razors to cut & take off that thick Scurf or Scab that covered my whole head & face. It was a complete mask! A fresh skin & fresh hair had grown under – my face was quite white & I thought I should carry the scars with me to the grave, but a few months after I became as usual.

Poor old Richard was also perfectly healed, but with many deep Scars. His face was covered with a perfectly new skin, grown over the flesh, for the flesh of his face had been burnt, but my Skin only had been burnt – his was roasted! But he had in his back two ugly ulcers that gradually eat into holes, near above the kidneys, & there was no means of putting him in any other position 'till it was too late. He died in much suffering on the 27th October, aged 62. His sons, scooped out a coffin from a large Spruce tree to put him in, & we buried him with our Silent prayers. A little building was erected over him & I engraved on a board the day & cause of his death, age &c. &c. When we left in the Spring, we again all assembled round the grave & once more offered up our imperfect Sacrifice.

The poor old creature was aware, & resigned to his fate. The 26th was very stormy, & the night was unusually dismal. About 8 o'clock at night we heard a strange, very loud & shrill cry, it was again repeated. Some thought it was the cry of a loon, tho' they had long since returned [south], some a bear, some an owl. Some of the women said it was one of the water deities. "What is all this talking about," said the poor old man. "It is my father who has sent to warn me to prepare, for I must die"! The next morning about 8 o'clock he breathed his last in great agony! May the Almighty God receive his Soul into grace, mercy, & peace.

Our Houses &c.

In the first days of November we moved into our /198/ houses. My own was about 15 by 24 feet, as I had Richards family with me. That of the men was 12 x 15, and a small store to put our furs &c.

I had the following men, vizt.

Frs: Richard, Sen[r]. as Interpreter, who died

Frs. Richard, Junr. - do.

Bpte: d° 　　}

　　　　　　　} these two were not hired, but assisted occasionally

Michel d° 　　}

Jos: Dalcour, from L'assomption
— Relle , « Laprairie
J. B. Welles, « Sorel.
Both the Richards & Dalcour, were married men, no children.

The story is now taken up by Nelson's own daily journal, which he began at the new post of Dauphin River, once his burned hands had healed enough for him to write.

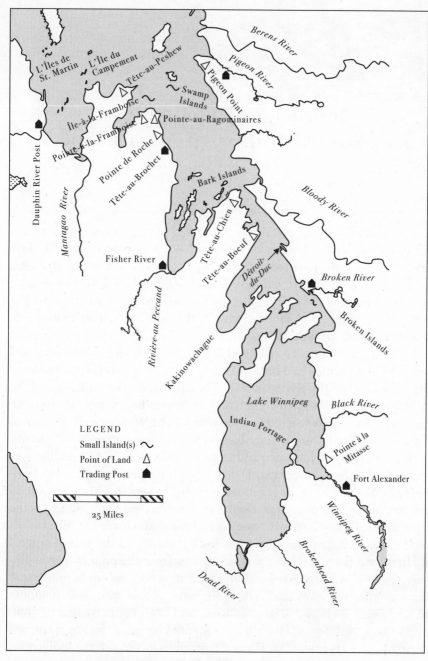

Map 5   Central Lake Winnipeg: Dauphin River and Tête-au-Brochet posts.

5

Journal at Dauphin River,
3 November 1807–31 August 1808

This is a small book of sixty-four numbered pages, 20 cm high x 16 cm wide, written on both sides of the usual Radway-type paper. The first eight pages are on four loose sheets, and the rest is on fourteen sheets, each 20 cm x 32 cm, which have been folded in half and nested so as to form a booklet. The pages are not fastened together in any way. No pages are missing, and the last page in this journal is immediately followed by the next in the series.

By the time Nelson's hands had healed to the point where he could write, he and his men had been at Dauphin River for several weeks, sleeping in tents while the post was built. The site was on the south side of the river, opposite the modern community of Anama Bay, about two or three hundred yards from where the river enters Lake Winnipeg. The larger of the two dwelling houses was for Nelson and his interpreters, the Richards, with their family of four men and boys and two women. The smaller was for Nelson's three voyageurs, Dalcour (with his wife), Relle, and Jean-Baptiste Welles. The trade goods were probably kept in Nelson's house to prevent thefts, and there was a small shed for storing the furs. Across the river, the freeman Charles Racette had a little house for his family.

The season began inauspiciously. Both Nelson and the elder François Richard had been laid low by their injuries from the gunpowder explosion. Nelson was recovering, but Richard, whose wounds must have become infected, soon died. The Indigenous people who were planning to trade with Nelson at Dauphin River had been badly treated by John McDonald, "le Borgne," the NWC partner in charge of the Fort Dauphin department, to the west. McDonald wanted to include all the Indigenous hunters on the west side of Lake Winnipeg within his own department, and would have seen Nelson's new post as an intrusion. Nelson soon learned that McDonald had established a post at Partridge Crop just west of Lake St Martin, some fifty miles by river to the west, and so he did his best to avoid encroaching on that post's hunters. Soon he was able to settle into a regular routine. He had his own small core of hunters, headed by Ayagon, the Ojibwe leader who had requested that the post be established. The river was full of lake whitefish, and there was an excellent fall fishery at the rapids about a league upstream from the post, so productive that it could also be used to support the Pigeon River post, on the other side of Lake Winnipeg. The winter passed quietly, and Nelson started making plans for improvements for the next year.

As soon as the breakup of the ice permitted canoe travel in spring 1808, Nelson and his men took his furs to Bas de la Rivière, where they were dried and repacked for the trip out to Fort William. He remained at that post for the summer, his bourgeois Duncan Cameron going out for the annual partners' meeting. The quiet of the summer was twice broken by a few days of intense activity. In June the canoe brigades came through with the furs from the NWC's wintering grounds, on their way to Fort William, or Lac la Pluie in the case of the Athabasca canoes. In late July and August, the same brigades passed through again, heading back to their posts with fresh goods. The wintering partners themselves kept a slightly different schedule, coming and going in their own "light canoes,"* which could travel more quickly on the water and over the portages because they carried only their passengers and their personal outfits. Nelson noted all these comings and goings, and mentioned many NWC partners and clerks by name. This part of Nelson's journal provides a rare glimpse of the summer activity at Bas de la Rivière, a kind of snapshot of the NWC's fur trade in action, when the company was at the height of its powers.

Shortly before the canoe brigades were to leave Bas de la Rivière on their eastward voyage, one of the Indigenous people at the post let slip that a conspiracy was afoot, to attack the brigades as they made their way up Winnipeg River. The plan, it was understood, was inspired by the teachings of the nativist preacher, the Shawnee Prophet. Though it seemed far-fetched, the threat had to be taken seriously, and the NWC partners consulted with the most influential Anishinaabe leader, The Premier, for reassurance. The Premier agreed to send his son with the canoes, as an agent to manage any negotiations that might be needed along the way. Nelson and his companions at Bas de la Rivière were on tenterhooks for weeks, until the first of the returning canoes appeared on 1 August, along with The Premier's son. No attack had been made, and the rumour had probably arisen from stories that had been heard about the Prophet's activities and influence in other quarters. Nelson appended a long endnote to his entry regarding this episode, which gives his own understanding of the Shawnee Prophet's teachings. This note is printed at the end of this journal.

The returning canoes also brought word of the death at Montreal of Duncan McGillivray, brother of William, and one of the Montreal agents of the NWC. And there was news of a visit to Fort William by a genuine nobleman, the Count de Chabot, which created a small sensation. This young man's brief sojourn in Canada caught the attention of several people. Louis-Guy-Guillaume de Rohan-Chabot, Comte de Jarnac, Vicomte de Chabot (1780–1875), lieutenant colonel in the British army, arrived at Quebec as deputy adjutant general in the fall of 1807, and left the colony a year later. Elizabeth Frances Amherst Hale, who with her husband John Hale, deputy paymaster general of the British army in Canada, socialized with Chabot at Quebec, and said of him that he "has brought the highest strongest letters of recommendation to us I ever read. He seems very Gentlemanlike nothing French abt. Him; his Mother is an Irish Lady & he was born in London & educated in England."[1] Chabot accompanied William McGillivray and William McKay, the NWC agents, from Montreal to Fort William in the summer of 1808. For the count, it was probably a tourist's adventure, while for William McGillivray it was a chance to show off his acquaintance with a man of high birth. John Askin junior, government storekeeper at Fort St Joseph near the NW corner of Lake Huron, noted on 18 June the arrival there of "Mr Wm McGilvery & McKay accompany [sic] by Count Chabot … from Montreal." Askin, who was struggling to advance his employment with government on the Upper Lakes, took the opportunity to ask the count to recommend him to the governor of Canada. After the return from Fort William to Montreal, McGillivray proposed Chabot for membership in the Beaver Club.[2]

Nelson closed his journal on the last day of August 1808, still at Bas de la Rivière, as he was awaiting the arrival of his bourgeois, Duncan Cameron, with trade goods and instructions for the next season of the Lake Winnipeg department. His next journal will carry on without a break.

1 Hall and Shelton 2002, 223, 233.
2 Quaife 1931, 606, 608. Proceedings of the Beaver Club, 17 September 1808, copy of original at McCord Museum; I am indebted to Warren Baker for this reference. Soon after his return to Britain, Viscount Chabot married the daughter of the Duke of Leinster, acquiring through her a great estate in Ireland, and became a notorious absentee landlord. For his reputation among the politicians of County Tipperary, see, for instance, Bond Head 1852, 303.

The Dauphin River Journal of 1807–08 is notable in that Nelson supplied explanatory notes to some passages, added later and found at the
end of the manuscript. For this edition, almost all of these have been
placed as footnotes where they are called for in the text. As already
stated, the longest of these, Nelson's explanation of the apprehended
conspiracy to attack the fur brigades, is printed at the end of the journal.

Journal.

The Commencement of this journal will be very incorrect; because
the explosion, or rather that accident which unfortunately happened
at Tête-au-Chien had so stupefied me, as well as a very sore hand that
I had, intirely prevented me keeping any exact account of our march,
or voyage 'till a little after our arrival at river Dauphine; – however I
recollect our encampments.

After our departure from Tête-aû-Chien with Mr. Du[n]can Cameron,
and Mr. Alexr McDonell (the day and date I do not recollect;) but being
two invalids each in our own Canoe we emcaped in the Isle à Bériö early
enough to have time to gether Pine for our burns. We were here detained
one day by the wind; after which we proceeded to the Tête-aû-brochet
where we remained for five or six days. Constantly wind bound; at
last we set off again but were soon obliged to put in near the Point a la
Framboise on account of the wind & rain: after having passed another
day here on account of a very high /2/ wind; we again set off, and
encamped pritty early, more on account of Poor old Richard's sickness
than fatigue. We Camped opposite to L'Isle du Campement.[3] The next
day we set off for the last time, & we very soon arrived at the River
Dauphine, where we found but one indian, and Old Rassette [Charles
Racette]; the other indians had followed Mr. McDonald to the Fort
Dauphine and Eyagon [Ayagon] was out with two young boys a Beaver
hunting. However there was enough of one to make his Complaints. He
told me that he had been very ill used by Mr. McDonald as well as the
rest of his friends. In the first Place they were asked to follow him up by
good accord, they answered not, which, I suppose displeased him. He
first menaced them, & then took all their things away (so as to be the

3 An island near the foot of the traverse across the mouth of Sturgeon Bay. This was
an important place on the route, the usual camping place for the brigades going farther
northwest.

more sure of them) even to their medicine bags. Beside this he told me many other things which are not worth mentioning. However he was very much displeased. But no sooner were we encamped than Old Cûl Fessé arrived with his son-in-Law, and their families. These made me still worse complaints – I get a little meat & about 30 fish from them; & two otters for which I gave two Quarts of mixed rum.

/3/ The next day which I reckon to be near about the second of the month Eyagon arrived with the two lads; and three Beavers that they had killed: they each paid one upon their debts. Now according to orders[4] gave them their rum as they were very impatient; first one Keg to Eyagon; and three other half kegs among the others. Last night about 10 O'Clock the men were obliged to take up the Net after having taken 35 white fish in it. This was 20 fathoms that the men took off a new net to fish at Tête-aû-Brochet to prolong their Corn[5] as there was no great appearance of our making much speed in our Voyage. Very just fears!! The men began to clear a place for building, the only Place as I am told where there is any proper wood.

Saturday 3 Novr. The men have raised the first house (my own) 22 feet by 15. This appears very large; and so it would if I had not such a large family [probably the Richards] to lodge with me. The men put out the Net again. Bad and rainy weather by showers.

Sund. 4[th]. They put up a part of the Covering catch plenty of fish.

Monday 5[th]. The indians being hardly yet sober, take debt & depart after I s[e]perated another Keg of mixed rum between them, the men finish Covering [my house].

/4/ Tuesday 6[th] Nov[r]. The men nearly finished raising their house; the first fine weather since the 2[nd].

Wednesday 7[th]. Eyagon being yet drunk Came back this morning for more rum, telling me that it was his Son who asked for it; I gave him three Quarts, when mixed made rum. The men cover their house.

---

4 Nelson's note (on pages 59ff. of the original manuscript): "Mr. Cameron's orders were; that on my arrival at this Place I should give one large Keg to Eyägon, & each an half Keg to Old Muffle D'orignialle & old Cû-fessé; and another half keg among the Young men for he expected I suppose that there would have been more indians than one; that is, Young men) but as there was but this one indian I did not think proper to create a kind of Jealousy for so little rum."

5 On the Great Lakes, hulled corn (maize) formed the bulk of the provisions issued for the canoes, but in the North, beyond Fort William, there was little or no hulled corn available. "Prolong their Corn" probably does not mean that Nelson's voyageurs were using hulled corn; rather, it may be Nelson's translation of a voyageur's expression, simply meaning to extend their travelling provisions, which were always limited.

Thursday 8th. Nothing extraordinary.

Friday 9th. The men begin the shop. This is now the third time since our arrival that we have heard Thunder. Poor Old Richard grows worse every day.

Satur 10th. The men finish the shop; and enter the goods. For the first time since our departure from Tête-au-Chien I venture to go out with the assistance of a Pair of Crutches; thoug[h] yet very soar & extreemly weake.

Sunday 11th. Mond. 12th. Bad weather (N wind) Francois Richard who yet doctor's his father & me told me that Yesterday afternoon that he found a small hole about the size of a buck-shot a little above his Father's rump it appears to be deep; but he could [not] Probe it, being yet too very tender, this may probably prove fatal to him!

Tuesday 13th. Eyagon arrived with some Moose-meat with the meat of three beavers, & the skins of two.

/5/ Wednesday 14th. Eyagon returns with a good deal of rum. – Very high wind. – Plenty of fish as usual.

Friday 16th. These two days the men are employed in getting wood for the flooring of my house. Poor old Richard grows worse & worse every day.

Satur 17th. They lay a part of the flooring. Bad weather.

Sund[–Mond] 18th. Finish the Flooring. Our Patient is worse than ever. There fell nearly 5 inches of snow.

Mond 19th!! Fine weather. Poor old Richard, at last after a long sickness departed this life about ten o'Clock: and after having suffered very much since about 8 O'Clock last night that his moanings were clearly heard at upwards the distance of an acre!!![6]

Tues 20th. Last night about 10 O'Clock La-Bessette (Cul Fessè's Son in Law) arrived with two thirds of the meat of a moose. One of Muffle D'Orinialle's wives came also with four beaver skins which she pays

6 Nelson's note: "He expired in extreeme great agony the thirty seventh day after that unfortunate explosion at Tête-au-Chien. All his children except the eldest weeped; but they soon hushed. The old lad did not weep but was very pensive not only I beleive an account of the death of his unfortunate father; but as if already experienced (or certain) of what will inevitably befal him should not his conduct be such as to be highly approved of by his masters. For, he has a very large family upon his own hands (we may say) & who cannot subsist otherwise than by his own extraordinary good behaviour; for, those whose age might enable them to be of some good, are so ignorant as to be almost a burden to themselves, except in the indian way of living, & the others are really helpless either through Youth or age & infirmities. Therefore, it would certainly be a hard matter to the Campany to maintain six people (for the young man has besides his mother, a wife & three brothers, one is no more than 8 years old) for the precarious service of one."

upon a Gun. I gave them two Quarts of HWines mixed with as much water; but it was not till after he got a good quarreling that he took it, he said for his reasons that there was not even enough for the women to drink & that Eyagon with the other indians asked for more; but this was a bad time that he chose /6/ for such arguments. About Noon the men buyried Old Francois Richard. I also attended at his funeral : but, with the aid of my Crutches. I got them to surround his grave with pickets (of split ash) to the heighth of a man.[7]

Wed 21ˢᵗ. With much difficulty, I can now make use enough of both my hands to continue making a Net that Young Richard begun a few days past besides 20 fathoms that Rassette makes for us.

Wedne. 22ⁿᵈ. Caught 54 fish. fine weather. Nothing new.

Thurs 23ᵈ. I finished the net, all including 76 fams. [fathoms] & got it set before sun Set –

Friday 24ᵗʰ. Fine weather; – Our fishing out of three Nets 154 including all kinds.

Sunday 25ᵗʰ. Caught 180 fish.

Tues. 27ᵗʰ. The fishing of these two nights past amount only to one hundred & Eight

Wednesd. 28ᵗʰ. Out of three Net we catch but 39 fish. Very stormy weather.

Thurs. 29ᵗʰ. Very Calm since yesterday yet did we not catch more than 51 fish. Had the fish always continued as plentiful as when we arrived we surely would in a short time have taken enough for the whole of our winter without puttin one single /7/ net under the ice whereas I am much affraid that we shall be obliged to fish the greatest part of the winter.

Friday 30ᵗʰ. Richard's being unwell D'alcour took the fishing; & Last night caught 111 of all kinds.

Satur 31ˢᵗ. Very fine weather. (South winds): Caught 214 fish. Fortier begins to chop his wood.[8]

---

7 The practice of surrounding individual graves with pickets, sometimes elaborately painted and carved, is still widespread in graveyards in the Canadian North. For a photograph of a graveyard at Little Grand Rapids in the 1940s, showing some of these surrounding fences, see Hallowell 1992, 76.

8 One part of a voyageur's duty, upon reaching the post, was cutting a certain amount of firewood for use during the winter. Nelson's journal entries for 29 October and 1 November 1808 give the amount required at his post as 16 cords per man. Sometimes one man would pay another to cut his wood for him. Women, though rarely mentioned, would probably have been cutting wood as well.

Sunday 1st. November. As this is the Toussaints or all-Saints the men keep hallow-day; that is, they refrain from all work accept [except] fishing. They took 168. Cloudy.

Mond. 2nd. Very high Westerly winds; & hazy weather; but 66 fish. It is remarkable that all winds except South Southwest or South East there are but very few fish to be had here; & the higher those winds blow the shallower the river is, when we then take plenty of fish.

Tues. 3d. Ice drifts down the river; but 47 fish.

Wednese 4th. Welles begins to chop. Fishing 317. do.

Thurs 5th. Calm weather. 234 fish in three nets.

Friday 6th. The river is ful of drifting ice. Caught 428 fish. The best fishing that we have yet had! Cold.

Satur 7th. Very bad hazy weather with a high Westerly wind; but 141 fish, what a great difference there is to yesterday's fishing.

Sund 8th. The river is taken intirely a-Cross. Caught 330 fish. Calm, & sharp weather.

/8/ Monday 9th. Novr A hard North wind broke up all the Ice; but 112 fish in our three Nets.

Tues. 10th. The men were obliged to breake up the ice to visit & take up the nets; Caught 105 fish. Very Cold. It snowd this afternoon; this is the first snow since the 17th of last Month. But it all went off a few days after –

Wednese 11th. The men set the nets Yesterday at the entrance of the Lake, but were obliged to take them up this morning on account of the ice with 127 fish in them.

Thurs 12th. Very raw, & bad weather. Richard & I Crossed the river a little above the houses; but the ice is not yet strong enough to set the Nets.

Frid 13th. Dalcour set a net this afternoon.

Satur 14th Took 36 fish. Richard also set a net before the house. Very fine weather, South wind –

Sund. 15th. In the two Nets we took 37 fish.

Mond. 16th. Very snow'y, stormy weather yesterday; Caught 42 fish this morning. Dull, overcast weather all day.

Tues. 17th. Dull weather. Caught 42 fish. We put out 4 lines.

Wednese 18th. We took 71 fish in our net; & six in our lines. Frs. Richard on his return from his traps found a place in the rapids where there /9/ were plenty of white fish; he killed 16 with a stick. About sun Set Eyagon arrived with one of his wives and a little boy; – they come for people to go to their huts for what little things they have. He Complains much of not being able to pay his debt, as well as the other indians owing to scarcity of beaver; & other peltries or I should say animals.

Thurs 19[h]. Eyagon remains, as being too tire'd. I gave him three pints of HWines after being mixed.

Friday 20th. This morning I sent Fr[s] Richard, Relle, Wells, and Fortier with Eyagon to his lodge. I gave Richard five Quarts of HWines (including what was for Eyagon) 1½ fathoms of tobacco, to give among the men; besides several other things of no value to trade with the women.[9] – It snow'd till near night; mild weather. No fish in our lines; but we took forty seven in our nets

Satur. 21st. Pritty clear weather. I went to the rapids with my spear, where I killed but 11; in our nets 53.

Sund 22nd. Cold weather with a NW. wind. In our Nets 47 fish. Nothing new.

Monday 23[d]. Cloudy weather this morning & mild. We took 43 fish in the Nets; & two in the lines.

Tuesday 24th. Very dull weath[er] & mild all day. In returning from my traps I stopp'd at the rapid, & killed four fish: our nets 47, & the lines but one.

A westerly wind, but very low –

/10/ Wednesday 25th. Nothing Extraordinary.

Thursday 26th. Snow'y weather as usual; though there is not yet above two inches upon the ground. About one O'Clock this afternoon Frs. Richard arrived from the lodges, with but very poor returns considering the time that they have had to hunt. They brought home but 43 Beaver skins, 12 otters, 1 red fox, a few martins, & a few rats.* – In our Net, 51 fish. lines two.

Friday 27th. Cloudy cold weather; fishing 57.

Saturday 28th. Fine Sun-shiny weather. I went to-day with the two Richard's to visit our traps. on our way up we stopped at the rapids, where Fr[s] killed 106 white fish. I continued towards my traps: I took two Martins; & on my return home about 3 O'Clock I stoppeded [sic]

9 Nelson must have meant trade objects such as beads and ribbons, which to his mind were "of no value" because he had no notion of the value they had for the women. But these items were always an important part of the fur trader's outfit, and desired both by Indigenous customers and by voyageurs with families. At Île-à-la-Crosse in 1786, the voyageur Joseph Landry purchased "75 Banches [bunches] Beads & 1 doz Rings," for which he was charged 28 livres in the NWC account book; presumably this was for his wife, or was needed for a courtship (Duckworth 1990, xxvii–xxviii). See Wilmott and Brownlee 2010, for an analysis of the material culture remains in two Ojibwe burials found in this region.

to spear more fish, as they were pritty plenty. I remained till sun set, where I killed 254 in so short a time

Sund. 29. Fine weather as Yesterday, only a little colder, Richard killed 146 white fish; & in our Nets 54.

Monday 30ᵗʰ. Mild weather. Having but one net now in the water, we took but 25 fish; & 224 more that Richard Speared. The men put out the second Net.

/11/ Thursday 1ˢᵗ Decʳ. Very snowy bad weather. I went up with Richard & Fortier to where our fish lie : On our way up we found a wolf taken in Richard's traps (steel); & a Fox. The men came up also to cover, & arrainge the fish till convenient to draw them to the house; including 333 fish that the men killed to-day we have now 1063 upon the ice at about one League and half from here. In our Nets 75 fish.

Wednese. 2ⁿᵈ. Snow'y & drifty weather fishing 52.

Thurs. 3ᵈ. Cloudy cold weather. While at my traps La Bessette arrived with another Young indian with orders from Eyagon that I should go to his lodge with plenty of Goods, & liquor to trade with a band of Strange Indians who have not as yet been to any Fort.

Friday 4ᵗʰ. At day breake this morning I set off with three of the men, Goods & nine Quarts of HWines.

Monday 7ᵗʰ. Pritty early in the afternoon we arrived at the lodges,[10] and about two hours after, Eyagon also arrived from Buffaloe hunting where he had been with his family & had killed four Buffaloes, & soon after we began to trade; what with Peltries, meat & Grease we had the load of us all. As to the Peltries we have near one hundred skins.

Tues. 8ᵗʰ. Fine but Cold weather, we remained /12/ here all day; and the indians informed us of their ill treatment from Portage La Prairie people; & at the same time they wish much to have some one to pass the summer, and to winter in this river; for they say that they are too badly treated by their own People, and are too pitiful. This is really the

---

10 There are no entries for 5 or 6 December, so it took three and a half days of winter travel to reach this band of "Strange Indians," far to the south of the Dauphin River post. The distance was probably at least 100 miles, given evidence of Nelson's snowshoeing abilities from elsewhere in the Journals. According to the entry of 12 December, the camp he visited was about three hours beyond Fisher River, and about a day and a half's journey from the site of Angus Bethune's previous year's post near the mouth of the Red River. This place must have been somewhere near the southern limit of the forest, as Ayagon was finding buffalo to hunt. So far south, this new band could easily have fallen in with the hunters who had been poorly equipped at Portage la Prairie, and who had plundered them as is explained in the entry of 8 December, and Nelson's additional note to that entry. Nelson does not name this band or any of its members, and it is not clear whether he ever traded with them again.

case with them; for I have never yet seen such Poor ragged, miserable People in my life.[11]

Wednesday 9th Dec[r]. We proceed now on our journey home.

Satur 12th. At Sun set we arrived home after a long, tedious & Cold voyage. We returned home from beyond the Fisher river about three hours march; & but one day & a half's march from Mr. Bethune's house last year at the entrance of the Lake. Since my departure Young Richard made two Slays, & taken plenty of fish in the Nets; but none above [at the rapids] as all was froze up.

Sund 13th. A North wind, Cold & snowy.

Mond. 14th. Bad weather as yesterday. Having but one Net in the water, (owing to the scarcity of thread for mending them) we took 20 fish.

Tues 15th. Very fine but Cold weather : fishing 25 white & one Pike. Monsoon.[12]

Wednesday 16th. Nothing new fishing 35.

/13/ Thurs 17th Dec[r]. This being the second day that the men began to build a fish house. Very Cold. Our fishing to-day 48 white fish & one Pike.

Friday 18th. The men brought up all the fish taken in the Nets; & put them in the house to the Number of 3080 exclusive of about 800 Common fish; that is, Pike, Pikeral; & Suckers: And all the fish we speared above, in the river. Weather more mild a little than yesterday! !!!

Satur 19th. Nothing extraordinary. Fishing in one Net 52 white & three others. Mild weather.

Sunday 20th Nothing new. Fine mild weather but it blew very hard last night, & a part of the day (**SW**).

Monday 21st. Tues. 22nd. Nothing Extraordinary. But plenty of fish as usual. Fine weather.

Wednese 23[d]. A little after Noon Etiene Charboneau arrived with the old Brochèt from their lodge which is opposite to L'Isle-Du-Campement. They are upon a hunting party being now twenty-Nine

---

11 This band perhaps planned to winter in Fisher River. Nelson's note: "Many indians at Portage La Prairie in Red River, were not allowed more than six skins upon debt; that is, one fathom of str[ou]ds & a Clout [breechclout] besides five skins in ammonition. Whether this was really the case or not I can't tell; but, I never yet have seen such a set of poor, miserable & ragged creatures; but when they fell in with our indians they (I mean our own people) according to their way soon made off with all their cloaths & became as naked as the former."

12 Nelson probably just means a heavy snowfall; it was much too cold for rain.

days since they left their Fort at Pigeon River. Fine weather. But 14 fish in the Net.

Thurs 24ᵗʰ. As I immagine that we will now have enough of fish for our winter I got the net taken up intirely. This last fishing amount to 32 including every kind.

/14/ Thursday 25ᵗʰ Decʳ As this is our Christmas we keep it holy; that is without working. The indian returns home, but Charboneau passes the day with us.

Frid. 26ᵗʰ. This morning I sent Fortier with Charboneau to the lodges with a little ammonition & three pints of HWines to get if he can two parchment skins to make us snow-Shoes (as I can't get any from our own indians; & t'is impossible to pass the winter without those Snow-Shoes.); & a little meat to pass New Year's day. Continually fine, mild weather, only that it snowed a little last Night.

Sund 27ᵗʰ. Nothing new. Weather as usual.

Monday 28ᵗʰ. Fortier arrived from the lodges; but he brought home much less than I expected – only two Rein-deer* Skins, & two bags of pounded meat. no fresh. It snowed very hard this morning; nearly six inches.

Tues. Wednes 30ᵗʰ. Nothing New, only windy weather, & Drifty. Westerly.

Thurs 31ˢᵗ or rather Friday 1ˢᵗ January 1808. Nothing new, only that Charboneau arrived with his two indians (who wished; & came of their own will). He brought me the tongue of a Moose.

Note. As I have known the commencement of this journal to be incorrect; consequently, it has been so all along, that is in regard to the date of the month; but now as I have learned by Charboneau that I am but one day a head of the right calculations I regulate myself accordingly. So instead of 31 Decʳ I say 1 Jany.[13]

/15/ Saturday 2ⁿᵈ January 1808. This morning I sent Fortier, Relle & Welles with Charboneau & the indians to their lodge to get a little meat, & a moose-skin for the soles of our Snow-Shoes. I gave the indians a small keg of Rum for the meat; & a little tobacco for two Moose snoutes. Stormy & bad weather this afternoon with a North Wind.

---

13 Nelson always had problems keeping his calendar correct. He was one day late on 2 November 1808, and again on 23 October 1809, as shown by his records of the two eclipses of the moon (see those journal entries). It was easy to make these mistakes at an isolated post when the clerk was the only one trying to keep track of the date, especially if the entries were not written up every day.

Sunday 3[d]. A little past noon Fortier & Welles arrived from the lodge; they brought home four limbs, three rib pieces & three briskets of moose. Relle remains for a moose-skin.[14]

Monday 4th. Relle arrives with the skin & two rib pieces which is all that comes to us. Cold drifty weather.

Tues 5th. Wednese 6th. Nothing new.

Thurs 7th. Fine mild weather. The men finish hauling their wood except Welles who has yet two Cords.

Friday 8th Satur. 9th. Nothing Extraordinary. Stormy weather this afternoon.

Sund. 10th. Very stormy bad weather : a westerly wind.

Monday 11th. Tuesday 12th. As our snow-shoes /16/ are now finished I prepare for sending to Mr. [Duncan] Cameron, who (as I have learnt by Charboneaus) is at lake d'ivrogne [Drunken Lake][15] – Very bad weather.

Thurs 14th. This morning I sent off Dalcour & Wells for the above mentioned place. Clear Calm weather but very Cold.

Friday 15th. Nothing new. Satur. 16th. For the want of Snow-Shoes, of Slays, and time it has been some time since anyone has been up to see the fish, so the wolves have had a good opportunity of eating what quantity they pleased, but Richard who has been up there to day tells me that they did not eat above twenty : he set his traps for them.

Sund 17th. Stormy bad weather; so that if Dalcour did not arrive Yesterday at Mr. M[c]Donell's at Pigeon river there is all appearance of his being degraded* to day.

---

14 The skin, which had been traded "for the soles of our Snow-Shoes" (previous day's entry), had to be tanned before use, and the process must not have been finished until the next day, when Relle returned. The skin would then be cut into long strips, *babiche*, which were used to thread the snowshoe frames. Women did the tanning of the skin and preparing and install-ing of the babiche, while cutting and bending the frames was apparently men's work. These snowshoes, badly needed for a winter trip, and for visiting the fishery up the river, were not finished until the 11th.

15 Nelson's note: "Mr. Cameron's intention was (last fall) as he told us, that he would winter at the entrance of Popular [Poplar] River, but I suppose his finding that the English had gone up as far as Drunken Lake (at about I suppose two Spring days journey up the same river) with the few indians that were in its vicinity prevented his wintering where he said. When Charboneau arrived luckily prevented a useless voyage; because I intended to send to the entrance of Poplar River whereas now I send to Pigeon river (instead of Blood river where Mr. M[c]Donell was to have wintered)." For the history of the HBC's expansion into this region, and for the locations of their posts, see Lytwyn 1986, 104–11.

Mond. 18th. Clear cold weather, a westerly breeze.

Tues 19th Wednes 20th. Nothing extraordinary. Weather as usual; wind North Northeast.

Thurs 21st Friday 22nd. Cold Cloudy weather with a hard, S.E. wind. Yesterday excepted. Nothing new.

Satur. 23^d. Early this morning Dalcour & Wells arrived here with Le Blanc one of Mr. McDonell's men to wait the return of Aurielle & one of Mr. Campbells men. A hard North wind. & Drifty.[16]

/17/ Sunday 24th. I sent Fortier off this morning to plant bushes at Certain distances to mark the road straight to the house; so as Aurielle (who has never been here) may not miss the road. Weather fine & Mild though an Easterly wind.

Mond 25th. Nothing new – Bad stormy weather.

Tues 26th. Very bad weather, Cold & Windy. Wind SE., & N.W. & N.E.

Wednese. 27th. Thurs 28th. Nothing new; only bad weather which has & always be bad.

Frid 29th. Satur 30th. Yesterday Young Richard killed a wolf. The weather being very mild I went as far as the island (about 3 Leagues distance); but could neither see any marks or signs of our People : I mean Rielle & Mr. Campbell's Men – a **South wind**. a miracle!!!

Sund. 31st A hard Westerly wind & very cold.

Mond. 1st February. Very find mild weather. Wind S.

Tues. 2nd A part of the day very fine; but the remainder bad & Stormy which prevented my sending off to Mr. McDonell's. The men brought from above 150 fish. Nothing New. –

Wedn 3^d. I sent D'Alcour & Fortier with Leblanc to Pigeon river; as there remains no mor appearance of Aurielle's or any other person arriving here. The men brought home 100 & odd fish. Relle & Swits.[17]

Thurs 4th. Nothing new: fine weather.

/18/ Friday 5th Feby 1808. Nothing Extraordinary; only fine weather with a hard South wind. The men draw fish every day from above.

Satur 6th. Very mild weather this morning. It rained, but this afternoon the wind turned North & Cold.

---

16 Nelson's note: "Mr. Cameron had already sent to Pigeon river & to Mr. Campbell with [a] letter for me & orders to pass by here absolutely, for finding himself so long without receiving any knews from here imagined, I suppose that we could not find where he was, or, that our Sickness, or burns proved fatal so as to intirely prevent our sending the men excepted."

17 Unidentified, unless this is for "Swiss," and yet another name for Jean-Baptiste Welles, whom Nelson often calls the Dutchman, the German, or L'Allemand.

Sunday 7th. Nothing new, but very bad weather hard wind.

Mond 8th. Weather clears up this afternoon; Yet blows Westerly. The Men (Relle & Wells) go for fish?? [*sic*]

Tues 9 Wedn. 10th. Nothing new. fine weather to-day Yesterday excepted The men haul fish as usual.

Thurs 11th. About three hours before day D'Alcour, & Fortier, arrived, Mr. McDonell sent Desrocher & Aurielle for fish.

Frid 12th. Nothing new. Fine weather these two days past.

Satur 13th. The two men load their slays with near two hundred white fish.

Sund 14th. Extreeme bad & Stormy weather with a very hard North wind prevented Mr. McDonells men setting out.

Mond 15th. The weather is very cold this morning, the coldest day that we have had yet this winter; therefore Mr. M^cD's men don't set out.

Tues 16th. Still cold but Old Desrocher is in such a hurry that 'tis impossible to prevent their setting out.

Wednesday 17th. Thurs 18th. This afternoon the weather grows a little milder; though not yet fit to travel on the Lake.

/19/ Friday 19th Feby. Nothing new. The weather is more mild than it has been these some days past. I immagine that Desrocher & Aurielle have not reached home 'till late to-day, as they were very heavily loaded, upwards of two hundred fish (white) – Sun Shine.

Satur 20th. A little after sun set I returned home from visiting my traps, I found Mr. Campbell had arrived here about ten O'Clock with two men (Belouin & Gendron): he came for an assistance of Goods, liquor &c. This is now the seventh day that he has left his Fort (at Kakinowachague)¹⁸ owing to too much Cold & bad weather – Nearly the same weather as Yesterday –

Sunday 21st & Mond. 22nd. Bad & windy weather has prevented their setting off to-day.

Tues 23^d. A little after sun rise they set off with what articles I could spare him. – He told me at the same time that he was much in want of a man to pass the remainder of the Year with him, I accordingly sent Younger Fortier, very mild weather, though a hard wind.

Wednes. 24th. Nothing new. Very mild weather. S. wind.

Thurs 25th Friday 26th. Very fine weather, though a hard South wind – The snow melts much.

---

18 Campbell's post in 1807–08 was apparently at the bottom of Washoe or Humbug Bay: see Appendix E.

Note Mr. Campbell has told me that old Muffle D'orinialle was within a day's march of his Fort; & that he was starving & had almost always starved since I were at their lodges. He had but very few skins; but had not traded any.

/20/ Satur. 27ᵗʰ Sun 28ᵗʰ Febry 1808. Nothing new. Fine weather yesterday; but to-day Stormy. Westerly wind.

Mon. 1ˢᵗ March - Very fine weather. South Wind.

Tues. 2ᵈ Wednes 3ᵈ Thurs 4ᵗʰ. Nothing extraordinary but very fine as has been for these some days past. S wind.

Friday 5ᵗʰ Saturday 6ᵗʰ. Cold bad weather these two days. N wind. Young Richard this day killed 3 large beaver & 3 small.

Sunday 7ᵗʰ. Fine mild weather. This afternoon Old Muffle-D'orinialle & his family arrived here with but few Peltries; & in a miserable starving condition. He had not seen Eyagon or any other indian since a few days after I left his lodge in Decʳ except his son-in-Law & Garcon-du-Morpion. This is the first of my indians that I have seen since the 8ᵗʰ Decʳ when I left their lodges; owing to the too great distance, difficulty in finding out the road; & a heavy body of snow that fell soon after my arrival home. I got but 40 Skins from the whole of them; & there were many martins –

Monday 8ᵗʰ. Out of 10 Quarts of mixed rum I gave Yesterday to the old man he but just recovers his senses.

Tues 9ᵗʰ. Yesterday & to-day are very cold, snowy & drifty a hard westerly wind. –

Wednese 10ᵗʰ Thurs 11ᵗʰ. Nothing new, but very Cold & a hard Westerly wind. So as to prevent old Muffle from hunting.

/21/ Friday 12ᵗʰ. About four O'Clock this afternoon Eyagon arrived from his lodge which is very near (that is, at th'other end of the bay). It is now one moon & an half since he, Cû-Fessé & his Son-in-law have seperated; they each took their own way.

Satur 13ᵗʰ. Early this morning I sent Relle & Wells a-head of Eyagon's women; & to bring each a load; for they have a good deal of Pounded meat. A little before noon they all arrived, Iägon gave me his furs which altogether amount to no more than forty-four Skins. I was obliged to give him a large Keg, in which I put no more than 7 Quarts HW.¹⁹

19 By a large keg, Nelson probably meant the 10-gallon kegs used to transport rum and high wines* from Montreal, so he was diluting his high wines almost sixfold. Assuming that the high wines were about 50 percent alcohol, the final concentration would have been less than 10 percent.

Sunday 14th Monday 15th. Nothing new, but fine weather as usual.

Tues. 16th Wednes 17th. The indians take each some debt and prepare to set off a hunting up the river.

Thurs 18th. Bad weather prevents the departure of the indians. The weather extreemly drifty & snowy; but soon clears.

Friday 19th. The indians set off today; and about noon Mr. M[c]Donell arrived from Pigeon River. He brought two men with him, & suffered yesterday a great deal in that hard gust of wind that passed yesterday morning. They were on a traverse of about three leagues from the iles-du-Maskquiege to the Tête-au-Pishew. They were taken on a sudden & nearly suffocated by the drifting snow which obliged them to shelter themselves behind their slays; but not without much anxiety fearing /22/ to freeze to death upon the ice & ne'er perhaps be found by any human being when to their great joy (after about an half hour's residence on the bare ice, one of them not being able [to] resist much longer on account of the piercing wind was oblige to walk about) they percieved the land not being being above fifteen or twenty acres distance.

Satur 20th. The worst part of his history I reserve for this day's Knews. And it cannot be without horor that I reflect on the cruel bar-barity of a Savage villain who after having been shown more kindness to than many other of his fellow <u>Brutes</u> has with one of his sons put to death three of our men in River ouinipique; and as if he not yet done enough to show (in appearance) in what contempt he held us, he killed & sacrificed one of their dogs. Mr. La Croix who is master of that post, being informed of this melancoly Knews, went in person to see how far this might be true & what was become of these unhappy men; & to bury them. But even this small gratis does not seem to have been granted them. The place was found where they were murthered, but this was all. For not the least appearance of the earth's being dug up appeared anywhere, unless he has had the care to thrust them under the ice (as is supposed from the vestiges that were seen) the better to clear himself from suspicion, if there yet remained any means. He has escaped with all his family, but it is supposed that he will be some-where detected.[20]

20 Alexander McKay, the NWC partner, paid a visit to the HBC's Thomas Miller at Lac du Bonnet on 28 January 1808, during which he reported "that He has had 3 of his men mur-derd in the Lake of the Woods" (HBCA, B.103/a/1, fo. 7r). The news took about eight weeks to find its way to Nelson at Dauphin River.

/23/ Sunday 21ˢᵗ March. Fine weather nothing new. Mr. MᶜD remains all day & I prepare to take a trip with him back.

Mond 22ⁿᵈ. Weather clears up this morning & we set off but were obliged to camp at the Islands about three leagues from here[21] on account of the rain, snow, & wind.

Tues 23ᵈ. We set off late & at dusk arrived at their house in about two leagues in pigeon river, considering the badness of the roads & other little circumstances I think that the distance of about 15 leagues is not bad going. –

Wedn. Thurs. Friday 26ᵗʰ. Mr. MᶜD. & two of his men conducted us near the entrance of the river, they returned, & we proceeded on our voyage; but a storm soon arising we were obliged to encamp at Tête-âu-Pishew.

Satur 27ᵗʰ. Yesterday's storm having rather increased we did not set off till late this morning, luckily the wind was Easterly which was in our backs. We arrived a little past noon at the house. The weather was so drifty & bad that at certain intervals we could not see the distance of an acre before us. I was almost surprised on my arrival here to find La Besette at the house with the Canoe +One of those five indians at whose lodges I had been in the month of Decʳ. He passes the Spring with us.+ who arrived late last night; their hunt from what they say I am afraid is not great. Their lodges are in the first lake (one days journey through the woods) where they & old Cu-fessé intend to make sugar.[22]

/24/ Sunday 28th March. The weather is if anything worse than these two preceeding days, therefore prevents the People from setting off. Old Muffle who by Lord Eagon's orders came Yesterday for people to go for more[23] meat to their lodges but having no men to spare I did not send, nor even gave them room [rum]; for, exclusive of near two kegs that they drank on their arrival here, Young Richard had given them a small keg while I was at Pigeon river, at Mr. MᶜDonell's, for the meat of about one Moose that he got from them. He is gone back not very well pleased.

---

21 The islands in the mouth of the present Sturgeon Bay.

22 The sugar maple does not grow in Manitoba, so the source was probably the Manitoba maple or box elder, *Acer negundo*.

23 At this point Nelson inserted the following: "I should have taken this, even though I gone for it myself; or had I been in as much want for it as last year; but (thank God it is quite the reverse) I rather wish that they should hunt wherewith to pay their debts; for I am afraid that some of them will remain greatly behind hand." Moose meat was bought as it came in, and was not used to satisfy the hunter's debt; for that he was expected to bring furs.

Monday 29th. As the weather cleared up last night at day break I sent off young Richard with Relle & Dalcour, a little HW, the remainder of the strouds* (2 fathoms), a laced Coat, 5 faths tobacco, 9 measures of Powder & a sufficiency of shot & ball. N. & N.E. wind.

Tues. 30th. In the course of this last night there fell near three inches deep of snow. Fine weather to-day but a hard W. wind.

Wednes. 31. The men arrived about Noon with a good load each; that is, in peltries, & meat. The weight of the Peltries amounted to 92[lbs] the greatest part was beaver except a few martins, some otters, 2 drest skins & a kind of Parchment. The men on their return here told me of having seen two Swans yesterday. This is the first game that we have seen this year except two eagles the 20th. Fine weather S.W.; & N winds. –

/25/ April 1808. Thursday 1st. For the beginning of a month nothing new has happened. – The weather is calm for once.

Friday 2nd. Nothing new this forenoon. About 4 O'Clock this afternoon Lord Eyagon & old Muffle arrived from above. They have but little meat, & less furs; for they have no more than about twenty skins altogether not one fourth part of what they latterly took upon debt. Very fine weather. Mild –

Satur. 3[d]. For about nine pieces of dry meat & a little fresh, besides those few skins of their debt, I was obliged to give three quarters of a keg of mixed rum for nothing. – From day breake till near noon there fell near six inches of snow; the weather is very mild.

Sunday 4th. My Lord [Ayagon] came this morning to see me, but he had the precaution of bringing a martin & two Parchment skins for which I was obliged to give about three quarts more he is very troublesome to get more. Fine weather the wind W. & N.

Mond. 5th. Yesterday afternoon Trempe & Braconier arrived from Mr. Campbells for rum tobacco & other things. The weather is very mild: & the indians all set off. –

Tues 6th. It rained a little this forenoon, but clears up about noon. The wind is from N. to E. to S. then to W. & back again always changing – Culèvé arrives.[24]

Wednes 7th. Unfavourable weather prevents Mr. Campbell's /26/ men's setting off, – as besides they wish to cut through a point of

24 This is the first appearance in the journals of any of the Mashkiegon band that began trading at Nelson's Dauphin River post in the fall of 1809. In 1808–09 they were hunting on the east side of Lake Winnipeg, and were probably the most important group trading with Alexander Macdonell at Pigeon River. This visit by Cul-Levé, one of the principal hunters in this band, may have been the first step in planning for the move.

woods. About Noon Cû Fessé's son-in-law arrived: he brought the meat of three beavers with the skins of four & three otters, all which he killed since three days past when he left his lodge to come this way. I gave him five quart of mixed rum, as his being with his two women. Wind continually changes as yesterday. fine weather.

Thursday 8th. This morning Trempe & Braconier set off for their home as do the indians for their own. The chief[25] purport of Mr. Campbell's sending here was for a little rum for him & tobacco for Alex[r] M[c]Kay Esq[r] #Brother to Mr W[m] M[c]Kay a proprietier of N. W. Co.# at Bottom of river ouinipique.

Friday 9th. This morning Cû-fessé's son in law set off for his lodge: I gave two Gallons of mixed rum for him & his father-in-law. This day we threw away below the point about five hundred fish (Pike, Pickeral, & Succors) being more than we can consume.[26] We seen a Swan this afternoon. Cold & hard wind N.

Satur 10th. About Noon the wind turns South. We seen three Bustards,* the first game this season. About noon one of Muffle D'orignialle's women & a boy arrived here; they brought 8 Pieces of dry meat two Moose-Snouts, & a parchment Skin. For this I gave them two & a half Gallons of mixed rum. Mild –

Sund 11th. Young Ricard Yesterday killed three Bustards. Nothing new for this days knews, only that it rained hard this morning. North wind this evening.

Mond 12th. Nothing new. Fine weather & a hard wind.

/27/ Tues 13 Wednes. 14th April. Nothing new, but a hard Westerly wind & rain this morning. Young Richard Killed two Cranes.

Thurs 15th. The men this day finished making a decent railing round poor old deceased Pere Richard. I thought rather to be named a house for it is made of large logs and a roof. I put a board at his head with his name & his supposed age (62 years) but his Cross shall not be put up till when we set off.

Friday 16th. This being Good Friday we kep[t] it as ordained. Cold weather. Wind continually changing.

Satur 17th. Nothing new. Changing wind.

Sunday 18th. According to some mistaken calculations unknown to

---

25 Nelson provides a long note to this passage, explaining the supposed conspiracy that kept the traders in a state of alarm all summer. Because of its length, this note has been left in place and is printed at the end of this journal.

26 With the mild weather coming, the frozen fish in the fish house would soon thaw out and rot.

me we have passed it according to the English Calendar either in the date of the month or the day of the Week, for in this Calendar it ought to be Sunday 17 April owing to some unaccountable mistake in the week or the month; however, I keep my old rule. Monsoon

Monday 19th. Young Richard & Dalcour go this morning to get La Bessette's Canoe in Monotagué river about nine leagues from this. The wind Changes so often, that is from W. round by North to the east & always so Cold that I for the future will not make no more mention of it except it happens to come again South.

Tues 19th [sic]. About 10 O'Clock My Lord [Ayagon] arrived with old Pin's son-in-Law to old Muffle D'orignialle. I got from his Lordship six Skins in beaver & three in martins, he is sorrowful for not drinking. Young /28/ Richard & Dalcour arrive this afternoon but have not the Canoe as the river or rather ice is nearly broke up & learnt by old Muffle when they seen that it was intirely impossible to reach the Canoes occasioned their return. They brought from his place the meat of three beavers with the Skin of one.

Wednes. 20th. His Lordship having arrived here without his Canoes set off with his family to bring them. Nothing new.

Thurs. 21st. Eyagon & old Muffle with his family arrive with their baggage, Canoes & the remainder of their debt. From old Muffle I got eight beaver & two otters, & from his two Sons about ten skin in Peltries. I gave them the rum that remains for the present use being about the third of a Keg. +This morning we threw 480 white fish away.+

Friday 22nd. A little South wind 'till about Noon & the weather so hot that the river breake's up & at evening pritty near rid of all the ice, 'tis now about eight Days since the snow is all melted in the woods. D'abour [Dalcour] goes for bark to mend his Canoe.

Satur 24th. Eyagon & old Muffule set off up the river in their [canoe] as the river is now intirely clear of ice. They go about 8 leagues in the river when they strike to the right over an old & short portage to fall on the upper part of La Riviere-du-Chemin-de-Guerier.[27] Old Muffle goes as far as the lake (Ouinipique) & my lord goes on the upper part. Hard wind.

Sunday 25th. Nothing new, but cold raw weather.

Mond 26th Tues 27th. Yesterday & a part of the night it rained. The wind is not hard, but from a cold quarter E. Fine warm weather to-day.

27 Ayagon and Mouffle d'Orignal were going to hunt on Warpath River, Ayagon taking the upper part, and Mouffle d'Orignal the lower part close to its mouth at Lake Winnipeg.

/29/ Wednes 28th April. An extraordinary incident has distinguished last night above all since October. While Young Richard was setting upon the wharf, Seignieur Rassette on the opposite shore, & straight [opposite] to Richard fired his Gun upon a musk-rat though he was a few feet above the level of the water & the river about 120 Paces broad, & fired very near in shore. Yet some of the Shot went at least fifteen feet above the level of the river one grain struck Richard on his forehead, pierced the skin & flesh & flattened itself on the scull-bone about two inches just above the right eye & another Grain gra[zed] his temple; – two grains also pierced Dalcour's Capot. The day before – Yesterday, the men put out a Net & take more fish than can be made use of. Fine weather & S. wind by spells.

Thurs 29th. My Lord & Old Muffle arrived here much sooner than they promised on account the water being so exceedingly low as to be impossible to navagate it. A hard S. wind & very warm.

Friday 30th. Very hot weather & it rained & Thundered by spells. My Lord killed but [sic] otters in his voyage: he gave them to me, mais en moyen Moyen de Moyennée, Old Muffle killed nothing & is pitiful!

Saturday 1st May 1808. Nothing new. –

Sunday 2nd. Old Cù Fessé; his Son-in Law, La Bezette & Cana arrived from above, – they have finished their hunt, & pass the remainder of the spring here in making Canoes &c. I gave them two Kegs of mixed rum, – it is the last. They made but few speeches Old Cù-fessé paid the remainder of his debt & gave me ten very large beaver, so that I may not speak with an empty mouth to /30/ Mr. Cameron in favour of those indians at whose lodges I were in last December. They made but little sugar & gave me less. It rains by showers.

May 3d. Stormy & bad rainy weather. North wind. Nothing new.

Tues 4th. About sun set Yesterday it began to snow, & snowed all day with a very high wind, in the afternoon the snow ceased but the wind continued as hard as before. Through Curiosity I measured the snow at different places in the woods & found it to be six inches and a half.

Wednes 5th. Weather is more mild than yesterday but did not prevent the ice taking in the river (intirely aCross) as thick as a Crown Piece. Richard begins to mend D'alcour's Canoe.

Thurs 6th. Nothing new, but frost.

Friday 7th. An uproar in the indian Camp has turned all upside down. It is occasioned by Old Muffle's women two of whom went to gather gum, but find a very uncommon large track in the woods bent outwards, they took it to be the Windigo.*

Satur 8th. A hard frost. Last night a Grand Counsel was held here by the indians where in they asked if it <u>Could</u> be true that all the <u>rum</u> was already spent & not a drop to be had for them! but when they found that there was none they returned in <u>Peace</u>!! Fine weather though a piercing Cold North & North East Wind.

Sunday 9th. A South-westerly wind & no frost though yet, there is in some places much snow upon the Ground.

Monday 10th. Nothing new. Bezette begins to make a Canoe. – North wind – fine weather.

/31/ Tuesday 11th May 1808. Yesterday after writing my Journal, about 4 O'Clock in the afternoon, we perceived a Very Great smoke ascending in enormous Clouds at E[ast] from this whence I suppose it to be as a kind of a Signal at Pigeon River. Richard finishes D'alcour's Canoe & goes with Old Muffle to Moncotgué river Monseigneur Rassette sets [off] also.

Wednes. 12th. Monseigneur arrives again with all his family he returned from his Campment that was about an half league from here. Though he was well apprised of this yet his obstinacy preponderated over our arguements.

Thurs 13th. Nothing new no farther than that we begin to make up our Peltries into Packs.

Frid. 14th. Another fright has again turned all upside down, obliged the indians to tie up their dogs mouths, to prevent them barking or giving warning; mother Rassette with her children stop here also (but the old man her husband being always conducted more by a spirit of fanatacism than any real courage remained at his tent), – All this was & much more was [sic] occasioned by little Michel Richard who being about one mile distant from here a-hunting said to have received a part of the Contents of a Gun load of Shot in his legs; he said that it was done purposely to shoot or kill him he thinks, & the more to verify this he says that he seen the smoke of the Gun & the wadding burning quite near him, besides a large black dog that came out of the bushes, with a number of other indeniable truths. All this was not wanted /32/ necessary to set them again. They passed the night, but 'twas not with the less anxiety but this morning finding that no one had yet come,[28] they thought that all was over. – We finish making our packs near six in number.

28 The larger concern was that the boy might have been shot at by a Sioux war party. This would have been unusually early in the season for war parties to be abroad.

Sund. 16th May. Richard & his brother arrive from their hunting party. Monseigneur [Racette] sets off again as the wind is south which makes a road close in shore but large enough for him to pass. He had not gone far when the wind turned N. & with such violence that it drove the ice back again with such fury as in some places to make it heap up in extraordinary large piles against the trees where he now lays up & blockaded.

Mond. 17th. Old Muffle's son-in-law arrived here for the loan of a steel trap; & he told me that Old Muffle's wife was arrived. This is such a singular piece of savage ferocity that I can't forbear making mention of it; & I dare say that no one has ever yet heard or seen of such a thing, except that it be in this lady herself. Muffle on account of some dispute with her, had beat her, that is, a slap in the face; she went out & sat at the lodge door disputing her right with her husband who was indoors. He menanced her that if she would not be quiet that he would give her such a beating as she had not yet had while with him. This with some other words put her in such a rage that she tore off her clothes & threw them into her husbands face & set off quite naked not so much as a shoe upon her foot only a small handful of hay which /33/ she held before her running towards the woods as hard as her legs could bear her. This so surprised them that she had a considerable distance upon them before any of them knew what step to take, at last, the old man at the head and the others afterwards, pursued 'till night when they were obliged to return without her. After two days search they gave over all hopes of ever seeing her again, thinking that she had committed suicide. However bad her situation with her husband was, she preferred it to death & even the state that she was then in. She slept out two nights and each night it froze very hard without fire or the least covering whatever except <u>perhaps</u> a little hay, & returned the third day in a miserable condition her flesh & skin tore in several places by running through the woods and swamps. This, to me, & I daresay to every one else will appear very strange; & it would appear the same to them also if they were not accustomed to such farces. For, if not in every drinking bout it's the next thing to it, that when she has a quarrel with her husband she makes no scruple of standing upright in the lodge & let her Clothes fall down to the Ground and remain as a statue quite naked before the children & all others 'till such times as a good drabbing from her husband obliges her to put them on again.

Tues. 18th May. The weather is rather milder than usual; & the ice melts much.

Wednes. 19ᵗʰ. This afternoon Welles who visits the nets took a very large sturgeon with several white fish. These are not the first though they are no way numerous.

/34/ Thurs 20ᵗʰ. An extraordinary large fire kindled by the indian women who were out raising bark for Canoes, but unperceived to them. It reached this a little past noon & continued burning with all the fury immagineable 'till a hard & unexpected storm with some rain drove it from here, otherwise we would have run great danger also of burning or Suffocating in the smoke which ascended the Skies in unspeakeable large Clouds. The wind & rain Continues 'till night. The ice breakes

Frid. 21ˢᵗ May. Yesterday's wind is as hard as ever; but in getting up this morning I was surprised to Yet find the Ground covered with the Snow that fell during the night. There appears no more ice upon the Lake, so now we have some hopes of setting off as soon as it may be Calm. The wind is N & N.N.W.

Satur. 22ⁿᵈ. Mother Rassette from her Camp has come to see us to day: They have nothing to eat & can't stir or move on account of the ice that has amassed in extraordinary large piles all along the woods. The wind falls & the ice appears again very Close & all in one Cake, therefore, I dont now expect to set off till nexth month. It has froze as hard this last night as any in the whole month of April. The wind is Easterly which drives the ice in.

Sund. 23ᵈ. The weather is Yet rainy & Snow'y (though there fell but very little of this last). The ice comes in but slowly.

Mond. 24ᵗʰ. The weather is fine about Noon; – & the wind turns to the E. The men embark in their canoe to see if there be no [any] road for us to get out of this tiresome hole, but find none. But very few fish.

/35/ Tues. 25ᵗʰ May 1808. The remainder of the ice, that is, that which is perceptible from here to the islands, is very close in shore. The whole band of raggy muffins are set off. Old Muffle with Madamme La Défarteuse²⁹ or the slave arrive here: he brings two brown Bear Skins, one Large black dº, five (fine) otters & eight rats, all which I take for twenty-two Skins. So now the old Gentleman only owes eight. A hard N.N.E. wind.

Wednes. 26ᵗʰ. We did not set off till late in the morning from our houses; & were obliged to encamp at about one league's distance in the

29 Literally "the stripper," that is, the Ojibwe woman who responded to her husband's threats by taking off all her clothes and running into the woods, on 1 May. Why Nelson gives the alternate name "the slave" is not known.

entrance of a small river at the foot of the traverse on account of a very hard N wind. See page [blank].

Thurs. 27th. Just at the dawn of day we set off & at about 9 O'Clock in the morning we were obliged again to encamp at L'Isle-du-Campment (exactly opposite our last Campment of last fall) on account of the ice being in appearance yet almost as strong as in last February. I conclude we are here for sometime. A few hours after our arrival the indians killed a (female) Moose, very fat considering the season. She had a young one but it could not be found. A very hard N. Wind –

Frid 28th. The indians were out a hunting after that Young Moose but could not find its track. Iägon speared a sturgeon. – Old Muffle with his Son in law & all his family encamped here to-day; – I got but 12 rats & an Otter from them; they are pitiful & they think that Monseigneur [Racette] will be here to-morrow.

/36/ Satur. 29 May. This is the second day that the men have put out a Net; we take plenty of red succors, & a few Pike. This is the only sort of fish we eat here except a Sturgeon that the indians (Iägon) killed, – he gave it to us – Monseigneur with all his family arrive here in an extraordinary pitiful & starving Condition.

Sund 30th. Last night the indians made Gonglerie or Cunjured. Old Muffle was the cunjurer not only because he was the only one able to do it, but on account of his wives & Children's sicknesses to know what was their sickness; & what medicine would be most proper for his giving them; he was told it & it was also done. I also asked the Mee-shee-Kain how long we were to remain Yet here. He said two nights, & that it would Yet be six before Mr. Cameron would set off from his fort – ????30 A Southerly wind the ice drives out fast.

Mond 31st. Young Richard & his family with Monsr Rassette set off a head. They Gum & arrange their Canoe as they made it narrower; because it went too slow, & made two oars [paddles]. About Noon we perceived a very large smoke at about A.E. [for Southeast] from this, which we take to be about beaver river (between Pigeon river & Tête-aû-chien). Very calm all day: the indians kill two Sturgeons.

Tuesday 1st June. We embarked about Sun-rise & having a fair wind we carried sail untill the Point, & on the S. side of it we found Richard & Rassette encamped; the[y] had killed a two year old Moose on their

---

30 Nelson was describing the shaking tent ceremony; for the fuller account that he wrote later, see Brown and Brightman (1988), 39ff. Jennifer Brown points out that "Mee-shee-Kain" was likely a mishearing of *jiisakaan*, the Ojibwe word for the shaking tent itself.

arrival here Yesterday. As there was yet too much ice in the bay to travel any distance we put ashore, but re-embarked about /37/ Noon (for the wind had already drove the ice far beyond any of the points); & at last encamped at Tête-aû-Peshaw. +[31]

Wednes. 2nd June 1808. A little after Sunrise we finished loading our Canoe & proceeded in our Voyage; but were obliged to put on-Shore about one league beyond (S.) having in vain attempted to Cross. The wind was fair, but too Strong – This traverse is about one league long.

Thurs. 3[d]. The wind having shifted & increased prevents our departure. It thunder's, lighten's & rains very hard but only for a short time this evening. The wind is E.S.E. but [sic].

Frid. 4 The weather is mild & more calm wherefore we set off & at L'isle-a-la-Fremboise we met, that is, Richard met a Canadian whom I suppose to be Old Hoole (for we passed on the N. side of this island; that is the east end & the old man on the west end which occasioned our not seeing him). He told Richard that there were free people in four or five Canoes coming behind. We put a shore at Pike-head [Tête-au-Brochet, Jackhead] where I think we remained near four hours & in the course of which time we set a Net & took many Pike & but two or three Pikeral & about 3 leagues beyond we met the three rather four Canoe loads of Free People, all bound to the Athabasca.[32] We encamped at the Islets verd.

---

31 The "+" symbol indicates that Nelson intended an endnote here, but there is none. The name means Lynx Head or Point; Ojibwe: *bizhiw*.

32 Peter Fidler, who was surveying his way northwards along the eastern shore of Lake Winnipeg, met these "free" Canadians (that is, not employed by the fur companies) on 31 May, and travelled with them until 2 June. He records the encounter thus: [31 May] "3 Large & 1 middle size Canoe met us 2 miles beyond last observation, they came from Red River along SW side – there are 21 Men of them all free except one Man, they are going to the Athepes cow to hunt Beaver – they put up 1½ mile ahead of us." [2 June] "The Man with the Canadian woman his wife, means to winter with Mr Tomison at Duck Lake in Churchill River – gave him a sketch to fine [find] it … These men Mitchel Alarie in particular has a Letter of recommendation from Mr Hugh Hen[e]y – added a Confirmation to it" (HBCA, E.3/3, fo. 58v). The man with the Canadian woman must be the famous Jean-Baptiste Lagimodière with his wife Marie-Anne Gaboury, almost unique in the northwest of that time as a woman of fully European descent. Michel Allary, a NWC clerk at Fort Dauphin in 1799 (Masson 1960, 1:62), presumably had been one of the many NWC employees laid off after the coalition with the XYC. Whether he succeeded in getting employment from the HBC at once is not known, but Michel Allerie, senior, was at Athabasca for the HBC in 1820–21, and at Edmonton House in 1821–22. In 1822–23, still on the Saskatchewan, he was listed as a freeman (HBCA Biographical Sheet: "Allerie, Michel"). Nelson missed meeting Peter Fidler by about three days.

Satur 5th. At the break of day we set off & encamped at river-au-Sang [Bloodvein River]. We found a large band of indians waiting Mr. Campbell's [sic: should be Cameron's] arrival.

Sund. 6th. The [wind] turns Easterly & is very high it begins to rain also. Nothing new.

/38/ Mond. 7th June 1808. In spite of all bad weather, wind & rain, Iägon [Ayagon] arrives here & encamps with the indians who are but at a small distance from this.

Tues 8th. Late this evening Old Muffle arrived & encamped with us. – An extraordinary storm.

Wednes. 9th. The wind turns S.S.W. & W & North & the weather Grows calm & fine. An indian arrived from Pigeon river, but the knews that he gave us was not Great but he told us to expect Mr. Cameron tomorrow, if the weather be Calm

Thurs 10th. Mr. Cameron arrived here about 8 O'Clock; & but a short time after his arrival all the indians came to see him. To mine; that is Ayagon he gave a Coat, hat, & feather; to Old Muffle he gave an Ilinoi Capot;[33] to Old Cû fessé, he gave 1 Blkt 3 pts & one fathom HB's Strouds (as payment for his present), & after a long speech he gave them one Keg mixed rum, 6 quarts of Powder Shot & Ball in pro-portion among them. To his own he gave two small Kegs of mixed rum with some very proper speeches occasioned their departure to their lodges in a very bad [temper];[34] tempestuous weather conducted by a hard N wind; though very calm this morning.

Frid 11th. Weather bound all day Satur 12th We set off very early as the wind abated some, & after having stopped for late breakefast & conducted by a fair [wind] we took up Mr. Campbell at river Casse & encamped at at [sic] our Campment of last fall on the Point of river aû Gavion.[35]

---

33 Cameron's gifts of a coat and a capot recognized certain hunters for their usefulness to his department. Willmott and Brownlee (2010, 81) cite a description of the "approved uniform for clerks" in the HBC in the 1860s as a "grayish blue cloth 'Illinois' capote with silver-plated buttons."

34 By "very proper speeches" Nelson meant speeches that rebuked the Indigenous people for bad behaviour, in particular for failing to apply themselves to hunting for furs. Though a new arrival on Lake Winnipeg, Cameron, as a veteran trader with Ojibwe hunters in the Nipigon country, understood very well the use of ceremonial oratory when trying to manipulate his Indigenous customers.

35 As already noted, Alexander Campbell had wintered somewhere near the bottom of Washow Bay, and left his winter quarters to wait for the rest of the Lake Winnipeg outfits at Broken River. Peter Fidler met him there on 31 May. Rivière Cassé or Broken River is

/39/ When we put a shore last night we took but [4 lines heavily crossed out] we met some Kay [*sic?*] & last of all Stopped at Bottom of river &c.

Sunday 13 June 1808. When we put ashore last night it was but to make Kettle when we immediately re-embarked, fearing that a small wind might prevent us reaching Fort Alexander[36] or bottom of river ouinipique; & we did not stop 'till the entrance of the lake (rather, river). Here we shaved & cleaned ourselves & reembarked lastly for the fort: – We met Mr. Alex^r McKay & Mr. Crebassa who came in a light canoe ahead of us.

Monday 13th June 1808 –

Early this morning Mr. Cameron sent off two light Canoes* ahead of Red river people as they are too heavily loaded to make any progress in their rout.[37] Between 9 or 10 A.M. Mr. Dorion [Louis Dorion] for [from] Pimbinat river arrived with four Canoes & two Batteaux's [bateaux*] all heavily loaded. He remains here sometime to mend & arrange his Canoes. /40/ This morning Tête-grise & at evening old Gagnian & Premiers eldest son came here for rum but were referred 'till tomorrow. We got three sturgeons from other indians. – Mr. Campbell & I were employed in untying & drying so many of our skins as were either damp or wet occasioned by travelling in too high a wind. Fine weather, but a very changing wind. –

Tuesday 14th June. Mr. Campbell & I continued working at our Peltries 'till near noon when the indians arrived. There was several fathoms of tobacco & 4 Kegs of mixed rum [given] to The Premier,[38] Tête-Grise, Oiseau rouge, & Gagnian besides another Keg given among the Young men.[39] During these ceremonies Mr. McDonald of Fort-Des-Prairies arrived with 11 Canoes including his own: he immediately took what was sufficient for his brigade & sent them all off except his

---

now Rice River, on the east side of the south basin. See Appendix E for a list of all these places.

36 This seems to be the earliest use of the name Fort Alexander for the NWC depot at Bas de la Rivière.

37 Nelson was beginning his summer posting at Fort Alexander. Most of the business at the depot was now sending off the canoes full of furs to Fort William. Cameron did not leave for the Fort William partners' meeting until 19 June, so the purpose of these light canoes is unexplained.

38 For The Premier, a kind of Grand Chief of the Ojibwe, see Appendix B.

39 This important visit from an influential Indigenous band required time and ceremony. They had arrived the previous day, and had been asked to delay their formal welcome until the post had dealt with the urgent matter of drying the wet furs.

own. In appearance there are good returns from that Department & in general in good health except himself who appears to be very ill.[40] The weather is fine & mild & the wind is South.

Wednes. 15ᵗʰ. Mr. Cameron sends off Mr. Ferguson to the Dalles but not to move untill his arrival there.[41] We make up 10 Packs to day. There were two batteaux's burnt yesterday for their Nails.[42] The weather is extreemly hot to day & it mists just about Noon –

/41/ Thurs 16ᵗʰ June. Before that we were up this morning Mr. Dorion set off but not to go at any great rate. We finished making up the remainder of our packs 12 in number. The weather is very hot today, & the wind is S.W.

Frid. 17ᵗʰ. Long after we were in bed last night Messrˢ MᶜLeod & MᶜKinzie from Athabasca; Mr. John MᶜGillivray from Slave lake; Mr. MᶜTavish from English River; Messrˢ. Campbell & Wills from Rat river; & lastly Mr. Huges from upper Fʳ. D. Prairies accompanied by Messrs Bethune, MᶜKinzie, & MᶜGillivray arrived in a very short passage through the Lake.[43] The returns from all these quarters appear

40 John McDonald "of Garth" was one of the partners in charge of the Fort des Prairies department, the NWC's name for the Saskatchewan River valley. McDonald could delay his own canoe because it was "light." He was on his way out to Montreal, to recover his health, which he did, and returned in 1809 to the Northwest. See biography by Livermore and Anick (1976).

41 Alexander Ferguson or Farquharson, see Appendix D. The Dalles (literally "tiles" or "slabs," probably because of the appearance of the rocky river banks) was a stretch of the upper Winnipeg River, the route through which all the outward canoes would pass. Duncan Cameron apparently meant for Ferguson to settle a post somewhere on the upper part of Winnipeg River, Portage de l'Île, where Cameron was "settling an equipment" according to the journal entry of 31 August.

42 When a bateau was too badly damaged to repair, the simplest way to recover the nails was to burn the boat and pick through the ashes.

43 The minutes of the Fort William partners' meeting in 1807 listed the "distribution of the Wintering Gentlemen" for 1807–08 (Wallace 1934, 246–7); it generally confirms Nelson's list here. These partners' full names are Archibald Norman McLeod, Alexander McKenzie (known as "The Emperor"; not the explorer), John McGillivray, Donald McTavish, John Duncan Campbell, John Wills, and James Hughes. The last three names in Nelson's list are of clerks who were probably being taken to the Fort William meeting as a privilege. For biographical notes on all of these NWC partners see Wallace (1934); for John McGillivray, see also McLean (1985), and for Donald McTavish, see Morrison (1983b). The other McGillivray, by elimination, must be Joseph, one of the twin sons of William McGillivray and his Cree wife, who was stationed at English River in 1806–07 (Wallace 1934, 219). The other two McGillivray clerks, Archibald and Simon, are otherwise accounted for in Nelson's journal of the summer's comings and goings. There were too many McKenzies in the NWC to identify with certainty the clerk mentioned here.

to have been good. This supposed conspiracy of the indians detains the Gentlemen here all day. Old Premier was sent for +See page 61. Where you will have an exact accounnt of this Plot.+[44] & old Roi being the only interpretor spoke to this indian according as he was ordered by the Gentlemen; which speech in my oppinion was very proper on this occasion especially. However, he denied all knowledge of it but cannot go with them out as he was asked but agrees to let his son go in his place. We this day finished pressing & marking our Packs. It rained several showers & a very high wind. Great preperations were made by the Gentlemen in going out, that is Guns & amonition, in case there should be some reality in this story.

/42/ Satur. 18th June 1808. The weather is such as to intirely prevent the departure of the Gentlemen: the wind was very high, & many heavy showers. We idled away our time uselessly though we had a great necessity of making good use of it. We had a dance last night, but soon left it over as all hands were tired & very sleepy.

Sund. 19th. The weather is yet very bad & cedes but very little to yesterday or the day before; but the Gentlemen all embark; Mr. Cameron is with them. They take old Roi & Premiers son with them; the former to interpret & the latter to appease the natives should there be any reality in the aforementioned. One of their loaded canoes (of 19 Pieces Cargo) sets off also. This afternoon & in very rainy weather Mr. Colin Campbell arrived here on foot from Point a la-Mitasse having a brigade of 6 Canoes Conducted by Cartier degraded* by the wind since Yesterday about 10. A.M.[45]

Monday, 20th. It rained successively the whole day through; but the wind has abated a little which has enabled C. [Cartier] to arrive here this afternoon: he sent 4 off & remained with one & his own to be the less embarrassed in the Portages.[46] Since Yesterday NonoCasse has lost his wife.[47]

---

44 See Nelson's extended endnote, printed here on pages 102–4, for the suspected conspiracy and how it was handled.

45 This brigade must have been from English River, the NWC's name for the Churchill. Colin Campbell, clerk, was assigned there in 1806, and so was Joseph Cartier, guide (Wallace 1934, 219). For Cartier, who had one of the longest fur trade careers on record, see Duckworth 1990, 141–3. For Colin Campbell, see the HBCA Biographical Sheet.

46 If the portages became too crowded, transport across them was slowed down, and packs could even get into the wrong canoe. Cartier, the guide, was doing what he could to minimize this "embarrassment."

47 She reappeared on the 28th.

Tues. 21ˢᵗ. It rained the most part of the day nevertheless Cartier set off. We were busy this day in taking the remainder of the inventory & remarking some of our packs from out of the Lake. In honour to Mr. Ferguson his woman early this morning brought forth a fine boy.

/43/ Wednes. 22ⁿᵈ. Cloudy weather with several showers of rain. Mr. MᶜKay set off with several men in a light Canoe to see what retarded our Canoes so much longer than we expected. We finished at last the remainder of our Packs. Crabassa's Step son[48] brought some moose meat which was paid in rum.

Thurs 23ᶜ. The weather is yet dark & Cloudy but clears up about noon. Our Canoes arrived from red river; they had met Mr. MᶜKay at Grand Maret; but continues his rout. We have been fixing the Garden to sow turnips.

Frid. 24ᵗʰ. The men are employed in mending their Canoes, & we sowed turnips. Cloudy & dark this morning, & this afternoon it thunder'd & rained by spells.

Satur 25ᵗʰ. This morning four boats* of red river arrived & at or about 11 A.M. Messrs. MᶜKay & MᶜDonell arrived in company with Mess Chisholm, MᶜKinzie & Caldwell.[49] Bercier is busy in weeding & cleaning the Garden. The weather is exceeding warm.

Sund. 26ᵗʰ. At 8 A.M. Eleven slave lake & rat river Department Canoes arrived in Charge of Mess Larocque & MᶜGillivray:[50] they remained but a few minutes & immediately embarked; & by which time our people were near ready to embark in five canoes loaded with

48 Thus, John Crebassa's country wife had been in a previous relationship, and had a son old enough to hunt moose, an important skill.

49 This was the brigade from Upper Red River, which Alexander McKay had gone to meet. John Macdonell was the partner in charge, with clerks Donald Chisholm, Charles McKenzie, and James Caldwell; this list was assigned to the department in 1806–07 (Wallace 1934, 220). For Charles McKenzie see Bishop 1985. Chisholm's and Caldwell's periods of service with the NWC were apparently short, and little is known about them: see entries in Appendix D. Note the use of boats rather than canoes in the Red River department to carry the pemmican, on a level river system that required no portaging. On their journey beyond this point to Fort William the Red River brigade used canoes like everyone else.

50 Slave Lake here means Lesser Slave Lake, in the Athabasca River department, where Simon McGillivray (one of William's twin sons) was a clerk. The canoes from Rat River, sometimes described as Lower English River, would have been accompanied by one of the English River clerks, Joseph Larocque (Wallace 1934, 219), for the arrangements in 1806–07. The NWC partners in charge of these departments had already passed in light canoes on 17 June.

ten Packs & 17 Kegs of Grease. Mr. McDonell enters his bulls* & Grease. Some of his C[anoes] that remained behind arrived at last.

/44/ Monday 27th June. To our great surprise this morning about 8 O'Clock we seen a canoe double the Point which we at first took to be either some extraordinary accident happen our Canoes, or, news sent to us by the Proprietors in regard of the intended **Ambush**; but we found it to be our own People who returned with Charboneau his [he] having fallen sick Yesterday: – he was obliged to re-embark there being no proper medicine here for his relief. Mr. McKay sets off about 10 A.M. Mr· McDonell's men are hard at work fixing their Canoes &c. An almost irresistible heat just about noon was Greatly allayed by an extraordinary N.W. wind, it lasted about two hours & then became as clear though not so hot as this morning.[51]

Tues. 28 Rassette & Richard set off; the former to pass the summer at blood river, & the latter with Mr. McDonell at Pigeon river. Nonocasse, who, these several days past found his woman has to-day brought us some fresh meat; he hunts in river aû Barbeu, but has seen nothing of Bousquet who promised not to go beyond that & to be back in a few days ready to set off with the whole Brigade. We now, & with all reason apprehend him of desertion.

Wednes. 29th. Mr. McDonell sends off 5 Canoes & all heavily loaded with Messrs. Caldwell & McKinzie on board. Hot weather.

Thurs. 30th. Mr. McDonell himself sets off to-day exactly at noon: he leaves Mr. Chisholm to pass the summer here, as besides his family – We had but [few] decent rooms; but one was employed by his family.[52]

/45/ Frid. 1st July 1808. The wind is from N. to E. is high & Cold. While we were busy in fixing & putting all to rights a brigade of four Canoes from Fort Dauphin arrived, pritty well seasoned with Packing Gum, & six Kegs of Salt.[53] Mr. McDonald [John McDonald "le Borgne"] himself did not arrive 'till evening a little after Lorrin & I had set two nets.

---

51 This wind blew down many trees at Rivière au Barbeu, making it impossible for hunters to follow an animal's track: see entry of 5 July.

52 John Macdonell's family consisted of his wife Marguerite Poitras (probably a daughter of André or Henri Poitras, the NWC interpreter at Fort L'Ésperance in the Upper Red River Department) and at least three children. When Macdonell retired from the NWC in 1812 and took his family down to Canada, his wife was soon baptized with all her children, and her marriage was celebrated, at the Catholic mission at Oka, Lac des Deux Montagnes. See parish register of L'Annonciation-de-la-Bienheureuse-Vièrge-Marie, Oka, entry of 30 January 1813.

53 Salt was one of the usual products of the Fort Dauphin department, taking advantage of the many salt springs in the region. I am grateful to Anne Lindsay for sharing her unpublished research on this topic.

Satur. 2ⁿᵈ. Raw, bad weather. Mr. Crebassa in attempting to hoist the flag broke the Halyards, for which reason we were obliged to take down the staff & put in another cord. At 3 P.M. Mr. McDonald sends off his canoes. Fishing for the first time is 28 in number.

Sunday 3ᵈ. The wind is S & S.E. 'till ten A.M. when it changes to the N where it now remains & blows with all the violence imaginable. The weather is Cloudy & misty 'till noon when it clears up. This day's fishing is 26.

Mond 4ᵗʰ. Nothing new, only that the weather grows more calm & finer towards evening. Lorrin & I set two nets & take a few fish.

Tues 5ᵗʰ. Within a few minutes of ten A.M., Mr. McDonald set off for Fort William; but, before this time Mesdammes Roi, Beaulieu, & Bourassa's wife set off for Red River on a visit but to be back the soon as possible. Old Mausgé & Bercier are employed in weeding the Garden &c. Morning fishing 18; & evening 28. This afternoon Nanofassé [Nanocassé] & Nanjôpe's eldest son arrived here in a starving condition, having been hunting at river au Barbeu where the wind of the 27ᵗʰ June upset & threw down so many trees as to be intirely impossible to follow any track whatever. They are intirely discouraged of hunting in that Quarter.

/46/ Wednes. 6ᵗʰ July. Fine weather. The indians that arrived yesterday were out a saining: they took but 3 small sturgeons which they gave us. We helped in cleaning up the Potatoe Garden. Morning fishing 10. Evening 7.

Thurs 7ᵗʰ. At 3 P.M. 10 Athabasca canoes arrived in charg of Mr. Arch. McGillivray & Guided by Blondin.[54] They set off at 4 having remained but one hour; all that the indians took in their sain [seine*] was but one Sturgeon; they gave it to us. Morning fishing is 15.

Frid 8ᵗʰ. Very fine & clear weather this forenoon, but after, we had several showers of rain when we transplanted some cabbage & 476 Onions. Except t[h]is nothing new. Fishing is 15.

Satur 9ᵗʰ. Clear & fine weather. The indians have been a Saining Yesterday & to-day but without the least success whatever. Morning fishing 3 Evening only 1.

Sund. 10ᵗʰ. Very warm weather. The indians were a hunting but [Nanjobe's son] having lost the flint off his Gun was obliged to return without killing anything, though he seen a Moose; & very near. Between

54 Archibald McGillivray was a clerk in Athabasca according to the 1806–07 arrangements, and Pierre Blondin was one of the guides (Wallace 1934, 219).

two & three P.M. Mr. R. McLeod arrived with his own canoe having left
15 others below;[55] at the Point-aû-Table all loaded of 25 Packs. There
is no knews of any particular consequence in his voyage. – About this
time the weather grows Cloudy and soon after begins to rain thund'r &
lighten with all violence imagineable 'till very late at night.

Mond. 11th. This morning the weather is fine & Calm; but is soon
/47/ succeded by a very thick fog, which, however, soon dissipates by a
little breeze. At 4 A.M. These fifteen Canoes arrive Guided by Delorme
; they take their provisions & other things they want & immediately
re-embark Mr. McLeod with them. Morning fishing 17. Evening 1.
The indians by a present of a few rats, a dresst skin & some berries, &
many promises, obtain a liquor to make a frolick.

Tues 12th July. The indians according to their promise now set off to
go a hunting (with all their families) to where Nanjobe's son missed
that Moose. The weather is fine & Calm. Fishing 15.

Wednes. 13th. The weather is extreemely windy from the S. & S.W. &
very cloudy; & it rains several showers. – The indians return, but with
no success whatever.

Thurs. 14th. The wind is from the S. & not so hard as Yesterday: but
the weather is very hot. Between three & four P.M. Old Mausgé's wife
bid an eternal farewell to this world. At 6 she was buried according to
the Roman-Catholic fashion; bein[g] thus baptized.[56] The wind is now
NW & in appearance we shall have such another storm as we had the
27th of last June.

Friday 15th. The weather is yet cloudy of the remains of Yesterday's
expected storm, which ceded but very little in anything to the former
but rain. Morning fishing 11, Evening 2.

Satur. 16th. The indians that have been here now this long time were
employed in making canoes. Mr. Campbell has hired them to hunt
for the fort as we are now out of all our good /48/ Provisions; & as

55 This was the rest of the Athabasca brigade, Pierre Delorme guide, except for four
lagging canoes that did not arrive until 22 July. The clerk accompanying Delorme's brigade,
Alexander Roderick McLeod, had wintered in Peace River. The journal he kept at Dunvegan
on Peace River in 1806 was printed by Wallace 1929, 122–34. For his biography see Williams
1988.
56 Mausgé was with Nelson at Dauphin River post in the summer of 1810. As no Catholic
priest had been in western Canada for almost seventy years, his wife must have been baptized
on a visit to Canada, or perhaps to Michilimackinac, where missionaries appeared from time
to time.

an encouragement has given them two Quarts of mixed rum.[57] About 9 last night the women of Red river being in a lodge near the back Gate were almost frightened out off their senses by some earth being repeatedly thrown upon their lodge. This they took to be some one who intended to killed [sic] us; & as if some formidable enemy had already taken possession of the Fort they could not be prevailed upon to sleep in their lodges. The women & children of the indians slept in the fort also; & their husbands laid in ambush & actually fired a shot as they say upon an indian, though I am more inclined to believe it was to increase the Panic than anything else. Fishing 15. Bad & overcast weather

Sund. 17th. Another fright last night occasioned such an uproar that Bercier & Lorrin made the tour of the fort upon one side & Mr. Crebassa & I upon the other; but we neither seen nor heard anything. – The indians set off with their families, baggage &c for another hunting part. Mr. C's & B's women set off also to gether berries. – The weather is very calm & warm. From about 8 'till noon-day a pike was seen swiming upon the surface of the water & would often in a manner as it were stand straight up upon the water: this is taken to be some very bad **omen**. Morning fishing 11, evening 15. –

Mond. 18th Cloudy weather &c. We were obliged to set up all night & keep watch in hopes of being able to detect the person or persons who has occasioned these frights for these several nights past: we /49/ did not go to bed 'till sunrise; but we neither seen nor heard anything. The wind is so high as to prevent our visiting the nets.

Tues. 19th July. The wind being yet very high we were obliged to take up the Nets wherein were 47 fish. Messrs. Campbell & Chisholm & I were obliged to draw rails[58] to make filling-in pieces to the fort as this important point was omitted by Mr. McKay; & in case of any future fear, fright, or surprise.

Wednes. 20th. Last night when we were going to bed a person, rather persons [outside] were heard to say "let us take notice & see; but I believe that there are women in this lodge" less than this was enough to set all a going; every one came running in the houses in such confusion as might have been an easy matter to have killed several in their

57 This entry shows that Alexander Campbell, who had supervised the Lake Winnipeg department for the xyc before the coalition, was left in charge of Fort Alexander for the summer of 1808.
58 This may mean to shape and smooth thin pieces of wood with a draw knife, so they could be fitted in between the palisades of the fort, to fill in gaps.

flight had there been any real ill disposed persons. However, be this as it may, the whole of us set up all night without sleeping a wink.[59] Messrs. Crebassa & Campbell each fired a shot as they suppose upon some one who attempted to set fire to the stores; & as a more convin[c]ing proof they think to have heard some one run towards the bushes. After Sun rise we went to bed. At 10 A.M. The White Partridge & Boiteu arrive from Tête-ouverte [Brokenhead] with some dryed meat; they get rum & sleep a little below this. All the women except Roi's wife arrive here.[60]

Thurs 21st. Les tripes D'ourx arrived from above: he brings no knews of any consequence except that all the indians starve. We are all employed in fixing our filling-in wood. Fishing is but 2.

Frid. 22nd. While we were yet all busy in working our wood & our /50/ four Athabasca canoes arrived here guided by Bouché le verd. He has been now 13 days in the days in the Lake most always wind bound. A Man in their brigade by the name of McKay being much swelled in his testicles of having overheated himself remains here in hopes of being cured. Despond's family & our indians &c, arrive in a starving condition, having not had the fortune of seeing even one track. Morning fishing 5, evening 3.

Satur. 23d. We are again all of us employed after the fort while Old Mausgé's busy in hoeing the Potatoes. Morning fishing 5, Evening 4.

Sund. 24th. Bad weather. Nothing new. Morning fishing 4 Even [sic]

Mond. 25h. After a dance that the indians had last night Despond's wife sets off to gether berries at Isle-a-la biche. Meanwhile Old N'anjôpe & his family arrived from black river what they brought was not worth much however they traded it for rum. At 2 P.M. Mr. Thompson[61] arrived arrived [sic] from the Rocky Mountain with only his own canoe; he

59 Summer was the time for the warriors to go to war, and it was possible that some enemies (Sioux, in this region) had crept up to the fort and were hoping to kill someone. It was also possible that some young men were just trying to contact women. No harm was done, and like many other alarms, the disturbances went unexplained.

60 This was the group that had left Fort Alexander to visit Red River on 5 July.

61 David Thompson, the explorer. Whether his wife, Charlotte Small, was with him is not stated, but Nelson rarely mentioned women. Crossing the easternmost range of the Rockies from Rocky Mountain House, Thompson had spent the previous year exploring the upper reaches of the Columbia River, wintering and trading for furs at a new post, Kootenay House. In the spring he came back across the mountains, and made the trip by canoe from the headwaters of the Saskatchewan to Lac la Pluie in forty-three days, where he arrived on 2 August. Two days later he was on his way west again, for another season of exploration in the mountains. Nelson records his brief appearance at Bas de la Rivière again, en route for the Pacific, on 11 August. See Tyrrell 1916, lxxxvi–lxxxix, for a summary of Thompson's movements in 1807–08.

remained but to take a few provisions & re-embarked. Morning fishing 8 Even.

Tues 26th. Having no nets in the water, Lorrin & I prepare a sain & having sained about 2 hours we came home with nothing.

Wednes 27th. Old N'anjôpe not half pleased in consequence of a quarrel with Mr. Campbell yesterday sets off in hopes of finding the HB's people at Broken river as well to get his wants from them as to make oats [collect wild rice]. We sain again, but take nothing. We at last finish this tiresome job of arrangeing the fort.

Thurs. 28th. Bercier cleans up the fort & old Mausgé works in the Garden. The star goes to find Crebassa's step son at isle a la biche.

/51/ Frid. 29^t July. After having sained again this morning without any success we leave all off as being a bad job. The weather is very smoky which we take to be some fire purposely kindled by the indians above. Lorrin & I set two nets – again.

Satur 30. We visited our nets & only took 1 fish. At 4 P.M. Bras Court's son arrived from red river with two women, he brought some meat, berries & a very few skins which they trade for rum.

Sund 31. Old Premier & all family &c arrive here in hopes of not now being long before he'll see his son. He brought some meat which is traded for rum. – At evening NanoCassé arrived from River-aû-barbeu (having been there a hunting since the 27) with the heart of a young moose that he killed to-day: he gives us the whole of it.

Monday 1st August 1808 – At 7 A.M. to the great pleasure of every one [a canoe arrived from up Winnipeg River], though we all remained in doubts 'till its arrival here when we were then certain & convinced of our foolish & false alarms proceeding from credulous & savage superstition. This Canoe was was [sic] for Athabasca with Mr. McGillivray & Harman; they left a brigade of ten other Canoes at the Portage. They gave us the news of Mr. McGillivray's unfortunate Death, as besides much appearance of a war with america.⁶² A Great

---

62 Until the first canoes came back from Lac la Pluie or further east, the people at Bas de la Rivière could not know whether the rumoured conspiracy to attack the canoes had materialized. The clerks in the Athabasca canoe were Archibald McGillivray and Daniel Williams Harmon, the noted fur trade journalist – the latter about to begin a two years' sojourn on Peace River. Harmon and McGillivray had met David Thompson in Winnipeg River on 29 July, and, as Nelson states, they arrived at Bas de la Rivière on 1 August, proceeding at once for their wintering ground (Lamb 1957, 11). They brought news that Duncan McGillivray, brother of William, one of the Montreal agents, had died in April at Montreal, after a long illness.

Personage is said to have come to Fort William by the name of Count de Chabot.[63] The Premier's Son arrived dressed like a Gentleman & a dirk &c by his side. Toussaint /52/ Vaudrie & Vandalle were sent from River-aû-Pembinat with a letter to the Gentlemen passants.[64] At the same time these men informed us of a party of Scioux having made an attack upon the fort; but whether this attack was really intended upon the Fort or upon the indians that were encampd very near it is intirely unknown to us. be this as it may, Mr Henry was not obliged to know their intentions wherefore he ordered his swivel to be fired having shot but twice, they heard the enemy cry & make a long speech afterwards they retired & several of them crying. The next day or some time after they found a saddle & bridle covered with blood.[65]

Tues. 2nd. Old Pin having arrived yesterday & brought much meat M. Cpb. [Mr. Campbell] gave him a small [sic] & returns now at this time Old Boiteu or Ca-wai-be-wee-tone arrived also he brought some meat & other things which he trades for rum. The men as the time now approaches go down below to mow but find the Grass so short (as the indians encamped there late this summer) that they are now obliged to mow behind the fort as the Grass is much longer; but; though not so fine as below.[66]

Wednes. 3^d. At 7 A.M. ten more Athabasca canoes arrived Guided by Bazil Nos & in charge of young Mr. McLeod after they took each 4 Bags Pemican [pemmican] they reembarked.[67] This evening NonoCassé

---

63 For the Count de Chabot, see page 60.

64 Alexander Henry, the NWC partner in charge of Lower Red River, had remained inland this summer, rather than attending the partners' meeting at Fort William. He sent Toussaint Vaudry and "another man" to Bas de la Rivière with letters on 27 July (Gough 1988, 327). The "gentlemen passants" were the partners en route to their wintering grounds.

65 Alexander Henry gives a long account of this incident, which began with the appearance of the Sioux war party across the river from the Pembina post on 22 July; see Gough 1988, 320–8.

66 The mowing was to get hay for the horses that Charles Oakes Ermatinger had procured from Red River in 1806, and were being used for ploughing: see pages 242–3 [excerpt from Nelson's letters of 1811–12, concerning agriculture at Fort Alexander].

67 The guide for this part of the Athabasca brigade, now going to the wintering grounds, was Bazile Nault, and the clerk with him was Alexander Roderick McLeod. McLeod's part of the Athabasca brigade had left Fort Alexander on 11 July, guided by Delorme, so the guide had been changed at Lac la Pluie; Delorme appeared on 8 August, guiding the brigade for Lesser Slave Lake or Athabasca River. This part of the Athabasca brigade took twenty-three days for the round trip from Fort Alexander to Lac la Pluie and back. In contrast, Nelson's journal entries show that the brigades for the nearer departments, such as English River, which were required to go out as far as Fort William, took about forty-three days on the

arrived; he brought the meat of one large bear & a small one. As Mr.
C. does not yet think proper to give him rum for this meat he intends
to encamp here tomorrow.

/53/ Thursday, 4ᵗʰ August 1808. [Because of] a scarcity of good
Powder, being alone (& other indians here) & an unwillingliness to
hunt without being imediately paid in rum, NonoCassé encamps here

Friday, 5ᵗʰ. Nothing new, only that the men are employed in mowing
& drying the hay.

Satur. 6. Premier's Youngest son was out a [hunting] but did not find
any-thing. We expect Mr. MᶜTavish hourly.

Sund 7. Bad & rainy weather all day Mr. MᶜTavish arrived here at 1
P.M. with only his own canoe & Mr. MᶜKinzie with him.[68] They both
have had a severe cold; but now recover fast. At 4 he sets off.

Mond. 8ᵗʰ. Mr. MᶜGillivray arrives here about 8.A.M. & about noon
Mr. J. MᶜTavish & young MᶜGil. arrive here also with five Canoes
Guided by Delorme[69] but after 8 of Mr. MᶜGillivary's Slave Lake
Canoes had, rather, were preparing to set off : they were Guided by
Bouché (Woa can).[70] And while Mr. MᶜGillivary was yet here, Mr.
Hughes[71] made his appearance but could not set off immediately as did
the other his canoes being behind. At Sun set all his canoes arrive, nine

---

round trip to and from Fort Alexander. These travel times show the advantage of allowing
the Athabasca canoes to turn around at Lac la Pluie, where there was a special depot for
Athabasca. These brigades had the farthest to go, and had to make the last part of their
inward journey at the very end of the canoeing season, so shortening their round trip by
about three weeks was a critical advantage.

68 Donald McTavish, normally in charge of English River, was assigned to Athabasca for
1808–09 (Wallace 1934, 254). Which Mr McKenzie was with him is unidentified.

69 John McGillivray, the partner in charge of Athabasca River department, or (Lesser) Slave
Lake as Nelson calls it. Mr J. McTavish must have been a clerk, but he has not been identified. "young McGil" was one of William McGillivray's twin sons by Susan, his Cree wife,
probably Simon who was listed as a clerk with John McGillivray in 1806 (Wallace 1934,
219). Delorme, the guide, had been in charge of part of the Athabasca brigade on the outward
trip: see journal entry for 11 July.

70 Jean-Baptiste Boucher, known as Waccan, was a celebrated man in the early history of
the fur trade in New Caledonia (now north central British Columbia), having first gone there
with Simon Fraser in 1806. According to Morice, he remained in that country for the rest of
his life (Morice 1905, 252–7). Nelson must have been mistaken in identifying the Lesser Slave
Lake guide in 1808, Bouché, with Waccan, however, as in August 1808 Waccan was one of
Simon Fraser's voyageurs, just returning from the famous expedition descending Fraser River
(Lamb 1960, 23, 128, 137, 153). For Waccan see also Duckworth 1990, 137.

71 James Hughes, one of the partners in charge at Fort des Prairies (the Saskatchewan). For a
biographical note see Wallace 1934, 458–9.

in number. Immediately after this he prepares a Canoe with five of his
men & Mr. Henry's two to go to the river au Pimbo [Pembina] –

Tues. 9th. Before day Mr. Hughes & his brigade set off as does the
other canoe that goes for Mr. Henry who is now to winter in lower
Fort-Des-Prairies.[72] Near Noon Mr. Crebassa sets off with his woman
& family to meet Mr. Cameron on the road & gather /54/ as many
indians as he can; & to be at the place where they intend to winter.
About 4 P.M. Mr. J. D. Campbell arrives here with two Canoes for
English river, and at Sun set eight others of his Canoes arrive (Guided
by Paul)[73] wherein were three for the Rat River Department.

Wednes. 10th. A little before sun rise this morning he sets off with
his two canoes the others having set off last night. This Morning
Mr. Crebassa's step son sets off to follow his mother : & Mr. Cpbl.
[Campbell] sends to Crebassa 6 quarts of HWines

Thurs 11th. At about 6 A.M. Mr. D[avid] Thompson arrives here
with only his own canoe for the Pacific Ocean: He is obliged soon to
reembark (though it yet blows very hard) & dry all his thing[s] below
as they all got wet & were being drowned & carried away by the wind
which blew with such violence at N & NW as to make the water raise
to an extraordinary heighth & carried off a great deal of the bark off
the stores. Alard's brother in law arrived from river aû-mort & brought
but very little of any thing with him. NanoCassé sets off for Broken
river, meantime he hunts Close here. Old Boiteu & his family sets off
likewise for river a mort.

Frid. 12th. Very fine & calm weather though very windy Yesterday.
Lorrin & I prepare to go to Broken river to see if the English be there
as well as if the indians have any thing; for we have not seen them as
yet since spring, but were obliged to encamp before we could reach
point a La Mitasse on account of very tempestuous weather (extraordinary high wind & rain).

/55/ Satur. 13. August 1808. We are here wind & weather bound all
day.

Sunday 14th. The wind having changed to another quarter & not
blowing quite so hard as Yesterday we re-embarked & before we

---

72 Since Alexander Henry had remained inland in 1808, the partners' meeting had to send a
special express to him by way of Lac la Pluie and Red Lake to inform him that he had been
assigned to Lower Fort des Prairies (Gough 1988, 327–8).

73 One of the English River guides in 1806–07 was Jos. M. Paul (Wallace 1934, 219). Joseph
Menon Paul was assigned to the Columbia in 1811–12, but was again at English River in
1812–19 (HBCA, F.4/32, 793, 974).

had yet reached the point-ala Mitasse we met old Chastelin's (now Fleurie's) wife who told us that there were no English & but few indians at Broken river with a few other things of no great consequence when we returned in company with her & at about 10 A.M. arrived at the fort. On our arrival I found that Mr. Cpbl. was preparing to send off Premier's son to River-aû-Mort with a small Keg of HWines & word to tell the indians not to pay any regard to what old Roi or Mr. D. McKinzie might say to them & not to follow either upon any consideration whatever; for there should be a fort from this place to winter there.[74] At night Red bird's son-in-law & his brother arrive from Tête ouverte: they bring but little, two skins all which they trade for rum.

Mond. 15th. A very hard wind prevents the indians's setting off. Mr. Chisholm & I lend the men a hand to make part of a stak [haystack].

Tues 16. It blows yet amazing hard; & the weather is clear though it rained, thundered, lightned & blew very hard almost the whole night. This afternoon the Mashkiegon,* of Premier's lodge arrived from hunting; he killed one large & a young Moose the latter of which he gave us, but for liquor.

/56/ August, Wedneseday, 17th. All hands went to-day & lent a hand to old Mausgé & Bercier to gether & put the remainder of the hay in a stack which was soon done. Gendre de l'oiseau rouge & his brother the Boiteu set off about midnight.

Thurs. 18th. A hard south wind & smoky weather which in appearance will not end or rather pass but in rain. Nothing new to-day unless it be my making of Candles (151 in number).[75]

Friday 19th August. Nothing new, unless it be our hourly expectations of the arrival of some strangers to give us knews; and Mr Campbell who repaints the houses.

Satur 20 Nothing new. Sunday, 21st. Nothing of moment this morning but this afternoon Premier's son arrived from his voyage to River aû Mort & spoke & done to the indians in such a manner as intices them to be here the seventh day from this date. Not long after the

---

74 Campbell was sending a message to the Indigenous people at Rivière-des-Morts, who hunted near the mouth of Red River, to ignore anything that the new partner in charge of Lower Red River, Daniel McKenzie, and his senior interpreter, Roi, might tell them, assuring them that the Lake Winnipeg department would maintain a post there in the coming season. See the Introduction for the attempts of the partners' meetings to prevent clashes between the Lake Winnipeg operations and the adjacent Fort Dauphin and Lower Red River departments, and Duncan Cameron's refusal to comply.

75 Candles made of buffalo tallow.

indian was [had] entered the room we discovered two Canoes doubling the Point-aû-Foutre upon whose arrival we found to be Mr. McDonell in C^o with Mr. [blank – must be McKinzie, see 23 August] each for their own department: their canoes will be here in about two days, but Mr. Cameron they left at the Portage des Chiens, so we need not expect them soon. –

Mond. 22nd. We hauled up a boat to dry & afterwards to burn it [to recover the nails]. – Having asked the indians to go a hunting to-day we could not prevent ourselves giving them liquor; but they set off tomorrow.

/57/ Tues. 23^d. August. 1808. Early this morning Messrs. McDonell & McKinzie's canoes arrive here 7 in number; & without any accident. About 3 P.M. Mr. J. McKay of HB. with 4 boats stopped here but M. Heney passed at some distance out in the river.[76] The Duck & Trout arrive also in comp^y with them; they are bound for the plains but we hope to make them return from this.

Wednes. 24th. A little after day set last night Mr. Cpbl. sent old Maûsgé Lorrin & I off in a small canoe with a small Keg HWine to go to the Red River as well to watch the motions of the English as to endeavour to [get] the indians peltries.[77] We encamped at the Portage Sauvage,[78] & early this morning we made it; but were soon obliged to encamp on acc^{nt} of a very high Westerly wind

Thurs 25. It blows yet very hard & the swells are very high nevertheless we embark & after a little abatement of the wind about 4 P.M. we reached the entrance of Red River where we met Bras Court's two sons & two other indians from whom we could not get more than 22 M[usk] rats & a small cub bear. We encamped at River au Mort

Frid. 26. On our arrival last night we found the indians so displeased (from several reasons; whither true or not I can't say) against us that they would not give us any thing whatever, not even to Mr. McDonell

76 John McKay of the HBC was again en route to Brandon House, while Hugh Heney was for Pembina.

77 Determined to assert the Lake Winnipeg department's right to trade at Rivière-des-Morts, Campbell sent Nelson and two experienced men to try to connect with the Indigenous people there before the partner in charge of Lower Red River, Daniel McKenzie, got there. As things turned out, none of the NWC people was well received.

78 A portage across the narrow neck of land that connects the peninsula on which the modern community of Victoria Beach is built. Nelson could use it as a shortcut, as he was in a small canoe, not fully loaded, whereas the Red River brigades, to avoid unloading and reloading, would take the longer way around the point.

(who happened to arrive about 8 A.M.) one M. rat; but a few pieces of bad, dirty, dry meat which he (to the great pleasure of us all) refused to accept. Mr. McKinzie about Noon arrived & immediately /58/ re-embarked, having received nothing, therefore, gave nothing also. About 4 P.M. the 7 boats of HB's people arrive & immediately trade for rum or trash all that the indians have & reembark. Having not been able to get even one rat* we returned with our rum & a dressed Skin & the mortification of seeing those vile, mean, wretches the E[nglish] have preference to ourselves. Before we encamped which was at river-aû-Diable we met Mr. McKinzie's two Canoes & boat.

Satur 27 At Sun rise we embarked, stopped some moments at river la Tête oûverte & encamped at the portage Sauvage without any thing new occurring

Sund 28 Early this morning we made over the Portage & inspite of a very hard head wind about noon we arrived at the fort, as well as Bras Court's two Son's &c.: their lodges & families are now at the Point a-la-Mitasse; & they contend to make oats [intend to collect wild rice] at Broken river en attandant l'arrivée of Mr. Cameron.

Mond. 29th. Pritty windy weather but Clear & warm. At noon young Richard & his family arrive from Pigeon River. His arriving before Mr. McDonell was occasioned by some small difference between them; but we soon expect Mr. M^cD. as well as Mr. Cameron

Tues 30th Nothing new. Wednes 31st About 4 P.M. Alard's brother-in law arrived from lake du Bonèt; but brings nothing except a little oats which (being a rarity) is traded for rum. Not above an hour after this Mr. McDonald of Fort Dauphin arrives having left his canoes at river blanche & Mr. Cameron at Portage de l'isle finishing an equipment. So, we may now soon expect him.

This Dauphin River journal concludes with a few endnotes that Nelson provided to explain or amplify some passages. All but the last of these have been incorporated as footnotes to the text above, each one labelled "Nelson's note." The last note, which is long and unusually interesting, is given below. Nelson, in explaining the context of the supposed conspiracy to attack the fur brigades on their way out to Fort William in May and June 1808, records his understanding of the system of beliefs that was introduced to the Anishinaabe world by the Shawnee Prophet, Tenskwatawa, after visions he experienced early in 1805. It was a nativist movement, characterized by abstemious behaviour and by a desire to return to pre-contact religious and cultural practices. As Nelson explains, the prophet's teachings spread rapidly, and were well established among the western Ojibwe by 1808.[79]

/61/ Nelson's note to his entry of 8 May 1808, on the supposed Indian conspiracy:

There was a confirmation made in his Letter of what Mr. McDonell informed me while he was here. But to give a more clear account of it to any strange person who may happen to read this journal it will perhaps be necessary to let him first know a little of the indian religion & their superstitions. They will believe almost any thing that regards their religion & are able to do many things to maintain it:

There has arisen a new religion among them; that is, they yet make sacrifices & feasts as usual with many other small trifles but none are allowed to make use of the drum & Woabanö,[80] they are to drink but seldom & then not more than one day & a night, nor are they allowed to smoke their tobacco with any kind of herb but the bark of Hard Rouge,[81] besides many other laws that are not worthy mention, except, that they must not go about at nights after the young women as they are accustomed to do. Any person who conforms himself to these is sure to be for ever happy both in this world & in the next, but, any one who should not do as is here mentioned, or Keep, or maintain

79 For the effects of the Shawnee Prophet movement in this part of the country see Peers 1994, 85ff.; she makes use of this note by Nelson, and also of accounts by Warren (1974) and John Tanner (James 1956). For Tenskwatawa himself, see Edmunds 1983.

80 This reference is to the rituals of the Waabanowiwin, a ceremonial practice that was becoming popular among some Ojibwe in the years around 1800, in preference to the older institutionalized Midewiwin. It was frowned on by the older generation, in part because its main purpose was apparently to do harm to enemies. See Angel 2002, 36–8. Nelson's remark seems to mean that the Shawnee Prophet also disapproved of this new practice, perhaps because it was a departure from the older traditions. The prophet and his followers rejected the Midewiwin too, but Nelson does not mention this.

81 Jennifer Brown suggests that Nelson meant the French word hart, referring to withes of the red willow or red osier dogwood. The bark, scraped and dried, was mixed with tobacco or other materials to make a smoking mixture. The use of this "kind of willow, termed by the French, bois rouge, in English red wood" for smoking is described in Carver 1778, 31. This teaching of the Shawnee Prophet may have been another attempt to go back to a pre-contact practice.

the whole of their old mode of worship inspite of these laws, is not to
expect the least regard from any person whatever; & soon shall die.
These with many others, some of which we know nothing, others but
very little, & the rest are so trifling & ridiculous that I forbear makin
the least mention of them. However, were none of them worse or
tended to no more evil than these, I have just mentioned all would do.
But, it seems that the person, or persons, who are the founders of these
laws /62/ had something else in view which as has been told at Bottom
of river Ounipique by an indian while he was drunk, but when he came
to his senses & having found that he had already gone too far made
a full declareation of the whole. He said (to avoid further question),
that in the first place all our Canoes were to be stopped coming down
Red river, to kill, pillage, & destroy everything that may be on board.
After this: that all our small outposts were to be done the same to,
particularly of the ammonition, which they will much want. That if the
pimican's being stopped coming down Red River should not intirely
prevent our setting from bottom of River O[uinipique], they are to be
stopped in three different places from thence to Lake-La-Pluie, to Kill,
pillage, & Massacre every thing; & latterly: that all our Canoes, boats,
vessels, water or land Carriages, be them whose property they may are
all to be intercepted on their road to Detroit, Michilmacknat, the Sault
& Fort William, either on this side or beyond wherever they can be
laid hold of on this side La-Chine. All this is to be done by the indians
'tis said & undoubtedly not them alone, for & can hardly immagine
that any band of indians whatever (almost) would dare attack such a
number of vessels as now sail upon the Lakes of Upper Canada without the assistance of some white People who in my opinion cannot but
be the instigators of this Plot. But I hope that with the Grace of God
& our own vigilance, that, all their malicious designs [designs] shall be
frustrated. /63/ But what can be their (real) motive for this is more than
I can immediately account for; for, certainly they can't by this intend
the conquest of Lower-Canada; nor, can they with any degree of hope
expect either to keep in their possession the Upper part of Canada
while the Lower yet remains in the hands of the English, these are but
frivolous observations at best & are worthy of but very little attention.
Be it as it may 'tis very well known that the natives of the inner part of
the Country cannot now subsist as in former times when but with the
use of their bows & arrows they could kill either large or small animals
even Game they could kill flying, but this is not the case now, they must
have Guns, ammonition, Goods, Knives, flints, fire steels & a number

of other things that I dont mention, which, without the use of all these, they, at least the greater part of them really cannot subsist. Except, (though in my opinion not very easily) they traffic with the Spaniards or, or [sic] & the Americans from the Missipi & even then many of them who remain in the interior would not be able to get any such articles as they should want.

All this was set of foot by a rascally indian who on a Sudden appearing before them (some where about Detroit) separated himself in two, that is, his right, & his left, but not till after he had harangued them & spoken to them a long time saying that he appeared now before them for no other purpose than to give them good advice & prescribe to them new Laws which they must all follow; & that he was the first person who <u>inhabited</u> the earth, therefor the Father of all who now dwell upon the earth, both black & white; & his reason for appearing /64/ to them in particular, was as aforementioned & that he was sorry very sorry to behold the pitiful condition that they are now in; & their Lands all over so barren; but, that before three winters should elapse all should return to its former state : & that he was sory to find that his white Children (us white People) should deal so very ill with his Yellow Children (the indians) & Yet to be all brothers : & after having concluded & began several times he finished with saying, take you one half of my body to the North, & the other to the South, put them up carefully in each their own box (to be made purposely), & carry them all round the (<u>indian</u>) world, so that every nation may see me & hereafter know me; & at a certain season are all to meet if not together at least by Great bands, & tell them as I have told you. And when all this shall be done he is to appear again & gives them further orders. – The most interresting part of this, or that which most regards our own safety is not yet very particularly known, no more than already mentioned & they were not to di[s]close it to any white people; for any person who should be guilty of it might be sure that he would die in a very short time with the whole of his family & relations, & be for ever damned!!! – 'Tis very certain however that no white person was allowed to see his vagabond Carcase; he passed this way, but he was only seen in his box at a distance & en passant. --

End of journal. The next Dauphin River journal carries on directly from this.

6

Journal at Dauphin River, 1 September 1808–31 March 1810, with an extract from *Reminiscences*

This is a book of fifty-four unnumbered pages, 31.5 cm high x 20.5 cm wide, without covers. It has been formed by folding fourteen sheets of Radway paper in half, nesting them to make a single gathering of fifty-six pages, and loosely stitching them together along the spine with thread. The last leaf in the gathering has been cut off, presumably to be used for some other purpose. At least one full sheet is missing between the tenth and eleventh of the fourteen sheets now present, producing gaps in the journal between 16 March and 10 April 1809 and between 25 September and 6 October 1809. The fact that this sheet is missing shows that the stitching together of the journal did not occur until after the full journal had been written.

The journal carries on directly from the journal of 1807–08, and continues through two trading seasons. In the transcript below, page numbers have been assigned, using square brackets to indicate that these are not present in the actual manuscript.

The trading season of 1808–09 at Dauphin River was a poor one, yielding only five packs of furs. The people Nelson traded with were the Cul-Fessé/Ayagon band of Ojibwe, and a new Ojibwe hunter, Cou-Fort, often referred to as Bras Court's eldest son, who had been persuaded to come to Nelson's post. His younger brother came along as well, and lived at the post through the winter. The low return of furs may have meant that the nearby hunting grounds were already largely trapped out, but the size of the Ojibwe hunting band trading at the post was really too small. The latest addition, Cou-Fort, having taken debt from Nelson in the fall, had also been seen at the Fort Dauphin department's outpost at Falle au Perdrix (Partridge Crop). In the end, though Cou-Fort brought Nelson some provisions in the spring and summer, his furs did not appear, and by the summer Nelson had accepted that Cou-Fort must be regarded as a Fort Dauphin customer.

Nelson's journal of the 1808–09 season shows an almost obsessive interest in the daily yield of fish, to the extent of recording those taken of each species, day after day. It was one way of filling up the journal pages – most of the time, there was little else to record. No Indigenous people at all appeared at the post between 8 November and 6 February. Besides provisioning his own post with fish, the staple food for men and dogs alike, Nelson was expected to supply Alexander McDonnell's post at Pigeon River, on the other side of Lake Winnipeg. There were frequent trips to Pigeon River, made dangerous by the need to traverse long stretches of open ice where storms might blow up without warning. It was indeed a hard winter. Nelson mentions several instances of frostbite, and storms were frequent.

On 2 November 1808 Nelson recorded a total eclipse of the moon, the correct date of which was actually 3 November. This error illustrates his difficulty in keeping his calendar correct, in the absence of any information from elsewhere.

In mid-March, while on a visit to Pigeon River, Nelson learned that Alexander Campbell, who was trading in opposition to the HBC in the Berens River headwaters, had given himself over entirely to drink, and with the breakdown of discipline his people were in danger of starving. Nelson himself accompanied an expedition to rescue Campbell and his party. Because the journal pages covering 16 March to 10 April are missing, Nelson's primary account of this episode is lost, but he recounts it vividly in his *Reminiscences*, and this account has been printed here to fill the gap.

In the summer of 1809, Nelson took his furs to Fort Alexander as usual, but rather than remaining there for the summer as he had the previous year, he returned to Dauphin River. There, he planted a vegetable garden and planned for the rebuilding of his post at a new site on the opposite side of the river. Again, the main activity of the summer was fishing, and Nelson commented that although they were working much harder at the fishery than previously, the returns were poor. He left the post again for Fort Alexander on 18 August to get the next year's goods, taking eight days on the journey because of the usual difficulties with high winds. After three weeks at the main post, he loaded his winter outfit and got back to Dauphin River on 26 September. The entries covering the next ten days are missing, but the main activity was rebuilding the post, ferrying the timber from the old buildings across the river, and so on. The new post was ready for occupation by the middle of October.

With the season of 1809–10, a new band of Indigenous people began to hunt in the territory around Nelson's post, and took debt from him. This was a group of Mashkiegons or Swampies from the east side of Lake Winnipeg, led by a hunter called The Belly. In past seasons, they had apparently traded at Pigeon River, but the NWC did not maintain a post there in 1809–10. This simplified Nelson's life, as he no longer had to send sleighloads of fish across Lake Winnipeg, on those dangerous winter journeys, to provision the Pigeon River post.

At 10 o'clock on the night of 12 November 1809, Nelson's wife, whom he called Mary Ann, gave birth to their first child, a daughter who was named Mary. Nelson records the event in his journal, but in curiously arch language.

Nelson was invited to Christmas at Fort Alexander, where Duncan Cameron brought the department's clerks together. It was a happy gathering, for which Nelson was very grateful. On his return, Nelson spent the voyageurs' holiday, New Year's Day, at his friend John Crebassa's post at Broken River. He paid for these treats when he encountered unusually harsh travelling weather between Broken River and his own post.

In mid-March, most unusually, Duncan Cameron himself visited Nelson's post. The purpose of this visit is not entirely clear, but he had particular Indigenous men whom he wanted to see, so he was concerned with how the trade at the post was getting on. When Ayagon appeared, he made him a present of rum, but also delivered "a very proper speech," a phrase that Nelson uses elsewhere to mean a rebuke to the hunters for not achieving what the traders expected.

The journal ends on a note of discouragement, with a hope to do better the next year.

------ *Journal for 1808 &c. &c. &c.* ------

September

Thursday 1st Septr. A very high wind all day, that with much difficulty Mr. McDonald's Canoe's arrive here, himself having arrived Yesterday (for Fort-Dauphin Depart.). And this evening Mr. D. Cameron arrives, with Messrs Seraphin Lamar, & Crabassay [Crebassa]. He left his Canoes at the Dalles.

Frid. 2nd. While Mr. Cameron was making the presents to the Premier and his band, – as also haranguing them (about 10 A.M.) his Canoes

arrive five in number having left two above with his own, which
make eight for the whole Depart[ment]. Guided by Old Bartrand dit
Desrocher [Durocher]. We put everything to rights in the stores in
hopes of unbaleing to-morrow. A very high wind yet all day.

Satur. 3ᵈ. It blows yet very hard. We begin to-day by undoing all the
bales & put each article seperately; & take an account of part of them
when we were obliged to leave off and prepare for a dance, which is
now the third, in honour to Mr. Seraphins wedding – Mr. McDonald
played the violin for us & Mr. Seraphin played the Flute alternately.[1]

Sund. 4ᵗʰ. The wind abates very much, and about Noon Mr.
McDonald sets off. The Premier & his band take debt & promise not to
be back 'till near spring.

Mond. 5ᵗʰ. About mid-day the indians finish taking what few things
more they may yet want & set off honor'd with the flag and several
shots, but above all a famous storm gathering just time enough to
conduct them home, however it soon clears up & becomes quite calm
at evening.

Tues. 6ᵗʰ. We are obliged to put out some things to dry that had got
wet yesterday in the stores. A few moments before breakfast Mr. Alex.
McDonell arrives having passed the summer at Pigeon river.

Wednes 7ᵗʰ. Messʳˢ Campbell, McDonell, & Crebassay fix & bale up
all their goods, each for his own post. The people fish as usual.

/[2]/ Septʳ Thurs. 8ᵗʰ. Before noon I put up all the Goods that are to
be sent in my Charge; & Mr. Cameron gives each our share of Iron
works &c &c &c. The Black smith is set to work.

Frid 9ᵗʰ. About dusk two of Mr. Ferguson's men arrive here with two
letters from their Bourgeois & orders to take back his wife & his two
Children who passed a part of the Summer with us.[2] Mr. Cameron
finishes giving us the remainder of our Equipment and about two hours
before sun set we all take leave of Mr. Cameron, & Mr. Seraphin &
encamp about half a league in the Lake: – Our arrangements are thus:[3]

---

1 The picture of fur traders dancing to the strains of a flute, rather than a fiddle, is fascinating.
Nelson does not describe the other two dances, but one must have been for Nelson's own marriage, to Mary Ann, the cousin of Duncan Cameron's wife. See the Introduction, pp. xiv–xvi.
2 Ferguson was apparently going to winter somewhere up Winnipeg River, perhaps around
Portage de l'Île, where Cameron had sent him in June.
3 This is an unusually full account of the personnel for the whole of the Lake Winnipeg district, apart from Fort Alexander, where the bourgeois, Duncan Cameron, was to winter. Apart
from naming all the men, Nelson also states whether they had wives and children, whose
presence was rarely mentioned, although they were a major aspect of life at the trading posts.

– Mr. Crebassay for Broken river with four men, Trempe (his woman), Brasconier, Sanssoussie, & Alard. – Mr. McDonell with four men Leblanc, Larocque, Charboneau, Belangé (a summer man), Desrocher (Guide), & [John] Inkster for Interpreter; their women are Mr. McDonell's woman & Child, Inkster's woman & Child, Désrochér's women & lastly Charboneau woman in all thirteen for Pigeon River; Mr. Campbell, his woman & two Children, Lorrin (interpreter), his woman & two Children. J Bpt. Larocque, L'Epine, Brilliére, Baudrie, & Rondeau, for Grand Rapid. For River Dauphine, Myself & woman,[4] Paradix, Longuetin, Ausger and Welles in all six. Mr. Crebasay returned to the Fort for his book of indian accounts. We met Young Richard & Mallioux at Pointe aû Sable who were sent to River-aux-morts in quest of Knews at the place, their reception at that Place has been more agreeable than mine was; the indians there are very impatient & wish much to have some of our people to winter there.

Satur 10th Sunday 11th. We were wind bound all day yesterday but we set off at the break of day sometimes bearing sail & at others, apaddling we encamped at the Tête-aû-boeuf (not in the Détroit) this morning we met Naganeckiejick & the Frisé on their road to Fort Alexander, we got a little meat from them & some more at their lodges at a short distance from there, I here found Bras Court's two sons, & as they were to come with me I left them a little rum & ammunition & embarked a few of their things incase they should give me the slip. It rained a little to-day.

Mond. 12th. We embarked early this morning & soon arrived at the /[3]/ Broken river where we found many indians, among whom were Tête de loup Cervier & Tête Grise our residence here being little wished we reembarked leaving Mr. Crebassay &c and about a league beyond, we met the Gaignan from whom we got a little oats (& a few dry berries) as our share from Mr. Creb. was but mean, though it was Mr. Cameron's desire we all should have at least a little. In spite of a very strong head wind we encamped at Détroit-du-Duc. This is the place where I met Ayagon with his women on his road to Fort Alex. from River Dauphine for People to winter at that place;[5] though there are at present but Cû-fèssé, & his son in law. So now if Bras Courts two sons were not with us that Post would consist but of three indians.

---

4 This is the only indication in the journal that Nelson had now taken a wife.
5 This encounter must have taken place in the summer of 1807, before the Dauphin River post was established.

What extraordinary returns might then be expected! – I give Ayagon a small keg of mixed rum & a little tobacco. he gives me a dress't skin & a little meat.

Tuesday 13th. Septr. Though it blew very hard 'till near day we reac[h]ed Tête-aû-Chien about 10 o'Clock A.M. we put ashore exactly opposite to the place where we were burnt by that Powder last fall. We here take breakefast & I go with three men to Blood River,[6] chiefly to bid "farewell" to Messrs Campbell & McDonell (as it is here where I take my road, rather where we seperate), though it was for an indian dog now in Rassette's hands, which I would have taken had not Rassette been so pitiful a wretch, he had a quarrel with me for it. Here Mr. Campbell sends Lorrin & Rondeau up this river in quest of Eatcho's band whom we we seen here last spring. – At Sun set set I arrived at Tête-aû-Chien where I had left Paradix to take Care of the Goods in my absence. Two of Ayagon's women arrive here, himself being gone to broken River to see Tête Grise his father-in-law.

Wednes 14th. I remain here all day waiting for Rassette who arrived about Noon. I traded with rather from him 97 rats, 1 bad otter & 2 Good minks he takes for 25 [skins] & a Cod line* upon debt from me. He is to winter at Tête au brochet.

Thurs 15th. We set off a little later than usual & having gone out of our way, towards Fisher river about two leagues owing to the stupidity of Welles,[7] we, after all, encamped at Tête-aû Brochet often bearing sail; immediately on our arrival we set a Net & as soon we take where-with for Supper.

/[4]/ September, Friday 16th 1808. I remain here waiting for my indians that are yet behind. The weather is dark, Cloudy, & misty with a very hard North wind. Being out to-day a hunting with Longuetin, I kill 22 ducks.

Satur. 17th. I was a hunting along the Lake but without success. The weather is bad & a hard N wind at intervals. In appearance we shall have an early winter; for but very few ducks are to be found & the Geese fly past in numerous bands.

Sund 18th. While I was to-day out a-hunting again Ayagon, arrived from Broken River; & at Sun Set Bras Court's eldest son arrives on

6 Bloodvein River, about six miles along the lakeshore from Tête-au-Chien.
7 Somewhere around the present Matheson Island, Jean-Baptiste Welles, who must have been acting as guide, mistook his direction and took the party to the southwest, into Fisher Bay, rather than taking the traverse directly across to Jackhead by way of Tamarack Island.

foot having left his wife & brother about three leagues from here with Ayagon's son & two women, as it blows too hard for them to come. I give Aya. another Gallon Keg of mixed rum to drink.

Mond. 19th. Aya.'s women &c arrive and keep up their frolick.

Tues 20th. Before day we embarked in a terrible shower of rain, but before we reached "La Pointe de Roche" we were obliged to put ashore on account of the wind. Here Aya. overtakes us, & takes for 60 skins upon debt & sets off so do I as the weather grows more calm & fine. A few minutes before Sun set we take the traverse of Tête-aû-Pishew with half only of our sail; & the more we advance the higher the wind blows, when at day set we arrived at Tête-aû-Pishew, every moment thinking to go to the Bottom which would certainly have been our fate had we retarded but two minutes, for, though we were very near shore & in shelter of the wind, it was yet with much difficulty that we could debark. As soon as we were on shore Paradix & I went to look for a small canoe that Ayagon gave me at the Pointe a la Fremboise & that we were obliged to loosen & let go to the favor of the wind.

Wednes 21st. As the wind abates some, about noon we set off and encamp near our Campment of Last March with Mr. A. McDonell about 3½ leagues from the mouth of River Dauphine.

Thurs. 22nd. At Sun rise this morning we set off with a very high E.N.E. wind which is favorable for us, and debark, & put all our things /[5]/ in the old (last Years) shop, we found no indians here, but Ayagon who was with us found several marks along the beach: however, about one hour after La Bezette arrives with his family on foot being about two leagues from this to the South. I give between them 6 quarts of mixed rum. It rains.

Frid. 23d. Though Ayagon sent his wife yesterday to Old Cu fessé's lodge, he is not yet arrived, wherefore, though in very bad weather I send Ausger & Welles who met the old man about one mile from this (with all his family) while he was busy in dressing a moose that he had just now Killed; the Greatest part of which he gives us. On his arrival here I according to my orders gave him a laced coat, a white shirt, Broyet [brayet], & leggings & about ½ keg mixed rum, with 1 quarter fathom tobacco.[8] To Ayagon 1 white shirt, a broyet, ½ keg rum. La

8 Nelson would have discussed carefully with Duncan Cameron how each of the Indigenous hunters expected at the post was to be treated, based on his previous year's hunt. Although it was Ayagon who had negotiated the establishment of the Dauphin River post the previous year, Cameron and Nelson had decided to assign the highest status to Cul-Fessé, the eldest in the family group, so it was he who was given the laced coat. For a detailed discussion of

Bezette 9 quarts mixed rum & ¼ fam. tobacco. The weather is bad to an extraordinary degree. Yesterday, the men pull down my old house & set a net wherein this morning we take forty white-fish.

Satur. 24th. The indians drink quietly. All day long we have had hail, snow, & rain each alternately with a terrible high wind N.

Sund. 25th. Calm & more fine than usual though we have had a hard frost last night. I set the men to work at my house, which I have to adjoin the men's house of last year, its length is 11 foot & breadth is 15. La Bezette being sober I give him what articles he wants to the amount of forty-skins upon Debt.

Mond. 26th. At the Sun's rising this morning Bras Court's two Sons arrive to whom I give 1½ Gallon mixed rum. About noon the weather grows more calm & mild for we have had a hard frost last night.

Tues. 27th. Fine weather as yesterday. I give debt [to] another indian.

Wednes. 28th. The remainder of the indians take debt & set off. All go the same road to the chemin du Guerier where each takes his own course.⁹ I give a Keg of mixed rum among them. Bad, rainy weather.

Thurs. 29th. Very bad snowy weather all day long 'till night when it Ceases & freezes very hard. Old Cu fessé comes for rum but is not received so well as he would wish, nevertheless I give him a little.

/[6]/ October 1808 Friday, 30th. The weather is clear this morning but soon grows dark & as bad nearly as Yesterday. I finish my net which is near 50 fathoms long but 18 mashes [meshes] high. As we have now near done our meat, we set an old net & take 37 [fish] before we go to bed.

Sund. 1st. October 1808. The wind is from E. to S.E. & blows very hard, & cold. The sun shines this morning, at noon is overcast, & at night is more Calm & mild; it rains. We take up the Net with 15 white fish. Yesterday I sent Paradix & Longuetin to bring across old Rassette's house¹⁰ to make my shop, & to day they rebuild it, while Welles, & Ausger plaister my room.

"chief's coats," given to leading Indigenous hunters to confer status and confirm trading relationships, see Willmott and Brownlee 2010, 60. A *brayet* is a breechclout or loincloth.

9 The winter hunting grounds were to be to the north and northwest of the Dauphin River post. Passing up Dauphin River, the Indigenous bands would reach the point where the river makes a sharp bend to the south, and a short portage from this point would bring them into the headwaters of the Warpath River. Ayagon and Mouffle d'Orignal had hunted there the previous spring, and must have concluded that there were enough animals to justify the whole band wintering there.

10 Charles Racette's old house, where he and his family had lived during the winter of 1807–08. Racette was planning to winter at Tête-au-Brochet this year.

Mond 2ⁿᵈ. It snows again all day.

Tuesd 3ᵈ. For these several nights past it has froze very hard Considering the season. Having had occasion to go to the rapids I found Ayagon & Cu-fessé to be yet there encamped. The weather is more fine & Clear than has been for some time past.

Wed. 4ᵗʰ. Yesterday we put out one of the New Nets & take 63 fish. Ausger & I split boards for my door &c. When busy working at my bed Ayagon comes for a small keg of mixed rum to pay old Cu-fessé for medicine that he got from him to put on his sore leg, occasioned, by a woman inadvertantly passing over it, though she did not in the least touch it yet it immediately began to swell.[11] To be the sooner healed of it he took the right hind leg of a Moose (for it was his right leg) & eat it, but I suppose his being now an old married man prevented it's having that salutary effect it once already had upon his hand while he (Ayagon) was young – Paradix mends & prepares an old Canoe for his voyage to Falle de Pardrie, – At noon Cloudy, & rains at night.

Thurs. 5ᵗʰ. It rained all night, & snows & rains a good part of this day.

Frid. 6ᵗʰ. We have had Sun-Shine, rain, & snow. The men knock down their old chimney & rebuild a new one. Old Cu fessé comes this afternoon & takes a robe & Gun upon credit. We put out a Net.

Saturd. 7ᵗʰ. The weather is 1ˢᵗ mild, but Cloudy, 2ⁿᵈ rain, 3ᵈ fine sun-shine. 4ᵗʰ a terrible from Nɴw, 5ᵗʰ Clear, 6ᵗʰ Rain & 7ᵗʰ Snow.

Sund. 8ᵗʰ. Yesterday Ayagon & Cu fessé come here & bring with them two large beaver for which I give them a little rum. Paradix & I finish the shop & put all to rights in it. The men nearly finish their chimney & lay a part of their flooring. As my fears at Tête-aû-brochet of an early winter, seem not to be altogether unfounded we begin by hanging up 8 white-fish & 7 Pike –

/[7]/ Mond. 9ᵗʰ October 1808. Very tempestuous weather, but clears up at night –

---

11 In the *Reminiscences*, Part 7, page 278, Nelson explains: "A woman, under no circum-stance is allowed to stride over a man, because of her periodical returns; & on that account are always considered unclean. When a man, & most especially a warrior, or a "Medicine" man, i.e. a Doctor or conjuror has swelled feet or legs it is almost invariably imputed to some woman having strided over him. On such occasions a rigid enquiry is made orally & by conjuring; & ceremonial Sacrifices are made. More than one woman has fallen a Sacrifice, i.e. been the victim of that indiscretion. The Montagne's, (Chippewayans of Athabasca,) I have been often told by my men carry this idea to the utmost extreme, insomuch that if a poor woman at these times by necessity be forced to cross the path or track of [a man], she acknowledges it when she gets home. The men make a làrge camp-fire over which she has to walk, to purify herself!"

Tuesd. 10th. It snows & drifts very hard all morning – our fishing is but poor.

Wednesd. 11th. I at last send off Paradix & Longuetin in Canoe for Falle de Pardrie but a hard frost last night freezing up the river intirely across & is intirely impassible either way – I keep them 'till another opportunity. I was up at the first rapids where I found Ayagon & Cu fessé very busy about nothing – Very cold all day.

Thursd, 12th. The weather is pritty mild. In the Course of last night there fell 9 inches of snow, for I found this depth exactly in several places, the wind is S. I now given the fishing business intirely into Ausge's hands who is the best able to do it as he can also mind them & to day's fishing is 53 white fish. The men at last finish doing all work that's to be done about the houses – We have seen a band of Swans going to the N. which gives us some hopes of yet having fine weather.

Friday 13th. I was out to day to look for wood to make slays & on my return home I found that Aya. & Cu-fessé were pulling down their lodges & intended to go a part of the way in Canoe as there is too much snow for the children to walk through – Sun-shine weather but cold. Our fishing is 188 but we were obliged to breake the ice before we could visit our nets –

Saturd. 14th. The weather is pritty mild – yet we have had several showers of snow; & the ice is now strong enough to bear a person for I walked some distance upon it – Paradix, Welles, & Longuetin begin to chop their wood. Fishing 168.

Sund. 15th. Cold weather, but sun shine. Nevertheless I take Paradix with me to the rapids (we drag a canoe upon the ice) & a few torches with each our own spear to spear what fish we may be able, for, our Nets are hardly able to maintain [us] in living, much less to put up a winters stock – In our Nets 75 white fish.

Monday 16. We return home this morning after having speared 313 white fish, & had we had conveniencies sufficient we might with all ease have speared 7 or 800; however I send Welles & Longuetin to hang them up during which time Paradix spears 266 others say more. This evening Ausger & I set two Nets under the ice which is now 2½ inches thick – what surprises me here, is, that the greatest of the Trees have yet all their leaves – Fine weather yesterday, but moreso today. Our fishing is 16 white fish in four nets: 313, 266, 579.

/[8]/ Tuesd, 17th. October, The wind is S & very hard & Cold – yet Paradix Ausger & I prepare for spearing more fish above. Net fishing is 8.

Wednes. 18. This afternoon we all returned home after having hung up 490 white fish that we speared with but few torches. A high wind, cold weather, a leaky Canoe & waiding up to our middle in water & ice, and our hands so benumbed by the ice continually coming on our spear handles as hardly to be able to hold them – Near night the weather grows bad, about which time Ayagon arrives with one of his women for People to go to his lodge for a part of a moose Old Cu-fessé killed yesterday. I immediately send off Longuetin & Welles with Paradix – Ayagon remains here drunk.

Thurs. 19th. Ayagon returns home. The ice is too bad to visit all our nets however we visit two of them wherein we take 14 white fish – and a few yards below this we have my new net, but as the ice is broken up & having no canoe we leave it to the favour of all weathers – Stormy weather at intervals – I finish my table.

Friday 20th. While Ausger & I were making all preparations necessary for spearing again this evening we were prevented from doing it by the arrival of our men (who bring all the usual meat of a moose except one shoulder), who informed us of the rapids being intirely stopped up with ice, so much so that they were often near drowning or being upset by large cakes of ice rolling down the Current with such fury as often to render it a Great task & were it not for Welles who set long poles upon the ice they probably would have drowned themselves – Now if some extraordinary fishing from under the ice does not relieve us I am much afraid we shall starve.

Saturd. 21st. Bad snowy weather all day & a North wind – I take Ausger with me to go for wood to make slays as I see there is not the least appearance of relaxation in this weather.

Sunday 22nd. Ausgé & I visit one of our nets with a Great deal of trouble where we take 14 fish, but there is the new Net I made near the lake which we have not the least signs of – I am afraid the ice has taken it off. However I make Aus. [Auger] set another one where the ice is much thicker. While busy at this net Bras Court's Youngest son arrives from La Bezette's lodge for People to go there for what little they have; he kills a swan near here which I believe has lost itself – It is very lean – The weather is mild, but Cloudy & Snowy –

/[9]/ Mond. 23d October 1808. At the breake of day I send off Aus. & Welles with but one quart of HWines and a small bit of tobacco to prevent there [their: La Bezette's family] being in so soon again – The weather is snowy & rainy 'till near night when it begins to clear up. Paradix & I visit the Nets & take 30. We afterwards go above to fix the fish with an oil Cloth to prevent the Crows and whisky Jack's eating of them – I see two fish in the ropes.

Tuesd. 24ᵗʰ. The wind is north & pritty cold towards evening, about which time A. & Welles arrive pritty heavily loaded in dry meat, & pounded meat – Bezette & his wife come with them more I believe to enforce Ayagon's desire of my going there than any thing else – Net fishing is 22 –

Wednesd. 25ᵗʰ. Mild weather & a little N wind – Early this morning I set off for the Lodges taking Longuetin, Welles, & Ausgé –besides a small keg of rum and a little tobacco – before sun set however, we arrive there & found only Bras Courts young son, at dusk the hunters arrived from whom I got 7 small Beaver & 2 large ones (with their Skins) – They drink quietly.

Thursd 26. Early this morning I send the men home with 5 Small & 2 large beaver, 3 bags of Pounded meat, 9 Martins, & 1 lynx, but I did not set off 'till near noon waiting for the women who were sent for two steel traps – I soon overtake the men & at Sun set we arrive at the house – The weather has been cold owing to a very high N wind. Fishing in our absence was 21.

Friday 27ᵗʰ. The sun shines but the weather is cold & the wind blows hard from S.E. Our fishing in the Net is 16. I take Ausger & Welles with me to look for that net which we suppose to be lost – however, after making a Gutter of about 60 yards long we find it with 19 fish – only two of them are eatable, the others are rotten.[12] – The water rises much by a N wind.

Saturd 28ᵗʰ. Very beautiful weather all day long, so that all the snow that was upon the ice melts & a good deal of what was in the woods. I was today at the rapids looking for air holes – I found two, & remaining about an hour I there speared 14 [fish] – A high wind prevents our spearing this evening.

Sunday 29ᵗʰ. Weather as yesterday. To-day's fishing is 13, & yesterday 10 altogether 23. Paradix now finishes chopping his share of wood 16 Cords –

/[10]/ Mond 30ᵗʰ October 1808. Welles & I having been 'till midnight in the rapids & Longuetin & Ausger whom I send to hang them up with a few that they killed amount to 263. In the Nets 4.

Tuesd. 31ˢᵗ. Very fine weather & a south wind which I believe will

---

12 This net had been missing since the 22nd. As fish immobilized in a net soon die, they must be taken out of the net every day or two, or they will spoil.

occasion the rapids breaking up a Second time, for much ice melts. I was up to-day to put up a few old traps & on my way there & back again I speared 38 & 14 in the nets.

Wednes. 1ˢᵗ November All Saints. I and the men remain at home, & they finish chopping their wood which all amounts to 48 Cords. Mild & Calm. Fishing is 10.

Thursd. 2ⁿᵈ. The wind breaks up much ice in this bay fishing is 10.

Frid. 3ᵈ. The night before last we had an Eclipse which began about midnight & lasted 'till near day, its effect was not Great, it did not become black but the Colour of Blood.[13] The weather is Clear 'till near noon when it grows dark & remains so all day – On my return home from my traps I met Ausger & Longuetin who were going to spear with each a few torches. I spear 20 fish, in the nets we take 14.

Saturd. 4ᵗʰ. About midnight they both return having speared 350 & to-day we prepare more torches for this evening (while Paradix & Welles hang them up) but are prevented by the arrival of Ayagon who comes with Bras Court's young son for People to go to his lodge for meat. The weather is very dark this morning, snow at noon, & a hard Westerly Gale at night. From the time of Ausge's arrival here 'till near noon to day it Thundered, & sometimes very hard – The indians who saw the Eclipse say that it is a sure sign of some accident befalling some of their Friends in some place or other. "I have often remarked this" says Ayagon. I give them some rum – & they are very troublesome.

Sunday 5ᵗʰ. Fine & Clear the wind is W. about 11 A.M. I send off all the men (& remain alone) with 6 quarts HWines & a little tobacco. I have told Mr. Ayagon & the other that neither they or any other of them should be back 'till such times as they may have wherewith to pay a good part of their debts. I told them more & Aya. in Particular that if he was to come, or send that he should not have even a pipe of tobacco from me – I hope these words may have their desir'd effect – Net fishing is 15 white fish.

Mond. 6ᵗʰ. Net fishing is 18. It snows & drifts very hard this evening. E. wind.

/[11]/ Tuesd. 7ᵗʰ November 1808. Just about noon the men arrive all well loaded, with 37 pieces dry meat 7 tongues, 7 snouts & about

13 A total eclipse of the moon, visible across most of North America and parts of the Pacific, occurred on 3 November 1808, totality beginning about 6 a.m. and lasting until about 10 a.m. Coordinated Universal Time (UTC). On Lake Winnipeg, at local time six hours earlier, the eclipse would have lasted from about midnight until 4 a.m., in agreement with Nelson's record, except that his calendar was wrong by one day, as he dated the event to 2 November.

10 lbs tallow. About sunset Bras Court's eldest son arrives – he has been always alone wherefore I hope he has made a pritty good hunt. In all the weather is pritty mild. Fishing is 13.

Wednesd. 8th. This morning I send of[f] Ausger & Welles to the indian's lodges I only send with them a little tobacco – & an awl, as it was for this that he come. I send no rum; because he [Ayagon] says that his child would be uneasy & cry were it to see them drunk. I went with the men to visit my traps & on my road there & home again I spear 177 fish. Net fishing is 7. Cloudy & high E. wind all day – I take 5 martins in my traps.

Thursd. 9th. To day I send Paradix & Longuetin to hang up the fish speared Yesterday – 950 they spear themselves & myself 140. Ausgé & Welles arrive at night having with them 2 Small Beaver & a fine Large Black Bear Skin with other things amount to 18½ Skins. Wind & weather as Yesterday. No net fish being busy elsewhere.

Frid. 10th. I send Paradix & Longuetin to put the fish they spear'd yesterday to rights rather in some order to prevent their being eat by the birds or Crows; but at the same time were it worth their while they should spear – at night they return having speared 450. – I get the Net taken up as it is not worth rotting for the few fish we take which to day are only 8. The weather is windy & overcast. Aus[gé] make a slay for Par[adix].

Saturd. 11th. In the Course of last night there fell several inches thick of snow & continues all day but not hard – Paradix & Longuetin make preparations for their voyage to Falle de Pardrie whither I intend sending them on monday if the weather be favorable, for I believe that near all the rivers & Lakes are take[n] sufficiently strong to bear a man.

Sund. 12th. I go to day to my traps where I take 10 martins & on my return home I spear two fish. Common fine winter weather.

Mond. 13th. Para. Long. & Ausgé go in train up to the fish where they Spear 68 – & bring home 15. Sun shine 'till night when it becomes overcast.

Tuesd. 14th. Paradix & Longuetin were ready long before day light but are prevented setting off this morning by a very heavy shower of Snow – however they set off this afternoon with a Letter addressed to the Gentleman in Charge of that Post for NWCº containing a list of the Names of those indians I have with me & the amount of the debts of each.[14] At sun set it snows very hard again, though it was fine at noon.

---

14 Nelson had been planning to send the men to the post at Falle au Perdrix (Partridge Crop) since 4 October, but was waiting for good travelling weather.

Wedn. 15th. The weather clears up, & a cold N wind prevails. I spear 17 fish.

Thursd 16th. Overcast & cold weather. I spear 79 fish.

/[12]/ Frid 17 November 1808. Pritty fine weather these two days running I speared 343 white fish exclusive of 28 I kill with a stick & catch in my hands in those same rapids where we Speared so many last year.

Satur 18th. Fine & mild this morning but soon grows bad & remains so all day. Aus-gé spears 55 fish – & I 62 as we each return from our traps.

Sund 19th. Yesterday I speared 11 fish with my knife –

Mond 20th. An extraordinary E wind & continually snowing since Satur[day].

Tues. 21st. The wind is now N & blows with much violence but is Calm & fine at night though it snowed this morning: so now I hope that Poor Parad. & Long. will be able to travel tomorrow; for the weather has been too bad to have made any progress

Wed. 22nd. A very fine winter's day. This afternoon Para. & Lon. arrive having left Falle de La Pardrie at the Eve that Mr. [Joshua] Halcroe[15] (who was master there) was to return to Fort Dauphin – There is not one single indian who winter's at that Post, few at Fort Dauphin, & less at Swan, or Elk river.[16] It was in some respects lucky that I did not send more early than I intended last fall, for I would not have found them, as it was with difficulty they arrived there through the ice. They left the river du Milieu at the same time with Mr. M^rDonald who remained there a long time in hopes of finding indians, at last embarked without any, at least very few. Longuetin unluckily fell in the rapids & froze his two great toes & two others I froze one of mine also being at my traps: however I take 5 martins.

Thurs 23^d. We were Greatly surprised this morning by the arrival of two of Mr. McDonell's men from Pigeon River whom he sends for Provisions as there is more appearance of Starvation than Good living there. He has sent Desrocher & Boulanger to fish at Tête-aû-Brochet. Except this there is no particular [news], unless, like myself but poor prospects of making any extraordinary returns. Fine weather this morning.

15 Joshua Halcro: see Appendix D.
16 Elk River or Rivière la Biche is now called Red Deer River, in the present Manitoba and Saskatchewan. Rivière la Biche and Swan River were regular outposts of the Fort Dauphin department.

Frid 24th. By far more beautiful weather than yesterday. Ausgé makes me a slay; & I prepare for going to Pigeon River, having an invitation from Mr. M[c]D. As the people went to day to the rapid, they spear 50 odd fish.

Sat. 25th. Para. & I go to the rapids; we there spear 34 fish. –

Sund. 26th. Fine weather all day – This morning I set off for Pigeon River & take Welles with me, We encamp at Grand Point about 6 leagues from the house. We take with us three Slays loaded with 51, 60, 50 [fish] – in all 161[17] –

/[13]/ Mond 27th. Nov[r] We encamp at Pigeon Point on the N side of the lake about 10 Leagues from Grand Point & four from the Fort in Pigeon river.[18]

Tuesd 28th. We arrive a little before breakefast time at Mr. M[c]Donell's where I had the pleasure of passing a fine day in pleasant Company –

[Sat] 2.nd [December] We remain here all this time –

Sund 3[d]. Before day light I set off to return home accompanied by Mr. M[c]Donell & two of his men. We very luckily fell upon the point of Tête-au-Pishew in a terrible storm from the N & NW –

Mond 4th. A little after sun rise this morning we set off in a terrible high & cold North wind. At Dusk we arrive at the house where I find all well Mr. M[c]Donell & Larocque were both very unlucky – the former froze his nose, the latter a Good part of his face

Thursd 7th. Yesterday & today we all go to the rapids where we spear 114 fish & bring a good many home. Very fine weather.

Frid 8th, Sat. 9th. Very tempestuous weather prevents Mr. M[c]Donell's setting off yesterday, but in recompense he sets off before day this morning loaded with 51, 32, 54, 41 in all 178 [fish] as the weather is really fine but it soon Grows bad & very tempestuous. I set the men to plaister my house on the outside.

17 Nelson's Journal, 18 February 1809, states that these fish were usually 4 to 6 pounds each, so the weight on each sleigh was at least 250 pounds.

18 This winter journey was dangerous, because of the long traverse over the open lake, where a sudden change in the weather could leave the travellers exposed to high winds and unable to see their way. This was to happen to Nelson and his party on their return trip. On this day, Nelson and his companions covered over 30 miles on snowshoes, mostly over the lake, by way of the present McBeth Point and Commissioner Island or islands to the south of it (Nelson called these the Swamp Islands) to Pigeon Point. This single day's journey shows what was possible in good winter weather. The distance also gives an idea of the length of Nelson's league, which was a bit short of the theoretical 3 miles. If McDonell's post "in Pigeon River" was 4 of these leagues beyond Pigeon Point, it must have been about 6 or 7 miles up that river. For a more detailed itinerary of this route from Dauphin River to the Pigeon River post see the journal entry of 6 March 1809.

Sund. 10[th.] Welles & Longuetin I send for fish [to the rapids], as I intend to have it now hauled all home they bring only 3 slay loads (1 trip) (consisting of 73, 44, 46) as it now serves to beat the road. Paradix & I enlargen the air hole & we spear 276 white fish. Fine weather yesterday & to-day –

Mond. 11th. Fine weather. The men bring home 9 loads of fish, 75, 51, 80, 60, 60, 60, 60, 42, in all 548; out of these Welles spears 42 fresh ones

Tuesd. 12th. Appearance of fine weather but soon Grows overcast & a high wind – Nevertheless the men bring the remainder of the fish off of the first stage we made last fall, 7 slay loads 71, 50, 80, 50, 90, 61, 50, fresh ones speared to day in all 452. I sent Paradix off this morning to go & live with Bras Court's Eldest son, he takes his usual train of artillery with him but I was surprised at night when I went with Ausgé & Longuetin to find him busy spearing of fish. He returned on account of his dogs not following him. There are but few fish –

Wednes. 13[th]. About midnight or a little after we return home having speared 420. The wind was to[o] high all night to spear many for our Torches were no sooner light than burnt out. Welles takes a rab[b]it in his traps; 'tis the second this year.

/[14]/ Thurs. 14[th] Dec[r] 1808. Nothing new. The men bring home 9 slay loads of fish 75, 75, 50, 72, 56, 50, 70, 57, 40 in all 545 –

Frid 15[th]. The People bring home 65, 49, 63, 61, 40, 40, 69, 63 – 450.

Saturd. 16[th]. We have speared near 200 fish – Fish hauling 63, 40, 50, 61, 45, 62, 65, 65, 41, 41, 70, in all 603.

Sund. 17th. Fish hauling is 65, 63, 40, 65, 65, 40, 75, 76, 40, 529

Mond. 18th, Tues. 19th. Nothing new the men bring home 56, 40 - 96 fish.

Wednes. 20th. Nothing new, Welles & Longuetin begin to haul their wood

Thursd 21st. Paradix & I went out a hunting – We found a beaver's lodge

Frid. 22nd. Para. & I go out a making of traps in the road we had been yesterday, & on our return home we found Inkster[19] & Boulanger an interpreter & man belonging to Mr. M[c]Donell who were sent for fish. Beautiful weather & little wind

---

19 John Inkster, interpreter, who was at Pigeon River now, but would be assigned to Nelson's Dauphin River post in 1809–10. See Appendix D.

Saturd. 23^d. The men go for fish & bring home 54, 66, 60, 63 in all 243

Sund 24th. I prepare all my letters both for Mr. Cameron & elsewhere as the Courriers will be soon off to bottom of the river (Fort Alexr).

Mond 25th Decr Christmas – Nothing new –^{20}

Tuesd. 26th. Inkster & Boulanger prepare their loads so does Ausgé whom I send to Fort Alexr. & Longuetin their loads are thus 40, 64, 40, 30

Wednes 27th. Before day light we all set off for Mr. McDonells, part of us by invitation & the others by obligation – The weather is sharp just at Sun rise, so that Longuetin freezes his nose & a Good deal of his Chin. Before we reach these first islands Ausgé is obliged to unload off his slay 16 fish & Belanger takes off 14 at the islands – We encamp about 1½ league from Tête-au-Pishew

Thursd 28th. At Dusk we all arrive at Mr. McDonells – but not before I had froze my nose in the first traverse this morning to Swamp islands. Old Desrocher arrived here about two hours before us from Tête-au-Brochet, where Seignieur Rassette resides, but according to all accounts he makes but a poor hunt.

Friday 29, Saturd 30. Very tempestuous weather these two days a N wind.

Sund 31st. Weather rather better –

Monday 1st January 1809 –

This is new year's day & Mr. McDonell gives a Genteel feast to all hands. And for the first Day of the year we have beautiful Weather. We dance at night and Ausgé sings for us as a mean substitute for the fiddle.

/[15]/ Tuesd 2nd January 1809. Ausgé and Le Blanc set off for Fort Alexander & I set off for home with Longuetin. Mr. McDonell sends Boulanger for fish & Desrocher and his woman come to live some time here. We encamp at the Swamp Islands late though we run pritty hard all day with a very hard South wind – It drifted very much.

Wednesd. 3^d. A few minutes before sun rise this morning Longuetin & I set off leaving Desrocher & th'other to come on slowly.^{21} We arrive a few minutes after Sun set at the house where thank [God] I found

20 This year, Duncan Cameron did not invite his clerks to Fort Alexander for a Christmas celebration, as in the previous year, but Nelson went to Pigeon River to join Alexander McDonell there for New Year's.

21 Durocher was much older than Nelson, and he and his wife could not have travelled as quickly as Nelson and his voyageur.

all as I had left it, well, We seen Eight Foxes upon the Lake working at Ausgér's fish –²²

Thursd. 4ᵗʰ. About an hour before day Old Desrocher arrived, he encamped at these first islands but set off about midnight rather sooner. Fine weather.

Friday 5ᵗʰ. Paradix Prepares to go to Mʳ McDonell's with Boulanger they have three slays between them loaded with 55, 50, 50 in all 155 [fish].

Saturd 6ᵗʰ. An extraordinary high wind all day but more so yesterday as prevents the men's setting off.

Sund 7ᵗʰ. Long before day light this morning Paradix & Boulanger set off, loaded as marked above – A high South wind all day –

Mond 8ᵗʰ. Nothing new – The wind as Yesterday this afternoon excepted

Tuesd. 9ᵗʰ. An Extraordinary high N wind & snow since last night.

Wednes.10ᵗʰ. Calm, but cold – This morning I get my chimney mended for it smokes too-much to be able to resist any time – I take Longuetin with me to go for two slays I split yesterday – Fine, sun shine all day

Thursd. 11ᵗʰ. Easterly wind all day with snow 'till near night when it ceases & becomes more fine. Old Desrocher & Welles set four lines for Pike for the dogs as at present we have nothing but white fish to give them – They take none

Frid. 12ᵗʰ. Clear & very cold with a North wind – They take Loches* 1 & Pike 2 in their lines.

Saturd 13ᵗʰ, Sund 14ᵗʰ. Pritty fine weather yesterday but very Stormy & bad today. I take a Carcajoux* in one of Paradix traps – In the lines yesterday we took but one Pike, but to day we take none which I take to be ow'n to the bates [owing to the baits] that are made of loches flesh. Unless this there is nothing new.

Mond 15ᵗʰ. It snows hard all day & the wind changes much; that is, often but the weather is mild. This afternoon Paradix, & Charboneau & his wife arrive from P. river this is the fourth day being degraded* one day in the swamp islands by the Cold.

/[16]/ Tuesd 16ᵗʰ January 1809. Fine weather this morning; but the weather grows bad & snows towards evening. This morning I give out a Net to be set by old Desrocher and the others. We take in the lines only 1 Pike & one loche.

---

22 The fish that Auger unloaded on 27 December because his sleigh was too heavy.

Wednes, 17th. This morning we visited the net & expected to make some extrordinary fishing but were disappointed as we did not take even one – This prevents my getting the lines taken up as I intended yesterday had the fishing been good. In the lines we take Loches 2 & Pikes 4. The weather is overcast & snowy all day

Thursd 18th. Very fine weather all day. Old Desrocher & I went to get wood for a slay but we could not find any. As our fishing yesterday was so poor I did not get the people to visit the Net. And in our lines we take 1 Loche & 1 Pike.

Frid. 19th. Yesterday according to my desire Welles & Charboneau prepared to set off for Pigeon River loaded with 50, 50, & 20 fish, but this morning long before day Longuetin prepares to go with Welles in Charboneau's place as this latter is too old to perform this trip so soon as they would wish. Fine weather all day. We visit the Net & take two suckers & in our lines two pike –

Saturd, 20th. Very fine weather all day. Nothing new, & no fish.

Sund 21st. An extraordinary high N. wind & bad weather. This morning I get my chimney put to rights again as there is no resisting in the smoke.

Monday. 22nd. As bad weather as yesterday.

Tuesd. 23d. The weather is rather more clear than these two days past but in recompense it is by far the coldest of any that we have yet had. However we visit the Net & take 2 small suckers & 2 Pike one of which is very large & in the lines we take three more Pike & all large. This day's employment for me is the beginning of a slay.

Wednes. 24th. The weather is Cloudy at intervals. This morning we had a little snow. I finish my slay, & Paradix a new bed.

Thurs 25th. While Desroché & Charboneau were visiting the Net (wherein they take 2 Pike & a Pikeral) Charboneau & I heard a Great noise upon the Lake resembling an extraordinary Clap of thunder we first heard it at about E.S.E. from this & left of at about NE.

Frid. 26th. At about one hour before day this morning Le Blanc & Ausgé, Longuetin & Welles arrive from Pigeon river whence they bring the knews of Bottom of river [Fort Alexander], Broken river, & river-aux morts where every one in appearance enjoys a good state of health as well as all the indians except old Premier who in appearance is drawing his last accounts. As I have done with this, I must remark a very extraordinary incident that took Place last night. It was between the evening Star & the one next to it that were so close to each other / [17]/ other (not being more that about 10 or 12 inches in the utmost asunder from each as appeared to us) & appearing so much more bright than usual, & in as manner bouncing to & from each other, as to excite an uncommon degree of curiosity in every one who beheld it; the more so as each star seemed to be upwards of twice their Common size. This gives me reason to relate what an indian from the N side of this Lake said in regard to the Moon. He got up in the Course of the night when it was yet very high but when he went out again after having smoked his pipe & made a fire (according to his accounts not near an half hour from when he went out the first time) he found just sinking below the Horison –

Yesterday we take 1 Large Pike in the lines. To day Old Desrocher pierces holes [in the ice] enough to pass a line for the setting of a Net I got today from Mr. McDonell. Very mild, but Cloudy.

Saturd 27th. Today Old Desrocher sets out the Net at the point in the Lake about 5 acres from here where the ice is about 3½ feet thick which renders it near two foot thicker than it is before the door in our water hole – The weather is very mild, in so much that it rains a very little this morning. Nevertheless it does not prevent Le Blanc and Charboneau from setting off loaded with 40, 43, & 41 [fish]; but at night it grows bad.[23]

Sund 28th. Fine & Clear but Cold, & drifts hard upon the Lake. Desrocher & Ausgé visit the Net of yesterday wherein they take 4 Large Pike & [from] the other one they take 4 Pikeral, 2 Suckers, & a Tullibie.*

Mond. 29th. Very fine weather all day. In the Net near the Lake 3 White fish, 3 Pike.

Tuesd. 30th. Fine weather. In the first Net, that is this one nearer the house, we take 3 Pike, 3 Pikeral, & 1 Sucker, & in the second 4 Large Pike.

Wednes. 31st. Nothing new this morning. Our fishing in the 2nd net is 4 Pike and 2 Pikeral. Towards the afternoon the weather becomes overcast. Having nothing at all to do our Common, rather, usual diversion is that of sliding, for which purpose we made a road to the ice & nearly reaching the opposite side of the river.

Thurs 1st February. This morning I send off Paradix & Welles to Lake St. Martin in search of Bras Court's eldest son who being near Fort Dauphin & there abouts, I am afraid tracks with those people.

23 The fact that Nelson lists three sleighloads rather than two probably means that Charbonneau's wife was returning with her husband to Pigeon River, and had charge of one.

– About 10 O'Clock A.M. Mr. McDonell arrives here with Le Blanc having left Pigeon River yesterday morning. – The weather was fine this morning but Grew very stormy after Mr. M^cD's arrival. fishing in the first net 2 Pike, 1 Pikeral, 1 Toulibie, in the second 5 Pike & 2 white fish.

Frid 2nd. Fine weather 'till near night when it grows stormy & bad.

Saturd. 3. Snow & drifty weather prevents Mr. McDonell's setting off. Yesterday's fishing in the second net was 3 Pike, 1 Pikeral; & today's was 2 Pike, 2 Pikeral, 1 White-fish.

/[18]/ February Sund 4th. The weather is mild & fine; so Mr. M^cD. sets off before day light loaded with 30 White fish. Being to-day up at my steel traps I found the track of a moose about ½ a league from the house, but misfortunately I have no one here able to go after it our fishing in the first net was 1 Pikeral & 2 White fish; in the 2nd, 2 Pike, 2 Pikeral, 1 Sucker & 1 white-fish. Very stormy at night.

Mond. 5th. Very clear & Cold all day. Fishing in the 2nd [net] P. S. W.f [=pickerel, sucker, whitefish] 2, 1, 3.

Tuesd. 6th. Very beautiful weather this morning but towards night it grows dark & windy. About noon Paradix & Welles arrive, having returned from the Lake without the least success whatever, though they spared no pains (they say) in looking for marks, tracks, or any other sign. While Para. was yet speaking of his voyage La Bezette arrived from his lodge about one Encampment beyond where I seen him last fall.[24] He seems to have made but a poor hunt, as well as Ayagon whom he seen about 2½ moons since owing [to] the scarcity of beaver & other small animals. Our fishing in the second net, or the one near the Lake is W.f. 2, doré* 1, Pike 1

Wedn. 7th. A very hard North wind prevails all day, which, with the indian's being a little sick in consequence of his being drunk all night, prevents our departure. Fishing in the 1st net is Wf 1, P 1, sucker 1, & in the 2nd is P 2, dore* 1, W.f. 1. It may not be improper mentioning here that of the white fish we take in our nets, there are at least 9 out of 10 that been speared in the rapids in the course of the fall; many of them are perfected healed & others are very near, thoug[h] in appearance they have been much hurt by the spear.

Thurs, 8th. Though the wind is yet very high (but fair) I set off with the indian [La Bazette] & take Ausgé & Welles, with a little rum. Early in the afternoon we arrive at his tent in a terrible storm which lasts 'till

24 La Bezette was the first Indigenous person to appear at Nelson's post since 8 November.

late at night. As they have but little meat I therefore get less from them; but in return I get near 60 Skins mostly in beaver.

Frid 9th. A little before sun rise we set off (except Welles whom I leave to go for a Cache that Ayagon & th'other indians made of Pounded meat last fall 9th Nov[r]), and on arrival at the house I was surprised to find Bras Court's Eldest son had arrived with his wife & child yesterday from Lake S[t] Martin where he has three moose laid up for me, besides about two others in dried meat – this, had I known yesterday would have prevented my getting, rather hireing Bras Court's young son to come and hunt for me at the house, as my stock of white fish is getting very short, the more so, as I am obliged to give Mr. M[c]Donell whatever quantity he may want of it (say them). The fishing in my absence has been but 1 Pike.

Saturd. 10th. About 8 O'Clock A.M. I send off Paradix, Desrocher, & Longuetin to the indians lodge for his Peltries, meat, &c. About 4 P.M. my hunter arrives & would have killed a moose on his way here but his Gun snapped too often. Welles he leaves at the Lodge waiting the retour de La Santé [the return of the health] of La Bezette to go for the Cache. Sun shines but it blows yet terrible hard from the same quarter as before.

/[19]/ Sund 11th Feb[y]. Fine weather today & yet hard wind which is favorable for Bras Court's young [son] who arrived yesterday to hunt for me here. Last night at about 6 O'Clock Larocque & Boulanger arrive from Pigeon [River] for Provisions as Mr. Campbell's arrival with them from Grand-Rapid has put Mr. M[c]Donell quite out. Early this afternoon Desrocher & Ausger arrive both heavily loaded with meat & about 30[lbs] of Grease.

Mond, 12th. Nothing new, further than that I prepare my Letters &c for Mr. Cameron as does Longuetin whom I send with Mr. M[c]Donell – Paradix's two dogs arrive here about noon having deserted from this old Lazy, dilartory wretch, as I ordered him to remain at the lodge to bring home a Cache of this indians which his own stupidity prevented him from seeing though he passed quite near it when I sent him to the Lake. Fishing in the 2nd net is P. 6, Suc 2, W.F. 1.

Tuesd. 13th. At day light Larocque, Boulanger, & Longuetin set off loaded with 50, 50, 40, & 20 [fish]. The young indian[25] returns home by the way of his brother's lodge as he has hunted all round here but with no success. I told him to tell Para. to come with his slay for the

---

25 Bras Court's young son, who had been hired to hunt for the post.

dogs, & at the same time to bring a little meat. The weather is very fine all day, & our fishing Consists of Pikeral 5, Suck 1, W.f 2, P. 1, Loche 1.

Wednesd 14th. Nothing new to day but fine weather.

Thurs 15th. As Old Paradix has not come yet for his dogs I send off Ausger & Welles. To-day I take a fine Grey fox the first (fox) I have ever yet taken.

Frid 16th. Para. A. & Welles arrive here about noon & a little after, all well loaded. Our fishing this morning is W 5, Doré 1, Pike 5, Para. & Welles prepare as I intend to send them off tomorrow.

Satur. 17th. Early this morning Para, & Welles set off for Bras Court's son's Cache that is where Ausgé & Welles went the 8th of last Nov[r], as well as two bags of pounded meat Welles left on the road from La Bezette's lodge to this place as he was too heavily loaded. – Just about noon in the Commencement of very bad weather, Boulangér arrives from Mr. M[c]Donell's with two slays for fish; but he is not to return 'till 4 or 5 days hence about which time his dogs may begin to grow into good order again as they are now very lean. Mr. M[c]D. is not yet off for Fort Alexander but will be off about the 20th. Today's fishing is P. 2, Dore 2, W.f 1.

Sund 18th. The weather Cleared up in the Course of last night but blows very hard from the North our fishing is P. 5, Carp* 1, & W.f. 1 whose length is 26⅛ inches & breadth 8⅜ inches weighing 11 [lbs] which is equal to two of (above) the common sort as they Generally weigh from 4 to 6 [lbs].

Mond 19th. After dusk last night Paradix & Welles return well loaded having taken the two bags he left on his way here from La Bezette's lodge. The weather is fine. Pike 3, Carp 1.

Tuesd 20th. This morning I sent Paradix to Bra Court's lodge. Tempestuous at night

Wednes 21st. Early this morning Para, & the indian comes for provisions as he starves at his lodge owing to his being often drunk. Fine weather except at night when it grows very bad.

Thursd 22nd. Bad weather all day. Fishing is about 5 of all kinds.

/[20]/ February, Frid 23[d]. This morning I send Welles with Boulanger to Pigeon river who are loaded with 50, & 26 in all 76 [fish] for that place. Though the weather clear'd up yet it blows hard from the S. & S.W. Yesterday's fishing was Pike 6, W.f. 4, Carp 3, Perch,* dorée or Pikeral 1.

Saturd 24th. Fine weather but a hard wind. Fishing in both Nets is P. 1, Carps 3, Doré 2, W.f. 1.

26th. Nothing new but pritty fine weather. Fishing today is Pike 3, W.f. 3, Carp 1.

Tuesd 27th. Rather stormy weather. Fishing but 1 Pikeral or perch.

Wednes 28th. Very fine weather, but as Cold. Fishing is P. 4, W.f. 3, Perch 1, & 1 Sucker.

March Thursd. 1st March 1809. Just at dusk last night Larocque & Welles arrived from Pigeon river where in appearance they do not make too good Chaire [cheer]. Paradix I send off this morning to Bras-Court's son's lodge for meat &c. Fine weather but a very hard S.W. wind.

Frid. 2nd. A Very hard S. Westerly wind with snow a part of the day prevent's Laroc's setting off – Fishing is 3 Pike, 1 White fish & a Carp.

March Saturd. 3[d]. Very tempestuous all day, much more so than Yesterday. A N wind.

Sund 4th. Very clear but Cold. At Sun rise Larocque sets off with Welles (whom I send to accompany him) loaded with 60 & 50 fish besides 110[#s] of pounded meat and thirteen[#s] of Grease with a little meat.[26] Paradix arrives only with 2 Shoulders & 2 rib pieces of a Young Moose. Fishing is 7 Pike, 3 W.f., 3 Carp & 1 Perch or dorée.

Monday 5th. Early this morning Longuetin arrives from Bottom of river [Fort Alexander] having left Pigeon river yesterday. Mr. Cameron's Letter obliges me to go to Pigeon river immediately to get the necessary knews from that place in regard to summering here as Mr. M[c]Donell is to set off to take Charge of Mr. Campbell's post at Grand rapid for [illegible]. Very fine all day but a N wind.

Tuesd 6th. Nothing new all day, only snow this morning & a terrible hard & Cold north wind 'till near night which renders travelling dangerous, especially in this part as there is but three traverses from here to Pigeon river. The first from here to the first islands are reckon'd three leagues, from thence to the big Point 3 more afterwards to the swamp islands far in the Lake we compute between 6 & [7], & then about 3 to Pigeon point, here is the last traverse. From Pigeon Point to the bottom of the bay at the entrance of the river near two & as many more to the fort which we expected to have performed to-day had the weather been proper.

Wednes 7th. Just as the Moon rose (about midnight) I set off with Ausgé & very early in the afternoon we arrive at P. river having had beautiful weather all day.[27]

---

26 The # sign is used here as an abbreviation for pounds.

27 Given Nelson's estimate of a total of about 19½ leagues (theoretically, 58.5 miles, which

Thursd. 8th. [Frid] 9th. We remain on account of a very high wind. Pitite Couilles arrives.

Satur 10th. Yet blows too hard & is Cold, Mr. M^cD. sends LeBlanc (& I send Welles with him) to the indians lodge at Tête-aû-Brochet, where the indians have killed 4 Buffalo – but have eaten all.²⁸

Sund 11th. In the Course of conversation last night with Mr. M^cD., having expressed my desire of seeing Little Grand Rapid, I this morning (about 10 O'Clock) set off in company with him. But as our notice was too short we encamped about 6 leagues where Mr. M^cD's woman relaces a pair of Snow-Shoes for me. Mond 12th. We encamp near Lac Rond, where we have plenty of snow – Mond [*sic*] 13th. We encamp above Portage du Cajin – Wed. 14th. We encamp near small Goose Lake – Thursd. 15th. We encamp in rainy weather in Carriboeuf Lake.²⁹

Several leaves are missing from the journal here; the missing portion must have included the entries for 16 March to 10 April inclusive. The gist of what happened can be supplied from Nelson's *Reminiscences*, from the account of his journey with McDonell to Little Grand Rapids. The whole of that passage is given here, to fill in the gap.

Reminiscences, Part 5, pages 210–18.

/210/ We had not yet in January had any news from Campbell therefore M^cD. by order of Mr. Cameron, sent two men in search of him. We knew he was to winter in some of the lakes above, but precisely where, no one could say; and he had promised to send information of his whereabout, success &c. as soon as the winter had fairly set in. He did not, & knowing the unremitted exertions that were required to

---

is very close to the true distance) for this journey, and a travelling time of about 14 hours, he and Auger averaged 4.2 miles per hour all the way.

28 Tête-au-Brochet was far enough south that some buffalo could be hunted, in contrast to Dauphin River where the only large animals available for meat were moose.

29 Lac Rond is still called Round Lake, a rare widening of Pigeon River. The rest of the landmarks Nelson gives do not appear on the modern map, but the route was up Pigeon River as far as Family Lake, then through that lake to Campbell's post.

/211/ keep soul "& body together" we became very uneasy. Therefore McDonell sent off one Laroque with another man, to search. After ten days he returned with most painful intelligence. That they were reduced to such [want] that some of them would certainly die if assistance were not speedily sent them.[30]

Campbells distress. My trip there.

M^cD. sent immediate information of this to Mr. Cameron; & after ten days received in answer that he should go & take the charge from C^a. [Campbell]. He wrote to me, informing me of what had occurred, desiring to see me the soonest possible for no time was to be lost. I accordingly set out about midnight with Augé & four Smart dogs and arrived about 2 P.M. at M^cD's.

He related the whole. Poor Campbell! had entirely given way to liquer, & though in his Sober senses, a sensible, prudent & able man, well loved & respected by his men & the indians, was now despised & disobeyed. Each one doing how, & as he pleased, things of necessity went very wrong. He was preparing to go up to take the charge. It was a very ticklish affair. C. was a high Spirited men: there was a secreet spite existing between them & the most trifling collision was sufficient to cause some very serious affair. But M^cD. was supported, he had rec^d positive instructions, and had right on his side. C. was without supporters, but unfortunately in the wrong: he had lost all claim to sympathy respect or Support. I, however, pitied him, so did McPhall,[31] another poor friendless & brow-beaten creature, who had been sent by Mr. Cameron to take M^cD's [place] during his absence.

M^cD. showed no small anxiety & apprehensions as to how C. might take the affair; for, if he were to "brindle up" one or the other would have to fall. I have been always fond of acquiring information, & seeing as much of the world & nature as I could, and expressing my sentiments in this respect M^cD. at last prevailed upon me to accompany him.

It was about the middle of March when we left McDonell's house with the following men,

---

30 Alexander Campbell, with two canoes and an outfit including eighteen kegs of liquor, had arrived at the post manned by the HBC trader John Slater (probably at Night Owl Rapids), on 27 September 1808, and built within 10 yards of the HBC post. Slater responded by building an outpost with a good view of all of Family Lake, while Campbell gave out large amounts of goods on credit and threatened to kill anyone who went to the HBC (Lytwyn 1986, 122–3).
31 John McPhail, clerk; see Appendix D.

J.B.Laroque   } and four trains, one for M^cD's
family
Frs. Cartier (LeBlanc)   } and 3 loaded as heavily as the dogs
J.B. Auger, (my man, a half breed } could draw, of dry provisions,
/212/ pounded & dry meat, Grease &c. &c. Our progress was necessarily very slow thus laden & encumbered.[32]

Our course was upon the river, frequently obliged to strike land to
avoid falls & rapids & sometimes open water. We met with few lakes,
& the river was hardly 50 yards wide. For the two first nights we had
plenty of wood, & brush (Sappinages) to put under us, but after that,
getting among those bleak & parched rocks, the country exhibited a picture vastly more dismal than the far famed Siberia. Rock after rock with
a swamp intervening, & but here & there a few Small Shrubs or Stunted
Spruce barely rearing their handsome green heads above the Snow. Every
thing was dreary & dismal in the extreem. In a few places we indeed saw
some larger trees, & occasionally a cluster or grove of green pine of 8
or 10 feet & from 1 to 6 ins. diameter, at the outside, contrasting most
beautifully with the pure white of the Snow for miles & miles around.
Yet, every object conveyed the idea of barrenness, solitude & wretchedness. It required all the energy Spirit & ambition of youth to seclude
ourselves for so many months in such regions. After the two first, & for
the other 4 nights we encamped out, we had great difficulty in finding
wood for the night, and we had to collect bits of bark & dry brush, &
occasionally a handful of grass or reeds or rushes to put under us. I shall
here relate a laughable incident that happened to us on the 4th night.

A North West meal

It happened on the fourth night we had to put up late in a low flat
point where were a few beach poplar trees, called by the men "liard."
It was dusk. I went to make a hole for water; but the ice was so thick
I had to give it up. Leblanc went into a small opening on one side of
the camp to fill the kettle with snow. Larocque warning him to be
careful lest he should gather lynx dung with it, as we [had seen] several
of those animals gamboling in the wood where we drew up to camp.
After several fillings of the kettle with snow to make water enough to
/213/ drink, Leblanc again filled for cooking. Our supper consisted of
a sort of porrige of a little pounded meat & some flour to thicken the

32 As Macdonell was to take charge of Campbell's post, he was bringing his family with
him, including small children, so the progress would indeed have been unusually slow by the
standards of Nelson, a strong and seasoned winter traveller.

liquor. All being ready we sat down & supped; but there being still some remaining, Leblanc & Laroque took a <u>tug</u> to see who could eat the most! Laroque gave up because it was not so good as at the first, & really had qualms & slight shiverings. This of itself was subject sufficient for many coarse & filthy jokes. Leblanc at last began to feel not quite right. Looking into the kettle we found at least a pound of lynx dung in crumbs in the bottom! Leblanc <u>restituted</u> as if he would throw out his Stomac, Laroque not so much so. We & Augé had only had the <u>broth</u> & were not so affected.

I have very often found the dirt of rabbits in our Snow water, but we never minded these trifles.

We had still three long days to travel. We reached a long rapid between two perpendicular rocks, about 60 feet broad, and about 100 yds long. The water was running down in large & violent swells. On the left, there was a narrow ledge of ice, like a shelf, of between 4 & 5 feet thick, & mostly two & three feet above the water. It was in some places full 12 feet broad, but in others again not more than four feet. We had to pass on this or make a great circuit over very high hills & rocks. We chose the former, & got safely past though the head sometimes became dizzy at seeing the water pass with such violence & so near us & we suspended on such a foundation.

The last (7th) day to avoid a great circuit we crossed a point of land, or rather rock. We happened to fall upon the river where the ice was but lately taken, between two rapids, the ice between 2 & 3 inches thick. But we were on a rock of some 10, or 11 feet high, & perpendicular as the wall of a house. Above & below, at the distance of perhaps 150 yards, either way, this rock gradually fell to the level of the river, but it was open water & without any possible means of getting to the ice; and where we were the ice did not adhere to the rock, for when with our poles we sounded the ice we beheld the water rising /214/ and falling on the edge of the ice, full proof of its weakness. McDonell at length, when he found that none of us would risk it without sufficient precautions, for if the first man fell through he would have to work out alone. So, while we were collecting dry poles to spread on the ice, he in a gust of passion, with the assistance of a long pole leaped as gently as he could upon it. The rock was about 10 feet high, and we had to let down our dogs & slays & immediately cross them over to the opposite side, about 60 feet, for the ice was cracking at every move, & before we had done our wading in the water two or three inches deep. All eventually got safely over.

A Sad Spectacle.

While crossing over that neck of rock just mentioned, we discovered two objects in the large open flat, on the opposite side, at the foot of the Grand Rapid, near the <u>Portage</u>, which is scarcely a mile from Campbells house. At first we thought they were two of the men coming down to fish; but seeing them stroll in such erratic courses we again thought they must be Rein deer (Carriboeuf)* for they were about a mile off, & we frequently lost sight of them in the clusters of low bushes that are dispersed over that flatt. Under this Supposition, we observed every precaution to avoid any noise, particularly of our dogs, lest we should alarm the Deer. When we got on the flat, it was sometime before we again got sight of them. We were lost in wonder what to think of them, their motions were so singularly erratic. Some of the party said "they must be the ghosts of some of those poor fellows who are wandering in this plain where, while living they so often fruitlesly sought a morsel."

We at length got sufficiently near to discern they were two of C.'s men. We called out; no heed was taken. When within a few feet Laroque calls out "Well Baudry, how are you?" He minded no more than if he were blind & deaf. Indeed all his faculties we[re] quite prostrated. When we got so near that Lar. put out his hand to him, at the same time accosting him in the usual coarse & familiar language of brother voyageurs, "Why d[amn] you, dont you see us? How are you?" He turned his head careless round. "Ah! what? est ce toi mon frere?" "What!" again rejoins Laroque, "is it you Beaudry? Are /213/ you dead or alive? Am I speaking to yourself or your Ghost?" "Eh, what-are-you-saying?" replied Baudry in such a drawling & Sepulchral tone of voice that alarmed us all.

He was warmly clad, but so filthy it was almost impossible to be more so. His beard of a reddish hue & nearly the length of his whiskers was full of the leaves of the balsam (Sappin), fish Scales, ashes, the spittle of his tobacco frozen in icicles in several places. His head not been combed perhaps since New Years day, also full of spruce & balsam leaves, fish scales & ashes; his eyes emitted a deadly glare & scarcely moving; emitting a most offensive odeur of <u>sour</u> smoke & fish – so strong & offensive that we had to keep several feet from him. The tout en Semble, his stare, voice, motions, language &c. &c. displayed a picture of idiocy & wretchedness indiscribable. He would certainly have died that day had we not most providentially arrived.

"I am very weak," he said. "We have nothing at the house to eat. We have been starving ever since the ice took (Novr 1st). We have not had not had one good (full) meal since we came to this frightful place, & surely we have tried our best & worked very hard. We must all die of hunger. Our bourgeoi[s] is quite disperited: he does not know what to do." He took full half an hour to say these few words, in broken sentences & long pauses as if his mind were bewildered & had hardly strength to articulate. His voice so sepulchral, hoarse, low & hollow as if he had neither lungs nor vitality!

About a quarter of a mile further on we found Lépine, the other object man we had seen. He was much stronger, his voice more natural & more life & vigour in his actions; but four or five days more would have completely prostrated him also. We gave them both a little pounded meat, not to fill them but to strengthen them a little and proceeded to the house, scarcely a mile beyond .

Campbell's house &c.

What we had seen in these two miserable objects above described, prepared for a scene of wretchedness & misery. It was indeed misery & wretchedness, but not at all similar to the two men. They were certainly much emaciated & reduced & weak & filthy; but they could have held out, with a few "God sends." This singular difference I fancy is to be attributed to various causes. Some men are naturally much stronger, & have more stamina than others; & from whatever cause I leave physicians to determine a less quantity of food nourishes more in some than a larger quantity /216/ does in others. Yet want, dire want was visible in them all, & in every thing about them; disorder, dirt, & a very bad odor.

Poor Campbell was much surprised & evidently displeased. I have reason to think that had his muscular energies not been so much reduced, he would have turned McD out [in margin "Campbell delivers up his charge"]. But he was a sensible man. He was well aware that McD. was a protège[33] & personally his enemy; he understood his position perfectly, & after making a few cutting observations on the business he peaceably gave up the Keys & his charge. McD, whatever were his feelings, treated him as kindly & as liberally as his circumstances permitted.

---

33 Nelson also saw Alexander Macdonell as a favourite of Duncan Cameron's, though he came to regard him as a friend. Macdonell was a member of a respected Highland family, well represented in the NWC's hierarchy: for his connections see Wallace 1934, 464. He was clearly destined for a partnership (which he achieved in 1814), while Alexander Campbell could see his prospects slipping away. From his position as senior clerk on Lake Winnipeg for the XYC in 1804–05, Campbell now found himself assigned to a small post with a difficult opposition and poor food supplies. His resentment of Macdonell would have been inevitable.

As is always done under such circumstances, he [Campbell] would send out his men, two by two, with two small nets, a few lines, nails or awls to make hooks, thread for Snares, a Gun & a little ammunition, to seek their lively-hood [in margin "How they endeavoured to save themselves"]. None of them were Successful but Laroque (not the one who accompanied us). He would frequently bring in a few fish, a hare, lynx or partrige, as he could get & spare. While we there he sent in a lynx & 2 or 3 fish. Every week he would send in more or less. Tho' very little yet by mixing the broth with rock-moss (tripe de roche)* they made out to keep themselves alive.

Their house was built on the borders of the Lake du Grand Rapide, a very considerable body of water; & in one part there was an excellent fishery, which, however, from some cause or other had been neglected, no doubt, chiefly from his frequent inebriety [in margin: "Description of country"]. The place was named from a beautiful rapid, thro' which the waters of the Lake emptied. It was not a fall nor a cascade, but a rapide running down in a narrow winding chasm between two very high rocks, or rather a very high rock split, as it were expressly to let the water thro', filled & covered with dwarf Spruce, giving the resemblance as if it came out of a cavern, so dark it was in the upper part.

In former times there were forests here, in this country too, tho' now so barren, as was evident from stumps we could still see in some places [in margin, "Supposed cause of its dreariness"]. But fires, whether natural, i.e. from spontaneous combustion as some say, or accidentally put by the indians in some extraordinary dry seasons, passed thro' different parts, scorched the trees that they fell; other fires again a few years after, when this timber was dry, burnt up even the moss which kept them moist & nourished them. So that in the Space of a few years, the Shade (afforded by the trees) being gone, with a very few /217/ exceptions the whole country displayed nothing but parched & burnt rocks, & in the numerous hollows only moss & water with a thick leafy bush, often difficult to get thro', in the Summer. A frightfully barren country; yet, in a few places landscapes the most beautiful the most fanciful imagination could conceive: but these are few & far between.

We slept there two night to afford time to Campbell to get ready to come with us. He had a wife & if I remember well, four children. This was a terrible lumber* to travel with in winter.[34]

---

34 As usual, Nelson preferred to travel as quickly as possible. See Journal, 6 May 1808, for the further complication that Campbell's wife gave birth on that date, so she must have been seven months pregnant during the journey.

The morning after we left McD. finding C. moving so miserably slow [in margin "Return home with Campbell"], I decided upon leaving him with two men to assist him & proceed on with Augé, my man.[35] C. was very averse & charged me with want of pity. But I told him that with so few provisions as we had two men less would be very favorable to him & he had still two men to assist him: our remaining could not accelerate his travelling; & as to starvation that was the very reason why we should leave [in margin "Leave him"]. I took about a pound of pounded meat each, & set off. I was loth to leave him, but our remaining only rendered the case worse. We encamped at night in that place where we had the feast (P.212). The next morning we were off early. But this being about the 20th March we had a great thaw (the first this year) & by ten o'clock we sank so deep every step & our Snow Shoes became so heavy we were very reluctantly obliged to put up. We had each our blanket & a tomahawk [in margin "a shift to collect Water"]. We made a Small trough & making large balls of Snow which being put on a stick, as it melted, dripped into the trough & thus furnished us water. At night the weather became cloudy & much colder. It was not more than midnight when we started. We reached a place that was called "La Chute blanche" – a very high fall, not much short of 150 feet high, rolling off an immense rock, very steep – whence, from the violent motion all is in a foam, obtains the name (of white fall) but which from the excessive cold, freezes completely over. We could not see the water but heard the roaring as of distant thunder. It was Auge's turn to lead, or break the road [in margin "The Wite fall"], & I told him of my suspicions, & advised him to keep close within the shore on our left; but he was a sour morose ricketty creature, growled out that he knew better: it was still a long while before day, & some broad flakes of Snow falling rendered the atmosphere peculiarly sombre. Scarcely two minutes after warning Augé, rising my eyes I saw no more

35 Macdonell's report to Cameron, his bourgeois, after he had arrived at Campbell's post and taken an inventory, is preserved as a transcript in the Selkirk Papers. Without Nelson's account it would be impossible to understand the context, as the letter is undated and the writer and addressee are given simply as "Alexr McD" and "D.C.E." [Duncan Cameron Esquire]. Macdonell mentions that Nelson had accompanied him, and reports, "the people of this post especially those at the House were in a shocking condition Campbell is without doubt a treacherous mean low lifed fellow." Also mentioned were the interpreter, Lorrin, who apparently had been assisting Campbell, and the HBC traders Slater and Thomas. In this letter, Macdonell had also to confess to having lost two kegs of high wines, which he had buried under the floor of his house at Pigeon River for safekeeping, but which were empty when he returned (Selkirk Papers, 9081–5).

of him. I was wondering what had become of him, and /218/ strech-
ing myself to see his "whereabouts" – down I went sliding, rolling &
tumbling from side to side – I immediately Saw where I was – a very
natural ejaculation – my God! – the fall! – It was soon over – I was
down at the lower end, & on rising I saw Augé hardly recovered from
his Surprise & fright [in margin: "a Slide down the edge of the fall"].
What is this? the fall? "voila une bonne glissade toujours" said he (at
all events it was a famous Slide.). We were on the very edge of the fall
& heard the water roaring & purling round us. We were soon off.
Comment is unnecessary; any one may imagine how we felt; but we
had not time to stay to look or talk; for we had full thirty miles yet
to reach the house [at Pigeon River], & had eaten the day before the
remainder of our scanty store. We continued walking as hard as if pursued by some ferocious enemy, & about 10 o'clock got to the house.
Those of the men who knew the distance we had come swore it was
the old boy (the d-l) who had carried us.

   The next morning before day light we resumed our march & reached
home in good time in the afternoon, where, thank God I found all well
[in margin "Reach home, all well. Campbell arrives"]. Six or seven days
after this C. arrived with his family to pass the remainder of the Season
with me, as I had abundance of provisions.

When the journal resumes after the gap caused by the lost pages, Nelson
was back at his own Dauphin River post.

/[21]/ April Wedn. 11th. To-day Ayagon arrives with all his things; &
there is but little water upon the Lake now.
   Thurs 12th. Yesterday I get the men to take up one of the Nets taking
much more fish than necessary; but very few whit-fish among them.
Old Desrocher & his Lady prepare to set off tomorrow for Pigeon
River having been here since the 4th of January. The first Game we have
seen this year were three Pelicans just about Sun-down.
   Frid 13th. Before Sun-rise Desrocher sets off. And Paradix & I go to
the river Monetàguée as there is but little Game yet arrived. Paradix
kills but one Goose & 2 ducks. I kill a duck also. We sleep here.

Sat 14th. Early this morning I return home & find all well but little of any-thing good to eat, having only nasty little ugly Pike with a few Pikeral, & Suckors. Ayagon was out a moose hunting with his dogs but Could not find any as they had set off Yesterday towards the Swamps where there is too much water to go through. Except this, there is nothing new, but a Changing wind.

Sund. 15.th. Fine mild weather. Longuetin & Ausgé gather gum. We loose the stand of our net.

Mond 16. Tues 17. The men gather Gum again to-day. The river is nearly free of ice except at this Point.

Wed. 18th. About 10 A.M. Welles arrives from Fort Alexr with our Letters &c. but very little news. He brings a Keg of potatoes and a little Parsnip seed for Gardening this summer. He left Boulanger at Tête-au Chien continuing his rout by that way to Pigeon river. He brings me from Rassete 3 Martins & 1 rat [?]. the river is entirely free above.

Thurs 19th. I get a Net put out as the river beyond the first point is nearly free of ice. Welles puts it out late in the afternoon & at Sun-Set we take 4 Suckors & 1 white-fish. except this nothing new

Frid 20th. While Welles was at the Net wherein he takes 9 White fish & many suckers, Le Blanc and Charboneau arrive from Pigeon river for a half Keg of HWines which I give them. They bring me a Strip'd Blanket & 2 Skains of Net thread – Ayagon goes a hunting to the Lake St Martin – We take down the old fish house.

Satur. 21st. Nothing new but very fine weather & a very high S wind. The river before the house is intirely free of ice 'till some distance in the Lake. We take but 1 whit-fish & plenty of Suckers. We put a fresh net out

Sund 22nd. This morning LeBlanc & Charboneau set off, so do Longuetin & Ausger who go to Pigeon river for bark to mend their Canoe, but they are obliged to return about half ways from the island as the ice is already too weake and bad that they would not probably be able to come back. Ayagon arrives this afternoon having returned but a short distance from beyond the Chemin de Guére as his little son was too loansome. He gives me 2 Swans, 8 Bustards* & 3 Large ducks. We take many fish among which 3 W.f. & one weighs 7½#s.

Mond. 23d. Welles returns from the Grand-Maret[36] where he had been yesterday to gather Gum, he finds but very little. Yesterday it snowed all day though not enough to Cover the Ground. Today it rains.

---

36 This Grand Marais was to the northward, about a day's travel from the Dauphin River post; see Appendix E.

Tuesd. 24th. It rains all day by showers, which prevents us putting up a flag staff that Mr. Capbl[37] and I cut down last friday by being too-Slippy. but [*sic*]

Wednes 25th. About noon after all or everything was fixed we put it up with much ease; it is about 53 feet long. The weather was this morning as yesterday but after noon it became fine & dry. A few w. f. is our fishing.

Thurs. 26th. I prepare for going to the Lake [St. Martin] a hunting with Ayagon. I take Longuetin with me also as I hope to see the indians. Fine weather this morning & 5 w.f. is our fishing.

Frid. 27th. Last night we encamped near the Chemin de guerre where we killed 1 swan & a duck, and to day about 3 leagues below the Lake where we kill 3 swans 1 crane & 3 geese. Besides a couple of ducks.

/[22]/ Saturd 28th April. We are obliged to encamp at the Lake & to make a lodge for the rain.

Sund 29th. We go some distance in the Lake in Canoe but leave it after & proceed on foot to opposite to the island where Cu-fessé &c makes sugar, but we were not able to go to them as the ice was too bad altho' we went a long distance in hopes of getting upon it. We fired several shots & called out to them, we were answered but the distance was too great to hear distinctly what they said. On our return home to the Canoe where we encamped I found in several places on the beach whild [wild] hops – Mond 30th. We encamp at Chemin-de-guerre to which place we killed 4 swans &c. Tues 1st May The wind blows as hard as it did yesterday but it is much colder for we had ice upon our paddles almost all the way home. On this hunting trip we killed rather brought home 11 Swans, 7 Geese, 4 Cranes & 2 ducks. All is well at home. The ice upon the Lake appears to be very weake now –

Wednes 2nd May 1809. The wind is E. all day & very Cold. nothing new only plenty of fish.

Thurs 3[d]. Nothing new only that Ausgé takes his Canoe out of its bed for mending. A hard S. Wind.

Frid 4th. It blows very hard S. & is very smoky which makes us think that the fire runs in the plains

Sat 5th. 'Till about noon it blows hard from the S. then turns NW. After this again towards night it is N which with some small showers

---

37 Alexander Campbell's arrival has not been mentioned previously, so he must have come on to Dauphin River from Pigeon River, along with his family, before Nelson's journal entries resume on 11 April.

of rain, besides one yesterday about noon, weakens the ice very much in appearance on the Lake as it comes in shore & goes out again as the wind happens to blow. Yesterday Ausgé took his Canoe across to mend it at old Rassette's house, but is prevented as it rains. 6 w.f. fine weather at night

Sund 6th. A little before about sun rise (for the weather was Cloudy) Mr. Campbell's woman was deliver'd of a boy. – Ayagon gives us a Sturgeon that he speared in the rapids. This is the first that we have seen this year. In our nets we take two Cat-fish* & several white-fish which is more than last year for 'twas seldom we ever took any W. fish & never a single Cat-fish –

Mond, 7th. Plenty of fish. The Men cross to the other side to mend their canoe to-day for the weather is more fine rather warm than usual altho' generally fine. Except this nothing new –

Tuesd, 8th. Ausgér finishes sowing [sewing] his Canoe. I set a net at the foot of the rapids

Wednes 9th. Ausgér put his Canoe last night in the water (river) to soake so as to band[38] it with more ease but as it rains to-day he is prevented. Wednes. 10th. Continually rains, but by Showers only. We take plenty fish.

11th Saturd 12th. As the weather is fine they band their canoe. About 4 O'Clock P.M. His Majesty Old Cu-fessé (without a nose),[39] His Lordship La Besette, & Bras-Court's youngest son (a common soldier in appearance) arrive here but very light, in the fur way. Having first been introduced into His Emperial Majesty's (Ayagon's) Lodge, they were permitted by the special love his imperial Majestey professes to any house where there is high wines to visit me, in which case I was obliged to act that part of un Grand Traiteur by distributing among them a little better than an half Keg of HWines one Keg & a half of which after being mixed was paid for in trifles & note [not?] dear. Ayagon was cloathed. The weather was fine all day & a Gentle Breeze shifting to every quarter. We take this morning 24 W. fish.

---

38 The meaning of "band" is uncertain. If "band" is meant, it may refer to putting bands of gum along the seams between the pieces of birchbark. If "bend," it may refer to forcing the gunwale rails outwards by inserting thwarts, which may have been removed when the canoe was laid up for the winter.

39 Cul-Fessé had apparently lost his nose since Nelson had last seen him. Noses were sometimes bitten off in drunken fights. See, for example, John Tanner's story about Peguis or Cut Nose (James 1956, 154).

Sund 13th. Nothing new but fine weather & the indians drink. Ausgé faraudes the Rinds of his canoe.[40]

Mond 14th. Very fine & warm weather the wind is E. Last night we took a Large Sturgeon in a Common fish net & a Cat fish also besides several w. fish & many Suckers –

Tuesd 15th. Nothing new but a very high wind (South), which drives the ice far out. Indians yet drunk

Wednes 16th. Early this morning, I send off Ausgé & Longuetin to the détroit of Lac St Martin to Bras Court's eldest son's lodge for what few things he may yet have as he owes me yet 37 Skins. A high S. wind, 22 white fish.

Thurs. 17th. I am busy to-day in making a small appartment of earth to put the Powder in more security [sic] than formerly. Paradix & Welles are employed in recovering the shop with Bark &c. to be more sure from fire. Ayagon kills 30 Cat fish & 1 Large Sturgin the half of which with 4 Cat-fish he gives us. Blows hard –

/[23]/ May Frid, 18[th.] 1809. Fine weather – Nothing new.

Sat 19th. Bad Stormy weather & a very high Southerly wind, nevertheless we yet begin to fix about the houses.

Sund. 20th. We had several showers of snow but melt as soon as it falls. It Clears up & becomes fine at night.

Mond. 21st. Altho' this is sunday we are obliged to fix my chimney, & room as we very soon now expect Pigeon River people here; for the Lake, that is, this part of it appears to be quite free of ice – for since yesterday the wind has turned north, but no ice yet comes; About 10 A.M. Ausger & Longuetin arrive from very near the Falle-de-pardrie without being able to find the least mark or vestige of him.[41] The

---

40 French *farauder*, to dress up. The "rinds" were the large pieces of birchbark forming the hull of the canoe (HBC journals routinely call birchbark "birch rind"), so Auger was painting or decorating his canoe.

41 Bras Court's eldest son, whom they had expected to find at the *détroit* (narrows) of Lac St Martin (see journal, 16 May 1809). Nelson had been worried that this man, who was new to his own post, was in contact with the Fort Dauphin people (see journal, 1 February 1809), and was doing his best to get his winter hunt, though the search was taking his men very close to the Fort Dauphin outpost at Falle au Perdrix (Partridge Crop). On the 22nd Nelson sent his men off on the search again, with instructions to go even farther west, and they returned on the 29th, bringing with them 11 skins of the debt of Bras Court's eldest son, much less than the half pack (about 30 skins or more) that Nelson had expected. They had met an engagé from Fort Dauphin living with another Indigenous band, confirming that they were infringing on the boundary of the adjacent department. Nelson did not see Bras Court's eldest son again until 6 July, upon his return to Dauphin River after delivering the season's

weather becomes pritty fine at night altho' it blew amazing hard this morning. Very few fish to-day.

Tuesd. 22nd. About 10 A.M. I send off Paradix & Welles upon a second tourne to look after Bras Court's Eldest Son & not to return but from the Manitobane unless he is at the (first) little Lake Vaseu beyond falle-de-Pardrie where all the indians here expect him to be – About Noon dark, Cloudy & soon after rainy weather with a terrible E.N.E. wind.

Wednes 23^{d}. Most extraordinary Stormy weather, that is, rain, rain-Snow, or melted snow & dry snow, for this morning there was about two inches thick upon the ground, & had it not melted a mesure there would have been upwards of one foot. Nevertheless towards night it becomes more calm so that that the men put two nets – we want to eat.

Thurs 24th. Very fine and calm weather, which makes us expect M^r McDonell (but he does not arrive). Mr Campbell & I plant Potatoes, the first I dare say that were ever brought to this place. I have here made a mistake & ought to have said that to-day I get two packs made and Friday 25th We plant the potatoes about ¾^{ths} of a Keg after being cut up into proper peices.[42] The weather is very Calm all day yet Pigeon River people do not arrive. Ausgé & L gum their Canoe.

Sat. 26th. The weather was very Calm 'til about 10 A.M. when it blows pritty fresh from the NE. This morning I dug up enough ground for the planting of a few parsnips. After this I go to the first bay of the opposite side of the river to chuse a proper place for building. This place here in some respects is handsomer but in return we are too much expose to every wind except the South which in the winter is rather too fresh – We have no wood here at hand for building & for fire; & we are s[h]aded from the Sun in the winter by a number of nasty small trees; & the water is very bad – but there, there is a small rivulet which plenty of good & Clear water – there is a fine view in the river & a pleasant one to the Lake. We have the Sun in our doors & are shelter'd from all winds except the S. & S.E. which Comes from the Lake, & enough wood to Build & to burn – fishing in the spring is not so near as at our present residence – having it at our door &c. – The

---

peltries to Fort Alexander. The man had some fresh moose meat for Nelson, but both would have been conscious that his winter's hunt was gone, most of it almost certainly traded to the Fort Dauphin department.

42 Growing root vegetables was a standard activity at established fur posts, and Nelson established gardens at both Dauphin River and Tête-au-Brochet. Alexander Henry, at his post at Pembina on Red River, frequently mentioned his vegetable gardening (Coues 1965).

distance between the two places is about 6 acres. A. & L. continue at their Canoe – The weather is Cold all day except this morning –

Sund 27th. I get the remainder of the packs made except a few peltries yet remaining in hopes that Paradix & Welles will bring enough to [make] about half a pack more which will make five & a half tho' they are not of exact weight I beleive as I put them to 80#s instead of 90 lbs as my stilyards* are too strong.

Wed. 28th. Yesterday it blew too hard & it was too cold for the indians to set off, but to-day they prepare after I gave them a sufficient quantity of ammunition &c. for their summer. They bother'd a little for rum, but I would not harken unto them tho' I have yet 1½ Kegs of HWines. The wind blows yet pritty high from the NE. Bras Court's youngest son remains with me for a passage to Fort Alexr & from thence to Lake Lapluie to see his father who is there! No signs of Mr. McDonell from P. river & of Paradix from FdP.

/[24]/ 1809, May 29th Tuesday. Very Beautiful & Calm weather. About 10 A.M. Paradix [torn] arrive from Falle-de-Pardrie where they found Chenette a living with Fort Dauphin indians where [torn] appearance they make pritty good returns as in every Post of that Dept. Beyond this are the Small Lake Vaseu they joined the indian [Bras Court's eldest son] from whom they got but 11 Skins of his. He is to hunt for some time in that Quarter & then to come down to the Lake

Wed. 30th. After our long & loansome expectations of Pigeon River people Mr. McPhall at last arrives near sun set with some difficulty through a great deal of ice that yeat [yet] appears to be & is in the Lake. Mr. McDonell arrived with his people from above the 6 of this [torn] & is now gone to Blood River to wait for us. They (Mr. McPhall) found our indians at the Grand Point a hunting Sturgeon.

Thursd. 31st. This Morning we take we take the different inventories & put all to rights for our departure of tomorrow. I put 1 Keg & 9 pints of HWines in Cache in our Potatoe feild, well fixed with barks & dry straw with a Little Ground. fine weather

Frid 1st June. Early this morning we all embark for Fort Alexr leaving John Inkster & Boulanger to remain 'til the arrival of those who are to pass the remainder of the Summer. We were obliged to encamp among the rocks before we could reach Tête-aû-Pishew. Blows hard all day.

Sund 3d. The wind having abated a little we set off & put a shore at a Point near Tête-aû brochet to make Kettle where we put out such of our things to dry as got wet in consequence of several heavy showers last night. We encamp upon the same spot as last spring, au detroit des islets verd.

Mond 4th. We were degraded 'till pritty late this morning by a very hard wind & rain. When the weather became more calm & settled we set off & put a shore at Tête-aû-Chien where I left my packs &c and proceeded to Blood River where Mr. M[c]Donell had arrived last night with a part of his own indians, Eatcho & several others &c from G. Rapid &c not being yet arrived.[43]

Tuesd. 5th. My men with two others go to Tête-aû-Chien for our packs & Canoe but Messrs. Campbell & M[c]Phall prefer waiting our arrival there. Ayagon &c all arrive. The Belly also arrives with his family, & is here time enough to be at the feast of the Baptism of Mr. Alex. M[c]Donell's boy whose birth day was yesterday.[44] As I was not present at the beginning I can give but very little information except what I got from those that were there. The begining was a speech immediately succeded by a Song and the ringing of some round bits of Copper fastened loosely to a stick to serve as belles[45] – the child had a stripe of vermillion put on his face from one temple to the other between the upper part of his nose & eyes the ceremoney was to be repeated with the rattling of belles & many other fanciful jests whenever the child should be sick to assure its recovery. Sugar, Pounded meat, Grease & smoking were given to the attendants & those invited – Ayagon was Preist, & God Father &c. – Many other things were done which I recollect not.

Wednesd 6th. Mr M[c]Donell gave liquor to the indians some of whom are yet tipsy – We have no strange News to relate altho' we are in a manner in a new Country – we take no sturgeon & we live (the men) upon d[ried] fish. The weather is fine sun shine, but blows hard.

/[25]/ Thursd. 7th June 1809. We remain here windbound to-day as we have since my arrival here, as well as for Little Cû-levé & some

---

43 In his letter from Grand Rapids to Duncan Cameron in March, already quoted, Macdonell mentioned the Indigenous hunters "Echo" [Nelson's Eatcho], Oscabas, "Puttute Garson" [Petite Garçon, presumably], "Nio Corbin" [Nelson's Nez Corbin] and "Lous" [Louse, Nelson's Morpion] (Selkirk Papers, 9081–2).

44 Evidently an Ojibwe naming ceremony. For another description see Peers and Brown (2000). This is the first mention of the The Belly, leader of a hunting band of Mashkiegons or Swampies who had been trading on the east side of Lake Winnipeg, but would be moving to Nelson's post on the west side for the next season.

45 Jennifer Brown suggests that these may be early examples of the metal cones that were later sewn onto women's dresses to make what are now called jingle dresses.

other of his indians who he has not yet seen. however, if the weather [improves] we shall embark tomorrow. Mr. McPhall who being loansome & want to smoke came on foot a long the beatch of this bay from Tête-aû-Chien (about one league & a half) bring us news of a light Canoe passing under a leif'd saild [reefed sail] towards Fort Alexʳ: but could learn no news from those quarters as they did not debark & as they were too far out in the Lake to be Known (as the traverse from one shore to another is a full good league).⁴⁶ But it must be reminded that this is by far, very far, the narrowest part of the Lake seperating it as it were into two different Lakes by this narrow of about one league or a little more in length – From this place to Fort Alex. it is about 25 or 26 leagues long, & from this place again to the other end of the Lake at Grand Rapid (the N end) is about or from 55 to 60 leagues more – The four men that I have (see the 9ᵗʰ Septʳ) get themselves bled by Mr. McD.

Frid 8ᵗʰ. Having been detained here several days in vain for Cû-levé & others of Mr. McD's indians we embark with a pritty high East wind which is fair for us as far as Tête-au-Chien where we take Mr. Campbell & proceed with a Land wind – We soon stop to take breakefast, & after this again we are obliged to stop for the Guming of Mr. McD's Canoe that got hurt upon some of the rocks when we reembark again & are obliged once more to put ashore (to Camp) at the detroit du duc for hard wind, about 7 or 9 leagues at utmost from blood river. We heard the report of two gun shots & see several very fresh vestiges which we take to be old Rassette with these indians for whom we were waiting – It is yet early & I think we wont set off to day.

Sat. 9ᵗʰ. We set off very early this morning with a Cold & hard wind besides Cloudy weather 'till in we came in the broken Islands where we run our Canoe full Paddle upon a rock which happily was smoothe, otherwise it would have taken off upwards of 1½ fms. bark; & in doubling the next point we found a letter addressed to me from Mr. Crebassa with a Keg of white corn we here found the old Brochet, but proceeded to the same island where we left Mr. Crebassay last fall. Here Mʳ McDonell's indians (those for whom we were waiting at Blood River) came & Got their due from. We eat here, & Gumed our Canoes

---

46 Probably a light canoe with one of the NWC partners from Fort des Prairies, as the Fort des Prairies brigade, under the direction of the clerk Colin Robertson, arrived at Fort Alexander on 12 June. The partner, if that is who he was, had already left for Fort William by the time that Nelson got there on the 11th.

then we continued to the Point beyond Mauricelle's river[47] where we encamped early. From the Sauteux's at B. R. we got some oats.

Sund, 10th. We set off before Sun-rise but were obliged to put a shore very early (at River au Table about 2 leagues) but sometime after-noon we reembarked as the weather Grew (quite) Calm (afterwards), & encamped at the island of the point de-la-mitasse (4 leagues from Fort Alex[r]).

Mond 11th. Just at day light we embarked with a fine breeze, which tho' was not very favorable for the sail yet we bore it some time. About 8 O'Clock A.M. we had the pleasure of being received by Messrs. M[c]Donell & M[c]Kenzie[48] (& Mr. Cameron) who have arrived here some days past with all their Canoes &c & an extraordinary Great quantity of Provisons & Grease, they seem to have made pritty good returns in the pack way also. Mr. M[c]Kenzie seems to be very ill of a dissentry [dysentery], Mr. Cameron appears to be indisposed also. There are many indians here. Mr. Crebassa made 11 Packs, Mr. Seraphim of River au mort made 9 & 10 Kegs Grease.

Tuesd. 12th. To-day we are employed among the torreaux's (Pemican) [taureaux*] and I was busy in remaking my Packs which amount to the pitiful number of five. We have had very hot weather by spells. To-day & at night the weather became very Cloudy & dark towards the NW which is a prelude to a high tempest which came on at Sun-Set – at which time a leather lodge took-fire which had been put up by Mr. M[c]Donell to get thoroughly dry & smoke – While we were busy here one Mr. Robertson[49] from Fort Des Prairies arrived leaving 7 Canoes the remainder of the brigade at the Point au Sable.

/[26]/ June. Wednes. 13th 1809. A Very high N wind Prevails all-day. Early this morning, Fort des Prairies Canoes arrived & immediately reembarked as did Mr. Robertson. Very hot to-day. Preparations on all sides without any result. Mr. Cameron sends off 2 Canoes to the Dalles loaded with 8 Packs, & 18 Kegs Grease – Mr. M[c]Phall is with them.[50]

47 Elsewhere Mauricette's River: see Appendix E.
48 John Macdonell and Daniel McKenzie, partners in charge of the Upper Red River and Lower Red River departments, respectively.
49 Colin Robertson, a clerk who was about to leave the NWC to work for the opposition, the HBC. He had just discussed the possibility with William Auld, the HBC's master at Cumberland House, and was now on his way to Fort William, where he would tender his resignation and go down to Montreal, armed with a testimonial from the agents. From there he proceeded to England, and was soon hired by the HBC, proving to be an energetic and valuable employee, and a thorn in the side of the NWC. See Woodcock 1988.
50 John McPhail (the usual spelling) is not heard of again in Lake Winnipeg after this. For what more is known of him, see Appendix D.

Thurs 14ᵗʰ. Nothing new, only that we are very busy about nothing, however we finish pressing & marking our Packs – they amount to 51, that is, those that are made in the Lake, River-aux-morts & this place. What an extraordinary [difference] is there between this present year & the last year that Mʳ Wᵐ McKay wintered here two years since!!! The number of Packs made in this Department were 167 – 67 Seven [*sic*] of which were made at this Post, which make 4 more than all those made in the whole Depᵗ this year! What does this depend upon! What occasions this! or who can give any plausable reason for this!

Frid 15ᵗʰ. Many preparations as usual, but no decision as yet. Very hot, but nothing else new.

Sat. 16ᵗʰ. Extremely warm (the therm. at noon was 94¾). All day & a very high S. by W wind. The indians are troublesome for liquor, but do not succeed, Messrs. Crebassa, Seraphim & McDonell take the inventory. Yesterday Mr. McDonell sent off his Canoes as did Mr. McKenzie

Sund 17ᵗʰ. Nothing strange but fine weather. The indians come & dance war dances before our house door; & Mr. Cameron gives them some tobacco & vermillion as he strikes at the Poteau saying that he was at two different battles & was wounded in one.[51]

Mond. 18ᵗʰ. About 10 O'Clock Last night Messrs. McTavish & Campbell arrive from Athabasca & English river & set off about 3 P.M. today. The knews from that quarter does not seem to be so good as last year in the pack way I mean.

Tuesd. 19ᵗʰ. Mr. Cameron sends off four of his Canoes being the whole & mostly loaded with Grease & Packs from Red River. Mr. Alexʳ McDonell goes to the Dalles. To night Tête-Grise, Gaignan, Tête-de-Loup Cervier, & old Nanjobe arrive from broken river – They are well received & four Kegs of rum & 4 fathoms tobacco are divided among them –

Wed 20ᵗʰ. We are all busy about our accounts – Fine weather. The indians are troublesome

Thurs. 21ˢᵗ. The indians make preparations for the Mietawie [Midewiwin*]. Nothing new

Satur 23ᵈ. About 9 A.M. Mr. Cameron embarks for Fort Wᵐ Loaded with thirteen pieces exclusive of his own things & lumber – we had

---

51 A warrior struck the post (*poteau*) to announce that he was about to tell of his achievements in battle. Cameron made his own contribution to the war dance, probably by referring to his service in a Loyalist regiment during the American War of Independence, before he entered the fur trade (Brown 1988).

a small shower of rain to-day but towards [evening?] we had a very heavy shower with lightning & some terrible Claps of thunder all which however subsided before sun set

Sund 24th. Altho' the weather is fine & Calm yet I dont get off. The indians are very busily employed at their meetaiwee in a lodge made for the purpose of Poplar branches (its length is about 80 feet).

Mond. 25th. About 8 O'Clock A.M. I set off in a small indian Canoe to go to the River Dauphine.52 The wind blows very hard & obliges me to put a shore at our old house53 from whence we reembark at about 3 P.M. & encamp at Black river, where we find that poor miserable & pitiful wretch Dubois.54

Tuesd. 26th. Wind bound all day – Dubois gives me some fish.

Wed. 27th. Late this morning I set off & encamp at the point of Mauricettes river after having been obliged to put a shore twice & paddle very hard, having a head wind. D. gives me 4 fish.

/[27]/ Thursd 28th June. 1809. A little after sun rise this morning I set off with a fair wind, but in doubling the point I met Mr John McDonald from Fort Dauphin with 5 Canoes loaded with 24 pieces each. – I am here some time but reembarking I encamp late at the Detroit de la Tête-au-Boeuf; having been obliged to put a shore on account of a great storm at the point of Tête-au-boeuf about 3 leagues from this.

Frid 29th. Windbound all day. Saturd 30th. The weather is a little more Calm wherefore I embark (leaving a mark at my encampment for Richard who overtook me where I was with Mr. McDonald), but was absolutely obliged to put a shore at Broken river where I took a part of the white earth55 & hid the remainder of a keg, & reembarked. This afternoon & soon met seven Canoes from Slave Lake but had not the pleasure of seeing Mr [John] McGillivray himself as he was bearing sail farther out in the Lake than I dared to go with My small Canoe

Sund. 1st July. Having encamped at the detroit du Duc I set off after noon, having left [let] pass several thunder storms & rain, & a beautiful south wind which was favrable to me in uselessly [sic] waiting for

---

52 Rather than passing the summer at Fort Alexander, as he had in 1808, Nelson was returning to his own Dauphin River post, which he was planning to rebuild on a new site across the river.

53 The old Bas de la Rivière post, which preceded the one that William McKay had built further upstream by levelling the old graveyard.

54 No further information; probably a Canadian freeman.

55 Perhaps to be used in whitewashing the new buildings at Dauphin River.

Richard, whom I now take to be a head having passed me in the night. However I leave a mark upon a piece of bark & encamp at about 2½ leagues from Tete au Chien.

Mond 2ⁿᵈ. I am obliged to put a shore in Les isles-aux-Ecorses for wind, & a little in hopes of finding old Desrochers wife there – They return & encamp with us at the Islets verds in our same encampment of the 3ᵈ of June.

Tuesd 3ᵈ. A hard N wind obliges us to put a shore at small Tête-aû-Brochet & the weather growing Calm we encamp at Tête-au-Brochet fective[56] where I find both the Mashkeegons* & Sauteux* of Pigeon river & Dauphine river waiting my arrival.[57]

Wednes. 4ᵗʰ. Altho the weather was very fit for travelling yet I could not set off till late on account of the indians who all had something or other new to tell me. About 5 O'Clock this afternoon I meet Mʳ Simon Fraser (a proprietor) with all his brigade consisting of 30 Canoes; & Blondin the Guide of them.[58] I encamp at the G. Point at our house (on account of a very hard head wind & was obliged to make all the tour of this Large bay)[59] where I found every thing in as good a Condition as Could be expected with both the men & the woman in very good health but loansome – A Short time after my arrival B[ras] courts Eldest Son arrived with his wife – he brought but very little of anything with him except the Greatest part of the meat of a fresh moose he killed to-day.

Friday 6ᵗʰ. The hottest weather that we have had this year by far. A S. wind. Bras Courts Son sets off to-day. I send Bellanger for pine bark to make me a lodge.[60]

Saturd. 7ᵗʰ. Boulanger goes for bark as usual. At night we set a net. It blows very hard.

---

56 Probably "effective," i.e., Tête-au-Brochet itself.

57 This Mashkiegon band, whose leader was The Belly, was taking its trade to Nelson's post this year. Nelson had met The Belly at Bloodvein River on 5 June, on the occasion of the ceremony to name Alexander Macdonell's baby son. The arrangement may have been agreed then, or it may have been negotiated during the preceding winter.

58 The Athabasca brigade, with Simon Fraser (the explorer), partner in charge. Fraser had made his historic voyage of exploration down Fraser River the previous summer: for him see Lamb 1960, Lamb 1976.

59 Sturgeon Bay. If the wind had not been so strong, Nelson would have made the usual traverse across the mouth of the bay.

60 The wooden cabins, tightly sealed for winter use, would be stifling in hot summer weather, and in any case the buildings were about to be taken apart and rebuilt on the other side of the river. Nelson was getting an airy bark lodge to live in for the time being.

Sund 8th. A terrible hard South wind all day. Boul. & I go & and make preparations for making a provision store & clear up some brushe from where we expect to build our new house. In the net but very few fish in the net [sic] & John puts out another one wherein he immediately takes 4 Cat fish. Last night & the night before though we fished with lines we took but one Cat fish each night.

/[28]/ July. Monday 9th. We take 22 Cat fish in our lines & but very few in our Nets tho' we have three out besides a Sturgeon Net. It is somewhat worthey of remark that this place is quite Changed for fish to what it was before, when we took whatever quantity of fish & almost of every kind we pleased but now, & tho' we take more pains than usual by far yet it is with great difficulty & the utmost exertions to give us but one meal a day – luckily I have pounded meat otherwise we should starve.[61] It rains by spells & blows very hard all day.

Tuesd 10th. Altho' there was appearance of very stormy weather all day yet towards evening Ayagon, Cu-fessé, & Bezette arrive with a better appetite than any thing else I give Ayagon 3 quarts of HWines, Cu-fessé 1, & Bezette ⅔ after being mixed.

Wednes 11th. The indians are yet drunk. At Last Frs. Richard arrives by the bay. 'Tis now five days since I arrived tho' I often lost very fine travelling weather [waiting] for him which I was obliged to make up by travelling in strong & dangerous head winds. His Canoe consist of twelve people (with their lumber) mostly women! Voici un beau temps pour les farreauxs de Cantines![62] the greater part of whom are to winter here. he comes also with the design of making them a house & to return with me this fall.

Thurs 12th. Dull weather & misty at times. The indians yet feel a little of their frolick & are troublesome for more but I agree with none of them in this point except Bezette to whom I give three good drams so as to enable him to undergo an operation in his eye by Frs Richard who takes rather cuts a piece of dead skin off his left eye which has rendered him quite blind of it since a few years past by some frozen

61 Nelson's ruthlessly extractive fishing at Dauphin River during his first two seasons there, when he was sending large quantities to Pigeon River, besides what he and his people consumed themselves, had seriously depleted the local fishery. His journal entry on 7 February 1809 shows his first hint of this, when he remarked that most of the fish being caught in the nets appeared to be wounded survivors from the fall spear-fishing season. This would have made him realize that the supply of these fish was not infinite.

62 The expression "farreauxs de Cantines" is puzzling, but the sense is that Nelson was worried about how he was going to feed all these people.

earth flying into both of them in working at a beaver Lodge. Richard after having thrusted a piece of soft leather made for the purpose, between the eye ball & the dead skin that Cover'd it almost intirely, then lifting or raising it with the wire of an ear bob already crookened & sharpened, he Clipped it off. He was Cured of the other eye by a dry branch as he went into the woods a hunting that ripped the skin of the eye & the remainder was Clipped by his wife on his arrival at his lodge at night, otherwise he would have been almost stone blind, as this morning he Could not see his hand at arms length unless brought close to his eye, & now he sees it but very imperfectly for it is almost full of blood & continuall[y] runs. but he will soon be done [recovered] yet I beleive that he never will see very well as there is yet a small pieces [sic] that Covers & sticks quite fast to the sight of his eye. I set a night line with 18 hooks!!!

Frid. 13th. Fine weather but blows pritty fresh from the S.W. The indians set off to go up the river to the first Lake (St. Martin)' where they are to pass the Summer except Ayagon who goes to Manitobanc Portage La Prairie to see his friend.

Satur Thours 14th. Nothing new only, that we live but poorly having but very [few] pigeons & very few bad fish.

Mond 16. It is pritty warm to-day though since some time past it has been Cold.

Tuesd. 17th. Nothing new 'till about noon at which time Le Ventre [The Belly] arrived from the River au Guerier, having lost his road in that direction, expecting to find our house there for he has not been here for many years past. His lodge is in the bay of Tete au Pishew / [29]/ with the Gendre (Laurrin's son in Law) who will not be here 'till some time hence. The Belley has brought me 1 Dressed moose skin & two beaver Skins with the meat of one, for all of which I give him 2 quarts of mixed rum.

At Sunset this day The Cou-fort, the Eldest son of Bras Court (an elder brother to the the one who wintered with me this last winter) arrived here with 13 Pieces of dry meat & about 40#s of Pounded d° [ditto] Conducted by La Bezette. So much for this day – but [sic]

Wednes. 18th. About 8 O'Clock this morning they set off – Altho' I had given the strictest orders that laid in my power, to every one of my indians, not to have to deal in any manner whatever with any of Fort Dauphin indians, yet neither would not believe until they had tried, now they return with shame, leaving all their things behind, except two dressed skins that I make him take home in spite of himself, &

1 Gallon of mixed rum with ½ fathom of tobacco &c, promising them (him) that any one of them whatever, except my own indians, who shall come down upon like errands shall be received just as he deserves.[63] No news from F.D. in Swan river, or Deer River, further than what Mr. McDonald has already told us, but they all deny however of having been enticed away by any of my indians, which I believe to be true. He informs us of a band of indians exceeding twelve men who are now in the Lake La poule-d'eau [Waterhen Lake] making the Grand Meetaiwee [Midewiwin], after which they are to Come down this way & disperse, some as far & others beyond Lac La Pluie, while there is . another band to disperse in both Red Rivers of [or?] their environs, & some others again to Fort Des prairies, that is, its lower part – Not long after noon, Messr⁵. Bezette & Cou-fort make their appearance, both drunk – having drank a part of their small Keg; & remain, having gone upon the opposite shore where they pass the night & drink the rest. They wanted to trade the two dressed skins but I refuse & turn them away without even a dram – The Belley sets off with his lady & encamps near here. We have several showers of rain this afternoon, & it rains all night –

Thursd 19ᵗʰ. Pritty early this morning the indians set off without Coming here. Jack Inkster & Boulanger go to Monotagué river a fishing & hunting for whatever they may get; for ever since my arrival here I may say that all we Can do with four & five nets is to get us one poor meal in the morning, & at night, when we don't have Pigeons we have nothing but dry Cat-fish to eat. The wind blowing too hard, the belly makes his appearance but returns again.

Frid. 20ᵗʰ. Wind & Calm, rain & sunshine succed each other all-day. Nothing new.

Satur 21ˢᵗ. The weather is not quite the same as yesterday. Inkster & Boulanger arrive with 4 Catfish, 12 Young (American) Geese & an old one with 3 small ducks. Richard & his brother were there also but they have not made much more than Inkster. It seems that all this bay is alike for fish not more in one place than in another.

Sund. 22ⁿᵈ. Inkster & I go to the rapids in a small Canoe in hopes of finding Catfish, but we had not the pleasure of seeing any or of any

63 Nelson had now accepted that Cou-Fort, the Bras-Court's eldest son, "belonged" to the Fort Dauphin post at Falle au Perdrix, although Nelson had given him debt the previous fall, and he continued to visit Dauphin River from time to time. The relationship was complicated by the fact that Cou-Fort's younger brother was living at the Dauphin River post, and had been hired to hunt for the post the previous winter.

kind whatever. What a difference between now & last November (the 9ᵗʰ). Fair & fine weather this morning.

/[30]/ Monday 23ᵈ July 1809. From about noon yesterday 'till this morning we have had very bad stormy weather, but today it is grown a little more Calm & reposed which however brings us nothing new or satisfactory, remaining here as if buried up where no one could find us at any rate I hope that this will not last long – Inkster & Boulanger are busy at the Nets, as they have been ever since & before my arrival here, yet is it with much trouble & difficulty that we can keep ourselves from starveing. We have set nets in every direction & in every manner, even by sowing [sewing] two upon each other which makes a double height, yet not more than otherwise – This mor[n]ing we take a Large Sturgeon in our small nets!! A Miracle-!!! Except this nothing new.

Tuesd 24ᵗʰ. Pritty fine weather this morning but after noon we have several showers of rain & some terrible Claps of thunder (& lightning.). Blows very hard.

Wednes. 25ᵗʰ. We have more rain this morning but at night Clears up & becomes fine. The wind was very hard from the N & NW which made the water rise about one foot perpendicular, which made us take many fish in our (5) nets – 50 in number.

Thurs. 26ᵗʰ. In Consequence of a very hard wind, Nez Corbin, Moose Eyes & Old Brochet remain here wind bound. They arrived at a late hour last night & wanted to return to-day but Can not – They bring me some meat & 9 fathoms of B[irch] bark.

Frid 27. The weather grows more Calm this morning (& quite so at night) Old Nez-Corbin tho'thers set off with 3 half pints of HWines mixed with tobacco & ammunition. They promise to be back as soon as they will have wherewith, for they only brought me two very small pieces of dry meat. their excuse for this is the want of ammunition.

Satur. 28ᵗʰ. At about 8 a.m. Le Ventre, Le Gendre, & Le Beson, Old Nez Corbins son (three Mashkiegons) arrive with the meat of 2 moose but dry, the Greates[t] part of which they give me when I give them rum in return. They are very troublesome for which they get some drubbings – The weather this morning is as the remainder of the day, very Calm & fine, but last night & some nights past it has been quite Cold considering the season – In our nets we take 53 fish (6 nets out).

Sund, 29ᵗʰ. The indians are yet drunk having traded the remainder of their rubbish – a fit of Jealousy taking possession of Lorrin's son-in-law he feigns poisoning himself with Poke-root (Carrot-a-Morreau)⁶⁴

64 Poke root or poke weed, *Phytolacca americana*, contains a number of toxic compounds in the roots, leaves and berries. In American folk medicine, it was sometimes used as a treatment

but not 'till after he had made several speeches to his Angel demanding
the muskatoes to eat him up immediately, but to begin by his nostrils
as it is the only place where he wishes to appear to be vulnerable.
Nevertheless (neither) the muskatoes (nor his angel) did not minded
[*sic*] him apparently for they would rest & bite upon every part of his
body where they could reach when he would start (at every bite) &
renew a part of his speech telling them that they were foolish & ought
to begin where he bid them (his nostrils) that they might soon kill
him & then have a general feast of the remainder of his "Charoign"[65]
When he found that they did not mind him he said I know very well
that some body sees me my angel tells me so (for he had seen young
Richard who was all this time close behind him attentively /[31]/ listening to him and observing his motions) wherefore he cannot agree to
my desire, but, however there are other methods he says & so I will try,
when he dug up some of this root which happened to be near him and
began to chew it, but he took great care not to swallow its juice nor
the root itself by slily spitting the whole out of his mouth in turning
his back towards Richard & returning his face again to him (Richard)
every time that he would take up more & daub his mouth well with
ground, which however he wiped off but was yet Cunning enough to
leave a little upon his lips & teeth so that he might be perceived by his
family, some time after his return home when he began at least feigned
to become stiff & motionless & foam at the mouth like a **Wild boar** –
they threw water upon 'till such times as he thought to be enough &
then came to his senses again & is not of course quite well – We have
several showers of rain to-day but appearance of plenty for tomorrow.

Mond 30th. It thundered, lightned, & rained very hard from the
breake of day 'till about 8 O'Clock when it leaves off during which
interval the indians set off again to return to Monotaguié river, but
it begins again by small small showers soon after they set off – I give
the indians one quart of mixed rum for nothing & trade the remainder of their meat – Yesterday afternoon the women of the fort here go
for some cold water in the swamps where they yet find plenty of ice
between three & four feet under the surface being nothing but light
moss –[66]

---

for chronic rheumatism, but when mistaken for edible plants such as parsnip or Jerusalem
artichoke it led to severe symptoms and sometimes death. See, for instance, Britton and
Brown 1970, 2:26.
65 French *charogne*, carrion.
66 The isolated permafrost zone, characterized by small islands of permafrost called palsas

Tuesd. 31st July. Nothing new, but very fine weather. But few fish as usual tho' 7 nets out.

August Wednesd 1st August 1809. Richard, Inkster & myself go for wood for the making of a sizeable Canoe, which is to be made the soonest possible. The weather is very smoky & calm 'till near night when it changes into a vey hard wind and showers of rain, which in appearance will last all night – some thunder & lightning also. Near Sunset, Cu-levé, Pitites-Couilles, Grand-Jeune-homme, & Dépouillé[67] arrive from Tête-au brochet with a little meat which they give me. They give us intelligence of three loaded canoes gone to Athabasca from Fort William they say that this is the third day they have passed at Tête-au-Brochet which is about the 30th of last month, much sooner than they ever passed at Bottom-of-the-River even – & according to their accounts it was the 28th that they [were] at Fort Alex^{r} (B. of river). This is the only news that we have. About 5 this afternoon the indians set off as the weather grew more Calm. 'Tis very extraordinary that we take no white fish yet, & but very few of others

Thurs. 2nd. I should have said this afternoon at 5 instead of yesterday when the indians set off. Rain is the only news we have to-day. about noon, when several very large Clouds gathered round us as if threatening destruction to all & every thing in their way, but all these except one pass in wind which however had no other effect except surprise in everyone who heard the terrible rumbling noise it made in passing over us & long afterwards 'till a terrible thunder storm with hail carried it apparently from our hearing

/[32]/ August Frid. 3^{d}. Nothing new appearance of rain – altho' we have none

Satur 4th Sund 5, Mond 6th. Nothing very extraordinary for these three days past except a very high South wind – To-day Richard lays the bottom of the canoe that is to be made here.[68] At night, at least

---

and peat plateaus, today does not extend farther south in Manitoba than the swamps at the north end of Lake Winnipeg. Aerial photographs show that substantial thawing of permafrost in that region took place between 1926 and 1967 (Thie 1974), so it seems possible that the isolated permafrost zone reached farther south, even to the Dauphin River area, when Nelson wrote in 1809.

67 Some of the newly arrived Mashkiegon band.

68 This was a small canoe, which was begun on the 6th and finished, except for the gumming, on the 11th of the month. François Richard was in charge of the framing, while the women sewed the seams and gummed the completed hull. Nelson used the canoe for his

near night Bras Courts son arrives here with his wife & Child, besides many dressed skins & a little dry & pounded meat also. He tells me many long stories. But now that he has a-banded himself with the rest of the Sauteux I see that he has become as great a hog as the rest. As I now find that the meat brought down here the 17th of last month by the Cou-fort belonged intirely to Bras Courts son who wintered with me, I no longer hesitate to trade it, for which I give him a bladder of very weake rum. Very hot all day at night the wind turns N.

Tues 7th. The wind Changed from S to N & now blows with terrible fury, & I beleive has frightned all the fish away tho' we have 6 nets out, we have taken but 18 suckors, 1 Dorée & 1_white_fish! About 8 O'Clock this morning this indian sets off with a letter that I give him to be delivered by his elder brother to whatever Clerk comes to trade at Falle-de-la Pardrie – We seldom have more rascally weather in the fall than we have to day, the water rises very much & lowers it in turns.

Wed 8th. 'Till about noon it always rains by showers, but after & near it Clears up, becomes fine & more calm. Richard with the women sow [sew] the great seams of the Canoe.

Thurs. 9th. Very fine weather all day; & does not blow very hard. About 8 O'Clock A.M. Lorrin's son-in-law, the Belley, Nez Corbin, & his son arrive here from Monotaguée river with the best of the meat of 4 moose, which they give me with some pounded meat in return for some mixed rum – They are very troublesome.

Frid, 10th. The indians are yet a little tipsy, & consequently want much to drink but they find themselves [i.e. recover?] they prepare for setting off with many menaces, but as they find that I do not pay much attention to them, they offer coming back again if I will give only each one pint upon debt which I absolutely refuse – They encamp round the first point of this river in the Lake about 10 Acres distant from here. It blows very hard from the S. we take 4 w. fish –

Satur 11th. It blows very hard but a the wind is Southerly & comes a little off (this) Shore the indians set off towards river aû-Guerier – I expect them back before I set off for Fort Alex^r (About the 18th). Richard at last finishes the canoe except the Gumming of it which will require about one day. Tempestuous in an extraordinary degree towards night.

---

trip to Fort Alexander a week later. For a detailed description of the building of a birchbark canoe, with many illustrations, see Adney & Chapelle 1983, 36–57.

Sund 12th. This morning Richard goes a hunting with his two youngest brothers (leaving the next eldest to fish for & take care of the
family) a hunting beaver on the North Shore of this bay to endeavour
to pay a few skins of his debt – We take 7 white & several other fish
in our nets – The white-fish appear to be coming now as the season
approaches – Contrary to usual they (appear) to be coming from the
Falle de Pardrie & Lakes above, instead [of] out of this Lake, when
they go to shallow rivers & rapids to Spawn. It blows very hard
towards night – & much appearance of very bad weather.

/[33]/ August Mond 13th. With the help of the women upon the other
side we Gum our small canoe. About 10 A.M. the wind begins to blow
with great fury & we have continual rain untill late at night – It blows
so terribly hard as to render all attempts for setting nets unavailing,
therefore we will have to live upon our stock of meat for a short time.

As I have nothing for this day's news I shall relate a piece of indian
superstition. When Bras Court's son arrived last July he killed a
(female) moose coming down this river which he gave me, the head
and all, but he desired that the ears might be hung up out of the reach
of dogs, for were they per-chance to get them he would not for a long
time be able to kill any more moose. Now that he is banded with
the other indians, he is almost every day a hunting but almost without effect, having killed but six moose in one months time, whereas
before his arrival here he never went a hunting but when he wanted
to eat, & had the good fortune of killing every time that he went
out. Now this he imputed either to us, or La Bezette's youngest wife,
whom he says dispised his medicine by leaving the head and skin
lying about in every direction, having seen it himself – because he had
given Bez. a whole moose.[69] I endeavour'd to impute it to his Gun
or ammunition or something else, but he is obstinate & will have
it to be owing to the ears for the last moose that he killed had its
ears "Cut" – a circumstance never known of before, for, altho' there
are many old indians yet living none of them has ever seen or heard
of the like. "This moose with Cut ears was sent purposely by some
Manitô to explain the cause of his (then &) future misfortune untill
he may find some means of appeasing their wrath & displeasure by
some sacrifice!!!" –

---

69 In Ojibwe-Cree belief, the animals expect their remains to be treated with respect and put
to good use, otherwise the hunter will not be successful. On this see William Berens's observations to Hallowell, in Berens and Hallowell 2009, 87.

Tuesd 14th Wed 15th. The weather was bad yesterday but to-day it is finer & Calm at intervals. Richard arrives from his excursion but without any success, as the weather was to bad that he could not set out his traps – I make preparations for my departure – It rains at dusk –

Thurs 16th. I take a General inventory of all the property in my charge & coppy it into the book. This afternoon old Nez-Corbin arrives with the Belley; they bring me some very fat meat & a little Grease, when I give them some rum in return & they go back. News, they found a very large encampment, seemed to have been employed by a number of our people bound to the North. This is all that they have to inform us with – Last nights rain continued 'till a little before day this morning but after Sunrise it is Clear, which however does not continue long as we have constant showers throughout the whole day – For these several days past the weather has been amazing Cold throughout the nights – morning & evenings & frequently in the day time tho' yet in the middle of summer. We had a Constant hard wind (I may say) from the W.S.W.???!!!

Frid. 17th. Nothing new for to-day, only that I am preparing for my departure tomorrow if the weather will permit, which I am afraid will not be the case as there is /[34]/ all appearance of very bad weather before that time : however all will be ready for another time. The weather has been very cold this late night insomuch that it froze pritty hard, I may say very hard considering the season. The leaves have all changed their Colours, & many are red & yellow – some (but very few tho') begin to fall. I sent Inkster to-day to the rapids to see how much the water had rise or fallen, as well could not exactly ascertain it here on account of the continual influx & reflux occasioned by the Lake &c. Having gone about one league from here so as to be the more sure he found it to have fallen just about 5 inches since the 20th of July, at which time we put a mark!

Saturd 18th. As the weather early this morning does not appear to be very fav'rable for our departure we take our time & set off somewhat late (from River Dauphine) & encamp at the Grand Point. As a Curiosity I have taken an exact account of every fish that we taken since the 12th of last month[+] merely to show the [difference] between the fall & summer. However, exclusive of 24 white fish, 5 Pike, 1 Pikeral, 6 Suckers, & 6 Laciesh[*] we have taken this morning, the rest, that is, from the 12th of last month untill last night, the total amount of our fishing comes to 1321 of [e]very different kind; & for Which quantity we made use of 237 Nets as may be seen by the columns below.[70]

/[35]/ Sund. 19th. At the breake of day we set off with a fair (& sometimes head) wind which however is very acceptable to me in particular as our Canoe is a perfect <u>Rasson</u>.[71] We encamp near little Tête-aû-Brochet about three or four leagues to the South of Tete-au-Brochet. at night we have some rain, thunder & lightning, last night also.

Mond. 20th. Very early we set off, but as the wind blows very hard we are obliged to encamp at a very early hour for the remainder of the day at the Foot of the Traverse from the main Land to L'Isle a Bériö – We hunt here but without as there is no Game (1 Goose kilt).

Tuesd. 21st. While Richard & I were out at some distance from home a hunting for wherewith to eat, the wind fell & we immediatley returned & embarked, & about 1½ hours before sun set we encamp in the Bay of Tête-aû-Chien towards Blood River where we (Wednes 22nd) this morning go; that is Richard & I on foot to get what news we can to Communicate on our arrival at Fort Alex[r] to the Proprietor of this Depart[ment]. Owing to the badness of the roads we did not reach there 'till near 10 A.M. where we found Cu Leve & Old Brochet just arriving from hunting, bringing with them some meat a part of which they give us. This is all the news we have, as the indians have neither seen black or white since thier arrival. We remain weather <u>bound</u> all Day –

Thurs 23nd. We set off early this morning with all the intentions of Great Travelles [*travails* = works] wishing to do more than can be done, however as the weather was proper (except the wind that came from every quarter but the right one to afford us a little relaxation from the paddle, except in the short traverse of Detroit du Duc) we encamp in the begining (N. end) of Broken islands.

Frid. 24th. We renew at an early hour the past fatigues of yesterday with a hard head (S.S.E. & S.W) wind, & can only gain the point of Mauricelle's river hardly time enough to encamp before Dark and heavy showers of rain 'till near day when we reembarked again (about 9 A.M.) but were not able to proceed the distance off one league for the wind. We put a shore on a small island in hopes of future good luck. (Saturd 25).

---

70 The table, which Nelson extracted from the journal entries above, and gives no further information about, is not printed here.
71 Jennifer Brown suggests that *rasson* means that the canoe rode very low in the water; cf. "au ras de l'eau" – nearly level with the water; "fortification rasante," a low fortification.

Sund 26th. We set off very early this morning & a little before Sun set we arrive at Fort Alex[r] having (general) calm or almost fair wind. Messrs. Crebassa & Seraphin who remained the summer were well as the rest of the men. Lorrin has been off these several [days] a head of the English (H. Bay's) observing their motions – News, are that Mr. Bethune was sent with Montreal people as far as this place with Goods for Mr. Thomson for Columbia as the distance of these new explored regions are far too Great for admitting their winterers carrying their returns (peltries) to Lac La Pluie even.[72] Good news in Canada!!![73] A Party of Cioux's [Sioux] were met about two days journey from River aû Pimbinat by a party of Crix's [Crees] & Sauteux, who were coming to River Pembinat to know the meaning of the extraordinary report that made them Cry last Summer (a shot being fired from a small Canon in consequence of their although [onslaught?] upon that Fort Last summer), but were answered by the Crixs' & Sauteux's saying "we have set off from our lands in quest of enemies who, every year commit great depredations upon our lands & even want if they could to prevent the white people from furnishing us with our necessaries – we have come this far – we meet you coming to war against us & our friends (the white) – so you must fight for your safety or be cut to pieces" – The Crixs & S. who had previously discoverd them had already made holes in the Ground so as to fight with more safety – So they did. Forty of their enemies were kill'd, & only four of themselves but several wounded –[74]

72 Normally the voyageurs in the canoes from Montreal would come only as far as Fort William, then return with the furs. Some would be hired to come farther, to Lac la Pluie, where the Athabasca brigades got their goods. In this case, some Montreal men were hired for a trip inland as far as Fort Alexander, so that canoes from the Columbia, with an even longer trip than those from Athabasca, could get their goods this much farther west.

73 Not explained further, but probably some family news in letters from Nelson's parents in Canada.

74 This was the next campaign in the annual wars between the Sioux and their Cree and Ojibwe enemies. Daniel McKenzie, the NWC partner in charge of Lower Red River in 1808–09, left a letter for his friend Duncan Cameron as he passed Fort Alexander, 8 August 1809, which read in part, "the Saulteurs & Crees of Red River have Massacred forty Scioux out of four hundred who were coming to attack my old Quarters; I am not sorry for this Wells must be on his Guard there is danger – He must absolutely remove the fort to some other Quarter." (Selkirk Papers, pp. 8546–8). The fort in question was at Pembina, where Alexander Henry, McKenzie's predecessor, had had trouble with Sioux war parties every summer. As Nelson states in his next day's entry, McKenzie himself was en route to a new station, in Rat River and Lower English River, while John Wills was to take over in Lower Red River (Wallace 1934, 260–1).

/[36]/ Mond 27th August 1809. Nothing new has happened this forenoon, but near night J. Steete of Hudson's Bay Cop^y pass here with three Barges or boats for Lower Red River or River aû-Pembinat[75] where he is to be a neighbour to Mr. Wells who is gone there this year, & Mr. McKenzie who was there last year is gone to Rat River. Lorrin arrives but a few minutes after, who tells us that he left Mr. McKay with four more Barges for Upper Red River (for the HB's Co)[76] & neighbour to Mr. John McDonald this spring from Montreal, Mr. J. McDonell being gone to English River Dept. as Mr. J. D. Campbell is gone on a visit to Canada.

Sund 28th. Long before day Richard & the Smith[77] are sent to River au-Mort to see after the English in case they put some of their people to winter there fine weather & very cold.

Wed. 29th. Nothing new 'till near night when Mr. J. McKay of HB's Co arrives with his four Boats for Upper Red River or Absiniboan River. He arrives here with Sail the wind being S.S.E. Last Saturday the Thermometer rose as far as 84. on Sund, 83½ & to day 85.

Thurs. 30th. Altho the weather was very fine 'till late last night yet to day it rains very hard but by showers, thunder & lightning also. At 9 A.M. J. McKay sets off in the middle of the rain to encamp near here where the other three boats went last night. wind is from SE. round to W. continually changing. The Ther[mometer]. is at 55.

Frid 31st. Very windy weather this day & some rain this morning. Past Noon M J. McKay of HB's comes here with his boat his son (lately from England),[78] young Baily & six men. being here about half an hour he asks to dance & dine which is accorded to him, & about 10 O'Clock P.M. he sets off – Nothing very extraordinary besides this only that Rassette arrives from River Noire & Le Dresseur from River La barbeu – Cold –

---

75 John Stitt of the HBC, formerly a trader for the XYC.

76 John McKay, one of the most effective of the HBC's inland traders. He had been stationed at Brandon House on the Assiniboine in every season but one since 1801. Nelson's references to him show that he made a point of visiting his rivals at Fort Alexander when he passed, probably out of mere friendliness. McKay was in failing health, and this was his last season; he died at Brandon House in July 1810. Some of the local NWC men helped to care for him at the last, a sign that he was well liked. See biography by McCloy (1983).

77 Here, Nelson mentions that there was a blacksmith at Fort Alexander, but does not name him.

78 John McKay's eldest son, John Richards McKay, was educated in England, and returned to Rupert's Land in 1808 as a writer for the HBC: see HBCA Biographical Sheet.

Sat. 1ˢᵗ September – The weather is fine. MᶜKay with his four barges set off. About Noon Alard's wife arrives from Black River where she had also been endeavouring to make oats or rise [rice] for her husband who is now for Fort Dauphin Department – About 5 O'Clock P.M. Richard and the Smith arrives from Dead River but the news they bring is of but very little consequence as they did not remain to wait the arrival of the English at that place.?!!! However they have for recourse the arrival of the Red Birds son in Law whom by his accounts is to be here in five days; & from whom we may probably have more Satisfactory accounts.

Sund. 2ⁿᵈ. About 7 O'Clock A.M. four men in a small canoe pass here for the HB's Com[pany]. The principal part of their loading being rum for which MᶜKay sent them to Osnaburghs house, afraid of being in want, as the Governor at Albany Factory gave him but very little at first. Fine weather the remainder of the day except a little shower of about 1½ minutes duration –

Mond. 3ᵈ. It rained in the beginning of last night pritty hard but soon gave over & became fine. About or a little after midnight we were awoke by the Cries of Charboneau's wife bewailing the sickness of her Child. All hands are anxious for the arrival of Mr. Cameron.

Tues 4ᵗʰ!! This forenoon Charboneau's child bid adieu! to this world after Great appearent suffering for two or three days only. Its death is said to be have been occassioned by a fall from its mothers bed while a sleep which broke two of its little ribs but was not found out 'till to day: a few minutes before it died – – We buried according to the Roman Catholic religion as it was thus Baptised.⁷⁹ It was born about the 3 of June 1809!!!!!

/[37]/ Wed. 5ᵗʰ Septʳ 1809. Yesterday morning Richard go went as far as b[page folded over] River a-hunting & to day he arrives with a very fat bear. Three indians arrive from lake Du Bonet but have not had the least sign of Mr. Cameron –

Thurs 6ᵗʰ. To day Mr. Crebassa sends off the indians with a letter a head of Mr. C. & to be bring back news immediately incase of accidents –

Frid. 7ᵗʰ. We at last to-day were gratified by the arrival of Messrs. Cameron & MᶜDonald. They were, that is Mʳ C. was misfortunate in the upper of River blance at Grand Rapid where lost 5 or 6 Pieces

---

79 In the absence of a priest, the baptism would have been performed by Charbonneau himself, or one of his fellows.

unfortunately & was nearly having some of his men drowned had it not been for other people who immediately embarked & took up the men & some other few articles that yet floated!!! This same place Grand Rapid is remarkable for Misfortunes for M[r] W[m] M[c]Kay in 1806 lost three men & 7 or 8 trading pieces –[80]

Sat 8th. We unbail all the Goods &c and receive our equipment & memorandums – Nothing new all day only that M[r] M[c]Donald's men set off long before day light.

Sund. 9th. Early this morning Toussaint Vaudrie[81] arrives here & was to proceed as far as Lac La Pluie where he was to serve as an Interpreter but Mr. Cameron finding it proper orders him to return from here. At about 10 A.M. McDonald sets off after having spent the night with us a dancing – Nothing new but calm.

Mond. 10th. Nothing new & we do nothing – Mr. Cameron is employed in writing letters to Red River by Vaudrie. All the men are employed in making a road straight down to Point au Sable through the woods –

Tuesd 11th. Both Ducharmes; Collish & Etiene free men are gone to Red River & Vaudrie sets off also –

Wed 12th. The men finish their road & are drawn out for the respective Post[s]. Tues 13th. We seperate rather say the Goods are divided &c.

Thurs 14th. The rest of our things are given out so that we have put all our things in a baggage at the Store doore &c – Now being out of my exact calculations[82] & to put myself right I shall begin to write.

Friday 14th September 1809. At all events we have last night had a dance that took us till near 12 o'clock P.M. As all preperations are previously made we embark each for our respective Post just at noone. Our Brigade consists of two Canoes & one boat viz. Mr. Seraphin with his boat for River aux Morts with 5 men: A. Bercier, – Mercier, Etienne Longuetin, B. Latour, Frs. Richard & himself, Seraphin. For

---

80 Nelson gives more details about this incident, which actually happened in August 1805, in the opening entry of his Lac du Bonnet journal, 29 August 1805.

81 Toussaint Vaudry was one of the most experienced men in the Lower Red River district; see Appendix C. Why Cameron would countermand an order from John Wills, the partner who had just taken charge of Lower Red River, is not explained, but there was some kind of antipathy between them: see D. Cameron to J.D. Cameron, Lac la Pluie 14 April 1813 (Selkirk Papers, pp. 8710–12).

82 By comparing his calendar with someone else's at Fort Alexander, probably Duncan Cameron himself, Nelson discovered that once again he was one day wrong.

Broken River one Canoe with 5 men: Frs. Trempe, – Braconier, – Alard, Perusse, & Dupuis & himself (Crebassa). For River Dauphine 6 men, Desrocher, Bpt Larocque, J.B. Aus-gé, Welles, Bellanger & Inkster (these two latter having remained in Land.) & myself (Nelson). We encamp at Sun set to the North of Black River where Rassette arrives with his family near nine O'Clock at night. He intends to winter (Free) at White River[83] where I am much uneasy about his life; much appearance of his Starving to death.

/[38]/ September Saturd. 15th. We set off at day breake & early in the afternoon incamp in the beginning of Broken islands (to the S. of the river) as Mr. Crebassay does not wish to arrive at night among his indians; as on his arrival he will be obliged to give them Rum &c for their oats [wild rice]; & on such occasions they are always very troublesome –

Sund. 16th. At 6 O'Clock this morning we arrive at B[roken] River where we find ...e[84] with the indians eagerly waiting the arrival of Mr Crebassa in hopes of drinking, which is impossible to be avoided altho' they will take very great care not to be too generous even in trading their oats with their traders; for of all all [sic] nations this band of Sauteuxs is I beleive the most hoggish. Having remained about a quarter of an hour with Mr. C. we proceed on our voyage with a reef'd sail, but are obliged to encamp at noon at Detroit du Duc on account of the wind. Here we have had a terrible storm with a few Claps of thunder but one in particular which I am sure fell not 6 acres from us; is clear but windy the rest of the day.

Mond 17th. We remain 'till near sunset when we embark in hopes of the wind being intirely Calm until we might reach at least Tête-au-Chien, but we were not half the Traverse before the wind took as fresh as ever which obliged us to encamp just at Sunset.

Tues. 18th. Just at sunrise we set off, sometimes with a fair wind & reef'd sail & sometimes Calm or head wind, untill half past Eleven when I reached tête-au-Chien where I found Cu Levé, Old Brochet, his step son; & Mr. Ventre [The Belly]. Lately arrived from River Dauphine where all was well except our dogs who having the same disease as those at Fort Alexander die by half Dozens. I get from these indians equal to a Keg and a half of wild rice, part of which was given upon

---

83 Presumably Rivière Blanche in Winnipeg River. "Free" means that, as usual, Racette had no contract with the NWC.

84 The name is partly lost at the end of a line. It might be Trempe, one of Crebassa's men: see Nelson's journal, 6 & 7 April 1810.

or for their ammunition Debt & some was traded for rum – I here give some things upon debt to those who cannot come [to] River Dauphin. 'Tis now five night since M[r] Fort Dauphin M[c]Donald has passed here.

Wed. 19th. Having encamped in the Détroit of Tete au Brochet in very calm weather last night, we set off before Day light this morning but were obliged to return to our encampment before we had reached half the traverse on account of a terrible gale of wind which kept us bound to-day (Wednese 20) & to-day (Thurs 21st). At last this morning we set off at Sunrise, as the wind had moderated but very little but had changed from S.E. to S.W. where it now remains & proves to be a Lee wind, which enables us to reach the Point a La Fremboise where we find Old Nez-Corbin his two sons; Petites Couilles; Lorrin's Soninlaw [Le Gendre] & Les Yeux de Males.

Satur 22nd. I gave the indians a little rum last night among themself & to-day I give them a large Kettle full of mixed ditto as the have given me about 2½ Kegs of rise with some pounded meat and grease in presents – Wind & weather bound all day –

Sund 23[d]. The weather grows a little Calmer & we set off very heavyly loaded, as to be much in danger from the least wind; however I encamp at the Grand Point – Before I left the indians this morning I gave them each some ammunition & tobacco upon debt – In ten days hence they are to be at the house –

Mond 24th. We set off early this morning, but had not proceeded above two leagues before we were obliged to put a shore [on] a small Island where after remaining sometime the wind changed, & I set off leaving 10 Pieces of trade [goods] en cache en attendant the first fine weather to go for it[85] – I arrived at three quarters past one at the house where I found Ayagon & his youngest Brother with old Cu-fèssé & La Bessette, Old muffle D'orignialle & all his family. They seen M[r] McDonald as he passed here but as he did not offer violence to them nor said anything amiss, I intend continuing my trade with them as usual.[86] I give out about 2 ½ Kegs of mixed rum among all

85 Because the heavily laden canoe was in danger of swamping in the wind, Nelson lightened it significantly before proceeding.
86 Nelson was continuing to worry about the fact that his hunters were working on the boundary of John McDonald's Fort Dauphin district. Dauphin River was not one of the five posts that the Fort William meeting had specified for the Lake Winnipeg department, and McDonald probably was expecting Ayagon and his band to transfer to his posts. He may not have realized that Cameron was going to ignore the partners' instructions, and send Nelson to Dauphin River again. Nelson had managed to inform Ayagon that he would be back this season.

these indians & Ayagon makes the proper speeches as I before hand told him of it –

[One or more leaves missing here, covering entries for 25 September– 6 October inclusive. The next page begins in mid-entry.]

/[39]/ certainly would not let slip so fair an opportunity of deceiving these indians with liquor to get their peltries; however, they have yet a fair opportunity for Belanger instead of keeping with Old Muffle has changed, & gone with Muffle's Son the Martin in quite a different direction, to Monotoaguée River which is to S of us & Grand Rapid[87] to the N. about fifty leagues from each other –

Sund 7 October. While we were busily employed in crossing & rafting the timber of our old houses across the river to our present one,[88] Old Cu-fesse, Bezette, Ayagon's Brother & Mapions Youngest son make their appearance, going now up this River, as there are too many indians agoing to the end of this Lake, where they now tell me that there is but little beaver – Pritty fair weather but it blows very hard

Mond 8th. Inkster & I are busy in fixing our nets; & the men cover the house with boards – Having bought a Canoe from LaBezette I am obliged to give him rum for it, besides a Couple of pints more to him-self & th'others for nothing they all set off & encamp near here – We encamp also near our new house (which is about 10 acres distant from our old one) yesterday. It froze hard last night

Tues 9th. As there is some appearance of Calm I send Desrocher & Inkster for the Canoe but [they] come back without it as it begins to blow all at once – We set out our net & an old one wherein we take 20 odd white fish –

Wed. 10th. Very fine weather. Inkster & I split other boards for our doors as those we have already split are not proper. We begin our

---

87 It is clear from the context that this was the Grand Rapids at the outlet of the Saskatchewan River, not Little Grand Rapids in eastern Manitoba.
88 The Dauphin River post was being rebuilt on the north side of the river, as Nelson had decided the previous spring.

fall-fishery to-day; that is we begin to hang up our fish, which number for to-day is 134 –

Thurs 11th. The night before last it froze, last night it did not, but the weather is very dull, 'till near noon when it begins to snow – for the first time this Year, & Continues all day – We put up of last nights fishing 152 white fish.

Frid 12th. Extraordinary bad weather yesterday & more so to day, that we even cannot visit our net in the river 'till night, when we take it up with only 50.

Sat. 13th. Finer weather than yesterday though we have some showers of snow – Altho' the weather was very bad these two days past yet the men finish our Chimnies & plaistering the inside of our houses – Ausger begins the flooring of my house or room – Cu-fessé &c remain encamped near here yet.

Sund. 14th. Laroque begins to make a Chimney in the shop which place Inkster now takes for himself;[89] & the shop will be built separate.

Mon 15th. Clear & Cold weather insomuch that there is ice upon the river enough to prevent our visiting the nets. Except this there is nothing new.

Tues 16th. Inkster & I finish my floor but not the dubbing[90] of it at evening I take up some of my Potatoes when Ayagon arrives with Old Muffle D'orignialles two sons, who come for Larocque to pass the winter with them as he is married to their Sister. Ayagon &c brought me twelve beaver Skins & the meat of five – Late at night Old Cu-fessé arrives here for people to go for a moose that was killed today by the young men. A very hard S. wind –

Wed. 17th. Early this morning I send off Laraque & his wife with Ayagon, after which I set off with Inkster and Bpt Richard for the meat – but as the road was bad I soon returned leaving th'other two to continue thier voyage in Canoe – Near sun set Black Legs, an indian from Mr. Crebassas at Broken River, arrives here for some meat & fish for himself, Old Gagnian & Tete-de loup cervier soninlaw, who are coming to hunt here as there is so much appearance of my making to great returns alone [sic].

---

89 John Inkster, who was now Nelson's interpreter, was asserting his right to a separate accommodation.

90 Dubbing means smoothing (perhaps with an adze or draw knife) or applying some kind of finish to a wooden surface: Oxford English Dictionary.

/[40]/ October Thurs. 18ᵗʰ 1809. Fine weather so that the river is now intirely free of ice. At night Inkster & Richard arrive with the meat: for they returned for it this morning having been here last night to sleep, as they had neither fire-gun or anything else to make any [fire] with – While I was busy mending the Net, Morpion's eldest son & Tête-de loup cervier's son inlaw arrive for rum – which I give him (4 quarts of mixed), but nothing for Ayagon except a good set down – for he sent word for half a Keg of mixed – Before they returned, tho' but a short time here, Moose Eyes arrives with some meat which I receive in return for some rum – He is alone with little Couilles opposite L'Isle du Campement – Yesterday I take up the remainder of my potatoes 15 Kegs the produce of one.

Frid 19ᵗʰ. We set out two nets wherein we immediately [get] plenty of fish –

Sat 20ᵗʰ. To-day we hang up 253 White fish taken last night – The men continue working at the houses – Rain at night –

Sund 21ˢᵗ. Extreeme bad weather, rain & N. wind. The water rises upwards of five feet, but at night as the wind falls & the weather Clears up it comes to its usual mark – It leaked very much in all our houses, so that I was obliged to put up my tent in my room Except [that] nothing new only that last night we took 40 white fish which we could not hang up as the water is half up the stage –

Mond 22ⁿᵈ. Calm & pritty Clear – The men finish the shop & we bring the remainder of our things over & put them in – We hang up 44 fish taken last night.

Tues 23ᵈ. The men Plaister the houses. Old Cu-fessé comes at night with his old wife & a martin to show me if it was in season:⁹¹ & after much bother I give him 4 quarts of mixed liquor – In consequence of the great rain these few days past, that the water has come so high that we take but very few fish.

Wed. 24ᵗʰ. About 2 hours before day there was an Eclipse of the moon.⁹² This forenoon La Bezette arrives here with his wife; & brings

---

91 Winter skins were much more desirable than summer or "stage" skins, so Cul-Fessé was wanting to know whether Nelson would accept martens as season skins this early in the winter. If not, it would be worthwhile waiting to set traps, so as not to waste the animals before their skins had reached their full value.

92 This partial eclipse (about 90 per cent at its maximum), visible in most of North America and parts of the Pacific, occurred between about 7:30 a.m. and 10:30 a.m. UTC, or about 2:30 a.m. to 4.30 a.m. at Lake Winnipeg, 23 October 1809. Once again, Nelson was one day out in his calendar.

all Ayagon's brother's things here with him, as the other is off since last night with Bezette's youngest wife. The indian now remains with me & is very uneasy about his future safety we take but very few fish; & the Cold of last night has put much ice in the river Inkster & I begin an ice house in the meat shop, but as we soon find a very large stone that fills the hole intirely we cannot go down about 5 feet

Thursd 25th. Again [sic]. This morning Ayagon's brother arrives, & after a little convervesation [sic] with La Bezette (wherein he had much fear) he returns to the woods & Swamps for the woman, but comes back soon without her, but returns again in the evening with all his things[93] – no fish in a manner – We two intirely finish the shop except part of its flooring – The men began yesterday to Chop their wood – Very fine & mild weather – 'Tis fit for travelling on the Lake.

Frid. 26th. Fine weather – Bezette sets off in a very poor & uneasy situation – We take up our new net & leave an old one yet down, for we take but very few fish – The men are employed at my Chimney & Inkster & I Fin[ish] splitting boa[rds].

Saturd. 27th. Very Calm & mild weather but dark – Bezette & his wife arrive here again in Canoe; for he reached his father in law, Old Cu-fesse's lodge (Who is now encamped at the other end of the first rapids where Inkster & Richard went for meat) last night, & he comes down to-day to inform me of the certain departure of Ayagon's brother – for he has all his shot & ball missen which he supposes to be taken away by Aya's brother. However long after his departure, which was in a real bad humour, Inkster found it in the Shop – Its having been left thro' mistake – I give him some rum on his promising to behave with sense & mildness

/[41]/ Sund. 28th October 1809. &c. – A Short time before day it begins to snow & continues all day altho there is yet but very little upon the Ground; for it rains by spells – The river is free intirely of ice & the water is pritty high, which occasions a very Great scarcity of fish. Except this & a North wind – there is nothing new –

Mond 29th &c. Tuesd 30th. Nothing new but dull & snowy weather. The river freezes intirely across last night but is not yet strong enough to bear a person. There is some ice also in the Lake – Last night which is now the third night running & the eighth time in different spells,

---

93 It seems that Ayagon's brother was persuaded to bring La Bezette's wife back to her husband, as Bezette and his wife were together two days later. Nelson would have been concerned about this affair because, unless settled, it could disrupt the entire winter hunting of this band.

that M[rs] Desrocher falls into fitts – she is subject to them, but every time except the first which was rather more serious than the rest has or have been feigned fitts to subdue the stubborn ill humour of her Old husband, whom she says is always quarreling and disputing her on account of the ill care she has of his things & other qualities? [sic]

Wed. 31st. Bad weather & the ice begins to be pritty strong so that Bpt Richard crosses several times to-day upon it on all-fours. LaBezette & his son arrive here to-day for a man from me to live with him a few days so as to enable him to go upon discovery for Beaver, as there is even not the least vestige of any near here – Continually busy at our buildings &c – A fish store is finished to-day.

Thursd. 1st November. Allsaints – Snowy & windy &c in the morning – Bezette returns – Nothing new except that we keep this holidy

Frid. 2nd. This forenoon Ausger sets off for LaBezette's lodge – He would take no provisions for himself to serve upon their discovery. Altho' I wanted to give him some. For this some time past it has snowed every day but the quantity that has fallen is yet but very little –

Sat 3[d]. Yesterday I handled a pair of spears but I beleive that they will be of but very little service – for I was at the rapids to-day where the water is exceeding [high?] & but very [few] fish – I speared but four – We put out our New Net??? [sic] a hard N wind & snow

Sund 4th. In visiting or overhauling our net we take 30 Wh. Fish –

Mond 5th. 31 White fish besides pike & a few others – Nothing new this morning only snow & a N. wind which (both) we have not wanted since several days past, altho' the ice was pritty thick (about 3 ins) in the Lake & at the mouth of the river especially yet the hard wind of yesterday has broken all up – Last Wedneseday night M[rs] Desrocher fell into her usual fitts, but I being in their room & seeing the old man (her husband) setting quiet & singing I told him everything of her Conduct which she overhearing made her fitts leave her in a sound sleep 'till next morning – She has not had them since but has been continually & is yet sick her head & stomach being both sore which is a prelude to Windigo & Cannibalism.

Tuesd 6. Bad snowy weather fishing is 44 – Ausger arrives from La Bezette's lodge with a little meat & word from the indians to go for more if we want any – but rum must follow otherwise they will be annannow-ise;[94] that is their trip will be useless for they will get nothing.

___

94 An Ojibwe expression, which Nelson defines in the following phrase. Baraga (1992, 276) translates "a useless person" as *ningot aianawewesid*.

Wed. 7th. I send off Ausgé this morning alone; & no rum – Old
Desrocher who was to see visit & make some traps to-day returns
before noon telling me that Ausger found a place where there were
many [fish] – upon which news Inkster & I go to the rapids & Welles
or Dutchman comes at night with some torches. But as the weather
is extreemly bad (snow & a terrible wind) that we wer[e] obliged to
make a lodge of Pine bushes to shelter ourselves – &c –

/[42]/ Thursd 8th November 1809 – Last night about 10 O'Clock
we return home upon very feeble ice having speared but 71 w. fish (at
the same place of last year) owing to the too great quantity of floating
ice drifting down the river prevented seeing the fish rightly as at the
same time it so disturbed the water that it was quite muddy whereas
it is Generally greenish & Clear – We take 36 in the net & take it up
to be mended.

Ausger arrives early this morning, considering the distance that is
about 6 leagues – he arrives without any meat, altho' he wanted to take
some but tells me he was prevented from it by the indians – Bezette
who had two moose tongues kept them for me expecting that I would
have sent some liquor, but finding the Contrary he told his wife [to]
cook them; for now they speake indian tho' since they were in the
lodge they always spoke English[95] – hinting at my sending no rum –
For near fifteen days past we have always had snow & dull weather
except today which is pritty Clear & very Cold – & Windy

Frid 9th. The Cold or frost of last night has froze this bay entirely
across in spite of a Continual hard N wind. The men go for wood for
their slays – The river is take[n] above but the water is very high owing
I suppose to some stoppage of the course of the Water

Sat 10th. Fine weather yesterday & a hard S wind; but finer weather
today for much snow melts & even some ice – We put out the Net; I
get my Chimney taken down in part to-day (& twice refixed) for it
smokes terribly!!!

Sund. 11th. I get my floor joined & or tightened – The weather is dull
but not very Cold – Yesterday afternoon it rained & some grains of
Snow fall to-day – Having put out our net last night we take 67 W.f.
this morning more than I have ever yet known for under thin ice

Mond. 12th. Except our fishing which for to-day is 76 we have
nothing new –

95 This shows that some Indigenous people could speak some English when it suited them.

Tuesd 13th. At about 10 O'Clock last night a stranger arrived[96]-!!!-
Lo! it was young.!!!-.......?? [sic] As my Chimney has been altered for
the worse instead for the better I get it taken entirely down to the very
bottom & Inkster rebuilt it before dark but now it does not smoke any
more! what a Cumfort.

At Dusk Larocque arrives with his wife & Child from the Détour
about 30 leagues from here[97] – The Old Gagnian with the rest of Mr.
Crebassa's indians[98] are still there in spite of that starvation which
obliged Old muffle D'orignialle to return – they stopped in several
rivers on this side of the Détour both going & coming, & in every one
of which there was plenty of beaver but did not even deign to work
even one lodge under pretext of their starving too much! They are to
encamp about 6 leagues or 8 leagues from here where they are [to] Kill
near 150 Skins the amount of their debts!! Dull weather but mild –
fishing is 67

Wed 14th. This last sunday it rained but since near day light (this
morning) it has began to snow, & continues with such a wind & force
that it prevented my sending Welles with some provision a head of
these half starved Devils – fishing is 60

Thursd. 15th. Welles set off early this morning & having gone as far
as the small river where he went to gather gum last spring (about 6
leagues from this) without coming up with them he put his fish, meat
&c up on a stage & returned here late at night

Frid 16th. yesterday fine sun shine weather but Cold, & today it is
dull /[43]/ and Cold – however I go to my traps for the first time this
year & put up 16 of them – On my return home I speared 140 fish
but weather growing too cold I was obliged to leave the place soon &
found Old Muffle D'orignialle arrived at the house having left his family behind – A few days past Larocque & this old fellow seen a man's
track bear foot,[99] & a womans with shoes on – upon the bare snow

96 This was the birth of Nelson's eldest child, Mary, with Mary Ann, whom he had taken
as his wife at Fort Alexander in September 1808. This child and her younger sister Jane were
baptized at William Henry (Sorel), Lower Canada, on 10 October 1816, shortly after Nelson
and his wife arrived there. The church register recorded her birth, correctly, as 12 November
1809, "at River Dauphine on Lake Winnipick" (Register of Christ Church [Anglican],
William Henry; images from Drouin Collection at ancestry.com).
97 Now Long Point, on the west side of Lake Winnipeg, some 80 miles north of the mouth
of Dauphin River, at least 30 leagues (90 miles) of travel along the shoreline.
98 That is, those who were expected to trade at John Crebassa's post of Broken River, far to
the south in the south basin of the lake.
99 Perhaps meaning a "bear paw"-shaped snowshoe, which would leave a distinctive oval track.

from whence I conclude that Mr. Louison is gone with his "wife" to see his brother in river au Guériér[100] –

Sat. 17th. There has fallen more snow between yesterday afternoon & this morning than we have had with all the former together – Yet old Mûffle returns to his family to show them the provisions Welles took to them last Mond[ay] – As the fear of **Starvation** in this Country is in some few respects a great help to our little authority the men go to spear fish at the rapids – but the place where I speared yesterday being very shallow & now consequently frozen up they make two holes in the ice where we spear'd so many last year & altho' there were many yet the depth of the water & force of the Current prevented their spearing above 6. Our fishing on Thurs. was 140; Frid, 30; all these are white fish as we [do not] Count the others

Sund. 18th. The weather Clears up & is amazing sharp & windy as the weather was too Cold to go through my trap road I stop at an air hole where we spear'd our fish two years ago, where I spear 111 by which time Inkster comes & Larocque soon after & spear including mine 763; Nez [nets] 32.

Mond 19th. Net fishing 47 – & spearing is 675 – About noon Old Muffle arrives with all his family; & very hungry – All their hunt together since they left me is 7 Large beaver 5 Small – 2 otters 10 Rats & 1 mink!!!! Clear, Cold & windy.

Tues 20th. Colder than yesterday – spearing is 625 – except this nothing new

Wed 21st. Very windy but Clear & Cold – spearing is 200

Thurs 22nd. While Ausger is employed in making snowshoe frames – Desrocher & Welles haul fish – so quick have they diminished – Calm

Frid 23d. Welles with three slays brings home 429 fish. As the fish have Grown so amazing scarce at this place Laroc. goes about have [half] a mile further up the river where he spears upwards of 1800 in a very short time, altho' he spears but [only] those that appear the largest & best!!!

Sat, 24th. Fish hauling all day – Laroc. & Desrocher are employed in spearing a few fish more & putting (the whole of) these famous ones in surety – It snows

---

100 Louison is not mentioned elsewhere in the journal by this name, so it must be an alternative name for one of the Indigenous hunters. Why Nelson put "wife" in quotation marks here is unknown.

Sund 25th. The number of fish brought home yesterday were 573, &
today, 625

Mond. 26th. Quiet all day except Ausger he goes for slay boards &
Laroc. to his traps.

Tues. 27th ??? Nothing new except very fine weather & the men haul
fish – Aûsgé has been very sick all night & is yet to day. He spits also
much blood. he strained himself yesterday

Wed 28th. Last night I gave him a vomit & this morning he threw
up a large worm Yesterday fish hauling was 476 & to-day 506. Fine
weather but nothing newer,

Thurs 29th. Old muffle D'orignialle sets off with all his family except
his second son the Sour[d] who waits the arrival of (his brother) the
Martin. I have some hopes that he /[44]/ will have some thing before he
comes in again as he has a good stock of dry fish &c, About 9 O'Clock
this morning LeBlanc & Brasconier arrive from broken river with a
letter from Mr. Crebassa & one from Mr. Cameron where we have for
News the sorrowful death of Mr. Angus McDonell at Eagle Lake in Lac
La Pluie Depart[ment], but a Clerk from Mr. Haldane at Montlagué.[101]
He was sent as a reinforcement to Eagle Lake but was most treach-
erously shot by a HB's man a Cowardly oatmeal eater;[102] but the

101 John Haldane was the NWC partner in charge of Monontague department, the trading
district lying north of Lac la Pluie and south of Lac Seul.

102 Nelson's reaction to this news was appropriate for a loyal Nor'wester, but the convincing account of the whole affair by the HBC servant James Tate (printed in Williams 1975,
106–50), shows McDonell's death in a very different light. An HBC party commanded by
William Corrigal was operating a post at Eagle Lake, north of Rainy Lake, in the fall of 1809.
Æneas or Angus McDonell, a young NWC clerk who had been sent to oppose the HBC here,
interfered violently with an Indigenous man who was trying to trade with the HBC. After a
scuffle in which McDonell wounded two of the HBC men with a sword, one of them, John
Mowat, shot McDonell dead. The NWC managed to get custody of Mowat and two other
HBC men, Tate and Corrigal, and took them down to Montreal to be tried for murder. Both
Tate and Corrigal wrote accounts of the whole episode, including the harsh treatment they
had received en route to Canada. In Montreal, they were able to make contact with business
associates of the HBC who assisted them with money and legal advice, but after long delays,
Mowat was convicted of manslaughter, and sentenced to be branded on the thumb and
imprisoned for six months. Corrigal and Tate brought countercharges against another NWC
clerk who had treated them cruelly, but the Montreal jury found no bill against him. The
clerk who was killed, Æneas McDonell, had influential relatives in Canada, and Corrigal and
Tate, and Lord Selkirk when he made inquiries at Montreal shortly after, were all convinced
that the courts had behaved with great bias because of the NWC's influence in Montreal. Long
after these events, during his time at Moose Lake, George Nelson had under his command a
voyageur named Paul Laverdure, who gave him an account of the encounter at Eagle Lake

proverb is almost right "il ny'a rien de semblamble a une vielle dans sa Lochete."!!![103] Ausgé is very sick yet, & having spent all my pep-permi[n]t & turlington[104] he grows still worse which obliges me much against my will to bleed him which I perform with the point of Pen knife!! It has snowed pritty heartily to day fish hauling to day is 314

Frid 30[th] Nov[r]. Fine weather – Ausgé grows much better – Old Desrocher puts up all the fish we have taken in the Net in the Store to the number of 700 (exclusive of what we have been eating all the while upon them) –

Satur. 1st December 1809. Desrocher & LeBlanc bring 90 fish from above, Mat [illegible word]. About 12 O'Clock to-day Cu-levé arrives from his lodge for people to go for his peltries & other things. He gives me news from all the Mashkeegons whom he left about 15 days ago, from the Martin & Boulanger also who, as they have made the best hunt he tells me, have about 4 or 5 skins each. The others, some are gone to beyond Fisher river to look out for buffaloe to make robes, & the rest amuse themselves with playing. What fine returns may I now expect from such fine hunters![105]

Sund. 2nd. I send off Inkster, Larocque & Welles each with a slay to his Lodge; & at night Moose Eyes arrives from the bay of Tête-au-Pishew with very few Peltries considering the time they have been out – Clear, Calm & Cold weather.

Mond 3[d]. More mild than yesterday a little. A bottle of HWines which I give to Moose Eyes to carry to his lodge finding it too little he drinks it at Baptist Richards house[106] across the river – Besides this nothing else

Tuesd. 4th. Moose Eyes [departs] & Baptiste Richard follows him but to make traps in the vicinity of the former's lodge– Broken River

---

that was probably much nearer the truth than what the NWC had put about in 1809. By the time he wrote his *Reminiscences*, Nelson had come to the opinion that the man who fired the fatal shot had acted in self-defence and should never have been punished (*Reminiscences*, Part 7, 279–81).

103 "Nothing is like an old woman in her …." The meaning of *lochette* is unknown.

104 Oil of peppermint and Turlington's Balsam were standard components of the fur traders' medicine kit.

105 This was the first news Nelson had received of his new band of hunters, the Mashkiegons. The Martin is mentioned separately because he was an Ojibwe, one of the more familiar Mouffle d'Orignal/Ayagon band.

106 Baptiste Richard, one of the elder François Richard's sons, was now old enough to have his own house, and probably his own family.

People return at last, after I kept them here longer than was necessary to give Mr. Cameron a full account of the news, prospects, & transactions of that place[107] – At night Old Mother Cu-féssé arrives with a little meat, & tells me that her old husband has got martins enow to pay the best part of his debt, but LaBezette has but very few & Morpion's son still less having nothing at all tho' are both much younger men than the former. However they yet have some hopes as they have 3 beaver lodges to work!!!

Wed 5th. The old woman returns to her home & Inkster &c arrive & except about 40 Skins the rest is trash. Old Muffle D'orignialle's son, who remained with me here some days, went with Cu leve to his lodge to hunt there the remainder of the year for his debt It snows hard today a N wind also.

Thurs 6th. Nothing new to day. Frid 7t. Early this morning Ausgé & Welles set off for Falle de Pardrie with a letter from myself to the person in Charge of that Post – by which I hope I may clear myself from these continual vile aspersions.[108]

Saturd. 8th. Old Cuféssé arrives near sun Set for People to go to their lodges for meat – I now take the opportunity of returning Bezette what he deserves – But all proves to be false – Ausgé has not yet forget lying!

/[45]/ (Frid [sic] 8 - a Miracle!) a few moments after old Cu-fessé arrives, Messrs Ausgé & Welles make their appearance – having lost themselves wishing to make the wise men in cutting this neck of land to the Lake (St Martin).[109] They have or had a very good excuse which they did not fail to make use of – for the weather was snowy & stormy yesterday.

Sund. 9th. Ausger &c. continue rather resume their route but by the river being the surest – Cu-fessé sets off & I send Inkster & old Desrocher with him with 3 pts HWines; & in answer to Bezette & Morpion's son who ask for ammunition, that when [they] will have paid me each their breech Clouts I shall give their wants – Baptiste Richard arrives from P. Couilles lodge. The only news is that they

107 LeBlanc and Brasconier, Crebassa's men from Broken River, had arrived with letters on 29 November.

108 That is, the criticisms of Nelson for trading with hunters who "belonged" to the Fort Dauphin department.

109 Following Dauphin River up to Lake St Martin, the traveller heads first northwest, then suddenly south, for a total distance of perhaps 35 miles, the route forming two sides of a triangle. Cutting straight across, west-southwest through the swampy bush, would save about 20 miles of this, but there was probably no trail to follow, and it was easy to get lost.

killed 2 Carriboeuf's yesterday; & now have two beaver lodges
to work

Mond. 10th. About 9 O'Clock last night Jack [John Inkster] &
Desrocher arrive with each a very heavy load of meat – A. & Welles
who necessarily pass at their lodge are said to travell very fast so I
expect tomorrow they will be near their journeys end.

Wed. 11th. Tuesday 12th. Wednes 13th. Thurs 14. Pritty mild weather
since some days past altho' we have had some days of snow. About 10
this morning The Bird a son of Old Muffle D'orignialle's arrives for a
man to go to their lodge for the meat of three large beaver – They have
killed but 5 since they left me!!!

Saturd 15th. Pritty cold & clear. Early I send off Larocque to his
father-in-laws' lodge for the beaver of yesterday110 – About noon or a
little after, Ausger & Welles arrive from Falle de Pardrie with a letter
from Mr. Halcroe with plenty of news but none of the best kind –
however they are all well, have more indians than are disposed to good
actions, and live well – At sunset Larocque arrives with the meat of
4 large beavers & 2 large & 3 small dry beaver skins, 9 martins, & 1
Carcajoux – Very mild & a high South wind.

Sund 16. Very mild insomuch that some snow melts – Nothing new
unless that I finish my Slay Cariole111 & prepare to set off tomorrow
morning early for fort Alexr.

Mond. 17th. As one of my dogs is missen [missing] since yesterday morning Ausge set off last night upon the road to old Muffle
D'orignialle's lodge, but he returned long after midnight having only
seen their tracks – Early this morning I go to the lodge myselfe where I
find only the Children the rest were out for meat upon some animal the
old fellow Killed yesterday – My dogs came here yesterday but went
off immediately to another quarter – About noon I arrive at home &
find him [Nelson's missing dog] arrived – but a few minutes only after I
had set off – Very beautiful weather

Tuesd 18th. A very hard south wind prevents my setting off before
day light. Baptiste Richard comes to show me the road by which Les
Yeux Demales came as it leads into that deep bay on the S other side

---

110 Jean-Baptiste Larocque's wife was a daughter of Mouffle d'Orignal.
111 A *cariole*, a travelling sleigh of the kind used in Canada, where a passenger could ride,
unlike the smaller sleighs used to carry goods and provisions, where the man ran along
behind. Both were pulled by dogs.

of Tete au Pichou.[112] Being loaded with fish provisions & encumbered with two slays we encamp before we reach the Lake.

Wed. 19th. We encamp between Pointe de roche & the Tête au Brochet.

Thurs 20th. Fine weather we strike off straight into the middle of the Lake to Tete au Chien being the shortest way & encamp about 3½ leagues from Tête au Chien. At our encampment of last night we hang up 9 fish & Ausge's snow shoes for our return home.

/[46]/ Frid. 21st. Having left one of our small Kettles & my snow shoes we reach Broken River in time to partake of a Good breakfast with my freind the reveren'd Doctor John Crebassa – (all is well here in appearance). Old Rassette was here too – Trempe & LeBlanc two of Mr. C's. men are arrived two days since from upper part of Fisher River where they seen the Martin whose whole hunt was 7 large beaver & 3 martins??? – which is now at Mr. C's[113]

Sat. 22[nd]. Rassette poor miserable old being set off about 10 O'Clock last night for his <u>own</u> home with a very heavy slay load of provisions for his numer[ou]s starving family. I pass the Day here & his holiness prepares.[114]

Sund 23[d]. Before day light we set off in Company with Mr. Crebassa who takes Braconier & LeBlanc. He has four dogs upon his slay & myself 3.

Mond 24. We set off from our encamp[ment] a little to the S of black River & arrive [at Fort Alexander] at haff past ten a few minutes before Mr. Cameron was ready for breakefast. We were received in the Kindest manner imagineable by our surely very <u>Generous</u> hearted Bourgeoi while we in our turns could only return our <u>wishes</u> & our hopes!!! We arrived here one day sooner than we otherwise would had it not been for false accounts – For here it is but the 23 & with us 'tis the 24th.[115]

---

112 Nelson was off on a Christmas visit to Duncan Cameron at Bas de la Rivière. The invitation must have been brought by Leblanc and Brasconier, the Broken River men who had arrived with letters on 29 November. The first part of Nelson's route was down the west shore of Sturgeon Bay, overland to Lynx Bay (the "deep bay on the other side of Tete au Pichou"), overland again to the west shore near Stony Point ("Pointe de roche"), south along the shore to Tête-au-Brochet, then across the mouth of Fisher Bay, which good weather allowed him to take in a single long traverse on 20 December.

113 Nelson had been expecting to get The Martin's hunt for his own post.

114 Nelson does not explain why he refers to John Crebassa in this way. Perhaps Crebassa was a more religious man than Nelson, or indeed than most of the fur traders in the Upper Country. The NWC partner John Macdonell, who was also religious, was known in the Northwest as "Le Prêtre."

115 Arriving at Fort Alexander, Nelson found himself one day ahead of the calendar as kept

Tuesd. (M. 25). Just about dusk last night as were going to set to dinner Mr. Seraphin arrives from river au mort, & at breakefast time this morning one Mr. Kennedy arrives (from Drunken river near river Blanche) a Gentleman who came in with Mr. Cameron last fall but was left behind in River ouinipique to be neighbour to the English if there were any there – but as there were none he came down late in the fall & is now a neighbour [to] the Honb^le Boar or Véra.[116] It seems now that the HB's &c begin to find out their errors but are not yet come to themselves going from one extremity to the other – Last fall their inland traders gave debts out to different indians at the usual rate but since then orders they have received by an express from the Governor at Albany being sent by two men in the very last season. They now take 5 martins insted of two for a skin; no Cased* or open'd Cats or Wolverines whereas formerly they took them at 2 Skins a piece; 2 red foxes now lately at a skin each in short the Change is extraordinary & portends a sad recompense for the troublesome & dangerous trade of this Country.[117] –The indians are so much displeased with the English that they promise to pay at the usual rate, that is, 2 martins for a skin 1 fox also, 1 cat 1 wolver[ine] at 2 skins each & what is remaining of their hunt to trade with the N West –

/[47]/ Frid 28. Sat. 29th. Sund 30. At last!! about noon Mr. Crebassa & I are obliged to take (our) leaf of our very kind Bourgeoi; & altho we have been here a long time it seems to us as if we had not yet passed one day, so agreable has all been to us. What rascality & villainy would it be in us were we to act but quarter as bad as some of our former freinds

---

there. This discrepancy agrees with his dating of the lunar eclipse on 24 October, which actually occurred on the 23rd.

116 "Honble Boar or Véra" must be one of the HBC's traders from Fort Albany, but he has not been identified, and Nelson's description or name for him is unexplained. For Alexander Kennedy, see Appendix D.

117 Nelson is describing a change in the HBC's "standard of trade," in which skins other than beaver had a fixed value relative to beaver skins. The official prices of goods were expressed in terms of beaver skins, and so were the other furs, so the accounting was done in a virtual unit of currency that the HBC called "Made Beaver." The Canadians used the word *plus* for the same thing, while Nelson simply used "skin." These radical changes by the HBC in the relative values of skins, which downgraded the value of martens by 60 per cent, and its refusal to trade cats or wolverines at all, would have been in response to instructions from the London Committee, which was trying to adjust for demand in Europe. As Nelson comments, the changes would have been poorly received by the Indigenous hunters.

(Poor Cal.),[118] or were we not to strive to our very utmost to deserve those kindnesses – Messrs. Seraphin & Kennedey set off for their respective homes two days after Christmass. My Poor & afflicted Freind Mr. Alexr. McDonell did not come,[119] & even, what pleasure could we have enjoyed!!! – – We encamp late at night at the Pointe au bateau.

Mond. 31st. Having set off about midnight we arrive [at Broken River] just time enough to partake of ragout's that were prepared by Trempe as he thought this to be New Years.[120]

Tuesd 1st January 1810. New Years & I pass all the day with my reveren'd Friend [Crebassa] in a much more plentiful manner than I thought this <u>poor </u>post of Riviere Cassé could afford. Every thing was made agreable to a degree.

Wed. 2nd. At Sun rise Ausgé & I set off pritty well loaded with goods &c which obliges me to walk all the way home. Altho the weather was fine this morning yet as soon as we got out of the islands a terrible N wind arose & obliged me to encamp at the same place I camped last fall, about 1½ leagues North from Detroit du Duc with frozen fases [faces].

Thurs. 3^d. Altho' we had plenty of wood we passed a very miserable night almost freezing to death with Cold & wind; & rose in the morning with near 6 inches of snow upon us that fell during the night – Very sharp & the hard N wind in our fases yet set off about sunrise – about noon 'tis finer & we put in at isles aux ecorses.

Frid. 4th. We set off late this morning with fine weather but sharp – & sometimes a South wind which was fair for us very early in the afternoon we arrived at our campment of the 19th – but we found all our fish eaten by the martins, even to the ends of Aus-gé's snow shoes that were hung up by the fish. As we have yet near two days yet to travel before we reach home I propose to leave the Goods well secured & try to reach the house in one day – I am obliged to give the dogs oats [wild rice] to eat –

---

118 Alexander Campbell, whose failure at the Grand Rapid last year would have been fresh in Nelson's mind.

119 This remark might suggest that Macdonell was still in Lake Winnipeg department, but he is not mentioned in the arrangements for 1809–10 (see Journal, 14 September 1809), and had been reassigned to Red River: see Appendix D. Perhaps Nelson and Cameron were hoping that, despite the move, Macdonell would manage to make it to Fort Alexander for Christmas. Perhaps he had intended to come, but had been prevented by illness, if that is what "afflicted" means.

120 Whereas Christmas was the time for the clerks and partners to get together for celebration, New Year's Day was the voyageurs' holiday. This year, Nelson managed to attend both celebrations at other men's posts.

Sat 5ᵗʰ. A most terrible storm arose about midnight from the ENE so hard & so cold that we were buried in the snow & had much difficulty to light our fire & still more trouble (from the Cold) to ty our slays & fix ourselves for the fire blew right upon us as we were almost upon the beach. Neverthless we set off with now a side wind & encamped at Tet[e] aû Pichou after having lost ourselves up on that wide traverse for the weather was so bad that we sometimes could not see three acres before us!!!

/[48]/ January 1810 Sund 6. Having had a very comfortable bed we did not rise 'till late – however I arrived at "my" home where thank God I found every one in health & all the rest was well. All the Mashkiegons have been in; & between them they gave but 97 skins in peltries, about one pack.¹²¹

Mond. 7ᵗʰ. This morning I send off Welles & Belanger to our camp at Tête-aû-Pichou for the Goods that I left there. Stormy & Cold.

Tuesd. 8ᵗʰ. Very bad weather 'till near night when it Clears up.

Wed 9ᵗʰ. Thursd 10ᵗʰ. About 8 O'Clock last night the men arrive safe with their load – As I was not here for New Years & the people about the [post] wishing to renew it we made a kind of a feast with a dance which was ended in a farce upon the German (Welles) who had a terrible desire for marrying, & having given him permission he bargained with old Desrocher for his wife who reserved only his dog but gave all the rest of her things. As this was a made up plot the bride remained in my room (pretending to be ashamed) 'till the others might have time to fall asleep – The bridegroom laid in his bed dreaming, snoring, coughing & rubbing himself &c when his future happiness entered & pretending first to drink threw a whole large Kettle full of Water & ice upon him & telling him, "here, take, this is to put you to your senses before you think of marrying again. You poor mean wretch you have but half a 3 pt Blanket & not a single sou to get even a clout for your woman, were she to wear one, no you shall never have me. This set the others into a fitt of laughter which aggravated Welles, but as he could gain nothing he joined the others in the "Couillionade"¹²² against himself –

Frid 11ᵗʰ. As we have now two sound axes the men begin to chop each six cords of wood en attandant les beau temps.¹²³

---

121 A pack of beaver would contain between sixty and seventy skins, so the Mashkiegons' hunt must have had many small furs, such as martens.
122 From *couillion*, a fool (a vulgar expression), so the process of making a fool of someone.
123 While waiting for good weather.

Sat. 12. The men chop; & the Weather is neither cold or warm –

Sunday 13th. Near Sunset Old Muffle D'orignialle arrives here with one of his women; & brings with him about 8½ skins – Since I left this for to go to Mr. Camerons our people had been once at his lodge & since then he killed 2 Carriboeufs – & 2 moose – I intend tomorrow to send Belanger for some of their meat &c. About 10 days ago one of his sons seen an encampment of old Cu fesé &c where there was a very long pole stuck up with a bark dish & four marks upon it (pointing towards Lake St Martins) from whence he supposes that there is some one of them sick – or by the pole that they go toward Leur Seucrerie.[124] – Good Winter weather & wind comes from every quarter.

Mond 14th. Nothing new only that I send off Boulanger with a bottle of rum for old Muffle &c &c &c!!!

/[49]/ Tues 15th January 1810. Larocque & Welles finish chopping 18 Cords of wood – Last night at sunset we had a heavy shower of snow but it did not last more than about 10 minutes – & to night 'tis the same – At sunset Boulanger arrives with 5 pieces of dry meat & about 20 ftm. of Cords[125] (a Shifting wind).

Wed. 16th. Nothing new only that all is quiet, & a S wind pritty hard.

Thurs 17th Frid 18th. I write a letter to-day for Mr. J. McDonald Proprietor of Fort Dauphin & one to Mr. Halcro (Clerk) at Falle de Pardrie whither I intend sending Ausgé, & Bpt. Richard who has a mind to go & see his Sister Halcro's wife.

Sat. 19th. Long before daylight they both set off. This is the only news, only very fine weather.

Sund. 20th. Appearance of very bad & Cold weather which however does not last long, for at night it becomes more mild & fine, this is all!!!

Mond 21st Tues 22nd. About 9 O'Clock A.M. Cu Levé, Pettites-Couilles, Brochet, Kieshkieman, Moose Eyes, Le Sourd, & his brother in law arrive with a little meat & but very few peltries – I seperate 46 Balls among them & give 1 Gallon of HWines with some water & a few other things. Belly & Son in law do not dare come,[126] Old Nez Corbin & his two sons were afraid to freeze, otherwise we would have seen all the Mashkiegon except Brochet's step Son – Fine expectations! What profits!

124 Cul-fessé's family's sugar-making place, an island in Lake St Martin.
125 Perhaps *babiche* (hide cords) used for stringing snowshoes.
126 Presumably because their hunts were poor.

Wed, 23ᵈ. About midnight they all set off. A little past noon Aus-gé & Richard arrive & bring me a letter from Mr. Halcro which contains but poor news – the only talk among the indians is – if you come once (more) to my lodge I'll pillage, if twice, I'll kill¹²⁷ – &c &c &c. No other news of any Consequence only that old Cu fessé is up in the upper part of warrior river a Starving-!!! [illegible] p returns.

Thurs 24ᵗʰ Frid 25ᵗʰ. Very fine weather with a shifting wind S.N.E.W.

Sat 26ᵗʰ. Cold weather & a N wind. Old Desrocher sets out 3 lines for Pike &c. – Sund 27ᵗʰ. The men set out our only net through curiosity for Gluttony – Old Desrocher takes in his lines, only a half starved Pike & a Loche – The men say that the ice at the mouth of the river is about one & a half foot thick, which is exactly half less than last year.

Tues. 29ᵗʰ. Early this morning I send off Inkster & Larocque to hunt after Cû-lèvé, Old Nez Corbin &c, & Le Gèndre &c, whom I expect to be in two perhaps three different bands, & not to be back untill they all be found not as I intend to put a man in Cû-levé's lodge – as they intend going towards the Manitôbane where I am afraid they'll be visited by the English¹²⁸ – which will be no augmentation to my packs – I give Inkster 2 quarts of HWines – & they take fish enough for their voyage – It blows very hard the NW. Lines one looke [loach].

/[50]/ Wednes 30ᵗʰ 1810. Nothing new. Net fishing none & lines, only one loche & a Pike.

Thurs 31ˢᵗ. Ausgé & I go to look for wood to make slays – no news, all is quiet.

Frid 1ˢᵗ February! Ausge & I again bring home wood for three slays. Near sunset Inkster & Larocque arrive here with – the Son-in-law, Belley, Old Brochet, Pitites-Couilles, Kieshkieman, Kieway koabow &c. They all bring a little meat with five martins & a beaver skin – News. The first day Inkster left this he arrived at the fish lodges where he found Cu-levé & the above mentioned indians – while Cû-levé was here his wife was brought to bed of a Girl but it died very soon after – Its head was nock[ed] in & the other Ceremonies were not

127 Halcro was trying to improve his trade by sending men to visit the hunters' lodges without invitation, asking for their furs. This practice, called going *en derouine*,* was not uncommon, but evidently was seen as an intrusion in this case. Nelson seems to have sent men to the lodges only when invited.

128 The nearest HBC opposition to Nelson was on the Assiniboine River, centred at Brandon House, whence men could be sent out in all directions to trade at the lodges. In Lake Manitoba (Manitobane), Nelson's hunters could come in contact with these HBC servants.

performed in a proper manner; & purposely as is thought.[129] Old Nez
Corbin was with one of his sons & the two Sauteaux* towards birch
lake where Inkster went, & on his return to the former lodges he met
young Brochet that I have not seen since fall – He had given his skins
to Trempe & others of Mr. Crebassa's men whom he seen about 10
days ago – The martin is the only one I have not yet seen, & he is upon
the upper part of White River[130] starving – Mr. Kennedey I suppose will
take care of him as he is near the English – I take up the Net for good,
for we take too few fish, today only 4.

Sat. 2nd. All the indians set off except Kieshkieman whom I keep
'till tomorrow to guide Ausgé (as far as their lodges) whom I send to
live with old Nez Corbin – I sent Belanger along with them to get the
martin's Kettle.[131]

Sund 3d. Ausgé & the young indian set off at the dawn of day –
Belanger arrives from the lodges & tells me that the indians drank the
best part of their rom [rum] near here – The weather is very fine, & the
snow melts.

Mond. 4th. Near night Moose Eyes arrives with his daughter & the
Kieshkieman to remain here near the house hunting large animals &
to make traps – he gives me a little meat for which I give him 3 pints
mixed rum.

Tues 5th Wed. 6th. Nothing new 'till night when Bezette arrives from
the Lake St Martin where he is encamped with old Cu-fesse – They
have but very few skins at their lodge – However as they are going
towards the Manitobane I am obliged to send Inkster and Welles for
what few things they have with a little rum. Moose Eyes was a hunting
to-day – he found many fresh tracks of moose but were all driven off
by the woolves last night –

Thurs. 7th. Early this morning I send off Welles & Inkster. Moose-
Eyes returns this evening from hunting with the heart & inside fat of
a Moose he killed very near here – Seen its track this morning as I was
looking for wood for a slay, but returned in expectations of the indian's
coming after & he killed it quite near where I chopped this morning –
fine mild weather but it blows a little.

---

129 Nelson apparently suspected that the infant had been deliberately killed. There may have
been some question as to the child's father.
130 Nelson said that Kennedy was stationed in the Rivière Blanche of Winnipeg River (entry
of 25 December 1809), so The Martin's hunt had ranged a long way from Dauphin River.
131 Perhaps it was in need of repair.

Frid 8. We go and bring all the meat – Inkster &c arrives at night bringing from Bezette only 7 skins & from old Cu fessé 12. Old Cu-fessé's /[51]/ wife comes for a little more liquor to make the devil & half his Generation for her old husband's sore legs – Inkster brings some meat which was killed by Cou-fort, one of Mr. McDonald's Falle de Pardrie indians – Bezette hid this from me – for he told me that it Old Cu-fessé that killed it; he even hid from me Cou-fort's being with them[132] – He, Bezette, wishes to have a man to winter the remainder of the year with him – & to agree with him I prepare Welles for that trip –

Sat 9th. Before midnight Mother Cu-fessé sets off – & near sunset this afternoon Old Muffle D'orignialle arrives for people to go to his lodge for meat that is very near here – He killed [a] moose yesterday & one the day before. I give him some liquor to drink with the other indians. This Poor old being has the same complaints as all the rest of the indians of this Post, which is, he knows not how to do to pay his debt – there is no beaver – & he trusted to martins, but he has not yet found one single place fit even to make a few traps.

Sund 10th. Before day light Welles sets off alone for the Bezette lodge – After sunrise I send off Desrocher – Larocque & Peter [Pierre Belanger] for meat. Very mild weather but snowy & drifty.

Mond. 11. Weather the same as yesterday but nothing else –

Wed 13. Belanger goes to old Muffle's lodge for my dogs that have deserted.

Thurs 14th. Yesterday old Muffle's wife came here to ask me if I had any objections to her husband's going up the river here a hunting, for in the different places they have run over since they left this last Novr they have given me but 15 martins in upwards of 200 traps; & where they are at present there are still less –

This afternoon old Nez Corbin arrives in snowey & drifty weather with a little meat & about 17 skins of their debts Mr. Ausgé was too lonesome which was the reason of the old man's Coming – Nothing new in that quarter.

Frid 15. The old man returns, & I am obliged to write a 2nd letter to Mr. Cameron – Sat 16th. A very hard south wind which makes some snow melt – Old Desrocher & Belanger, whom I send with him set off For Fort Alexander – I expect them back in 15 days – Near Sun set this evening, Cù-levé, Le Gendre, Belly, Pittites-Couilles, & Old

---

132 La Bezette was afraid that Nelson would refuse to accept the meat if he knew it had been killed by Cou-Fort, whom Nelson now recognized as one of the Fort Dauphin hunters.

Brochet's step son arrive all with a little meat but Still less Peltries – I make Candles.

Sund. 17th. Our arrivals of yesterday got in a pet last night on account of my refusing them som rum – Their making use of some language that I was not very fond of obliged me to have recourse to a method that soon stopped them; & had it not been for Cû-lèvé, I should not have given them a single dram, whereas I was obliged to give a half Keg of liquor among them for to encourage Cû-lèvé; for altho' he appears not be very dishearten'd, yet a refusal at this momment is sufficient to prevent him paying his debt, that amounts to no less than 24 skins – it has obliged me to boar [bore] open a new keg of HW. which leaves me but one more.

/[52]/ (Saturday 17 Feby) The mashkiegons had left this but a few moments when old Muffle D'orignialle encamped here with his whole brigade – Having previously prepared Ausgé he set off for Old Nez-Corbins lodge – Yesterday & today we have had a very hard South wind & mild but to-day the snow melts very much even in the riv[er] & on the Lake –

Mond. 18th. The wind is north & the weather is Cold.

Tuesd 19th Wed 20th Thurs 21st. Yesterday the wind was S.E. & very hard – snowed some also – To-day the weather is Clear but windy & Cold – About noon Ausgé arrives from Nez Corbins &c's, lodge – he brings me 15 martins & a fox which is all that they have killed since.

Frid. 22nd Sat 23d. Nothing new only that Mr. Moose Eyes is at the Richard's[133] house – & this evening I give him a sort of a lesson of what will happen to him if he does not take care of himself.

Sund 24th. Old Muffle D'orignialle at last raises camp up the River – We have nothing new, which is a poor sign for packs! –

Mond 25. Cold Drifty weather, & that's all – Tuesd 26th. I begin with Inkster to repair my table & make a couple of chairs.

Wed 27th. Amasing bad & drifty weather much similiar to that I [experienced] beyond the Tête-au-Pichou (the 5th of this last Jany.) & the wind from the same quarter.

Thurs 28th. Worse weather than yesterday. Old Muffle D'orinialle's son comes here for people to go for meat – his father killed a moose to-day.

March Frid. 1st March 1810 – This morning I send off Larocque & Ausgé for meat – About 3 P.M. Old Desrocher arrives from my same

133 The house where Baptiste Richard and his family were living, across the river from Dauphin River post.

campment at Tête-aû-Pichou: he brings me Mr. Cameron's Letters with one from each of the Clerks of this Department. Mr Cameron sends me 40 [#s] twist tobacco 10[#s] balls & 1 Keg of HWines! (besides other articles). European news the latest tells us that Russia is again at war with the Devil[134] where he commanded in person at [that] battle (that was fought by both parties [that] seem'd to be pritty equal – Plenty other news of different kinds.

Sat- 2nd. Last night Larocque & Ausgé arrive.

Sund 3[d] Mond 4th. I prepare to send to Falle de Pardrie. Mr. Cameron's Letter.

Tues 5th. Early this morning LeBlanc & Baptiste Richard set off & I prepare Ausgé & Larocque for a trip to the other (say North) end of the Lake in quest of Mr. Crebassa's & my indians – for I am afraid that Messers the oatmeal cakes[135] have already paid their respects to them.

Wed 6th. Very bad weather which prevents the people setting off except this nothing new unless I say that I cannot walk – for having cut my leg about 10 days since & yesterday knocked it against a stick so hard that it bled much & is swollen very high.

Wednes 7. Bad weather again – Frid 8[th]. Early this morning Larocque & Ausgé set off but this is all

/[53]/ March Sat. 9[th]. This morning LeBlanc & Baptiste arrive but have no news from those new people & they have none as yet from Mr. M[c]Donald – Mr. Halcro speakes of h[e]aring of Welles but does not know where he is with the Bezette – they bring 4 pieces of meat from old Muffle D'orignialle's lodge, whom they seen at War road river Portage.

Sund 10[th]. Nothing new. Mond 11[th]. After Dusk last night Ayagon arrives here with his Brother who eloped with La Bezette's wife – They are now upon the warrior's river near the Lake – They have not as many furs as we might have expected – Altho' they went at a great distance & besides have worked the lodges that old Muffle D'orignialle

---

134 Napoleon Bonaparte, long at war with Britain and the rest of Europe. Nelson's information was wrong (France was at peace with Russia until 1812), but this may have been a garbled account of Napoleon's campaign against Austria, which culminated in his victory at the Battle of Wagram in July 1809. News of that event could have reached Lake Winnipeg by way of a winter express in March 1810.

135 The HBC men, so called by Nelson because of their supposed diet.

left near the Détour last fall.[136] Besides this nothing new old [*sic*; only?] that I give them to drink.

Tuesd 12th. This morning I send off Inkster & LeBlanc to Ayagon's lodge – Fine weather.

Wednes. 13th. Very fine weather. About 10 O'Clock this morning – Mr. Cameron arrives here accompanied by Messrs Crebassa & McDonald from the Dalles – There is no news of any particular consequence At Night Inkster &c arrives with very near 2 Packs.

Thurs 14th. To-day I sent off The Bird Old Muffle's son to Ayagon's lodge as Mr. Cameron has a desire of speaking to him.[137]

Frid 15- Saturd 16th. About noon to-day Larocque & Ausgé arrive from their jaunt but have been lucky enough not to find the least vestiges or markes of any one whatever – Late this evening Ayagon & old Muffle D'orignialle arrive – Mr. Cameron treats them to some liquor & makes them a very proper speech

Sund 17. Mond 18th. Last night Mr. Cameron gave a Parole* to Ayagon for the other indians which I hope will be attended as it deserves – To-day Old Muffle & his sons pay me a few skins of their debt –

Tues 19th. About Sun rise this morning Mr. Cameron is off & leaves me here Old Longuetin or Jérome in the place of Ausgé whom he takes along with him to prevent any future dissentions among ourselves on women's accounts. Blue beefs.[138]

Wed 20th. Old Desrocher crosses this bay to make traps, & Ayagon sets off for his lodge with a little rum from Mr. Cameron & some from myself.

Thurs 21st. Very beautiful weather since Monday – This morning we fill our ice house (about 5 foot square & as many deep) with ice. Old Desrocher arrives from the other side without finding the least track except those of indians whom I suppose [must] be Pitites-Couilles going to the Grand Pointe ready to cross at the first notice.

---

136 See *Journal*, 13 November 1809, for the beaver lodges found on the lower part of Warpath River, whose mouth is not far from Long Point (the Détour).

137 Cameron was probably coming under more pressure from the NWC partners to abandon Nelson's post at Dauphin River, because of the continuing conflict with the Fort Dauphin department. As it was Ayagon who had first asked that the post be established, Cameron may have wanted to consult with him about the effects of this step.

138 Nelson uses this expression again in his Journal entry for 25 July 1810, where he calls Durocher's wife a "blue beef." It is a crude reference to a woman, which may refer to sexual inexperience. See also Nelson's journal for 27 December 1818, when he calls Welles's woman "a piece of fresh beef."

Frid 22nd. Old Muffle D'orignialle & his family set off to encamp where he had been making traps all winter hoping there to be able to pay the rest of his debt in martins –

/[54]/ March 23^d Friday 1810! Nothing new but very fine weather – one of Old Muffle D'orignialle's women comes here to-day – but returns immediately.

Saturday 24th. Nothing new but overcast weather at night –

Sunday 25th. Pittites-Couilles & old Brochet arrive this morning from their lodges that are near that Portage I made in going to Fort Alex^r near Tête-aû-Pichou.[139] – they have about 60 skins in different Peltries among them – The son in law [Le Gendre] in making a bait for foxes nearly killed himself, for his knife hav^g slipped runned about 1½ inches in, under his left breast. Showers of snow all day

Monday 26th. About 2 O'Clock P.M. I arrive at their lodges & take what few Peltries they have after which I give them 3 quart of HWs mixed.

Tues. 27th. Having sent off LeBlanc & Longuetin very heavily loaded, but almost only meat – I remain some time behind with Inkster to know when & where I may find them, should I happen to be in necessity of sending to them – 'Tis surprising to see what trouble these people give themselves at present & to what little purpose – they have near 1200 traps between them all some reaching as far as Tête-au Brochet – others in the Bottom of this bay & others again as far as Tête au Pichou, yet between them all I could hardly get 100 marting [martens] from them – A few minutes after my arrival at the house, Welles arrives from Partridge Crop having left Bezette's lodge but a few days before where he been starving & doing almost nothing – for Bezette & Cû-fesse between them have just 9 skins! – – – News from swan river is that La Loge the murderer of Mr. McDonald's men last year has Killed two two [sic] indians & intends to Kill twenty more (indians or white people) when he deliver himself up – He says that he is afraid of the white, but he laughs at the indians.[140]

---

139 See journal entry of 18 December 1809.

140 In the *Reminiscences*, Nelson has an extended account of The Lodge, who murdered two of the Fort Dauphin voyageurs when they were sent to his lodge *en derouine*; was captured by one of the NWC clerks, Cuthbert Cumming; but was allowed to escape by other NWC men because they were afraid of him. After further murders, The Lodge was finally shot dead by a clerk (*Reminiscences*, Part 7, 282–3).

Wednes 28. Thurs 29. Inkster & I make a Caryole as I intend to pay a visit to Mr. Crebassay, if I can have time.

Friday 30th. Terrible snowy & bad weather – which last all day.

Saturday 31st. This morning I send off Longuetin & Welles with a little tobacco & 2 measures of ammunition, the first to stay with the son in law & the latter with Cu-Lèvé – Old Desrocher arrives from his traps with his wife & nine martins – he set off on Thursday – Nothing new or promising to fill this last sheet of my Journal – As it began so it ends – Altho' I have left nothing undone for the interest of my Employers (such as appeared to me just & reasonable) yet I have done nothing worthy of their regard – However – I leave this old & now worthless thing, to begin a new one wherein I hope to have something more pleasant & interesting to show – Geo Nelson at River Dauphine Lake ouinipique Depart[ment] under direction of D. Cameron.

End of journal. The next journal carries on directly.

7

Journal at Dauphin River and Tête-au-Brochet, 1 April 1810–1 May 1811

This journal is similar to the previous one of 1808–10, in this case composed of 13 folded sheets of Radway paper, nested so as to give 52 pages, each 20 cm high x 16 cm wide. The sheets are not fastened together, but nothing has been lost. This journal carries on directly from the previous one.

As the trading season of 1809–10 came to an end, Nelson delayed sending off the winter's trade as long as possible. Many of his hunters had not yet paid their debts, and he hoped not to close the year's books until he had got in every possible fur. Apart from a brief trip to Crebassa's post at Broken River, perhaps hoping for instructions from Duncan Cameron, he remained at Dauphin River until the third week of May, waiting for the appearance of the Mashkiegons, who were on the east side of the lake, and also for a party of Ojibwe who had gone north to the neighbourhood of Long Point. The Mashkiegons arrived in a group on 20 May with their spring hunt, and two days later came news that the hunt of the northward group of Ojibwe had been poor. Nelson then finished packing all his furs, fourteen packs this year, an excellent improvement on the five packs of which he had been so ashamed in spring 1809. He dispatched these furs to Fort Alexander on 8 June, with his most experienced man Durocher in charge, and his last two able-bodied canoemen were sent there on the 13th. Nelson himself remained at Dauphin River for the summer. With him were his wife and baby daughter, one voyageur (the old man Mausgé), and the family of François Richard, his interpreter.

Nelson occupied himself in fishing for day-to-day subsistence, planted potatoes, and sowed parsnips and peas. Provisions were in short supply. Nelson hoped that the Indigenous people would bring in meat, but he had almost no trade goods left to pay for it, and the hunters were not interested in selling on credit. By early August it was clear that the post would soon run out of food completely and Nelson decided that he should take his family to Fort Alexander. He and his wife set off in a small canoe on 13 August, no doubt with little Mary in the bottom of the canoe, leaving François Richard and Mausgé in charge of what remained at the post.

Barely had they begun their journey when at the Île-à-la-Campement, on the far side of Sturgeon Bay, they happened upon the brigade for Athabaska River, en route to their winter quarters. The NWC partner in charge, John Macdonell, informed Nelson that the axe had finally fallen on the Dauphin River post – the Fort William partners' meeting had firmly decided that it was to be closed. Nelson was to move to a new site at Tête-au-Brochet, still on the west side of the lake but farther south, and significantly farther from the Fort Dauphin department's border. This news had come to Nelson by accident, from a man he knew only slightly. There was no letter from Duncan Cameron, his own bourgeois, to explain what had happened, to offer comfort or encouragement, or to give instructions for the new season. Nelson went back to Dauphin River to pick up his one voyageur, the reluctant Mausgé, and with the usual delays for weather the little party made its way to Fort Alexander. Old Mausgé was no longer a strong canoeman, though Nelson thought he was doing his best. In spite of this handicap, they reached Fort Alexander in two days.

Two days later Duncan Cameron appeared in company with the Fort Dauphin bourgeois, John McDonald, and Nelson was sent with McDonald, to return to Dauphin River and have some kind of consultation with the Indigenous people there. If he had behaved decently, McDonald would have taken Nelson and his little family into his own canoe, but he left them to paddle their own rickety vessel, keeping up with the Fort Dauphin brigade as well as they could. Nelson did not mention it in his journal, but for a clerk like him to have to paddle under such circumstances was an insult, whether calculated or not, if not an outright humiliation. At Dauphin River, they found no one on the plantation. No doubt, all of Nelson's hunters knew that changes were in the wind, and were staying well clear of John McDonald's harangues. After a brief delay McDonald's canoes went on to their wintering grounds, taking with them Richard, Nelson's interpreter, who would now become part of the Fort Dauphin establishment. Nelson was left with one voyageur, Allard, to make his way back to Tête-au-Chien for the usual Lake

Winnipeg department rendezvous. There was no one at the rendezvous yet, so Nelson carried on to Broken River, where on 16 September he met Duncan Cameron with the Lake Winnipeg brigade. For Nelson and his wife it had been four weeks of useless canoeing up and down the lake, with plenty of time to reflect on how he was being treated, and what future the NWC could hold for him.

Duncan Cameron's behaviour towards Nelson during this awkward period was nothing to be proud of. He was probably downcast by the partners' meeting, which had forced him to give up his project of developing the Dauphin River post, and he may even have fallen into a depression. This would explain his apparent lack of action (he spent almost a month at Fort Alexander before proceeding to the departmental rendezvous) and in particular his failure to communicate with Nelson directly as he should have done. As the two men went back to Tête-au-Chien together, we can imagine the uncomfortable silence that hung between them. They reached the rendezvous on 19 September, and after the usual ceremonies with the Indigenous people waiting there, and distributing the winter's goods into the canoes, Nelson left the next day for his new wintering location, at Tête-au-Brochet.

Tête-au-Brochet was about two days' paddle farther away from the Fort Dauphin department than Nelson's old station, on the other side of a large, multi-bayed peninsula that separates it from the present Sturgeon Bay and Dauphin River. There had been a post at Tête-au-Brochet before, most recently in 1806–07. When Nelson examined the site, he found no better place to build than where the old, decaying buildings stood, though much of the nearby wood had been cut down by the previous occupants. Living conditions were different than at Dauphin River. There was no equivalent of the great fall fishery at the rapids above the latter post, where as the weather grew cold Nelson and his men could spear thousands of lake whitefish and hang them up to freeze. Instead, Nelson built a *puise* or fish trap, in which many pike and pickerel were taken. Once the buildings were finished two men were sent overland to Dauphin River to bring back the remaining potatoes from the garden there. Later, expeditions were sent to Dauphin River to spear whitefish at the rapids, but few were taken, and it was reported that the usual high population had failed to appear as usual.

In the spring, Tête-au-Brochet proved to be on a goose flyway, and during April there was a good goose hunt which brought a welcome supply of rich meat.

Nelson found himself trading with much the same Indigenous hunters as he had at Dauphin River, with the Mashkiegons in particular, though the Ayagon/Mouffle d'Orignal band still appeared from time to time. The season began ominously for everyone, with starvation on everyone's lips. The great Ayagon himself could hardly feed his family, and news came in December that they had struggled to come in from the hunting grounds as far as Dauphin River, where they had lived upon Nelson's whitefish. The shortage of provisions extended as far as Fort Alexander itself, for twice during the winter Duncan Cameron sent men to Tête-au-Brochet to get as much meat as Nelson could spare.

On 6 December, Duncan Cameron surprised Nelson by visiting him at Tête-au-Brochet, accompanied by two of his voyageurs. For the bourgeois to visit a peripheral post in mid-winter was very unusual. It may be that Cameron had decided that he owed Nelson a private explanation for what had led to the sudden closing of the Dauphin River post in August, and for the careless way in which Nelson had learned of it. Nelson tells us little of the visit, except that Cameron was able to correct a four-day error that Nelson was making in his calendar. The bourgeois was obviously not very well, perhaps suffering from dysentery brought on by the poor diet. Cameron returned to Fort Alexander on the 13th, having given the usual invitation for Christmas. Nelson was so eager to attend that he set off on the 21st, arriving at the central post before any of the other clerks. They all had a fine time, remained until after New Year's, and were joined for a few days by John Dougald Cameron, one of the clerks from the Nipigon department.

Early in April Nelson made an extra trip of his own to Fort Alexander, for an unknown purpose, but it would have helped to relieve the tedium of the season. Back at his own post, the Indigenous people came and went, but they seldom had any furs. Nelson vacillated between opinions as to the reason. Sometimes he thought that the hunters were doing their best, but that the country was exhausted. Sometimes he suspected that they had all conspired to disappoint him, resentful of the move of the post from Dauphin River. By the first of May 1811, when the journal ends, he had made up only three packs, and had part of a fourth, as miserable a return as he had ever achieved on Lake Winnipeg.

❋

1810 April Journal

Sunday 1st. Altho' I finished my last journal in as poor a manner as Could be (in regard I mean to trade) yet I begin this one with much worse. Welles arrives this afternoon from Cu-lèvé & Pitites-Couilles' lodge, having left Longuetin there who is not to be back [here] but with them in some days hence – Lorrin's soninlaw [Le Gendre] is gone with his family towards Tête-aû-Brochet to fish – & pay his debt what may – The others have steered different Courses also but what they will do God knows! – The fall of snow of Friday last has been the heaviest of any we have yet had this winter – there fell very near a foot Deep – No appearance of spring as yet, which in truth I wish would not come on these two months to come – Welles who arrived from Falle de Pardrie the 27th of March tells me that the People there seen a Swan & a duck many days before

Monday 2nd. I prepare for a visit to Mr. Crebassa's near sun set. Old Nez-Corbin & the Sourd arrive [from] their lodge on the upper part of Monotàguée river – They have nearly the amount of their debts – between 45 & 50 skins – Very fine weather.

/2/ Tuesday 3d April 1810. A little after sunrise I send off old Desrocher to Nez-Corbin's lodge – and sometime after I set off myself, leaving the Sourd at the house who intends to go & rejoin his father [Mouffle d'Orignal] who is towards Warrior's river. We encamp at Tête-aû-Pichou – LeBlanc & Boulanger are with me.[1]

Wednes 4 Thurs 5th. Yesterday the weather being very warm we were obliged to encamp about noon in "l'isle ronde" opposite to Tête-aû-Brochet. At sunset we set off again but having lost ourselves in an island – the night being very dark with a high wind & some rain, obliged us to return a part of the way & encamp about midnight under a large Epinette [pine tree]. At day breake to-day, finding that we were upon the right road, we were again obliged to put up at about 10 O'Clock – We see crows.

Frid. 6th. At about 8 or 9 this morning we arrived at Mr. Crebassa's [at Broken River]. – Trempe is off several days since to Mr. Cameron's with old Premier (& band's) hunt –

Satur. 7th. Near or at sunset Trempe & Perusse arrive from Fort Alexr – According to the winter express* there is Good news all over

---

1 The voyage was on foot, over softening spring snow. Lake Winnipeg would not be free of ice for two more months.

the North except at Slave lake where Mr. John McGillivray had the misfortune to loose his guide last fall. – two other common men also are dead!! Nothing strange at Fort Alex^r except that Mr. [Duncan] Cameron means to leave the Country this year for Good – Sund. 8th. I write a letter to Mr. Cameron & one for Mr. Seraphin – which Mr. Crebassa will take there.

Mond 9th. At about 8 O'Clock last night I set off, but as the wind was very high & the night dark we were obliged to encamp near Detroit du Duc – about 5 league from the house.

/3/ Mond 9th. We encamp about 3 O'Clock P.M. in Mr. C[rebassa's] Campment which was about 10 yards from our pine where we put up last Wenese^day night.² Here I find Mr. Crebassa's tea pot that was forgot –

Tuesday 10. At day breake we set off – & pass near Tête aû-Brochet to see if the son in [law; Le Gendre] or any others were there but seeing no marks we continue our route to Tête aû-Pichou where I find Cu-lèvé & P.C. [Petites-Couilles] having spent some time here in arranging their debts &c. I set off & encamp pritty early at the Grande Point for it was pritty fine travelling.

Wednes 11th. Having set off at the breake of day I arrive pritty early in the morning at the house where I find all the men & a few skins from Old Nez Corbin's &c, & the Youngest of old Morpion's sons who had been in some days past & paid but 13½ skins the hunt of a whole winter! – At the entrance of the river as we were coming in we seen two Geese going to the South – "This is all."

Thurs 12th. Inkster & I tie up 380 martins ready to put in the packs – The weather is Cold –

Friday 13 Satur 14th. LeBlanc & Longuetin go a piece up the river for a Cache of fish that Bezette & Cu-fèssé made last fall – They bring home 108 being all that were there. This morning also I sent off Welles & Boulanger to Lac St. Martin to look after Bezette &c. – Much snow melts.

Sunday 15th. About 2 O'Clock this morning Old Brochet his step son & Kieshkieman arrive from their lodges with about 10^lbs of meat for ammunition &c. As they have a few martins am obliged to send Larocque with them but I give no rum – At Day breake I send off Inkster & Longuetin to Tête-Aû-Brochet to [look] after the other indi-ans, & Longuetin is to go with Pitites Couilles for his cache of oats in river Chebanagen. To day Richard kills a goose & we see several others with a swan. A high S. wind.

---

2 The place where Crebassa had camped on his return from Dauphin River in March.

/4/ Monday 16th April. Nothing new 'till about noon when
Morpion's young son arrives for people to go for a Moose. At Sunset
Larocque arrives, being obliged to return at a small distance from
beyond old Nez Corbin's lodge, for according to his account they did
not wish him to go, he brings me 2 Carriboeuf Skins with some martins
& a little meat – Larocque seen Pelican's & ducks – A South wind.

Tues 17th. About 9 O'Clock last night Welles & Boulanger arrive
from Bezette's lodge in their sugar island where they are to pass the
remainder of the season³ – Bezette's hunt is 6 martins, 5 foxes, 3 Dresst
Skins, & 1 fisher. Cû-fèssé – 9 martins.

Wednes. 18. About noon Desrocher & LeBlanc arrive from
Mor[pion]'s lodge with each a very heavy load of meat. Fine weather
& it thaws much.

Thurs 19th. This morning, while or rather a short time after the men
put out a net, Longuetin arrives from Chebanagon river whither I had
sent him for oats – Near sunset Inkster arrives having seen Soninlaw
[Le Gendre] &c at Tête-aû-brochet, but he brings but very little of
anything from them – Soninlaw, Belly, & moose Eyes intend to Cross
the Lake into little beaver river where according to their accounts they
are to work miracles!!

Good-Friday 20th. The men visited the net last night & took 25
fish of different kinds (except whitefish). This morning they take 17
of the same kind but we take up the net as the current is too strong –
Yesterday I killed a Goose, & to-day old Nez-Corbin brings me 5 more
with two Swans & a beaver; a few moments after this the Sourd & the
Bird arrive & bring me about 20 skins in martins, they also bring me 7
Carriboo tongues.⁴

/5/ Saturday 21st. To day the weather is very rainy & cold, yet Welles
set off about midnight for Old Muffle's lodge & arrives about noon
with a little dry meat & 6 Carriboeuf skins quite wet – Near night
Tabishish (old Nez Corbin's youngest son) sets off but his father
remains here drunk upon 3 pints of HWines that I gave him –

(Easter) Sunday 22nd. Old Nez Corbin sets off with a very little
ammunition that I give him – to-day the wind is N consequently Cold
& it snows pritty hard all day – the men say to have heard thunder
yesterday.

---

3 This band's sugar island was in Lake St Martin.
4 These two men were brothers, sons of Mouffle d'Orignal, and must have brought with
them an invitation for Nelson to send a man to their father's lodge.

Mond. 23ᵈ. Cold & snowy yet Larocque goes to set traps for beaver in a <u>small</u> river at some distance from hence.

Tues 24ᵗʰ. Clear weather today & not very cold. This morning Old Muffle brings me an otter & 6 rats – He comes to borrow a Canoe from me to hunt about in a small river 'till such times as he can make his own.

Wednes 25. Old Muffle returns home with my canoe & Larocque goes to his beaver lodge – This is all & no more for today except that I sent Belanger to live with the Soninlaw [Le Gendre], Belly & Moose Eyes, who make their hunt in Pigeon River.⁵

Thurs 26ᵗʰ. This morning Larocque arrives with a beaver & at about 10 O'Clock to-day I send him & LeBlanc to the Détour [Long Point] to wait for & hurry on the Morpion's oldest son as son [sic] as he may arrive there – Longuetin goes with them as far as Muffle's lodge to gather gum – The river begins to breake up a little altho' the weather is cold. At night Morpions son arrives but returns again.

Frid. 27ᵗʰ. Young morpion encamps here but brings nothing with him except two Swans – Jack [John Inkster] who was yesterday a hunting comes home to day, having slept at Old Nez Corbin's lodge. He brings me but 2 swans & a Couple of Geese, for the old fellow amuses himself at hunting game only.

Satur 28ᵗʰ. Towards morning it snowed a little but soon melts again. About noon La Bezette arrives here with his wife & one of his Children. He brings me two beavers, a Bearskin & an otter dᵒ [ditto, i.e. skin] besides a little new sugar – He left Old Cu-fessé in their sugar island.

Sunday 29. Nothing new, but cold weather, & much ice drifts down the river – This is all –

/6/ Monday 30ᵗʰ April. This morning I send off Inkster with Welles to the Monotagueé river for the soninlaw's canoe that I bought. About 8 o'clock this morning it began to snow & continued very hard 'till near noon when it left off & clear'd up so that Bezette set off with 3 pints of HWines that I give him – About 2 P.M. Morpion or Weaga comes to trade me some rum for an otter a Cat & a martin, but I place this to Old Nez Corbin's acᵗ [account] as it or they come from him.

---

5 These Mashkiegons had told Nelson of their plan to hunt around the Pigeon River post on 19 April; having traded there in previous years, they would have been familiar with the possibilities for furs. The NWC did not occupy Pigeon River in 1809–10, so at Dauphin River Nelson was able to extend his trade to the other side of the Lake.

Tuesday 1ˢᵗ May. Last night the river was free 'till near Richards hut about 6 acres from us, but this morning it is barred again with new ice of last night sufficiently to bear dogs. I send Longuetin for the small canoe that Desroché & Larocque left at Montaguée Point last fall (in Novʳ). Pritty clear weather. The River is clear.

Wednesday 2ⁿᵈ. Cloudy weather but not Cold as the wind is partly south – Inkster & Welles arrive here with old Nez Corbin (& their Canoe 6 Geese & 3 Swans) who comes for Iron hoopes [sic] to make arrow Spears.⁶ At night we set out a net near the mouth of the Lake

Thurs 3ᵈ. Old Nez Corbin returns – we take but very few fish as the Current is so strong as to make the net lie straight [parallel] with the river's bank.

Frid. 4ᵗʰ. We take up our net but with very few fish – Inkster & Baptise [Baptiste Richard] go a hunting to the Lake St. Martin above, Pritty fine weather

Satur 5ᵗʰ. The weather is pritty warm – We put out the net again but before the Door as we think that there is less Current; at night we take a few fish –

Sund 6ᵗʰ. This morning we take 31 suckers & 2 white fish, the first that we taken this **Year** here – & at night only 2 suckors – Inkster & Baptiste arrive – They [took] only 9 Geese, 1 Crane, 2 Cormorants, & 1 Loone. They seen but 6 swans but could not get at them – and they say that but very little ice is melted in the Lake above, being all at the entrance of the River – Yesterday & today the weather is pritty fine but wind is N

Monday 7. Tuesday 8ᵗʰ. Nothing new since these two days past –

Wedneseday 9ᵗʰ. About 10 this morning old Muffle D'orignalle /7/ arrives here with his family – he gives me but 8 skins upon his debt. About 5 this afternoon Ayagon's son-in-law arrives here with his wife & 16 skins in peltries: he left Ayagon's family at the Portage du Guerier, for Ayagon himself was gone to Lake Sᵗ Martin to see Cu-fesse his fatherinlaw.

Thurs 10ᵗʰ. This morning he [Ayagon's son-in-law] returns, & as he tells me that he is a going immediately to the Portage La Prairie I give him a little powder &c with some tobacco [and] 5 pints of HWines. About 3 P.M. he arrives again with Ayagon to whom he gave his rum – he [Ayagon] of course is drunk and absolutely wants me to give him his rum & Clothing – &c – Much ice breakes at the mouth of the river, in the Lake I mean

---

6 Iron hoops, discarded from liquor kegs, could be cut up to make arrowheads.

Friday 11th. This morning Cu-lèvé & moose Eyes arrive from Tete-au-brochet but what is their mission God Knows – they say that there is much water yet upon the ice & that it is strong – being no where broke. Saturday 12th. This morning Cu-Lèvé & Moose Eyes return, but I am afraid for them as the ice Yesterday shoved much upon the shore. Except this we have nothing new.

Sunday 13th. Yesterday Ayagon's son-in-law set off for the Portage La Prairie to be one of the warparty. This morning Welles & Boulanger fight a rugh & tumble, & a pitch battle. It appears that Boulanger's army was not of sufficient strength for that off Welles. Ayagon (my father) invites the women to sow [sew] a twelves skin lodge for him.[7]

Monday 14th. A very high south wind. We begin clearing ground to-day to sow or plant some potatoes near the Lake – Old Desroché also begins to arrange his can° [canoe] – With the fish we took yesterday & to day in our net we take 3 Cormorants – Welles & Boulanger fight again but Boulanger got so well pounded that I was obliged to bleed him

Tuesday 15th. Nothing new. Wednesday 16th Early this morning we finish a piece of Ground which we suppose to be sufficient for the sowing of our five Kegs of Potatoes – I give two Carriboux skins to be cut up into a twine to make a drag net* for sturgeon – The weather is very warm

Thursday. 17th. A fine South wind 'till about 8 a.m when it turns to the north – Inkster works, indeed nearly finishes the above mentioned net.

/8/ Friday 18th May 1810. Inkster finishes the net in spite of some showers of rain that prevent Old Nez Corbin's returning to his lodge that is round the Point towards Mônôtaguée river – Morpion's young son is in the river yet but is to be in in a short time – the old fellow came here today upon account of some smoke that was occasioned by our burning the brush round the house – he took it to be a signal for his immediate arrival – They kill two bears in Monotaguée river and a few otters, but a scarcity of Powder prevents their Killing some beaver that they seen very close – Inkster takes 5 fine large sturgeon in the new leather made sain [seine].

Satur 19th. Very fine weather but nothing new.

---

7 A twelve-skin lodge was unusually large, probably because Ayagon, who had five wives, had to accommodate a large family. Jennifer Brown suggests that this was a *zhaaboondawaan* or "long lodge," with three fires and an entrance at each end, like that owned by the father of the Berens River Ojibwe, Fair Wind, around the turn of the last century (Brown 2017d, 301–2), but made of leather rather than of a frame covered with sheets of birchbark.

Sunday 20th. This forenoon (about 9 O'Clock) the Mashkiégons arrive all in a brigade, except Lorrin's soninlaw & his brother the Belly who are at bloody river doing what, God Knows! – As these Gentlemen now expect a treat as they are all together – I prepare myself for it by getting a flag hoisted to the end of a pole on their arrival with a few shots in honor to it. To the Mashkiégon's I gave 2 Kegs of liquor & to the Sauteux's 1½ with three Coats & a belt between them, & two flags – When I gave one to Ayagon I told him that it was not for him to trouble the White people for rum or anything else like it when incited to it by the young men – that this flag did not hold rum – it was given him merely as a mark of his being a Great man so that the other indians might look upon him as such also, with other indian parables that finished the speech –

Mond. 21st. We begin sowing our Potatoes, & the indians are very Drunk – Yesterday while the indian women were cutting their lodge poles, they seen a man in the woods who run off as soon as he was perceived; 'tis said that one of his shoes fell off his foot – a fright.

/9/ Tuesday 22nd. We finish sowing our potatoes five Kegs – The weather is yet very fine – After sunset Larocque & LeBlanc arrive having left old Gagnan; & the other indians are a little beyond the River aux sables[8] – They came upon the Lake the 12th of May, so long were they in their hunting. They had been far beyond the Grand Rapid but they had no success as the English who wintered there last year got the whole of what few furs were there – There are no English there this year[9] – The hunt of these four indians is but very little according to the mens accounts – They are to be here as soon as the ice will begin to leave the shore a little – for it is yet very strong in that quarter as the men tell me, but here, in this bay there has been no appearant ice since sunday morning – Ayagon is yet very drunk & has nearly killed one of his women on account of his war pipestem that was lost – This he tells me is occasioned by the woman's going into his (leather) lodge contrary to their laws. The manito is or was so angry at this that he took away the stem – & planted the Greatest part of his arrows in the Ground through revenge –[10]

8 See note to entry of 10 June 1810.

9 Nelson must have been referring to a post established by HBC traders from York Factory, at or near Grand Rapids, on the outlet of the Saskatchewan River into Lake Winnipeg, in the season of 1809–10.

10 The taboo that was violated was not entering the lodge, which had no special importance. The woman must have disturbed Ayagon's possessions in some way, thus displeasing the spirit and bringing on the stated result.

Wednes 23ᵈ. Nothing new. Thursday 24ᵗʰ. We begin today to make our peltries up into packs – We have some showers of rain.

Frid. 25ᵗʰ. We finish making up our packs – we have twelve of them, 5 of which are beaver – This afternoon Old Cû-fessé arrives here with Bezette, Cou-fort, Mangeekiejick & Old La Graise d'ourse accompany him here from Falle de Pardrie, & upon their account I expect to get another rub or two from Mr. McDonald, for I am certain that he will blame me for this altho' I am as free now as I was formerly from this imputation nevertheless this will not clear me in their Eyes. They bother me much for liquor but I mind them no[t].¹¹ –

Satur 26ᵗʰ. It rains several showers very hard to-day & the rest of the day is dull & overcast with a North wind renders it cold. /10/ Last night Ayagon's brother arrives here with his stolen woman he brings me near 20 Plux's [plus] in different Peltries. Today he sets off with his brothers & nine other indians for war – I sent Inkster & two men with them as far as the rapids with 10 Pints of mixed Rom [rum] as he has not yet had his due – Not long after their departure I give Old Cu-fessé ½ Keg of mixed rum as his share with a shirt, & to Bezette I give 3 Quarts of rum also – they drink, drink & drink.

Sund 27ᵗʰ. Weather something fairer than usual – Ayagon having whiseled [weaseled?] his brother out of the rum that I sent him yesterday came back last night & got drunk with the others who were very troublesome to me upon his account, & the other warriors being displeased at their being left behind by their leader came back in great discontent this morning & will not return with him upon any consideration whatever.

Monday 28ᵗʰ. Ayagon resumes his route with the Bras-Court's son & Graise d'ourse & old Muffle's two son's with another lad – the Mashkiegons will not go – We press our packs to day.

Tuesday 29ᵗʰ Wednes. 30ᵗʰ Thurs. 31ˢᵗ. Nothing new for these three days past, except it be that the weather is very warm & a hard South or southwesterly wind drives the ice to the other side of the Lake. So now in a few days we may expect these indians whom Larocque & LeBlanc seen this spring – Old Desrocher gums his canoe – Old Brochet with a few others set off towards Mônôtàguée river, Richard & his family goes with them – Old Desrocher sends off his wife with her mother Old Brochet's wife.

11 Some of these men – Cou-Fort for certain, and probably Mangeekiejick and Graise d'Ours, whose names have not been mentioned before – "belonged" to the seasonal post of Partridge Crop, in the Fort Dauphin department, so Nelson was doing his best to avoid trading with them.

Frid. 1st June. Yesterday we make or clear some Ground to sow turnips &c – & Yesterday again I get 3 quarts of peas sowed /11/ which is the first attempt towards gardening that was ever made in River Dauphine – The wind is very [high] today, nevertheless Larocque & LeBlanc go in Canoe for eggs towards that little river where Old Muffle D'orignalle passed this last winter – They seen not the least appearance of ice towards the north, except a little in the bay which was yet strong enough to bear them up – they bring home about 2½ Kegs of eggs of Gulls or what [sic].

June. Saturday 2nd Sunday 3d. Longuetin & Boulanger go for eggs in other islands near where Larocque &c went, but there were none as they tell me – They say that there is yet plenty of ice in that quarter – Old Nez Corbin & Cû-lèvé with the rest of the Mashkiegons set off for Pigeon & other places, & are to be back about the Middle of July – A hard south wind.

Mond. 4th. We put up a flag staff to-day & hoist our flag for the Kings birth-day. Nothing new, but a little rain.

Tues 5. Wednes 6th. Yesterday morning we had some snow & last night it froze pritty hard – Nothing new –

Thurs. 7th. As I am afraid that Mr. Cameron may be uneasy about the peoples of this place, I undertake to send off all the men except two, whom I keep to wait the arrival of those indians we are now waiting for – A very hard S wind.

Frid. 8th. It rained last night & a little this morning, therefore old Desroché could not set off before near 8 O'Clock with near 14 Pack containing the following Peltries, 355 beaver skins weighing 482lbs, 307 rats, 44 fine otters 18 Common, 13 Cased Cats, 1078 martins, 18 minks, 53 drest moose skins, 33 Parchments, 11 Grey foxes, 29 red, 3 Cross do 2 swan skins, 1 wolf, 8 Dressed Carriboeuf Skins, 3 do Parch[ment], 8 Fishers, 4 Wolverines, 9 Large Black bears, 2 do brown & 1 Cub.

/12/ Frid 8th June. Bad weather, that is, several showers in the Course of the day, with a high wind, has obliged our people to encamp I am afraid at the Grand Point –

Satur 9d. Very fine weather & some fresh breezes, but yet I beleive that our men have gone at least as far as Tête-aû-Brochet, if not in the isles aux écorses.

Sund 10th. As Old Gagnan & the others do not arrive yet I send off LeBlanc & Belanger to go as far as Rivière aux Sables if they meet them not before or see not any vestiges on the beach. At Sunset They

arrive having met the indians at the Grand Maret.[12]. Very fine & Calm.
I suppose our men to have gone to bloody river & returned again to
Tête au Chien &c.

11th Mond 11th. This morning LeBlanc & I sow a few turnips. About
noon Old Gagnan & Morpion's son arrive – I give near half a keg of
mixed rum to Morpions son; & 8 quarts of d° to Gagnan &c – Very
beatiful & quite Calm weather all day.

12th Tues 12th [sic]. The indians are busy telling stories to each [other]
& loose [lose] another very fine travelling day except about noon when
it blows rather hard, but not enough to prevent travelling.

13th Wednes 13th. About 7 A.M. Gagnan &c, (LaBezette & La Graise
D'ourxe) set off for fort Alexr or Broken river. Morpion's son goes to
the Tête-aû Brochet to wait his father's arrival there from Fort Dauphin
by this river – Le Blanc & Boulanger set off for fort Alexander also.
It was very calm this morning & this evening also, but the middle of
the day the wind was very hard – Nevertheless I suppose our men to
have arrived at Fort Alexr today at least unless they have travelled
remarkably slow, for the weather since last Friday has been in all very
beautiful Canoe travelling weather.

/13/ Thurs 14th June. As I am now quite alone only with my lady
& Child I shall keep an account of my employment. Yesterday after
the men went away I went for Paddles & today I am obliged to make
myself a (pine) bark lodge, for the Muskotoes & heat in the house
are (both together) insufferable – At night I put out a night line of 12
hooks – Calm in the morning & at night but not in the day – I lend
my saine to the indians who begin to kill some sturgeon –

Frid. 15th. Nothing new except stormy weather.

Satur 16th. The indians all set off for up the river & I remain now
quite alone; & work a little about the house.

Sund. 17th. These three days past I have been employed in fishing &
mending &c that were very much broken.

Mond. 18th. About 8 A.M. while I was busy in hoeing up the weeds
in my potatoe Garden, Old Muffle & Cu-fèssé arrive with the meat of
a very bad She moose they killed yesterday – they souffle[13] themselves

---

12 This was the party of Ojibwe who had been hunting far to the north, in the direction of
Long Point and Grand Rapids, but with little success.
13 Literally "blow or puff"; here, it means that Old Muffle and Cul-fessé were boasting of
what they had done, expecting to be rewarded.

for they expect to get some rum – they get neither rum nor tobacco as I am quite out of both –

About three this afternoon Francois Richard & his family arrive with plenty of Good news all over except from here, for there are excellent [returns] in the department in General <u>except here</u>. Lorrin it seems has taken his daughter from Richard, which poor fellow renders him really down hearted: I am afraid that this will be of hurt to the Company – he is an excellant interpretor, well beloved by many of the indians & feared by many others – so much so that if he takes it into his /14/ head to leave the Service & go for the English the Company I am certain will perceive of it – he is very sorry & even (often) Cries – Lorrin would have done much better had he kept himself quiet[14]

Tues 19th. About 4 P.M. Mr. McDonald of Fort Dauphin depart's canoes arrive. He remained for a few days at Fort dauphin on account of the indians but will soon be here – He has made 100 Packs!

Wednes 20th. Pritty early this morning Mr. McDonald arrives & Mr. Cummings a Clerk with him.[15] He remains here but a short time which prevents my writing to Mr. Cameron as I would wish; however, I write to Mr. Crebassa who is to summer there, & according to Mr. McDonald's opinion I have sent Richard to Fort Alexander for a little of the most necessary things that I want here – in case the English should pass here as the indians tell us they will – I doubt not but that I will be blamed as reproached for sending Richard in this manner where his woman is – but these things were well weighed beforehand.[16]

Thurs 21st. Nothing new. Frid. 22nd. Satur 23. To-day I go for birch bark to make a lodge, as I am obliged to Keep my tent always up in my room on account of the Muskotoes that are much more numerous this year than ever I knew of before.

Sund 24th. Nothing new –

14 It later emerged that Lorrain had given this daughter to Duncan Cameron himself, the partner in charge of the Lake Winnipeg department.

15 Cuthbert Cumming is recorded as a clerk for the NWC in Fort Dauphin department in 1806, and in 1812–20. He was made a chief trader after the merger with the HBC in 1821. See biographical note by Wallace 1934, 220, 435; HBCA, F.4/32, 206; and HBCA Biographical Sheet.

16 Nelson realized that it would cause trouble to send young Richard to Fort Alexander, so soon after her father had taken his wife away, but at this point Nelson was alone at his post, and had no other fit man whom he could send on this errand. Also it appears that John McDonald, the NWC partner, had approved the plan.

/15 June Monday 25th. Very fine weather. Old Mausgé hoes up the Potatoes, at least begins to do it – I go for bark again Yesterday, rain; & it rains again this morning & evening –

Tues 26th. As it blows now pritty hard I am obliged to put out a night line – It rains almost all day

Wednes. 27th Thurs 28th. Rain all day yesterday & pritty often to-day the weather is also cold, considering the season – This is all my news – for a trader (in this Country) ought never to expect to see indians about his house with anything when he [is] out of things himself – which is the case with me at present – If I had rum – I should not mind being out of fish (for we take but very few now) for the indians would give me meat enough –

Frid. 29th. I go for bark again – There is much water now in the woods & but few muskotoes considering the amazing number that were before. – There are but very few Horse flies also – however I suppose that all these will gain vigour & life again – that it be once more almost dangerous going in the woods (for fear of being devoured by them.).

Satur 30. As we take no fish at least but very few here in the river, I and old Pérè [father] Maus-gé set a net about half a league out in the lake where there are no more than between 4 & 5 fathoms of water. Almost fine weather

Sund 1st July 1810 – Nothing new –

Monday 2nd. Young Michel Richard & I going towards Monotaguée river see several Moose upon the beach & in the water both going & Coming home but could not get at any at all, except one that was pritty far out in the Lake. Altho the road we had or were /16/ obliged to go by (to keep out of its sight & smell) was exceeding bad, we remained a long time upon the beach expecting that it would come to debark, but finding that it was too long we went out after it above our middles in the water – We fired, but the swell prevented our taking a right [aim]. The moose at long last took the fright & our now being upon the shore prevented its debarking – altho it endeavoured after having swam along distance – It at last began to be bewildered & turned & kept turning about very slowly 'till it got out of sight in the Lake – Had we been nearer the fort or house rather we would have gone for a canoe & drove it in shore – but we were too far.

Tues. 3^d. Nothing new only that it blows pritty hard.

Wed. 4th. Old Maus-gé finishes hoeing the potatoes.

Thurs 5th. Yesterday & today – travelling weather by spells.

Frid. 6th. It was very tempestuous all night & blows very hard today.

Satur 7th Sund. 8th. Nothing new, only that the weather is always windy, which I am afraid will add not a little to Richard's natural dilatoriness – We take but very few fish altho' we take the Greatest pains with our nets &c – If Richard gets nothing at Fort Alex[r] I am afraid that we will be pinched for our "aliment" [food] for indians are never too much in a hurry to bring provisions to white people except when they are very sure of being several times paid immediately – Altho' we trust them large debts in the fall (& often but poorly paid) they cannot find the way of doing the same with us when we are out – They will do that for any free man but not for trading people – so strange are the manners of these cursed wretches![17]

/17/ July Mond. 9th. This afternoon Francois Richard & his brother arrive – Rassette & his family also stop here empassant [*en passant*] for the English river where he intends to go to see his son in-law Mr. Robert Henry. &c.[18] – News at Fort Alex[r] is, that M[r] M[c]Donald arrived there in three days from here (the 23[d] of June) with all his canoes – Then he found several of the gentlemen of the Concern with Mr. Cameron – Richard gets not his wife as he expected for she was long before then donnée'd to Mr. Cameron; & she says to have left Richard for ill treatment & jealousy, however he brings his son with him; & I don't know what has passed upon his brains but he is now quite gay, so that I am even surprised, for he was really dull when he first came –

He seen all the Mashkiegons at Tête-au-Brochet but could not get one rascal of them to come there altho' he done his utmost as he tells me – But, why should they come here? what is to entice them here! is it two fathoms of tabacco with not a Grain of ammonition or rum that is a sufficient allurement for these rascally vagabonds – Old Mausgé gathers pine bark to cover the mens house –

---

17 Nelson was forgetting that he was a representative of the NWC, so the Indigenous people would have seen him as having great resources behind him, unlike them or the freemen, who were entirely dependent on their own efforts. See also the experience of the Methodist missionary, Allen Salt, with the Rainy Lake Ojibwe in 1854–55, upon which Jennifer Brown comments: "The Ojibwe had learned ... that [white men] could not be assumed to participate in the generalized reciprocity of the Ojibwe moral universe; they had to be bargained with" (Brown 2017c, 248).

18 Racette had wintered in the Rivière Blanche in Winnipeg River. The fact that a daughter of his was the country wife of the NWC partner Robert Henry, then in charge at English River, is new information.

Tues 10th. Nothing new. Wednes. 11th. As I have nothing to do (as well as not too much to eat) I begin to make a bed room out of Inkster's room by taking down the partitions & replacing them.[19] –

Thurs 12. Frid. 13th. As it has been a kind of a rule since sometime past that when we have not rain every day it is every other day therefore we will not be surprised if it rains to-day – & except this nothing new.

Satur Sunday 15. We were lucky enough this afternoon to take a sturgeon in our net & a good number of other fish, otherwise we should have been obliged to go without supper (so well furnished are we in provisions).

/18/ July Mond. 16th. Tues 17th. Francois Richard & his brother go out a hunting in Canoe today: They arrive at night with a Carriboo that they killed – The women say to have seen some fire on the opposite side of the bay here – I hope that it is some indian Coming here. Very fine weather to day & pritty Calm –

Wednes 18th. A terrible high N.N. West wind which makes the water rise very high here in the mouth of this river – it rains by showers almost all day.

Thurs 19th. Wind & rain 'till near night when it clears up. Francois goes off with his two brothers to gether [gather] eggs &c in the islands.

Frid. 20th. I gather red pine bark to cover a room of mine – Old Cufèssé arrives from Lake St. Martin's having left the other indians about 8 days since, who go somewheres into Manitoban Lake a Moose hunting, for where the[y] have been the moose are now pritty scarce & amasingly lean, on account of their being too many **Horse** flies & muskatoes that eat up thier backs which obliges them to keep in the water all day long which occasions their being so very lean – Old Cu fessé gives me 3 pieces of dry meat & a dry snoute & head – a shower of rain to day again.

Satur 21st. It blows very hard 'till near night when the Richards arrive: they bring only a few small geese & 4 Large ones for the water & wind last Wednesday was so high & strong as to overflow many islands & drown all the young Cormorants & Gulls, & Gull eggs – lying in heaps along the bushes of the islands a little rain this morning.

Sunday 22nd Monday 23^d. Very warm weather.

Tues. 24th. Old Muffle D'orinialle & his band arrive this morning – they bring me some fresh meat & some dry meat also – He has not

---

19 Nelson must have known that John Inkster would not be returning as his interpreter, but he did not yet know that the post itself was to be abandoned.

seen Ayagon since he left Old Cu fèssé which is now many days ago.
however, he is to be down here this fall time enough to drink, otherwise
he would not be a "Pillieur."[20]

/19/ July 25th. Amasing warm – Old Rassette sets off at last Poor old
being "Pour la bonne aventure" – Cu-lêvé, Belly, & old Brochet with
Mrs Desrocher a "blue beef" arrive – but as I am not much in the tune
of keeping des mangeurs de pain en trahison with me (besides these
I already have) she prepares to set off for her indian home again[21]
– Mashkiegons – Nez Corbin & his two sons are gone towards the
Poplar river in quest of the English – Pitites Couilles is gone towards
Tête-aû-Chien, Moose Eyes is in the deep bay of Tête aû Pichou –
These that are arrived to day bring nothing with [them] alledging a
scarcity of ammonition (which is a very good excuse for those who
dont want to act well. Old muffle's son, the Sourd has been out a
hunting to day with Bpt Richard – He killed a hee [bull] moose that is
terrible lean; he got within the reach of ten foot when he shot him – the
Poor animal was so troubled with muskatoes & flies that It did not
perceive or even hear the indian –

Thurs 26th. It rained in the morning but was Calm & fine in the
afternoon when all the indians here set off for Monotaguée River.
(where they are to work great faiths? [feats] & wonders).

Frid. 27. Satur 28th. Moose Eyes arrives here this afternoon from
Monotaguée river & sets off again imediately for his lodge that is in
the bay of Tête au Pichou – He gives me plenty of indian news & I give
him English answers such as I hope will keep at least some of his generation back, that is from going to the HB's people.

Sunday 29th. LeSourd & the Soninlaw arrive here with a rotten moose & tell me par sur le marché that I must expect no more
meat from them as they intend to cross the lake towards (I mean in)
Chebànàgôn river to make oats; but I am afraid that this is a kind of
oats they are agoing to make me eat – however, if they make me eat the
oats they shall eat the Chaff ("Ils mangeront la balle").[22]

20 Perhaps a joking reference to the Pilleurs or Pillagers, a division of the Ottawas who had
a reputation for stealing traders' goods.
21 For another example of the expression "blue beef," see journal entry for 19 March 1810.
The woman was hoping to stay at the post, but Nelson was not willing to have another
mouth to feed, and may have been wary of having an unattached woman so close to his voyageurs. He sent her back to her relatives.
22 "They will eat lead," roughly. Nelson was annoyed that these Indigenous people were
leaving him, but having no goods nor rum, could offer no reason why they should stay.

/20/ Mond. 30th. Nothing new, except I say that we have had very beautiful (Calm, Clear weather) since Rassette left this – We saine this evening & altho' the sturgeons jump pritty often yet we cannot [catch] one – We begin by untieng [untying] a sturgen net to make it over again with larger mashes m[eshes]; for as it is now we cannot take anything in it –

Tues. 31st. Very fine weather. We hear several gun shots towards the islands mais nous ne scavons qui que ca veu dire23 – I whitewash my Cabinet with some yellow earth that I got yesterday at the rapids –

Wednes 1st August Thursday 2nd. This afternoon my Father's brother (Ayagon's brother I mean) arrives here with plenty of pounded meat & some dry meat, with a few peltries also – He gives no news from above.

Friday 3d. Last night between eight of us we finish both undoing & remaking up the sturgeon net of 39 fathoms & to day we set it out. If we had nothing now to eat but the fish out of our nets I'm thinking that we should begin to get long teeth.24

Satur. 4th. Ayagon's brother & the other young man return (I should say yesterday for they arrived on Wednes.) To-day The bird & another boy of Old Muffle's come here; they want to borrow my leather25 so that they may kick me to hell with my pint of powder & thirty balls & ½ fathom tobacco I gave their old father expecting that he would hunt for me here as he promised – I am happy to find now that they starve & cannot kill anything, however I give them 5 fathoms of line & a hook.

/21/ Sund 5th August – Very Clear & warm & it blows very hard to day – Cû-lèvé & old Brochet's step son arrive here on a visit only – I get from them 1 Dressed & 1 parchment skin – Old Cû-fèssé told these indians that if he had seen anything at the house here with or of which he might of expected payment, that he would have given me more meat &c – Now I think that this deserves something – & this something he shall surely get if I can see him this fall – Now is his turn & he makes a good use of it – then shall be my turn when I shall make a better turn of … it26

---

23 The shots were taken to be a signal, "but we don't know what they mean."

24 By "long teeth" Nelson presumably was referring to rodents, whose teeth must be worked continually to keep them from growing too long.

25 Perhaps the net for netting sturgeon, which had just been remade, and was composed of leather cords.

26 Nelson was complaining that Cul-Fessé, who had promised to hunt for him this summer, was refusing to give any meat on credit, now that Nelson was out of rum.

Mond 6th Tuesday 7th. Nothing new 'till this evening when the Coû-fort & Graise d'ourx arrive – the former from broken River & the other from Red River – News!! Mr. Thompson for the Columbia encamped the day before yesterday at the isle du la [sic] Campment (about 6 leagues from here) with four canoes as last year, they returned from Fort Alexander – Montreal people having come as far as there[27] – In this part of the Country all goes pritty well – A new company of traders also is formed for the North – In Canada there has been a terrible sickness all winter of which many people died – a Complaint taking them only in the head & stomack which puts a period to their lives before 24 hours & even in the Course of one night!!! If this be Genuine I am sore afraid that there be morning [mourning] for me![28] –

Wednes. 8th. We take so few fish here that I am resolved to set gon [get going?] next Mond. or Tues. at furthest, for the little meat that I have here will be eaten up & up before the 18th If I wait 'till that time – I am [afraid] that starvation will attend this place this year at Evening we have a most terrible thunder, lightning, hail, wind, & rainy weather for about a hour –

Thurs 9th. Nothing new only that yesterday morning the Cou fort &c continue their route up the river –

Frid 10th. – Satur 11th. To-day I take the inventory which however requires no long time – Fine weather & very Calm.

Sund 12th. It blows very today but it may perhaps Grow calm by tomorrow –

/22/ Monday 13th August 1810. This morning I set off with my lady for Fort Alex[r], taking my Cassette[29] & a few clothes with me, leaving the rest in Charge of young Richard & old Mausgé. I come as far as L'isle du Campement where I meet Mr. John M[c]Donell who goes this year to Slave Lake in the place of Mr. John M[c]Gillivray.[30] – He tells me

---

27 See note to journal entry of 26 August 1809 for the explanation of this new policy for shortening the trip of the brigades for the Columbia. For a summary of Thompson's explorations and travels during 1809 and 1810, see Tyrrell 1916, xc–xciii.

28 Nothing more is heard about this supposed new company. Perhaps it was a misunderstanding, but there were probably always rumours like this circulating at Montreal. The news of the fatal disease in Canada made Nelson concerned about his parents, brothers, and sister there.

29 A cassette was the fur trader's box, containing personal papers and other small possessions.

30 John Macdonell "le Prêtre," after many years in charge of the Upper Red River department, replaced John McGillivray as the partner in charge of Athabasca River (which included Lesser Slave Lake) in 1810, McGillivray being assigned to Athabasca itself (Wallace 1934, 264).

that the Post of River Dauphine is given up to Fort Dauphine[31] & some other news but of no consequence to the Comerce of the Country. This obliges me to go back to the last islands & make a fire & fire 4 Gun shots as a signal of my wanting the people with me, but as no one came I was obliged to set off (Tuesday 14th) leaving my box & provisions en Cache expecting to be back again to night, but again old Maus-gé's being very sick & begging of me so hard that I am obliged to retard, expecting that he will be ready for early tomorrow –

Wednes 15. Rain prevents my setting off & Thursd. 16th the wind – At last Frid. 17th I set off at sun rise & encamp at the point a la Framboise from whence I beleive the indains to have set off only to day, for Mr. McDonell told me that he seen a brigade of them there – Old Mausgé is very sick to night for he forced himself a good deal to day.

Satur 18th. At the Pointe de Roche I meet Mr. Daniel McKenzie for Rat River Depart[ment], this Gentleman is always sickly but I beleive particularly so at present – I meet his two loaded Canoes opposite to Tête au Brochet where I put ashore to make Kettle, but the wind rising obliges me to encamp with Old Cufesse & Morpion, who are not over fond of having a post here as is said. However there pleasure is not much consulted now a-days.

/23/ Sund. 19. I am obliged to encamp about one league from Tête au Brochet. Altho' I set off very early (Monday 20th) we travel this afternoon a little piece again – Tues 21st. At sun rise we had already gone some distance but obliged to put ashore twice on account of the wind Nevertheless we encamp pritty early near (about 3 leagues from) Detroit du duc –

Wednes 22nd. We put out again before day light & were very early obliged to encamp at Detroit du duc as at the same time we kill a bear (cub) The weather is Clear but very windy.

Thurs 23d. We pass at Broken river where I found a bear with two young ones but having no more powder than to prime my gun I was not able to fire at it, altho' it made some attempts to get at us but was at last afraid – we nevertheless kill a small one with a stick – we meet six indian canoes going to make calls –

31 Nelson now learned, through this accidental meeting, that the annual partners' meeting had determined that he was to give up the post that he had worked so hard to develop over the past three years. The journal entry of 18 August seems to show that Nelson had been told that his new post was to be at Tête-au-Brochet, since he comments there that two of his Indigenous hunters were not happy about the prospect.

Frid 24th. We bear sail all day & encamp opposite to black river, from whence we set off this (Satur 25) morning & soon arrive at Fort Alexr in spite of a very high S. E. wind & rain – we seen 4 boats of English pass for the two red rivers – Good News in Canada[32]

Sund 26th. We remain all day & Mond 27th Mr. Cameron arrives here with Mr. McDonald of Ft. Dauphine depart[ment].

As the affairs of the Company require obedience at all times Mr. Cameron sends me with Mr. McDonald together in case that we might see some indians & know whether the present or future situation of affairs should require that the post of river Dauphine be thrown away or not – So, after a very few days we embark & encamp near point au /24/ Battau but Mr. McDonald's 4 Canoes continue – The next day we encamp at Tête aû-Chien having lost some time at Broken river with some indians who come to make oats – Mr. McDonalds Canoes are here – Having passed the night here we continue, but the wind being too high we encamp early at Tête aû brochet in which river I go up a hunting & kill but 9 ducks We are obliged to remain over night, & this evening which is sunday we set off & encamp late at night at Tête aû Pichou – we remain here all Monday & Tuesday morning we set off & encamp about noon about 5 leagues from our house – The four Canoes that are behind come up with us here – Wednes. – 5th of Sept. In spite of a terrible high wind we arrive at the house where we find Richard with plenty of white fish, but no indians have been here since I left this the 17 of last month –

Now, as we have seen no indians, Mr. McDonald cannot judge what step will be necessary – Richard & his family prepare & Thurs. 6 They set off with their new Bourgeoi[33] who leaves me here only with one man to take all our things & dogs in an old large rotten bark Canoe – Frid 7 We put up our things ready & Satur 8th Alard & I set off leaving a few of our things behind with three dogs – We encamp after having rowed [paddled] very hard at the Grand Point – Here we pass the night, but our canoe breaking we were obliged to gum it, during which time the wind changes, yet we set off but are obliged to encamp at about 1½ leagues distance, where we are wind bound till night, when the wind ceases & we /25/ reembark, resolved to travel all night but

---

32 The "two red rivers" were the NWC departments of Lower Red River (the Red River itself) and Upper Red River (the Assiniboine). The good news from Canada was probably in private letters for Nelson from his family, delivered to him at Fort Alexander.

33 Young François Richard was now formally reassigned to the Fort Dauphin department, where he remained for the rest of his career: see Appendix D.

near 10 O'Clock we find a fire on the beach which proves to be old Muffle D'orignialle who crossed to-day from Maskieg islands where he leaves Cu-Lêve, Little Couilles, & old Brochet. They Could not Cross as the wind is too high – I am obliged to encamp here – but this morning the Wind turning fair I set off leaving a little rum & ammonition with the old fellow – We encamp at the last Bark Islands which place we reached with a good deal of trouble as the wind changes some with our course –

Tues. 11. Wednes 12ᵗʰ. We remain degraded by a most terrible wind & rain 'till near this night when we set off & encamp at Tête aû Chien expecting here to find Mr. Cameron, but are mistaken, for he is not yet arrived – Thurs 13ᵗʰ Frid 14ᵗʰ We are wind bound till this evening, when Cu-lèvé & Pitites-Couilles arrive expecting to find Mr. Cameron – Satur. 15. I set off again alone with my man for the Sourd Man being lazy, which makes me row alone while Alard steers. We nevertheless encamp at Detroit du duc having been degraded about three hours to-day with Old Poivre & the Duck, who were making oats at Broken [River] from which place they set off the 6 days now past as well as old Cu fesse & Bezette who make no oats either – Sund 16 being wind bound here Mr. Cameron at last arrives with our canoes bearing a high sail which retards the loaded [canoes] 'till late – We again set off with Mr. Cameron but soon again encamp as night & very black weather comes upon us.

/26/ Monday 17ᵗʰ of September. We arrive pritty early at Tete aû Chien, where we yet find the indians who arrived here but a few moments before us from hunting in Bloody river – They bring a few ducks & Geese, with them – Mr. Cameron makes them a speech suitable to the present occasion³⁴ – They all three set off with their present of 8 quarts of rum & 1 fathom of tobacco.

Tues 18ᵗʰ. Wind bound. Wed. 19ᵗʰ. Wind bound all day – To-day old Nanjobe & the Ducks wife come here but as the former is half dead – & the latter's conversation is not pleasant, they are both refused debt –

Thurs 20ᵗʰ. Mʳ Cameron leaves us last night, & this morning before day we set off & altho we were degraded a little time we yet arrived pritty early at Tête-au-Brochet where I find Ayagon & his brother

---

34 Cameron would have explained the decision to abandon the Dauphin River post and set up a new one at Tête-au-Brochet, a plan that the Indigenous hunters would not have received well.

– St Germain his son – & his nephew[35] Old Muffle [and] his family;
the three mashkiegons, Old Morpion himself & his young son – I give
3 Kegs of mixed liquor among them – Ayagon met Mr. McDonald at
Falle a la Pardrie from whom he got a letter which he now gives me –
St Germains woman [women?] are at River Dauphine feeding upon my
Potatoes –

Frid 21st. We go to chuse a place for building but find none so proper
as at the old buildings altho the wood is greatly ruined –

Satur. 22nd. We chuse a place for building & begin by choping some
wood for the buildings.

Sund 23d. I give debt to the indians who are not in the humour of taking so much as formerly – As they want /27/ to set off immediately I give
two Kegs of mixed liquor among them as an incentive to make them pay
their debts – St Germain left this yesterday; I give him no debt –

Mond. 24th. As the Mashkiegons are in the humour of setting off
I give them a two Gallon Keg of mixed Liquor & one fathom of
tobacco to give to old Nez-Corbin & the rest of his Friends – Old
Desrocher [Durocher] sends his wife with them – I wanted much to
send a man with them, but their Canoes were either really too small or
they did not much relish the proposal, for they refused a man[36] – This
evening I traded a Canoe from old Muffle D'orinialle – & some skins
from some others –

Tues 25th. The Indians Grow sober & all set off. Old Muffle &
his family go up this river[37] – Ayagon, Bezette, & Cu-fèssé set off
for Dauphine River & Warrior River but finding I suppose that rum
would be too far from them, they come back & encamp near us – Old
Morpion & his young son go towards bloody River – Now we may
pritty near judge what kind of a hunts they will make from the different quarter they have chosen – I am sore afraid that the returns this
year will be less than those of even last year –

35 Nelson's undependable punctuation makes this list difficult to parse, but it should probably read "St Germain, his son, and his nephew."
36 The Indigenous people on the west side of Lake Winnipeg had probably not decided yet
whether to continue to trade with Nelson, now that his post was so far east, or whether they
would go to the Fort Dauphin outpost at Partridge Crop. Taking only a little debt, and refusing to take Nelson's man with them, kept their options open.
37 Jackhead River drains several lakes, notably three, now called St David, St George, and
St Andrew Lakes, from which, in small canoes, it would be possible to get farther west and
south, but Mouffle d'Orignal may have been content to remain among those lakes until
freeze-up.

Wednes. 26th. It rains & blows amazing hard this morning but about noon it leaves off, that is, it grows clear but the wind continues very hard yet –

Thurs. 27th. This morning Ayagon & his brigade set off – I give him a little liquor

Friday 28th. Early this morning Ayagons brother /28/ arrives with a Couple of parchments for liquor & permission or orders from his brother to trade his lodge that he left in my Charge[38] – I therefore give him some more rum & positively forbid any of them coming upon such errands in future unless with something to give me in return – The weather is fine & pritty mild – Desrocher, Alard & I finish covering our old new shop – The other men finish my Chimney.

Saturday 29th Septr. St Micheal [St Michael's Day] – very Cold & raw weather – nevertheless we work at our other Chimney.

Sund 30th. This morning Moose Eyes & Kishkieman arrive from Pigeon river where he left The belley & old Nez-Corbins young son – waiting for news – Old Nez-Corbin & the Soninlaw were off two days before this to go to black river to see the English – They are determined not to have any more dealings with our people for they say themselves to be too pitiful with us – I should now be glad to know how I shall fix with these Cursed wretches – now that I have several places to send to at once & not one person proper to understand the indians language[39] – & have but one small Canoe & the large one –

Mond. 1st October 1810 – Very Calm all day with some rain by showers – No one arrives yet which renders me a little uneasy concerning their future behaviour – The men plaister both our houses today –

Tues. 2nd. I get nine dressed & parchment skins (but all bad ones) sowed up into bags besides 5 bale cloths & three other bags to put all potatoes into that are at River Dauphine – I intend to send for them the first fine Calm weather –

Wednes 3^d. It blows amasing hard from the North & the weather /29/ is very Cold, which I b[e]lieve has driven off all the game into the small inland lakes for I was out a hunting to-day but seen but very few ducks & nothing else – Longuetin & Alard plaister the shop

---

38 This must be the large leather lodge that Ayagon had made the previous year. Getting rid of this bulky possession may have been a sign that Ayagon was thinking of moving farther west.

39 John Inkster, Nelson's interpreter of the previous season, had been reassigned, and François Richard had gone to Fort Dauphin, and no replacement had been provided.

– Larocque dubs <u>off</u> my floor – Desrochér makes a few floats for our net – Welles begins Choping – & I myself after my hunting excursion begin to make my window sashes – Cold!

Thurs- 4ᵗʰ. The first snow that we have had this year was last night tho' we've had new ice several times before this – nothing new again to-day – except that it very Calm indeed – almost a miracle.

Frid 5ᵗʰ. As it is yet very calm this morning I send off Larocque, Longuetin & old Desrocher in the big canoe to river Dauphine for the few potatoes & other things that may yet be remaining there; but at night they all return here again for they had but just reached the Point-aû-Ragominaires when a terrible [storm] with rain, hail, & snow obliged them to put ashore, & at last put all their things upon a stage & come back – The water here in this little crick [creek] rises very high, occasioned by this ras-cally weather – I begin to make a net today.

Satur. 6ᵗʰ. The wind was & is yet so high that last night it drive down a middle size pine upon our lodge & would perhaps have done us much hurt had not Laroch [*sic*]

Sunday 7ᵗʰ. Much finer & Calmer weather than we have had since many days past – It is such that with some difficulty people might travil upon the Lake – We work at every thing.

Mond. 8ᵗʰ. Early this morning Larocque, Longuetin & Alard set off (for old Desroché [Durocher] has had such a sore back that I was obliged to put a blistering plaster of about 9 inches long & 14 broads upon it – it has had the desired effect I beleive) from here on foot to take their Canoe en passant – Larocque's woman is very sick & I give her a <u>purge</u>. A very high S.E. wind drives our men with a fine sail to near River Dauphine – bad weather at night.

Tues. 9ᵗʰ. The greatest part of about 4 inches of snow that fell during the last bad weather melts to day by a soft rain & sun shine weather – The night before last the river took intirely across but came free again the same day.

/30/ Wednes 10ᵗʰ. Nothing new but cold bad weather as has been for these many days now past – I work at the new net. It rains –

Thurs. 11ᵗʰ. Old Desrocher & I finish our net of 70 fathoms long (for the Poor old fellow can now begin to stand a little) while the Dutchman (Welles) works at my chimney that smokes or at least did smoke most terribly – Cold & raw, & snow & rain, & hail & fair weather, all at once & each in their turns such is to-days weather –

Frid 12ᵗʰ. Amasing Cold (but clear in the afternoon) this morning that when I visit the net the ice would grow upon my hands I take

27 – Lawyers (Pikeral) Pike & suckors – I enter my house today having passed the fall in a leather lodge[40] –

Satur 13th. A miracle for Tête-aû-brochet – we take 4½ Whitefish this morning in our nets – the other half was eaten by a large otter that old Desrocher seen near the net. People have been seldom known to take any white fish here I believe – Very fine fall weather – that is, Clear & not too warm.

Sund 14th. News by baskets full – While Old Desrocher & I were takeing our usual morning regale upon this well tasted, high flavor'd & substantial Pike – Pikeral we hear several Gun shots which prove to be old Nez-Corbin & all the Mashkiegons together, coming to hunt on this side of the Lake. Nez Corbin, Soninlaw & Brochets stepson who were at Sutherlands at Black river[41] seem to have had no great encouragement from the English from (what is usual among them) an untimely diffidence, owing I beleive more to laziness than anything else – for surely, had he given them the least encouragement, I should have found myself here in a sweet Pickle – whereas now I only wait till such times as I be sure of my hold, when I hope to retaliate upon this pusil-lanimous band of rascally vagabonds – They, the indians, tell me of having seen Peruse pass at Pigeon Point with Mr. Dougald Cameron's woman & family[42] who is /3 1/ now travelling as fast as the weather & fear of starvation will allow (them) in quest of her husband who prob-ably winters at Loon lake near Nepigon – They were very scarce of provisions & had but very little ammonition remaining. They are badly off, for in this miserable Lake much precaution is necessary as there is little or no game in it & pritty near as much fish!

The Mashkiegons had been here but a few moments when Ocs young son arrives here with some meat & two little Boys belonging to the Duck – They give me for news that Old Nanjobe died four days after they left us at Tête-aû-Chien! They left all their Children very sick & but little hopes of their recovery –

40 Ayagon's leather lodge of the previous season, which he had sold to Nelson.
41 Donald Sutherland, one of the HBC traders from York Factory, spent the four seasons 1807–11 near the mouth of Great Black River (now Mukutawa River), in the north basin of Lake Winnipeg. See his sketch map, HBCA, B.16/e/2, fo. 3d, 4; reproduced in Ruggles 1991, Plate 27. This was now the only HBC presence on the lake.
42 John Dougald Cameron had been a clerk in the Nipigon department for some years, but in 1811 he was put in charge of the Lake Winnipeg department. Louis Perusse, a Lake Winnipeg engagé, may have been a close relative of Nelson's wife, which would explain Nelson's interest in this news: see Appendix C.

Mond. 15ᵗʰ. About 9 O'Clock last night our people arrive from River Dauphine with 50 kegs of Potatoes, the produce of 5 Kegs sown – we should have had upwards of a hundred Kegs had not Sᵗ Germain & his cursed band fed near a month upon them which is much more than half the Garden they pulled up – Mashkiegons are drunk & the Devil is at play some times among them – Morpion &c return after I give a little debt out for the Duck – hazy & misty.

Tues 16ᵗʰ. Brochets step son being out yesterday a hunting towards the small Lake above seen several white fish in the rapids near here. Today I send the men to set a net wherein they immediately take 3 besides other fish – The remainder of the indians take debt and set off with a little Courage rum that I give them as usual – Very cold – in short usual weather.

Wednes 17ᵗʰ. Cû-Levé, Brochet, His step son, & Mr. Belly come down this way; the three former going into the bay of Tête-au-Pichou – & the latter towards small tête au Brochet. The wind is high & the weather Cold & hazy I get them to dam the river at the usual place intirely across leaving a small hole with a bed of small hoes [holes?] for the fish to come in at – This is called [a] puise – I call it pond [pound] – or fish cage.

/32/ Thurs. 18ᵗʰ October 1810. Yesterday in our whitefish net we take two – last night 3 & this morning 5 – & this afternoon I send Desrocher & Larocque to set a net near the Lake as this white fish comes from above – Old Brochet fixes the door of our pond or cage in such a manner as to prevent the fish going [out] when in⁴³

Frid. 19ᵗʰ. Very Cold, We take many fish in our pond last night, but only one white fish in our net above & a few pike & Pikeral very windy prevents the Belly going off as he has a very small canoe – The men rebegan [began again?] to chop yesterday.

Satur. 20ᵗʰ. Remarkably fine weather for the season; for it is warm & we have plenty of summer flies – Yesterday 180, today 190 fish in our pond or Puise, making altogether 370.

Sund 21ˢᵗ. As fine weather as yesterday we take 330 fish.

Mond 22ⁿᵈ. Having previously prepared Larocque (his whore & bastard)⁴⁴ & Alard set off for River Dauphine with our four nets to put 3,000 whitefish [in] as they are easier brought home being lighter &

---

43 The entry points for the fish trap were funnels made of sticks, wide at the outer ends and narrow at the inner, so that the fish could come in easily but not find their way out.

44 This is an unusually contemptuous remark for Nelson to make about a "country" mar-riage, and one wonders what provoked it.

together c'est à dire ils sont enfilé[45] – The weather turns bad & snowy immediately with a terrible NNwest wind which makes the water rise here to such a degree, that altho' our Pond is in a considerable long (& pritty steep) rapid, yet it within a very few inches eaqual with the upper part of our dam – Larocque is surely wind & weather bound. I pity him on account of his Child for he has no tent & but very few blankets. We take last night 290 fish (besides a cat fish which is the first we take here – altho' the place is mean & scabby we take enough white fish to eat) making a total of 997 fish-!!! say 1,000.

Tues. 23ᵈ. Pritty mild today – we hang up 300 fish.

Wednes 24ᵗʰ. Pritty cold this evening – Old Nez Corbin & his woman arrive here in Canoe with 20 Ducks that he gives me – I have never yet in my life seen any thing to eaqual these ducks for the fat. This old fellow tells me that Pittites Couilles, Moose Eyes, Kieshkieman, The Soninlaw [Le Gendre], & Mr. Belley (for he has gone up this river unperceived by /33/ us & Contrary to what he told me) are gone to a small Lake that is at some Distance from here – He tells me also to have heard the Sauteux's fire several times, which he takes to be upon Monotagueé river – for the Distance is not great across land to go there – What difference between these people! 'Tis now but a very few days since the Mashkiegons have left me – yet before they leave their Canoes to go up inLands they have gathered these few ducks to give me – as they imagine not to kill any large animals this sometime yet to come – The Sauteuxs or Mr. Ayagon & his band have been by far better treated by me than these others, yet they have not had the heart to bring me the least mouthfull of anything, altho' they've passed the fall quite near me & have killed many large animals besides a great quantity of game, as appears by their campments – I shall probably pay [repay] this in my turn – We hang 250 fish.

Thurs 25ᵗʰ. It snowed amasing hard all night & a part of yesterday, & to-day I give old Nez Corbin 7 half pints of mixed rum, but he drinks them here with the old women – Last night's snow & Cold has filled up our puise in such a manner that we have not taken near 50 fish! –

---

45 Nelson was sending men to fish at the whitefish spearing place in Dauphin River, which in the previous seasons had been his main source of food for the winter. The total weight of 3,000 whitefish, if about the amount that Nelson caught at Dauphin River in previous seasons, would be about 6 tons, so many trips would be needed to bring them all closer to the post. There, they would be hung up to dry on cords passed through the gills (enfilé = threaded).

Frid. 26th. Nothing new only that we take 100 fish more. The ice upon the river below here is almost strong enough to bear people upon it. Nez-Corbin who does not set off ' till this morning, from here is obliged to leave his canoe at a small distance from us & go home a foot – Cold & nasty –

Satur 27th. We go upon the ice – We take 144 fish –

Sunday 28th. Cold but fine weather, that is Clear & sunshine – I go down to the Lake upon skates & find that considering the season & even the Climate of this place there was a good deal of new ice gathered in this bay, besides great quantities of it that appear'd toward Mashkieg islands & outwards –

Mond 29th. Clear & Cold & Nothing new – Having taken 100 fish yesterday besides 150 today makes altogether 1154 & the other 1000 Exclusive [sic] –

/34/ Tuesday 30th October 1810. Nothing new.

Wednes 31st. Very fine weather & we take plenty of fish.

Thursday 1st November. Nothing droll we keep holiday.

Frid 2nd. Pritty cold yet fine weather & very calm, which certainly makes the Lake take much sooner than it would otherwise – I was yesterday below (at the Lake about 10 or 15 acres from here) & walked upon its ice tho' not far, we see ice out in the deep as far as the eye can extend; yet not sufficiently strong to bear people upon it – This I suppose is why Laroque & th'other don't come for I'm certain that River Dauphine bay is not yet taken, but I think the river D[auphin] is so.

Saturday 3d. Nothing new – Sunday 4th. As yesterday.

M.5 T.6 W.7 Thurs 8 Frid 9 & Saturday 10th. Nothing new all this week past, except I relate that yesterday about sunset on coming home (having been out all day for wood for trains) I seen a <u>white</u> <u>Crow</u>. The weather has been pritty fine this week past – except today that it begins to snow very much. The ice is pritty strong upon the Lake now for I walked a good piece upon it – It is taken in every direction as far as the eye can extend – No one comes yet –

Sund 11th. There fell in the Course of last night near a foot of snow, but today the weather is Clear, Cold & Windy – We yet take many fish, particularly what the french call Laciesh.*

Mond. 12th November 1810. 'Tis or at least to night it will be a year since our Stranger [Nelson's daughter Mary] arrived!

Tues 13th. Very fine weather & that's all the news.

Wednes 14. Windy. Thurs 15th. Windy – Cloudy & Cold.

Frid. 16ᵗʰ. Most terrible stormy weather. The wind blows with so much violence (all day from the North) that our Chimnies smoke so much that we're obliged to have our doors continually open which is the cause of our enduring no small addition of cold & snow & smoke, smoke & smoke to almost all eternity I beleive a pritty large red pine tree fell upon our house last night but likely it was the /35/ small end, otherwise I beleive Mr. Welles would have felt a little of its weight for it fell exactly over his bed –

Saturday 17ᵗʰ of November 1810. Nothing new.

Sund. 18ᵗʰ. Larocque not yet arriving obliges my sending off Old Desrocher & Longuetin with five slays & almost all the dogs. I'm much uneasy about Larocque – Very fine weather.

Mond. 19ᵗʰ. South wind & hard. Long before day Desrocher &c. set off – Tues 20ᵗʰ. A little snow yet fine weather –

Wednes 21ᵗʰ. By rights the men are to arrive to day, third out.

Thurs 22ⁿᵈ. About half past 3 this afternoon – Our **whole brigade** arrive with not near 200 fish, whereas they ought to have brought at least 300, but Larocque's woman being sick & unable to walk occasion's this in part, & besides there being but very little snow towards Dauphine river & none whatever to come as far as the Grand Pointe (about 6 leagues) makes all so slippy that neither dogs nor people can hardly walk upon it –

I'm sorry to find that I'll make much less this year than even last. Ayagon, his Brother, Bezette, Cu-fessé & Muffle D'orignalle with all their families have left R. Dauphine now 8 days past having been driven there by hunger; & would I daresay have died alltogether (unless the flesh of one had made food for the other), had it not been for the 350 fish my men hung up there in my old shop when they went for the potatoes – for there were no fish at all in the rapids this year as usual, they arrived at my old house hardly able to stand much less to walk – their dogs even (but 5 remaining I beleive out of upwards of 30 that they had) they were obliged to carry up the hill some days after their arrival It has cost the life of one of Old Muffle's Daughters – to such extremes were they reduced – They were arrived 4 days when Laroque arrived & he was 8 days going from here – so it was about the 25ᵗʰ of last when the indians arrived – Laroque the 30ᵗʰ.

/36/ Friday 23ⁿᵈ November 1810 – Very fine weather Long before day light I send off Welles & Alard with all the Dogs & slays again for more fish – & at the same time give them a bottle of rum & some amonition & tobacco for Ayagon with as much for Old Muffle & orders

for his eldest son to come here – a small bit of tobacco to old Cu-fessé
& Bezette to learn them to speake a little better of one[46] –

Satur 24th. Nothing new. Sunday 25th. As yesterday.

Monday 26th. I make a slay to make me a Caryole.

Tues 27th. Pritty fine weather, & this is all – all all! –

Wednes 28th. Pritty early this forenoon old Muffle D'orignialle's
second son (Le Sourd) arrives With Alard &c and near 300 whitefish – They bring a few skins with them – It seems that Old Muffle's
Daughter did not die altogether by starvation altho' I daresay that it
Greatly contributed – her death seems to be occasion'd by the same
disease as old Nanjobes, a kind of dysentry & discharge of blood thro'
the nose, ears, mouth (& eyes) – This disorder or sickness seems to be
prevalent (& catching) all over the Country.[47]

Thurs 29th. Nothing new but very mild weather.

Friday 30th. Between midnight & daylight I send off Larocque &
Longuetin to River Dauphine – The young indian [Le Sourd] goes with
them I give him some rom to cry for their departed relation (Daughter
& sister) Exceeding mild weather –

Satur. 1st December 1810. Nothing new for today but very mild
weather, "Nous tracassons [travaillons] a notre petite ouvrage
d'ordinaire."

Sund. 2nd. Very Drifty & Cold from the North yet our People arrive
with 350 fish. They bring me two Cased Cats* that were put in the
house by some of our indians (they made this trip in 2½ days –

/37/ Monday 3d. At dusk yesterday Cu-Leve & Brochets step son
arrive from their lodges this morning, that is in the bay of River
Monotaguée – They appear not to have starved any since last fall : their
hunt however is not Great – This morning I sent off Welles with them –
The weather is Clear but has not been so cold all this year as it is to-day.

Tues. 4. I send off Desrocher & Alard before day to Fisher River in
quest of Old Morpion &c. (see 14 october) I am rather uneasy about
them – At Broad day light I send off Laroque & Longuetin for fish to
River Dauphine – Very Cold, I remain alone only with the women

Wednes. 5th. Amasing Cold I am almost afraid that our Dutch[man]
Welles is frozen as he is not yet arrived –

---

46 Nelson added "Curse them," but crossed it out.
47 The symptoms suggest a viral hemorrhagic fever, signs of which should be traceable elsewhere in fur trade records, but are scarce for these years. Hackett (2002) does not mention
any such illness in 1810, but also notes the paucity of the records.

Thursday 6th. About 2 hours after Welles arrives this morning from Cu Leve's lodge (with 3 bladders of bears Grease, 6 or 7 Pieces of dry meat, & about 20 skins in Plux's [*plus*] or furs), Mr. Cameron arrives bringing with him Fleuri ronds & Baptiste Latour from Fort Alexander this being the third days travelling from that place – News – none of any extraordinary, except that <u>Mr.</u> Heney passed last fall at Fort Alex[r] in a light boat from Albany Factory to surperseed Poor old John M[c]Kay in the service of the HBay's Company. What rascally treatment is here – Heney no longer able to find any Employment in any service whatever in this Country on account of his theivish, roguish Principles, deserted by every one & not daring to return to Canada (where his Character is well known) for fear of being branded, was taken up by M[c]Kay merely upon Charity's sake when he immediately fell to work upon planning his benefactor's ruin, & finally accomplished by going to England with Vincent, who both making their Complains (both against M[c]Kay, & Mr. Hudson [Hodgson] the Governor of Albany factory) to a Company almost /38/ as ignorant of the (transactions of their servants in this Country as I am of the Court of S[t] Cloude – where in appearance they were listned to – since both M[c]Kay & the Governor were both surpseeded. In my opinion if Heney & Vincent dont give their employers un Coup de pied de Cochon (before a very long time) it will be more owing to the want of some <u>ingredients</u> than any real want in themselves Particularly Heney[48] –

Frid. 7. Late at night Desrocher arrived from Fisher river, but could find no satisfactory marks[49] – Laroque & Longuetin arrive with 4 slay loads of fish –

Satur. 8. By some unaccountable mistake I find Myself four days behind hand in date with Mr. Cameron for it is now according to his account, & as I find myself by the age of the Moon, to be very exact.[50]

48 John Hodgson had been the HBC's chief at Albany since 1800, and was indeed replaced by Thomas Vincent in 1810; for a biography see Brown (1987a). Whatever Hugh Heney may have told Cameron he was going to do, he did not displace John McKay, as that officer had died at Brandon House on 6 July 1810 (McCloy 1983). Heney was not a success. In charge at Brandon House in 1810–11, he had to deal with hostility from his own men, and when assigned instead to the less important Pembina House in 1812–13, he fell out with Miles Macdonell, governor of the Red River Colony. Heney left the country for England with the HBC's fall ship in 1813: see HBCA Biographical Sheet.
49 Durocher had been looking for marks or signs that Old Morpion might have left around Fisher River, as he had not been heard from since he left Tête-au-Brochet on 15 October.
50 Although Nelson was often a day wrong in his reckoning, this was a remarkable error, probably explained by his habit, when there was little or nothing to record, of writing up his

Wednes. 12th Thurs. 13th. About 2 O'Clock this morning Mr·
Cameron sets off leaving me an invitation for Christmass – Mr.
Cameron appear'd to be very unwell while here which I beleive is in
some measure why he set off so soon – He has very fine weather.

Frid. 14th. Rien de nouvau or nothing new. We are making preparations for our intended journey.

Satur 15. Very Cold weather & drifty – Nothing new –

Sund 16th. This Morning early I send off Laroque & Alard to Cu
lèvé's lodge for meat if there be any there for our new-Year's day; for I
dont expect to get any from any of my other indians before that time.

Monday 16–Tues. 18th. It blows very hard & drifts much

Wednes 19th. Very fine but pritty cold this evening. Laroque is not yet
arrived –

/39/ Thursday 20th. We wait anxiously 'till night expecting Laroque's
arrival – but he does not come.

Frid. 21st. About midnight (last night) Laroque arrives very heavily
loaded – & we consequently prepare for our departure & set off.

Satur 22 Sund 23d. I arrive this evening at Fort Alexr where I find Mr.
Cameron with all his family in the best of health & spirits – No one is
yet arrived here except myself – therefore no news

Monday 24. Very bad weather.

Tues 25th Wednes 26th December Thurs 27th. While all hands were
busy dancing Mr. [John] Dougald Cameron arrived with two men &
Bousquet from Lac-Du-huard about 10 O'Clock last night. No news
of any Consequence unless I remark the old Predominant Complaint
of this Department – "Starvation," consequently the indians are doing
nothing – which is particularly the case this year in this department
– even at Mr· Crebassa's at White river,51 where there are plenty of
Moose, his hunter is almost dead with hunger –

Tuesday 1st January 1811. Mr. Crebassa having arrived here last
Sunday, We passed Newyear's pritty merrily – Cold –

Wednes 2nd. We all prepare for our Departure

Thurs 3d. We set off a little before day & having mistaken our road
in bad weather we encamp near midnight. Frid. 4th. To our Great
surprise this morning we found ourselves about 3 leagues from Red
River having travelled our backs towards Mr. Crebassa's for more than

---

journal several days at a time. He now seems to have consulted an almanac, perhaps one that
Duncan Cameron had, to check his dates with the phase of the moon.

51 Perhaps a joke, as Crebassa was wintering at Broken River as usual.

three leagues – We resume our road & very late we arrive in Company with his grace at his house – Now being very tired as well as our dogs I remain here all day to-day (Satur the 5ᵗʰ) when Mr. Creb's hunter arrives with his family for something to eat!!

Sund 6ᵗʰ. Pritty fine weather & at day light we set off & camp God Knows where – Mond 7ᵗʰ We set off & camp at about 7 leag[u]es from our house in the same place where we camped the 21ˢᵗ having left 8 pike, upon which we fed our dogs who are much in want –

/40/ Tuesday 8ᵗʰ January 1811. Very Cold & windy which prevents our setting off very early. However having wrapped ourselves in our Buffaloe robes & Blankets we arrive pritty early at our own home (Tête-aû-Brochet) here I find all well – The Mashkiegons have been in, & between 6 of them have not given me half a pack their hunt Consists of 10 bear skins, 2 beavers, 4 otters, 4 martins & 2 Cased Cats – What fine hopes for a New Year!!! I found Old Gagnan at the house, Laroc having gone for him the day before yesterday to small beaver Creek where he was starving almost to death he remains a few days to fatten – The Coldest weather this winter was Sunday the 30ᵗʰ of Decʳ – at break of day the thermomiter was 32½ below o. Clear & Calm – 'till about 3 in the afternoon when Mr. Crebassa arrived – His men did not freeze –

Wednes 9ᵗʰ. We pass a kind of new years day here again among ourselves – Thurs 10ᵗʰ. This morning altho' the weather is bad I send off Laroc & Alard to Cu Levé's lodge for meat, if he has any, & if not to try & kill some –

Friday 11. Yesterday very bad & drifty. To-day worse 'till noone.

Satur 12ᵗʰ. Very fine Clear & Cold. Cu Lèvé & little Couilles with Kieshkieman arrive – They bring me a little meat & only a small bear skin – Now we may see that there only wanted this junction between the Creatures to make nothing for some time – I hope that they shall soon reseperate – Laroque whom I sent off last Thurs will I suppose sleep to night at these lodges.

Sund. 13ᵗʰ. This morning I send these indians back after having made an agreement with Cû-Lève to kill me a few moose – The weather being pritty Cold they all come back rather tipsy of the rum I gave them this morning but prevent them from drinking here – Cold, Clear.

Mond 14ᵗʰ Before day light they reset⁵² off, & about 10 O Clock (dᵒ) Larocque & Alard arrive having slept at the Lodges & not less troubled for their rum – Colder

/41/ Tuesday 15ᵗʰ January 1811. This morning I send off Alard to live with Cu-Lèvé & incase he kills meat to bring me some & the news.

Wednes. 16ᵗʰ. Nothing new but calm & clear weather – how long it will last I know not – Old Gagnan who is yet here appears to have no great desire of leaving this so soon – The men draw wood all day.

Thursday 17, Friday 18ᵗʰ. Very fine weather & a south wind. The men finish drawing all the wood, which amounted at first to 44 Cords.

Saturd. 19ᵗʰ. Alard (& Mr. Belly) arrives for people to go for meat, two moose that Cu lèvé killed yesterday. He brought me the two hearts that are exceeding fat – I have not yet seen their eaqual for fatness.

Sund 20ᵗʰ. This morning long before day I send off Old Desrocher, Longuetin & Welles with 4 slays for the meat, but as that gang of Créve faims⁵³ are yet abanded [sic] with Cu leve, they eat some, therefore the slays were not so loaded as I expected – A little after sunset and about 3 hours after the men arived, Messrs. Cûléve & LeGendre arrive – They bother me so much that I could not refrain from Giving them at least a little rum, which they Carried to Gagnan's lodge, which induced the old fellow to bring me two large beaver skins to trade, which I refused not a little to the Displeasure of our old Gentleman – I however gave him half a pint of HWines. Here may be seen a true indian Character – offer to trade his debt with me & promising that he would tell nobody.⁵⁴ The weather has been so warm yesterday & today, that much snow melts even in the woods.

Mond 21ˢᵗ Tues 22ⁿᵈ. Yesterday the two indians went off & to night Brochets step-son arrives with his Lady, & Gendres mother comes for her "virgin" Daughter Le Bateuse and La miquene or Ladle⁵⁵ – I send off Alard this morning to live with Cu Lévé again. fine weather.

Wednes 23ᵈ. The old women set off except this nothing new.

Thurs 24ᵗʰ. Yesterday Brochet's step-son set off late at night.

---

52 This is the third example in this journal of Nelson inventing new verbs by putting "re-" in front of a familiar verb rather than saying "again." This quirk does not appear in the earlier journals.

53 French, crève-la-faim, down-and-out, starveling.

54 Nelson regarded old Gagnan as "belonging" to the Fort Dauphin department, and therefore refused to trade furs with him.

55 These references are obscure.

Friday 25th Saturday 26th Sund. 27th. Old Gagnan at last prepares for his hunt – they set off with 6 Slay loads of Furniture & Pike they Encamp about a mile from this – fine Weather but Cold –

Mond. 28th. Five of Mr. Cameron's men arrive here with each a slay for meat I have so little that I am afraid not to be able to load them as they require – however what is they shall have – Alard arrived but a few /42/ minutes before Mr. Cameron's people arrives. He brought me 2 loads of meat which help a little, Cu Lèvé & Old Brochet return immediately with a small keg of mixed rum that I give them Old Gagnan also comes upon a visit.

Tues. 29th Wednes 30th. Having previously prepared their loads & letters they set off for Fort Alexr – The Belly arrived yesterday with his lady &c, & today he sets off with three loads of fish to make traps; for he says that there are many martins where they now are – but he is such a liar there is no relying upon what he says – Nothing new except this more than than usual.

Thurs 31st. Early this morning I send off Laroque & Welles to River Dauphine for fish. That is, if the indians & Wolverines have not yet eat them all. I sent off Alard also to remain at Cû lévé's lodge but he met old Brochet near here who was coming for fish as they have not yet killed any thing since the 26th. Very mild – I put up our Peltries under cover of Bear skins for the number of mice here is really extraordinary.

Frid. 1st February 1811. Nothing new, but very mild weather Francoise (Desrocher's former wife) & Moose Eyes's Daughter return to their lodge. The old Brochet yesterday took a pike in Laroque's traps that were set for otters up this river – Alard & I split a birch for a slay.

Satur 2nd. Amazing mild but dull; it even rains – which is a sort of a miracle here; for I have seldom known it to rain in this Country in the winter – Lorrin's & Gagnan's sons-in law (for Old Gagnan since yesterday is encamped with the Mashkiegons) come for people to go for meat – I immediately send Longuetin & Alard off, they arrive about dusk pritty well loaded. Larocque & Welles also arrive about sunset with 190 fish they would have brought more, but the old shop where they put up their fish last fall taking fire, after they were in bed burnt one slay & three dog-harnesses intirely up they were therefore obliged to come home only with 3 slays – The fire took by negligence as usual; for as they arrived there pritty late they were obliged to make use of flambeaux's [torches], & some of its Coals I suppose falling between the flooring took fire, but was not percieved (for as we suppose after they had done loading they inadvertently put a slay over the fire) 'till it had taken to the roof also.

Sund. 3ᵈ. Wellès is employed in making new harnesses as it is his <u>own</u> that are burnt –

Mond. 4. I send Welles & Longetin for fish & Alard to Cu Levé's lodge.

/43/ Tues 5ᵗʰ February– The weather was fine yesterday but is very dirty & bad today altho' it is not Cold.

Wednes. 6ᵗʰ. As bad weather as Yesterday if not worse, yet poor Alard arrives with a little meat in spite of a foot of snow at least that fell.

Thurs 7ᵗʰ. Altho' the weather (yet) keep Chorus & time with these two days past, yet I send off Laroque with Alard for a little more of the meat that Alard left behind (for bad roads); because I am now so well acquainted with indian oeconomy – that altho' Cu-lévé killed two Moose only these few days past that but a very short time longer would be sufficient for them to give too good an account of the remainder – There has fallen & is yet busy falling so much snow that I am much afraid that our people will have enough to do [to] bring home at the utmost 20 fish per slay – As luck will have it they have plenty to eat, if L'enui does not drive Longuetin intirely mad, for his lady has such a share in his thoughts at present as almost to deprive him of the <u>whole</u> or rest of his senses!!

Frid. 8ᵗʰ. Almost as bad weather as these few days past. Laroc &c arrive with the rest of the meat which is not much – Cu Lévé is preparing very large snow shoes as it is very inconvenient without them there having fallen much above a foot of snow at this boute [sic] – I go for a slay in the woods.

Satur 9ᵗʰ. The weather is rather Colder & worse than usual; but yet Alard begs of me to let him go a head of the men with their snow shoes – I agree to let him go – he sets off without even a blanket or provisions but quite unknown to me.

Sund. 10ᵗʰ. This evening the men arrive with 200 fish upon 5 slays the quantity of snow that has fallen towards River Dauphine is really extraordinary as the men say – but perhaps their ennui makes it appear more. Alard found them in their Campment at Grand Point about sunset yesterday – the distance is about 11 leagues – Cold & snow'y.

Monday 11ᵗʰ Tuesday 12ᵗʰ. Pritty Cold but Clear & no wind at least not much.

Wednes 13ᵗʰ. About noon to day Old Nez Corbin arrives here with his youngest son from a place they call Monatàguée Lake somewhere or other on the upper part of Monotâgueé River – Ayagon & his brother are with them – But from appearances their hunt appears not to be much – CuLèvé arrives with his wife & Desrocher's "Defunt"[56] A few moments after they bring me a little meat – a moose that he killed this last Monday weather is very Cold – Old Nez Corbin left his lodge Night before last.

/44/ Thursday 14th Feby. 1811. The weather being so amasing cold that the indians dare not set off (as well as the men) I give them a little rum to drink here – Friday 15th. This morning however they set off; for the both the weather & wind have Considerably abated, altho' it is yet extreemly Cold Cu Levé sets off also – I send Alard to live in his lodge a few days, expecting him back very soon with some meat – for I am much afraid that I'll not have wherewith to load Mr. Cameron's people when they will be in again – Satur 16th Nothing new – Cold & windy – Sunday 17th. The weather is rather warmer than usual.

Monday 18th Tuesday 19th. This morning Larocque &c &c arrive & bring me consequently the hunt of these indians amounting to 42 skins[57] – Ayagon's hunt alone last year amounted to more than all this together. How rapidly are these places diminishing in every thing!! I am afraid that I'll not make 10 packs here this year, & yet make as much indeed more expences than were required to make 20 & 30 only but a few years past – The country grows poorer every day, but does not diminish the indian's wants. Far from it, the latter increases as the former diminishes – & I should not be surprised in a very few years hence to hear that some (rather many) of our indians, & in this department particularly, pass the winter in the neighbourhood of some good fish Country & go naked unless cloathed from charity or with rabit skins – & worse than this, I expect almost next year that the Company themselves will will [sic] be obliged to take care & feed some indians or see them starve at their door – Here is a fine opportunity for enlarging upon this subject any person who chuses, mais moi il faut que je me laise [for me, I must leave it].

Ayagon arrived a few minutes after the men for a little amonition, & to get his gun arranged – He made me a speech as pitiful as it was true upon poorness of the Country & their inability of maintain[in]g their families (from us). /45/ To-day (Wednes. 20th) he returns – I give him a little liquor & some tobacco; & encourage him as much as my duty & abilities will permit.

56 Durocher's former wife, known as Françoise.
57 This was the hunt made by Nez Corbin and his band, and Ayagon and his brother, at Montagao Lake: see journal entry of 13 February.

Thurs 21st. Very Mild – Near day (this last night) Laroque who was in bed with his woman & both awake got such a fright as to become intirely speechless & motionless for some time – it proceeded from the apparition of an unknown person in the house who going (with his back turned (to Laroc) towards Desrocher's bed & in a stooping position immediately turned & fell upon him as he was wishing to turn himself in his bed so as not to see it – His (Laroc.) wife was obliged to call out to Welles to make a fire – Be this as it may – the poor man passes a miserable day –

Frid. 22nd. Nothing new – mild weather – Satur. 23d. Desrocher who goes to Little Tête-aû-Brochet about 1½ leagues from this to make traps fell upon an indians track but just passed – as the track came towards the house Desrocher followed it when to his surprise (the track coming out upon the Lake near his own of the morning) the indian returned upon Desrocher's road as we suppose to enquire of Des. what may be his news – I suppose this to be the Belly as he was to remain to make traps, where he was at the time Longuetin & Alard went for meat the 2nd of this month, & the others were to make traps in Fisher river bay. Mild.

Sund. 24th. Since yesterday it begins to melt before our doors.

Monday 25th. Tuesday 26. Nothing new. Mild Dull weather.

Wednes 27th. Thurs. 28th. For the last of this month the weather is cold & stormy, yet the sun shines. Longuetin sleeps out with his Lady a making traps. Larocque & his Lady arrived yesterd. having slept out one night also upon the same errand.[58]

Friday 1st March 1811 – As Alard does not yet come, I send off Welles in quest of him – it is now 15 days that he is with Cu-Lèvé, which makes me think that they are either starving or some accident has happen'd him – I know not what keeps him from coming – About 2 hours after Welles sets off, Latourelle, Latoure & Rondo arrive from Mr. Camerons for meat – But all that I have here together is not able to load one slay – What a distance are these people come for nothing! News in their quarter appears pritty good in the pack way at least – particularly at Mr. Crebasssa's as le Blanc says who is come with Mr. C's men.

/46/ March. Saturday 2nd. Nothing new.

Sunday 3d. Very bad weather. This afternoon Welles arrives having slept out these two nights & continually travelled to no end, for he

---

58 These errands may have also been a chance for some marital privacy.

could not find out Alard. However – this trip was yet useless, for Poor Alard arrived with old Brochet about sunset, having left the lodge this morning – Cû lévé has not yet kill'd a moose since he left this (the 15th of Feby.), Altho he gives himself much trouble – he was off again this morning but was to sleep out – Longuetin arrived yesterday from his traps having slept out last night with his wife!! –

Mond. 4th. Very Cold & pritty windy from the North, yet Mr. Cameron's men set off with two moose thighs & 14 Pieces of dry meat – which is all that I have got –

Tues 5th. This morning Old Brochet sets off & Alard goes again with them. I give them a little flour, rise, Potatoes & 7 whitefish – The weather is Clear & pritty warm considering.

Wednes. 6th. Thurs 7th. Alard arrives this evening bringing me 2 ribs a Briscet & the snoute of a moose that Cu-lévé killed in that terrible bad weather last, people are to return in four days.

Frid. 8th. Having nothing to-do I take Alard with me to make traps we travel about 2 leagues in the woods from the house but do not see a single martin track – How this place has diminished – but a very few years since, when Ferguson & Campbell winterd here (1806–7), there people took plenty of martins – but I dont beleive that we will take a hundred here between us all, this year, altho' the people make traps at a Great distance from here, What will become of the indians in a (very) few years – may it please God that I be out of the Country before that time.

Satur 9 Sund 10. Very mild (& fine) for the season.

Mond 11th. Nothing new today. I send off Welles to Cu-lévé's lodge with a bottle of HWines & ½ fathom tobacco. Laroque & Alard with my permission go to make traps. The weather is exceeding fine & mild. Much snow melts. /47/ Last Thursday Longuetin & Welles arrive from Pigeon river, having sent them yesterday – they bring no news from that quarter – they saw neither vestige, track or anything else as they tell me – how far this may be true depends upon themselves Desrocher – about 12 or 15 days since (see 23 of Feby) seen a fresh indian track as he told me – last Wednesday I sent off Larocque upon that track but as he could not find Desrocher's path was obliged to come back – the next day (Thursday) I sent Derocher with him, but this track turned out to be his own, so stupid is this old fellow that he did not know his own road or even snow shoes track –

Tuesday 12th. Very mild – indeed rainy – Larocque &c arrive – taking already four martins in their traps since yesterday – all appearance of a crust if it freezes.

Wednes 13th. Welles arrives but today, Cû-lèvé is yet in his unlucky-ness – however the day before yesterday he shot a large (she) moose, & altho it threw up much blood yet he was not able to get it – he intends returning after it – It has rained pritty hard a Good part of Yesterday & last night but not yet sufficient to make a Good Crust

Thurs 14th. Old Desrocher goes to sleep out a trap making –very mild –

Frid. 15th Satur 16th. Exceeding mild all day – the snow melts much – Welles with my permission goes to sleep out also – he has a gun & a little amunition in case he should fall upon the path leading to the Mashkiegons which he is to follow; for I want to know what they are about; & to get some meat from them if they have any – – Quite late this evening Le Sourd & one of his brothers arrive from River Dauphine at which place they have encamped the day before yester-day: they appear not to be over stocked with furs – Cu fessé is a little beyond There are people again this year at the Falle-de-Pardrie & in all apperance are doing exceeding well – Richard & his family are there – Mr. Halcroe is master[59]

Sund 17th. Very mild.

Monday 18. The weather being too bad they remain – We seen 2 wolves quite near the house.

Tues 19th. Early this I send off Larocque, who is to return from Old Muffles today Welles whom I send also is to go to old Cu fessé's near Lake St. Martin; & in the mean time is to Carry a letter to Mr. Halcro from me – The wolves & Carraboux's[60] breake almost all the mens traps.

Wednes 20th. Larocque arrives quite late at night with the hunt of Old Muffle his five sons & La Bezette amounting to 84 skins, W[t] 51[lbs]. Desrocher & Alard sleep out.

Thurs 21st Frid. 22nd. Nothing new, Desrocher & Alard arrive. Larocque has sore eye.

Satur 23[d]. I send off Alard to Cu-lèvé's lodge to see for meat if there be any – for I have nothing at present to receive Mr. Cameron should he come – Larocque & Longuetin go to sleep out a martin hunting – but altho' they went several leagues from this they could not so much as find one single track – they consequently come back.

59 Joshua Halcro was again the master at Partridge Crop, but he was now benefiting from the skills of young François Richard, whom Nelson respected as an interpreter and hunter. Halcro's wife was Françoise Lorrin, whose sister had once been married to François Richard, before her father took her away and gave her to Duncan Cameron. For Halcro, see Appendix D.

60 Probably an error for *carcajoux*, wolverines.

/48/ Sunday 24ᵗʰ March 1811 – This afternoon Alard arrives with a good slay load of meat of Carriboeuf principally. Brochets step son arrives also with his wife & Kieshkiemann: they also bring me a little meat & a few peltries – but the hunt of these indians this year is shameful; & one would be apt to think from their doings that they act in this manner purposely! – Brochet's step-son, Moose-eyes, & Kishkiemann had pitched off together in the beginning of February towards Monotagueé river & beyond – within perhaps three short leagues of River Dauphine: they killed between them 6 Carriboeufs & one moose – hardly any martins. Le Sourd being yesterday a moose hunting fell upon their road & followed it to Cu levé's lodge, where he arrived just as they were pitching thier tent. He reports that the German [Jean-Baptiste Welles] had a sore leg – but whether he was yet at their lodge or not I could not learn.

Mond 25ᵗʰ. I send Alard back to live with Cu Lèvé a few days. Fine but Cold.

Tues 26ᵗʰ Wednesday 27ᵗʰ. I arrived at the house (here) having been out to make a large trap for the wolves. I found that Mr. Cameron had arrived but just a few moments before. Mr. Crebassa & Seraphin were with him – Everyone is well but the shabbiest returns ever made in this department will be this year, unless the indians change much in almost every respect, particularly their hunting.

Alard arrives this afternoon from Cu levé's lodge with the meat of a Carriboeuf he killed yesterday – he sends me word that I am not to expect any more meat.

Thurs 28ᵗʰ Frid. 29ᵗʰ. Nothing new, we impatiently wait Welles' arrival – it obliges me to send Larocque after him.

Saturday 30ᵗʰ. Early this morning Larocque sets off. Old Nez Corbin & one of his twins arrive here – their lodge is at no great distance from here. He brings me 4 Pieces of dry meat – Between them all they have 35 skins in furs. Old Morpion who has been at this lodge 5 days since, asks for people to go to the Fisher River at the entrance of which he will be in 6 days hence – he has made by far a better hunt than any of my other indians this year – It is 30 skins.⁶¹

Sunday 31ˢᵗ. Altho' Welles does not arrive Mr. Cameron sets off at broad day light – I shall take him the news of Welles's retardment as soon as I shall be informed of the occasion of it: Old Nez Corbin & his son return.

---

61 Nelson would have been relieved to have news of Morpion, not having heard anything of him since mid-October, although he had sent men to look for him on 4 December.

Monday 1st April 1811. About 9 O'Clock this night Welles &
Larocque arrive – Larocque met him yesterday – Near Lake St Martin
coming home – his retardment was occasioned by Mr. Halcroes not
arriving at his place 'till the day before yesterday – he was on a visit
to Mr. McGillis[62] at Fort Dauphin – No news of any particular consequence in those quarters – the 20th of March they killed several swans
& bustards at Falle de Pardix.[63]

Tues 2nd. I send off Alard this morning to see after his dogs that
left /49/ us yesterday, & as they are accustomed to go often to
Cu-Lèvé's lodge I send Alard there – This afternoon he arrives having met old Brochet about half ways from their lodge with his dogs
& a little meat. I therefore prepare immediately for my departure
– Kiewaykoabow one of old Nez-Corbin's son's arrives with 30 odd
skins, the whole of their peltries.

Wednes 3d. Before day light I set off taking Alard & Longuetin with
me 4 dogs upon my slay or Caryole & 6 upon the mens – We went at
an extraordinary rate 'till Tete au-Chien (about 8 leagues from here)
when we with some difficulty proceeded about 4 leagues further to Mr.
Camerons encampment from my Place[64] – our slays were quite worn
through[65] we were therefore obliged to put a sort of runners to them –
Here Ausgé & Bétourné arrive, Mr. Crebassa sends them for meat at a
little distance from here.

Thurs 4th. We arrive at Mr. Crebassas [at Broken River] – and about
2 hours after his hunter the eldest of deceased Nanjobe's sons was
brought here dead – he was killed by his own brother who is a little
younger than himself – he received two stabs in his stomach & another
full in his heart – this was occasioned in a drunken frolick – he [the
murderer] immediately set off to where two of Mr. Crebassa's men
were about one league & a half in the woods & beyond the lodge
– he then asked for meat saying he was hungry & told the men that
his brother had been stabbed by another indian, & as they were yet
quarreling he came off, but while he was yet speaking his own brother
in law arrived & snapped his Gun twice in the stomack of the other,

---

62 Angus McGillis, a longtime clerk in the Fort Dauphin department. The other McGillis in
the NWC, his brother Hugh, was a NWC partner, stationed at Fond du Lac this year (Wallace
1934, 264–5, for the arrangements for 1810–11).
63 The appearance of these birds (Canada geese) was an unusually early sign of spring.
64 Duncan Cameron was not here; this was the place where he had camped on his route
back to Fort Alexander in December.
65 Probably because the recent melt had exposed rocks on the trail.

who sat just as quietly as if nothing at all was going on, altho' the two men were struggling with the indian for the Gun who immediately let his hold & seized his knife, but was again misfortunately or fortunately prevented by the men, when he began to cry & make the Greatest lamentations saying "French people let me kill that dog – he has killed his brother; he must die; he ought to die" – the other all this time remained quite quiet untill little Le Blanc sent him off.

Frid, 5th. At two this afternoon we arrive at Mr. Cameron's log [lodge, i. e. Fort Alexander] where we were received in the most polite manner – 'tis surprising to see the Great difference in the weather between these two places – here every thing has the appearance of a pritty advanced spring whereas at Tete au Brochet we see all as if we were yet in January – We seen a Gull today.

/50/ Mond 8th. We are now degraded by fine weather – what a difference between this weather & that of last Christmas.

Tues 9th. About 9 A M. we arrive at Mr. Crebassa's, having taken our leave of our very kind & good Master Mr. Cameron about 11 last night[66] – We should have arrived about day light this morning had the Lake been good but there was such a depth of water that we were often apprehensive of upseting in our Caryoles – Then eat Geese the first that I have tasted this year –

Thurs- 11th. About 10 O'Clock last night I set off & early this morning we encamp at the same place where I slept with Ausgé &c we met LeBlanc near here returning home with rather better than 30 beaver skins he had traded with Old Morpion's eldest son[67]

Friday 12. Good Friday About 9 this morning I arrive at home where I find all well with a little appearance of spring. Pilles-Cauilles [Petites Couilles] & Le Ventre [The Belly] are here – the former remains here intirely, for his wife has such a sore knee as not to be able to walk[68] – the other comes upon an errand – a little before day in the Isle a la Cache or birch island I found Lorrins son in law & old Gagnian going to bloody river.

Saturday 13th. Nothing new: today Cu Lévé & his brigade arrive leaving their things at the point a la Fremboise from whence they intend to take the traverse to Mashkieg islands & then to Pigeon River

66 The purpose of this visit, at an unusual time of year, is never stated.
67 Le Blanc was one of Crebassa's men. Thus, Old Morpion's son had given his trade to Broken River.
68 See entry of 19 April for more on this woman's injury.

where they mean to live upon Sturgeon & pay the remainder of their debts in rats [muskrats] if they can.

Sunday Easter – 14th April – Nothing new but mild weather.

Mond. 15th. Larocque sets off to make his spring hunt towards the Rivieres aux Sables near the Detour where he spent last spring; & I doubt not but that he will yet make a hunt eaqual to the best of my indians, so careless are they become this year about their debts & future arrangements – but each shall be recompensed according to his due – Lorrin's son-in-law arrives here – he tells me that his lodge is now at the Pointe aux Lievres near Tête-aû-Chien & bloody river – he tells me that there was a great firing there yesterday & last night – he thinks it is /5 1/ some new indians that are but lately arrived there – this makes me prepare Old Desrocher & Alard with some goods silver wares &c to trade with them if there be any – however I doubt much of it at present, for our women tell us that at the lodges here he told the women he came in a fright, thinking it was N'anjobe's son who had been to kill old Gagnian & the others[69] – Old Nez Corbin arrives this afternoon with Kiewaykoabow [his son] & their women – they bring me 13 Geese & 1 swan & 7 otters & 2 martins – He tells me that he has heard Ayagon fire several times, near where they left their canoes last fall with old Muffle D'orignialle – I suppose I may expect this Gentleman in soon for he is no enemy to HWines

Tuesday 16th. I send off Desrocher as aforesaid & Welles to Fisher river in quest once more of Old Morpion – for he did not see him the first time he went[70] altho' he went some distance up the River – I ordered Longuetin last night to go with the German [Welles] but I was surprised to find this morning that he was yet here – his reasons were – that Welles would not have him go – Cû Lèvé &c &c set off!! What wonders to be expected!

Wednes 17. At Day light this morning Desrocher arrives & prooves my suspicions to be but too true, for there was no one there nor did the indians fire hardly a single shot – what a Confounded rascal this must be.[71]

Thurs 18th Altho' the wind was Sout[h] almost the whole of Good

---

69 Some kind of feud, but nothing more is heard of it. Perhaps it explains why Gagnian, whom Nelson regarded as one of the Fort Dauphin hunters, had spent the winter so far to the east.

70 See entry of 4 December.

71 Durocher's expedition had been based on Le Gendre's false report of a new Indigenous hunting band towards Tête-au-Chien.

friday which [wind] according to the mens account ought to last 40 days yet the weather was very raw last evening & freezes pritty hard during the night.

Frid. 19th. Welles arrives about noon from Fisher River – he has made this trip without success – he could not find out the indian. During this afternoon old Nez-Corbin's two twins both arrive one brings me 6 Geese & 2 Swans – the other comes to live with Pitites-Couilles as this indian's wife is extreemly sick & reduced of a small gash with the corner of an ax she gave herself on the knee this winter, & is not yet healed – the wound is stopped up, is blue, Green & yellow & black, while matter gathers upon her thigh & leg, & renders it extreemly painful – Yet this poor woman endures it all with less trouble & pain than one would think; being in a damp (rather wet) place hardly anything to shelter them, & the least gust of wind covering her head (particularly) with smoke, ashes, feathers, chips, & God knows what – besides this I say this poor woman has a Child of about a month & a half old which she must nurse & suckle.

Satur 20th. Nothing new – the ice is sufficiently strong for us to skate, both this morning & this evening.

/52/ Sunday 21st April 1811. Pitites Couilles & KiewayKoabow [one of Nez Corbin's sons] go a hunting. Nécowatch returns to his fathers lodge – very cold for the season.

Mond 22nd. I send off Longuetin & Welles to Old Nez Corbins lodge for a load of Geese – this even[ing] Longuetin arrives with 5 – Welles remains to be home tomorrow as the men are out a hunting – Pitites C. & Kieway &c arrive they bring 3 Geese & 1 Otter – the whole of their hunt.

Tuesday 23. Welles arrives with three Geese, the indians being unsuccessful yesterday. It snow'd during the course of the night & part of this morning –

Wednes 24th. Very cold & this is all – Wind, north-North East & East.

Thurs 25th. Pitites Couilles & Kiewaykoabow give me each 2 Geese –

Friday 26th. Old Nez Corbin arrives here with his family (that is his wife) he intends making a canoe – for it will be yet sometime before the small lakes above here will be fit for hunting rats [muskrats], which is their only resource for the remainder of this season –

Saturday 27th Sunday 28th. Nothing new – the old Story.

Monday 29th. Old Morpion not yet arriving, & fearing some accident happening him I send Alard once more to Fisher River &

Kiewaykoabow with him with orders to search in every direction for him Little Couilles sets traps in an island out here for beaver.

Tues 30th. The weather was very mild yesterday & today. Many flocks of wild Geese pass. We made up some of our peltries yesterday into two packs.

Wednes 1st May. Today made up three packs & have yet rather better than one more yet remaining, exclusive of about 70^{lbs} weight at Mr. Crebassas – What miserable returns for such a number of indians as I have here! It is scandalous; & I now firmly beleive that it was a made up bargain between them last fall not to do anything this year – because they had no one to winter at their fav'rite place River Dauphine. I gave out upon debt last fall 960 skins[72] among the whole of them; & except Cu-fèssé & LaBezette every one of the others were able only with little exertions to pay the whole of their debts & trade something besides. But the stubborn & obstinate temper of an indian is able, indeed prefers rendering himself & family pitiful in the extreme, if he thinks by that means of injuring only a little those whome he supposes to be authors of his troubles & miseries – Some of my indians deserve to be starved; & if an opportunity offers I may perhaps do it.

Nez Corbins young son arrives from Monotàgueé river where he has been a spring hunting; but as that river is not yet free of ice he only bro't me 2 otters & 2 swans – He says that Le Sourd returned yesterday from there with three otters & 2 swans, but was to be back in a very few days with a Canoe. Kiewaykoabow & Alard return from fisher river, but as there was so much water in the woods, they could not reach the first forks of the River – they consequently bring no news, either of vestiges, marks or signs – &c. &c., as this began, it ends –

End of journal.

---

72 That is, trade goods valued at 960 *plus* or beaver equivalents.

8

Summary of Nelson's Letters to His Family, 1811–1812, with an extract from *Reminiscences*

Although Nelson remained on Lake Winnipeg until 1813, we have no journals for the next two years. Seven long letters from Nelson, to his parents and siblings at Sorel, do survive among the Nelson Papers from this period, amounting to about 18,000 words, but they have little information about his fur trade activities.

The first letter, to his sister Rebecca, is dated "Lake Ounipique June 4th 1811," and was written at the end of his first season at Tête-au-Brochet, a few weeks after the last journal ends. The letter is on a single sheet of Radway-type paper, folded to make four pages each 20.5 cm high x 16 cm wide. Most of this letter was about food. At one point, Nelson rather spoiled his description of how plentiful the whitefish were by likening their numbers to maggots in a carcass. He was starting to think of a future outside the fur trade, for he expressed the hope that the family had managed to buy a farm for him, in which case he would come down as soon as he could. This letter was written in time to go out to Fort William with the canoe brigades, and then down to Canada.

The rest of the letters, written during the season of 1811–12, are addressed to his parents. Someone had pointed out to him that, although there were very few opportunities for sending letters to Canada from the Upper Country, there was no reason why letters could not be written whenever time permitted, then kept until they could be sent. This realization triggered a spate of letter writing. Nelson wrote three letters between 3 November and 22 December 1811, then another dated 9 February 1812. They are all on a single gathering of seven sheets of Radway-type paper, folded and nested to make a booklet of 28 pages, each 31.5 cm high x 20 cm wide.

These letters show that he had passed part of the summer of 1811 at Fort Alexander, and was again wintering at Tête-au-Brochet. He had little hope of success in trade, for the country was trapped out. The letters go on at length about various subjects, sometimes almost as a stream of consciousness, in which Nelson lost his train of thought, had no compunction about admitting it, and went on to something else. Most of the contents are philosophical musings, but along the way, he mentioned that his interpreter (unnamed) had been in the Upper Country for some thirty years, and had a good store of anecdotes. Some of these probably ended up in Nelson's *Reminiscences* later. He expressed the view that very few who entered the fur trade made a fortune out of it, but that most ended up indebted to the company to the extent of several years' wages.

George Nelson and Mary Ann's second child, Jane, was born at "Pike head River" (Tête-au-Brochet) on 10 November 1811, though the event is not mentioned in the letters. We know her birthday from the record of her baptism, at Christ Church, William Henry (Sorel), following her father's return to Canada in 1816.

In a "footnote" to one of his letters, Nelson provided an account of developments at Fort Alexander, which includes information not otherwise available. This account is printed below.

The country was very rich in animals of all kinds, but in after years, they began to be more scarce, & the Indians consequently withdrawing to a greater distance, & fish being very scarce, rendered it almost as terrible as before; but in the year 1805 Mr. Charles Ermatinger saved 15 or 18 Kegs of potatoes he got from red river, which have now so increased with, turnips, (Choux de Siame)[1] &c. &c. & barley, that with a fishery lately found, they begin to shift pretty well. Two years ago they began to sow a little wheat; & they have last winter eat two or three times of country flour, made in a pepper mill. We begin to hope of having plenty of flour soon, for they intend to sow about 2 Kegs of wheat this year.[2] Pease also thrive pritty well & so does oats; but <u>we</u>

---

1 Rutabaga; literally, Siamese cabbage.
2 In a letter to John Dougald Cameron, dated 14 April 1813 at Lac la Pluie (Rainy Lake, where he was now the bourgeois), Duncan Cameron offered congratulations on "your success in making the First Mill and grinding flour in the North West" (Selkirk Papers, pages 8710–12). When William Laidlaw, acting for Lord Selkirk, captured Fort Alexander in January 1817, he noted the following garden produce stored there: 41½ bushels wheat, 55

apprehend that the Montreal party will not allow their carrying on agriculture with their trade, a (wise) political <u>motive</u>, for you see they eat bread as much as they please & don't feel our trouble. The winter partners are pritty stubborn when they take a point in hand, [so] we all hope they will gain. In the spring of 1806, M[r] Ermatinger got a fine house raised in the English fashion, with two stores 60 feet long d° for in this same winter he got 2 horses from Red River. A Couple of years after a cart was made & in the spring of 1810 a plough was made which is very expeditious for the sowing of 30 & 40 Kegs of potatoes. Last fall their crop was 600 & odd Kegs of Potatoes, 16 or 18 of pease, as much barley, 3 of wheat from only a very few quarts of seed. (Timothy was sowed in 1809 or 10 but is trash.) besides cabbage, turnips, Shoux de Siame, beets &c &c. .... In the winter of 1807 M[r] W[m] M[c]Kay made 64 Packs here, which to us is really astonishing. His brother M[r] Alex[r] M[c]Kay wintered here the year following, but being accustomed to another mode of trade & with other indians made but very little (not even 20). The Country is now too ruined & the indians too rascally to make any more <u>miracles</u>. T'was this year that it received its name of Fort Alexander, for 'twas before called Bas de la rivierre ouinipique, as it here discharges itself into the Lake, & this being too long a name M[r] M[c]Kay calls [it] Fort Alexr from the number of Clerks in this department by the names of Alex[r].

Nelson's fourth letter to his parents is dated 9 February 1812, with additions to 17 February. Nelson had gone to Fort Alexander for the usual Christmas visit with the new bourgeois, John Dougald Cameron. There he met his former fellow clerk Alexander Macdonell, "an old acquaintance of ours ... a young Gentleman from the Upper settlements (of Canada), who came from the Forks of the two red rivers on a visit to Mr. Cameron also." Nelson decided to accompany Macdonell back to the Forks, to see the country. Rumours had reached the NWC traders about the Earl of Selkirk's intended colony at the Forks – the first colonists were already wintering at York Factory on Hudson Bay, and would make their appearance in Red River late in August – and much of this letter is devoted to Nelson's doubts about how such a colony could possibly succeed.

---

bushels barley, 34 bushels peas, 25 bushels unthreshed oats, and 250 to 300 bushels potatoes (Selkirk Papers, page 4572).

Two more letters complete the collection. One was begun on 12 May 1812. In it he replied to family letters just received, commented on the family news, and discussed, in a rambling way, his own hopes for entering commerce in Lower Canada, and his sisters' prospects for marriage. The last letter, dated 29 May 1812, reported that he had reluctantly agreed to stay one more year in the country. He had been putting in a vegetable garden at Tête-au-Brochet, and told an anecdote about one of his best hunters, Nez Corbin, "a good old man," who wanted to get some seed potatoes, and seemed to expect that with those he could grow all of the good things that the Europeans had to eat.

All these six letters would have been sent out to Fort William at the same time, and would have reached his parents as a single package in the fall of the year 1812.

EXTRACT FROM *REMINISCENCES*

The only part of Nelson's *Reminiscences* that clearly relates to the years 1811 and 1812 is a passage containing a vivid description of Nelson's friend and customer Ayagon. This leads into a long account of an incident that began in the summer of 1811, after the last journal ends. Nelson got into some kind of confrontation with the Mashkiegon leader The Belly, and, according to Nelson, "shamed him." This then led The Belly, according to rumour, to plan revenge on Nelson. The passage quoted below (*Reminiscences*, Part 7, 288–92) begins with Nelson's description of Ayagon.

... Spring came at last, & with it my indians. Those of them who hunted on the West Side of the Lake had all came in and departed except /289/ Ayagon, who, I had many reasons to wish him not to be present when the Swampy's [Mashkiegons] come in. He was a very sensible & prudent man & very proud, Grave & reserved, as the Sauteuxs generally are, yet sociable. He conversed freely & kindly with the other tribes, always very careful to avoid offense either in his language or his manners & deportment; for, as he often told me "they are an ignorant, weake & frivolous people; but it is not their fault; they have had no opportunity of meeting with other people. How then can they know how to act with strangers; but they are good tempered & kind hearted & they have many Sensible men among them. They have always been in peace with their neighbors, we cannot wonder their being timid: we should not therefore consider them cowards & treat them with contempt. I dont like that & I often tell our people how wrong it is to despise them. I make it a point to associate as much as I can with them, to encourage them" &c.

But in the Summer of 1811 he was in Blood river, where there was a straggling family from the Nepigon Countries, bold, haughty & turbulent when they durst. They were five men, with their families, tall, stout, strapping, active fellows, with fine pleasant & open countenances; but from envy or Some other cause, left their own lands & were continually rambling, over a vast extent of country. They got some liquor, & while frolicking, one of their Sons, a fine lad too of 17 or 18 years of age stabbed Ayagon below the Shoulders, near the Spine. This very naturally created a great rumpus. The father & uncles expressed very great indignation. But he (Ayag.) calmed & pacified them by saying, "he has not killed me, compose yourselves. I will not retaliate on you for I see you are also surprised & indignant, & I know it sometimes happens that a Sensible father has a foolish Son. But bring him here that I may Speak to him & see what could have led him to such a wicked & wanton act."

. He became, however, very angry when he found him not coming, for the moment he committed the act he scampered off & could no where be found. "I am very near getting angry! what is the reason he does not come? Is this a premeditated thing? Has he any accomplices? Where are they? Let them come & look me in the eyes."

All the others Surrounded him & expressed their Sorrow & indignation in such manner as pacified him. "I am very sorry for this," continued he: "and I thought too that my language, manners & all my actions were such as to show how desirious I am to live in friendship with all people. It is a Strange way to shew ones courage. A coward & a very dangerous man may be struck in the back; but a man always strikes in the face (before). It is a sad way to begin life (a career)." And I was told this young fellow might be in among the others. Besides this, there was a rumour that the /290/ "Belly" had invited all these indians (& such of their friends as could) who were present last year when I "shamed" him, to come & see the revenge he intended taking of me. And some reports went that Ayagon had told the "Belly" he was a coward – he should have revenged himself at the moment as he had his "dag" in his hands at the time. This I positively denied for I was too well aware of his (Ayag's) prudence & discretion; but as to the rest, there was reason to apprehend. Ayagon had only a brother in law with him, quite a youth. I therefore wanted to hurry him off but all I could do was of no avail; I had to give him rum & he got drunk as a Sow. He often hinted to me when sober, but in a very delicate manner & when in liquor, plainly, that any offence or injury done to me, he would consider it as done to himself & resent it accordingly. But being much annoyed with his frequent repititions (in liquor) I imprudantly said "yes! it seems so indeed since you told the Belly he was an "old wife" that he did not retaliate." I was alarmed & sorry indeed that I had been so indiscreet. He got pale as death, his nose pinched & lips quivering "what? – my Son? can you be so ignorant, so silly as to believe such a report? Well, I intended leaving before they came in, merely to please you; but now I shall not move 'till they come & we shall see if that stupid, old wife's tongue will dare to repeat those words to me. I did not think you could harbor such thoughts of me. It shall be explained." With a great deal of trouble & intreaty we got him to bed. But he Strictly, & peremptorily ordered his wives (and he had five) to awaken him if the indians did come. But I also forbid them to awake him.

A few minutes after he retired the cry of "here, they are coming" was made. Our little river was completely covered with Canoes – there must have been, altogether not far short of Fifty families. It was one of the largest assemblages of indians I had ever seen in the out Posts. I was far from being sure as to the result, but being now driven to the wall, I had to abide, & "wore my usual old face," leaving all to Providence, and, taking my chance, to avail myself of every circumstance, & fall, if to fall I were doomed, as a man Should. Durocher & Jean Lonctain were sound, but the other four! some of them hardly knew if they were on their head or their feet.

I made them encamp to the East of the house about 80 yds off; Ayagon was to the W., so that I was between them; & I put people to watch to prevent any of the Strangers going to Ayagons. Indeed, the most of them were in terrible dread of him, not excepting the "Gros Blanc."

Their furs were bro't in, counted, & accounts Settled. I gave them each a "glass," & sent my men to take their breakfast, for it was early in the morning; & I would neither implicate my men in my difficulties, & I scorned to have it said that I trusted to their Support as so /291/ many of our "high-flyers" were in the habit of doing. I then gave another round & began to address them. First "I salute you all & am really happy to find you all collected with me once more after so arduous a winter as we have passed. Your children, their mothers

& yourselves, all well. I am thankful that I see you all again. I here give you each a little rum to enjoy yourselves together; & I hope you will drink, talk, play, & sing & dance quietly & peaceably together as friends, as people so intimately connected as you are should do. Go therefore to your tents, & I hope I shall not be pained by hearing of your strife. Go to your tents quietly & in peace.

"But now, after expressing my thanks for seeing you all here so well, & for your exertions this winter, I have something further to say. It has been told me that the number of strangers who come over to this side this year, are come by special invitation of the "Belly," not only to see the vengeance he intends wreaking on me because I "shamed" him last year, but also to assist him." When I got thus far several of the oldest & most respectable of them surrounded me, taking & shaking me gently & kindly by the arm "Dont believe those reports: we also have heard of them; & we carefully searched out the Source; they are fabrications, the dreams of old women disordered in their minds. If there were any truth in them we should have found it & we would tell you of it. They are mistakes, they are lies. They are all lies."

After some further conversation, to explain the reasons why I "shamed" the Belly & of the reports that were spread, they went off to their tents. The House was so full that many of them could not come in. I thought I should be smothered. Old Durocher, suspect-ing my intentions, & returned just as we were finishing our mutual explanations.

They soon got gay, singing & dancing & made such a racket that Ayagon got awake & he came Staggering along just as I was engaged talking with one of those who were said to have come expressly to assist the Belly. "Ah! they are come .... nothing can happen better – here we are all three – when did I tell you (addressing himself to the indian) you should retaliate & stretch my son on the ground (Kill me)? – You are a man – you said it & (of course) can repeat it. I am a man also & with my knife will prove the contrary. Come! explain this satisfactorily immediately." I was in a regular "pickle." The indian denied positively all knowledge of it; and I with great difficulty stopped him. "Hah!" uttered with a mixture of Surprise, pity & disdain, "it is you then who fabricated this Story – I did not think you a liar."

/292/ Sometime after, when he had become considerably Sobered, he went to the other lodges. The moment they saw him they called out Ayagon! & fled. He went to the next, where they were fighting, all pell-mell, the same cry was uttered Ayagon! & away they fled also. In the third lodge likewise. He came to me evidently hurt. "I must be terribly frightful or a very bad man that they all shun me so!" I could not but feel sorry for him: & I am certain it was owing to the terror they were in of him that the remainder of the day passed off so quietly. They had already had several battles & perhaps blood might have been shed.

Thus terminated another wintering, which, at particular intervals looked gloomy enough, & particularly the last few days. We fared well, had abundance of fish & sometimes meat.

I measured the ice several times this winter & found it from five feet eleven to six feet two inches thick, in the lake. In the river it was upon an average four feet thick.

When the ice broke up in the river, i.e. in the rapid, about the middle of April, we speared what fish we wanted, and only at the moment we required them. The rapid, below the Basket,[3] was litterally swarming with carp & pike. We would select such as suited our fancy & spear them. From the time the ice broke up in the rapid untill the 17ᵗʰ June, the day we left, about a month and a half, the rapid was constantly swarming with them: it was a beautiful sight to see them all by pairs & so closely or densely clustered that throwing the Spear at random we failed not bringing up one & turning three & four & sometimes as many as seven & eight upon their back or side. When we wanted a treat we took only the heads of the carp, and the intrails or gut of the pike, which turning inside out, with all the fat & tied at both ends, made a really good morsel.

We also often made pancakes of the roes which we crushed or bruised with a handful of hay or grass & then strained thro' a coarse loose rag. Fish oil served us in lieu of butter or lard. It was also in this manner we made "Egg-nog," stirring the roe smartly while pouring in the rum, & afterwards sweetened. I found no difference between Egg-nog made of fish roes or fowl eggs.

There was another little river to the South of us a few miles where the bears frequented for the fish. They would go in the water, & in the course of a night throw sometimes upwards of a hundred on the beach. One of my indians, Tishshewy, the uncle of the Girl who passed the winter alone in the Snow, mentioned at P. [blank] killed 3 or 4 bears there this Spring.

This is the end of the last surviving part of Nelson's *Reminiscences*.

---

3 The *puise* or fish trap constructed in the fall of 1810.

As explained in the Introduction, Nelson was assigned to Pigeon River, on the east side of Lake Winnipeg, for the season of 1812–13. No further information about this season has survived, but the site was presumably the old post that Nelson had visited in 1808 and 1809, and had supplied with fish from Dauphin River throughout the winter. In 1813 he was transferred from Lake Winnipeg, to the district of The Pic, to the north of Lake Superior. Three short journals survive from that part of his career, which are not printed in this volume. In 1816 Nelson took his little family home to William Henry, Lower Canada, where his parents and siblings lived. Perhaps short of money, in 1818 he returned to the Northwest fur trade. His wife and children remained at William Henry, and he would not see them for five years.

9

Lake Winnipeg Journals, 1818–1819: Introduction

Nelson's posting for the NWC, following his return to the Northwest in 1818, was again at Tête-au-Brochet, and for that season we have a sequence of three more journals. The first, which has become separated from the rest, is now held at the Archives of Ontario. It consists of forty-eight numbered pages, each 20 cm high x 16 cm wide, arranged in a loose stack. The paper is another example of the Radway paper; one page has an almost complete impression of the Britannia oval watermark, and another bears the watermark "RADWAY/1816." The period covered is from 21 September 1818 to 30 April 1819.

Two more journals, both in the Nelson Fonds at the Toronto Reference Library, follow this, each covering a period of a few weeks during the year 1819. Both are copied into the same book: six half-sheets of Radway-type paper folded in half and nested to make a book of twenty-four pages, 20 cm high x 16 cm wide. The earlier journal, which Nelson entitled "Journal B," has entries between 1 May and 8 June 1819. It begins at one end of the book, and completely fills twelve pages, ending in mid-sentence. Immediately following is an obvious change in ink, with which is written the phrase "and Here end the whole for this Route at least. 1819–20–21 g. nelson." Apparently Nelson was recopying this journal from somewhere else, and either had lost the end of it or had tired of copying it. There are four blank pages in the middle of the book. Starting at the other end, and upside down relative to the first journal, is another, with entries between 1 August and 15 September 1819. It fills seven pages, and ends a quarter of the way down the eighth.

Although the journals of 1818–19 are still in the form of daily diaries, like those Nelson had kept during his previous sojourn on Lake Winnipeg, the contents are often more private than in the earlier journals. His description of his own depression (entry of 26 March 1819), and his musings on Larocque's jealousy (entry of 7 May 1819), are perhaps the most striking examples. There is also specific mention of another "diary" (entry of 12 January 1819), which may have been an official record of daily activities that the NWC expected him to keep, but this has not been found.

It was perhaps only in a private journal that Nelson allowed himself to give full vent to his feelings. The general tone is much less optimistic than what he wrote during his earlier years on Lake Winnipeg. Nelson was older now. He was lonely, his family far away in Sorel, and during his two years in Lower Canada he had probably got used to the relative comforts available there. A few of those comforts he had brought with him: his journal entries give exact timings for his journeys, so we know that now he had his own watch. He also had a few panes of glass for his windows, which would greatly improve the amount of precious winter light entering his house.

The 1818–19 journal begins at Fort Alexander, where Nelson was preparing to set off for his winter quarters. His new bourgeois was the NWC partner, Duncan McDougall, whom he had met only that summer. Besides Fort Alexander itself, three posts were to be occupied in the Post of Lac Ouinipique. One was at a place called Grand Equierre or Grand Equisette on upper Winnipeg River (assigned to Joseph Lorrin, the old interpreter), and another was at Little Grand Rapids, east of Lake Winnipeg (assigned to John Crebassa). Nelson was to re-establish a post somewhere on the west side of the lake, in opposition to an HBC party that was expected there. He had five voyageurs, two of whom, Larocque and Welles, had worked with him before, while a third, Vandalle, had just been transferred to Lake Winnipeg after seven seasons in Fort des Prairies.

Nelson and his party, which included women and children and numbered twenty-nine in all (besides fifteen dogs), set off from Fort Alexander on 22 September in a boat, rather than canoes. The boat, some version of the famous York boats later used by the HBC with such success, was an improved technology, better suited to the incessant problems of wind on Lake Winnipeg. It took the party five days to reach Tête-au-Brochet, where Nelson found about fifteen Indigenous men, who clearly hoped that the post would be built there. The season was advancing, so he agreed, and started building for the winter.

Throughout that season, Nelson was worried about a possible HBC opposition. The HBC from York Factory had established a post on Lake Manitoba in the fall of 1815, increasing the pressure on the NWC's

Fort Dauphin department. The first post to be built was at a place called Big Point, on the western shore of Lake Manitoba, which could serve the Indigenous people all round the lake, even as far as Lake St Martin, near the edge of Nelson's territory. A post in this region, eventually known as Manitoba House, would be maintained by the HBC for many years, and it would be here that the Canadian government's Treaty No. 2 with the Ojibwe, covering the southwestern part of the present province of Manitoba, would be signed in 1871. In the fall of 1817 another post was built on Lake Dauphin, in direct opposition to the NWC's main Fort Dauphin post, and in the fall of 1819 the third post was established alongside the NWC at "the head of Partridge Crop River," just west of Lake St Martin.[1]

At Tête-au-Brochet, George Nelson was already anticipating this expansion. On 21 October he sent two men to Dauphin River, the site of his old post of 1807–10, with instructions to build a small post alongside the HBC if they found them there. The men returned on 2 November, with the pleasing news that there was no HBC post at Dauphin River, though they had heard that the rival company had left two men at Lake St Martin to fish, and a post might be established after freezeup. A week later, two young Indigenous men brought news that the HBC were indeed building on Lake St Martin, but this was far enough west that Nelson could leave them for the Fort Dauphin department to worry about. He would be spared the unpleasant duty of daily, head-to-head competition, now a routine aspect of these last, bitterly confrontational years of the struggle between the companies. Some men enjoyed the confrontation, but Nelson did not.

Although some of the Indigenous people who traded with Nelson at Tête-au-Brochet this year were familiar to him from his previous sojourn on the Lake, there had been many changes. We hear no more of Ayagon, nor of the other Ojibwe who were part of his extended family. Ayagon, at least, was probably now hunting in the Fort Dauphin department – he certainly was there by the next season. Most of the Mashkiegons were still in the district, but the largest band of them was headed by a new man whom Nelson calls Red Breast or L'Estomac Rouge (Red Stomach). In the end Nelson was not greatly impressed with the hunting prowess

1 The history of the HBC's posts in the company's new Manitoba district, up to 1820, is given in Peter Fidler's "Report of the Manitoba District 1820," HBCA, B.51/e/1, fo. 13r, v. The journal of the first HBC season in the district, "Manitoba Lake Journal Book 1815 & 16," by Donald Sutherland, is HBCA, B.12/a/1.

of this band. His best single hunter was another new man, Nez d'Argent (Silver Nose). It is likely that some of these new figures had been young men or boys when Nelson was keeping his earlier Lake Winnipeg journals. Then, he had had no reason to mention them particularly, but now they had grown up.

In the fall of 1818, and again in the following spring, Nelson often got ducks and geese from the Indigenous people. Evidently the post was on a migration flyway, unlike Dauphin River, where ducks and geese were rarely mentioned. The *puise* or fish trap that Nelson had built in 1810 was reconditioned, and yielded thousands of fish. Women and children from the large Indigenous camp farther up Jack River were constantly taking large quantities for themselves, to Nelson's chagrin.[2]

Since Nelson's departure from Lake Winnipeg in the summer of 1813, there had been important changes in the region, most of them the result of Lord Selkirk's new colony. This colony, usually known as the Red River Settlement, had been established at the Forks of the Red and Assiniboine Rivers beginning in 1812. The story of this settlement is a complex one, with wild swings in fortune and a long list of actors. The colony had been established with the encouragement and assistance of the HBC, and it was immediately caught up in the struggle between the two fur companies. The NWC soon recognized that the colony – and the new authority represented by its administrator, the Governor of Assiniboia – was a serious threat to its business, and it made several attempts not to weaken, but to extirpate the entire settlement. By the time Nelson returned to Lake Winnipeg, Lord Selkirk had taken steps to protect the colony, and it was clear that it would survive. But there had been many ugly incidents (notably the killing of twenty-two colonists and HBC men at Seven Oaks in 1816), and the NWC and the HBC were locked in a death struggle.[3]

George Nelson seems never to have visited the colony at Red River, but he was well aware of it, and saw some of the effects it was already

---

2 According to Peter Fidler, discussing how property rights were understood by the Indigenous people he traded with, "A particular spot in a river where a fishing wear is erected is the exclusive property of those who erected it no longer than the fishing season is over after the Ice sets in – next spring it is common & free to any whome the first to make the necessary repairs as the wear is generally greatly damaged by the floating Ice in the fall but in the Spring is totally swept away by the driving Ice, drift wood & high water" (HBCA, E.51/e/1, fo. 18r). Since the NWC had not operated the *puise* at Tête-au-Brochet for several years, it was probably regarded as common property.

3 For details, see the accounts cited on page lxin62.

having on the Northwest. The intensified hostility between the two rival companies meant that he had to worry, not just about losing furs to the HBC, but about outright attack. Using the supposed judicial powers of the Governor of Assiniboia, that company had taken to arresting NWC people, and removing them from the country: Duncan Cameron, Nelson's old bourgeois, had suffered this fate at Red River in 1815. The most notorious incident of this kind was yet to occur. In June 1819, the Governor of Assiniboia, William Williams, set an ambush at Grand Rapids, where the Saskatchewan River reaches Lake Winnipeg, and captured four NWC partners and eight engagés on their way to the partners' meeting at Fort William. As it happened, Nelson was able to pass a quiet winter at Tête-au-Brochet without disturbance from the HBC, though he was always on his guard. The fact that the Indigenous people trading with him could easily divert their hunt to the rivals on Lake St Martin moderated his behaviour – he no longer felt able to deal out a "good basting" to a troublesome customer as he had in the past.

Two other aspects of Nelson's perception of the country also arose from the presence of the Red River Settlement. First, he recognized that the population of the colony was a source of serious diseases, endemic in the Scottish Highlands from which many of the settlers had come, but new dangers to the Indigenous population. In the opening entry of his 1818–19 journal, he notes the arrival of two voyageurs from the Forks, with news that scarlet fever "was again agoing to begin to rise. God help us I say!" Although Hackett had not encountered references to scarlet fever in northwest Ontario before the 1840s, when well-trained physicians, who could recognize it, began to be available in the country, he points out that this disease had been well established in North America for more than a century, and that some epidemics of "sore throat" mentioned in the Northwest from the 1770s onwards may well have been scarlet fever (Hackett 2002, 187–8). Nelson's reference to a return of the disease at Red River in 1818, implying an earlier epidemic, appears to be new information.

Second, Nelson now recognized the mixed-race population of the country, the Métis, as a distinct component within the fur trade work force. He refers to these people as *brûlés*, that is, the *bois brûlés*, or "burnt woods." This was a term recently adopted by the Métis themselves, as part of the development of their racial and political identity that accompanied the NWC's recruitment of them into the war against the Red River Settlement. After the sudden death of the NWC partner in charge of Lake Winnipeg, Duncan McDougall, Nelson was indignant that the senior of the two clerks at Fort Alexander, Roderick McKenzie, had not been allowed to take over the post for the rest of the season, but had been superseded by someone else sent from the Red River Department. The reason for passing over young McKenzie, Nelson was sure, was that "Mr. McK. is a brulée."

In the case of Roderick McKenzie, there was more behind the decision than race. McBean, the partner in charge at Red River, would not have wished to leave the Fort Alexander post in the hands of an apprentice clerk in only his fourth season. Moreover, as Nelson later learned (see entry of 22 January), McKenzie had begun an affair with the wife of Potvin, one of the men whom the NWC had sent down to Upper Canada to give evidence against Lord Selkirk and the HBC. There was no knowing how much trouble this would cause. Rather than letting McKenzie remain at Fort Alexander, McBean directed that he be sent to the other posts in the Lake Winnipeg department, as Nelson stated, "to be kept about between Crebassa and me."

The death of Duncan McDougall, the partner in charge of the Post of Lac Ouinipique, at Fort Alexander on 25 October 1818, was probably a surprise to his peers, though McDougall may have sensed it was coming, as he added a codicil to his will one week before. Nelson did not learn of the death until 17 December. The news occasioned a remarkable outpouring of feeling for a man, whom, as Nelson says, he had only known for a few weeks.

The journal entry on 1 February 1819 lists all the furs that had been traded up to that point. To each item, Nelson attached a superscript to give its equivalent in beaver – what the NWC called a "*plus*" and the HBC "made beaver." Thus, this inventory provides us with the NWC "standard of trade," the company's official guide as to what goods were to be given in trade for each fur. This standard of trade was as follows: large black bears, cats, and silver grey foxes, two beaver each; small bears, otters, and red foxes, one beaver each; martens, fishers, and wolverines, half a beaver each; and minks one quarter of a beaver each. The beaver equivalent for the 82 muskrats is illegible in the entry, but to make the total that Nelson gives, 193½ beaver, the 82 muskrats must have been worth 8¼ beaver, so the value of a muskrat skin, rounded off, was one tenth of a beaver. Actual beaver skins were worth one beaver if "large" and half a beaver if "small." The entry of 2 February adds the fact that a dressed deer skin was worth two beaver, and Nelson allowed three beaver for a bear skin that must have been unusually large. It will be noticed that very little of the trade inventoried at the Tête-au-Brochet post was actually beaver; most of the skins he traded were martens.

Nelson was not invited to Fort Alexander for Christmas, as in the old days, but the young clerk Roderick McKenzie arrived at Tête-au-Brochet on 21 December, and Nelson did his best to act as host. To Nelson's surprise, there was no letter from Charles Hesse, the clerk who had been sent to take over the department after McDougall's death. McKenzie returned to Fort Alexander on 12 January, where his reappearance finally elicited a letter to Nelson from Charles Hesse; two voyageurs arrived with it on the 22nd. It was a formal, flowery missive, whose main purpose was to remind Nelson that young McKenzie was to be kept away from his paramour, the wife of the absent voyageur Potvin. Nelson characterized the letter as "in the true Spanish Stile, i.e. of lovers." Hesse's command of English was probably not great, and he may have composed the letter in French first, and then translated it into English. Nelson, like many English speakers of the time, found the French style of *politesse* ridiculous, and used the letter as an excuse to express his resentment of Hesse.

Perhaps to clear up any misunderstandings, Nelson himself paid a visit to Fort Alexander, leaving Tête-au-Brochet on 15 February. All he says of his reasons is that it was "from motives I cannot now communicate." He returned home on the 25th, accompanied by young McKenzie who was to take charge at Tête-au-Brochet while Nelson made a visit to John Crebassa at his remote post at Little Grand Rapids. The influence of Cupid upon McKenzie was still too strong, for on 1 March Nelson recorded that "mad after his sweet-heart, I allow [him] to return; because I am confident he would fall sick."

He then bestirred himself for one of his heroic winter journeys, the visit to John Crebassa at Little Grand Rapids. It was a hard three-day walk up Pigeon River, which Nelson reckoned as about 200 miles. News had been received that Crebassa was having little success against a strong HBC opposition, and Nelson would have remembered how an earlier attempt at the same place, by the pitiable Alexander Campbell in 1808–09, had ended almost in disaster, Nelson and his fellow clerk Macdonell having to rescue Campbell and his family from starvation. To his relief, Nelson found Crebassa and his men in good health, subsisting mostly upon an unusually plentiful supply of rabbits. They were invited to the house of the HBC trader, Donald Sutherland, for dinner on one day, and reciprocated the invitation the next.[4] Nelson was back at Tête-au-Brochet on 18 March, having travelled twelve hours a day in the coldest weather of the winter, "for we travelled like men escaped from the Gibbet." In his absence, young McKenzie had appeared again, this time with letters bringing news that the court cases in Canada between Lord Selkirk and the Nor'westers, over the attempts to destroy the Red River Settlement in 1815–16, had ended in acquittal for the NWC.

Nelson made one more winter journey in this season, a short trip to Dauphin River to see some of his Indigenous hunters. The overland journey took him about eight hours, across the neck of the great peninsula separating Sturgeon Bay from Tête-au-Brochet, in contrast to the summer canoe journey of two days around the peninsula. Nelson's journal ends on 30 April. He was in a state of some suspense. He had sent men to Fort Alexander, and they had not returned, making him wonder whether HBC men had fallen upon that post and taken the Nor'westers prisoner. And he had yet to hear from many of his hunters, so the season's yield of furs was still in doubt.

The next journal, Nelson's "Journal B," carries on directly from the last one, without a break. Nelson's men finally returned from Fort Alexander on 22 May, to his great relief; they had been absent an entire month. By their own account they had tried three times to come home, but were prevented by the rotten state of the ice, succeeding only with difficulty on the fourth attempt. The last of the Indigenous hunters brought in their furs on 2 June, and Nelson set off in his boat for Fort Alexander with the season's returns on the 6th. On the last day, while Nelson was awaiting a fair wind, he took his leave of the Indigenous people at the post, and they began a Midewiwin initiation ceremony, some of which he observed before the change in the wind obliged him to depart. He tells us that he appreciated what he did see of the ceremony, "having now a far better idea of their Theology, & understand their language also much better than I did 13 years ago when I saw them the first time."

This brief journal ends in mid-sentence, with the entry of 8 June, when Nelson and his party were partway on their road to Fort Alexander. The next journal does not begin until 16 August.

---

4 Late in the season, Sutherland reckoned that he had traded twelve packs of furs to the Nor'westers' two (Lytwyn 1986, 147–9).

10

Journal at Tête-au-Brochet, 21 September 1818–8 June 1819

✳

Monday 21nd September. To day I got my men to grind me about 5 Pecks of wheat, which they finish at 4 P.M.[1] I propose leaving this [Fort Alexander] tomorrow (please God nothing intervenes to prevent me) for Tete au-Brochet. Old Lorrain left this at 10½ a.m. for the Gr^d. Equisitte in the upper part of this river. Mr Crebassa left this on Wednesday last, being detained in the River by hard winds; he goes to [Little] Grd. Rapid. <u>Boss</u>-cassé [?] arrived here this morning from La Grosse Isle as does <u>old Gagnon</u> & his band this evening at dark. M^r McDougal's men were employed in digging holes to day to plant the Posts of the new Stable. Very fine weather, but I fear it will not last long as it blew hard from the East today.

Larocque & Paradix arrived last Saturday night from the Forks, where it would [seem] as if that unfortunate Scarlet fever was again agoing to begin to rise. God help us I say!

Tues^d 22^d. We take our departure from Fort Alex. at 4½ P M. for Tete au Brochet. Encamp at [time left blank] in the mouth of the small river near the old XY fort.[2] I have with me five men, Larocque (his wife & 6 children), L'ullemand [Allemand, i.e., German] Welles (wife & 3

---

1 Nelson's men would have used the grist mill at Fort Alexander, and wheat grown on the plantation there. It is possible that some may have been purchased from the Red River Colony, which had its own wheat and its own grist mill by 1815. In 1822, when the colony's mill broke down, some wheat was sent to Fort Alexander to be ground there (Kaye 1981).
2 Evidently most of the day was spent loading the boat, and collecting all the people and dogs, so Nelson did not go very far before camping. The old XYC fort was close to the mouth of the Winnipeg River, and the "small river" near it must be one of two unnamed streams that fall into the main river on the same side, below the present Fort Alexander settlement.

children) and Vandalle (wife & 4 children), Paradix & Plante, and a little boy I take with the inclination of sending him to Canada.[3] I have passengers Boisverd's wife & 3 children, & a foolish indian boy, making, including myself 25 persons & 15 dogs.[4] Mother Beaulieu & her daughter encamp with us at night to winter at Tête au Brochet.

/2/ Wednes 23ᵈ. September 1818. As the wind blows a head I took net out of the bales, which we soon set, but the wind falling we embarked at 2½ P.M. taking 3 white fish. We encamped at 8 in the Riviere Noire. It was quite calm till dusk when we hoisted our sail a small breeze arising. Welles put out the net again. Much appearance of wind.

Thursd 24ᵗʰ. A high wind all day a head, that keeps us snug enow [enough] in our encampment. We fortunately took 7 nice Pike & a Pikeral in our net which we took up to dry, & put it out again at 2 P.M. We are very much in want of this & fine weather for we have not for more than 4 days of Provisions. Larocque went out a shooting & found in a small island a few yards from us a <u>Cache</u> belonging to some indians we suppose from the flying of the ducks to be in that river. Upon examination they prove to be a medicine bag & another small bag of the fine chaff or dry[g] of rice – not being worth anything for us I leave it & keep what I would have put in its stead. Great up. [?] 7 /rmo.../ iven.[5]

Frid. 25 Last night Larocque on his return from hunting brought home 5 Pike & 2 Pikeral out of the net; & this morning, Welles took 3 Pike & 2 Pikeral. We set off at 4¾. hardly day. We had a slight sail the most of the day, which with our oars brought us, at 6 to the entrance of Broken river where we saw some indians, I suppose Gagnon & his band. We put out the net tho quite late.

Saturd. 26ᵗʰ. A nice south wind, somewhat high by spells but thank God we got on charmingly. We put up at 6¾ on the N. side of Isle á Beriau. A few acres across this on the S. shore is where I encamped in

---

3 An apparently mentally disabled boy whom Nelson found at Fort Alexander, and was concerned about, probably fearing that he would not be able to take care of himself. On 19 October, at Tête-au-Brochet, the boy left the post, attempting to return to Fort Alexander, but did not get very far before he was found and brought back. What happened to him after that is not mentioned.

4 The correct total is twenty-nine persons. As the entry of 27 September shows, this large party was travelling in a boat, which not only had a great capacity but was less dangerous on the windy lake than the canoes that Nelson used in earlier years. This would have been a version of the York boat, which was so useful to the HBC throughout the first half of the nineteenth century.

5 A few illegible words.

1807, the 18 or 19 of this month a few days after our Keg of Powder blew up & burning some of us so severely! The wind was too high so the poor /3/ old woman (whose Canoe had been of so much service to us) could not follow us; & I did not leave her anything to eat! But I hope she will soon come up with us. If it pleases God that the wind remains in the same quarter I expect to be in Good time at Tete au Brochét. But I fear the arrival, lest the HB's be there & have the indians be drunk, in which case I will have abundance of trouble, reproaches, threats & God knows what from the drunken indians, but God have mercy on us.

Sund 27th Septr 1818. The wind being still high, from the same quarter, I embark at 6¼, the wind driving us on furiously. At 8 put ashore to breakefast at Petitie téte-au-brochet, where we shave, & as I expect to find the indians in a short time I put up my flag – the first time I ever did to arrive among indians. At 10 we pushed out, at 11 were saluted by the hoisting of a flag & Guns firing from their church[6] – I put ashore for a moment & proceeded immediately to the River, which is about one mile further. Here as the water is very low, we were obliged to unload all & drag up our boat. L'Estomac Enuye & Cu-levé with all the rest came to see me, about 15 of them in all. I gave them a large treat of rum & send them off. They all appeared exceedingly well pleased, & in answer to my speech to them, promise to behave well. They wish me to build here, but I am told the English are to be in River Dauphine, in that case I shall be obliged to go there along side of them – a measure I hate, but there is no alternative. The indians killed 2 moose & they gave me the 2 rib pieces & a brisket & thigh of an old male, & in the rutting season too, I found it very good & sweet, but tuff [tough]. It is now 5 years past, & more that I have eaten fresh meat (moose).[7]

Mond 28th Tuesd 29th Wednes 30th. The indians have been very troublesome these last 2 days, but particularly yesterday.

/4/ Wednes. 30th Septr 1818. I was several times very near basting [beating] some of them, but the opposition keeps me as much in order as it incourages them however today I got them to finish. The Belly on his return home stab'd his wife in the thigh. Very calm all day & rain towards evening. Mother Beaulieu arrived last night; & Boisverd's wife

6 "Their church" was probably a large Midewiwin lodge, erected during the previous summer.
7 Nelson means that he had not tasted moose meat since he left Lake Winnipeg in 1813 for The Pic district, where apparently moose were not hunted.

set off for Ft Dauphin yesterday.[8] I got 7 Grey Geese from 2 of my indians today. We put out our net only a few hours this afternoon, which gave us fish enough for three & four times our number.

Thursd. 1st October 1818. I began today by giving debt to some of my indians, but the rain this afternoon put a stop to us.

Frid. 2nd. If we had a beautiful warm rain last night we had a most excessive cold one today, with a furious North wind; but about 2 P.M. it ceased in some measure & I proceeded to give debt to others of my indians, & by dint of solicitation I give them their Encouragement Rum. Three canoes, of four that went a hunting up the river last Tuesday, arrived to night. They killd a mouse [moose] with some Ducks & Geese. I got some of the meat & 5 Geese with 3 ducks.

Saturd 3[d]. Set off from our encampment this morning at 6 to go to our old houses, a few acres above, which I propose repairing by degrees; for the non arrival of the HB's puts me far back for several reasons. I got the old shop repaired sufficiently to put in my goods in safety before night. At night Le Nes d'argent arrived from above with only a few ducks & Geese, 4 of which & 10 Ducks he gave me. I gave him his anticipated Rum. A beautiful day.

Sund 4th. I had a good deal of trouble today with some of my indians, & was near giving a hearty basting to the Nes d'argent for attempting to break in my shop. I [did] not, all however went well. Beautiful weather.

/5/ Mond 5th Octr 1818. Frisé & Nes d'argent set off to hunt in Fisher river. The rest of the indians Encamp here on their way up this river where the most of them intend wintering.

Tuesd. 6th. Cu Léve sets off for the Sandy rivier, far beyond river Dauphine to hunt.[9] Old Tete Grisés Son, Laseur en Rond [Le Jour en Rond], Le Cancre, set off for River Dauphine & the bay of Tête-au-Pichew. One of L'Estomac roughes [Rouge's] sons follows them, to take or marry one of Tete Grises daughters.

Wednes.7th. At last at noon today I am debarrassed of all my indians; they take their departure for their hunting quarters up here in this river.

8 Mother Beaulieu and her daughter had been following along behind Nelson in their own canoe; they were to spend the winter near Nelson's post. Nelson had brought Louis Boisvert's wife and her three children this far on her journey to Fort Dauphin, where her husband was stationed. How she travelled the rest of the way is not clear; perhaps Madame Beaulieu loaned her canoe.

9 This Sandy River was north along the west shore of Lake Winnipeg, almost to Long Point.

I pity the Poor wretch who, having tasted of the sweets of civilized life is obliged to serve in this Country!

Last night at 9½ old Gagnon with Two Canoes arrived here, with a Good deal of meat for comnition of [ammunition and] other things they want & are Short of. I equips them again, & they set off for their lodges in Bloody river. Mr. McDougall [Duncan McDougall] may suspect me of decoying them; but it is false. A few showers today. Yesterday I put two men to man the old house Ausgé made me in 1811.12 & 3 others to split wood for the planing of it. This afternoon I got the chimney posts planted.

Thursd 8th. It began to rain last night & continued all day by intervals. The Frisé arrived a little after 12, with better than the meat of one moose, two snoutes & a tongue, from the bay of River aux Pécans, where he is now encamped. He returned with near 2 Galls. of mixed Rum I give him, & desired me to tell the Siffleu (Groundhog) to go to [there?] & pass the winter with him, so that he (Frisé) might encourage his daughter to remain with him (the Siffleu) which she is now averse to.

/6/ Frid. 9th Octr. 1818. Rain again till late this afternoon nevertheless the men repair their old house. It was made for me in 1811 but now mostly rotten, & hut [put?] the covering on it, working during all the Rain. This Evening the Siffeu came here, on his way to the Frisé's, his father-in-law. His wife came to see us today & I told her what her father had Said. Very cold indeed.

Saturd. 10th. Make my Chimney eaqual with the Roof & begin by clearing the rubbish of the mens house. A beautiful day. The indian sets off.

Sund 11th. A furious NE wind all day & some drops of rain which from the great cold makes me apprehensive of snow, & induces me to shelter my self in my old House; tho' a great deal of rain being thunder all the afternoon.

Mond 12th. The weather is exceedingly mild & calm. Finish my chimney & roof & lay a part of my floor.

Tuesd 13th. Nearly finish my floor, while the other men finish the covering of their house & plant their Chimney Posts.

Wednes 14th. We had some frost last night. Cold & windy all day. Great numbers of Geese & outerdes [outardes*] fly home, besides 3 or 4 flocks of Swans. The men begin & finish their chimeney today & finish the Room their house. I make & hang my door.

Thurs 15th. We had some hard rain & snow about 9 P.M. last night, the first this year, but a furious frost, insomuch that there was ice all along the beach of our little river here. We begin today, before the weather becomes too cold to repair our "Peige" or fish basket.[10] At night the Belly arrives brings me all the best pieces of 3 moose he lately killed. He is alone, The Red breast & others are together, but are starting & in another place, on this side. We bar the River intirely across & make a temporary basket.

/7/ Frid. 16th October 1818. At 1½ A.M. L›assiniboine arrived here with 18 ducks & a savour for Rum. I gave him 9 pints & sent him off, for I was great displeased at being thus disturbed. We intirely finish our basket today. We took near 500 fish in our temporary basket of yesterd[ay]. A beautiful morning, but very cold & raw when past 10.a.m.

Satur 17th. I got my house plaistered inside, & my hearth made. The men lay the greatest part of their floor & enter their house this evening. Vandalle who has a little "hanger"[11] at the end of mine lays his floor too today. I put up two of my windows only for want of Skins.[12]

The foolish boy I brought with me disappears this afternoon. He has frequently, but this morning particularly expressed a great "ennuie" [longing] for bas de la riviere. On examaination we find his traile on the beach of the Lake leading that way. He has only a thin bl[an]ket & broken [torn] leggings: & it is very cold.

Sund 18th. Early this morning I send off Vandall & Plante to look for the fool. At our fire of 27 Septr about 3 leagues from here they found him lying down & shivering. They got home at 12. At 2½ P.M. La femalle de Carriboeuf arrives with one of her Sons, & he brings me 29 Ducks, & a Marchment[13] the belly Sent me. Last night mother Beaulieu [...] arrive, apparently in disgust. Rain & melted snow all day.

Mond 19th. Very cold. La F[emale] de Carriboeuf & mother Beaulieu set off this morning. The men Palister [plaster] their houses.

Tuesd 20th Rather milder today, hasy towards evening. Yesterday morning I get The square [...] building put up at the basket for our

---

10 This was to improve the *puise* or fish trap, a low dam with holes in it below the water line, that Nelson had first constructed at Tête-au-Brochet in the fall of 1810. The "fish basket" (*piège*, trap) was probably a tapering basket, open at both ends with the narrow end inwards, so that the fish could go upstream easily but would find it difficult to return, so that they were trapped in the pond above the dam.

11 French *hangard*, a storehouse; here, probably a lean-to built up against the side of Nelson's house.

12 On 19 December, Nelson installed two window panes in his house; why he did not do so at first is unexplained. He had not received a further shipment of goods, so perhaps the glass was buried in his outfit, and not discovered until now.

13 Probably a sheet of parchment leather, made from moose hide, to put in a window.

fish; & this morning we hung up 360 laciesh. The men works at different things. Larocque makes his bed as I send him off tomorrow to River Dauphine to see after the HB's if they be there or not; & give him a letter for Mr. /8/ Cummings[14], in case he be at Falle de Perdrie, or at some other place in opposition to HB's. He is likewise to spear me 2 or 3 fish; & to make a small house if the HB's be at the mouth of this river near them, so that I may have people to watch them. About 4 P.M. Le Jour en Rond arrives with his wife from the bottom of the bay of Téte-au-Pichew, where he tells that by the frequent firing they hear at River Dauphine they suppose the HB's to be there, & that he saw the tracks of an indian on the beach not far from here. I believe him, but still I don't think that there are People at River D., & the track I take to be one old one.

Wednes 21st. At the Dawn of day Larocque sets off (wth Paradix) leaving his family here. Very mild, hasy almost all night. Le Jour Rond leaves this about 10 a.m. with all the fish we took last night, near 600. L'Estomac Rouge arrived a little past noon with 49 ducks for which I gave him ½ a Keg of rum he returns immediately. He tells me that there is a great deal of snow where they are. About 7.P.M. Le Frisé & Nes D'argent arrived from fisher river with 2 Canoes full of Geese [...ing] 88 of the four Sorts of Geese, but principally the white [...] 2 Swans, 26 ducks, & one bag of Pounded meat, with 3 Parchment Skins. I has been very calm all day, but very cold to night. [I] make, & sleep in my bedroom.

Thurs 22nd. At 10 The two indians returned with rather better than 4 Qu[ts] of HWines I give them. It was so calm & cold last night that I was obliged to send my men to carry their canoes to [...] Encampment, as here it was frozen up. This even/9/ing four brats from above come to take fish in our basket, & how can I help it?

Fri'd 23[d]. Yesterday it was rather windy, but to day most beautiful weather. The Children of yesterday, tho' [I] followed them and [took?] the fish, yet they remain to take more.

Satur 24th. Those four whelps return about 10 a.m. "The Boy," old Gagnon son in law, arrives here with some dry meat to pay for part of the amunition they got from me, & to get some rum. They are from Beaver River, just opposite to us on the East side of the Lake. They are going to Bloody River now. I get 7 skins from him. He returns about 3 P.M., his wife & one of old Gagnon's came with him. L'allemand

14 Cuthbert Cumming: see note to journal entry of 20 June 1810.

[Jean-Baptiste Welles] makes his Door & hearth. Vandalle goes for a [...]

Sund 25th. Very fine weather, but the wind is North, & the moon near its change; we may therefore soon expect a change. We made very good haul of fish last night, near, if not above 700 but principally laciesh.[15] We have now 943 Laciesh & 372 Pike, Pikeral & Carp.

Mond 26th. Very low dull weather this morning & evening & much appearance of rain, but the weather was truly delightful from about 10 to 4. We made a famous fishery last night, say 1000 Laciesh & 126 Pike we hung up today. As my Shop is very small I get my men to refitting an old building that is now [...] thrown down & was formerly my shop. For fear our dam should give way I got two supporters put to it.

Tuesd 27th. We had some rain last night, but the weather was very fine today. Hang up 1960 laciesh besides 100 Pike, & other fish.

/10/ Wednesd. 28th Octr 1818. A Thick hoar frost & a very high S.E. wind today. Hang up 1360 Laciesh & 120 Pike and others.

Thursd 29th. Hang up 1180 L. & 160 Pike &c. The weather is most delightful indeed. About 4.P.M. Tête Grisés son & family all arrive, with Le Jour rond from Tète au Pichew bay, where they have been starving, & are now on their way to the Red breast's up this river, for the doctoring of one of their woman that is very sick indeed. Not long after, five women from Red breasts band came down for fish.

Frid 30th. After 12 a good deal, the indians set off. L'estomac Rouge, with la Ventre & le Gendre arrive, they bring me a few ducks for that confounded Rum. My expences in every thing I have here, is Shameful. I finished my third Keg to day, & have not received the nature of 20 Skins, meat excepted, yet. They return very soon. The women who came for fish carry almost all off, tho' I daresay there was 2000 or more this morning – we hung up but 260 L. & 80 Pike &c. The weather most delightful today.

Satur 31st. Hang up 580 L. & 80 Pike &c. Welles & Vandalle began chopping their cord wood. Plante is working for me. Very fine weather still.

Sund 1st November. Hang up 1000 L. & 70 Pike &c. The wind is Southerly, (but very hi & cold).

Mond 2nd. Hang up 860 L. & 130 Pike &c. But I am afraid Master

---

15 It is interesting that the principal fish caught in the trap at Tête-au-Brochet were Lake Winnipeg goldeye (*laciesh*), followed by pike, whereas at Dauphin River the greatest catch was of whitefish.

Welles plays me some dirty [illegible word] /11/ there, 'Tis now the 3ᵈ
or 4ᵗʰ time I have thought so of him, & I must try to find it out. Wind
the same as yesterday. Weather fine. This Evening mother Beaulieu, her
daughter, & the other [woman] came down for fish, & amusement. At
6.P.M. (dusk) I had the pleasure of seeing Larocque & Paradis arrive.
They gave me the pleasing news of there being no HB's at River le
Dauphine, & that they left two men only in Lake Sᵗ Martin to fish, but
that they were to send people on the first ice to winter there. This latter
part I am inclined to consider as false, because the only advantage they
can derive from it, is to serve as a store for those who may travel back
& forward, & to haul to their own lodgings.

Tuesd 3ᵈ. Rain all day. Nothing new.

Wednes 4ᵗʰ. Hang 1220 L. & 20 Pike. The women return, & carry
off all the best fish of here. Larocque & Paradix begin to chop their
cord wood, as Plante did on Monday, & the others have last Saturday.
The weather is dull but not cold.

Thurs 5ᵗʰ. Hang up 1300 L. & 100 Pike. Cold & hazy.

Frid 6ᵗʰ. Hang up 240 L. & 7 Pike. The weather is Cloudy & very
cold; & our little river was frozen over.

Saturd 7ᵗʰ. With the help of 2 of my men I bend two slays today,
one for me & an other for Larocque; I attempted one yesterday for
Vandalle; but the wood was so bad I broke it. No fish, not even sufficient to Eat.

/12/ Sund 8ᵗʰ November 1818. Both yesterday & to day we had a
very high S. wind, which rendered the weather much milder. We take
but very few fish, i.e. eatable ones. Great numbers of small Pike, not
much bigger than young snakes, fall in our basket; very few good
Pike & no Paciesk [laciesh]. This, however, I attribute to the taking of
the ice & the clear nights. The same thing, only far worse happened
to me here in the fall of 1811 for we did not take any fish till long
after the ice took.

Mond 9ᵗʰ. I was surprised this morning by the arrival of two young
indians of mine from River Dauphine, whither they had taken allard's
wife. They told me that the HB's went up that river with only one
boat, instead of 3 as Larocque told me, but there were four Clerks
or masters on board; that there were [no] less but an interpreter &
2 men in Lake Sᵗ Martin, but that more were to come on the first
ice; that Fras Richard was at Falle de Perdrix, and Mr Cummings in
Lake Manitâbane. This news set me to rights – I am happy of it. This
Evening they embark for the rest of their band, that are up this river.

I made i.e. bent Vandalle's Slay today, & went to look for another one for myself, but uselessly. Snowed this afternoon.

Tuesd 10ᵗʰ Cold, Cloudy, but no more snow. L'allemand finishes chopping all his wood 13 Cords including 6 for me. All the others have likewise finished /13/ last week chopping my wood, 30 Cords between them, but they all have some yet to chop for themselves.

Wednes 11ᵗʰ. Tho' there is not yet one inch of snow on the Ground, I went out to make traps, 11. L'allemand & Laroque went likewise, the latter brought home one. This Evening <u>Tête-Grisé's Eldest Son</u> & his <u>2 younger brothers</u>, <u>Paskhew</u>, & <u>2 of Red breast's sons</u> arrived here. They have been out a hunting since yesterday, but have not seen the back of one moose.

Thursd 12ᵗʰ. I cross upon the ice this morning, opposite this place, the only spot where it is sufficiently strong to bear a man, but it is still very weak. The indians return this morning by an other road, in quest of moose. I went to day with Paradix for Slays upon L'allemand's Road. We split & squared two. I observed plenty of ice to day in the Lake but it was so thin & weak, that the least breath of wind is sufficient to breake it.

Frid 13ᵗʰ. I went out again to day to make traps; I made 8. There is as yet so little snow on the Ground as not to be able to discover them (tracks) but with the greatest difficulty.

Satur 14ᵗʰ. It began to snow last night & continues still to day. There may be now about 2 inches deep on the Ground. This evening <u>the old woman</u> & a <u>parcel</u> of <u>brats</u> came from the lodges above to get a few articles they <u>left en cache</u> here, as they intend soon to Pitch off to where /14/ they may kill moose. They brought me the brisket & the two rib pieces of a very fat moose, killed sometime ago.

Sund 15ᵗʰ. They all return. Very mild.

Mond 16ᵗʰ. Very mild still, but it grew cold towards Evening. The men plaister all our buildings today. I took a martin in my traps; they are very scarce.

Tuesd 17ᵗʰ. I bend Paradix' slay today.

Wednes 18ᵗʰ. I put out a Gun today & a large trap for the wolves, four of these Chaps hovering about & last night, the men say they drove the dogs into our doors. I heard them but did not see them.

Thurs 19ᵗʰ. Larocque took a most beautiful Silver grey fox in his steel trap today. The Wolves draw off, for we hear no more of them. They broke all L'Allemand's & Laroque's traps.¹⁶ Rather sharp. We can now

16 Steel traps, strong enough to resist an animal's struggle when it had not been killed

travel pritty surely upon the river; but in the Lake there is only a little thin ice.

Frid 20th. I bend an other slay for Vandalle today. Cloudy, a little snow. I am very happy to observe that the fish begin to come again. I fancy it was owing to the clear moon light nights & the taking of the river, that they left us for so long a time.

Saturd 21st. Very fine & mild weather till evening when it began to snow. Between 3 & 4 P.M. Le Jour Rond & L'oiseau arrive from the Red breast's for people to go for meat. They killed 4 moose the day before yesterday. They are Pitching off into the interior.

/15/ Sund. 22nd. Novr. 1818. A thick snow all night & day prevented my sending the men off. I went to see the Lake today; & as far as I could see there was ice with snow on it; but this high North has already broken it much, & I am afraid will intirely destroy it or at least render travelling very disagreable this winter upon it, for the wind blows furiously towards Evening.

Mond. 23d. Weather mild & Calm, & becomes quite clear, & rather sharp by noon. At 6 a. m. ½ an hour before day light I send off the men i.e. Larocque, Welles & Vandalle. Paradix & Plante lay the flooring of my Provision store. At Dusk, Les Jambes Noires, Pahkon & La Chemise de cotton arrive here bag & baggage, starving like lusty fellows & bawling out Eat Eat. They seperated about 8 days ago from the Red breast & took the left, in hopes by being only a few they might make out; but that has been their hunting Ground all summer & fall, & besides three other families have pitched off on that road only a few weeks before. I am very sorry for this because they tell me there are plenty of martins & a good few otters in that quarter.

Tuesd. 24th. At 10 a. m. The men arrive, they bring but the ribs, briskett, snoutes & 2 tongues, but all so lean that tho' I boiled a brisket for about 3½ hours, there was not the least particle of Grease to be found in the Kettle. I never eat any so lean. They had a great deal of trouble to get to the lodges. They were near losing Welles & 2 Slays &c by sinking. /16/ They likewise lost the Powder. About 12 Tete Grises Eldest Son arrived. He comes for people to go for meat, a female moose one of Red Breasts young sons killed yesterday. A heavy snow all day.

---

outright in the jaws, were still a novelty, and Nelson notes several cases where a fine fox was caught because of the new trap. The trap also held onto a large wolf whose tracking down is described in the entry of 8 December.

Wednes 25th. Early this morning I send off Vandalle & Paradix for that meat. The most beautiful Fox I ever saw in my life was one Laroque took in the course of this last night. It is so black that it resembles a beautiful Cub – it shines like a Crow. I took also a very handsome silver Grey one. The snow that fell this last night shows us the Lake to be fast, as far as we can see.

Thurs 26th. My two men arrive, they bring me the 4 limbs, 2 ribs, brisket, & half of the rump. Very fine weather.

Frid. 27th. Those indians who arrives here on Monday night return, loaded with dry fish. Most delightful weather, & but moderately cold.

Satur. 28. Sund 29th. I went to day to see the Lake, I went about ½ a mile upon it, & tried in several places its thickness, where there was no snow it was about 5 ins. Thick, but where there is snow not more than 3½ or 4 [inches] tho' all taken at the same time; but it appears that snow lying on it prevents its thickning so fast.

/17/ Mond 30th Novr. Very fine weather still. The men haul wood again today. Last Saturday they hauled 12 Cords for me, & now they haul some for themselves.

Tuesd 1st Decr 1818. I send off Welles early this morning to the lodges for dressed skins, and <u>Babishe*</u> to net me snow shoes.[17] He is to wait till he can get enow of them all say 4 or 5 drest skins, & 1 cut up.

Wednes 2nd. Nothing new. Thurs 3^d. About noon today Welles' dogs arrived – it appears they run away from him.

Frid 4th. I make preparations for sending to Mr McDougall's the news of this place. Paradix & Vandalle are the men I send. Beautiful weather.

Satur 5th. About day light, or very near, I send off my men. About 9 The weather grew cold, & at 10 we had snow with a furious wind & bitter cold all day. After breaking 3 or 4 pair of show shoes I at last succeeded in bending a pair to my fancy. Welles is not yet arrived.

Sund 6th. The wind ceased about noon, but the cold is near about the same. Welles' not coming put me very much out of the way; & I am afraid will injure me. I was for sending last Thursday in quest of <u>Cû-levé</u>, but for this reason I could not. Tomorrow please God I send after him [Welles]. Larocque seems to be very anxious – he seems to think him dead, i.e. drown'd on his return (as the latter end of the 2nd river is very bad & dangerous), but I apprehend no such thing. His dogs in that case would have come here with at least a part of their

---

17 Netting snowshoes was women's work. As Nelson's wife was not with him this year, he may have employed Welles's wife to do it.

harness on them; but they came quite naked, & both together. But W. can remain there still a month.

/18/ Mond. 7th Decr 1818. At the dawn of day I sent off Plante & Wm Pritchard, a scorched stump (brulé*) in Welles care to look after him (W.). I sent Larocque too as far as the first lake. At dusk, they arrive (except La. Who got home about 3½ P.M.) and W. tells me he lost himself, & did not reach the lodges till the fourth day, having stupidly followed a small band (four) who seperated from the rest so as to hunt with more success. This is a lie & I am sure of it.

Tuesd. 8th. Most bitter cold, i.e. in comparison to what we have had. About 3½ p. m. I was surprised to see Le Nez d'argent arrive. He left his lodge about midnight, which is upon this side of Fisher River. They have made [out] not much better than all my other indians together. The Frise is gone on to a place called Birch Lake in quest of other & Le Gendre, Belly & Assiniboine are with him. The 3 last were starving & had nothing about 15 or 18 days since. Messrs Blacklegs & Co. about 7 days en camped with this band, N d'A [Nez d'Argent] & brother. Yesterday I took a large Grey fox in a steel trap in the first joint of the fore paw, & the Gentleman travelled about 2 miles through a most thick wood.[18]

Wednesd. 9th. I send off Larocque & Plante about 2 hours before day to River aux Guerriers in quest of Cu-levé & Cancre. I do this being afraid of the HB's paying them unrequested respects in that quarter. I sent 4 meas. Powder, 3 lb [?] Shot & 42 balls. 1 quts of spirits, & 2½ ftms tobacco. I was obliged to day fix up my chimney as it smokes so dreadfully. I done it one way yesterday, but it became worse.

/19/ Thurs 10th Decr. At 1½ after midnight & of course 5 hours before day light, I send off Welles with the indians. I of course remain alone with the women. Why have the women of this country so great a name for being light-tailed?[19] Very cold.

Frid 11. Satur 12th Sund 13th. Still very cold – my men must have a very disagreable travelling – the air is so cold & sharp. My Employment since I am alone, is to provide myself dry wood being in my Green wood, water, cook, & attend i.e. empty the fish basket morning & evening, which is no trifle of a joke, to chop the ice in the

18 The fox, once caught by the leg, managed to drag himself and the trap over this difficult terrain before succumbing, or before Nelson caught up with him.

19 Nelson may have been expressing indignation at an undeserved reputation for the local women, or, his wife absent in Canada, he may have made a sexual invitation that was repulsed.

current, clean it &c. I began copying some rubs [?] for Stenography from a manuscript lent me.[20] The weather is clear. We have however had snow almost every day this week but very little at a time.

Mond. 14 Tuesd 15th. I was very much surprised this morning, a few minutes after sun-rise, by the arrival of young Frisé. He went with M. Crebassa last fall to Grd. Rapid, but being disgusted with that part of the country & the indians, he left it & came near the Lake here in cane [?] time. He is now near my old house in Pigeon-River[21] with one of old Nez Corbin's Twin-Sons. From his accounts Crebassa has made but a very indifferent Fishery, if indeed he has taken any at all. It appears likewise that the HB's have such influence over that superstitious & incestuous set of indians as to prevent them in from going openly to C's. Creb. had given out but very few debts owing to the few indians that dared to go to see him.

Wednesd. 16th. Welles returned this forenoon with a very moderate load from the indians. He brought me however between 50 & 60 lbs of Grease; he left 3 slay loads still behind.

/20/ Thurs 17th Decr 1818. This morning near 3 hours before day the Frisé returns home. He is to guide my men if necessary to Mr Crebassa's, & the appointed time & place is 9 nights & in Pigeon River, at the first falls. About noon I had the pleasure of seeing my two men arrive from Fort Alexander; but they brought me the most melancholy accounts, – the death of our head, Mr Duncan McDougall the 25th Octr, a Gentleman for whom I had the most perfect esteem, & who, I am sure, was worthy of more. I did not become acquainted with him till late in July this year, & it was not till late in Septr that I had the means of knowing anything of him, & then only during a very few days. His generous, open, & truly candid & honest behaviour has intirely won my affections. Exclusive of this, our dispositions, our sentiments were so congenial that I will regret him most sincerely. From his confidential communications to me, I am sure our esteem was reciprocal, more than is commonly to be found at present among brothers. I have lost him, & I may safely say, I lost my only Friend! He is gone! Let the God of Peace & mercy have compassion upon his Soul!! He had his failings, as well as other men, & he was so

20 Nelson was copying some kind of shorthand dictionary. It may have been this that put him in mind of inventing the substitution code that he used in his coded journal in 1820.
21 This is the only indication in the journals that Nelson had once wintered in Pigeon River, on the east side of the north basin of Lake Winnipeg. As noted previously, this must have been in the 1812–13 season.

fully sensible of it that they were the sole of his last days. Why is our
state so weake! O Lord! Let my end be as truly devoted & Christian
as his has been!

/21/ Thurs 17th Decr 1818

Messrs McKinzie (the son of he who was confined by L.S. [Lord
Selkirk]) & Bell were with him.[22] Mr. McKinzie, being the elder clerk
of Course had the charge of the place after this. According to his duty,
he sent word to Red River, [to] Mr McBean, my former master in the
Pic Dept, [who] winters at River Qu'appelle, & it seems he is the head
master of that Dept: & of course, in consequence of this melancholy
accident, he has an eye at present over this; & from reports as appears
from his letter to me, he sent down a Mr Hess to take the charge from
Mr McKenzie who is to be kept about between Crebassa & me. This is
another convincing proof to me how true the first maxim I ever formed
& adopted is, that a mans only friend is his own good conduct; and
after that, a good pouse [?], or a long [alone?] in the world. Mr. McK. is
a brulée* & appeared to me to be a fine young man, & his men say the
same. Were I in his place, i.e. young, free & independent I should not
allow my Eyes to close before I should have an ample explanation of the
whole. Poor & needy what shall I do when my character is destroyed?

Larocque & Plante also arrived this afternoon from River aux
Guériers, where they found my two indians, & brought home 30
skins, all in martens, except one beaver. The Wolves destroyed their
traps is their but too just complaint Laroque tells me.[23] He also tells
me that all my fish at River Dauphine are perfectly rotten & uneatable even by the dogs!!!

/22/ Frid. 18th. Saturd. 19th. At 2½ a.m. I send off Larocque with
Vandalle & Welles for the remainder of those Provisions. The weather
was delightful yesterday & part of this forenoon, it became snowy
afterwards, but mild. Mr McKenzie altho' expected yesterday is not yet
arrived. I put two pieces of Glass in two of my windows today.

Sund 20th. A high E wind, & snowy, but mild.

Mond 21st. At 9 a.m. Mr McKenzie arrived with two men Jos: Bergé
& La Course. They brought me no letter, Mr Hess not writing to me.
I forgot to mention that my men arrived in good time yesterday, say

22 Roderick McKenzie and John Bell; for both, see Appendix D. Roderick's father was
Daniel McKenzie, one of the NWC partners who was arrested by Lord Selkirk at Fort William
in 1816.

23 Not the strong steel traps, but traps of weak materials that the wolves would break to
steal the baits.

about 1½ P.M. They broght me a good deal of Pounded meat about 600 lbs wt besides some Poor miserable dry meat.[24] They saw one of the indians who had come to see the things [?].

Tuesd 22nd Wednes 23d. Thursd. 24th. I prepare my men today to leave this for three different quarters, say Laroque & La Course for Mr Crebassa's, Bergé & Plante for Bas de la rivière; & Welles with Paradix for Falle de Pardrix. The weather was remarkably [warm] yesterday – it is rather more Cold today

Friday 25th. We all pass Holyday together, but let us look out for tomorrow.

Saturd 26th. At 3. a. m. Larocque & Claude Lacourse set off for Mr Crebassa's. I give them about 4 lbs grease & 16 quts of rice. I send Welles & Plante off to Falle de Perdrix.

/23/ Sat 26th Decr. 1818

About an hour before day I send Bergé back to Fort Alexander & Paradix along with him. Nothing new besides this.

Sund. 27th. Mond 28th Tues 29th Wednes. 30th. All very quiet during this interval. I passed my time very busily in endeavouring to make Snow shoe frames but to no purpose – I broke them as fast as I brought them in. I was <u>much</u> surprised by the arrival of Welles who returned from about 8 miles up River Dauphine he told me there was too much water on the ice, & now, of course they could not make any head way for the want of snow shoes but this is a lie. He had one, or two, greater reasons for it one is that he was afraid of not being back for New Years &c &c, or, & which I think is the most likely, Jealousy. He has got a piece of fresh Beef nearly as large as a steam-boat, & just as handy, i.e. can go head wind, up rapids &c &c and <u>bring-to</u> roundly, he, I fancy was afraid that she might give <u>passage free</u> to some distressed traveller;[25] but oh! Yea! However, a mad dog lives all over & every thing, even rotten wood or iron for the want of better stuff. He brought me a few fish as a specimen of those Larocque speared for me, & which he said were absolutely uneatable. Some of them were indeed rotten, but some are very good.

Frid 1 Jany 1819. Pass this foolish day [New Year's Day, the men's holiday] together.

24 The dried and pounded buffalo meat would have been prepared at Red River, and may have been brought to Fort Alexander by Charles Hesse to improve the supply of food in the Lake Winnipeg department.

25 Nelson is talking about Welles's wife or woman. The phrase "piece of fresh Beef" looks like a variant of the phrase "blue beef" that Nelson used to speak of some of the voyageurs' women in 1810 (see journal entry of 25 July 1810).

Saturd 2nd. At day light send off Welles & Plante again with only one Pair of snowshoes. Vandalles wife was delivered of a female child about 2. a. m. I make another pair of snow shoes, being determined to succeed in making them properly.

/24/ Sund. 3 Jany 1819. Mond. 4th Tuesd. 5th. No News.

Wednes 6th. Very cold indeed, but no other News.

Thurs 7th. A furious Southerly wind & snow. La Roque & La Course arrive this Evening, at dusk. They bring but Poor news from that quarter. It is merely by the dint of application that they do not starve there. Mr Crebassa's wife had taken 1000 rabbits, his 2 daughters 850, Brisebois 1000, &c. Fortunately for them, because the indians of that quarter wont see them, & even menaced them with their lives. The HB's have a most compleat ascendancy over them; but indeed Poor Crebassa has some men, who it appears are men [only] because they are not females.

Frid 8 Sat. 9th Sund 10th. A heavy Snow till 2 P.M. when we have a most furious <u>wind</u> & cold. Mr McKenzie prepares to return to Fort Alexander tomorrow, with La Roque whom I send to bring Paradix back.

Mond 11th. The wind is terribly hi from the N.N.W. & the weather is colder by far to day than it has been yet this winter. I took Vandalle with me to get a slay for himself.

Tuesd 12th. Mr McKenzie, with La Course & La Roque set off about 2 hours before day this morning, the weather being too bad yesterday. At 2 P.M. <u>Two of my indians</u> arrive, two of the three that came here starving last Novr 23^d. They are upon Fisher River, towards the head of it. <u>Old Frisé</u> & <u>the Belly</u> are with them. They have been eating well, but that is all. I had a long conversation with them explaining them what they have to /25/ expect next year if they do not behave well this year. This is what they did not expect, & the explanation of it, from what they said appears to have been very proper. There is a widow they tell me that arrived at their lodges the day before yesterday from the upper part of <u>River-au-Mauricette</u>, near four days march for a young man from where they are now. She left an <u>indian family</u> with whom she was, to look for <u>her</u> <u>mother</u>. She left there in the first quarter of last moon (& the present one is past its full) with her child she carried on her back, & without provisions. She was obliged to set snares to live. This however, is but a very trivial circumstance in comparison to many things of the like nature that happen here in this country. Many of them would be much doubted were they even seen by People who are not accustomed to see misery but as she is in the civilised world, where she is termed.

Wednes. 13th. At about 4 a. m. (2½ hours before day) the two indians return. I send Vandalle with them, but sorely against his grain tho' he does not complain, because he is a peevish cowardly thing with the indians. He had orders from me to wait 2 days for Welles. Welles at last arrived at 10 a. m. he brought me 12 skins from one of my indians that was hunting near the HB's in Lac St Martin where he was most hospitably treated both going & coming. All quiet, & all is well in those quarters. The weather grows much milder.

/26/ Thurs 14th Jany 1819. At day light this morning I send off Welles & Plante to join Vandalle. Cold. Nothing new.

Frid 15th. We had snow both of these days, but not sufficiently to make the weather mild.

Sat. 16. Sund. 17th Mond 18th. This Evening my men arrive, very heavily loaded, but only in dry & Pounded meat, with some Grease. I got 44½ Skins from them 7 in all, but the Frisé & his son killed 39½. If unfortunately they should continue so lasy the rest of the year, I am afraid I will not make 4 Packs here. Clear, but Cold.

Tuesd. 19th. Wednes. 20th. L'assiniboine, the son-in-law of Old Lorrain's son-in-law [Le Gendre], arrived about 3½ P.M. He is with his father in Law, a little beyond the last Lake above here, & left the lodge this morning. News: he tells me that he has 23 skins, his F.in.L. 12, & Boitineau's daughter 1½ (i.e. 3 martins) because she has nothing but a drest skin to cover herself with. The 5 martins I got from Le Jour-Rond (an indian with the Frisé at present) he stole out of their traps, besides a quantity of meat he found hid in the ground. He also stole ½ of a Green moose from the Red Breast: he & his father in Law are pitching towards the fort with my consent. In the last quarter of last moon they met with the Red Breast. He had but little or nothing, & was starving, informing that they were to come here for fish if they did not soon kill. They had all seperated. Tete-Grises Eldest son & family were on /27/ on one of the branches of Monotágué River, towards L. S^t. Martin. The Souffleu, who left his brother to hunt out & pass the remainder of the winter with his mother, was going with her, one R Breasts son, & Capot verd. One of those indians that arrived here on the 9th Novr was towards the mouth of Monotagué River, round which & in that large Point of Tete au Pishew [they] are to hunt 'till spring. Capot Verd was to go to the HB's in L. S^t. M. to pay them 4 skins he took from them in debt last fall. If unfortunately for me, they go, & that the HB's have any sense, they will keep my indians in good order for the remainder of the season. <u>Red Breast</u> himself, was on one of the southern branches of that River. The indians, he tells me, all speak well of the <u>Savard</u>,[26] & are fond of him, if this be so, why then do they not hunt better?

Thurs. 21ˢᵗ. This indian returns alone. I send no one with him as I have no slay, i.e. that is, my men have broken all their slays in their last trip, they were so heavily loaded, & there being so much fallen wood.

Frid 22nd. I get my house white washed today in the inside, as it was becoming very cold.[27] This afternoon Laroque arrived with Paradix. They brought me 2 pritty good loads of one thing or another. Nothing new, unless I mention the old story, i.e. the indians complaining of starvation & making no hunt. Mr. Hess wrote me this time, apologizing for not having done it the first time; but it is in the true Spanish Stile, i.e. of lovers. I will here give an extract verbatim, "Mr Nelson youll know I had particularly order to dispatch Mr Rodᵏ McKenzie to your Eimable Person to Remain with you /28/ at the same time to assist M Nelson to Go about to the Indian tents for furs Sir I don my duty as far as to Send You the Young Gentleman I shall not be blamed for the Great man the young Gentleman was Sond back I do not know for What Sir youll know that Mr McBean will not be Pleased Mr McBean is Vext at the young Gentleman So forth." No stops or any thing Else, but plenty capitals & bad spelling. – but this is nothing – it is very pardonable considering all things – Please God I will pay him a visit & see more about him. — <u>Eimable Person</u>!! In other respects, it appears that young McK had but two faults, one & the first he assumed too much after the charge of B. de la R. devolved on him, the other his too open & unpardonable connections with Potvins wife, a handsome young half-breed at F. Alexander (her husband is now as evidence in Canada for the Compy. ɴw. In short, there is but little difference between them two now, & her & her husband last Summer.

Sat. Sund. 24ᵗʰ. Fine weather & mild.

Mond. 25ᵗʰ. A very heavy snow & south wind till late in the afternoon. At day light I sent off La Roque & Paradix to River Dauphine in quest of my indians (<u>Angce</u>) & from thence to river aux Gueriers after <u>Cu-levé</u> & <u>Cancre</u>. I went to see my trap today that I kept out a long time, but found it off, & only one place where he [the animal] had tumbled. The snow

---

26 This passage specifies the chosen winter hunting grounds for five Indigenous bands, and gives an idea of the area over which the furs they traded with Nelson were expected to come. Savard (a "wise one") must be a term for Nelson himself.

27 Apparently a house was warmer, or was felt to be so, if it was whitewashed on the inside.

since 2 a. m. being so heavy I could not discover anything to a certainty, however, by the gnawing of a branch I /29/ supposed it to be a wolf; & by a track in the woods, which with much difficulty I found, I perceived the trap did not drag much. I returned home, took breakfast & prepared for a push. With a great deal of difficulty I found his track leading into the woods. I had 3 dogs with me, but none of them were anxious to follow the track, they kept playing near me. At last one of them pushed off & soon came up with him, it was a wolf, a very large one, but lean.

Tuesd. 26th. This morning at day light I send off Vandalle, Welles & Plante to the Frisé's on Fisher river for meat, which he said I was to get in Ten nights.

Wednes 27th. Thursd. 28. Snow all forenoon, yesterday & today see Diary.28

Frid. 29th. Snow again. Tho' we have had snow so frequently this week, still there fell but little in depth.

Sat. Sund 31st. My men arrive about 2 P.M. they bring a shee-moose & an old Rotten Bull (Buffaloe) – the only animals they have killed since they were last on Fisher River. At 4 P.M. Laurrin's son-in-Law [Le Gendre] arrived. He is two Encampments on this side of where they were when his Son-in-Law came. They've killed 3 female & 1 male moose since then. He comes for People to go for two of them, in fresh, & near two others in dry, meat. I got some more information from him concerning L'Estomac-Rouge. It appears he had not even Power suffi- cient to stop his own children from going so near the HB's. I prevailed upon this man to send his son in law [L'Assiniboine] for him to come here, so that I may speake to him.

/30/ Mond. Feby 1st. 1819. It was broad day light before the indians returned. I sent my 3 men with him. The weather is most delightful these two days, see [...]. I took an acct of my Furs today in the shop, not including mine or those of Laroque, vist:

274 martins 137; 5 L. Blk bears 10; 4 small do do 4; 22 otters P. & Com. 22; 5 beavers L. & Small 3; 82 musk rats [...]; 1 Cat Prime 2; 3 Fishers 1 1/2; 2 Red foxes 2; 3 minks 3/4; 2 Wolverines 1; 1 Silver Grey 2. Amounting to 193 1/2 as paid for them to the indians, making Rather better than a Pack; about 100 lbs in all I suppose.29

28 Nelson was apparently keeping a diary, and his journal was extracted from that.
29 The small superscript numbers attached to each item in the inventory are the equivalents in beaver, so this entry gives us the NWC standard of trade. See introduction to this journal.

Tuesd 2nd. A most Charming day. My men arrive a little before sun set and bring me 47 martins [23] ½, 5 otters [...] 1 Drest Skin [2] 1 L. Brown Bear [3], making in all 37½ Skins.[30] A miserable hunt for near 3½ months, but they all assure me that they will pay. They brought me a few Pieces of dry meat besides a whole fresh moose; & being a female, & with young is very fat. They left another one there which they are to go for very soon.

Wednes. 3[d]. Thurs. 4th. At day light I send off Vandalle & Welles (L'Allemand) for the moose they left behind. This is the Eleventh day that Larocque is off for a trip I expected him to take no more than 7 or 8 days at the very furthest to perform. I am afraid something has happened /31/ them: it is true La Roque is a very Prudent man, respected by the indians but Paradix is just the reverse.

Friday 5th. About 12, Vandalle & Welles arrived. They brought me the moose, it was a small one. L'Assiniboine was not yet returned, it was supposed that they were pitching off towards Le Gendre's. I had the pleasure to see La Roque & Paradix arrive here about 1½ P.M. They brought me 87 skins, a most famous hunt if we consider all things properly. They went to see three of the HB Indians that were on the upper part of the right branch of River aux Gueriers. They brought me only 15 martins and a small Cat – the indians not willing to trade by any means & were near killing them & taking (i.e. robbing) them of their rum; but they left the lodges in the night, & one of the indians pursued them a piece to get their rum, but he failed! They wanted to kill my men to revenge the death of one of their friends whom they say old Rassette killed, because his daughter eloped with him. The Swan promises himself a parley with them on this subject – we shall see I hope, how far he says truth. Angce gave my men but 2 martins. Cu-Levé, Cancre, & Cie-Sec gave 78 skins, a Glorious hunt. Oh! My God, if all my indians would pay me as well I should be a happy man, for this year at least.

I have now in the shop, say Packed up on Monday   193½
                          From Gendre & band   37½
                          Cû-levé & band   87 –
                          L'allemand's wife   2¾
                                              329¾

---

30 The beaver equivalent of the otters in this entry is illegible; from the previous inventory, it should be five beaver. The total value of the skins in this entry would thus be 33½ skins or *plus*, not 37½, as Nelson states.

which may make me about 1½ packs![31] The same quantity in Beaver
would make me near 6 Packs!

/32/ Saturday 6 th Jany [*sic* – should be February] 1819. The Weather
is most remarkably mild. The Thermometer rose 7 degrees above freezing Point. The Weather has been remarkably mild for many days past.
Drissly today.

Sund. 7th. Send off Vandalle, Welles, Plante & Paradix, to the Frisé's
for meat, in Fisher River, before day-light. The Red Breast does not
come, I fancy he considers as being insulted by my sending to tell him
that I wanted to see him, to give him advice, & will not come. Very
mild still but the wind changed to the N.W. & app. of cold.

Mond. 8. Tuesd. 9th. Wednesd. 10th. This Evening at dusk my men
arrive with each the half of a moose. No news. Welles broke his slay
intirely & with much difficulty brought his load here.

Thurs 11. Frid. 12th. Satur 13. Before day light this morning I sent
off Larocque to Le Gendre's, to enquire of Red Breast he returnd about
1 P.M. telling me that they were heavily loaded with meat & were
pitching towards us very quietly; & that none of them had been to the
HB's, nor had even any intention towards it. I am very happy at this
news. I make preparations for a visit to Bas de la Riviere from motives
I cannot now communicate.

Sund 14th. Expect to leave this tomorrow, please God, for Fort
Alexander.

Mond 15th. Leave this at about 2 hours before day & Encamp at
Detroit-du-Duque at 3 P.M., a distance of 16 leagues, 2 hours before
sunset. I took Paradix & Ant. Vandalle with me. On Tuesd. 16. /33/ we
set off at 2 a.m. & encamped at Pointe au Batteaue at 3 P.M. (16 more
leagues), having stopped 1¼ hours at noon, to eat. On Wednesday 17
set off at 3, & at 8½ a.m. arrive at Fort Alexander (8 leagues) where I
found all well thank God, & quiet. On Tuesday 23d I returned, taking
Mr. McKensie with me to keep charge of my place during my absence
to Mr. Crebassa's. Fleuri & Bergé two of Mr Hesses men came with me
for meat; & Bapt. Carribouef, whom I got for Paradix as I was afraid
the indians would kill him for his brutishtry. We en camped very early
at Pointe au Mauricette, 11 leagues & set off on Wednesd. 24th at broad
day light as it snowed, which continued without much intermission
all day. At noon the wind was furious from the N.N.W. (in[...] forces)
& it sleeted very hard at 4½ P.M. we put up near detroit du duc (our

---

31 The total of the numbers given is 320¾, not 329¾ *plus*.

campment in going), which we could not reach from the excessive badness of the weather, tho' not more than a mile & a half from it. On Thurs 25 (Feby 1819) the weather was beautiful indeed. We sett off a few minutes before sun rise, & arrived at my house a little after sun set, where I find all well & quiet thank God, but Larocque was alone, L'allemand & Plante were gone to river au Pecan [Fisher River] to Nes d'argent's lodge, for meat & 60 skins in furs he killed since Decr 20th. At Tête aux Chien I met 2 of old Gagnan's sons returning from our house, where they had been 3 days waiting for me. By their account we slept only a few acres from their lodge last night. They have done by their account but very little. L'Estomac Rouge has not been yet in.

/34/ Friday 26th Feby 1819. This forenoon two of L'Estomac-rouge sons came in. They left their lodges yesterday, near monotagué river; they likewise have done but very little. Welles & Plante arrive a little after sun set with two very good loads of green meat, besides 65 skins in furs, & ten they left at the lodges, being over & above what he owes me – see what a man can do when he chooses – this indian alone, has done more than all the band of Red Breast put together.

Saturd. 27th. At day light I send off Laroque & bapt. Carriboeuf to Red-breasts lodge.

Mond 1st. Last night after 9 my two men arrive, bringing two very good loads of meat, & 65 skins in furs. Tête-Grises's Son & family &c were not yet arrived. I must of course send again. This morning a little before sun rise I send off Fleurie & Bergé, with half an animal & 1 bag of pounded meat. I send Welles with them as far as Detroit du duc for some of old Gagnan furs. Mr. McKenzie mad after his sweet-heart, I allow to return; because I am confident he would fall sick [otherwise]. Cupid is a dreadful antagonist.[32]

Tuesd. 2nd March. Before day light I send of all my men (Laroque, Carriboeuf, Vandalle & Plante) to the Red Breast's again, after the others.

Wednes. 3d March. About half after two [?] my men arrive, bringing me 44 Skins in furs, but plenty /35/ of meat. I was much surprised to find they brought back my rum, all except about 2 quts. This is a wonderful thing among this nation (Sauteuxs). Carriboeuf would not give them more, because they Paid so little of their debts. Welles arrived this evening, having seperated from Mr McKensie & th'others this morning,

---

32 Contrary to instructions, Nelson was again letting Roderick McKenzie return to Fort Alexander, where he could continue his affair with Potvin's wife.

late at Detroit du Duc. He brought me a few skins & the meat of a Carreboeuf.

Thurs 4ᵗʰ. The men rest, & their dogs more so.

Frid. 5ᵗʰ. Early this morning I send off Vandalle, Welles, & Carriboeuf, to Fisher River for more, that which Welles left there.

Satur. 6ᵗʰ. In good time this afternoon my men arrive, bringing me the whole of the Buffalo, tho' nearly rotten, notwithstanding it had been cleaned & put upon a stage; but it was so completely wrapped up on account of the squirrels, mice & martins that no air could get to it. They brought me some dry & Pounded meat.

Sunday 7ᵗʰ. About 2 P.M. Nez-d'argent & another indians arrive from Fisher River. They bring me 33½ skins in martens – this makes 112 skins N. d'argent has killed already.

Mond 8ᵗʰ. The indians return with a little rum I give them & 21 skins in Goods they traded. I took a most beautiful Black [fox] this last night in my trap.

/36/ Tuesd. 9ᵗʰ March, 1819. I make preparations to leave this to morrow for Grd. Rapid to pay Crebassa a visit. I take 2 Slays as heavily loaded as I can, of dry provisions for him. This afternoon Le Gendre, Belly, & Assiniboine came in again, they bring me about a dozen more skins. They pitched quite near in here, about a mile from this. They come as they tell me to fill their bellies (having starved for a long time past) & to get rum to honor the birth of a daughter of his (Le Gendre's) born 5 days ago.

Wednes. 10ᵗʰ. About half an hour before day I set off for Mr Crebassa's, taking Laroque & Carriboeuf, Welles & Plante, the two latter with each a heavy load of meat (dry & Pounded) for Mr Crebassa. We en camped about 12 or 14 miles in Pigeon River. We had very bad wether from 10 to 4. After that it became more mild & fine.

Thurs 11ᵗʰ. Set off about an hour before day, & at about 1½ miles above the 5th Falls (about 24 or 25 miles) we fell upon a road, marked as at a little above it struck off into the woods, & apparently going [in] a straight course, in our direction. I followed it, supposing it to be Crebassa's step-son pitching off to see his mother. We went on heartily & encamped after sun-set in their 6th tent, from the /37/ river. This was a great day, for we travelled hard & stopped but seldom, & then only for a few moments to let the dogs breathe. We were uneasy, afraid & very anxious. I intended this to have been the last day Welles & Plante were to come with me, but not knowing where we were (except we went always in a N.E. direction, being assured it would shorten our

road a great deal if we could fall on the river) I found myself obliged
to keep them till such times as we found or came up with the indians.
Very Cold, & a furious N. Wind.

Frid. 12th. As it still blew very furiously we did not start 'till broad day
light (6 o'clock) lest we should loose our road. We had the pleasure a few
minutes after 7 to find another hut where they had killed several Rein-
Deer (Carriboeufs) & had remained several days, for the Poles were quite
sooty, whereas the others were hardly singed (remaining but one night in
each). 'Till this place they appeared to be living on rabbits only, & apparently but very few of them. Travelling very smartly, we arrived at their 4th
lodge at 11 P.M., which place they had pitched off this morning. We kindled a fire, made water to drink & staid 'till near noon, so that they might
have time to finish their building before our arrival. We reached their tent
at 1 P.M. & found to my surprise it was old Nez Corbin & his youngest
Son, with an HB Man. There was only the old man's wife, the others were
gone for meat. They arrived a few hours after, & to my inexpressible pleasure found that I was but at one days Journey from Crebassa's straight, &
the Son promised to go with me. They had a great deal of meat, /38/ some
of which I bought for my dogs with rum; as I was short of food for them.
The weather very cold indeed & a furious Wind.

Satur 13th. We set off at 3¼ a.m. & at 2½ P.M. arrived at
Crebassa›s, where I found them all well, living well but only on rabbits
of which there are surprising numbers in this quarter, & a few fish. He
lives on Good terms with his neighbor, but furs are very scarce, consequently the returns are, or at least will be very poor, on either side. I
made my other two men put up their loads on a stage & ordered them
to return from this place (where we slept).

Sund. 14th. Mr Crebassa's neighbor[33] came & took dinner with us as
we did on Mond. 15th. I found him, like all Englishmen, plain, honest
& very open.

Tues 16th. We set off at day light to return home & before sun rise
met 3 of Crebassa's men just getting home with the loads they were
sent for (that I tooke up for them).

Wednes. 17. Thurs 18th. A few minutes past noon I reached home,
but not till after I had suffered much from the bitter cold we had
(certainly far the coldest weather we've had this year) & excess of
fatigue; for we travelled like men escaped from the Gibbet. I reckon
the distance to be near 200 miles. We travelled at the Rate of a good

33 The HBC trader Donald Sutherland; see Appendix D.

trot from 4 to 4, & this day from 2 to 12¼, very seldom stopping. I found all well, thank God. The day I left home Mr McKenzie & Bonhomme Hense (Tous^t. Vaudrie)[34] arrived /39/ with letters from Bas de la Riviere, an express from Upper Canada giving us the pleasing intelligence of all our people in the two Canadas being liberated & his Lordship not daring to appear at Court.[35] It is further reported that on his return to England by the United States, he was there detained & obliged to give security for his appearance, in 3000 Dollars.

Frid. 19th. <u>Four women</u> arrived from <u>Red Breast</u> lodge. They tell me that their men are doing their utmost to pay their debts; & will be in here in a few days.

Satur 20th. Nothing new, very cold.

Sund. 21st. Two of the women Return, they are with the <u>Siffleu</u> on their way to Fisher River; & encamped on the large lakes behind here from whence they came here.

Mond 22nd. A furious wind all day, & a little snow last night. I sent Bapt. Carriboeuf & Vandalle to Mr Crebassa's with the Expresses.

Tuesd. 23^d. We put out a net today, because Vandalle allowed the Indians to carry off almost all our fish. The few remaining are very bad. Sharp weather, but more Calm.

Wednes 24th. In our Net we took but one Pikeral, but it was a very large one. The Net was too much twisted. I measured the ice today & found it exactly 4 feet thick, another very convincing proof of the mildness of <u>this</u> Winter.

/40/ Thursd. 25th March 1819. The cold to day was very moderate, but the wind was truly terrible. We all remain quiet.

Frid 26th. Our net gave us 10 Pikeral, 4 Pike & a carp. Since some days past I am become as excessively lonesome that every become tiresome to me. I try every thing I can conceive, but all in vain. I took a long walk this afternoon to pass my time & on my return I found a <u>young indian</u> at the house come from the Bay of Fisher River about 18 miles from here. He comes from <u>Nez d'argent's lodge</u> for people to go for a moose he gives me. They killed it in that furious wind of yesterday. It had two young ones with it, one of them escaped. It was very

---

34 The reference is unclear, but it may mean that Toussaint Vaudry had brought the letters from McKenzie and Hesse at Fort Alexander.
35 A summary of the result of the various trials of NWC men on charges brought by Lord Selkirk over their treatment of the colony at Red River.

big with young; it had 3 young ones – two were of the natural size, but the 3ᵈ was about the size of a barn root [?], had the hair & all the other marks of having been for several in the Embryo [*sic*]. This, altho' ridiculous in appearance, is notwithstanding a strict fact.

Satur 27ᵗʰ. I send Laroque & Welles for the meat. They come back a few minutes past noon. This afternoon One of L'assiniboine's wives & Boitineau's daughter came in, on a visit.

Sund 28ᵗʰ. These two women return & at 2 P.M. The Belly arrives – he brings me 3 martins & the tongue with the snout of a young moose. The Poor devil has passed the winter without a Kettle & is come for one. At 3½ P. M. Vandalle & Carriboeuf arrive, an amazing quick Journey, all is well there.

/41/ Mond. 29ᵗʰ March. The Belly returns.

Tuesday 30ᵗʰ. Nothing new, only that I am making preparations to go to see Cu-levé & Cancre in R. Dauphine.

Wednesd. 31ˢᵗ. Set off about half an before day & arrived at R. D. About 4 P.M. a few acres in the River I found Angce (i.e. again, once-more, &c). Poor miserable wretch! To tell a wealthy man of a civilised world how this creature with his wife & two young daughters have passed the winter, would be only to hunt for the name of a Liar. They [have] only one blanket of 2½ pts between them to cover all four at night; a most miserable hut, part hay & part bark, with holes big enow to let in Crows & only one very small tomahawk between him & his wife, i.e. to make traps & chop their fire wood! Shoes & snow-shoes of a piece with the rest; & their food was the remains of my fish, so bad Rotten that it was uneatable to us, tho' God knows [we are] not too delicate in our taste either. He is far from being the only one living in this manner. There are many so, & many worse; & yet it is from such poor miserable wretches that great fortunes, & of course Ease, plenty, & Luxury come! I got 27½ Skins from him, by far more than from many of those who pass for good hunters.

I found the Cancre there, on his way to me, to give me the pleasing intelligence of their being on this river, about 6 leagues up, a starving, & having made no hunt, & the little they have has been mostly traded from them by the HB's of Lac Sᵗ Martin. I encamped at the foot of the rapids, about 2 miles in the river.

Thursd. 1ˢᵗ April. Set off at day light, & at 7½ arrive just as they were pitching off. I found several of the /42/ of the HB indians there. I got but 30 skins from them all. I staid 'till noon, & returned to our encampment at 3½ P.M. I saw a white headed eagle to day, the first seen by us this year, were at the house on Sund. 21ˢᵗ ultimo.

Frid. 2nd. Return at day light, & at 3 P.M. arrive at the house, when, thank God, I found all well. The Cold 'till 10½ a.m. was so great to our feelings that we had work enough to keep ourselves from freezing when we retired to our slays for a few moments to rest. I found Welles; Carribeuf has left the house this morning for Fort Alexr with the letters I had given them. I found the Belly with all his family at the house. They come in starving.

Saturd. 3ᵈ. Two young men came in from Nez-d'argent lodge, they bring me only a few furs, & want people to go for about 12 or 15 more, they have there.

Sund 4ᵗʰ. Tho' this be Palm Sunday I am obliged to send, for fear some others should come in. I sent Larocque & Plante & they came home at 8½ P.M.

Mond. 5ᵗʰ. Tuesd. 6ᵗʰ. It has thawed pritty well these 3 last days. We had a little snow just at day light this morning. Belly sets off to visit his traps.

Wednes 7 Thursd. 8ᵗʰ. I was very much surprised this morning, between 8 & 9 to see the Young Frisé arrive with two of Mr. Crebassa's men, Jos. Vandalle & Beaucampe. He /43/ sent them to the Frisé's lodge for more meat, but as he had not a sufficiency to load them, they came to me for the remainder, according to his order. All is well there.

Frid. 9ᵗʰ. Good Friday, Lorrin's son in law & Gang arrive. They encamp a little below – they come to prepare a stock of fish as the hunting of moose is become extremely difficult from the rustling of the leaves.

Saturday 10ᵗʰ. Nothing.

Sunday 11 Easter Sunday Apl 11th 1819, and a fine Sunday it is to us. In the first place we had very fine weather all day; but not too much thaw, & some snow before day. Now Prepare – after much solicitation I gave some rum to these indians who got drunk & the Frisé (who Viewes himself upon being the same as we ourselves) went & drank with them, & gave them all a good hearty basting. They kept me up all night. At 10 a.m the Older Frisé arrived with his Son. I got 40 Skins from them. At 11, Old Gagnon's Eldest Son & son-in-law came in also; they brought me 14 Skins & some meat. At 5 my men arrived from Bas de la riviere with one bag of Shot & 50 lbs of flour, & that's all. All is well there; but they were very near burning down twice in the big house by the fire catching in the Kitchen. James Grant a Proprietor of the (NW) Company at R. River was very ill, & indeed nearly despaired of.[36] At Lac La Pluie /44/ likewise they (our people) were near burning down: and McPherson, clerk for the HB's Co. there & formerly a neighbour of mine, two years was unfortunately drowned in crossing (in Canoe) at the foot of the Falls, with one of his men & an indian, on the 24th Feby.[37]

Mond. 12th 1819. Early, before day, I sent off Crebassa's men, giving them a bag of Grease (about 70 lbs), 3 quts Salt, & some cords, &c. &c. I prepared & Packed off also, all my indians, giving them a little rum; but they went & drank it at the Lodges with Le Gendre &c. The weather was Cloudy but mild consequently we expected rain.

Tuesd. 13th. When I got up in the course of this last night, I was much surprised to find a deep snow on the Ground; & it snowed 'till near ten a.m. leaving us about 8 ins. deep of fresh stuff. This Snow will play the deuce with the few Game already arrived. The first Game heard of this year was by the Frisé in Fisher River, an outerde,* on Good Friday; & one on Sunday by Gagnans Gang. We, here, on Sunday, saw a flock of Pellicans flying over the houses.

Wednesd. 14th. It was not 'till today that the Frisé & Gagnan's band return; because the[y] got drunk with the other indians & lay'd all night in the snow without shelter; & one of them slept upon the ice, /45/ having only his blanket as a shelter; but he was drunk, & that is sufficient. They came in yesterday morning dripping wet, & laughing at their narrow escape.

Thursd. 15th. I was surprised by the arrival of Tête Grise's eldest Son. He came with his brother & brought me 36 Skins between them.

Friday 16th. Bapt Carriboeuf, one of my men, whom I brought with me in exchange for Paradix, fell into fitts last night. He suffered exceeding & strained beyond belief. We were 5 of us holding him, &

---

36 James Grant survived, and retired from the fur trade in 1821: see Wallace 1934, 450, for a biographical note. His account in HBCA, F.4/32, p. 424, confirms that he was at Red River in 1818–19.

37 Donald McPherson, hired by the HBC in 1811 as a writer, had advanced to the rank of master, in charge at Lac la Pluie, by the time of his death. Nelson's information on the date and manner of his death is confirmed by the Lac la Pluie journal for this season (HBCA, B.105/a/6). See HBCA Biographical Sheet, "McPherson, Donald." McPherson had been the HBC trader at Manitonamingon Lake, in The Pic district, in opposition to Nelson, in the fall of 1813. He appears frequently in Nelson's journal for August-November 1813, and also in another journal for January to June 1815, somewhere in the same district. Thus Nelson and McPherson were "neighbours," but rivals, in 1813–14 and 1814–15.

notwithstanding we sometimes had a great deal of trouble to keep him
down & prevent him from biting himself. He fell five different times
between 9 & 12 this morning when he fell asleep. I watched with Mr.
McKenzie till 2 a.m. & then went to bed. When I got up at 4½ a.m I
was much surprised to find Laroque›s wife off. We hunted hi & low far
& near, & was not found till this afternoon with Le Gendre where she
had been. It appears to have been from Jealousy, by her account, & by
his [Larocque's] because she would not listen to his Embraces, altho'
kindly sollicited for upwards of 20 days past. At last he got angry &
threw her out of bed; & she got up & walked off, by his accounts.
By my account, I beleive it is Jeaslousy, because his eyes shew it, &
to make us beleive he is not so, he asked me once this winter "what
Jealousy was" how it is made; what is it like?" &c &c.

/46/ Satur. 17th Apl: 1819. Between 8 and 9 last night Carriboeuf had
two dreadful returns [of his seizures]; particularly the first, which lasted
near half an hour, the second only 12 minutes. Today he feels much
better, has not that head-ache or that inclination to vomit.

Sund 18 Mond. 19th. I was very much surprised last night by the
arrival of an indian (Moniâ) from Bas de la Riviere. He brought me
a letter from Mr Hess being the Copy of one from Mr McBean. The
indian is on a visit to the younger Frisé. A son of one of Red breasts
wives (who arrived here on Saturday, the day Tête-Grise's Son's
returned) killed a duck & a Goose which he sent me.

Tuesd. 20th. L'Assiniboine & Red Breasts son each kill a Goose which
they send me. The Belly leaves this today for the Lakes above & Red
Breast's son's go with him.

Wednesd: 21st. Moniâ goes off to the Frise's lodge i.e. in quest of it. I
give him the letter as it contains useful information, & knowing him &
Frisé to be as trusty, & more so even than many of our own men. Having
at last Prepared a sufficient quantity of fish. Mr. McKenzie prepares to
return tomorrow & I send Vandalle & Plante with him for things I want.
I was very desirous of going myself; but as Laroque was very uneasy
lest Carriboeuf should relapse, /47/ & that I expect some of my indians
whom I wish much to see, I find myself obliged to remain.

Thursd. 22d. At 1 a.m. they set off. On the 20th Two of Femelle de
Carriboeuf's sons came in, they brought me 16 Skins & returned again
immediately. I heard FROGS sing this evening, the first this year; & the
fish began to go up our river, a good sign.

Frid. 23d. Two old women, unbanager [?] & Femelle de Carriboeuf
came in to day, they brought me 5 drest Skins & 2 martins, they return

immediately, being from the 2nd Lake above most delightful weather. Carriboeuf, by my leave, goes to pass a few days with <u>the Gendre</u> & <u>his son in law</u> in the small Lakes behind us, to gather gum. <u>Mother Beaulieu</u> also sets off with them today.

Satur 24th. Sund 25th Mond. 26 Tues 27 Wednes 28th Thurs 29th. <u>Two young lads, the sons</u> of those women that came down last Frid: brought me in 8 Geese, 1 Swan & 2 ducks. I give them a little ammunition & they return again immediately.

Frid. 30th. Le Gendre came in today with 10 Geese* & 2 oies* besides an otter & a few rats. I give him a very little amunition & he returns immediately. Very frequent showers of snow /48/ all day, but none remains 'till late this afternoon, & when it left off there was half an inch deep. It is now several days since the snow is all melted in the woods, only on the brink of the Lake where it collected into large banks there is yet & will be for many days to come a great deal.

I begin to feel uneasy about my men. I am afraid that the HB's have been paying us some unwelcome visit at Bas de la Riviere; but God help us I feel very lonesome & tired of my winter tho' I passed a very peaceable, easy & quiet one. But let us be ever so well off, there is still one thing that we always want , & always will want. Friday 30th Apl. 1819. G. N.

Tete au Brochet, Lake Ounipique
In the NW Co Service

❈

End of journal.

Journal at Tête-au-Brochet, 1819

The next journal, which Nelson calls "Journal B," continues on immediately.

Journal   *1819*
B

May Saturday 1ˢᵗ. Between 9 & 10 last night, some time after I had
been a-bed I heard two hearty wraps at my door, on looking to see, I
found it was Red Breast with three of his sons. This is their 3rd day
from Monotaqueé river. They bring me a few furs, about 40 skins. By
his account my man was well, but was soon to pitch off.[1]

Sund. 2ⁿᵈ Mond 3ᵈ. We have had very bad weather these some
days past, & this morning, there was at least 4 ins. of snow upon the
ground, all the old snow being gone a long time ago, except on the
borders of the Lake; but the most of it melted before night.

Tuesd 4ᵗʰ. My men not being yet arrived, puts me very uneasy, & this
afternoon I send off the Red Breast & his family with about ½ lb. of
Powder, all that I can spare him.

Wednes. 5ᵗʰ. Early this morning I sent Laroque for L'Assiniboane,
who is 7 or 8 miles from here, & prevail upon [him] for ten skins, to
go with Carriboeuf in quest of our people to Bas de la Riviere. I see
but two reasons that can detain them, either that the ice was too bad

---

1 Jean-Baptiste Welles, who did not reappear at Tête-au-Brochet until 2 June.

for their return, or the HB's have been paying us some unwelcome visit there, & detained my men /2/ lest they should bring me information. The Red Breast said, the night before he left this, that in <u>thinking</u> (not dreaming) of my men,[2] he saw one with a strong beard, & bloody mouth enter my house, & then went into Vandalles; by which he supposes there is bad news. Vandalle has a very strong beard, & the bloody mouth alludes to words giving <u>bad news</u>. I send off Carriboeuf to sleep at the indians lodge, as it is on their road. They are also properly instructed how to act, lest this delay be occasioned by any of the 3 distressing reasons.

Thurs 6th. The ground, in consequence of these late snows & rains &c. &c. became very wet; but the hard frosts we have at night & (moderately) warm weather we have in the day, has dried it up greatly. Pike, Suckors &c. enter our river in abundance & numbers of them are killed only for a little Grease [a few words in code].

Frid 7th. Nothing new, further than that <u>the</u> time passes very heavily with me. The only man I now have here with me, to keep me company &c. is Laroque; &, than him, few are more Jealous, & jealous of me too into the bargin. We speak precious little to each other & I never visit them as I used to do. This man, two or three times in the course of this winter asked me to give him a <u>definition</u> of jealousy. I did, & accompanied it with two or three accounts of Jealous people, with remarks of my own; because, though he spoke & acted as one absolutely ignorant of that Hellish passion & that I was greatly inclined to beleive him, still I knew he was jealous, & that his behaviour was only to /3/ <u>pump</u>. Poor unfortunate creature! miserable, truly wretched is he who is troubled; nay, rather, Tormented with this most dreadful disorder. How just, very just is the saying "My Jealousy burns like a <u>consuming</u> Fire."[3] It deprives a man of all things, & his reason – it is something of the nature of Hydrophobia. Nothing is pleasing, nothing can you relish, all goes against you. The heart becomes weak, beats & appears as if it would melt. Even to the recollection of past pleasures seem to increase the rage or melancholy; according to the nature of the disease. He told me some days ago, when he spoke to me on the

2 Nelson had come to understand a distinction the Indigenous peoples made between dreams and waking visions, and to respect both phenomena as potentially useful sources of information. Here, he emphasizes that Red Breast believed that a waking vision, rather than a dream, had come to him.

3 This aphorism is probably inspired by Deuteronomy 4: 24, "For the LORD your God is a consuming fire, a jealous God," but I have not traced the exact source that Nelson quotes.

subject, as relating to myself, that he would <u>set a mark</u> on her, & one she should bear all her life, if he perceived any thing, by which I supposed he meant to slice a piece of her nose; but it appears, it is an ear she has to lose. She appears to me, & all my men to be a remarkably sweet tempered woman; she has no will of her own & is ready to do all <u>she can</u>, but that is very little; & she is handsome & remarkably fair (having only ¼ native blood). On the other side she is slow, awkward, dirty, & some say, light, before she came with this man; & if that be the case, he is just now on the track to make her become ten times worse; for he scolds & quarrels every moment of the day. And I say that a woman that is thus treated, unjustly does well to pay her husband, if she can; but she deserves punishment if she plays on him first.

/4/ Saturd 8.th May 1819. Most Beautiful weather & no appearance of my men yet. I am very lonesome indeed, having only two old women for company & two whelps. My man passes the day with his gang below.

Sund. 9th. It appears that he enjoys a little more ease there than here & I am happy of it. I went to day about 10 miles below (ie. towards F.A.) to see either after my men or the indians, but returned without anything. I found the ice exceedingly bad insomuch that in many places I bored it through with a small stick I carried in my hand; & was frequently very near sinking, tho' far out from the beech [beach]. At 4.P.M. Carriboeuf arrived. They returned from beyond Broken-river a little, the ice rendering their continuation dangerous, if not impossible, there being large spaces where there is no ice at all. I hope that this is the only reason that has prevented the return of my people. Vandalle is a very great coward upon the ice. Carriboeuf left the dogs & slay, for the poor brutes [the dogs] were absolutely unable to walk their feet were so worn out by those numerous points of ice. I suppose we may bid them <u>Good-bye</u> also.

Mond. 10th. Nothing new, only that the wind is South, & blows smartly. I hope in three weeks to be away from here. Well, I pity Laroque, tho' I have no great mind to do it. I spoke to him this forenoon; & he candidly acknowledges his failing, without, however, wishing to cure himself of it. He is a <u>cully</u> [a dupe, or cuckold], I now find; but merely through his own fault; /5/ and indeed he deserves to be much more so. He went with her to <u>tap</u> Birch trees on the other side, where there are but a very few, instead of doing it all round the house, where there are numbers. But there she is more safe, as we have but one Canoe & he keeps it there.

Tuesd 11th May. A furious southerly wind all day which make the ice turn of all colors. This Evening we had a pritty good Concert of Muskatoe Musick, Thunder & Lightning; and as it is the first this year, I remark it accordingly. This Evening also the rapid below was swarming with Laciesh, yesterday two only were seen; & this is a good sign for our speedy departure.

Wednes. 12th. The wind was N. this morning & cold; & blowing very high, it drove the ice out a good deal. As it begins now to move, I am in hopes it will soon be off. This Evening we had some grains of snow, & a hard frost.

Thursd. 13th. The wind continued the same way, and as high. The ice of course is a great way out. By climbing into a tree I found there were large spaces open & free so far from the shore as not to be discernable but from a height. My good hopes increase much. L'assiniboane & his two wives arrive here at 7 P.M. to dry fish as he says; but the Swan thinks it to be to get at some of our women, & he is not always mistaken. The weather is very Cold indeed.

Frid. 14th. L'Assiniboane returned this morning. The weather still is very cold.

Saturd 15th. I sent off Laroque & Carriboeuf yesterday for a Canoe, left in the second lake above by the indians; & this /6/ forenoon they returned with an old, & almost useless thing, five or six others remaining, but were cut up by Red Breast's family on his return from here. There were two old women who passed the spring in these Lakes above with each a son, quite young lads (one about 12, the other 15 years' old) & maintained themselves upon ducks & geese they killed with their arrows, being too short of ammunition. One of them came down this afternoon, & the other will be here soon to dry fish.

Sund 16th. A most beautiful day. Bapt: Carriboeuf had yesterday all the symtoms of a return of his dreadful fitts. Having but one man with me I became very uneasy, for 4 men have enow to hold him, & keep him from tearing himself to pieces. As it always takes him, first with a sickness at the stomach, & an inclination to throw up, & a great pain in the temples, I thought it might proceed from a foul stomach; & being easily worked [persuaded] I gave him about 4 Grs. of Tar: Emet.[4] On taking it, the inclination increased much, but soon subsided. I gave him about 4 Grs: more with the same effect, only that the inclination to

---

4 Tartar emetic (potassium antimony tartrate) is still used to treat certain non-bacterial infections, such as schistosomiasis, but the antimony is a poison, so Nelson was right to be concerned when the repeated doses failed to induce vomiting, but remained in the body.

vomit seemed to subside; but being much afraid of the consequences if it should remain upon his stomach I gave another small dose, but I was surprised to find it had no effect further than intirely taking away his inclination to vomit. Then I made him drink warm water, as I became seriously apprehensive for the consequences, tho' I did not shew it. This brought on a little return, but as it also soon subsided, I then gave him another dose of about 6 Grs. This made him throw up a little; but as he soon began to throw up blood (which he tells me /7/ always happens when he pukes) he gave over; & some time after began to eat. This Evening he felt himself only exceedingly weak (another sure indication of its being a return) & on going to bed I gave him 20 drops of opium. There might have been in all, from first to last, at a very moderate computation 16 Grs. of Tar:Emet. & about 2 or 3 spoonsful of cold water to each dose : & it is good, because others have found the effects of it. He went to stool 6 times.

Mond 17th. The wind was Northerly again today, & drove the ice in to us again. The other old woman encamped here this afternoon. I got but 16 rats from them.

There is something strange going on, for Laroque has resumed, today, his old custom, & allowed his wife to go with Carriboeuf & the others to gather berries; & this afternoon he left her to go & put out his traps for rats; & again, he went alone to his sugar-bush for the Kettle he left there. The funniest of the business is, that I woke him up to take care of his child when I went to the Lake where his wife was. There is a great deal of hypocrisy in his composition, & it is this I beleive that makes him turn to his former custom. Jealousy is a dreadful disorder, & I sincerely pity those who are visited by it, let them be right or wrong; because it deprives them of rest & reason.

I am particularly happy to find that those medecines I gave to Carriboeuf have had the desired effect, & seem, at least to have restored him for this time to his usual strength & Gaiety.

Tuesd. 18th Wednesd. 19th Nothing new.

/8/ Thursd. 20th May 1819. Le Gendre with his son-in-law & their families, encamp here today. I got but 16 rats from them. They complain of the other indians having been before-hand with them; & as there was no fish above, they were obliged to come here to live. They saw the Belly a few days who said he would be in the tenth day, say night.

Frid 21st. Hear several Gun-shots towards Pigeon River. The ice drives continually to the Southward, the wind for this long time past having been almost always from the NW. to the E. & not sufficiently high to breake it much.

Saturd. 22nd. Between 5 & 6. P.M. I was very agreably surprised by the arrival of one of Mr Crebassa's men with an indian from Pigeon river. They arrived there yesterday, starving as if it had been for a wager. He sent me a Keg of rum, and wants Laroque to help them in repairing their Canoes &c. A few minutes after I had the pleasure of seeing my two men arrive also. They left this the 22^d. Apl. but would have been back long ere now had the ice permitted. They left the Fort [Alexander] the last (& fourth time they attempted it) the 15th May, having a great deal of trouble amongst the ice, & some danger. All is well at Fort Alexander thank God.

Sund. 23^d. About 10.a.m. I send off Laroque with the indian, & he takes all his family with him. Crebassa's men came in Canoe to La Pointe de Roche, about four miles from here, where the ice prevented their coming further.

/9/ Mond 24th. Rainy. Misty, almost all day, the wind increasing a little from the N. clears the lake a good deal to the South of us; but there appears still to be much ice out in the middle; indeed, it seems not to have moved there. We haul up our boat to fix it for our departure.

Tuesd. 25th. Early this morning I send Vandalle & Plante for the remainder of their things. They return late, a little before sun set. Le Gendre goes with his family to get me some bark. L'assiniboane goes also a hunting in Tete-au-Pishew bay. The Lake clears of ice intirely here.

Wednesd. 26th. I put 10 new ribs into the boat, the old ones being very indifferent. Le Gendre arrives, brings me five fathoms bark.

Thurs. 27th. I sent Le Gendre & Carriboeuf for gull eggs, in the outer islands. They brought but a very few, & 5 Geese they killed. L'assiniboane also arrived a little before sun set, he brought me 9 Geese; & tells me he <u>thinks</u> to have heard firing at T[ête]. a. Pishew, & that there was no ice there.

Frid 28th Satur 29th Sund. 30th. Early this morning I sent off Le Gendre with his wife & younger children in quest of Red Breast & my other indians in that quarter. I was also surprised by the arrival of Nono-cassé's son. He came from riviere au-Gavion (a little beyond Broken-river) where he left his father & several others. He found my friend Crebassa still at Tête-aù-Chien, but was waiting for fine weather to set off. The Belly, <u>mother-Fleurie</u>, & two young indians from Bas-de-la-Riviere arrived here also. They left Frise /10/ with Nez-d'argent & his family in an island in Fisher-River-Bay, waiting some signal from me to come.

Mond 31st. I sent off Belly, & three other indians in two Canoes for Eggs. They returned this evening with but a very few, & a sturgeon which they give me.

Tuesd. June 1ˢᵗ. Nothing new.

Wednes 2ⁿᵈ. This Evening I had the pleasure of seeing all my indians come in, with Poor Welles, but I did not get 20 skins from them – so contemptible a hunt! At 11 last night, Frisé, Nez-d'argent & Brother came in. I got about 30 skins from them also. They being altogether I gave them their rum; but it was 11.P.M. before they all left me, & went to the mouth of the river (about 10 or 11 acres from this) where they begin to drink.

Thursd 3ᵈ. A smart rain the most of the day, but remarkably mild. My indians, tho' a great many of them, & many wranglers among them, drink more quietly than I ever knew any indians yet, even amongst near relations. There were a few quarrels, but of no consequence, & occasioned by a dirty devil of a fellow.

Frid. 4ᵗʰ June. Frequent showers 'till noon then it became more clear & fine. Some of my indians are yet drunk; the men, a few only.

Saturd 5ᵗʰ. I assembled my indians today, they being sober, in a smoking-feast, & gave them my opinion of their conduct, past, present, & future. I also deal out all /11/ my amunition & tobacco amongst them, & prepare as fast as I can for my departure.

Carriboeuf, last night at dusk had a sudden return of his fitts, twice only, but not so severe as the former times. It seems to have been occasioned by straining. In moving our boat to caulk & grease it, it was near slipping & hurting, perhaps several of us. We had already raised it to the height of our arms, & coming down some, so suddenly seemes to have driven his left elbow into his short ribs. The pain all day was great. I bled [him] this morn. but the vein being small, & the skin black, & in the dark I did not make the orifice by any means large enow, I got but about a Gill. After-noon I tried again in the same arm, but to no purpose, then in the other (left arm) when I got a pint bowl full. It made him most excessively weake & he fainted, & was near falling into fitts again. Towards night, he had a little more ease thank God.

Sund 6ᵗʰ. At 10½ A.M. I took my departure from this place, i.e. my wintering Ground, Tête-au-Brochet, & encamped about 1¼ miles from the house, the wind being very high from the S.S.W. & of course nearly in our teeth. I went to see my indians & bid them a farewell; & I am happy to be able to say that they all, even to the women expressed much uneasiness about my not returning. This is a great consolation to me in spite of all. I, thank God, passed a very easy, quiet, & happy winter; but I unfortunately lost my master an irreparable loss to me. See Decʳ. 17 1818.

/12/ Mond 7ᵗʰ June 1819. My indians being very busy in preparing for the Meetaywee [Midewiwin], to initiate two men & a woman

in their <u>Brotherhood,</u> <u>confirmation,</u> or whatever it may be termed. I
passed a part of the night in looking at them, having been invited; &
to day I went to see them go through the <u>initiation,</u> but unfortunately
the wind changed of all of a sudden to the N.E. & I took my leave of
them just as they began their prepartory Dance and speeches, which I
admired a good deal, having now a far better idea of their <u>Theology,</u>
& understand their language also much better than I did 13 years ago
when I saw them the first time.

The wind being very high, & our boat exceedingly leaky I was
obliged to put up in an island at the foot of the Traverse des isles aux
Ecorses, & about 10 or 11 miles from the house.[5]

Tuesd. 8th. Rain almost all night & the wind still very high; but by
coasting the island a couple of miles it shortened our crossing a good
deal & brought the wind much fairer for us. At 2.P.M. we were upon
the Traverse, & at 4 we were over, after being near swamped ten times,
the wind increasing to a terrible pitch & being much on our left made
us take in many swells, and to make bad worse, we found ourselves
obliged to lower our sail & to row a good piece ahead to avoid breaking on a stony ridge that prevented our running under the island as we

The journal ends here in mid-sentence, and the remainder, if it continued, has been lost. It is also possible that Nelson copied to this point, and
then stopped. Further down the page, and carrying over to the bottom
of the next leaf, is:

and Here end the whole for this Boute at least. – 1819–20–21.

G.N.

This was clearly written at a different time, as the pen is freshly re-cut.

---

5 The traverse, across the mouth of Fisher Bay to the Îles-aux-Écorces (Bark Islands), was
hazardous because of the wind, but Nelson could now attempt it in his boat, whereas the
canoes he used in the 1807–11 period would have obliged him to await better weather.

12

Journal from Fort Alexander to Cumberland House, 16 August–16 September 1819

Nelson presumably reached Fort Alexander without incident, and there he may have spent the next ten weeks. During the gap before his next journal begins on 16 August 1819, the NWC had sustained a serious blow in its struggles with the HBC. In mid-June, at the portage giving passage around the Grand Rapids, where the Saskatchewan River falls into Lake Winnipeg, five NWC partners and eight engagés were ambushed and captured by Lord Selkirk's Governor William Williams, commanding some of the demobilized soldiers whom Selkirk had brought up to Red River two years before. Williams justified his actions by claiming that there were warrants for the partners' arrest for previous incidents in the ongoing war between the companies. One NWC partner, William McIntosh, managed to escape, and made his way to Fort Alexander, where Nelson would have been among those who heard the news.

The rest of the prisoners were taken to York Factory, whence one NWC partner and four of the voyageurs were sent to Moose Factory on James Bay, and thence overland to Canada. Another two of the captured partners were sent to England aboard the HBC's fall ship. The last partner in HBC custody, Benjamin Frobisher, still suffering from a blow to the head sustained when he was captured, and now further impeded by a bad cold, was apparently singled out for special severity. He was to be kept a close prisoner at York Factory for the winter, along with the two remaining voyageurs, Turcotte and Lepine. These three contrived to escape, stole a canoe, and made their way by water and land, over the course of about six weeks, to within a few days' walk of a NWC post on Moose Lake, where none other than George Nelson was in charge. By now it was late in the season, and the three were not well prepared for winter travel in the woods. So close to rescue, Frobisher could go no farther. The two voyageurs left him by the fire, reaching Nelson's post in four more days, on 24 November 1819. Nelson sent a rescue party for Frobisher at once, but he was found dead. He had managed to keep a journal during his captivity and escape, which was recovered. Samuel H. Wilcocke, a Montreal journalist and propagandist, used the journal in a highly coloured account of the whole episode that he wrote for the NWC in 1820. This account may not have seen the light of day at the time, but it found its way into the Masson collection of fur trade manuscripts, and Masson printed it (Masson 1960, 2:179–226).

Nelson's next Lake Winnipeg journal begins at Fort Alexander. He had received orders from Archibald Norman McLeod, a NWC partner who was now one of the Montreal Agents for the company, to proceed to the Cumberland House department, and accordingly set off in one of the canoes destined for the English River department on 16 August 1819. He was leaving familiar territory, and was worried that, not knowing the Indigenous people or the nature of the HBC opposition at his new post, he would be at a disadvantage, as he was during three seasons in The Pic department in 1813–16.

This journal describes Nelson's canoe journey from Fort Alexander to Cumberland House. The first part, as far as Grande Pointe (now Saskatchewan Point) was familiar, for he had gone over the route many times when he was trading at Dauphin River, but everything to the north of this was new. His detailed account is one of very few that describe this section of the fur traders' great canoe route to the Northwest. Alexander Henry the younger's description, as he made his way from Red River to the Saskatchewan in August 1808, also gives a good description of the route. Henry was in a small boat, which was better able to deal with the winds on Lake Winnipeg than the canoes in which Nelson was travelling.[1]

On 1 September, at the foot of Grand Rapids, Nelson met a freeman named Lemire, who was on his way to Swan River, in company with an HBC interpreter. Lemire told Nelson that "our gentlemen," the NWC partners whom Governor Williams had captured in June, had all been sent down to Canada by way of Timiskaming, which would mean that all were safe. Williams had promised that all would go to Canada for trial, but as things turned out, he had changed his mind. Only one partner was sent to Canada, along with four of the voyageurs. Rather than using the shortest route from Moose Factory, by way of Abitibi, Temiskaming, and the Ottawa River, these prisoners were dispatched by a longer route, by

---

1 Coues's edition of Henry's journal (Coues 1965, 450–75) annotates this route exhaustively.

Brunswick House, Michipicoten, Sault Ste Marie, Penetanguishene, and York. They did not reach Montreal till the end of November. Wilcocke, who wrote the account of the death of Benjamin Frobisher, believed that the longer route was meant to delay the Nor'Westers' arrival until after the conclusion of the Quebec Court of Oyer and Terminer's session on 21 October, thus delaying their access to justice (Masson 1960, 2:206).

Nelson reached Cumberland House on 9 September, where he found a Mr Fraser in charge for the NWC, awaiting Nelson's arrival so he could proceed to his own wintering post. Nelson would take over at Cumberland until the partner William Connolly, who was to manage the post for the winter, arrived on the 11th. Nelson assisted in unbaling and preparing outfits for the other dependant posts, and on 16 September the journal ends as he was about to set off for Moose Lake, his new wintering assignment.

August, Monday 16th. Having received a letter from A. N. M[c]Leod Esq.[r] ordering me off to Cumberland House Department, I set off this morning at 5.45 in an English River Canoe leaving M[r] Bell [John Bell] in Charge of the Fort 'till the arrival of the Gentlemen who <u>are</u>, or <u>is</u>, to winter there. This is a jaunt I am far from relishing; & am much afraid it will have the same consequences as that of '13-14-15. &c. &c.[2]

The weather was beautiful indeed, & had also a very fine & moderate wind, but were obliged to put up at Pointe au Battau at 11-45' we were so deeply sunk. At 4 P.M. re-embarked again, the wind falling some, at 6 spoke some indians at R. au Foin but got nothing from them & encamp at 6-45 a short distance beyond.[3]

Tuesd 17[t]. At 2-40' we embarked again. At 4-20' met old Raçette's family going to B. d. l. R. [Bas de la Rivière] all very ill & Complaining much. I gave them a note for Mr. Bell [at Fort Alexander], as they are now at the Company's Charge, the father being taken down as witness to what passed at Grand Rapid between the two Concerns. At 8 we found some indians fishing a la Grosse isle; we exchanged some Pemican for a few, small fish. They told me a part of their band was

2 Archibald Norman McLeod, formerly a NWC partner, was now one of the company's so-called agents at Montreal, but had probably come up to Fort William in 1819 to attend the partners' meeting.
3 Nelson is now reporting exact times (as he did not do in his earlier journals), showing that he had now supplied himself with a watch.

out for the meat of three moose (the mother & 2 young ones) they had killed yesterday, but [we] had not time to wait. At 11-20' stop to breakfast in Broken islands. At 12-25 Push off. /2/ At 1-10' P.M. breake our Canoe, but at 2-25' were on the water again. Encamp at 7-15' about 3 miles N. of Detroit du Duc for fear of a storm that was threatning us for a long time past. We had a most delightful calm day, only that it was rather too warm. We had sail for a few minutes.

Wednesd. 18th. The wind very still, as also the swells, the relics of a most furious [storm], which with little intermission lasted all night. At 1-10' P.M. the wind changing, & coming now off the shore, we put out, but at 1-56' were obliged to stop 'till 5-32, but shipping too much water we encamped at 6-45, travelling about 6 miles altogether.

Thurs 19th. Weather much more moderate. Set off at 4-20'. At 10-30 put ashore in a small island to breakfast, at the foot of the Traverse of Isles aux Ecorses where we remained all day, the wind being too high for us, tho' indeed very moderate. Here the men drove home the timbers of the Canoe to stiffen it.

Frid. 20th. Embark at 1-18' A.M. At 8 I stop a few minutes at T. au B. [Tête-au-Brochet] to see if I could find any marks, so as to counter-Point in case of the HB's. but found no one, nor any thing. At 2 40' put ashore on the N. side of Tête-au-Pishew the wind springing up quite suddenly. Here I saw a fine large indian dog, lost by some one or other, but he ran from me. At 5-28 we re-embarked, & encamped at Grd. Pointe, at the foot of the Traverses of St Martin islands at 8-15'. This Place is reckoned at half the Lake & I compute this much of it to be 150 miles from B. d. l. R. [Bas de la Rivière].

Saturd 21st. The wind rose about midnight, at 8 a.m it blew very hard, & had some rain with it; but towards night it was dreadful indeed.

Sund 22nd. Wind very violent all day, but rather more moderate towards night.

/3] Mond. 23d Augt (1819). Set off at 4-31' a.m. but at 6-20' were obliged to put up in a small island about 3 miles distance, where I had hid some things in 1810.[4] At 6-15' the wind abating some we embarked on the 2nd traverse, & at dark (7-52') put up in another island about 4 miles off, there being every appearance of another fine storm.

Tuesd. 24th. Quiet all day, the wind blowing blowing most violently all day; we also had frequent rain. This is a fine large island, about 3

4 See journal entry for 24 September 1810.

or 4 miles round. I encamped here in 1809 in the winter with Mr A. McDonell.⁵

Wednes 25th. The wind fell a little about sun rise, but is still too hi. We prepared to set off at 10 but did not embark 'till 2-57', & at 5-35' we encampd on the main land, Thank God, but not without much fear, as the swells were hi & every other indication of a renewal of the tempest. I compute this to be 15 miles from G^rd P^t. We have now no more traverses, & have the land always on our left, we therefore expect soon to be over the Lake.

Thurs. 26th At 1.9 a.m. we put out once more the wind falling a good deal, but as the bays tho' narrow, are very deep, the men had much pulling. We put up at 5-52' at the G^rd Maret - I reckon this day at 15 miles.

Frid 27th Embark at 3-35', tho' more appearance of storms, & the wind is exceeding cold. At 9-30' put ashore at the Grande Pointe the wind veering more to the N.E. made the doubling of it dangerous. At 1-50' put out again, but at 4-28' were obliged to put up in earnest at 4-28' – say 34 miles.

Saturd. 28th. Frequent showers. Quiet all day.

Sund 29th At 5-56' a.m. with much difficulty we got off, being obliged to load on a low, shallow & exposed beach. Still very Cloudy & much appearance of more bad weather. We /4/ had frequent sail today. But at 2-6' a.m. were obliged to encamp at P^t aux Renards, as the wind by our Course then becoming a-head – say 32 miles.

Mond. 30th August. We passed a very uncomfortable night indeed, the Point being quite low, nearly level with the water, & not a single spear of hay & the wind very hi all the while. But at day light we embarked & went to the bottom of the bay, about 3 miles, where the neck of land is not more than 2. acres across to the Lake,⁶ where we had more shelter. A skunk paid us a visit last night. Frequent rain & a furious wind.

Tuesd. 31st. The wind changing to the S.W. abated the swell, so that we embarked once more at 4-12" a.m. & had a fine sail 'till 8-12"

---

5 Probably Little Sturgeon Island, the largest island in the group. Nelson and Alexander Macdonell did travel together from Pigeon River to Dauphin River in December 1808, so this must be the trip referred to. In his entries for that trip, Nelson does not state exactly where they camped on the night of 3/4 December 1808; it may have been on this island.

6 Nelson is describing the present Gull Bay, which is partly protected from the main lake by sandbars.

when we were obliged to encamp at the Detour.[7] This being a very long & narrow point, our course was in a manner treading back our steps again. The wind became quite a head – say 30 miles good measure.

At 5-8', the wind & swell falling we put out again & travelled very well 'till dark; but then we began to make Zig-Zags[8] & every appearance of stormy weather we encamped in a rascally Point opposite isle aux Muffles at 11-30' P.M. Say 24 miles.

Wednesd. 1ˢᵗ Septʳ 1819. At 4-25' a.m. we were again upon the water, & stopping a few minutes at isle aux-Chevaux (6 miles) we with much difficulty doubled the last Point and entered river DuPas at 9.22' (45 miles from Detour) we breakfasted at the foot of the descharge [décharge*] at 10.a.m. & the men carried up their half load, but I remained behind to watch over goods as we found some fire on our arrival, which in the evening, we find to be one Le-Mire, an old Free Canadian, just arrived from Pike river, going to Swan River with one Turner an HB interpreter. He informs us that /5/ our Gentlemen were well & had been well treated; but were off some time since for Canada by Temiskaming.[9] We Encamped about 4 P.M. at the upper end of the Portage of Grand Rapid, the wind & rain coming on heartily.

Thursd 2ⁿᵈ Septʳ. A most dreadful wind all day & frequent rain. Many large trees were driven down with a violence I little expected. We had a very uncomfortable time of it.

Frid 3ᵈ. Wind & rain nearly the same still. At 11-35' we embarked, the rain subsiding, though we had frequent showers still. We encamped in Lack travers (about 9 miles) having had much trouble to get in from the violence of the 7ᵉ wind. We embarked old Lemire, to as far as Lac Bourbon where his freind Montreuil is waiting for him.

Satur 4ᵗʰ. The wind fell a good deal towards day, & became quite calm at 5. At 3-48" a.m. we set off & arrived at the entrance of Lac Bourbon at 8°-11', where we find old Martin, a free Canadian, but much interested for the NW. He was sick & starving, & of course could not assist us. Montreuil had some fish, but would not let us have any unless we laid cash down. Martin told us that all our People, 36 Canoes of them, altogether, passed here the 20ᵗʰ last mo. At 10°-49' we re-embarked, having Gumed our Canoe, & the weather being Calm

7 The Détour is the present Long Point, which juts out almost 30 miles from the west shore, thus adding about 60 miles to the canoe journey.
8 In a canoe it is important to keep the bow heading into the wind or away from it, so safe progress against a side-wind can only be made by the equivalent of tacking.
9 The NWC partners whom Governor Williams had captured at Grand Rapids in June.

we encamped at the upper end Lake Bourbon at 7-15' P.M. I reckon 9 miles from G.R. to L. Travers, 9 miles from there again & 45 the Lake. Now it is reckoned 60 miles to the Pas, & 60 more to Cumberland Lake. All appearances of fine weather.

Sund. 5ᵗʰ. We set off at 4-16'. At 6 we took leave of L.B. and enter R. du Pas. At 10-35 stop to /6/ stop to breakefast in l'isle au Festin, in Lac Vaseu, at 11-38' push out again & encamp at 6-35' in an island. Great numbers of Geese & Ducks. We had frequent sail & rain today.

Mond 6ᵗʰ. At 5-10' set off, because we had a heavy shower of Rain. Breakfast at 9-25'. At 10-55' push out & encamp at 6-44" (about 1 mile above a barge of HB. people going down to Moose Lake, with a horse) in Petit Chenaile. More rain again today.

Tuesd 7ᵗʰ. From 2 to 8 a.m. frequent showers. At 3-15' set off. At 7-28' stopped at the Pas where we find some of our women of Fᵗ Cumberland. From them we got some fish which we eat here, & embarked at 9-32'. We encamped at 6-20'. We overtook another old woman of the house returning above with a son of hers.

Wednes. 8ᵗʰ. Weather extremely foggy. Set off at 4-9'. At 8-11' breakfast & push out at 9-21'. At 5-43' leave R.D.P. & enter Petit Chenail, 24 miles from the house. We encamped at 6-30'. We had a fine sail some places but a fine rain too.

Thursd 9ᵗʰ. Very cold & foggy. Set off at 4-9'. At 9 arrive in Lake Cumberland, when we clean ourselves & at 10-35' arrive at the house [the NWC post of Cumberland House] where we find all well & quiet. Mr. Fraser being prepared, having received previous notice, left us at at 1 P.M. All very quiet here & on a very amicable footing. Weather fine & calm.

Frid. 10ᵗʰ. Two indians arrived last night, but brought nothing with them. Morning & Even wind. In the middle of the day a fine calm, but rain this morning.

/7/ Saturd 11ᵗʰ September 1819. The Whooping-Cough is here amongst the people, & I am afraid the measles too will get amongst them after this. They all look pitiful.[10] Several indians since my arrival here, have come in to the HB's. & I suppose with furs or provisions, because they are drinking & make all our indians here drunk also.

We had a dew last night eaqual to a good shower. Very fine & Calm all day, but appearance of rain to night.

---

10 There were serious epidemics of both whooping cough and measles in the Northwest in 1819–20: see Hackett 2002, 137ff.; also George Nelson in Brown and Brightman 1988, 50, for a Cree explanation of the spread of disease in 1819.

This Evening between 4-30 & 5 P.M, we had the pleasure of seeing Messrs. Conolly, Cameron & Bethune arrive.[11] They bring no news of any particular consequence.

Sund 12th. A Furious wind all night & day. Messrs. Bethune & Cameron make preparations for their departure from this as soon as the wind falls.[12] M[c]Kay the Guide [of the] English River Canoes arrived here about noon for their provisions, & returned soon after Messrs. Cameron & Bethune depart also this afternoon, the wind falling a little.

Mond 13th. Derouin, the Interpretor of this place arrived from his tourney [*tournée*, tour] in River Maligne whither he had been to take care of some of the indians of this place. This Evening our remaining three Canoes arrived all in good order.

Tuesd 14th. We unbaled & assorted today, & made up Mr Cardin's equipment or outfit for the Rat River quarter. Yesterday a Canoe with two HB men arrived at their fort here. We cannot learn anything further than that they are of the party sent to winter in opposition to M[r] Cardin, & that they left their people, waiting I beleive, above Riviere Maligne. A Warm day, the first for this very long time Past. Almost all the women & Children of this place are very sick of the Whooping Cough.

/8/ Wednesd. 15th Sept[r] 1819. This Morning between 9 & 10.a.m. M[r] Conolly sent off M[r] Cardin's Canoe for Lac des Graines. This afternoon a man by the name of Normand, the man who went with M[r] Cardin (the day I arrived here) to follow the HB's arrived. He informs that the HB's winter in Lac de la Roche, upon this side of Lac des Graines, about 9 miles.

We made up all my bales, 6 in number, for Moose Lake & prepare, please God, to Set off tomorrow. Fine & warm today, but a high wind.

Thurs: 16th [nothing entered]

End of journal.

11 The NWC partners William Connolly and Angus Bethune. Cameron is probably the partner John Dougald Cameron, who was stationed in English River in these years (Van Kirk 1985).

12 William Connolly would remain at Cumberland House for the winter, as the partner in charge. See Peel 1988.

13

Journal from Cumberland House to Fort William, 3 June–22 August 1822

George Nelson spent the next two seasons, 1819–20 and 1820–21, in charge of a NWC post on Moose Lake, a large, multi-bayed lake located to the north of Cedar Lake and the delta of the Saskatchewan River. There is no journal for the first of these seasons, during which a notable event was Nelson's part in the sorry episode of the capture, escape, and death of the NWC partner Benjamin Frobisher, already mentioned. Perhaps the NWC took charge of Nelson's journal, and took it down to Canada in the spring, to be used as evidence in preparing Samuel Wilcocke's account of the Frobisher affair.

A surviving journal does record parts of Nelson's activities in 1821. It is a small book of 76 pages, 20 cm high x 16 cm wide, formed of folded half-sheets of the usual Radway-type paper, roughly stitched together. It starts at Moose Lake on 19 April 1821, continues as he took his winter trade to Cumberland House, and covers the summer and early fall, when Nelson remained at Cumberland, where he was to winter. This journal runs to 47 closely written pages, most of which are in code, using an original cipher that Nelson had invented. It is a straightforward substitution code, letter for letter, which Sylvia Van Kirk has deciphered.[1] The most important event recorded in it was the fact that the NWC and HBC had agreed to an outright merger. This news reached Cumberland House by way of Lake Winnipeg on 24 June 1821. Nelson called the news "very pleasing information," and said that it was a great surprise. This journal is not printed in this volume.

Copied into the same book, and following on immediately after the first journal, is a second one, which begins on page 48, at Cumberland

---

1 Van Kirk 1984.

House on 3 June 1822. This document, which Van Kirk has called the Canoe Journal, describes a canoe journey that Nelson took through Lake Winnipeg, Winnipeg River, Lake of the Woods, Rainy River, and the chain of lakes, rivers, and portages all the way to Fort William, then back again as far as Fort Alexander.

The Canoe Journal runs on to the end of the booklet, and then continues in a different format. The rest of the journal is written on two full sheets of Radway paper, which has the usual Britannia watermark and also the watermark "RADWAY/1818." The two sheets have been folded in half, giving eight pages (32 cm high x 20 cm wide), and each page has then been ruled so as to subdivide it into four equal rectangles or "pages," giving 32 small "pages" in all.

1821–22 had been the first trading season without opposition, since the two companies were now joined, and Nelson found himself one of eight English-speaking traders who were wintering at Cumberland House. The bourgeois in charge of the post was Chief Factor Alexander Kennedy, an experienced HBC man, and the four others whom Nelson names were all drawn from the ranks of the old opposition – Governor William Williams; the clerks James Swain and Donald Ross, and a Mr Boulton.[2] For Nelson, so many educated companions, all English-speaking, would have been a rare treat, and his natural friendliness would have served him in good stead.

Nelson left Cumberland House on 3 June 1822, in company with four other canoes, all fully loaded with twenty-five packs of furs apiece, doubtless the proceeds of the trade at Cumberland House and its dependent posts. It was an early start, and it would be good luck indeed if Lake Winnipeg were free of ice so early. The brigade called at The Pas, and at Moose Lake, Nelson's old post, where he commiserated in his heart with George Flett, his old HBC opponent there. Flett had worked hard to improve his post, only to have it abandoned after the coalition – a plight with which Nelson could identify, having the same thing happen to him at Dauphin River in 1810.

Nelson's instructions were to carry on from Fort Alexander as far as Fort William with a canoe load of provisions, to assist canoes coming up

2 For Kennedy, see HBCA Biographical Sheet. Swain must be the HBC clerk James Swain, junior (his father, James, senior, having returned to Scotland in 1819), although the HBCA's Biographical Sheet on him states that he wintered at Lac la Ronge in the Île-à-la-Crosse Department from 1821 to 1823. The HBC clerk Donald Ross later spent many years in charge at Norway House; Wallace (1934, 496) has a brief note on him. Mr Boulton, who was to accompany Governor Williams to Moose Factory, was perhaps his secretary.

from Montreal. It was a routine task, but this was a valedictory journey, over the river highway that had been central to the Northwest fur trade since La Vérendrye's time. Now, with the amalgamation of the two companies, and the HBC bringing all the trade goods in and furs out through Hudson Bay, it was about to become a very minor part of the fur trade network, though for decades it remained the only direct route from the Northwest to Canada. Nelson must have recognized the significance of what he was doing as he wrote this journal, for he made a careful description of all the portages and other features, and he sprinkled his account with anecdotes and traditional stories. The Canoe Journal, in its way a requiem for the old North West Company, is a fitting end to this volume.

During his journey to Fort William, Nelson was overtaken by four interesting characters. On 1 July, while the brigade was pausing at the Lac la Pluie post, Samuel Black and Peter Skene Ogden arrived in a light canoe manned by ten voyageurs, bound for Montreal. They had no guide, and Nelson assigned one of his men to take them through the next, most complicated part of the route. These two NWC clerks had been explicitly excluded from the settlement with the HBC because of their violent behaviour through the years of struggle with the other company. Now they were being exiled from the fur country. The HBC's governing committee would permit both to re-enter the company's service in 1823, and both would do important service as explorers in the Northwest.[3]

Black and Ogden must have covered the rest of the route in a leisurely fashion, for they did not overtake Nelson with his brigade of heavily laden canoes until 9 July, in Kaministiquia River, almost at Fort William. With them now was a second light canoe with two more former Nor'westers, Cuthbert Grant and one McDonell. Like the other two, Grant had played all too prominent a role in the violence offered to the HBC, in his case in the war upon the Red River Settlement. Grant was also going into exile at Montreal, though Governor Simpson was probably already planning to bring him back once the initial feelings against him had subsided. Once he returned to the Northwest, Grant was employed by the HBC for about thirty years, under the title "Warden of the Plains," to maintain a sort of government over the Red River Métis, from his home at the White Horse Plain.[4]

Identification of Grant's companion, whom Nelson calls "All: McDonell," is uncertain. He cannot have been Allan Macdonell, a

3 For Black, see Woodcock 1988a; and for Ogden, see Williams 1985.
4 For Cuthbert Grant, see Woodcock 1985.

partner in the NWC since 1816, who became a chief trader in the HBC, and was in charge of the Swan River department in 1821–23.[5] Most probably he was Alexander Macdonell, who had been Nelson's fellow clerk on Lake Winnipeg in 1807–09 before he was transferred to Red River. There, in 1816, he was responsible for organizing the Métis force that took part in the incident at Seven Oaks at which so many HBC men and colonists were killed. This involvement would explain why he was travelling with Cuthbert Grant, and why he too was leaving the Northwest. Alexander Macdonell did not return, but entered political life in Canada (see Appendix D).

Black and Ogden took Nelson into their own canoe for the last day of the journey, and they arrived in Fort William on the afternoon of 10 July. Nelson remained until the 21st, and then began the journey back to Fort Alexander. At this point his journal still has dates, but the entries are simply descriptions of the portages as he encountered them. For almost all he gives the name of the portage, the quality of the landing, the length as he measured it, and the derivation of the name, presumably provided by the voyageurs or perhaps sometimes his own imagination. The journal takes him back to Fort Alexander, where he apparently arrived on 22 August. It does not continue beyond that date.

Nelson was to spend one more winter in the Northwest, this time at Lac la Ronge, a post dependent on Île-à-la-Crosse in the present northern Saskatchewan. It was during this winter that he composed the long and valuable essay on Ojibwe and Cree myths and religion, which has been edited by Brown and Brightman (1988). The next year he was one of the clerks who were laid off as a part of George Simpson's post-amalgamation efficiencies, and he left the fur country for good.

The last item in the Canoe Journal, apparently an afterthought, is an account of two Swiss emigrants, a carpenter and a blacksmith, who had come out to Red River with the HBC ships the previous fall. They had had such a difficult experience in the colony that they had decided to make their way back to civilization in Canada. Nelson and his party met them in Winnipeg River, near the Chute d'Esclave [Slave Falls], and were dismayed to see how poorly provided they were, in equipment, provisions, and information, for the long voyage through the wilderness that they sought to make. Already they had rejected the advice of a priest who had encountered them in Lac du Bonnet and warned them how unwise they were. A journey from Red River to Canada was no

5 Wallace 1934, 465; HBCA Biographical Sheet.

place for amateurs. Now they were surely at the end of their tether, and Nelson persuaded them to return with him to Fort Alexander, where John McLoughlin, the bourgeois, undertook to keep them until spring. One wonders whether somewhere there is further information about this hapless pair, and what happened to them next. Presumably they had come to Red River in response to some encouraging letter from one of the demobilized soldiers already settled there, and had not realized how completely cut off from the world they would be.

In editing the Canoe Journal for this volume, no attempt has been made to annotate the many place names, which Nelson lists along the canoe route between Fort Alexander and Fort William, or to add them to Appendix E. Already in print there are several contemporary accounts of the canoe routes between Lake Winnipeg and Lake Superior,[6] and a lively description of them, as they were in the 1950s, was published by Eric Morse (Morse 1979, 71–88). The routes are familiar to many recreational canoeists today, but Nelson's account will be a welcome addition to what is known.

June 3ᵈ 1822. Every thing being previously arranged, at 9 a.m. I take my departure for Ft. William; 5 Canoes, containing 95 Packs of 90 lbs ea. This is much earlier than we are used to leave this place but it is considered necessary to be out as early as possible. 2½ bags Pemican pr Canoe & two nets in case of accidant. Governor Williams had left this on Tuesday last, with Mr Boulton, for Moose Factory;[7] & there remain still (waiting the arrival of the Saskatchewine people) Messrs Swain & Ross, & my worthy Bourgeoi Mr Kennedy, of whom I shall long think with the greatest regard. I passed this winter in a manner far beyond my expectations, & even my wish; so pleasant & comfortable as if we

---

6 For the older route by way of Grand Portage (used up to 1803), which joined the Fort William route at Lac la Croix, see John Macdonell (Gates 1965, 96–107); Alexander Mackenzie, 1801, xlviii–lxi; and Alexander Henry the younger (Gough 1988, 6–15). There is also a less detailed description by Harmon (Lamb 1957, 23–7), and later accounts by various authors. In his edition of Henry's journals, Coues drew detailed information about the Fort William route from the unpublished surveys of David Thompson (Coues 1965, 8–35; 217–18, n. 18).

7 William Williams, who had been appointed resident governor of the HBC's territories in 1818, was transferred to Moose Factory as governor of the Southern Department in 1822. George Simpson then became governor of the Northern Department. For Williams, see Smith 1985.

had all been nearly related to each other. Including the Governor, there were 8 of us.

Tuesd: 4th. At 2½ a.m. were upon the water, & encamped near Sun Set, a little below the 'Pas, notwithstanding a very strong head wind. Saw two bands of Indians from whom I got 11 Geese, 3 white-fish & some Eggs, for which I gave them a note to be paid by Mr Kennedy. I remained a long time with Constant[8] to take in his furs &c. Poor wretch! He excites my pity & compassion, tho' his former conduct but little deserves it but it is "the nature of the /49/ beast," & what can be done? He complains much of Eskataye (his step Son) & tho' he does not confess it, still his language shews how much he is in dread; & I must own, not without the greatest reason: for surely that lad will be his death if his brother is not before hand with him, i.e. does not <u>kill</u> him <u>first</u>, if which there is no lack of inclination among the three. How can it well be otherwise seeing the stalks from which they spring. To take him out of harms way, I allow'd Gamache to hire him.

Wednesd. 5th. Embarked whilst it was yet dark. At 2. P.M. reached Moose Creek where we left 2 men to take care of the packs & proceeded to the Fort, at which place we arrived at 3½ P.M. & found all well. Too, a walk with Mr Heron[9] round my old premises (of Moose Lake fort) & entered the furs, mens accts. according to order. Here Mr Heron made about 80 Packs, a great deal indeed, but a fourth less than I expected.

Thursd. 6th. Rained very hard all day. My good old neighbor, Geor: Flett[10] is still here, poor of [sic] Creature I pity him. He has done a great deal of work himself to bring the place to some order, profit, & comfort & the moment that he was to have reaped the benefit another steps in, a mans feelings, however humble his sphere, ought never to be play'd with, and the old man has no Philosophy, & not too much discretion.

---

8 Constant is a prominent character in the part of Nelson's coded journal that covers the spring of 1821 at Moose Lake. He had worked for the NWC for many years, though he wanted to retire and settle down at The Pas, and was hoping to be released from his latest contract. Nelson considered him a good trader, but a troublesome employee: "He certainly has talents, but they are most ill applied."

9 Francis Heron, an HBC clerk, was in charge of the Moose Lake post in 1821–22, the first year after the coalition. See Wallace 1934, 457; HBCA Biographical Sheet.

10 George Flett, in charge of the HBC's Moose Lake post before the merger. Flett remained at Moose Lake as assistant master for one more year, then retired to the Red River Settlement. See HBCA Biographical Sheet.

/50/ Frid. 7th June 1822. Left Mr Heron after Sun rise a little. At
the mouth of the Creek we stoppd to Gum our Canoes & breakfast.
About 9½ a. m. we were off & encampd at 5 P.M. at pointe a Martel,
in Lac Bourbon as the people had some Cedar wood to gather for their
Canoes. The wind was strong a-head. This Pointe is so named from a
theiving runaway raskal by that name, who was here put in Irons many
years back.

Satur: 8th. Embark very early again, under sail & had crossed Lac
Bourbon about 10, where finding some Indians from whom I got 4½
Sturgeon for another note, to be paid by Mr. Kennedy. We encamped at
the lower end of Grand rapid early in the afternoon. Here we have our
Canoes to repair, & several packs to dry, from the quantity of water
we all shippd today. Saw snow and ice in many places to day; & I am
inclind to think that Mr. Williams is still in the Lake bound by the ice.

Sund: 9th. All hands working hard at the canoes & Packs. Take
plenty of Pike in our nets. Jaques & Sayre went a spearing sturgeon. I
bro't home 4 beautiful, & large ones. I forgot to remark that from the
scarcety of provisions Normand had been sent (by Mr Kennedy) with
his family to procure, & dry fish of all kinds for the Passants.[11] We
came up with him yesterday here.

/51/ Mond: June 10th '22. A very hi wind with frequent showers of rain,
& this evening frequent showers of snow. In spite of the Cold & badness
of the weather Martin Lavallé went a spearing & bro't 3 sturgeon.

Tuesd: 11th. About 10. a. m. Messrs Cardin & Middleberger arrive
with the 3 Cumbd Boats arrive [sic], the first is to pass the summere
here with Normand, the latter, to proceed to Bas de la Rivière with the
remainder of the Cumberland Musk Rats. Several Indians also arrive
with their trader Turner. Wind very hi with showers of Snow & Rain.
Get but one Sturgeon today.

Wednesd: 12th. Very uncomfortable weather still. Get 6 Sturgeon that
Marin & Bellanger kill. I also employed 2 indians for the same purpose; they got 2, but kept them.

Thurs: 13th. We at last got off this morning, tho' the weather was
uncommonly thick & foggy. When we got fairly into the Lake we
hoisted sail, but the wind soon becoming too hi. for us we put ashore;
but the Boats continued.[12] About 11 a. m. the wind abaiting, we pushed

---

11 Passants means the men of the canoe brigades who were to get on as quickly as possible,
and be fed as they passed Grand Rapids.
12 The boats stood farther out of the water than canoes, and could tolerate more wind.

off once more, but as [the wind] intirely fell we were obliged to take to
ye paddle. Doubled that terrible long point Le Detour a little before sun
Set, & encamped about 11 P.M. at P^{te} aux Renards, i. e. in the bottom
of ye bay. From here, across land to where we put ashore this morning, it is scarcely 5 miles, tho' at least 50 by water. This forenoon saw
several large fields of ice, & about ye point a great deal of small ice, &
the water & air very cold. /52/ There was not even the appearance of
Budds upon the Trees, tho' in River du 'Pas (Saskatchewene) the leaves
were half [out] when we came by. We were all shivering with cold when
we put ashore. We overtook the Boats at dusk & they put up a little
beyond us: they appear to us, who are accustomed to smart Travelling
uncommon slow & unweildy things.

Frid: 14th June. Set off very early, carry a little sail, but becoming
Calm paddled to Gr^d Maret, where we put ashore early to Gum our
Canoes that from the coldness of the water crack & breake a good
deal. The Leaves here were large.

Saturd: 15th. Set off about 2 a. m. & carried sail for a few miles; but
the wind increasing too much we were forced to put ashore & had the
mortification to see the Boats ride with ease. Here vegetation is very far
advanced; & every thing looks beautiful.

At about 6. P. M. the wind falling we re-embarked; gathered a few
Eggs at ye [foot?] of the Traverse & proceeded, the men singing &
yelling all night. They expected to put a shore at the other end of the
Traverse but finding themselves disappointed they cursed McKay (the
Guide) most heartily.

Sund: 16th. We did not put ashore 'till about 5. a. m. as the wind
increased too much, at Tete-au-Pishew. Here we remained 'till /53/
about 9 or 10 a. m. when becoming [calm] again we set off, & a little
before Sun Set encamped in the Bark island. From Tete au Pishew we
kept in the middle of ye Lake – we had one Traverse of about 18 miles.
We hunted for Sturgeon & Eggs but found none.

Mond 17th. Embark at the dawn of day, & discovering some fire
on the Rocks of Tete-au-Chien we proceeded for it, where we arrived
a little before Sun Rise & found Govr. Simpson, Mr McDonell, &
Mr Miles.[13] They left Bas de La Riviere yesterday morning (in a light
Canoe) & encamped here at a late hour. Provisions uncommonly

---

13 George Simpson, who had just taken over from Williams as governor of the HBC's
Northern Department, accompanied by McDonell and Robert Miles. This may have been the
only occasion on which George Nelson met Simpson, at least in the Northwest.

scarce & the regulations & orders in consequence are strict & severe.
Mr. Williams had crossed the Lake amidst the ice in that Terrible bad
weather that detained us at Grd. Rapid.

We breakefasted at noon at Detroit au Duc, where we met Mr.
Clarke from Montreal (& Mr. McMurray from Bas de la Rivière)
who comforted me a little with the news of all my friends below
being well.[14] Stopp'd a few minutes in Broken islands to gather Rock
Moss [*tripe de roche**] to make <u>Bouillon</u> with our <u>Toreau</u> [taureau*].
Encamp in the Detroit de la Tête de Boeuf at Sun Set. We met besides,
several Canoes from Lac La Pluie for Norway House,[15] manned with 3
& 4 men. Extremely sultry all day.

Tuesd: June 18th. It must have been early in the night, for I had had
but little sleep /54/ when I heard the cry of "ils partent," repeated with
sacre's & Crapeauxs without number. However we loaded too, & put
out after the other 4 Canoes that had left us. The night was uncommonly dark – we had not a cloud, a star or anything to regulate our
Course by for this Traverse (which is 4 or 5 miles) but unremitted
flashes of lightning sometimes in the NW & at others in the S.W. A very
smart hard breeze, but still scarcely ruffling the surface of the water,
with a distant dismal growling that was far from rendering our situation either pleasant or comfortable. The people paddled hard & all
hands listening if we could hear anything of the other Canoes. At last
we saw a light, as that proceeding from a pipe, & sometime after heard
calling, very frequently repeated, which was a signal to keep together.
We joined at length, & put a shore still long before day, having crossed
the Bay. We were not very long ashore before it began to rain & blow
furiously. However, this either did not last long, for about 10 a. m. we
were off again. A few miles beyond, we found the Lake extremely agitated, a sign of there having been a dreadful tempest very lately tho' we
did not get any of it. We saw about noon 3 Sails, which we take to be
/55/ the Boats. A little after Sun Set we encamped at the old X.Y. fort,
at the mouth of River Winnipic with the Boats, that had arrived but a
few minutes before us.

14 John Clarke, who after a complex career was returning to the Northwest at the rank
of chief factor, to take charge of the HBC post at Fort Garry: see Brown 1985. For Thomas
McMurray, former NWC partner, see Wallace 1934, 483. They brought Nelson news of his
family in Canada.
15 Norway House, founded by the HBC in 1814 close to the outlet of Lake Winnipeg, had
been chosen by Governor Simpson to replace Fort William, as the inland supply depot and
summer rendezvous of all the senior traders in the newly amalgamated HBC.

Wednesd: 19th about midnight we were again overtaken by one of those furious storms that so frequently occur in this part. It was as sudden as violent; & inspite of all exertions the men could not keep the packs from wetting. The water rose several feet and buried most of the small things in the rubbish & drift-wood, which we had much difficulty to find, & some were entirely lost.

We arrived early in the morning at the Fort (of Bas de la Riviere) where, such a reception!! – one of the Boats running upon a Stump, broke a hole thro' one of its boards. Provisions uncommonly scarce.

Thursd: 20th. About noon sent off 5 Canoes with 22 Packs each, & 5 & 6 men Pr. Canoe; because Mr Chs: Ross, a Clerk from Lac La Pluie[16] arrived yesterday with several Canoes, the crews of which return from this. The orders for the Provisions were half a bag (about 40 lbs) pemican & 25 lbs of Flour (as it was termed, but what I call, & truly too, badly bruised wheat) Pr. Canoe! I do not remember when I felt so much grieved at being obliged to send men off for such a distance & so ill provided. It requires seven days of fine weather & extreme hard pulling to reach L. L. Pluie, but it is a journey of ten days commonly. They grumbled & growled a good deal, but at last they set off in their usual good /56/ good humor singing & yelling to aggravate the more a few obstreperous characters amongst them. The Boat people with Mr. Wm. Mittleberger left this also today; but being <u>Europeans</u> they would not be imposed upon, & <u>soon</u> succeeded in getting what they considered (tho' indeed but little still) as reasonable, & somewhat more than double to the Canoes, tho' they have but the Lake to travel thro' (about 300 miles).[17] Towards evening I left this place also & incamped at the 1st Eaux qui remuent,[18] amongst miriads of Musquetoes. Mr. Dease[19] palmed Gen. Cameron (a half breed, clerk) upon me: & our provisions were 7 lbs. Pemican & 7 lbs. of <u>fine</u> Flour, for the mens flour was uncommonly coarse, & <u>not</u> sifted.

16 For Charles Ross, see HBCA Biographical Sheet.

17 Almost all the HBC servants before the amalgamation in 1821 were from Orkney, and they had a reputation for insisting on routine, in contrast to the Canadian voyageurs, who could usually be persuaded to accept unusual challenges as they travelled. Mr Mittleberger's boats were returning north, probably to Cumberland House.

18 Nelson gives a systematic account of all the portages between Fort William and Lake Winnipeg at the end of the journal.

19 Mr Dease was apparently in charge at Fort Alexander during Nelson's brief visit. Four sons of Dr John Dease, of Montreal, entered the fur trade; see Wallace 1934, 435–6. This was probably John Warren Dease (1783–1829), who was in charge at Lac la Pluie in 1816, and was soon to be transferred to the Pacific slope as a chief trader for the HBC.

Frid. 21st. Embark at 2-5' a.m. Haul up the two Descharges of
Beaubien & Minette; carry across the Portages of 2d Eaux qui remuent;
the 3ᵈ do; Terre Blanche, Roché du Bonet, & Bonet; where we breakefast
at 8-30'; but at 11-20', two Canoes manned with Lac La Pluie men, not
being yet near ready I set off with Canoes leaving McKay [the guide] to
wait for them. At L'Ense du Bonet we waited again 2¼ hours, when at
last these slow motioned devils arrive. Wee put up at 5 P.M. at the upper
end of Lac du Bonet. We had a strong fair wind that aided us a great deal
between the Portages. These Lac La Pluie gentry are accustomed to travel
in the orkney style, i.e. not to breake their necks, of course, being obliged
to keep up with us works /57/ up their Bile in such a manner as aston-
ishes them, & they faint like an old Grey Horse my father had, under
their loads. Indeed, even these men, to one unaccustomed to such sights,
seem to do more than ever was meant for human nature; but how much
more so the others, who, rise at dusk in the morning & untill near sunset, are either pulling on their paddles, or running with 180, or 200 lbs
wt. on their backs, as if it were for life or death; never stop to take their
meals peacably, but with a piece of Pemican in their hands eat under their
load, or when they stop "aux Pipes" i.e about every 2 miles, seldom, however for even 4 minutes, when any clerks or masters are in the Brigade,
they commonly stop to breakefast every day about 9 or 10 o'clock. Such
work is more than enough to kill any men, & 20 years service here commonly knocks up a man. And what is their gain! ruin & beggary!

There is a part of the fable of Hercules, so very applicable to this
point, that the author [of] it would seem had these people in view at
the time. It is true that the whole of the verse is not perfectly applicable
to all, but the difference I think is not very great: it runs thus,

"Vast happiness enjoy thy gay allies
"Youth of Follies, an old age of Cares
"Young yet enervate; old, yet never wise
"Vice wasts their vigour, & their mind impairs
"Vain, idle, delicate, in thoughtless ease
"Reserving woes for age, their prime they spend
"all wretched, hopeless, in the evil Days
"With sorrow to the verge of life they tend
"Grieved with the Present, of the past asham'd
"They live, & are despis'd: they die, nor more are nam'd"²⁰

20 These lines are part of a verse rendering by Robert Lowth (1710–1787), Bishop of

/58/ whilst we were at the (Portage de) Bonet awaiting the remainder of the Canoes, about 20 Canoes or more of River ouinipique indians arrived, almost all 2 men Pr Cano going to <u>war</u>! in the upper part of Lower Red River, upon the Cioux's [Sioux]. By the <u>Head</u> of the Colonists, a sort of peace had been patched up between the Sauteuxs & Sioux's & the latter with their chiefs came every year to the Forks (of Red River). There were enough of the young of each party inclined of themselves to breake the peace, & for the 2 or 3 last years the visits became very unwelcome & a great degree of animosity was shewn reciprocally, inspite of the endeavours of the <u>Elders</u>; but the behaviour of the Sioux's shewed a generosity & bravery above all danger. It was at last reserved for a Cowardly [man] to begin, by killing a Sioux in one of these Embassys, & tho' there was no great danger he could hardly get off with himself, so much was he overcome by fear. This same rascal in the Summer of 1808 or 9 killed a very fine young indian, & I believe a distant relative of his. This fellow had left Bas de la Riviere some days before the young man, & was going as he said to Red River. He encamped about 12 or 14 miles from the House, & watching a fair opportunity, whilst the lad was approaching a moose & had but just a moment before left another boy he had taken with him, was shot: the other lad saw him fall, but could scarcely believe he had been fired at till he saw his friend lying breathless. The other always denied the charge, tho' it was known there was no one within many miles but himself.

/59/My Canoe being so lumber'd, 14 Packs, 11 Grown people, besides our private lumber, I here left one of my Boxes, which I hid, & I will take it when I can.

Satur 22nd. Off at 3 a.m. At 7 got to the first Portage of River Blanche (about 12 miles) & at 10½ my Canoe got up all the Portages of this river (Blanché). There is about 5 miles long, in which space there are 6 Portages & 3 Descharges, the access to almost every one of which is very dangerous, & requires great caution & adroisse.[21] As my Steersman is

---

Limerick, of a speech by the Sophist philosopher Prodicus of Ceos. It tells a fable in which the young Hercules is presented with a choice between virtue and vice. First published in 1747, the poem, entitled "The Choice of Hercules," was widely republished over the next century, particularly in anthologies intended for schools.

21 Coues 1965, 32 n. 36, gathered together several descriptions of the portages of the Rivière Blanche of Winnipeg River, and noted that there was a great disagreement as to the lengths of the portages, no doubt because of different water conditions when the various authors went over the route. As noted previously, the entire Rivière Blanche has been subdued into a chain

yet a novice I had many a good alarm. We breakefasted here; & as the two Lac La Pluie Canoes make us lose more time than our Provisions warrant we leave them to come on as well as they can. Mr Cameron angled here & took one small fish, another one broke the hook. As McKay broke the stern of his canoe by the Line's breaking in a narrow & Cliff [?] gut way, I left him & encamped alone at the Barriere.

Sund: 23^d. Embark at 4, at 6 cross Chute aux Esclaves where we take a Pikeral & kill Pigeon. At 9½ had crossed 2 other Small Portages & Pointe de Bois, where McKay & the others overtake & breakefast with us. We here lose our tracking line, but in a manner that makes me suspect that some one has thrown it in the River, or stolen it. We left this place at 1 P.M. leave Pointe de Bois; at 2¾ P.M. cross Chute a Jacqueau (about 10 Mile) just in time to cover our Packs & get under our Canoes just as a furious Thunder came over us. Here we remain'd an hour & at 5 whilst under a smart reef'd Sail Met Dr. McLaughlin with a /6o/ Capt. Bulger, appointed Governor by Government of the Red River Colony, & Mr. Halkett, 3 Canoes.[22] Exchanged a few words, caught a Letter from my Father Flying, & seperated on account of another furious storm. We put up on the Point of a Rock where under shelter of my Cloak I read my poor old Father's letter. By it I learn thank God that all is well now at home; but the silence regarding my Dear Mary [Nelson's wife] I fear means no good! After the shower was over we returned to McKay who had put up behind us in a nasty swamp.

Mond: 24th. At 2-50' a.m. Embark, at 7-40' crossed Portage de l'isle (30 miles from C. a Jaqueau) where we breakefast. About 6 we passed Mr. McMurrays house at Grande Equierre, where Poor old Lorrain was killed 2 years ago. I do not remember if I ever mentioned the death of his murderer. It was thus: Joseph Lorrain, a half breed son to the old Man, promised to revenge his Father's death. In the spring of ye same year, this Indian with several others arrived at the Fort of Bas de la Riviere. Lorrain went down to the beach & told the indian to get out of his canoe, which he did. Then Lor. took him by the shoulder with one hand, & with the other, in which he held a knife, gave him 3 stabs to the heart, saying "Dog! You kill my father cowardly, & hast

---

of placid lakes by the Seven Sisters Dam and Hydroelectric Generating Station, begun in 1929.

22 John McLoughlin, NWC partner, now a chief factor in the amalgamated company, who became known as "the Father of Oregon"; Andrew Bulger, governor of Assiniboia 1822–23; and John Halkett, Lord Selkirk's executor (Selkirk died in 1820) and a member of the governing committee of the HBC.

rendered my Mother & all of us pitiful: I promised to revenge his death, but I do it bravely, & like a man. Thou diest." He fell, & never uttered a word. There were a /61/ great many indians present, & murmured a good deal, Mr. Dease got them all assembled & made a very appropriate Harangue to them, which, if it did not convince, at least silenced them for the time. This wretch had been protected by Poor Old Lorrain from some of these same indians who were absolutely bent upon killing him for the murder of another, which he pretended was accidental. Such is indian Tradition. At 9.39' we embarked again & put up near Sun Sett at the Pins (9 miles below the Dalles). We hauled the Cave, which at low water is two Descharges, but this year, only one. Terre Blanche (Port.) about 8 acres above, Decharge a Charette, 1 mile; 3 acres to Terre Jaune Port. & about 3 miles to the Grand Descharge. We had all day a very smart sail which is the reason why we came such a long piece, but the weather was very cold. Saw an indian canoe with 3 people in it – [they] told me they had a few pike at their Lodge, but as we had no time to spare I gave them a bit of Tobacco & proceeded.

It is scarcely possibly to imagine a more ugly & a more handsome river than this. The beach is most uncommonly irregular, being broken in an infinity of places, leading into extreme deep bays, Lakes, rivers or Creeks, a vast number of Rocky islands & points, some truly beautiful & Picturesque, & others parched, frightful, hideous Rocks: but the main Land (if it may be so called) seems as one immense large Shore or Rock (for many miles) with a vast number of Cracks & crevices, in some of which are beautiful Groves /62/ as if planted by the Hand of Man, so regular & beautiful; but these a precious few – mostly only nasty dwarf willows, or Birch, thro' which in all directions for a great distance back & 2, or 300 feet high appear these black, grey, or red Rocks, become so by the heat of the Sun or fire. Yet, generally speaking, the indians live well. There are Moose, plenty of Rein deer,* & some Bears with here & there a solitary Beaver. Plenty of Partridges (Grouse, some call them) some Lynx, & abundance of Rabbits. It is a singular fact that in these Barren Rocks the Moose are much fatter than in the common woody Country. The reasons assigned by the indians, & which I think very just is, that the fire running often, every year new willows &c sprout up, which, being tender (it is their natural food) they are uncommonly fond of, & roam but little except [when] disturbed. I have found this to be the case in all Rocky Countries, in some of which there are more moose than a person accustomed to better places would imagine. There is also abundance of fish in some places, but these they must procure as well as they can; very rarely a net being given them.

About a mile above Portage de l'Isle is the road leading to Albany Factory, the route thro' which Govr. Williams & Mr Boulton passed, a few days before me.[23]

/63/ Tuesd: June 25th 1822. At 2.43' a.m. we were off again, & at 8.30' had crossed Portage du Rat, where some indians we had seen a little before came to us with 3 fresh sturgeon & some dry dᵒ, for which I gave them a Bottle of wine some amunition & a bit of Tobacco. They liked the wine, because it was <u>chiefs</u> Drink, but they'd have prefered rum & had I had any to give them I dare say I should have had more from them. At 2-25' P.M. we re-embarked (but the wind was dreadfully strong) in Lac de Bois (which the White in their fondness for Perverting, or rather proud ignorance, do denominate. The word is Cree, & signifies "Lake of the Islands," & well it may, for I dare say there are between 1500 and 2,000 & some very large). We carried sail, & tho' but one reef, yet were near upsetting several times. Towards night it grew calm. We put up at 7¼ P.M. We gathered a good few Eggs in a small rock island; there were a great number of Gulls & the eggs were good; particularly to <u>us</u>; for eating is something more than a fashion.

Wednesd: 26th Embark at 2.30 a.m. & cross <u>Portage du Lac des Bois</u> at 5, where we found an indian from whom we got 2 large Pike for a little ammunition. a beautiful calm till 7, when a fine breeze spring up, we carried sail till 10, but the wind veering a-head we put up in an island. Near Sun Set we re-embarked again, but after 3 miles travelling put up in another island at the foot of this Noted Traverse. Jos: Bellanger, a /64/ smart, active half-breed, killed me 14 Pigeons, which with some more Gull Eggs we gathered this evening made us a good supper & had something remaining for our breakefast tomorrow. One of the Pigeons was uncommonly fat, as much so as the fattest duck I ever saw, it [w]as perfectly covered, even to the first joint of the wing. In the island we put up this forenoon the men saw several Turtles, basking in the Sun. Except in Red River, this is the last place going to the interior, where, I know, we find any. In Some parts in the interior of

23 This water route went by way of the English River and Lac Seul, over the height of land to the headwaters of the Albany River, and down to Fort Albany on James Bay. This route was the means by which, for many years, the HBC traders from Albany reached their wintering grounds on the Red and Assiniboine Rivers, Lake Winnipeg, and the lands to the east of that Lake. Near the end of George Nelson's first sojourn on the lake, the HBC began to supply these regions by the much shorter route from York Factory.

River Ouinipique, the indians say there are some, but many <u>fabulous</u> stories attend them.

Thursd: 27th. Very stormy all night, particularly towards day, when the rain ceased, but the wind blew violently 'till noon. We did not set off however till 5½ P. M. allowing time for the <u>swells</u> to fall in the Traverse, which is one of the most dangerous from Montreal to Athabasca. It may be about 7 miles broad, but whether from the shallowness or current (which by the bye we don't perceive) the swells soon become large, i.e. short & deep, & of course very dangerous.[24] <u>Our</u> people have often been detained 4 & 5 days: sometimes 6 & 7; but in 1817, Some of our Canoes were detained 22 days notwithstanding the great anxiety of several of the (NW) partners to get on! In all <u>these</u> Lakes, /65/ when the swells soon <u>rise</u>, they also fall almost with the wind, Lake Superior, & a few other <u>deep</u> places excepted; but it is not the case here. The wind had fallen nearly to a dead calm for near 3 hours when embarked, still we shipped a great quantity of water; the wind indeed had increased a little.

On entering the Traverse we saw an indian lodge, to which I went & found a very stout Sauteux bathing in the waves & Sand. He gave me a few eggs, which was all that he had; & told me that the Red River people had passed only 5 days ago! How must these poor creatures have suffered from hunger! We put up at dark about 4 miles up Lac La Pluie River. Find the water hi. & some few musquetoes. We gathered 7 or 8 doz eggs on a couple of Small islands we debarked upon for the purpose.

Frid: 28th. Set off at 2.10' a.m. About 6 saw a young Bear, but that was all we got, as he had crossed the River & entered the woods long before we could <u>reach him</u>. Put ashore at 8 (at Rapid River) to cook our miserable breakfast. Sayre went to the foot of the Falls, saw a few sturgeons, but too far out; & another man lost his fishing line, angling. At 9¼ were off again, /66/ & hoisted sail for a few minutes in one of the bends of the River. Weather clear, calm, & uncommonly hot. Met a few indians from whom I got a little dry & Pounded Sturgeon, & some sturgeon oil, for which I gave one of my old Shirts, 8 ins. Tobacco, 4 loads amunition & Tecier's Blanket Capot, a great deal more than all was worth but we had no alternative. Saw a few more indians at

24 The traverse, from the southernmost tip of Bigsby Island to the NE end of the Sable Island, is a little over 4 miles. The prevailing SW winds, working on the most open part of Lake of the Woods, can generate high swells that hit the canoes sideways. Vessels much larger than a north canoe, and higher in the water, can have great difficulties crossing this traverse in a moderately high wind.

the foot of the Long-Sault, from whom we got a little more Sturgeon with a great deal of difficulty, as they also complained much of hunger. Here we haul up the Canoes, but the line of my Canoe consisting of the halyards (or Sail lines) of the other Canoes, broke, but fortunately without any damage. It began to rain just as we were getting to the upper end of the rapid, & continued for about an hour with terrible violence, thundering & lightning most dreadfully. We had not had time to unload, & our only shelter except 2 or 3 old oaks were each other. However, calm ensuing we pursued our course a few miles more & put up after Sun Set just [as] another dreadful storm was coming down. We were forced to put up in a nasty wet, narrow beach, scarcely broad enough to put our cargoes, but not sufficient /67/ for my Tent, part of which was on the side of the Hill, so that all night long the water was running under us, sometimes 2 or 3 inches deep. I had gathered a few small sticks on which I curled myself under my Cloak. We however got Tea, only by the perseverance of Tecier, who, poor old creature was as hot for it as ourselves. Many of the men were worse off than me, for they had no shelter but their Canoes, & as the beach was so very narrow most of them passed the night, litterally in the water & the lower side of their Blankets buried in the mud, leaves, & rubbish, by the waves of the river breaking upon them. In spite of this & the miryads of musquetoes our sleep tho' short, was sound: what will fatigue not do? I have had many most uncomfortable nights since I've been in this country, but this one beats them all. Not the least part of our body but was dripping wet.

Saturday 29th. As 2.15' we were off again, & carrying sail from 10 a.m. under double reefs, we arrived at Lac La Pluie Fort, thank God, safe & sound at about 4 P. M. A Mr. Rodk McKinzie[25] was master here, & treated us most hospitably; & we made decent amends for last time. A short distance above our last night's bed we hauled up Le Rapide du Manito, half load, /68/ & which is dangerous when the water is hi. as this year. Camarere (my bow-man) in reloading let drop his paddle, which he went for in a small canoe taken at the indian lodges (of whom we found several, but got nothing). In running the Rapid with Bellanger he kept too near the swells – in an instant the canoe was upset & they under water. Camarere, fortunately for him,

---

25 Roderick McKenzie, master at Lac la Pluie. Wallace (1934, 479) has a few notes on each of four fur traders with this name, but more research would be needed to establish which one this was.

got a hold of the canoe, so did B. but as they could not both stick to it, B. generously left it to the other & shifted for himself. It was awful to see them, & every soul, even to the indians, thought them both lost. Cam. holding the Canoe & sweeping round in the eddies as swift as a Top, & sometimes hauled in a manner under water by the whirlpools, whilst B. sometimes turning also like a Top, and others dragged suddenly for near a minute at a time, to the bottom; & then rising nearly his whole length out of the water, as if thrown up, & springing for life, again carried down, for several times running, at last he got into a large smooth Eddy just as the men in one of the Large Canoes was coming to him; but would not Embark as Camarere was still in great danger. They both, thank God, got safe, B. to land, Cam. in the L. Canoe.

/69/ We saw a good many indians at La Petite Fourche; but being under a heavy sail, we would not stop.[26] Two of them came out to us, & complained of hunger, tho' they had some Sugar. They are Pilleurs,[27] from the American Territories on the Fon[d] du Lac. These two Rivers, i.e. Petite et Grande Fourche, both take their rise in the Fon du Lac territories & fall into Lac la Pluie river 7, or 8 miles apart.[28] The entrance of both is beautiful, & I am told by those who have been to their Sources that they are the same all along. The soil on the banks of L. L. Pl. rivier is generally excellent, & there is abundance of Sturgeon in the River, but not so much other fish as one might expect. At the foot of this River, immediately on entering Lac de Bois is a long, low, narrow sandy island, called "Isle aux Sables" it may be said to bar the river almost about the middle of it are a great many Sandy Hills, something in the form of Cones, roofs of Houses, & various shapes, thus formed by the drifting of the light, white, sand, which it is the only soil in this island, a smart [small?] part excepted of the East End, where grow a few oak & some other Trees. The first years the white [man] travell[g] this Road, this Island was a rendez-vous of the indians, & a sort of tributing place, where, independent of trade, they always compelled them to give presents, & the last year preceding the

26 Nelson is now backtracking, to describe the place where the Rainy River ("Lac la Pluie River") enters Lake of the Woods, and to tell an anecdote. His story of the local Ojibwe, taking advantage of this strategic point at the foot of the dangerous traverse to impose a tax or tribute on fur traders, adds to our understanding of the control that the Indigenous people sought to maintain over this part of the canoe route to the Northwest.

27 Pillagers or Makandwewininiwag, a band of Ojibwe living around the headwaters of the Mississippi.

28 Now Big Fork River and Little Fork River.

Small-Pox (see Sir a. McK. Journal) it was with great /70/ difficulty
they got past.[29] The fur trade was then but just in its childhood, and
almost every Gentleman was a Company. Envy, Jealousy, hatred, was
mutual, of course there was no unanimity, & the indians, tho' barba-
rous, knew perfectly well how to avail themselves of these advantages:
& this year (I forget precisely what year, but it was immediately preceding the S. Pox. see Sir A: McK. Jour.) they detained these Traders 7
days. During their stay there were many quarrels & battles, but very
few lives lost. However, by dint of Presents, Promises, &c they were
allowed to depart but fully warned that the ensuing Spring they should
not pass! These poor insignificant wretches, tho' they were scarcely
able of annoying of themselves, yet found means thro' the Cupidity of
the white of obtaining all they required, i.e. their necessities & respect:
the latter, however little we may relish, we cannot deny. Yet there were
Men among the white, spirited & disinterested enough, but their voice
was borne down by those other Fellows. Now we pass peaceably, &
seldom stop but to eat Sand Berries, of which there are immense quantities & are delicious when fully ripe.[30]

Sund: 30th June. The men working at their Canoes & drying our
Packs. The indians, or somebody, had the bare-faced impudence to roll
one of our Packs into the branches & took near half the Rats out, tho'
not 50 yds from the tents & almost in a plain.

/71/ Monday July 1 1822. Finish our Canoes &c &c take our provisions & make every preparation for our departure tomorrow. Mr.
McKenzie it is true had not the means of giving us much, but Still his
kindness & attention in every thing he was able made full amends. I
have left young Cameron here.

This evening at Sun Set Messrs. Black & Ogden arrive in a light Canoe
& ten men, the first from Athabasca, the latter Columbia. All well. As
they had no body knowing the Road beyond this I left one of the men of
our Brigade to guide them. I should have accompanied them but my Bow
& Steersman I don't like to trust to. I have seen enough of them.

Tuesd 2nd. At 2-10' a.m. we set off, & soon got into the Lake, being
about 3 miles above the Portage where we mended our Canoes. At
7 Put ashore to cook Rice for our breakefast. At 9-10' off again &

29 The imposition of tolls upon strangers travelling through the lands of Indigenous peoples
was common. See Dickason 1997, 82–3, 103, 131, for examples on various waterways.
30 The end of June was too early for any berries to have ripened in this part of the world,
but wild cranberries, which ripen in the fall, hang on the bushes until spring, and are sometimes known as sand berries. I'm grateful to Jennifer Brown for this information.

encamped at Sun Set in the upper end of Lac Lamecan (i.e. Nàmé-káàn, i.e. where Sturgeon is "made" dried, &c &c). We found a Solitary Indian at the South End of the L. La Pluie, from whom Dorion, for 4 Prs Shoes, traded about half a Gallon oil. A little before we put [up] we found St Pierre, with one McNabb with 3 Canoes of Provisions for Norway House. I took half a (9 Gall) Keg of Rotten Grease from them to season our oats (rise) /72/ for we had been but sparingly supplied with Sturgeon oil for that purpose. We had alternately Sail & head wind most of the day. Lac la Pluie is reckond 18 leagues long, very broad in some places, & some islands; & is full of Shelving nasty rocks almost all the way thro'.

Wednesd. 3^d. Embark at 1.48' with frequent Sail through the remainder of Lake Lamican & Vermillion Lake. At 7 enter River La Croix & at 8.45' had crossed the last Portage to enter Lac La Croix, where we breakefasted. Here we remained till 12 a.m. drying some of our Packs that had got wet yesterday. We encamped at 5 P.M. at Portage de l'Isle, the first Portage on leaving the old Grand Portage Road. The water is very hi this year, hence we come on so well. In the summer of 1804,[31] the water was so low that we took the best part of two days to get thro' River la Croix, tho' scarcely above 12 miles we were obliged to make half loads & carry even to the Canoe in some places, the bed of this river in one or two places being perfectly dry! There are plenty of Turtles in this river I am told. It is small, & winds a good deal.

Thursd. 4th. Mc Kay somehow overslept himself so that it was 2½ a.m. before we set /73/ off At 7 had crossed several Portages & désjarges [*décharges*] & breakefasted at Portage Des Grosses Roches. We had scarcely time to cover our Bagge & Pitch my Tent when a terrible Thunder storm passed by us: we however [got] only part of it. McKay & the others came up with us at 8. At 10 the weather clearing up & entered Lac D'Esturgeon, thro' which we carried sail almost all the way. This to my fancy is a handsome (in Summer) lake. It is narrow & about 18 miles long, has a few Islands but the sides are not so much broken with hidious rocks as in the winnepeek. The banks here seem to be but one solid Rock with a few small openings into handsome little Bays, & are for the most part covered with Pines (Epinettes) & Cypress, which with the few Poplars & Birch intermixed give a

---

31 In 1804, Nelson passed over the route on his way from the Folle Avoine department to Lake Winnipeg. We do not have his journal of this trip, but he evidently remembered some details vividly.

beautiful shade, particularly where there are some smooth low points of Rocks. After this we crossed a few small Lakes or Ponds, Portage des deux Rivieres & P. des Morts. These two Portages are made to avoid an immense long circuit that we otherwise should be obliged to make, I believe near a days march &c in Lake-way. The last of the two is a handsome dry one, with a nice Lake at each end, & so named from a man (or two) who died, & are buried here from <u>ruptures</u> &c they got in the other Portages. The other one (P. des 2 Riv) is undoubtedly the worst of any I have yet seen. It is so called from a rivulet that must be crossed at the foot of a nasty wet hill, over which there is a <u>Country</u> bridge, that is saying enough! It is astonishing to me that the men do not hurt & even kill themselves, running /74/ as they almost always do with 2, 3 & sometimes 4 Parcels of from 84 to 100 lbs wt. each. It is commonly very muddy, with nasty hills, from one of which oozes a spring exactly in the middle of ye road, & which, from end to end is filled with fallen Trees, Stones, Stumps, and Ponds knee deep, & choked up with willows, alternately, or altogether. None but good, true, sure-footed Beasts of Burden like the Canadians can do it: a horse trotting would soon breake his neck, & a dog, either, drown in the mire or rip out his Guts, but a Canadian smiles at the idea till he is over, & then <u>wonders</u>!

I found an indian & a boy a hunting. They were starving as they told me from the want of ammunition. They saw a Bear & Carriboeuf today but are not so expert with their bows as the Moose Lake Ind. They had 4 or 5 small birds unfledged, with which they intended to make their supper & bait a few hooks for Pike!!! We encamped early (at 6 P.M.) at the further end of the Portage des Morts.

Frid: 5th. We had another dreadful Thunder Storm this last night, but to day the weather was fair & excessively warm. Embarked upon Lac du Dorée whilst there were yet plenty of stars, & having some sail we entered that nasty Creek (Riviere) des Francois (to avoid the Long Port. of that name) at 7. At 10 we had crossed Petit Port. des Francais at the upper end of the Creek, where we breakefasted & remain'd till 1.50' P. M. Drying our Packs. Hauled up some /75/ nasty shallow Rapids, cross a couple of Lakes rivers <u>Descharges</u> & encamp at dusk at Port. La Penté. Lucier & Gamache made a small hole in their Canoe from the Knot of a Tree, but no further injury.

Satur: 6th. At 2.10' were off again. At 5 entered Milles Lacs, handsome enough in many places. Breakefasted between 7 & 9 as also to dry a few Rats, & Pitch our Canoe. We had left our landing but a short time when I met Mr Frs: Grant, 4 Canoes loaded with Corn & Grease for Norway House, from Ft. Wm 11 days. We were very short [of provisions], but as his orders were positive I did not like to insist [on taking any], so that I push'd on to put out our 2 Nets at the further end of Port. La Prairie, in a small Lake.

Near the East end of the Lake met one Loranger, a petty Trader,[32] bound to Red River, as he says: but I fear the poor creature will make no great Spate of it this year. Three or four days ago he had the misfortune to lose one of his men: they were ashore in River des Chiens preparing a breakefast for the Red R. people, when a number of Pigeons lighting near them, this man called for Lorangers Gun, another Sharped [?] brute of a fellow in endeavouring to take it out from under the Bars of the Canoe, kick'd the Cock some where, when giving it another pull it went off, & the Contents, upwards of 40 Grains of shot, lodged in his lower belly & groin. He survived but a very few hours.

In Milles Lacs this Last winter, a./76/ Mr. Cadotte,[33] equipt & sent in for this winter as a Trader, left three men with some trading Pieces here. In the month of February I believe, three indians come to their House. In the forenoon just as the Fisherman returned from his nets, the master one Beaulieu went out to see his fortune, leaving one man in ye house with them. He was scarcely out when he heard the report of a Gun, & dreading something he ran into the house, but met the 3 inds. running out, with their Guns in their hands & giving the "Death Cry." He saw his man weltering in his blood, & heard another shot, which wounded the fisherman. Seeing his only 2 men fall he ran into his own house, & his wife, the only help mate he now had loading his Guns for him, he began firing & crying, or yelling rather, as they did, which kept them in the woods, where they watched him 2 nights & 3 days, & at last returned [to their lodges]. One man was killed outright, the other with difficulty recovered. It is not known what could have been their motives – say it was their distresses, being destitute of almost all their necessaries, but principally amunition. This however, is but a sorrowful plan, & I am more inclined to attribute it to villainy & its consequences – the desire of plunder. That they will escape I have not the least doubt, & be more than connived at till they have murdered several of ourselves. Such is the Policy of the Indian Trade from the very first. "Poor fellows."

32 An independent trader, hoping to take advantage of the concentration of people at the Red River Colony.
33 One of the Cadottes of Fond du Lac (Warren 1974; see index).

The journal immediately continues in a different format – eight full sheets of Radway paper folded in four, with four numbered pages to a side (the order is upper left, upper right, lower left, lower right). The dates covered are 6 July–22 August 1822. Pages 10–32 begin as a table listing the details of all the portages from Fort William to Cumberland House (not printed here, as there is a much more detailed account later on). Following the table, the journal continues.

/1/ July 6ᵗʰ Sat 1822}
"Poor Fellow! He is a good Indian – I know him very well. – I can't conceive how it happened. I may say any thing to him I please & he never minds it: he must have been instigated, urged on by the others." Such too frequently are our excuses. We do not, can not, or will not, perceive that if the case has not befallen ourselves it is merely because the opportunity did not offer. Cadotte had a Glimpse of him in Lake Superior & made for his tent (one of them I mean) but he dreading his vengeance very justly, made off to the woods. C. pursued him some time but in vain, then returned to his tent & destroyed his property. This indian (the only one of the three) I knew in '14-'15.[34] He was then a boy, an excellent lad & a very good hunter, a few years back he killed his own brother, & a couple of years before, in an <u>indian Duel</u> killed an indian – this now being his third, & perfectly sober each time – But as I said above, such has been, is yet, & I am afraid will be for a long time to come, the Policy of Indian Traders. We might as well say "he has not killed me"!!

/2/ Sund: 7ᵗʰ. Set off again very early, but it was sometime before we could get thro' this nasty winding river (de la Savanne) from the vast quantity of fallen Trees, which in many places, almost completely choke it up.

Crossed Portage de la Savanne (40 acres long) Portage du Milieu, & Portage de la Prairie, & Portage de l'eau froide, all within a short distance of each other, & making near 5 miles of Portage, between them. It is difficult to say exactly where is the proper <u>height</u> of <u>Lands</u> here at the South End of Port. La Prairie is the source of one river,

---

34 This refers to Nelson's second season in The Pic district, north of Lake Superior.

oozing, or rather a spring, running out of the ground, in a valley; at the N. end is a small round Lake, about 400 yds broad (& perhaps 1,000 long, entirely surrounded with a swamp – it is apparently very deep & a miry bottom, & without any visible communication (or source) with any stream) to Portage du Milieu, at the N. end of which is another Lake, very irregular, shallow, & in some places muddy, 'till the small creek that leads to Port. de la Savanne (perhaps 1½ miles distant from each other). Here, the current, which by the /3/ by the bye, loses itself in that long Swamp we carry over, runs to the N. & of course falls into Hudsons Bay at York Factory. At the North end of Portage de la Savanne is the river of the same name, taking its rise I am told in a Lake, a few miles above the Portage.

In the Lake between Port. La Sav. & Port. du Milieu, the Indians take some excellent white fish, but only after the Voyageurs have passed some time; because the noise we generally make, they say frighten the fish, the Lake being very shallow. Neither the Ind. or white, can say from where they [the fish] come. At a few acres from the S. end of Port. La Prairie, is another (short) Port. to avoid a creek full of stones & trees, & a little to the S. again on the route Ft William are 2 or 3 small Lakes, where we put out our 2 Nets in hopes of getting a few fish.

Mond: 8ᵗʰ July '22. We took but 2 or 3 fish. McKay with the rest of the loaded Canoes overtook us, & we also left the place at 12. a. m. We took up our nets as we passed, but not a single thing in them, at 2 P. M. we had entered Riviere des Chiens, a /4/ nice large River, taking, as I've been told, its rise not far from Lake Nepigon. We encamped at 5 P. M. behind the brigade, for we had been retarded at Port. a Jourdain, Gumming our Canoe &c. I was very sorry for it as the other 3 Canoes had broken one of their Kettles, & had but one between them. About 3 P. M. we were overtaken by a furious, but short, Hail storm, & put up early to shelter ourselves in time from another.

Tuesd: 9ᵗʰ. Embark at 2. a. m. Frequent showers of rain during yᵉ day, overtook McKay on entering Lac des Chiens, a handsome, deep, clear (water) but irregular Lake, with very hi lands all round. At 2 P. M. all hands had crossed the Portage & the poor creatures had not yet had their breakfast. It is now 2 or 3 days since they've been upon short allowances, & they have scarcely one meal between them. They keep running & racing however as before, laughing & damning les Bourgeois, & at each other; but they are all pale & weake, & play that merely to hide the gnawings of their Stomacs. as my Canoe was considerably /5/ less loaded than the others, I proceeded a head to put out our Nets in hopes of getting a breakefast for tomorrow. We took a carp immediately on putting out ye nets; & McKay came up with us at Sun Set.

A Little before Sun Set Messrs Black & Ogden (in one Canoe) & All. McDonell & Cuthbert Grant (in another) overtook us at our Encampment. Of this I was very glad, because I was much afraid they had lost themselves, as the road is difficult enough, & they had no Guide. After Sun set I got my breakfast with these Gentlemen.

Wednesd: 10th. Messrs Black & Ogden had the politeness to give me a passage in their Canoe & we arrived, thank God, safe at 4 P.M at Ft. Wm where I laid in a good stock of bread & fresh butter. The morning was very cold, & a heavy Fog prevented our settling off 'till late. Still we ran down several large & long rapids in the thickness of the Fog. I could not sufficiently admire the _adroisse_ of our Bowsman in avoiding the numerous stones; how quick & exactly they made the most acute angles in spite of the /6/ mist, strength of the current & the velocity with which we went, for sometimes all the crew Paddled, one time in particular, they had 3 very acute angles to make to avoid several Large & sharp stones, & so near each other that it seemed impossible to avoid being dashed to atoms even on the first. But they ran perfectly light, only a few men in each Canoe. We were looking on with the greatest anxiety & wonder. They shipped some water in the terrible swells, but did not even touch one stone. We had a great many rapids to run to day & several Portages to make. Below the _Mountain_ however, we often ran upon the stones, but they are so terribly numerous, that it is even a wonder how they escape at all.

Whilst we were breakefasting, & cleaning ourselves at the Mountain, McKay again came up with us, as these light Canoes had a few quts [quarts] Corns remaining it was given to my People.

A few miles below the Mountain we saw a couple of indian tents, /7/ drying of Sturgeon, at my request Mr Bl[ack]'s Canoe drew up & I asked of them (being Sauteuxs) if they had any fish, & to carry all they had to my men that were starving at the Port[age] & that I would pay them handsomely on their arrival at Ft. Wm. An elderly woman that was looking on replied in a most vociferous manner "Tut, tut, you are cheat Pa dog; you always cheat the Indians. Thus by that fair & insinuating manner of speaking you have, but you shall not cheat me. I know you too well: the whole of ye traders, but particularly you, you cheating, smooth tongued Dog: I know you, I know you, Say no more." Then addressing herself to the rest of the generation (of vipers) "He thinks I don't know him; nor his manner of cheating; but I am well aware of him, & his great cunning will be of no use here" with a deal of other stuff that came rattling out so quick that I could scarce understand the half she said. This broad side astonished me beyond measure, & tho' I am seldom at a loss to answer these Termagants, yet so /8/ sudden & unexpected was this salute, & the laughing of Messrs B. & Og. that I was completely silenced, & did not answer a syllable, but told the men to pull out. However as we were going off she said that "Towards night I'll send the children, because the men must not suffer on your account." I was still phased [fazed], & promised to pay well. It was a long time before the Gentlemen (Particularly Mr Og.) forgot this business. A few days after she came in & being at breakefast with one of the Gentleman's woman, saw me pass & called out "Hisht! My Payment you: I am on the Ground & you shant cheat me." I gave the Bitch a little of her own lingo; but being no more young & heedless, I durst not go too far, for fear of getting the whole Fort about me. Upon enquiry for I have not even yet any recollection of having ever seen her, she claimed this abuse as a previlige: 'are you not so & so &c &c well & what have you got to say? am I not to speake to a relative? come hold your tongue, & say no more, for I have still /9/ "still plenty in store for you: but the best for us both is to make peace!" I began to think so too, & ordering her a couple of quarts of rum, left her. This old harridan (for she is one in the fullest sense of the word, excepting a few years yet in her favor) is a relative i.e. cousin of a woman that thro' courtesey to her has been used to stile me "Nee-nim" brother in law, & as there is no end to relationship among the Indians, she also calls me thus! The Devil take such acquaintances.[35]

A few miles below this again, we found Monsr (or Messire) Provenché, now a Bishop, on his way up to Red River from Montreal.[36] We remained but a few minutes & one of his men during the time gave me a Letter from home.

35 Peers and Brown (2000) explain this episode as an example of the vigorous teasing or joking that Ojibwe women and men, related as cross-cousins, sometimes used towards one another. Nelson was taken by surprise, and embarrassed in front of the others, but knew enough of their kinship practices to figure out that she was entitled to this behaviour. See also Brown 2017b, chapter 8.

36 Joseph-Norbert Provencher (1787–1853), a Roman Catholic priest who had been sent to the Northwest as a missionary in 1818. Called back to Montreal in 1820 as the plans for the mission developed, he was now returning with the title Bishop of Juliopolis in partibus. He worked tirelessly and with imagination for the Red River community for over thirty years, and was designated Bishop of St Boniface, the francophone community on the east bank of the Red River opposite the Forks, in 1847 (Lemieux 1985).

Thursd 11th July. My Men arrive! Poor creatures & quite famished.

/10/ List of the Portages &c as they are met with from Fort William to Cumberland House, & their lengths Names &c which I measured with a Cod-Line (i.e. Canoe tracking line), allowing about 1/10, so that if they were remeasured with a Chain, I think they would be found near 1/5 longer.

July 1822

Sund 21. Left Ft Wm with 21 Pieces, my lumber & that of another clerk, 4 Men, & a Free man. The Brigade, consisting of 3 Canoes, off yesterday.

Mond 22[37]. Port du Paresseux 275 <u>Paces</u>. Fine, flint stones. So termed from a lazy dog that had not carried a Canoes cargo (25 Pieces) over, in near 4 days. To avoid a shallow rapid part of the river.

Port. de la Montagne, 1380 yds, the hill, (which resembles rotten slate, very steep, & cut in the Rock by the NWC to avoid the old Road (of the French) & which is almost Perpendicular) 120 yds to avoid a tremendous fall[38] where there is a most beautiful, shifting, & perpetual Rain Bow. Its name from the hill.

June 23 Ecarté, 795 yds. From a man that lost himself for near 2 days, I am told, in it; & many yet miss the path in consequence of the immense number of large stones, lying from one end to the other, except where there are a few bridges to avoid the mud &c. Made to avoid a long succession of frightful falls.

/11/ June 23. Roses Des. 210 yds, haul up the Canoe with a few Pieces, this year 1/3d load, water being hi. From the wild Rose.

P de l'isle, 54 yds. Lower end nasty landing, upper end safe, but the departure very dangerous as we must double a pt. of Rock, projecting far in the river & very near the fall indeed. At this Pt there is a strong current. Fine, made in a small island.

Racoursé, 163 yds. Lower end requires caution & dexterity from the strength of the current, eddies, & whirl-pools, upper end safe, with caution. Some years, maniacs, such as Iroquois, & some very few Canadians run, never without a fright, & sometimes the <u>hurt</u> with it.

Epingles, 187 yds. Landings safe, & nasty carrying from the stones & moss, to avoid a bad fall. Name, from the stones at the lower end that are sharp as knives & yet no avoiding treading upon them.

37 The journal now becomes a detailed description of the canoe route west from Fort William to Cumberland House.

38 The present Kakabeka Falls.

Wed 24. 8 Descharges, one or 2, perhaps of 200 yds. & a great many rapids. At low water carry half the cargo over them all, but this year, ye water being hi, hauld up, the full loads.

Petit Port. des Chiens, & it is un Chien de Portage[39] only 77 yds, over a solid Rock, the surface smooth, but /12/ uncommonly unlevel, several yds of slanting rock, now perpendicular up, or down, with of course many deep hollows, as the surface is smooth & slippy the men frequently slide on their back sides, or fall on their faces, with from 160 to 200 lbs & run they must. To avoid an awful fall, named from the next one above.

Thurs 25. Grd P. des Chiens 2640 yds. Landing safe, upper end in a beautiful Lake, lower in a large basin. From the beach to the brow of the hill 1020 yds, the last 120 extremely steep. From the brow of this hill Lake Supr (to the S.) might be very easily seen, but the immense intervening hills prevent; but the view is very grand, at either end, for at both ends there is a steep hi. Hill. The walking is beautiful & dry, & shaded by Poplars & Cypress. To avoid a long succession of Falls & dangerous Rapids. Name, from an immense large Dog killed & buried by the Sioux's in former days, just on the brow of the S. hill. The place is still visible, but far exceeding the size of any animal I ever saw. Its head was placed either to the W. or E. according as either the Sioux's or Sauteux succeeded. Ind. tradition, my informant an half breed clerk.

/13/ Saturd 27 July

P. a Jourdain, 127 yds, covered with lar. round stones (as in L'Ecarté) except where there are bridges to pass over the water & mire. To avoid a very strong Rapid, which is frequently run, with almost empty canoes. Name [from] Jourd. a Guide, breaking his canoe here.

Sun 28. P. d'eau Froide, 150 yds. Fine, landings on bridges from the swamps on the edges. Name, from the water being excessively cold, uncommonly clear & transparent. To avoid a narrow Creek, full of stones & trees.

P. La Prairie, 4100 yds, beautiful cypress country, but 2 nasty long & steep hills. This Port is about 300 yds from the last & about 100 more to the left, is the source of part of the St Lawrence waters, issuing in a large Spring from under Ground, in a fine valley between 2 steep hills. Name, from the clear & open country at both Ends, particularly the N. end. Men here carry across land, into a small Lake, about 400 yds, where we find

---

39 Nelson's joke, "a dog of a portage."

Mond 29 P du Milieu, 754 yds. except a short ridge in the middle, the which is a bog & swamp, which is passed on bridges. Name, being between as we might say, the height of Land, & P. La. &c. &

P. Savanne, 2370 yds. Excepting 150 yds, the whole length of it is a bridge, of 2, 3 & 4 logs, sometimes laid lengthways /14/ at the N. end of this Por. We go down the current (see the Jour.) as from Ft. Wm, we came up to Port La Prairie.

August Sund 4. P. du Baril (or McKays P.) 396 yds, up & down a very hi. hill from beach to beach, the hill being about the middle, landings beautiful & safe, in two Lakes. It is I believe, across land, or to avoid a long, bad, small river. Name, some accident happened to a Keg of liquor belonging to Mr Wm MKay.

P. de la Pente 470 yds fine, with a couple of Bridges. S landing in a lake, N in a small rivulet. To avoid this rivulet that is too shallow, full of stones & trees &c. Very long, some low water years it is upwards of 1200 yds, except the Canoe, which is always 470 or 500 yds. Name, from the most part of the road being in the side of a hill.

Mond 5. Des Pins. 50 Paces, very fine, between two Lakes. This year we let down the Canoes, but at very low water carry all. To avoid a short rapid & narrow. Name, from the fine large fir trees.

A good many shallow & narrow rapids now occur, which at low water give an infinite deal of trouble.

Petit Port des Francais 442 yds. Another very hi. hill in the middle, to avoid a small creek, full of rapids /15/ and falls, & a great quantity of fallen timber. Name, in contra-distinction from Grand Port. des Francais, about 3000 yds, to avoid the river des Frs which, being narrow, shallow, very crooked, & terribly full of fallen timber, & willows, is impassible at low water. The Grt Pt is fine except for 5 or 600 yds at the N end, which is a very bad swamp, & has several hi' hills. I cannot say why it is called P. des Frs. but I suppose from some accident befalling that people their first years, & prior to the conquest of Canada. At N end, a handsome small Lake.

Tues 6. Port des Morts, 556 yds, fine & dry, landings beautiful, in 2 handsome Lakes. Name from one or two men who died here of rupt[ur]ing. Across Land, from Lake to Lake.

Deux Rivieres, 694 [yards]. Landings good, i.e. safe, but the road is infamous, blackguard & villanous as can be. It is either in mud, knee deep, over stones, sticks &c trees, up or down hills. Immediately at the foot of one hill is a bridge to cross the creek that passes in the valley. It is long since in ruins, & tho' constantly wet from a spring oozing out of the bank, directly in the middle of the road, & of course uncommonly dangerous, yet the men must run over. Even a dog would pace it with /16/ caution & dread. These 2 last Port. are made to avoid a very long circuit in Lake way, which, however, prudent people, would prefer, but Canadians are made for Beasts of Burden, & are sure footed animals. Name, from the creek that passes thro' it.

At 5 or 600 yds is a short Detroit, between two Pts of Land, where from the shallowness, stones & trees, the canoes at low water are carried by careful men.

Wed 7. P[ortage des] Grosses Roches, 363 yds, fine enough. In going to the interior run the Canoes with a few Pieces, but out going carry all. Landings, safe & fine. Name from the stones. This is the first P. in Riv^r maligne.

P. Rocher des Pins, 193 yds, fine; landings, with caution, safe enough. Name, from the Rock, & beautiful Fir trees.

Des. de L'isle, 197 yds, indifferent, upper land[ing] requires caution. Name, from an island, in which some fool-hardys go.

Petit Rocher, 34 yds, Landings safe, but very bad, being very shallow & full of rocks. Name, from the rock; to avoid a fall.

Port. de l'Isle, 86 yds, beautiful, fine large Firs, upper end very /17/ dangerous to arrive, but particularly to set off from the upper end, for the Portage is on an island, not 2 acres long, on each side of which is a frightful fall, that requires resolution & dexterity from being driven in by a pretty strong rapid only a few yards [away]. On each side of another small island, & immediately opposite the falls, but fortunately the suction is not great. Name, from the island. This is the last Port. in R^r maligne, so called from its shallowness, & the great number of sharp shelving rocks & stones all over it. A little below this, we fall into Lac la Croix (by the Soteauxs, Fir Lake), where is the old Grd. Portage Road, but abandoned since 1804, being, I am told on the American Territories. It is a fine, handsome, easy route, in comparison of the infamously blackguard one we now go.

Thurs 8. 1st P[ortage] La croix, 189 yds, fine, landings good & safe. To avoid [a] small nasty creek, full of rapids, falls, & trees, an outlet of this Lake (la Croix). Name, I know not why, because we are fond of perverting everything.

2nd P L. C. 248 yds, fine enough, landing bad, but safe, to avoid a fall. 3d d. d. [ditto] 58 yds, beautiful, to avoid a fall. Landing good & safe.

Frid 9. 1st Port. Neuf. 139 yds across land, into a small creek, fine enough, landings safe.

/18/ Aug Frid 9

2ⁿᵈ P. Neuf 226 [yards], most of it very muddy, landings safe. Here I saw an infinite number of Leaches, of different kinds, & some beautiful ones, sporting in the water & even debarking on the stones. These 2 Port. are made to avoid a long circuit, leading by "La chaudiere des Frans" (a Port.) into Lac la Pluie, at hi. water; but when low we can't pass this way. Name, because it is a later discovered Road.

Suñd 11. P. du Lac la Pluie, about 180 yds. I did not measure it; fine, landings good & safe. It is here that the voyageurs call "le bout tes Terres" – probably by the French, their first years in this Country long prior to the conquest of Canada, & it being the utmost length they had as yet discovered, perhaps thought it the only part, or whole of the interior: because it would appear by Carvers Travels, not 60 yrs back that the great Lakes below this were branches of the Sea, i.e. considered as such from the reports of the Indians. But this is too ample a subject for my present time & pasm [?] discuss at present.

We here follow Lac La Pluie river, from one end to the other, large & deep, & abundance of sturgeon. Several places are truly beautiful & picturesque; & the soil in general excellent. The current is even & strong excepting in two places. The first, Le Manitô, is a dangerous rapid to the incautious, at hi water; the other, Le long Sault, from the length of the rapid, requires caution, but not dangerous. At its out let, is the Lake of the woods /19/ Lac des Bois, to avoid a long circuit, has a Portage, this year, about 100 yards, some years it is paddled over, & at others again is at least 600 yds, long, muddy the S. Landing.⁴⁰

Satur 17. Port. du Rat, 126 yds, moderately fine, being in an almost continual Rock; the landings safe. To avoid the river & falls, name is indian, & signifies a root the muskrat is fondest of. It is said the Boundary line passes here.⁴¹ From this place to Lake Winnipeeke, the

---

40 Now called French Portage Narrows, where two deep bays meet or almost meet (depending on the height of the water), providing a sheltered passage for canoes across the Aulneau Peninsula.

41 Because of the language of the 1783 Treaty of Paris, which was based on inaccurate information about the geography west of Lake Superior, the boundary between British territory and the United States was still unsettled in 1822. The final puzzle was applying one phrase in that treaty, which specified that the boundary must run to the "north west angle of Lake of the Woods." The fur traders suspected that this point would turn out to be Rat Portage itself, so that this critical portage would end up either on the boundary or even within American territory; Nelson's remark reflects this suspicion. The Boundary Commission's surveyors reached Lake of the Woods in 1823 and 1824. Their key problem was to locate the "north west angle," a geographically vague concept interpreted to be the point at which

French term Riviere ouinipique. The ind. have no name for it, only certain particular spots. It is a very ragged river, for there is not, for a long distance, 3 miles that can be called its beach: it is full of breakes, inlets, deep bays, Parched rocks & islands, which renders the navigation or Canoe extremely difficult to be learnt.

Sund 18. Grd. Des[charge] 156 yds. Fine, run some of the cargo, but requires dexterity. In outgoing, track up, a part over a hi. steep rock.

P[ortage] Terre Blanche, 114 yds. fine, in dry weather, but otherwise, muddy. To avoid the Falls in the river. Name, from the Grey earth.

Des[charge] Rocher a Chaurette, about 15 yds landings on a small rock; run & track up, part of the load. Name, a Guide broke his Canoe, & lost some things here. The fall is short, & very steep, so that in running I have tho't the water above, would have filled the canoes.

/20/ Augt Sund 18

P. Terre Jaune, 248 yds, very bad & in wet weather. To avoid falls. Name, the Yell[ow] Clay

La cave, is 2 Small Des[charges] at low water, on a smooth fine rock, name from the deep hollowness when the waters are low.

P[ortage] de l'isle, 52 yds. run, or let down the Canoe, but carry the cargoes, fine landings, safe, but bad. Some maniacs run this Rapid, but are almost as sure of a decent fright, & sometimes lose their lives as they deserve. Name from the island.

Mond 19. Chute a Jaqueau, 72 yds, a smooth rock, but very uneven, as if deep channels, but the Canoes must race here too, as they do all over tho' they many times full with their loads; & it is a wonder they don't drive their guts out at their eyes: a few Groans, some Grunts, spitting blood, Mon dieus, & Batems [baptême, a mild religious oath], & they are well again, they are good beasts of burden. To avoid a beautiful large fall. Landings at low water good & safe, but not so at hi. water. Name, from a Slave by that name drowned in running it.

P[ortage] Pointe de Bois, 297 yds. Landings, safe & good, uncommonly bad in wet weather. Name, because it cuts a long Pt [?] & avoids a great many frightful falls

---

a straight edge, oriented SW–NE and sliding towards the Lake from the NW, first contacted a point on the lakeshore. David Thompson, now employed by the British side of the Boundary Commission as a surveyor, located three possibilities for this point, one of which, the present "Northwest Angle," was chosen. This placed most of Lake of the Woods within British territory (now Canada), and set the fur traders' minds at rest about Rat Portage (information from David Malaher).

/21/ Mond 19. P[ortage] Petit Roché. 70 yds, fine, upper landing good enough, but uncommonly dangerous, as we must pass immediately above, & within a few feet of a tremendous fall, but fortunately it has scarcely no suction. It is but a few yards from the last Portage. Name, being on a rock.

P. Roche Brulé. 66 yds, fine rock, safe landings, to avoid more falls. There is hardly 2 miles between these 3 P. & I verily believe there is 150 feet, if not 200, of falls, perpendicular, they have an awfully grand appearance, the river here being very broad.

P. Chute aux Esclaves, 600 yds, but in hi. water double. Landings very dangerous & difficult, walking, on fine handsome rocks. Name, a slave that was dashed to pieces.

P. Barriere, 134 yds, let down the Canoe, some fools run, but they often meet with what they deserve, i.e. death. Landings good & safe, but requires a little care walking, a fine rock.

Tues 20 1st P[ortage] Lee-nà-wâ, 120 yds
    2 [second]   38 [yards]
2. Des[charges] run some of the lading
/22/ Tues 2d. 3d Port. of the Pinàwâ 82 yds
4th " " or Enfant Perdu 452 yds. Landings safe, to avoid falls. Walking, over rocks, Green woods &c. Indian tradition, & not very remote, says a child was lost in one of the Large Crevices in the rocks of this Port. The child was heard crying for a very long time, but could never be found.

5th do do Glissante, a beautiful rock (26 yds length) smooth as Glass. Over this, in the bed of the river, passes a few inches water, & we must pass more than half the bredth of the river within 10 feet of the fall, but there is no danger, scarcely even from willfulness.

16th [should be 6th portage] do do 17 yds, another smooth rock, & pass again very near the head of the fall, but no danger.

A little below this, about 15 miles, we fall into Lac du Bonet. These Port. and route is taken when the water is sufficiently hi, to avoid La Riviere Blanche, which is full of danger & death on every side. Many people have lost their lives by that route. It is unavoidable at low water, but is much less dangerous. There are 7 Portages, & several descharges within the space of 5 or 6 miles; from which some people think the name is given, as the foaming for the waters of the Falls, rising like large steps one /23/ above the other, as far as we can see (it is certainly a grand sight), looks as white as snow. But the name is indian (& as with most other names of places, the French or Cands. have perverted) & is given by them to a handsome river, falling in a cascade immediately below the last Port. in going to the interior, on the left in consequence of a fish resembling, & with it I believe is, the Rock Bass – as near as I can make it out, means the "white mouth" (fish) or "white water'd mouth" (fish) because some of their idioms are absolutely uninterpretable. The mouth of this fish does indeed seem as if whitned by too much soaking; & most of the Sauteux names, whether of things, or of places are descriptive: so that by the mere name the thing (& cause &c) is often known & understood, without ever having seen or heard of it before, so appropriate are they.

The Pinàwâ, is also an indian name, & descriptive (i.e. Tà-pee-nà-wâ wee (or o') see-pee) the Leeward river, or more properly perhaps, "the river sheltered from the wind"; & indeed it is, for it would require a half dozen West india hurricanes together to be wind bound in it. It is narrow, winding & completely sheltered, from the woods & Grass: still there are some handsome spots in it; & this the Mus-quetoes give us ample information of when the weather is warm & overcast.

/24/ P. Ense du Bonet, 37 yds very fine & handsome. Landings good & safe, with caution, because at the upper end we pass within a few yds of the fall that would drive every thing to destruction. Name from the Lake, again most strangely perverted. This was one of those numerous fav'rite places where the Indians formerly used to exact toll from the passing traders – their choices were certainly judicious: they could live by bands; & the Canoes must all pass close to their tents or ambuscades. They still ode [?] about the same spots, but the white [men] are too numerous, & they could not live out half a season without their supplies. They are now, most of them more wise & prudent, tho' I think yet as haughty & independent spirited as ever. This Lake (Du Bonet) has 3 outlets, each broad, & near to one another.

Roché Brulé, 148 yds. Fine Landings good & safe, name from the Rock, to distinguish it.

Le Bonet, 1290 yds, one half in a beautiful rich meadow interspersed with a few old oaks, the rest in the woods, very bad in wet weather. Landings good & safe: to avoid 5 or 6 Beautiful falls. Name, indian (Cris) but it never occurred to me to ask from cause, tho' I believe it is from some warriors Caps.

/25/ P[ortage] Rocher du Bonet, 210 yds, walking, a clean, long & smooth Rock. From the last Port. to this about ¾ mile is an immense strong current, eddies & whirlpools, & as the succion is very great, there is some danger in coming to it. Lower landing difficult, from the great motion of the water & a fall.

Thurs 22. Terre Blanche, 278 yds, very bad in wet weather. Landings good & safe. To avoid a fall, or rather number of cascades, when the water is very hi, some few very dextrous hands run down, but quite close to the shore, where there is but little water to drown. Name, the white, or Grey clay or mud.

About 25 years back, a number of Indians firing upon & wounding some of the people (& I believe killed one), at L'Ense du Bonet, a few days after 2 or 3 light canoes, passing were saluted in like manner, Messrs A. N. McLeod & Wm McKay, ordered their men to pull with all speed to the Tents, whereupon all ran off, but 2 aged men were taken, bound & put on board the Canoes with an intention of making an example of them, on coming to this Portage (Terre Blanche) one of them had the courage to try for his life, being loosened, he accordingly [jumped] out of the Canoe & swam off, diving like a loon, making for the fall, & every time he rose out of the water cried hoo, hoo, hoo, imediately an exasperated or pursued Loon: the canoe made /26/ for him but to no effect, he got into the fall & tho' he kept up for a long time, he was at last lost sight of: the canoes encamped merily by a small island that happened to be at the head of the fall. The other was taken to Bas de la Riviere Fort, & the halyards of the Flag staff put round his neck, but he begged so earnestly that his life was not only granted, but received a full Chiefs Clothing, with many Provisos on both sides. His name was Le mauvais Chef, & a bad one he was too; & his wife the quintessence of Bitchisms: he had a good many sons, most of them yet alive & great villains. Since that time, they've never stopped canoes, tho' frequently murdered & Pillaged in the winter: I mean the inds. in general of this river.

1st Des Eaux que Remuent, or Port[age] des chenes, 132 yds, fine in dry weather, upp[er] landing very dangerous; for we must unload on a point of rock very near a most tremendous & aw[ful?] fall, & the suction very great: yet some beasts go within a few yds to shew their dexterity. Lower Landing, good & safe enough with caution, but the rock is smooth & very slippery & the eddy very great. It is a small bay, perhaps 50 yds across & about 100 deep, & seems as if formed by the immense violence with which the water from the upper fall rushes into it, across the Bay is the /27/ 2nd des Eaux qui Remuent, 280 yds but at low water, about 400, as then the people pass round the Piont

in those beautiful smooth rocks. Walking thro' the point good only in
dry weather, the landing, from the stones, or fragments of Rocks that
lie in the water, & covered with a green, slimy moss, is very indifferent, particularly as the eddy is very strong & very irregular: sometimes
rising about 2 feet, & immediately again falling, just as much, below
the natural level of the water. People therefore must be very cautious,
otherwise they would fall & perhaps be carried with the Canoe into
this terrible Gulf. But I never heard of this having happened – it is only
miraculous. Lower landing good & safe. Then 2 Port[ages] are made to
avoid a terrible fall. The river is somewhat more than 100 yds broad,
& the water carries rushing down the whole breadth in some places, in
beautiful declivities & in others by cascades, & being broken in some
places by large blocks of Rock, precipitates over them & crossing (the
different streams, or columns of water) each other forms such dreadful
billows, & dashes at Certain intervals, the water so hi. as to astonish
even those much accustomed to such sights. It is almost impossible to
conceive any thing more grand & terrific. It has, above all the [world?]
been always a subject of amazement & Terror to me: there are many
of the falls higher, & have a much more grand & beautiful appearance, but this one, to me, has Grandeur /28/ Majesty & terror blended
together. I always considered it as one of the wonders of nature.

Thurs 22. Dec[harge] a Minette or Millette, about 50 yds, run it with
ease & safety at hi water, but not Low we carry all even to the Canoe,
the Portage is on a low rock in the mid. of the river. A man, by his
presumption being drowned, with several others, he considered it as
too insignificant & ordered his sweet-heart into the bow of the Canoe:
it took a sweep round, caught a whirlpool, & upend. We haul, or carry
up, accord as the water is hi, low.

2nd Des[charge] de l'islette, or Beau-Bien, 157 yds run full load at
low water; but at hi water only a few pieces & by another road. Name
from the Rock or island over which we carry. About the year '98 or '99
Monsr. Beaubien[42] from the easy apparent motion of the water insisted
& made his Guide run it absolutely against his will. The consequence
was as foreseen, & told him by the Guide that the crooked tops of the
swells would either fill their canoes or the eddy, which is very large &

---

42 One Beaubien was a partner with Gabriel Atina Laviolette in an opposition company
trading to the Northwest in the early 1790s, bought out by the NWC in 1796 (Lamb 1970,
458). He probably left the country after this, so Nelson's estimate of the date of this incident
is a few years too late.

violent, with the whirlpools in it, would upset, or engulf, i.e. <u>suck</u> them down, several people were drowned, & much property lost. Not half a mile below is another terrible fall, & if the most of them did not go in, it was owing to the eddy, that kept them turning round, 'till one Canoe, that had passed safe, gathered them up.

/29/ Augt Thurs 22

3d des Eaux qui Remuent, 240 yds, very fine, upper landing good & safe, lower very difficult, & somewhat dangerous from the smoothness & slippyness of the Rock & extraordinary motion of the water. It is well named L'eau qui remuent, for they do so with a vengeance; but the Canadians are made for this Country.

There remains now but one other small Impediment in this river, a Des[charge] which we always run full load, & track up.

From this last Portage to the Fort [Alexander], somewhat better than 6 miles, & about 3 more to the Lake Wenepeek, an ind[i]an Name (we née peig, or winepieg) signifying Dirty water, from an odd mishap that befell their God, Noah, or Adam, for it is difficult to say precisely which of the 3 it is they mean.

Sir Alexr M' Kinzie is certainly in a great error in his admeasurement of the distances between almost all the Portages of this River.[43]

I shall refer to the 16° sheets, inclosed with this, for a few other remarks & fill up the remainder of this sheet with something else.

D. or Des. signifies a descharge, or place where we take out part, more or less of the lading, according as the water is hi or low. This year, as the water was hi we ran down, or tracked up, full load, in several of them.

P. or Port: a Portage, sometimes of the whole, /30/ and at others, the Canoe is let down, &c.

The dates &c are those on which I passed at the different Portages, in the course of our route in from Ft. William.

When we had finished the Portage of Chute aux Esclaves, which this year was very long & bad walking thro' water, sometimes nearly to the middle, & a very strong current, MKay (the Guide) allowed the men about 2 hours rest, for tho' it was scarcely past noon, yet from the running & straining of the men, we had already come the actual distance

43 Mackenzie, 1801, xlviii–lxi, gave a detailed account of the canoe route from Grand Portage to Lake Winnipeg. The first part of Nelson's route was different, since he began at Fort William and used the new canoe route that had been introduced in 1803; but from Lac la Croix westwards the routes described are the same.

of a days Journey. Here we breakefasted about 3. In the afternoon two
Poor wretched Swiss came up. They came last autumn from Europe, by
the way of York Factory, & of course had not the least knowledge of
this Route. Yet they had suffered so much last winter in Red River that
they were determined upon the trail at least; & accordingly set out in a
small /31/ Canoe & some <u>dry fish</u>, a Soldiers musket & a little amunition. Their Guide, the information of others & a Pocket Compass!
A Priest, or Eaclesiastique, overtook them in Lac du Bonet, & done
all he could to send them back. But they had taken their measures, &
were determined to succeed or die. "Car si nous avons a mourire, il
vaut mieux mourire en nôtre enterprise, qu'a cette R. R. Car là, on est
assuré de y' mourrire, quand ça serai que pour l'extortion de ceux qui
ont un peu a vendre, la faim, le maltretment, & le desespoire. En notre
Route, peut etre rencontrerors nous quelque gens a qui notre situation
excitera la misericorde, et il nous pront charité. Dieu, asisse, ne nous
[word] sera, pas mourrire de mama! A L'egard du chemin, nous ne
pouvent pas beaucoup nous cloigner, car nous savons que la Route est
au Lac de l'Est; et si nous marchons trop long tems sans trouver de
ces nombreuse marques qu'il y à sur les Points Gallets (rocks) et isles,
nous reviverons, et reprendrons une autre cours. Peutetre aussi nous
trouverons des /32/ Sauvages, qui nous meneront un bout, ou nous
ferons une Carte."[44] It is wonderful how they got this far even, but
they were just upon entering the worst part of the route, full of deep
Bays, acute angles & very long rocks &c &c. We at last succeeded
with them, made them <u>throw away</u> (leave) their old rotten Canoe, &
gave them a passage to Bas de la Riviere, where I was happy to find
that Dr McLaughlin approved of our measures, & intended to solicit
their remaining 'till spring. They were both mechanics, Blacksmith &
Carpenter. The latter, blind in one Eye, Poor creature! fell in a fitt just
as we were going to run a strong rapid. It was perhaps owing to grief,

---

44 "For if we must die, better to die in our enterprise, than at that Red River. For there, one
is assured of dying, whether it shall be by the extortion of those who have a little to sell, or
hunger, maltreatment, or despair. In our route, we may meet some people in whom our situation will excite mercy, and give us charity. God ... [sentence garbled]. As for the route, we
cannot greatly mistake, for we know that the way is to the Lake of the East, and if we go too
long without finding those numerous marks that there are on the rocky points and islands, we
will recover, and start again on another course. Perhaps also we will find some Indians, who
will take us to our goal, or give us a map."

despondency, & indigestion; tho' indeed he had not eaten much, but his extenuated Stomach was but ill calculated to digest even that light food, Corn. They were extremely well pleased with our treatment of them & appeared very grateful; for they thanked us all very often: they were pity & misery itself. They had been infamously imposed upon, & in Red River had to pay £7-10s. for a shoulder, a thigh, or a rump, of Buffaloe!!!

Dec 14th
1822 S. [?] river G. Nelson.

✳

End of this journal.

Appendices

Glossary and Special Terms in Nelson's Lake Winnipeg Journals

Words that appear in this glossary are marked with an asterisk (*) in the text at their first appearance.

ACRE: Nelson used this old Canadian linear measure, stated to be equivalent to 208 feet, the length of one side of a square piece of land having the area of one English acre. It was very similar to the French measure, the *arpent*, said to be about 192 feet.

AGRÈS: The equipment with which a fur trade canoe was furnished, consisting of a cod line, oil cloth, sail and halyards, sponge, baling kettle, hatchet, canoe awl, tin pan, gum, birch bark and wattap (spruce roots, for sewing) (Duckworth 1990, 191 n 28). The last five items were used to repair damage to the canoe.

BATEAU: *See* boat.

BOAT: Although the NWC depended mostly on canoes, because of their speed and ease of portaging around the many falls and rapids on their transportation routes, boats were also used on parts of the network where little or no portaging was required. Both Nelson and Alexander Henry occasionally use the voyageur's word *bateau* for these boats, which would have been undecked and could be propelled by oars and a sail. In the Red River district, comprising the Red and Assiniboine Rivers, the NWC's most important product was pemmican, brought down in the spring and stored at the depot at the bottom of Winnipeg River (later called Fort Alexander), for the use of the canoe brigades. John Macdonell's Red River journal for 1793–95 shows that boats, as well as canoes, were in use on the route from Fort L'Esperance on Qu'Appelle River to the depot in his time. Alexander Henry, junior, was using boats as well as skin canoes during his nine seasons at or near Pembina on the Red River proper. The boats were probably built at the wintering posts, required caulking and repairs every spring, and were often replaced. Nelson mentions Red River boats being dried out and burnt at Fort Alexander, at the end of their journey, to recover the iron nails. The size of these boats increased over time. In spring 1795, the two boats from Fort L'Esperance were initially laden with 138 and 137 *taureaux* or bags of pemmican, of 90 pounds each, but this proved too much, and 100 taureaux had to be sent back to the fort (McGill, John Macdonell Journal, 1793–95, 28 April & 15 May 1795), for a final capacity of 88 and 87 *taureaux* per boat, or about 7,900 pounds each. In spring 1808, Alexander Henry had a "long boat" built at the Pembina post which he dispatched for Fort Alexander on 1 June, laden with 282 taureaux, besides 224 "pieces" (packs of fur); 42 kegs of grease; two pairs of cart-wheels; and other items. He also had a second boat, laden with 107 pieces, 5 kegs of grease, 1 pair of cart-wheels, and other items (Coues 1965, 441–2). If the taureaux, pieces, and kegs were all of the standard portaging weight, 90 pounds, the cargo of the "long boat" must have been well in excess of 49,000 pounds, and the smaller one more than 10,000 pounds. The larger boat, a veritable leviathan, would have been difficult to manage, and useful only on a downriver trip when the water was high, but Nelson confirms the safe arrival of the two boats, with the rest of Henry's brigade, at Fort Alexander on 13 June.

Boats, as opposed to canoes, were not in routine use on Lake Winnipeg during Nelson's first sojourn on the lake, from 1804 to 1813, but when he left Fort Alexander in September 1818, to re-establish the Tête-au-Brochet post, his entire party and their possessions (including dogs), twenty-nine persons in all, made the trip in one boat. This was probably about the dimensions of the famous York boats used by the HBC throughout its commercial empire, later in the century, that is, about 6,000 pounds capacity. Nelson and his men were able to lift and turn this boat in the spring, though with difficulty, before caulking it for the outward journey.

Besides the NWC boats, Nelson occasionally mentioned the boats used by the HBC's traders from Fort Albany to supply posts as far west as Brandon House on the mid-Assiniboine River. These vessels, usually regarded as the precursors of the York boats, could not be too large, as they had to be dragged on rollers around numerous falls and rapids along the route through the Canadian Shield. Nelson sometimes used the epithet "barge" for these boats, probably to express his contempt for a vessel that was so much slower than the NWC canoes.

BOURGEOIS: The voyageurs' expression for the head of a department, or (depending on context) a boss of any kind.

BROCHET: English, pike; *see* fish.

BRULÉ, or BOIS BRULÉ: A Métis, child of a white father and an Indigenous mother. Ojibwe equivalent *wissakodewinini*, literally "half-burnt-wood man" (Baraga 1966, 421). Another word, around the Great Lakes, was *chicot*, said to mean "half-burnt stump" (Peterson 1985, 64 & n 65] but this is not found in the Canadian Northwest.

BULL: *See* pemmican.

BUSTARD (French, *outarde*): *See* geese.

CARCAJOU: Wolverine.

CARP: *See* fish.

CARRIBOEUF, CARRIBOUX: The woodland caribou; Nelson sometimes uses reindeer* to mean this animal. As a trade animal it was useful for its skin, when tanned using traditional Indigenous methods.

CASED CATS: Generally believed to be bobcats, though raccoons (Canadian French *chat*) may be meant. Cased meant that the pelt had been turned inside out, so the fur was on the inside. The term open cats is also met with, presumably meaning that the fur was on the outside.

CATFISH: *See* fish.

COD LINE: Light rope on which hooks were fastened and baited to fish for pike. It could also be used to drag a canoe up a rapid from the shore, called "tracking" the canoe.

DÉCHARGE: A place where canoes were partly or completely unloaded, but the canoe itself, with any load remaining, could be pulled up a rapid using a line from the shore, with one or two men aboard it to steer.

DEGRADED (*dégradé*): Prevented from travelling by the wind or weather.

DEROUINE: The fur traders' practice of visiting their customers' camps to get the furs, rather than waiting for them to come to the post. The tactic was often used when traders from different companies were competing for the same furs. Indigenous people resented these visits, not just because they prevented them from bargaining for the best price, but because they were intrusions on their homes.

DOGS: Although dogs were an important part of the trading post community, they are mentioned very rarely in Nelson's journals. Each of the wintering voyageurs, and Nelson himself, had his own dogs. On winter trips, two dogs pulled each sleigh, sometimes more – Nelson's "cariole," which he built for himself in the early winter of 1809–10, was pulled by three dogs, and his fellow clerk John Crebassa was once pulled by four. When Nelson and his party of twenty-nine people, including five voyageurs, their families, and some Indigenous people, left Fort Alexander to re-establish the Tête-au-Brochet post in September 1818, they also had fifteen dogs with them, or between two and three dogs per working man. When the dogs were pulling sleighs, the loads were heavy: from Nelson's figures, a typical load of at least 250 pounds of whitefish per sleigh can be calculated. The dogs were not tied up when not working, for several times Nelson mentions that some had run off, sometimes to return on their own, sometimes to be sought for at the lodges of nearby Indigenous people. Evidently they were allowed to have their own lives, much as dogs in First Nations communities are treated today. This informality is to be contrasted with the treatment of dogs during the heyday of the HBC fur trade, two and three generations later, when dogs were worked mercilessly on the sleighs, tied up when idle, and kept starving. In Nelson's day, some dogs were highly valued, and probably not just for their working ability. On one occasion, Nelson tried to get an "Indian dog" from the freeman, Charles Racette, "which I would have taken had not Rassette been so pitiful a wretch, he had a quarrel with me for it" (*Journals*, 13 September 1808). And when Jean-Baptiste Welles thought he had made a deal with his fellow voyageur Durocher, to buy his wife (this later turned out to be a joke played on Welles), Durocher "reserved only his dog but gave all the rest of her things" (*Journals*, 10 January 1810). This curiously ambiguous remark may mean that some dogs were regarded as the women's property. When times were hard, the dogs would suffer first, and might become food for humans. Thus, in the early winter of 1810 Nelson heard that Ayagon and his band were starving, that only five of their thirty dogs were still alive, and that the surviving animals were so weak that they had to be carried up the riverbank (*Journals*, 22 November 1810).

DORÉ: *See* fish.

DRAG NET: *See* seine.

ENGAGÉ: NWC term for a man working on contract, usually a canoeman or voyageur. Interpreters and clerks were specified as such.

ÉCRIVAIN: Writer, a literate man assigned as assistant to the master of a post to keep records and accounts. Except at the busiest posts, the master was his own writer, unless he was illiterate, as was the case at Lac du Bonnet in 1805–06, when George Nelson was écrivain to the post master, Périgny.

EXPRESS: *See* winter express.

FAWN: A skin bag full of wild rice: *see* wild rice.

FISH: The most prominent fish in Nelson's journals are sturgeon and whitefish.

STURGEON: the Lake Sturgeon, *Acipenser fulvescens*. The traders caught sturgeon in Winnipeg River in the summer and fall using the seines (large-mesh nets), or traded them from the Indigenous people. The fish spawns in late spring, which is when a few sturgeon were caught at Nelson's Dauphin River post. Lake sturgeon were once common, and an important food fish for all, but the population was sadly depleted by commercial fishing in the late nineteenth and early twentieth centuries. They then suffered a further blow with the construction of dams on the main rivers, which prevented their access to their spawning grounds (Stewart and Watkinson 2004, 45–7).

WHITEFISH: the lake whitefish, *Coregonus clupeaformis*. At the Dauphin River post, Nelson's men speared them by the thousands at a spawning ground two miles upriver from the post, below a rapids, hung them up to freeze, then brought them to the post where they were the mainstay of the food supply for men and dogs all winter. Typical fish weighed 4 to 6 pounds; the largest taken weighed 11 pounds. Besides feeding his own people, Nelson sent sleighloads of frozen whitefish to the NWC post at Pigeon River. According to Stewart and Watkinson, "Among Aboriginals and European fur traders and settlers, whitefish was said to be a fish that could be eaten as a steady diet without growing tired of it" (2004, 163).

OTHER FISH: During the winter of 1808–09, Nelson's journal made unusually detailed records of the fish that were caught for the post. Using Stewart and Watkinson's (2004) excellent descriptions, these may be tentatively identified as follows:

CARP: probably the quillback (*Carpiodes cyprinus*); the common carp is an introduced species, not present in Manitoba in Nelson's time;

CATFISH: five species known in present-day Manitoba, family *Ictaluridae*;

DORE: doré jaune or walleye (*Sander vitreus*);

LACIECH: goldeye, or in French *laquaiche aux yeux d'or* (*Hiodon alosoides*);

LOCHE: burbot (*Lota lota*);

PERCH: yellow perch (*Perca flavescens*);

TULLIBIE: cisco (*Coregonus artedi*);

PIKE: (French: *brochet*) the northern pike (*Esox lucius*);

PICKEREL: presumably the same as doré (*Sander vitreus*); walleye is usually called pickerel in Manitoba and northwest Ontario, and is marketed under this name;

SUCKER: any of five species found in Manitoba; the commonest is the white sucker, *Catostamus commersonii*.

FOLLE AVOINE: *See* wild rice.

GEESE: Nelson's terminology for geese is not clear, and perhaps not consistent. Like some other fur traders, he sometimes used the word "bustard" for goose, or its French equivalent *outarde*. These terms actually refer to a European bird, but it is widely accepted that in a Canadian context *outarde* meant specifically a Canada Goose. In his journal entry for 14 October 1818, Nelson distinguishes between "Geese & outerdes," while at 21 October 1810 he talks of "four sorts of geese," one of which he calls "white." On 30 April 1819 he mentions "10 Geese & 2 oies." In present-day Manitoba, in spring, the Canada Goose and Snow Goose are abundant, the Cackling Goose is common, and the Greater White-fronted Goose is fairly common (*Checklist of the Birds of Manitoba*, PDF at www.naturemanitoba.ca, retrieved 24 September 2017). These may have been the "four sorts of geese" that Nelson mentioned.

HIGH WINES (Nelson usually writes HWines or HW): a distilled spirit (not actually wine), much used in the fur trade. *See also* rum.

LACIECH: *See* fish.

LEAGUE: Nelson's usual measure of distance. It was a voyageur's term, supposedly equal to three miles. By comparing Nelson's estimates of distance with the modern map, it appears that his league was indeed very close to three miles: see note to *Journal* entry of 26 November 1808.

LIGHT CANOE: A canoe that was well crewed but not loaded to capacity, usually because it was transporting a NWC partner who wanted to travel faster than the main brigades. Fast travel from inland posts to Fort William was essential so that the partners could attend the summer meetings.

LOCHE: *See* fish.

LUMBER: Nelson uses this word for baggage, personal possessions, and perhaps even families who had to be transported – anything not directly connected with trade.

MASHKIEGONS: Swampy Cree, or people of the muskeg, based in northeastern Manitoba and the Hudson Bay lowlands. One of the main bands trading with Nelson on Lake Winnipeg was Mashkiegon.

MIDEWIWIN: The Midewiwin ceremony, often a feature of the large spring gatherings of the Ojibwe. *See* Angel 2002. Nelson was invited to a Midewiwin initiation ceremony in late June 1819 at Tête-au-Brochet, but had to depart before it was finished, though he felt that he had now acquired enough knowledge of Indigenous religious practices to understand and appreciate what he saw (*Journals*, 7 June 1819). Angel 2002, 91, has a description of a Midewiwin lodge, and a photograph.

MILIEU: An engagé who paddled in the middle of the canoe, as opposed to the more skilled and better paid positions of devant (bowsman) and gouvernail (steersman).

MIXED RUM: *See* rum.

NET (*rets* in French). The conventional fishing nets were very long. Nelson, young Richard, and Racette made a net of 76 fathoms length in October 1807, and Nelson made another that was 50 fathoms long but 18 meshes broad in September 1808 (*Journals*, 23 October 1807, 30 September 1808). Nets were made in the fur country, using twine that was sent up for the purpose. Nelson was adept at the task. For fishing, the nets were set in place, and usually visited daily to remove the catch, before the fish spoiled. In winter, a special technique, involving drilling a series of holes in the ice and passing the net from one to the next with a long pole, was needed to set nets under the ice and retrieve them.

OATS: In Nelson's usage, wild rice; French, *folle avoine.*

OIE: Swan, in Nelson's journals probably the tundra swan, *Cygnus columbianus.*

OUTARDE: *See* geese.

PECCANT: Traders' French for the fisher, *Pekania pennanti,* a fur-bearing animal of the weasel family, highly valued in the fur trade. The French name is said to be taken from the Abenaki language.

PEMMICAN: The fuel on which the NWC fur brigades ran. It was the most important commodity produced in the Upper Red River department (centred around the forks of the Assiniboine and Qu'Appelle Rivers), where bison were plentiful. To make pemmican, bison meat was cut into thin strips and dried in the sun, then pounded to a powder, and packed into a bison skin bag. Bison fat was melted and poured into the bag until it was full. Sometimes berries were mixed in for flavour. The solidified mixture was a very concentrated food, rich in calories. Because there was almost no water in the mixture, it was slow to decay, and could be kept for long periods. A bag of pemmican was known as a *taureau,* or "bull," perhaps because it was fancied to represent an entire animal in processed form. The pemmican made in Upper Red River was brought down the Assiniboine and Red Rivers to the depot at Fort Alexander, and stored until issued to the long-distance canoe brigades travelling between Fort William and the fur countries of the far Northwest. A dependable supply of Red River pemmican was crucial for the NWC's operations, and in 1814 the attempt by Miles Macdonell, governor of Lord Selkirk's new colony at Red River, to forbid the export of all foodstuffs from the district precipitated the NWC's attempts to drive out the colony.

PERCH: *See* fish.

PICKEREL: *See* fish.

PIKE: French, *brochet; see* fish.

PLUS: The Canadian traders' term for the value of a traded skin or fur, in terms of beaver equivalents. Nelson usually called a *plus* a "skin"; the HBC used "Made

Beaver" for the same thing. The list giving the values of different furs, relative to a large beaver skin, was called the Standard of Trade, and occasionally it was modified from one season to the next, reflecting changed market conditions in London, where the furs were sold. For examples of Nelson's calculations of the values of different furs in *plus* or skins, using the NWC's standard of trade, see *Journals*, entries of 1 & 2 February 1819, and notes.

RAT: Muskrat, the cheapest pelt in the North American fur trade.

REINDEER: Nelson's usual word for woodland caribou; he also used *carriboeuf*.

RICE: *See* wild rice.

RUM: One of the staples of the fur trade, usually used as a gift rather than traded or sold. The rum was brought up in concentrated form, as it came from the distiller, in kegs of about 90 pounds weight, the usual weight for packages to be portaged. Small quantities could be doled out in glass bottles or phials (*fioles*), but it was usually diluted with water to about the concentration found in modern strong beer or wine; this was called "mixed rum."

SEINE (saine): Or drag net, a large-mesh net used to catch sturgeon by casting it and dragging it through the water, unlike the common net which was set in place and visited daily to recover what had been caught.

SAUTEAUX: Or *saulteurs*, people from the Sault Ste Marie area. A French term for Ojibwe, whose first contacts with the French were in that area in the 1600s.

STILYARDS: Steelyards, a weighing device, an unequal-arm balance. In his journal entry for 27 May 1809, Nelson remarked that the packs he was making up at Dauphin River were too light (80 rather than 90 pounds) because "my stilyards are too strong," that is, not properly calibrated.

STROUDS: The common woollen cloth used in the fur trade, *drap* in French. Though unglamourous and rarely mentioned in the journals, this item made up the largest part of a fur trader's outfit, and has been called "the major staple of the trade" (White 1987, 171; see also Willmott 2005).

STURGEON: *See* fish.

SUCKER: *See* fish.

SUCRERIE: Place for making maple sugar. The Mouffle d'Orignal/Ayagon band had their sucrerie on an island in Lake St Martin, and resorted there in the late spring, just before the ice became too soft and thin to travel on it. Once on the island, they would have to remain there until the ice had cleared, and then leave by canoe: see Nelson Journal, 29 April 1809. A family's maple-sugar-making place was not intruded upon by others, to the extent that the implements, such as bark dishes, could be left safely from one season to the next (Peter Fidler's Manitoba District Report, 1820: HBCA, B.51/e/1, fo. 17v).

TAUREAU: *See* pemmican.

TRAVERSE: A crossing over an unprotected stretch of open lake, either in summer or winter. If the wind was too strong, canoes, or winter travellers, would have to wait at the foot of the traverse.

TRIPE DE ROCHE: Various lichens of the genus *Umbilicaria*. When scraped from the rocks, *tripe de roche* was a last-ditch resort when real food was impossible to get. When boiled it yielded a glutinous material that was believed to give some nourishment. See Leighton 1985, 18–19.

TULLIBIE: *See* fish.

WHITEFISH: *See* fish.

WILD RICE: Voyageur's French *folle avoine* (literally, "foolish oats"); Nelson sometimes uses "oats" and occasionally "rice." An important cereal crop, which grows abundantly in shallow lakes, known as rice lakes, especially to the east of the south basin of Lake Winnipeg. The grain was harvested in the early fall, as it is still, by moving through the plants in a canoe, and beating the grains into the bottom of the canoe with sticks. The fur traders often purchased wild rice in small skin bags called *fawns*, either because they were actually made of fawn skins, or because of a fancied resemblance to the small body of a fawn.

WINDIGO: A cannibalistic monster or a human who has become a cannibal. For Ojibwe windigo stories, see, for instance, Berens & Hallowell 2009, and Brown 2018, chapters 10–12.

WINTER EXPRESS: The NWC had a regular winter express, by which reports from all the different fur trade districts were sent out to the depot on Lake Superior, in some cases even to Sault Ste Marie, to meet the company's Montreal agents on their way up for the partners' meeting. The first year of the arrangement may have been 1798–99, for which we have Alexander Mackenzie's detailed description of the operation of the winter express, with summaries of the news it brought (Lamb 1970, 474–81). A memorandum in the NWC Minute Book for 1806 shows a much tighter schedule (Wallace 1934, 218–19). Individual departments collected their own reports to join the main parcel, as Nelson shows in his journal entries of 3 and 8 January 1806.

Indigenous People Mentioned in Nelson's Lake Winnipeg Journals

Most of the names that Nelson records are nicknames, usually in French. A few of them are quite vulgar. Others are mentioned only as the son, brother, or son-in-law of someone else. Nelson does record a few individuals using what appear to be Ojibwe or Cree names; these seem to have been younger men, who perhaps were not yet familiar enough to the traders to have been given nicknames.

ALLARD'S BROTHER-IN-LAW: probably Ojibwe, from Rivière-des-Morts, mentioned 11 August 1808. Presumably brother-in-law of the Lake Winnipeg voyageur, Pierre Allard.

ANGCE: hunter, probably Ojibwe. One of the Indigenous hunters who traded with Nelson at Tête-au-Brochet, 1818–19. Nelson found him, his wife, and two young daughters at Dauphin River on 31 March, along with the Cancre.

L'ASSINIBOINE: hunter, probably Mashkiegon, in spite of his name. He is prominent in Nelson's 1818–19 journal, where he is called "the son-in-law of Old Lorrain's son-in-law," that is, son-in-law of Le Gendre.

AYAGON: also spelled Eyagon, Eagon, and Iägon. Ojibwe, a member of the Mouffle d'Orignal band; while not the eldest, he was probably the leader, and it was he who asked for a trading post to be established at Dauphin River in 1807. Nelson had a special regard for Ayagon, whom he once called "my father," though he also called him "Lord Ayagon," "My Lord," and the like. Ayagon had five wives, one the daughter of Tête-Grise, and another a daughter of Cul-Fessé. By 1810 he had a son-in-law (name unknown) who was old enough to hunt for himself. Though an able man, Ayagon was prone to drunkenness. In Nelson's

Reminiscences there is a long passage about Ayagon, printed in this volume (pages 244–8), which makes clear, much better than many incidental references, the respect that Nelson and the other Indigenous people had for Ayagon, and how much his friendship meant to Nelson. Ayagon continued to trade with Nelson after the post was moved from Dauphin River to Tête-au-Brochet in 1810, but neither he nor any of his band are mentioned in the journal for 1818–19. By then, they had moved farther west, and were trading on the eastern fringes of the Fort Dauphin department. Brown (1985a, 2) convincingly identifies Ayagon with Iahcoo, who is mentioned in the following passage from Peter Fidler's Manitoba District Report for 1820: "Iah coo generally Trades with the Nor West Company, and resides in general about the Partridge Crop and the vicinity he is a good fur hunter, quiet, but a confounded beggar – he is generally clothed every year ... by the NWCO, and has about six or eight followers" (HBCA, B.51/e/1, fo. 16r).

AYAGON'S BROTHER: Ojibwe. In the fall of 1809, Ayagon's brother eloped with the wife of La Bezette, another member of the same group. He was still with his "stolen woman" in the spring. Peace must have been made, as both Ayagon's brother and La Bezette were with a group that survived on whitefish that Nelson's men had hung up to freeze at Dauphin River in October 1810. Nelson's *Reminiscences* describe a war party, sent against the Sioux (apparently in the summer of 1811), which was led by "two noted chiefs – 'Grants brother in law' of the Crees' & 'The Black Robe' (Ayagon's brother) of the Sauteux's" (*Reminiscences*, pp. 287–8). The Black Robe, or La Robe Noir, also known as Mechkadewikonair, signed the Red River land use treaty with Lord Selkirk in 1817. Brown (1985a, 2) suggests that this man was also the same as Blue Coat, who, according to Peter Fidler's 1820 Manitoba District Report, was the brother of Iahcoo [Ayagon]. Blue Coat had been recognized as a chief by the Red River colony in 1817, and was living around the HBC's Big Point post near the southwest corner of Lake Manitoba. Fidler said that he was about 42 years of age in 1820, and in spite of his recognition by the Colony, was no more than a tolerable hunter, and "has little authority amongst his countrymen" (HBCA, B.51/3/1, fo. 16r).

AYAGON'S SON-IN-LAW: Ojibwe, hunting for himself in 1810. In May of that year he went to Portage la Prairie to join a war party.

BATEUSE, LE [*sic*]: (perhaps meaning the woman who was beaten). Probably Mashkiegon. Virgin daughter of Le Gendre's mother, whom her mother came to get at Tête-au-Brochet on 22 January 1811.

BEAULIEU, MADAME OR MOTHER: Apparently an Indigenous Elder. Together with Mme Roi and Bourassa's wife, she left Fort Alexander to visit Red River in July 1808, "but to be back as soon as possible." She accompanied Nelson's brigade to his winter post at Tête-au-Brochet in fall 1818, travelling in her own canoe with her daughter, and spent the winter near the post. She was presumably the wife or former wife of a clerk or voyageur named Beaulieu, who has not been identified. Voyageurs of this name have been found in Athabasca at this period.

BELLY, or LE VENTRE: Mashkiegon, one of the leaders of the band that began hunting around Nelson's Dauphin River post in 1809–10, having come from the east side of Lake Winnipeg. Le Gendre was his brother. Nelson had some kind of disagreement with The Belly in the summer of 1811, which led to Nelson "shaming" him, and The Belly spoke of taking revenge, but did not do so. He was part of the trading force at Tête-au-Brochet when Nelson returned there in 1818, though he seems to have lost his leading role to a new figure, the Red Breast.

BEZETTE, LA: (probably *La Besette*, "Penis": *see* Bergeron 1980); Ojibwe, son-in-law of Cul-Fessé. In October 1809 his youngest wife eloped with Ayagon's brother, putting La Bezette in fear of his life: *see* Ayagon's brother.

BEZON, LE: Mashkiegon, son of old Nez Corbin.

BIRD, THE: Ojibwe, son of Mouffle d'Orignal, trading at Dauphin River in 1809–10; Possibly the same as L'Oiseau, part of the Red Breast's band in 1818, but the latter band were Mashkiegons, not Ojibwe.

BLACK LEGS: Probably Ojibwe, trading at Broken River in 1809; Possibly the same as Jambes Noires.

BLACK MOOSE: *See* L'Orignal Noir.

BOITEU or Ca-wai-be-wee-tone: Trading at Fort Alexander in summer 1808; his brother was Gendre de l'oiseau rouge, i.e. Red Bird's son-in-law.

BOITINEAU'S DAUGHTER: Living with Le Gendre's band in 1818–19, when she was reported to have "nothing but a drest skin to cover herself with" (*Journals*, 20 January 1819); In her article on "Fur Trade Families in the Lake Superior-Rainy Lake Region," Jean Morrison described an application to the US Department of the Interior, for land and tribal entitlement, made in 1932 by

Laura Bottineau Gray of the Red Lake, Minnesota, Indian band. This document stated that her ancestor was a "full-blood Chippewa Indian" named Margarette Ahdik Songab, who was married three times: (1) to a "full-blooded Indian," Pewanakum; (2) to the NWC partner, Peter Grant; and (3) to Charles Bottineau, a voyageur (Morrison 2003, 97–8). Charles Bottineau was one of Alexander Henry's voyageurs in 1803, with a wife and "squalling infant" (Coues 1965, 226). Boitineau's daughter may have been a child of this voyageur.

BOSS-CASSÉ: Probably Ojibwe, arrived at Fort Alexander from La Grosse Isle, 21 September 1818.

BRAS COURT ("Short Arm"): Ojibwe. He was based at Lac la Pluie, but he and his family sometimes hunted much farther to the west. Thus, "Old Bras Court" traded at the NWC post of Alexandria, on the upper Assiniboine River, in March and April 1801, accompanied by two of his young sons, and also "the Young Premier" and "Mitchel's Step Son" (Gates 1965, 161–2, 173, 175–6). The "old Bras Court" arrived at the Lac la Pluie post on 7 October 1804 "with his Son and Michel Alarics wife," who may have been Bras Court's daughter. His son went to the XYC house, while Bras Court took some debt and departed (Gates 1965, 213). Michel Allarie had been a senior clerk in the Fort Dauphin department in 1799–1800 (Masson 1960, 1:62; Gates 1965, 157, 163–4). The sons of Bras Court were among Nelson's regular customers at Dauphin River in 1808–09, particularly the eldest, Cou-Fort. In May 1809, Nelson gave passage to Bras Court's youngest son in his canoe as far as Fort Alexander, whence the young man would continue on to Lac la Pluie "to see his father who is there." These references show that Bras Court's family ranged across three NWC departments, from Lac la Pluie on the east to Alexandria on the west.

BRAS COURT'S ELDEST SON: *See* Cou-Fort.

BROCHET ("Pike"): Mashkiegon, one of the hunting band, headed by The Belly and Le Gendre, which began trading at Dauphin River in the fall of 1809. The Young Brochet and the Brochets' stepson were also members of this band. Brochet's wife was the mother of Françoise, who was briefly married to Nelson's voyageur, Durocher.

CANA: Ojibwe, a companion of Cul-Fessé who appeared at Dauphin River, 2 May 1808.

CANCRE, LE ("The Crab"): Ojibwe, associated with the son of Tête Grisé and

Laseur en Rond. He was trading with Nelson at Tête-au-Brochet in 1818–19, but also with the HBC post at Lake St Martin (*Nelson Journals*).

CAPOT VERD ("Green Capot"): Ojibwe, one of Nelson's young customers in 1818–19, but also trading with the HBC at Lake St Martin (*Nelson Journals*).

CARRIBOEUF, LA FEMELLE DE: Presumably the wife of Baptiste Carribouef, one of Nelson's voyageurs in 1819. She and another woman, with their young sons, were apparently associated with the band of The Belly, the leading Mashkiegon. They spent the spring of 1819 in the lakes up behind Nelson's Tête-au-Brochet post, "& maintained themselves upon ducks & geese they killed with their arrows, being too short of amunition." La femelle de Carriboeuf and her companion, whose name seems to read "Unbanager," came to the post with dressed skins and two martens, 23 April 1819.

CAYEN LE NOIR: Part of the band, probably Ojibwe, that traded with Périgny and Nelson at Lac du Bonnet in 1805–06: see Grosse Tête. Cayen le Noir was brought in to the post on 25 September, very sick, and died soon after. His brother, L'Orignal Noir, buried him near the post. "Cayen" is often a corruption of "Cadien," i.e., Acadien, but why an Indigenous person would be called this is unknown.

CENDRE, LA ("The Cinder"): A Court-Oreille, trading near Bas de la Rivière in September 1805.

CHEMISE DE COTTON ("Cotton Shirt"): Probably Mashkiegon. Trading at Tête-au-Brochet in 1818–19.

CIE-SEC: *See* Oie-Sec.

COU-FORT ("Strong Neck"): Ojibwe, eldest son of Bras Court; in the fall of 1808, he and his younger brother came to the Dauphin River territory, where it was hoped that he would be a useful addition to the roster of hunters trading at that post. By the end of the season, it emerged that he had given most of his hunt to the Fort Dauphin outpost of Falle-au-Perdrix.

COURT OREILLES ("Short Ears"): A band of hunters of this tribe was hunting in Winnipeg River in the fall of 1805, when Nelson traded a sturgeon from them. One was called La Cendre. They were among the members of various Algonquian groups who had moved into the Lake Winnipeg basin during this transitional period; others were Ottawas and Nipissings.

CREBASSA'S STEP-SON: Probably Ojibwe, the son of John Crebassa's Indigenous wife. Nelson mentions him at Fort Alexander in the summer of 1807, and again on the east side of Lake Winnipeg in March 1819.

CUL-FESSÉ ("Spanked Ass"): Ojibwe, one of the principal hunters in the Ayagon/Mouffle d'Orignal band, trading with Nelson at Dauphin River, 1807–11; Nelson sometimes calls him "Old Cu-fesse," and once mentions "Old mother Cu-fessé," presumably his wife. La Bezette was his son-in-law.

CUL-LEVÉ ("Raised Ass"): Mashkiegon. A leading member of the Mashkiegon band that moved from the east side of Lake Winnipeg to Dauphin River in the fall of 1809, and became some of Nelson's most important hunters. Cul-Levé visited Dauphin River on 6 April 1808, probably to discuss the move. Cul-Levé was still one of the best hunters for Nelson at Tête-au-Brochet in 1818–19.

DÉFARTEUSE ("Stripper"): Ojibwe woman, also called "the slave," part of Mouffle d'Orignal's band; Nelson describes how she dealt with her husband's threats by stripping off her clothes, and on one occasion ran naked into the woods, where she stayed in the cold for two nights (*Journals*, 17 May 1808).

DÉPOUILLÉ: Mashkiegon. The name refers to the large fat deposits on the back of a bison. He visited Dauphin River with Cul-Levé and others of that band on 1 August 1809.

DRESSEUR, LE ("Trainer"): Probably Ojibwe. Arrived at Fort Alexander, 31 August 1809.

DUCK, THE: He and his brother were part of the band, probably Ojibwe, that traded with Périgny and Nelson at Lac du Bonnet in 1805–06: see Grosse Tête. At the beginning of the season, his little son died of burns suffered when he was playing with a powder horn in the fire. The Duck apparently wintered well to the east of Lac du Bonnet, as on a visit to Ducharme's post on Lake Winnipeg, on 8 March, Nelson found that Ducharme was getting meat from him. In August 1808, Nelson heard that The Duck was accompanying the HBC people to Red River. Nelson met Old Poivre and The Duck on Lake Winnipeg in September 1810; they had been harvesting wild rice. The Duck's two little boys arrived at Nelson's new Tête-au-Brochet post, with the Morpion's son, on 14 October, with news of the death of Old Nanjobe.

DUCK'S BROTHER: *See* The Duck.

EATCHO: Ojibwe or Mashkiegon. Trading on the east side of Lake Winnipeg in 1808 and 1809. He is the "Echo" who is mentioned in Alexander Macdonnell's undated letter to Duncan Cameron (Selkirk Papers, 9081–3; this letter must date from March 1809, as it describes Nelson's trip to take over the post at Little Grand Rapids from Alexander Campbell).

ENGLISHMAN, THE OLD: Part of the band, probably Ojibwe, that traded with Périgny and Nelson at Lac du Bonnet in 1805–06; *see* Grosse Tête. L'Orignal Noir, another member of the band, was camping with him during this season. The name is not explained, but he may have been called this because, like the famous English Chief at Athabasca, he was known to have traded with the HBC ("the English").

ESTOMAC ROUGE: *See* Red Breast. Estomac enuye, mentioned 27 September 1818, was probably the same man.

FLEURIE, MOTHER: Perhaps Mashkiegon, as she was travelling with The Belly, and had news of others of that band, on a visit to Nelson on 30 May 1819; Nelson met her on Lake Winnipeg in August 1808, when he called her Fleurie's wife, "formerly old Chastelin's," that is, once the wife of the former NWC clerk, Louis Chastelain. Her second husband was the Lake Winnipeg voyageur, Louis Fleurie, but the relationship may have ended by 1819, as she was living with some Indigenous people.

FRANÇOISE: Ojibwe or Mashkiegon woman, formerly the wife of Nelson's old voyageur, Joseph Durocher; "Old Desrocher & his Lady" were camped at the Dauphin River post from January to April 1809. She was the daughter of "Old Brochet," and was subject to fits, though Nelson suspected that these were often faked to manipulate her husband. In February 1811 Nelson, now calling her Durocher's former wife, notes a visit by her and Moose Eyes' daughter to the Dauphin River post. A few days later Durocher's "defunct" visited again along with Cul-Levé and his wife; as Cul-Levé was a Mashkiegon, she may have been as well.

FRISÉ, THE ("Curly"): Part of the band, probably Ojibwe, that traded with Périgny and Nelson at Lac du Bonnet in 1805–06; *see* Grosse Tête. He was wintering with Griffes d'Ours and Grosse Tête in the headwaters of Masqua River in December. On 11 September 1808, Nelson met The Frisé & Naganeck-iejick at Tête du Boeuf on Lake Winnipeg; they were en route to Fort Alexander. These references may be to a different man than The Frisé with whom Nelson traded at Tête-au-Brochet in 1818–19, as that man's hunting companions were Mashkiegons. In October 1818, Nelson reported that The Frisé was trying to convince his daughter to marry a young hunter, The Siffleur.

FRISÉ, THE YOUNG: Probably Ojibwe, perhaps the son of The Frisé with whom Périgny and Nelson traded at Lac du Bonnet in 1805–06; in 1818–19, he first hunted around Crebassa's post at Little Grand Rapids, in the hard East Winnipeg country, but "being disgusted with that part of the country & the Indians," he moved his hunt to Pigeon River, and traded with Nelson at Tête-au-Brochet. A man from Fort Alexander, Moniâ, came to Tête-au-Brochet on 19 April 1819 to visit "the young Frisé," the older Frisé's son, suggesting a continuing connection with the hunter of Winnipeg River.

GAGNIAN (OR GAIGNAN, GAGNON): Sometimes called Old Gagnian; apparently a member of The Premier's band, which included the Young Premier, Tête-Grise, Oiseau Rouge, Tête-du-Loup-Cervier, and "old Nanjope"; but Gagnian also camped with other hunters, including the Mashkiegons. He was at Fort Alexander in June 1808 and June 1809. He tried to trade with Nelson at Dauphin River in the season of 1809–10, but Nelson regarded him as a Fort Dauphin hunter, and refused; he also suspected him of taking debt at the Broken River post. In 1810–11, Nelson did equip the Old Gagnian at the new Tête-au-Brochet post. Gagnian was one of four hunters who went far north along the west shore of Lake Winnipeg, "far beyond the Grand Rapid," but found that any furs had been trapped out by HBC men who had wintered in that country two years before. Gagnian returned to the post, starving, in early January, but soon set off again in a different direction, and spent the rest of the winter with the Mashkiegons. In spring 1811 Nelson learned that Nanjobe's son was believed to be trying to kill Gagnian, which may explain why Gagnian had spent the winter so far east. The Old Gagnian, his son, and son-in-law traded again with Nelson at Tête-au-Brochet in 1818–19.

GENDRE, LE, or the Son-in-Law: Mashkiegon, brother to The Belly (Le Ventre). His name was used because he was the son-in-law of Joseph Lorrin, the Lake Winnipeg interpreter. These two family connections placed him at the centre of a kinship network that involved several of the most important Mashkiegon hunters on the lake, but also the NWC partner Duncan Cameron and the clerk Seraphin Lamarre, both of whom were married to Lorrin's other daughters. Le Gendre first appeared at Nelson's Dauphin River post on 28 July 1809, accompanied by two other leading Mashkiegons, The Belly (Le Ventre) and Nez Corbin's son Le Bezon.

Henceforth he and the rest of the band were regular customers, though they still spent some time on the east side of Lake Winnipeg, and once made an inconclusive attempt to trade at a temporary HBC post at Broken River. His wife is mentioned in the journals only once, in an episode when Le Gendre pretended to poison himself with poke root to impress or alarm "his angel" (*Journals*, 29 July 1809). Le Gendre was still in the district in 1818, and traded with Nelson at Tête-au-Brochet in 1818–19, although his prowess as a fur hunter had been eclipsed by new men, Red Breast and Nez d'Argent.

GENDRE'S MOTHER: Presumably the mother of Le Gendre. Accompanied by "la Miquene or Ladle," another old woman, she came to Nelson's post "for her 'virgin' Daughter La Bateuse," 22 January 1811.

GENDRE DE L'OISEAU ROUGE: *See* Red Bird's son-in-law.

GRAISSE D'OURS ("Bear Fat"): Apparently Ojibwe, sometimes called "Old Graisse d'Ours"; he made an appearance at Nelson's Dauphin River post in May 1810, along with Cul-Fessé, La Bezette, and some other Ojibwe, stayed at the post for a few days, then went off with Ayagon on a war expedition. He returned from Red River the following August. Nelson was cautious about trading with these visitors, as he knew that some of them "belonged" to the Fort Dauphin Department.

GRAND JEUNE HOMME ("Tall Young Man"): Mashkiegon, visited the Dauphin River post, 1 August 1809, along with Cul-Levé, Petite Couilles, and other Mashkiegons.

GRIFFES D'OURS ("Bear Claws"): Part of the band, probably Ojibwe, that traded with Périgny and Nelson at Lac du Bonnet in 1805–06; *see* Grosse Tête. He was wintering with The Frisé and Grosse Tête in the headwaters of Masqua River in December 1805.

GROSSE TÊTE ("Big Head"): Part of the band, probably Ojibwe, whose members were Périgny and Nelson's main trading customers at the Lac du Bonnet post in 1805–06; other members were Cayen le Noir (who died in September 1805) and his brother L'Orignal Noir; The Duck and his brother; the Frisé; Griffes d'Ours; the Old Englishman; and the Trout. This band harvested wild rice at the Pinawa in the fall, then wintered south of the post, up Little White River (now Whitemouth River).

GROUNDHOG: *See* Le Siffleur.

IÄGON: *See* Ayagon.

JAMBES NOIRES ("Black Legs"): Probably Mashkiegon, as he and his companions, Pahkon and La Chemise de Cotton, had been hunting with the Red Breast, the Mashkiegon leader, in November 1818, but were unsuccessful and came in to Nelson's post, starving; two of these three appeared again on 12 January 1819, having had more success. Perhaps the same as Black Legs, who traded at Broken River in 1809.

JOUR ROND, LE ("The Round Day," apparently): Mashkiegon, trading with Nelson at Tête-au-Brochet in 1818–19; in January, Nelson heard that he had stolen martins out of traps belonging to Le Gendre's band, and also meat from them and the Red Breast.

KIESHKIEMAN: Mashkiegon, a young man. Traded with Nelson in 1809–10 and 1810–11. Not mentioned in 1818–19, unless he was now going under a different name.

KIEWAYKOABOW: Mashkiegon, son of Nez Corbin, probably one of his twin sons.

LITTLE COUILLES: *See* Petites Couilles.

LOGE, LA: Probably Ojibwe, in the Fort Dauphin department. In March 1810, Nelson heard news from Swan River, that La Loge, an Indigenous man who had killed two of John McDonald's men the previous year, had now killed two Indigenous men, and vowed to kill many more. In his *Reminiscences*, Nelson has an extended account of The Lodge, who murdered two of the Fort Dauphin voyageurs when they were sent to his lodge *en derouine*. Cuthbert Cumming, one of the NWC clerks, managed to capture him, but other NWC men allowed him to escape because they were afraid of him. After further murders, The Lodge was finally shot dead by a NWC clerk (*Reminiscences*, pages 282–3).

LORRAIN'S SON-IN-LAW: *See* Le Gendre.

MANGEEKIEJICK: Probably an Ojibwe hunter associated with the Falle-au-Perdrix outpost of Fort Dauphin department; He visited Nelson at Dauphin River on 25 May 1810, along with La Bezette, Cou-Fort, and La Graisse d'Ours, but

Nelson regarded some of them as Fort Dauphin hunters, and was reluctant to trade with them.

MARTIN, THE: Ojibwe, son of Mouffle d'Orignal; Nelson's man Pierre Boulanger was hunting with him in October of 1809. The Martin trapped seven large beaver in the upper part of Fisher River, but he took them to Crebassa's post at Broken River. In February Nelson heard that he was now "upon the upper part of White River starving," that is, Winnipeg River.

MIQUENE, LA, or LADLE: Indigenous woman; she and Le Gendre's mother visited the Tête-au-Brochet post in January 1811.

MONIÂ: Probably Ojibwe; he arrived at Tête-au-Brochet on 19 April 1819, looking to visit the younger Frisé, and brought a letter to Nelson from Charles Hesse at Fort Alexander.

MOOSE EYES: Mashkiegon, also called Les Yeux Demales; he traded at Nelson's Dauphin River post in 1809–10 and 1810–11. Along with Le Gendre and The Belly, he made his spring hunt in Pigeon River in April 1810. In February 1811, Nelson heard that he was hunting in Monatagao River, well west of the Tête-au-Brochet post. His daughter was living with Françoise, the former wife of Joseph Durocher, not far from the post that winter.

MORPION ("Louse") also called Weaga: Mashkiegon; sometimes called "old Morpion"; he had two sons old enough to be hunting for themselves in 1809–10. In his undated letter to Duncan Cameron (about March 1809), Alexander Macdonell at Pigeon River reported that "Nie Corbin & Lous" were sending in for people to go for meat that they had killed. These two must be Nez Corbin and Morpion.

MOUFFLE D'ORIGNAL ("Moose Nose"): also called Old Muffle; Ojibwe, one of the older generation of the main band trading at Nelson's Dauphin River post. Two of his sons, The Martin and Le Sourd, were old enough to hunt on their own in the season of 1809–10, while a third, The Bird, was still living with his parents. In 1810–11, five sons all contributed to the family's hunt. A daughter of Mouffle d'Orignal was the wife of Nelson's voyageur Jean-Baptiste Larocque, and in the fall of 1809 Larocque and his wife camped with the family, which hunted as far north along the Lake Winnipeg shore as The Detour (Long Point), but returned to Nelson's post for lack of food. Mouffle d'Orignal and his family are not mentioned in Nelson's journal for 1818–19; he may have died, or, like

Ayagon, another member of his band, had moved farther west into Fort Dauphin territory.

NAGANECKIEJICK: Probably Ojibwe; a companion of The Frisé; Nelson met the two of them, going for Fort Alexander, on Lake Winnipeg, 11 September 1808.

NANJOBE OR NANJOPE: Probably Ojibwe; Old Nanjobe and his family were hunting around Fort Alexander in the summer of 1808. Nelson and Duncan Cameron met him at the Lake Winnipeg narrows in September 1810; he was "half dead," and was refused debt for the ensuing season. Four days later, Old Nanjobe was dead, reportedly of "a kind of dystentry & discharge of blood thro' the nose, ears, mouth & eyes," an illness that was widespread all over the country (*Journals*, 28 November 1810). The family's troubles continued, for next April one of Old Nanjobe's sons was killed by his own brother, stabbed in "a drunken frolick" at Broken River post; his brother-in-law attempted to shoot him in revenge, but the traders managed to prevent it.

NECOWATCH: Mashkiegon; mentioned in Nelson's *Journal*, 21 April 1811, returning to his father's lodge: from the context, probably one of Nez Corbin's twin sons, the other perhaps being Kiewaykoabow.

NEZ CORBIN ("Raven's Nose"): Mashkiegon, once called "old Nez Corbin"; he was one of Nelson's better hunters at Dauphin River in 1809–10. In the fall of 1810, Nez Corbin and his family tried hard to make contact with the HBC traders, first at Poplar River and then at Black River, and Nelson heard that "they are determined not to have any more dealings with our people." Nez Corbin, Le Gendre, and Brochet's stepson got little encouragement from Sutherland, the HBC trader at Black River, however, and they were soon back trading with Nelson at Tête-au-Brochet. Nez Corbin was still on the lake in 1819, but did not trade with Nelson, who came upon him near Pigeon River in March, "where he is with his wife, his youngest son and a HBC man." He had twin sons, whose names were apparently Kiewaykoabow and Necowatch; two other sons were Le Beson and Tabashish.

NEZ D'ARGENT ("Silver Nose"): Mashkiegon, one of the best fur hunters at Nelson's Tête-au-Brochet post in 1818–19; the name may mean that he had a silver nose ring, or even that his nose had been bitten off, and replaced by a silver one. He is not mentioned in the Journals for 1809–11, so, like Red Breast, he had become an important member of the group in the interim. He was hunting in Fisher River in 1818–19, and produced over 150 skins during the season.

NONO-CASSÉ (the second word appears to be French, "broken," but the meaning is obscure. The name appears once as Nanofassé): Probably Ojibwe, hunting around Fort Alexander in summer 1808. Nono-cassé's son visited Nelson at Tête-au-Brochet in May 1819, having left his father and others at Rivière-au-Gavion, on the east side of Lake Winnipeg. Nelson's *Reminiscences* tell a sad story about Na-no-cassé, an excellent hunter, whose canoe was trapped in ice in the fall of 1811. In trying to free themselves, his wife and children were all thrown under the ice, where they drowned. Na-no-cassé dived under the water, where he could see their bodies lying, and drowned beside them. His mother-in-law, and a young man who was courting his daughter, survived and told the story. This episode cannot be reconciled with the fact that Nelson had news of Nono-cassé in 1819, but Nelson says that the drowning occurred while Duncan Cameron was in charge of the Lake Winnipeg department (*Reminiscences*, 284).

OISEAU ("The Bird"): Mashkiegon, part of Red Breast's band; probably not the same as The Bird, son of Mouffle d'Orignal, as that man was an Ojibwe.

OISEAU ROUGE: *See* Red Bird.

ORIGNAL NOIR ("Black Moose"): Part of the band, probably Ojibwe, that traded with Périgny and Nelson at Lac du Bonnet in 1805–06; *see* Grosse Tête. His brother, who died in September 1805, was Cayen le Noir. Later in the season, L'Orignal Noir was camping with the Old Englishman, another member of the band. He did not stray far from the post, as he sold moose meat to the traders from time to time during the winter. On 20 January he was encamped at the foot of The Parches, on the Winnipeg River about six leagues from the post.

PAHKON or PASKHEW: Probably Mashkiegon, part of Red Breast's band, trading with Nelson in 1818–19; Nelson's orthography is uncertain enough that these two names are likely the same.

PETITES COUILLES ("Small Balls"): Mashkiegon, trading at Pigeon River in early 1809; in the summer of that year he shifted his hunt to Nelson's post at Dauphin River, along with the rest of the band led by The Belly. He is not mentioned in Nelson's journal for 1818–19.

PIN, OLD ("Pine"): Probably Ojibwe, at Fort Alexander in August 1808.

PREMIER, THE: Ojibwe, also known by the Ojibwe word Nitam, "First or the First" (Baraga 1966, 305); one of a series of four hereditary chiefs given this title, based at Rainy Lake (Waisberg and Holzkamm 2001, 5–6). The Premier and his sons are frequently mentioned in the fur trade literature, hunting at different times as far west as the Fort Dauphin department. The NWC regarded this family as important political agents in keeping peace with the Ojibwe through whose territory the fur brigades passed. Nelson's journal at Dauphin River tells us of a crisis in which The Premier played a central role. In June 1808, the NWC brigades had just made their usual pause at that post, when a rumour spread that some Indigenous men were planning to attack the canoe brigades on their way out to Fort William. The supposed conspiracy had been inspired by the anti-European teachings of the Shawnee Prophet. The NWC partners, highly alarmed, consulted The Premier, who denied knowledge of such a conspiracy, but agreed to send his eldest son with the brigades, to see them safely through the most exposed part of the route. The episode makes clear the important position that The Premier occupied in the fur traders' eyes, and the prestige that he enjoyed because of this. Nelson heard in January 1809 that "Old Premier … in appearance is drawing his last accounts," but he was apparently still alive in April 1810, when one of the voyageurs at Broken River had gone to Fort Alexander "with old Premier (& band's) hunt." It seems likely that the Old Premier did die soon after this, and that the leader called The Premier who signed the Selkirk Treaty in 1817 was his successor.

RED BIRD, or Oiseau Rouge: Probably Ojibwe; this man himself does not appear in Nelson's journals, but must have been well known, as another Indigenous man was known as Red Bird's Son-in-Law.

RED BIRD'S SON-IN-LAW, or Gendre du Oiseau Rouge: Probably Ojibwe; one of his brothers was Boiteu. He and his two brothers, who were trading with the opposition NWC, were very troublesome to the young Nelson, trading for the XYC, at his Rivière-aux-Morts post in 1804–05; and when Nelson returned to the post in 1806–07, now as a NWC clerk, he had more trouble with these men. The cause was apparently that in 1804 some of the children of the Red Bird's son-in-law had died, and the NWC, then opposed to Nelson, had convinced the father that the XYC people had caused the children's death by sorcery.

RED BREAST, or Estomac Rouge: Mashkiegon, traded with Nelson at Tête-au-Brochet in 1818–19; he is not mentioned in Nelson's Lake Winnipeg journals in 1811 or earlier, so he had risen to prominence in the interim. Nelson regarded him as one of the leaders of this band, perhaps more influential than The Belly and Le Gendre, although he was not one of the best hunters of furs.

RED STOMACH: Probably Ojibwe, traded with Périgny and Nelson at Lac du

Bonnet in 1805–06. Early in the season, his women offered the traders rotten meat, which was refused. Soon after, Red Stomach took pains "to vindicate the lost Character of his women," and took considerable debt, 86 skins' worth beyond an original amount, for the winter. Red Stomach spent the first part of the hunting season with the small Nipissing band, in the country southwest of Lac du Bonnet, but separated from them in December. Nelson visited him at his lodge twice during the winter. It is unlikely that he is the same as the Red Breast who traded with Nelson at Tête-au-Brochet in 1818–19.

ROI, MADAME: She accompanied Madame Beaulieu and Bourassa's wife on a visit to Red River in July 1808.

SIFFLEUR, LE ("Groundhog"): Probably Mashkiegon; one of Nelson's hunters at Tête-au-Brochet in 1818–19. His wife was a daughter of Le Frisé, but she wanted to leave Le Siffleur, and Le Frisé was trying to persuade her to stay.

SOURD LE ("The Deaf"): Ojibwe, second son of Mouffle d'Orignal; one of Nelson's hunters at Dauphin River, 1809–11.

ST GERMAIN: Apparently an Indigenous man, or perhaps a freeman, whom Nelson found with several others at Tête-au-Brochet in September 1810, awaiting the building of the new post. There were several St Germains in the fur trade, who might have been this man's father. Nelson did not give him any debt, so if he was an Indigenous man, he was probably regarded as belonging to the Fort Dauphin department. Apart from another reference to his band eating Nelson's potatoes, St Germain is not mentioned in the journals again. He must be the "Son German" or "Son Jerman," usually accompanied by sons or a son-in-law, who traded at the HBC post on Lake Manitoba in the season of 1815–16 (HBCA, B.122/a/1).

STAR, THE: Probably Ojibwe; at Fort Alexander in July 1808.

SWAN, THE: At Nelson's Tête-au-Brochet post, 1818–19; in February, he promised to organize a parley over the dispute arising when Charles Racette killed an Indigenous man who had eloped with his daughter. In May, The Swan told Nelson that L'Assiniboine had visited the post "to get at some of our women, & he is not always mistaken."

TABASHISH: Ojibwe, youngest son of Nez Corbin; One of Nelson's hunters at Dauphin River, 1809–11.

TÊTE DE LOUP CERVIER ("Lynx Head"): Probably Ojibwe, one of the hunters trading at Broken River, along with Tête Grise, 1808–09; Nelson tells an anecdote of "old Tête-de-loup-cervier," who raised a black bear cub with his family in the spring of 1810, but ceremoniously sent him away in the fall when they went to their hunting grounds. There was a joyful reunion with the bear the following spring, and he stayed with them for three years, swimming after the canoe, until one of the NWC men shot and ate him (*Reminiscences*, 283–4). His son-in-law appeared at Dauphin River in October 1809.

TÊTE GRISE ("Grey Head"): Probably Ojibwe, at Fort Alexander in June 1808, and at Broken River that fall; a daughter of his was one of Ayagon's wives. In October 1818 one of Red Breast's sons was going to marry a daughter of Tête Grise, presumably the same.

TÊTE GRISE'S ELDEST SON: Probably Ojibwe, one of Nelson's better hunters at Tête-au-Brochet, 1818–19. He and his brothers were closely associated with Red Breast.

TRIPES D'OURS ("Bear Guts"): He arrived at Fort Alexander "from above," i.e., up Winnipeg River, 21 July 1808.

TROUT, THE: Part of the band, probably Ojibwe, that traded with Périgny and Nelson at Lac du Bonnet in 1805–06; *see* Grosse Tête. In December he was wintering in Little White River. In August 1808, The Trout was accompanying the HBC brigade into Red River.

WEAGA: *See* Morpion.

WHITE PARTRIDGE: Probably Ojibwe; he and Boiteu arrived at Fort Alexander from Tête-ouverte with dried meat for rum, 20 July 1808.

YEUX DE MALES: *See* Moose Eyes.

Voyageurs Mentioned in
Nelson's Lake Winnipeg Journals

The following sources have been routinely used here:
Searchable database of voyageurs' contracts (in the notarial archives at Montreal), at the Centre du patrimoine website of the Société Historique de St Boniface, Manitoba: www.archivesshsb.mb.ca/en. Many of the contracts for the relevant period were calendared in the *Rapports des Archives nationales du Quebec* for 1942–43 and 1943–44, but the abstracts at the Centre du patrimoine are much fuller and more informative. Most contracts were with McTavish, Frobisher & Co., the Montreal agents of the NWC, or their successors, McTavish, McGillivrays & Co. Several others were with Alexander Mackenzie & Co., the Montreal agents of the XYC, and a few, dating from the 1790s, were with other minor companies. For several of the voyageurs whom Nelson mentions, no contract has been found. It may be assumed that all voyageurs had written contracts at this period, but most of those that survive are copies in the records of the notaries of Lower Canada. Contracts executed in the Upper Country rarely survive.

1805 list: List of NWC and XYC employees in most departments, including "Lake Ouinipique," following the coalition of 1804; MS 472, MASS 2357.31 (Masson Collection), McGill University Libraries, Rare Books and Special Collections Division; cited from the website http://digital.library.mcgill.ca/nwc/toolbar_ 1.htm. The XYC men are annotated "AMKC," for Alexander Mackenzie & Company, the Montreal agents for the XYC, who would be responsible for assuming those men's debts. The names on this list, but not the wages and debts, were printed in Masson 1960, 1:395–413; there are some misreadings, altered spellings, and rearrangements in his version. Wages are expressed in livres and sous (20 to the livre); the livre, though no longer represented by an actual coin, was the usual money of account in the Canadian fur trade. It was valued at one-twelfth of the pound Halifax that was used as current money in Canada (Duck-worth 1991, 178).

1811–21 Accounts: NWC Grand Ledger of Men's Accounts, 1811–1821; HBCA, F.4/32. Personal accounts for most of the men employed as winterers by the NWC during the ten seasons ending 1812 through 1821 (the Columbia Department is not included). Most of these were engagés, with contracts and regular wages, but some freemen are also listed, and also some Iroquois who had come to the Northwest as fur hunters, with payments for specific errands or for fur trade produce supplied. The accounts in F.4/32 are summary accounts transferred from other account books (now lost) kept in the departments. The titles of those books are given in abbreviated form, however, so there is usually some information about where a man was stationed. Thus, the "L.O. Book" or "L. Oui. Book" was that kept in the Post of Lac Ouinipique (Lake Winnipeg); the "F.D." Book was kept at Fort Dauphin; the "R.R. Book" at Red River; and so on. Partners, clerks, and interpreters might also have charges in the "Petty Ledger," probably a book kept for sales at Fort William, where goods were much cheaper than inland. Dates given in these accounts refer to the previous year, so, for instance, 1812 means wages or expenditures for the season or Outfit of 1811–12. For those men whose accounts begin in 1811, there is a balance (usually a debt owed to the NWC) which must have been transferred from the previous Grand Ledger, now lost.

ALLARD, PIERRE: Engagé, Lake Winnipeg department. *1805 list*: Pierre Allard, Lac Ouinipique, debt 219 livres, wages 350 livres; 1 yr left on contract. *1811–21 Accounts*: debt 777 livres 17 sous in 1811; charged for "sundries" at Lake Win-nipeg 1812–15, 1819–20, and at Red River, 1817–19; wages 350 livres 1812–16, 1818, 250 livres 1817, 300 livres 1819–21 (HBCA, F.4/32, 13). "Alard" was with John Crebassa at Broken River, 1808–09, 1809–10, and with Nel-son at Dauphin River, 1810–11. Although the NWC accounts book shows that he remained in Lake Winnipeg, his whereabouts are not always clear. Nelson's journal mentions that two of his Indigenous hunters had taken Allard's wife to Dauphin River in November 1818. Nelson also mentions Allard's brother-in-law, an Indigenous man from Rivière-aux-Morts, at 11 August 1808 (*Nelson Journals*). Pierre Allard & Louise Vivier, daughter Geneviève Allard was married at Pembina, North Dakota, 23 January 1849.

L'ALLEMAND: a nickname for Jean-Baptiste Welles.

AUGER, JEAN-BAPTISTE: Engagé, Lake Winnipeg department. Nelson often spells his name Ausgé or Ausger. Not found in *1805 list*. *1811–21 Accounts*:

Jean Bte Auger, debt 1,581 livres in 1811; charged for "sundries" at Lake Winnipeg, 1812; Michipicoten, 1813–14, and Lac la Pluie 1815–16, 1818–20; wages varied between 350 and 600 livres in different years, but employed in each year from 1811 to 1821 (HBCA, F.4/32, 12). With Nelson at Dauphin River, 1808–09, 1809–10. In March 1810 Duncan Cameron took Auger away to Fort Alexander because of trouble over women "among ourselves" – no details are given, but Auger had spent almost all the winter working around the post. Among his skills was canoe building (Nelson Journals). He built a house for Nelson at Tête-au-Brochet in 1811–12 (Journals, 7 October 1818). Nelson took Auger, "my man, a half breed," on his trip to Grand Rapids in March 1809 (Reminiscences, 211). There were several fur traders named Auger or Augé in the Michilimackinac trade in the 1760s. One Augé was an NWC clerk in Upper Red River in the 1790s. This man was probably a Métis son of one of these.

AURIELLE, JOSEPH: Engagé, Lake Winnipeg department. 1805 list: Jos Aurialle, Lac Ouinipique, debt 1,008 livres 14 sous, wages 500 livres, 1 yr on contract. Not found in 1811–21 Accounts. Aurielle or Rielle was one of Alexander Macdonell's men at Pigeon River, 1807–08 (Nelson Journals).

AUSGER, AUSGÉ: See Auger.

BARTRAND DIT DESROCHER: See Durocher.

BEAUCHAMPS, PIERRE: Engagé, Lake Winnipeg department. 1811–21 Accounts: Pierre Beauchamps, charged for "sundries" in Montreal Engagés' book, 1817, and at Lake Winnipeg 1818–20; wages 350 livres 1818, 450 livres 1819–20 (HBCA, F.4/32, 69). "Beaucampe" was one of Crebassa's men at Grand Rapids, 1818–19 (Nelson Journals).

BEAUDRIE, MICHEL: Engagé, Lake Winnipeg department. 1805 list: Michel Beaudrie, Lac Ouinipique, debt 342 livres 14 sous, wages 350 livres; 2 yrs left on contract. 1811–21 Accounts: Michel Beaudrie, debt 960 livres 8 sous in 1811; charged for "sundries" at Lac la Pluie, 1812–14; wages 400 livres, 1812–14 (HBCA, F.4/32, 101). Evidently he left the fur country at the end of the 1813–14 season. Baudrie was one of Campbell's men at Grand Rapids, 1808–09 [Nelson Journals].

BELANGER, PIERRE: See Boulanger.

BELOUIN. Engagé, Lake Winnipeg department. 1805 list: Nicolas Belloin, Lac

Ouinipique, debt 222 livres 10 sous, wages 450 livres; and Joseph Belloin, Lac Ouinipique, debt 365 livres, wages 450 livres; both with 3 yrs left on contracts; either of these could be the man mentioned by Nelson. No one of this surname in *1811–21 Accounts*. Belouin was one of Campbell's men at Kakinowachague, 1807–08 (*Nelson Journals*).

BERCIER, ALEXIS: Engagé, Lake Winnipeg department; according to Nelson's *Reminiscences* he was from the St Lawrence suburb of Montreal, so he is probably the Alexis Bercier, of Montreal, who contracted with McTavish, Frobisher & Co. on 18 January 1791 to go "où ils jugeront à propos" (ANQ *Rapport* 1942–43, 291). In 1805–06, he did some errands for the NWC on Winnipeg River. He was a summer man at Fort Alexander in 1808, and wintered with Seraphin Lamar at Rivière-aux-Morts in 1809–10 (*Nelson Journals*). In his *Reminiscences*, Nelson tells an anecdote about his involvement in helping to level the old graveyard at Bas de la Rivière in 1807, where William McKay had decided that the new fort should be built. *1805 list*: Alexis Bercier, Lac Ouinipique, debt 934 livres 10 sous; 2 yrs left on contract. *1811–21 Accounts*: Alexis Bercier, debt 471 livres 12 sous in 1811; charged for "sundries" at Lake Winnipeg, 1812–13; wages 300 livres, 1812–13. Apparently free after 1813, but in 1819 he was paid 500 livres for "the trip to York," and was charged for sundries at Fort William and Sault Ste. Marie (HBCA, F.4/32, 89). This trip was probably to give evidence against Lord Selkirk at York, Upper Canada. Alexis Bercier (died 1840) and his Saulteau [Ojibwe] wife Josephte (died 1853) had six children who appear in Métis genealogies.

BERGER, JOSEPH: Engagé, Lake Winnipeg department; Perhaps the Joseph Berger, of La Prairie, who contracted with McTavish, Frobisher & Co., 4 March 1793, for 3 years, to winter in the North, as a *milieu*,* wages 600 livres. *1805 list*: not found. *1811–21 Accounts*: Jos Berger, charged for "sundries" at Lake Winnipeg, 1812–15, 1818–19, and at Red River, 1815–18, 1820; wages 350 livres, 1812–16, 1818–21 (HBCA, F.4/32, 88). Bergé was at Fort Alexander, 1818–19 (*Nelson Journals*).

BÉTOURNEZ, PIERRE: Engagé, Lake Winnipeg department; Pierre Bétourné, son of Pierre Bétourné, inhabitant of St-Constant, and Marie Lanctot his wife, was born 21 September 1781, baptized the next day (Laprairie baptismal register). Pierre Baytourné, of La Prairie, contract with McTavish, Frobisher & Co., 26 November 1801, to go to Grand Portage as a *milieu*, wages 230 livres; and another contract 19 March 1802 (replacing the first), for 1 year, to winter in the North West as a *milieu*, wages 900 livres. *1805 list*: Pierre Bétournéz, Lac

Ouinipique, debt 1518 livres 15 sous, wages 600 livres; 2 yrs left on contract. *1811–21 Accounts*: Pierre Betourné, charged for sundries at Lake Winnipeg, 1812–14, at Red River, 1815, 1817–21, and at Fort Dauphin, 1816; wages 450 livres, 1812–14, 1816–21, and 500 livres in 1815 (HBCA, F.4/32, 92). Bétourné was one of Crebassa's men in 1810–11 (*Nelson Journals*).

BLONDIN, PIERRE: Guide of the Athabasca brigade; Nelson notes his arrival at Fort Alexander, 7 July 1808. On 4 July 1809, on Lake Winnipeg north of Tete-au-Brochet, Nelson met Simon Fraser's brigade of 30 canoes, "Blondin the Guide of them." Pierre Blondin is named as the guide on the bill of lading for an Athabasca canoe in 1806 (Winterburn 2003, 65), and Alexander Henry notes his arrival at Fort Alexander, with six canoes from Peace River (part of the Athabasca district), on 20 June 1806 (Coues 1965, 278). Pierre Blondin was one of the two guides assigned to Athabasca in 1806, the other being Pierre Delorme (Wallace 1934, 219). *1811–21 Accounts*: Pierre Blondin, credit balance of 823 livres 13 sous in 1811; wages 1,000 livres, 1812; charged for sundries per Petty Ledger, and for a payment of 450 livres cash paid to Claude Blondin (presumably a relative in Canada), both in 1812 (HBCA, F.4/32, 33). As his account ends with 1812, he presumably retired after that season.

BOISVERD, LOUIS: Engagé, Lake Winnipeg department; Louis Boisvert, of Mascouche, contract with McTavish, Frobisher & Col, 28 December 1792, to go "dans le Nord" (ANQ *Rapport* 1942–43, 315). *1805 list*: Louis Boisvert, Fort Dauphin, midman [*milieu du canot*] with 2 yrs to serve, debt 1,268 livres 10 sous; wages are not given for this department. *1811–21 Accounts*: Louis Boisverd, charged for sundries at Fort Dauphin, 1812–21; wages 350 livres 1812–21 (HBCA, F.4/32, 86). Boisverd was not a Lake Winnipeg engagé, but Nelson took "Boisverd's wife & 3 children" in his canoe from Fort Alexander to Tête-au-Brochet on 22 September 1818; she then set off for Fort Dauphin, presumably to join her husband (*Nelson Journals*).

BOUCHÉ LE VERD: Guide of four Athabasca canoes that arrived at Fort Alexander, 22 July 1808, after thirteen days on Lake Winnipeg, mainly windbound.

BOUCHE (another): Guide of eight Slave Lake canoes (Athabasca River department), accompanied by Mr J McGillivray, clerk; arrived at Fort Alexander 9 August 1808. Nelson adds the parenthesis (Woa can), identifying this man as Waccan, well known in the fur trade of north central British Columbia over many years. In May/August 1808, Jean-Baptiste Boucher, known as Waccan, was one of the nineteen voyageurs who accompanied Simon Fraser on the famous exploration that proved that the Fraser River was not the Columbia. The party returned to Fort George only on 8 August (Lamb 1960, 23, 128, 137, 153), so Waccan cannot have been guiding the Slave Lake canoes in that year.

BOULANGER, PIERRE: Engagé, Lake Winnipeg department; Pierre Boulanger, of Trois-Rivières, contract with McTavish, Frobisher & Co., 15 November 1802, to go as a *milieu* to Kamanistiguia "pour hyverner dans les Limites des Robeska" [Athabasca], wages 700 livres. *1805 list*: Pierre Boulanger, Lac Ouinipique, debt 666 livres 4 sous, wages 350 livres; 2 yrs left on contract. *1811–21 Accounts*: Pierre Boulanger, debt 790 livres 4 sous in 1811; charged for sundries at Nipigon, 1812; "deserted to HB" (HBCA, F.4/32, 104). Belangé or Boulanger was with Alexander Macdonell at Pigeon River, 1808–09, and with Nelson at Dauphin River, 1809–10. Boulanger and Welles fought twice in May 1810; Boulanger lost both times (*Nelson Journals*). This may be why he transferred to the Nipigon department in 1812, but soon left for the HBC.

BOURASSA, MICHEL: *1805 list*: Michel Bourassa, steersman and hunter, in Lower Red River department, 2 years of contract to serve, wages 500 livres, debt 1,577 livres 5 sous; *1811–21 Accounts*: Michel Bourassa, debt 1,119 livres 5 sous in 1811; charged for sundries at Fort des Prairies, 1811, 1814–15, 1817–20; wages 500 livres plus 337–10 "allowed for hunting," 1812; 500 plus 207 "by animals killed during the winter," 1813; 450 livres, 1814; 550 livres, 1815–17; 700 livres, 1818–19; 800 livres, 1820–21 (HBCA, F.4/32, 63). Bourassa's wife, along with "Mesdammes Roi & Beaulieu," left Fort Alexander 5 July 1808 on a visit to Red River, "but to be back the soon as possible" (*Nelson Journals*).

BOUSQUET, CHARLES: Engagé, Lake Winnipeg department; Charles Bousquier, of L'Assomption, contract with McTavish, Fraser & Co., 10 February 1797, for 3 years, to go to Nipigon or Lake Superior, wages 500 livres. *1805 list*: Charles Bousquet, Lac Ouinipique, debt 275 livres, wages 450 livres; 1 yr left on contract. In the *1811–21 Accounts*, Charles Bousquet was shown with a debt of 332 livres in 1811, considered a doubtful debt; he was charged for "sundries" in the Lake Winnipeg book in 1813 (HBCA, F.4/32, 783, 1058). In June 1808, Bousquet went hunting from Fort Alexander, promising "to be back in a few days to set off with the whole Brigade," but did not return, and Nelson concluded that he had deserted. Perhaps the same Bousquet who was with Mr Dougald Cameron on his Christmas visit to Fort Alexander in December 1810 (*Nelson Journals*). There was a Charles Bousquet, a clerk at Fond du Lac in 1799, wages 900 livres, but this was probably a different man.

BRANCONIER, JEAN-BAPTISTE: Engagé, Lake Winnipeg department; Jean-Baptiste Branconier, son of Baptiste Branconier & Josse Bevois, born/bap 16 December 1780, Notre-Dame-de-Montréal. Baptiste Branconier, of the Montreal St Laurent suburb, contract with McTavish, Frobisher & Co., 22 December 1802 for two years, to go to Grand Portage ad "Dependances du Nord." *1805 list*: J-B Branconier, Lac Ouinipique, debt 892 livres 15 sous, wages 400 livres; 2 yrs left on contract. *1811–21 Accounts*: Jean Bte Branconnier, debt 610 livres 12 sous in 1811; charged for sundries at Lake Winnipeg 1811–15, in Montreal engagés' book, 1819, and at English River in 1820; wages 350 *livres*, 1812–19, 400 livres 1820–21; credited 225 livres for animals (that is, as a hunter), in 1816 (HBCA, F.4/32, 91). Braconier [*sic*] was one of Campbell's men in 1807–08, and was with Crebassa at Broken River, 1808–09 and 1809–10 (*Nelson Journals*). Jean-Baptiste Branconnier was at Fort Gibraltar in April 1816, when Colin Robertson captured it for the HBC; was sent to Hudson's Bay and then to England; and appeared as a witness in the Semple case at York, Upper Canada, in October 1818 (Amos 1820, 142–3). There was another Jean-Baptiste Branconier in Nipigon department 1813–17, then at Red River in 1818–21 (HBCA, F.4/32, 129).

BRILLIÉRE [*sic*]: Engagé, Lake Winnipeg department; one of Campbell's men at Grand Rapid, 1808–09 (*Nelson Journals*). Not found in *1805 list* or *1811–21 Accounts*.

CARRIBOUEF, BAPTISTE: Engagé at Fort Alexander, February 1819, whom Nelson exchanged for Paradix, whom he was afraid the Indigenous men would kill; he spent the rest of the season with Nelson. He was subject to seizures that Nelson attempted to treat [*Nelson Journals*]. Not found in *1811–21 Accounts* under this name, but the surname looks like a nickname. His wife was perhaps La femalle de Carriboeuf, an Indigenous woman associated with the band of Red Breast, a leading Mashkiegon.

CARTIER, JOSEPH: Guide for the NWC's English River brigade; he had one of the longest fur trade careers on record. Nelson notes his arrival at Fort Alexander with six canoes, 20 June 1807. For a biography, see Duckworth 1990, 141–3.

CHARBONNEAU, ETIENNE: Engagé, Lake Winnipeg department; Étienne Charbonneau, of Boucherville, contract with David & Peter Grant, 12 December 1794, for 2 years, to go as a *milieu* "dans le Nord (à la Rivière Rouge)." The Grants were a rival company of Northwest traders who were partially absorbed by the NWC in 1796, and Charbonneau was probably kept on after that. He was a *gouvernail* or steersman for Alexander Henry in Lower Red River in 1800–01 (Coues 1965, 49–50). *1805 list*: Etienne Charbonneau, Lac Ouinipique, debt 1,748 livres, wages 400 livres; two yrs left on contract. *1811–21 Accounts*: Étienne Charbonneau, debt 1,265 livres 10 sous, 1811; charged for sundries at Fort des Prairies, 1812; wages 350 livres 1812, 400 livres in 1820. During this last season, part of his wage was paid directly to his wife (HBCA, F.4/32, 191). Charbonneau was with Alexander Macdonell at Pigeon River, 1807–08, 1808–09. His wife was with him in the latter season, and she accompanied him on a winter trip to Dauphin River to fetch fish in January 1809, but Nelson did not send him back because he was "too old to perform this trip as soon [quickly] as they would wish." A child of theirs died at Fort Alexander, aged about three months, in September 1809 (*Nelson Journals*). The *1811–21 Accounts* suggest that Charbonneau retired from the fur trade in 1812, but returned for one more season, 1819–20. On 19 October 1812, Étienne Charbonneau married Marie Louise, aged 18 yrs, "metise des pays hauts," at Boucherville, Lower Canada, she having been baptized the same day; by this marriage they legitimized a boy aged 15 months, who had been baptized three weeks earlier (Boucherville church register). Marie Louise must have died within a few years, as Étienne Charbonneau, "veuf de Marie Alex de cette paroisse," married again in 1822, at St-Constant (St-Constant church register).

COURNOYER, JEAN-BAPTISTE: Engagé, Lake Winnipeg department; Jean-Baptiste Cournoyer, of Sorel, contract with Alexr MacKenzie et Compagnie (then acting for the XYC), 20 & 26 November 1802 [two contracts], as *gouvernail*, wages 800 livres, to make a round voyage between Montreal and Lac la Pluie. *1805 list*: J.B. Cournoyer, Lac Ouinipique, debt 962 livres 15 sous, 500 wages; 1 yr left on contract. Cournoyer was with Ducharme on the upper part of Winnipeg River in 1805–06. During the winter an Indigenous man carried off his wife, but he and a companion pursued the couple and brought her back (*Nelson Journals*; and *Sorel Journal*, 72). Not in *1811–21 Accounts*.

DALCOUR, JOSEPH: Engagé, Lake Winnipeg department; Joseph Dalcour, of Terrebonne, contract with William Grant (one of the most important fur trade suppliers), 2 February 1787, to make a round voyage between Montreal and Michilimackinac as a *devant*, wages 280 livres. Joseph Dalcour, of La Mascouche, contract 5 January 1796 with Alexander & James Robertson, the Montreal suppliers of David & Peter Grant, to go to the North as a *milieu*, wages 1,000 livres; and again 19 January 1796, with McTavish, Frobisher & Co., for the same duties. The replacement contract probably represents the takeover of the Grants' rival enterprise by the NWC, which took place early in 1796. Joseph

Dalcour, of Terrebonne, contract with A. McKenzie & Co. 21 December 1802, to go to Grand Portage and the North as a *milieu* or *devant*, wages 1,400 livres. The large annual wages paid to this man are remarkable. *1805 list*: Jos. Dalcour, Lac Ouinipique, "AMKC" [Alexander Mackenzie & Co., i.e. XYC], debt 928 livres 5 sous, wages 500 livres; 1 yr left on contract. Not found in *1811–21 Accounts*. Nelson states that Dalcour was from L'Assomption, Lower Canada, and that he had a wife by 1807, but no children (*Nelson Reminiscences*, 198). One of Nelson's voyageurs at Dauphin River, 1807–08. Perhaps the same as Joseph Delcour, *devant*, who with his son Jean-Baptiste, a *milieu*, wintered with David Thompson in the Rocky Mountains in 1809–10; was leaving Fort des Prairies for the Columbia on 8 July 1810, and was with Thompson again on the Columbia in September 1811 (Coues 1965, 610).

DELORME, PIERRE: Guide of the Athabasca brigade; Nelson notes his arrival at Fort Alexander with a brigade of fifteen canoes, 12 July 1808, accompanied by Mr R. McLeod, then a young clerk assigned to the Athabasca department. They proceeded onwards towards Lac la Pluie, the depot for the Athabasca brigade, where they would have delivered their furs and taken on new goods. On 8 August, Delorme was back at Fort Alexander with five canoes, along with J. McTavish and "young Mr McGil," probably Simon McGillivray, one of William's twin sons. Pierre Delorme, of Beauharnois, contract 8 May 1784 with John Gregory, as a *milieu*, wages 500 livres, to winter "au Poste de Michilimakinac et Limites." Gregory was a partner in the firm of Gregory & McLeod, a rival company to the NWC, in which the famous explorer Alexander Mackenzie was a partner. The two companies merged in 1787, and Pierre Delorme was one of Mackenzie's voyageurs on his famous trip to the Arctic Ocean in 1789. Perhaps this experience established a personal loyalty to Mackenzie, as on the post-1804 list he is found on the list for Athabasca River as "Pierre Lemay Dit De Lorme AMKC," wages 750, debt 1526 livres, one year to serve on his current contract. Delorme and Pierre Blondin were the two guides for Athabasca in the arrangements for 1806 (Wallace 1934, 219). *1811–21 Accounts*: debit balance, 1,426–10 in 1811; charged for sundries in ARiv book, 1812–19, and in LLP book, 1820–21: wages 800 livres, 1812–21 (HBCA, F.4/32, 265). There was another Pierre Delorme in Fort des Prairies 1812–20 (F.4/32, 291).

DEROUIN: Interpreter at Cumberland House, 1819; not found in the *1811–21 Accounts* under this name.

DESROCHER: *See* Durocher.

DUBOIS: Apparently a Canadian freeman; Nelson met "that Poor miserable & pitiful wretch Dubois" on Lake Winnipeg in June 1809, gave him some rice, and left him at Mauricette's River.

DUNORD, FRANÇOIS: Engagé, Lake Winnipeg department; *1805* list: François Dunord, Lac Ouinipique, "AMKC," debt 515 livres 9 sous, wages 450 livres; 1 year left on contract. "Little Frans Dunord" was one of three voyageurs drowned in Rivière Blanche section of Winnipeg River, with William McKay's brigade on the way inwards from Lake Superior, in August 1805 (*Nelson Journals*).

DUPUIS, FRANÇOIS: Engagé, Lake Winnipeg department; François Dupuis, of Maskinongé or Berthier, contract with A. McKenzie & Co., 20 December 1802 (an earlier contract of 7 November was cancelled) to go to the Northwest, for 4 years, wages 1,000 livres. *1805* list: François Dupuis, Lac Ouinipique, debt 720 livres 15 sous, wages 500 livres; 1 yr left on contract. "Dupuis" was with Crebassa at Broken River, 1809–10, but probably left the service soon after, as he is not in the *1811–21 Accounts*.

DUROCHER, JOSEPH: Engagé, Lake Winnipeg department, also known as Bertrand *dit* Durocher. As a young man, Durocher had wintered with Indigenous people at Fort des Prairies in the year of the smallpox epidemic, 1781–82; he saw a man kill his wife in despair, then stab himself to death (*Sorel Journal*, 61). On 29 July 1799, writing to William McKay from Grand Portage with instructions for the conduct of the Lake Winnipeg department, William McGillivray stated that he was sending Durocher to show McKay the road to Lac Rouge, where McKay was to establish a post. McGillivray further says "Durocher is only hired for this year – you know he is a Slipping Chap – he might give some trouble here next year – as he knows the road to the English River I have no doubt but they'd made a Guide of him – he is also a piece of Trader – to Avoid this you must fall on some means to keep him late in the Country or to pass the Summer altogether. His Engagem^t is for Nipigon but he could not bear the idea of going there & is very happy at going in this way – I tell him you will send him to Winter Where you please" (NWC Letterbook, LAC, MG 19 B1 vol. 1, 86).

At this time the NWC was trying hard to prevent the XYC from hiring any men who could guide their canoes into English River, and thence to Athabasca. In Nelson's time, Durocher was the guide for the Lake Winnipeg canoes, making the trip out to Fort William and back each summer. He wintered with Alexander McDonnell at Pigeon River in 1807–08 and 1808–09, but was transferred to Dauphin River in January 1809, with his woman or wife, as the supply of provisions was better there. He was with Nelson in 1809–10 and 1810–11. His wife, known as Françoise, was from among the Mashkiegons, the daughter of Old Brochet's wife, and much younger than her husband. Nelson referred to her as a "blue beef," apparently a vulgar term for a newly eligible woman. The relationship was not happy. She was subject to convulsive attacks, but Nelson suspected that some of these were faked as a way of dealing with her husband, who constantly complained about how she took care of his things. Durocher sent her back to her mother at the end of May 1810, after which she occasionally reappeared at Nelson's Tête-au-Brochet post, along with other Mashkiegon women. *1805 list*: Jos^h Durocher, Lac Ouinipique, debt 817 livres 10 sous, wages 600 livres, 1 yr left on contract. Jos. Durocher, guide, Lac Ouinipique, is in the NWC arrangements for 1806 (Wallace 1934, 220). *1811–12 accounts*: Jos. Durocher, credit balance of 150 livres in 1811; charged for sundries in Lake Winnipeg Book, 1812–14; wages 600 livres, 1812–14; retired in 1814 with a credit balance of 1,500 livres 15 sous (HBCA, F.4/32, 307).

DUTCHMAN: A nickname for Jean-Baptiste Welles.

FLEURY, LOUIS: Engagé, Lake Winnipeg department; Louis Fleury, of Maskinongé, contract with McTavish, Frobisher & Co., 27 February 1797, to go "dans le Nord-ouest" (ANQ *Rapport* 1942–43, 381). *1805 list*: Louis Fleurie, Lac Ouinipique, debt 250 livres, wages 350 livres; 1 yr left on contract. *1811–21 Accounts*: Louis Fleurie, charged for sundries at Lake Winnipeg, 1812–15, 1818–21; at Lac La Pluie, 1816; and at Red River, 1818. Wages 450 livres, 1812–16, 1819; 112 livres 10 sous 1818 ["By Wages from Rd R ... deserted to HBC"]; 350 livres, 1820; 300 livres, 1821 (HBCA, F.4/32, 370, 356). Nelson met Fleurie's wife, "formerly old Chastelin's," coming from Broken River to Fort Alexander, August 1808. Perhaps the same as "Fleuri Ronds," an engagé who accompanied Duncan Cameron on a visit to Tête-au-Brochet in December 1810 (*Nelson Journals*).

FORTIER, PIERRE: Engagé, Lake Winnipeg department. *1805 list*: Pierre Forcier [*sic*], Fort Dauphin, midman [*milieu de canot*], credit balance of 24 livres, no wages given. Not found in *1805 list*, or *1811–21 Accounts*. One Fortier was with Ferguson at Tête-au-Brochet in 1805–06, and with Nelson at Dauphin River in 1807–8. With Nelson also in 1807–08 was a "younger Fortier" whom he sent in February to spend the rest of the winter with Alexander Campbell at Kakinowachague (*Nelson Journals*).

FORTIN, PIERRE: Engagé, Lake Winnipeg department. *1805 list*: Pierre Fortin,

Lac Ouinipique, debt 222 livres 10 sous; no wages given; 1 yr left on contract. He was with Nelson and Perigny at the Lac du Bonnet post in 1805–06; Nelson calls him Fertin or Firtin (*Nelson Journals*). Not in *1811–21 accounts*, so had probably left the service.

GENDRON, LOUIS: Engagé, Lake Winnipeg department; Louis Gendron, of Châteauguay, contract with Alexander Mackenzie & Co., 1 March 1803, for 3 years, to winter in the North, wages 800 livres. *1805 list*: Louis Jeandron, Lac Ouinipique, "AMKC," debt 2,731 livres 10 sous, wages 400 livres; 1 yr left on contract. He was with Campbell at Kakinowachague in 1807–08 (*Nelson Journals*). Not in *1811–21 Accounts*.

INKSTER, JOHN (JACK): Engagé and interpreter at Lake Winnipeg department. *1811–21 Accounts*: John Inkster, debt 116 livres 8 sous in 1811; charged for sundries in Petty Ledger 1811–12, and at Lake Winnipeg, 1812; wages 450 livres, 1812; notation "drown'd in August 1812" (HBCA, F.4/32, 478). Inkster, whom Nelson sometimes called "Jack," was Alexander Macdonell's interpreter at Pigeon River, 1808–09, when he had a wife and a child; and he was Nelson's interpreter at Dauphin River, 1809–10. He is not mentioned in Nelson's journal for 1810–11. His Orkney name and his qualification as an interpreter suggest that he was born in Rupert's Land of an Indigenous mother (few Orkneymen ever mastered Indigenous languages), so his father was probably an HBC servant. I have not been able to identify him in HBC records, unless he is the John Inkster who was with the HBC's John Mackay at Brandon House in 1805–06, and was sent further up the Assiniboine to establish a branch post (HBCA, B.22/a/13, entries of 2 & 7 October 1805, 5 May 1806).

LACOURSE, CLAUDE: Engagé, Lake Winnipeg department. *1811–21 Accounts*: charged for "sundries" at Lake Winnipeg, 1818–20; wages 350 livres, 1818; 450 livres, 1819–20; 700 livres, 1821. Apparently stationed at Fort Alexander in 1818–19, but made winter journeys to Nelson's post at Tête-au-Brochet and to Crebassa's at Grand Rapids [*Nelson Journals*].

LAMBERT, ANTOINE: Engagé, Lake Winnipeg department; Antoine Lambert, of Yamaska, contract with McTavish, Frobisher & Co., 7 January 1803, for 3 years, to winter in the Northwest, wages 750 livres (ANQ *Rapport* 1944–45, 344). *1805 list*: Ant. Lembert, Lac Ouinipique, debt 2,040 livres 3 sous, wages 500 livres, 1 yr left on contract, "AMKC." *1811–21 Accounts*: Antoine Lambert, debt 1,479 livres 7 sous, 1811; charged for sundries at Lake Winnipeg, 1812–15, 1818–21; at Red River 1816–17; wages 450 livres 1812–16, 400 livres 1817,

450 livres 1818–21 (HBCA, F.4/32, 585). Lambert accompanied Paul La Croix on a visit to Ducharme's post, March 1806 (*Nelson Journals*).

LAROCQUE, JEAN-BAPTISTE: Engagé, Lake Winnipeg department; not in *1805 list*. *1811–12 accounts*: debt 1,357 livres 11 sous in 1811; charged for sundries at Lake Winnipeg 1812–16, 1818–19; Montreal *engagés'* Book, 1817; Red River Book 1818, 1820; wages 450 livres, 1812; 500 livres, 1813; 450 livres, 1814; 500 livres, 1815; 300 livres, 1816; 400 livres, 1818; 550 livres, 1819; 400 livres, 1820–21; he was also paid for sundries (433 livres 10 sous plus 290 lives 3 sous) in 1816, and 52 livres 10 sous in 1821 (HBCA, F.4/32, 582). The reference to the Montreal Engagés' Book must mean that he was in Canada in 1816–17. This man was either the Larocque who was with Campbell at Grand Rapid, 1808–09, or the one who was with Alexander Macdonell at Pigeon River in that season (their first names are not given). Baptiste Larocque was with Nelson at Dauphin River, 1809–10, and at Tête-au-Brochet in 1810–11, and again in 1818–19. He is one of the principal characters among Nelson's engagés, useful at many tasks. By the fall of 1818 he and his wife had six children. Towards the end of the season of 1818–19, Larocque became concerned about whether his wife was faithful. In passing, Nelson notes that she was very handsome, and one-quarter of "native blood" (*Nelson Journals*).

LAROCQUE, —: Engagé in Lake Winnipeg department; Nelson mentions two engagés of this name in the department in 1808–09, one with Campbell and the other with Alexander Macdonell. One must have been Jean-Baptiste Larocque (see previous entry), and this is the other. Perhaps the Pierre Larocque of the *1805 list*, Lac Ouinipique, debt 736 livres 15 sous, wages 400 livres, 2 yrs left in contract; or the Charles Larocque of the *1811–21 Accounts*: debt balance of 2150 livres 10 sous in 1811; charged for sundries at Lake Winnipeg, 1812–14, and at Red River, 1815–16; wages 350 livres, 1812–16; "deserted to HB" (HBCA, F.4/32, 588).

LATOUR, BAPTISTE: Engagé, Lake Winnipeg department; B. Latour was with Seraphin Lamar at Rivière-aux-Morts, 1809–10 [*Nelson Journal*]. Not found in *1805 list*, or *1811–21 Accounts*. One Jean-Bte Latour, of l'Isle Jésus, contract 17 April 1804, for "les dépendances de Détroit" (ANQ *Rapport* 1944–45, 390).

LATOURELLE, JEAN-BAPTISTE: Engagé, Lake Winnipeg department; Jean-Baptiste Latourelle, of Berthier, contract with McTavish, Frobisher & Co., 25 August 1800, for 2 year, to winter in the North, wages 1,000 livres. *1811–21 Accounts*: Jean B La Tourelle, debt 358 livres 15 sous in 1811; charged for sundries at Lac la Pluie, 1812–14; wages 350 livres 1812–14, plus "allowance for playing the fidell," 50 livres, 1812–13; paid off, 1814 (HBCA, F.4/32, 596). One of Cameron's men, 1810–11 (*Nelson Journals*).

LEBLANC, —: Engagé, Lake Winnipeg department; One of Alexander Macdonell's men at Pigeon River, 1807–08 and 1808–09, and with Crebassa at Broken River, 1809–10, but from March 1810 onwards Leblanc was at Nelson's post at Tête-au-Brochet for the rest of the season; again with Crebassa, 1810–11 (*Nelson Journals*). His first name is never given, and there is no Leblanc associated with Lake Winnipeg in the *1811–21 Accounts*.

LECOMTE, FRANÇOIS: Engagé, Lake Winnipeg department; François Hebert *dit* Lecomte, of St François-de-Sales, contract with McTavish, Frobisher & Co., 13 March 1792, as *gouvernail*, for one year, wages 1,000 *livres*. François Lecomte, of Montreal, contract 17 April 1794 with Todd, McGill & Co. to go to the Mississippi [ANQ *Rapport* 1942–43, 338). *1805 list*: François H. Lecompte, Lac Ouinipique, debt 643 livres 18 sous, wages 500 livres, 1 yr left on contract. Le Comté [*sic*] was one of Ducharme's men on Winnipeg River, 1805–06. Not in *1811–21 Accounts*.

L'EPINE, —: Engagé, Lake Winnipeg department; one of Campbell's men at Grand Rapid, 1808–09 (*Nelson Journal*). There is no Lepine or L'Epine associated with Lake Winnipeg in the *1805 list* or the *1811–21 Accounts*.

LONGUETIN OR LONGTIN, ÉTIENNE: Engagé, Lake Winnipeg department; with Seraphin Lamar at Rivière-aux-Morts, 1809–10 [*Nelson Journals*]. Not in *1805 list*. *1811–21 Accounts*: Etienne Longtin, credited with amounts from the Columbia Outfit, 1813 & 1814; charges in Montreal Book, 1814 & 1815; Cumberland House Book, 1815; "To J. M. Bouchers Adventure at LLP," 1815; and for sundries in Athabasca River Book, 1816–17, and Athabasca Book, 1817. Wages 700 livres, 1816; 600 livres, 1817. Cash paid "his Brother" £100, equal to 1,200 livres, 1816. Paid off 1817 (HBCA, F.4/32, 637).

LONGUETIN or LONGTIN, JEAN: Engagé, Lake Winnipeg department. *1805 list*: Jean Longtin, Lac Ouinipique, debt 198 livres 12 sous, wages 450 livres, 1 yr left on contract. *1811–21 Accounts*: debt 640 livres 11 sous in 1811; charged for sundries at Lake Winnipeg, 1812; at Nipigon, 1812–14; and at Red River, 1815–20. Wages 450 livres, 1812; 550 livres, 1813–14; 450 livres, 1815–16; 100 livres, 1817; 450 livres, 1818–19; paid off 1819 (HBCA, F.4/32, 587). With Nelson at Dauphin River, 1808–09; he may also be the Longuetin who as with

Nelson in 1810–11 (*Nelson Journals*). In his *Reminiscences*, Nelson mentions that Jean Lonctain was one of his men at Tête-au-Brochet in 1812.

LONGUETIN, JÉROME: Engagé, Lake Winnipeg department; Jean-Évangeliste Longtain dit Jérome, of St-Constant, contract 29 March 1799 with James & Andrew McGill "pour aller dans tous endroits indiquées" (ANQ *Rapport* 1943–44, 381). Not in *1805 list*. *1811–21 Accounts*: credit balance of 803 livres 12 sous in 1811; charged for sundries in Athabasca Book, 1812–14; wages 600 livres, 1812; 700 livres, 1813–14; paid off 1814 (HBCA, F.4/32, 498). "Lonquetin (or Gerome)" was assigned to the Lac du Bonnet post, 1805–06. In March 1810, Duncan Cameron brought "Old Longuetin or Jérome" on a visit to Nelson at Dauphin River, and left him there, taking away Auger "to prevent any future dissentions among ourselves on womens accounts" (*Nelson Journals*). Either this man or Jean Longtin was the Longuetin who was with Nelson at Tête-au-Brochet in 1810–11.

MAILLOUX, CHARLES: Engagé, Lake Winnipeg department; *1805 list*: Charles Mailloux, Lac Ouinipique, no debt or credit recorded, wages 350 livres, 1 yr left on contract. *1811–21 Accounts*: Charles Mailloux, credit balance of 44 livres 10 sous in 1811; charged for sundries in Nipigon, 1812–14; wages 550 livres 1812–13, 450 livres 1814; paid off 1814 (HBCA, F.4/32, 733). Nelson met Mallioux [*sic*] and young Richard coming from Rivière-aux-Morts in September 1809 (*Nelson Journals*), so he was probably transferred from Lake Winnipeg to the Nipigon department in 1810 or 1811.

MAUSGÉ, —: Engagé, apparently, Lake Winnipeg department; "Old Mausgé" was a summer man at Fort Alexander, 1808; his wife died 14 July 1808, and, having been baptized a Catholic, was buried according to those rites. Mausgé was with Nelson at Dauphin River in summer 1810, and, though sick, assisted in the unexpected move of the post to Tête-au-Brochet in August (*Nelson Journals*). Perhaps the François Maugé, of faubourg St Laurent, Montreal, contract 20 February 1789 with Gabriel Cotté to go to Nipigon (ANQ *Rapport* 1942–43, 274). Not in *1805 list* or *1811–21 Accounts*.

MERCIER, —: Engagé, Lake Winnipeg department; Mercier wintered with Seraphin Lamar at Rivière-aux-Morts, 1809–10 (*Nelson Journals*). Not in *1805 list* or *1811–21 Accounts*.

PARADIX, FRANÇOIS: Engagé, Lake Winnipeg department; with Nelson at Tête-au-Brochet, 1818–19. *1811–21 Accounts*: charged for sundries in Montreal *Engagés' Book*, 1816; at English River, 1817–18; and at Lake Winnipeg,

1818–21; wages 450 livres 1817, 350 livres 1818–21, plus 50 livres for "Trip to Grand Rapid," 1820 (HBCA, F.4/32, 772). Early in the season, Nelson learned that the Indigenous people would not deal with Paradix, and even threatened to kill him, having discovered that he was stealing things from them (*Nelson Journals*; *Reminiscences*, 278–9).

PARADIX, —: Engagé, Lake Winnipeg department; "Old" Paradix was with Nelson at Dauphin River, 1808–09. *1805 list*: Culbert Paradis, debt 55 livres 5 sous, wages 450 livres, 1 yr left on contract; and Fran⁵ Paradis, credit balance 114 livres 10 sous, wages 300 livres, 1 yr left on contract; both at Lake Winnipeg. Either could be Nelson's man. Neither appears in the *1811–21 Accounts*.

PÉRON, GODFROI: Engagé, Lake Winnipeg department; Godfroy Perron, of La Prairie, contract 1 March 1793 with Myers Michael & Co., as a *milieu*, to go for one year to the Mississippi, wages 460 livres; and Godefroy Perron, of La Prairie, contract with James & Andrew McGill, as a *milieu*, to go to Michilimackinac, wages 170 livres. Both contracts probably refer to the same man. *1805 list*: Godfroi Pairon [*sic*], Lac Ouinipique, debt 559 livres, wages 400 livres, 1 yr left on contract. With Ferguson at Tête-au-Brochet, 1805–06 (*Nelson Journals*). Not in *1811–21 Accounts*.

PERUSSE or PERUCE, PERUZE, LOUIS: Engagé, Lake Winnipeg department; *1803*: Louis Leruce purchased goods totaling 262 livres 10 sous at Fort William, 1 & 31 July (Account book of men's purchases, in North West Company Papers, Baldwin Collection of Canadiana, Toronto Reference Library). *1805 list*: Louis Péruze, Nipigon, debt 453 livres 5 sous, steersman, wages 550 livres, 1 yr left on contract. *1811–21 Accounts*: Louis Periffle dit Peruce, debit balance of 1066 livres 7 sous, 1811; charged for sundries at Nipigon, 1812, and at English River, 1813–14, 1816–18; wages 550 livres (1812), 600 livres (1813), 530 livres (1814), 480 livres (1815), 600 livres (1816–18) (HBCA, F.4/32, 805, 1001). With Crebassa at Broken River, 1809–10. Not in *1811–21 Accounts*. See Introduction, pages xv–xvi, for the possibility that this man was the father of Mary Ann, George Nelson's wife.

PINAULT, PIERRE: Engagé, Lake Winnipeg department; Pierre Pinault of Trois-Rivières, contract 29 April 1793, as a *milieu*, with David & Peter Grant, to go "dans le Nord (la rivière des anglais excepté," wages 1,200 livres. *1805 list*: Pierre Pinneau, Lake Winnipeg, debt 926 livres, wages 350 livres, 1 yr left on contract. Not in *1811–21 Accounts*. Pinault was with Perigny and Nelson at Lac du Bonnet, 1805–06 (*Nelson Journals*).

PLANTE, —: Engagé, Lake Winnipeg department; There are eleven men named Plante in *1811–21 Accounts*, but none was associated with Lake Winnipeg. Plante (given name not found) was with Nelson at Tête-au-Brochet in 1818–19.

POTVIN, LOUIS: NWC engagé or freeman, Lake Winnipeg; Louis Potvin, of Yamaska, contract 29 April 1793 with McTavish, McGillivrays & Co., as a *milieu*, to go to the Nord Ouest, wages 1200 livres. *1811 accounts*: Louis Potvin, debit balance of 238 livres 11 sous in 1811; charged for "sundries" at Lake Winnipeg, 1812–15, 1818, and at Red River, 1816–17; wages 350 livres, 1812–18; in 1818 he was paid his balance owing, 252 livres 17 sous, in Montreal (HBCA, F.4/32, 803, 1000). In 1818–19 Potvin was down in Canada giving evidence for the NWC, and his wife, "a handsome young half-breed at F. Alexander," was having an affair with the clerk, Roderick McKenzie (*Nelson Journals*).

PRITCHARD, WILLIAM: NWC engagé or freeman, Lake Winnipeg; Nelson sent him on an errand from Tête-au-Brochet in December 1818. In the entry, Nelson described him, "a scorched stump (brulé)," his version of the well-known term for a Métis, *bois brulé* (*Nelson Journals*). He was likely a son of the NWC clerk John Pritchard, who had joined the XYC in 1801, was taken over by the NWC in 1805, and left its service for the HBC in 1814, settling at Red River. John is known to have had at least one son with an Indigenous or Métis woman, and William could have been another, about 10 years old in 1818. After John Pritchard married a woman from the Red River Settlement in 1816 (Judd 1985), his first family may have been left to its own devices. In 1818 Nelson described William Pritchard as "in Welles care," which may mean that he was the stepson of Jean-Baptiste Welles, and that Welles had now taken Pritchard's mother as his wife. William probably continued to make himself useful around Lake Winnipeg as he grew up. He was hired by the HBC in 1826, aged 18, and remained in the company's service until 1835 (HBCA Biographical Sheet).

RELLE, —: Engagé, Lake Winnipeg department; Relle was with Nelson at Dauphin River, 1807–08 (*Nelson Journals*). In his *Reminiscences*, 198, Nelson does not give his first name, but says he was from Laprairie. Not identified further. There are four men of this surname (Relle, Rhel, or Rhelle) in the *1811–21 Accounts*, but none is associated with Lake Winnipeg. He cannot be the same person as Joseph Aurialle, who was at Pigeon River in 1807–08.

ROI, —: Interpreter at Fort Alexander, June 1808, whom the NWC partners employed to converse with the Old Premier about the rumoured Indigenous conspiracy; in August 1808, he was sent to try to draw the Indigenous hunters away from Rivière-aux-Morts, where the NWC no longer wanted to maintain a post; at this time he was apparently associated with the Lower Red River department. His wife was likely the "Madame Roi" who left Fort Alexander along with Mme Beaulieu and "Bourassa's wife," for a visit to Red River, in July of that year [*Nelson Journals*]. The surname is very common, and from this slight information there seems no basis for identifying him with any of the various men named Roi or Roy in the fur trade literature.

RONDEAU, LOUIS: Engagé, Lake Winnipeg department; Louis Rondeau, of Lanoraie, contract 23 January 1802 with McTavish, Frobisher & Co., as a *devant*, to go to Grand Portage, wages 400 livres. *1805 list*: Louis Rondeau, Lac Ouinipique, debt 167 livres, wages 350 livres, 1 yr left on contract. *1811–21 Accounts*: debt 1,016 livres 5 sous in 1811; charged for sundries at the Columbia (1812), at Nipigon (1813), and at Athabasca (1814–20); wages 450 livres, 1812–14, 500 livres 1815, 400 livres 1816–19, 600 livres 1820–21 (HBCA, F. 4/32, 823, 1044). Rondeau was with Campbell at Grand Rapid, 1808–09, and with Cameron at Fort Alexander in 1810–11 (*Nelson Journals*); the *1811–21 Accounts* show that he was eventually transferred to Athabasca.

ST DENIS, EUSTACHE: Engagé, Lake Winnipeg department; *1805 list*: Eustache St Denis, Lac Ouinipique, debt 840 livres 16 sous, no wages or contract given, "AMKC." One of three voyageurs drowned in Rivière Blanche, coming inward with William McKay's brigade, in August 1805 (*Nelson Journals*).

SANSFAÇON, PIERRE: Engagé, Lake Winnipeg department; *1805 list*: Pierre Sansfaçon, Lac Ouinipique, debt 38 livres 10 sous, wages 450 livres, 1 yr left on contract. One of three voyageurs drowned in Rivière Blanche, coming inward with William McKay's brigade, in August 1805 (*Nelson Journals*).

TREMPE, FRANÇOIS: Engagé, Lake Winnipeg department; *1805 list*: François Trempe, Lac Ouinipique, "AMKC," debt 486 livres 14 sous, wages 500 livres, 1 yr left on contract. With Campbell, 1807–08, and with Crebassa at Broken River, 1808–09, 1809–10 (Nelson Journals). Not in *1811–21 Accounts*.

VANDALLE, ANTOINE: Engagé, Lake Winnipeg department; an unusual number of notarized contracts have survived for one or more men of this name. Antoine Vandalle (fils), of Sorel, contract 13 September 1800 with Alexander Mackenzie & Co., as a *milieu*, to go to Grand Portage and winter, wages 230 livres; Antoine Vandalle (son of Augustin Vandalle), of Sorel, contract 8 November 1800 with "La Nouvelle Societe du Nord" [the XYC], as a *milieu*, to go to Grand Portage,

wages 230 livres; Antoine Vandalle, of Sorel, contract 8 January 1801 with the
same, as a *gouvernail*, to go to Grand Portage, wages 400 livres; Antoine Vandalle, of Sorel, contract 5 November 1802 with A. McKenzie & Co., 5 November
1802, as a *gouvernail*, to go to Grand Portage, wages 400 livres; Antoine Vandalle (fils), of St-Ours, contract 17 December 1803 with Alexander Mackenzie
[& Co.], as a milieu for 2 years, to go to Grand Portage et les dependances du
Nord-Ouest, wages 800 livres; and Antoine Vandalle, of Sorel, contract 7 January 1808 with McTavish, McGillivrays & Co, as a *milieu*, for 3 years, to go
to the Nord Ouest, wages 700 livres. Probably two different men are involved
here, one (the *gouvernail*) more senior than the other (the *milieu*). It seems that
the younger Antoine began his career in the canoes that went from Montreal to
Grand Portage and returned, but in 1803 began to winter in the Northwest. The
fact that he signed a contract in Montreal in 1808 shows that he left the Northwest in 1807–08, but then returned, very likely for good. *1805 list*: Antoine
Vandal, Lac Ouinipique, "AMKC," debt 308 livres, wages 400 livres, 1 yr left on
contract. *1811–21 Accounts*: credit balance 683 livres 13 sous in 1811; charged
for sundries at the Columbia, 1810–11; at Fort des Prairies, 1812–18; and at
Lake Winnipeg, 1819–21; wages: 550 livres (1812), 400 (1813), 425 (1814),
400 (1815), 350 (1816), 425 plus 17 livres hunt (1817), 350 plus "short for wages
last yr 25," also for gum 9 (1818); 350 (1819–21) (HBCA, F.4/32, 878, 1017).
Antoine Vandalle was with Nelson at Tête-au-Brochet, 1818–19. Nelson says that
he had been in the country for many years, and had a wife and four children; a
fifth, a daughter, was born at the post on 2 January 1819 (*Nelson Journals*).

VANDALLE, JOSEPH: Engagé, Lake Winnipeg department. *1811–21 Accounts*:
Joseph Vandal, charged for "sundries" in the Montreal Engagés' Book, 1816; at
Lac la Pluie, 1817; at Red River, 1817–18; and at Lake Winnipeg, 1818–21; wages
300 livres (1816), 200 livres (1817), 350 livres (1818–20), 450 livres (1821)
(HBCA, F.4/32, 912). Thus he first hired with the NWC in 1816. Joseph Vandalle
was one of Crebassa's men at Grand Rapids, 1818–19 (*Nelson Journals*).

VANDALLE, PIERRE: Engagé, Lower Red River department; not in *1805 list*.
1811–21 Accounts: Pierre Vandal, debit balance of 709 livres 10 sous in 1811;
charged for "sundries" at Fort des Prairies, 1812–18; wages 450 livres (1812),
400 livres (1813), 425 livres (1814–16), 450 livres (1817–18), 500 livres (1819)
(HBCA, F.4/32, 875, 1073). Pierre Vandle [*sic*] was in the crew of a boat with
Lower Red River returns, sent from Pembina to Fort William, 1 June 1808 (Coues
1965, 430, 442). Vandalle and Toussaint Vaudry came to Bas de la Rivière from
Pembina, 1 August 1808, with a letter to "the Gentlemen passants," i.e. the partners returning from the Fort William meeting (*Nelson Journals*).

VANDALLE, —: Engagé, Lake Winnipeg department; Vandalle was one of Ducharme's men in Winnipeg River, 1805–06 (*Nelson Journals*). Possibly the same as Antoine Vandalle.

VAUDRIE, TOUSSAINT: Trader and guide, Lower Red River department; Toussaint Valdrai, of St-Constant, contract 13 June 1794 with Pierre Gamelin, for Michilimackinac; Toussaint Vaudrain, of St-Constant, contract 27 February 1800, for Temiscaming (ANQ *Rapport* 1942–43, 340; 1943–4, 404, 428], Toussaint Vaudril was one of the men who accompanied David Thompson from Upper Red River to the Missouri River, to visit the Mandans, in November–December 1797 (Coues 1965, 301). Alexander Henry mentions him often in his journal at Pembina, once he came under his command in 1803. He was an effective trader, capable of supervising a small post. He wintered at Rivière-aux-Morts in 1803–04 and 1804–05, at Portage la Prairie in 1805–06; at Rivière du Milieu (on the Assiniboine), 1806–07; and at Grand Fourches, Red River, in 1806–07 (Coues 1965, 215, 225, 236, 259, 267, 276, 422, 424). Vaudry accompanied Alexander Henry as interpreter on his trip to the Mandan villages in July 1806 (Coues 1965, 292). *1805 list*: Toussᵗ Vaudrie, Lower Red River, guide, debt 253 livres 3 sous, wages 750 livres, 1 yr left on contract. Henry sent Vaudry to Bas de la Rivière with letters, 26 July 1808 (Coues 1965, 438); Nelson notes his arrival with Vandal on 1 August (*Nelson Journals*). *1811–21 Accounts*: Toussaint Vaudrie, credit balance 973 livres 19 sous in 1811; charged for sundries in Petty Ledger, 1811–13, 1815–17, and at Red River, 1812–17; wages 600 livres 1812–14, 500 livres 1815, 600 livres 1816–17; credit balance transferred to Montreal, 1,946 livres 15 sous, in 1817 (HBCA, F.4/32, 877). Thus he retired to Canada in 1817. Toussaint Vaudry was at Fort Gibraltar when Lord Selkirk's Des Meurons soldiers captured it on 10 January 1817 (Douglas 1954), and he was a witness at the trial of the Semple case at York, Upper Canada, in October 1818. In his testimony, he stated that he had been "upwards of thirty years" in the Red River country (Amos 1820, 132–4; he also made a brief appearance at another trial, ibid. 344). There is also an account for Toussaint Vaudrie Jr (HBCA, F.4/32, 914), presumably a son, who married Marie Anne Crebassa, presumably a daughter of Nelson's friend, the NWC clerk John Crebassa; their daughter Marie, born about 1818, married Romain Lagimodière, one of the children of Jean-Baptiste Lagimodière and Marie-Anne Gaboury.

WELLES, JEAN-BAPTISTE: Engagé, Lake Winnipeg department; Nelson also calls him the Dutchman, the German, and L'Allemand. Perhaps he was the son of one of the Hessian mercenaries who had stayed in Canada after the American War of Independence. He was from Sorel (*Nelson Reminiscences*, 198). *1805 list*: Jean Bte Welles, Lac Ouinipique, debt 525 livres 10 sous, wages 350 livres, 2 yrs left on contract. *1811–21 Accounts*: Jean Bte Welles, debit balance of 1,067 livres 10 sous in 1811; charged for sundries at Lake Winnipeg, 1812–15, 1818–21; at Lac la Pluie, 1816; and at Red River 1816–17; wages 400 livres (1812), 450 livres (1813–16), 400 livres (1817), 450 livres (1818–21); in 1813–14 he was paid 130 livres for a trip to Fort William (HBCA, F.4/32, 884, 1018). Welles was with Périgny and Nelson at Lac du Bonnet, 1805–06; with Nelson at Dauphin River, 1807–08, 1808–09, and 1809–10, and at Tête-au-Brochet, 1810–11. He is one of the most prominent characters in the journals for those years, doing all kinds of tasks, including frequent winter journeys to set traps, or to fetch meat or furs from Indigenous lodges. In January 1810 he was the victim of a practical joke when he attempted to buy the wife of "old Desrocher." He and Boulanger had fights on two successive days, the following May, both of which Welles won. When Nelson returned to Lake Winnipeg in 1818, Welles was again one of his men, and by now he had a wife and three children (*Nelson Journals*). See entry for William Pritchard (above) for indications that Welles's wife was the former wife of the NWC clerk, John Pritchard, and thus that Welles's children were stepchildren.

WELLES, SAMUEL: Engagé, Lake Winnipeg department; Samuel Wells, of Masquinongé, contract 6 April 1801, with Louis Belair for Jean-Marie Boucher (agent for McTavish, Frobisher & Co.), to winter 1 yr in the North (contract in Yale University, Beinecke Rare Book Library, WA MSS S-2357; cited from online finding aid). *1805 list*: Samuel Wells, summer man, no debt listed, wages 450 livres, 1 yr left on contract. Not in *1811–21 Accounts*. Sometimes called "the Negro," he was with Perigny and Nelson at Lac du Bonnet in 1805–06 (*Nelson Journals*). No further information.

APPENDIX D

Clerks, Freemen, and Partners

This list is limited to men who served the NWC in the Lake Winnipeg department, or at least appear frequently in the Nelson *Journals*. Other NWC clerks,
mentioned only once or twice, are identified in footnotes to the journal texts,
and are not listed here. General sources are the same as in Appendix C.

BELL, JOHN: NWC apprentice clerk; John Bell, of Argyllshire, Scotland, contracted with the NWC on 6 June 1818, to serve six years as an apprentice clerk in
the Northwest (Beek Repertoire, ANQ-M, Calendar p. 145). He would have proceeded at once in the canoes for the fur country, and he was at Fort Alexander in
the fall of 1818, when his bourgeois, Duncan McDougall, made his will (which
Bell witnessed) and soon after died. Bell was taken over by the HBC, served in
the Lake Winnipeg district 1821–24, and was made a chief trader in 1840 (Wallace 1934, 425–6). *1811–21 Accounts*: charged for "sundries" in Petty Ledger,
1818, 1820–21, and at Lake Winnipeg, 1820; wages "⅙th of £100," 1818 (the
salary of an apprentice clerk), 200 livres 1819–21 (HBCA, F.4/32, 979).

BETHUNE, ANGUS (1783–1858): XYC & NWC clerk, later partner; for biog-
raphies see Russell 1980, 1985. Son of John Bethune, a prominent Presbyterian clergyman in Canada, and Véronique Waddens, daughter of the fur trader
Jean-Étienne Waddens. Nelson's writings provide new information about the
beginnings of Bethune's fur trade career with the XYC. In 1803–04 he wintered
on Lake Winnipeg, possibly at Pigeon River, and was so starved that he was
reduced to crawling on his hands and knees (*Nelson Reminiscences*, 209). The
next year he was sent "to the S. Side of the Lake" (*Sorel Journal*, 56); Alexander Henry, junior, locates him at White Mud River, in opposition to the NWC's
Toussaint Vaudry (Coues 1965, 259). After the union with the NWC, Bethune
remained on Lake Winnipeg at first (Wallace 1934, 220), wintering in 1806–07

near the southwest corner of the Lake (*Nelson Journals*, 12 December 1807). For 1807–08 he was transferred farther north, probably a sign that he was being groomed for a partnership. Nelson noted his arrival at Bas de la Rivière, along with the partners from Athabasca, Slave Lake, English River, Rat River, and Upper Fort des Prairies in June 1808. Bethune was in the Fort des Prairies department in 1810, and was transferred to the Columbia in 1813–14. *1811–21 Accounts*: credit balance of 3,506 livres in 1811; charged for sundries at Fort des Prairies, 1812, 1813; at Montreal, 1814; and at English River, 1820; salary: 1,200 livres, 1812–14; transferred to Columbia, 1814 (whose accounts are not included in this source) (HBCA, F.4/32, 73). For the rest of his career, including his role in negotiating the amalgamation with the HBC, see Russell 1980, 1985.

CALDWELL, JAMES: NWC clerk; From his name, he was likely a relation of the Montreal merchant James Caldwell (1760?–1815; LaBrèque 1983), but no proof has been found. This man wintered at the Hair Hills, Lower Red River, apparently for the XYC, 1804–05; his opponent was the NWC clerk, Michel Coloret dit Langlois (Coues 1965, 259). *1805 list*: clerk and summer man, 4 yrs to serve on contract; no wages or balance given. Clerk in Upper Red River, arrangements for 1806 (Wallace 1934, 220). In July 1806 he accompanied the NWC clerk Charles McKenzie on the latter's fourth trading expedition to the Mandan villages on the Missouri River (Wood and Thiessen 1985, 269–96; Coues 1965, 345–6, 403). Caldwell and his bourgeois Mr McDonell, with the rest of the Upper Red River brigade, called at Fort Alexander on 25 June 1808 on their way out; he embarked with the canoes, 29 June (*Nelson Journals*). Caldwell is not heard of again in the fur trade records, and may have left the Upper Country for good in 1808.

CAMERON, DUNCAN: NWC partner; see Introduction for an account of his early career in the fur trade, and his period in charge of the Lake Winnipeg department; and for a general biography, Brown 1988. There are many letters addressed to Duncan Cameron in the Selkirk Papers. One, from Daniel McKenzie, on 15 January 1809, is addressed to "D. Cameron Esqr. of Lochiel," evidently in fun, as it gives Duncan the title of the chief of Clan Cameron (Selkirk Papers, 8543–5). These letters were probably seized at Red River when Cameron was arrested by the HBC in 1816, and came into Lord Selkirk's hands. *1811–21 Accounts*: charges for sundries in the Petty Ledger, 1811, 1813–16; at Lac la Pluie, 1812–15; at Red River, 1816; and in the Athabasca book, 1815. Also some small charges including a subscription to the Quebec *Mercury* newspaper in 1815 and 1816. The credit side shows payments to him as a NWC partner "By McTavish McGillivrays & Co." in 1812–17, and in 1818 a small credit "By Captain McLean" (HBCA, F.4/32, 222).

CAMERON, JOHN DOUGALD (1775?–1857): NWC clerk and partner; for a biography, see Van Kirk 1988. He and his elder brother Ranald Cameron were sons of Dougal Cameron, a British soldier who had fought in the Revolutionary War, took his discharge in America, and settled at William Henry (Sorel), Lower Canada. George Nelson's letter to his sister at Sorel, 4 June 1811, states that Dougald Cameron, then his bourgeois on Lake Winnipeg, was "the son of old Mr Cameron your neighbour." [John] Dougald Cameron contracted with the breakaway fur traders, David and Peter Grant, to go "dans le Nord" on 10 January 1794; his brother Ranald was also hired (ANQ *Rapport* 1942–43, 330). The brothers must have been taken over by the NWC when the Grants' company was absorbed in 1796, and they were assigned to the Nipigon department, where Duncan Cameron, a clansman, but probably not a close relative, was in charge. John Dougald Cameron remained in Nipigon until 1811, and is mentioned often in the journals of HBC servants in the district. On 18 July 1809, William McGillivray wrote him about his prospects for advancement, and two years later wrote again to promise him a partnership in 1814 (Selkirk Papers, 9166–9). In his journal for 14 October 1810, George Nelson noted a report that Mr. Dougald Cameron's wife and family, with one Peruse, had been seen at Pigeon Point on Lake Winnipeg, travelling as fast as they could in quest of her husband "who probably winters at Loon Lake near Nepigon." The reference to Peruse in company with John Dougald Cameron's wife is interesting, given that Nelson's wife, whose surname was apparently Peruse, was related to Duncan Cameron's wife (see Introduction, xv–xvi).

John Dougald Cameron's wintering place was indeed at Loon Lake (which is unidentified), as he arrived at Fort Alexander "from Lac-Du-huard" for a Christmas visit that year (*Nelson Journals*). In 1811 he took charge of the Lake Winnipeg department, replacing Duncan Cameron who had been moved to Lac la Pluie. There are many letters addressed to John Dougald Cameron in the Selkirk Papers, which must have fallen into Lord Selkirk's hands during his trip to Red River in 1816–17. Following the amalgamation of the two companies in 1821, Cameron was appointed a chief factor, took charge of various posts, and did not retire until 1846. *1811–21 Accounts*: charges for sundries in Petty Ledger, 1811–20; and in the books from various departments, 1812–20, confirming his movements as known from other sources; also various other charges, including "To Cash paid his sister 300#" in 1812. Credit balance of 634 livres 2 sous, 1811; salary 1,200 livres, 1812–13; paid by Seraphin Lamar in 1813, 900 livres; and his shares as a partner, to be paid by McTavish McGillivrays & Co, 1814–21, confirming that he became a NWC partner in 1814 (HBCA, F.4/32, 212).

CAMPBELL, ALEXANDER: XYC and NWC clerk; this was probably the Campbell who traded for the XYC in 1802–03 at Portage la Prairie (Coues 1965, 221).

Alexander Campbell was chief clerk for the XYC on Lake Winnipeg in 1804, when he "went far into the interior on the east side" (*Sorel Journal*, 56). He is in the NWC arrangements for 1806 as a clerk in the Lake Winnipeg department (Wallace 1934, 220), and was in charge of Fort Alexander in summer 1807 (*Nelson Reminiscences*, 186). Ferguson and Campbell wintered at Tête-au-Brochet in 1806–07 (*Nelson Journals*, 8 March 1811). Campbell wintered in 1807–08 at a place that Nelson calls Kakinowachague, probably at the foot of the present Washow or Humbug Bay; he visited Nelson at Dauphin River, in order to get more trade goods, late in February. In June 1808, Duncan Cameron proposed to "court martial" Campbell for drunkenness, but George Nelson denounced the proceedings as unfair, and Campbell remained in the country for one year more (*Reminiscences*, 204–7). The chance that Nelson's support gave him was not well used, for in 1808–09, Campbell, put in charge of the remote post at Little Grand Rapids, east of Lake Winnipeg, lost complete control of the situation. Nelson had to make a long winter trip to the post to take charge of it, bringing Campbell, his heavily pregnant wife, and their children back with him to Dauphin River. Campbell was sent down to Montreal in the spring. Nelson later heard that Mr Ogilvy (one of the old XYC partners) had given him employment, but that he continued to drink to excess, and died a few years later (*Reminiscences*, 227).

CARDIN, PIERRE: NWC clerk; *1811–21 Accounts*: Pierre Cardin, clerk, charged for "sundries" in the Montreal Engagés' Book, 1816; at Cumberland House, 1817–20, and in the Petty Ledger, 1818–21; salary 240 livres (stated to be ⅕ of £100), 1817–21 (HBCA, F.4/32, 236). The salary marks him as an apprentice clerk, but with a five-year contract rather than the usual seven. Nelson mentions a clerk named Cardin who wintered in 1819–20 in "the Rat River quarter," equipped from Cumberland House, and opposed by the HBC. This must have been Pierre Cardin.

CHASTELIN, LOUIS: NWC clerk; Nelson and Lorrin met "old Chastelin's (now Fleurie's) wife" a short distance south of Pointe Mitasse on 14 August 1808. The only Chastelin known in the fur trade at this period is Louis Chastelain, a clerk at Lower Fort des Prairies. In 1799 his wages were 1,800 livres, one of the highest salaries in the Northwest (Lamb 1970, 459; Masson 1960, 1:62). He had probably been in the service of the NWC for several years by 1787, when the Company owed him £197.18s.10d.; by 1799 this amount had grown to £296.1s.7d. (Wallace 1934, 80–1, 105). Alexander Mackenzie passed a pleasant evening with "my fellow Travellers," including "Chatland," at Lac la Pluie, 8 July 1790 (Lamb 1970, 442). "Monsieur Chatellain" was in charge of the NWC fort on the South Branch of the Saskatchewan in the summer of 1794, when it was briefly attacked by the "Rapid Indians" (Gros Ventres, Atsina: see Malalney 2005); the nearby HBC post was overrun at the same time, and all but one of their people killed (Lamb 1957, 97–8). Chastelin had probably retired by 1808, explaining why his wife was now married to another man.

CHENETTE, FRANÇOIS: NWC clerk. *1805 list*: in Lake Winnipeg department, debt 2,072 livres. He is not listed in the NWC arrangements for 1806, so probably was not retained after his contract expired. On 29 May 1809 Nelson heard that he was "a living with Fort Dauphin indians" at Falle-au-Perdrix. This suggests that after being released by the NWC he was attempting to lead the life of a freeman.

CHISHOLM, DONALD: NWC clerk. *1805 list*: clerk, Upper Red River, five yrs to serve; no wages or balance given. The long contract suggests that he was an apprentice clerk on a seven-year engagement, which would have begun in 1803. At Upper Red River in arrangements for 1806 (Wallace 1934, 220). He arrived at Fort Alexander from Red River on 25 June 1808, with his bourgeois Mr McDonell, and remained there for the summer (*Nelson Journals*). In a letter to Duncan Cameron, dated at Fort Alexander 8 August 1809, Daniel McKenzie wrote: "I beg leave to recommend Mr Chisholm to your patronage should he deserve it. His uncle is parson McKenzie of Knockbain a most worthy character & a man to whom I am under obligation" (Selkirk Papers, 8546–8). This recommendation might indicate that Chisholm was being transferred to Lake Winnipeg, where Cameron was in charge, but Nelson does not mention him again. He is not in the *1811–21 Accounts*, and had probably left the fur trade. Chisholm's uncle was presumably Roderick McKenzie, minister of the united parishes of Kilmuir Wester and Suddy (commonly known as Knockbain), who wrote the description of his parish for the *First Statistical Account of Scotland*, 12:262–78.

CREBASSA, JOHN: XYC and NWC clerk; Probably the closest of Nelson's friends in the fur trade. Jean Baptiste Crebassa was baptized at Notre-Dame de Québec, 26 March 1777, the son of Sieur Henri Crebassa, *négociant de cette ville*, and Marie-Angélique Tanquerelle, his wife. Another son, Henry Crebassa, was the Sorel notary who recorded George Nelson's first contract with the XYC in 1802. John Crebassa appeared on Red River on 21 September 1801, with two canoes and ten men for the XYC, and opposed the NWC partner Alexander Henry at Pembina in the seasons of 1801–02, 1802–03, and 1804–05 (Coues 1965, 188, 221, 259). His whereabouts in 1803–04 are unknown. When news arrived at Pembina in early 1805, of the amalgamation of the NWC with the XYC, Crebassa

did not believe it at first, and persistently told the local Ojibwe Indigenous people "that the report concerning the coalition was false, and that next year the
X. Y. would be stronger than ever, with double the number of canoes, etc."
When at last he had to accept the truth, and send the rest of his property over to
Henry's fort, "he got himself despised by the natives, and in the end had a narrow escape for his life from Pegouisse [Peguis, the famous Ojibwe leader], who
certainly would have murdered him had I [Henry] not interfered" (Coues 1965,
257). *1805 list*: John Crebassa, Lac Ouinipique, clerk, 1 yr left on contract,
no wages or debt listed. Following the union with the NWC, Crebassa spent
one more year at the Grandes Fourches post in Lower Red River department,
1805–06, and he was one of several "passengers" sent out to Lake Superior on
10 June 1806 (Coues 1965, 276, 281), probably because their contracts had
run out and they were not being continued in the service. Crebassa is not in
the list of arrangements for the departments in 1806 (Wallace 1934, 219–21),
and likely did go down to Canada, but he returned to the Northwest in 1807.
He was stationed at Lac du Bonnet in 1807–08 (*Reminiscences*, 199; HBCA,
B.103/a/1), at Broken River in 1808–09 and 1809–10, and Fort Alexander in
1810–11. Although Nelson sometimes referred to Crebassa as "his holiness" or
"my reverend Friend," presumably because he was unusually religious for a fur
trader in the Northwest, it is clear from the *Reminiscences* that he was a valued
friend. Nelson entrusted him with his journals when he left Lake Winnipeg in
1813. *1811–21 Accounts*: John Crebassa, credit balance of 3,466 livres 6 sous
in 1811; charged for sundries at Lake Winnipeg, 1812–15, 1819–21, and at Red
River 1816–17; salary 1,200 livres (1812–17), 1,500 livres (1819–21). Among
other charges is a donation of 18 livres in 1819 towards "Church in Glengary"
– presumably St Raphael's, the first Catholic parish in Upper Canada (HBCA,
F.4/32, 213). As noted in the Introduction, the apparent transfer of Crebassa to
Red River in 1816–17 may not have been real, as there are indications that the
Lake Winnipeg department was combined with Red River, likely for reasons of
economy, for two seasons. Two letters from Archibald McLellan to Crebassa, at
Fort Alexander, dated 8 October 1816 and 2 January 1817, show that although
his account may have been in the Red River books in that season, he remained
on Lake Winnipeg (Selkirk Papers, 8597–8, 8599–600). A letter from Crebassa
to William Morrison, dated from Bas de la Rivière, 22 July 1816, says that Crebassa was staying inland for that year, but hoped to get to Fort William in 1817,
and perhaps to Canada, "as I am always unwell it seems to me that the Country
will no longer agree with me" (Selkirk Papers, 8887). The fact that he was not
paid a salary in 1817–18 suggests that he did spend that season in Canada. Crebassa and George Nelson both returned to Lake Winnipeg in 1818, evidently as
part of a process to strengthen or re-establish the trade on the Lake.

For the season of 1818–19, Crebassa was at Little Grand Rapids on the upper part of Pigeon River, where he had little success against a well-established HBC trader, Donald Sutherland (*Nelson Journals*, 7 January 1819; Lytwyn 1986, 148–9). In 1819–20 he apparently took over Nelson's post at Tête-au-Brochet (HBCA, B.51/e/1, fo. 17v). Crebassa had a wife in the Northwest, an Ojibwe woman whom he called Susanne; her son, "Crebassa's stepson," is mentioned in Nelson's journals in 1808 and 1819. Crebassa evidently left descendants in the Northwest, for the Métis land scrip applications include those of two daughters of John Crebassa, French Canadian, and Susanne, Sauteaux: Maria (born about September 1803 at Pembina, wife of Louis Galarneau), and Marie Anne (born about July 1807 at Fort Alexander, widow of Toussaint Vaudry) (Métis Claims No. 679, 800). The birthplaces and dates agree with Crebassa's known movements. It is not known whether Crebassa continued in the HBC service after the coalition, but he was a witness at George Nelson's wedding at Sorel, Lower Canada, in January 1825, and in 1829 he was living as a merchant there. Susanne, his country wife, had either died or been left in the Northwest, for he married Léocadie Leprohon at Notre-Dame-de-Montréal on 12 May 1829, and they had at least one child, born at Sorel. Jean-Baptiste Crébassa, esq., *marchand à Sorel*, died on 20 June 1843, aged 67, and was buried two days later at St-Jean-Baptiste, Nicolet (church register).

DESFOND, —: NWC interpreter; he was Nelson's interpreter at Rivière-aux-Morts in 1806–07, said to be an excellent man, but a drunkard. He is mentioned, apparently as a voyageur, at Fort Alexander in summer 1808.

DORION, LOUIS: NWC clerk. *1805 list*: Lower Red River department, Louis Dorion, clerk & summer man, credit balance of 923 livres, wages 1,000 livres; 1 yr left on contract. *1811–21 Accounts*: credit balance 4,256 livres 10 sous in 1811; charged for sundries in Petty Ledger, 1811, 1813, 1815–16, 1818–21, and in Nipigon Book, 1817; also "Cash paid Susanne," 60 livres, 1816; wages 960 livres 1812–15, 1,200 livres 1817–21 (HBCA, F.4/32, 313). During Nelson's last season for the XYC, on the lower Red River, the NWC clerk opposing him was Louis Dorion, whom Nelson describes as "a quiet & decent elderly man"; they passed the winter "without any broils" (*Sorel Journal*, 58). Dorion is frequently mentioned in Alexander Henry's journal for Lower Red River; in 1802–03 he wintered at "Bear's Head River" (unidentified) without any opposition; in 1803–04 at the Forks of the Red; and in 1805–06 and 1806–07 at Portage la Prairie (Coues 1965, 203, 422). Dorion was at Pembina River in 1807–8 (*Nelson Journals*, 13 June 1808), replacing Alexander Henry, the NWC partner who was transferred to the Saskatchewan this year. Although the NWC Grand

Ledger shows that he remained in the NWC's employment through to 1821, his whereabouts are not indicated, except for Nipigon in 1816–17. He signed a new contract with the NWC on 24 April 1816, to winter three years as a clerk (Beek Repertoire, ANQ-M, Document No. 2227).

DUCHARME, COLLISH: Freeman on Lake Winnipeg and in Red River; Nelson notes on 11 September 1809, "Both Ducharmes, Collish & Etiene free men are gone to red river" (*Nelson Journals*).

DUCHARME, DOMINIQUE: NWC clerk; he may have been the Ducharme who wintered for the XYC at Park River, Lower Red River district, in 1803–04, opposing the NWC's John Cameron (Coues 1965, 234, 245). Not found in the *1805 list*, but Nelson says that Ducharme and Meniclier were assigned to establish posts in the upper part of Winnipeg River in 1805–06, and Dom: Ducharme is listed as a clerk, Post of Lac Ouinipique, in the NWC arrangements for 1806 (Wallace 1934, 220). He is not in the *1811–21 Accounts*. In his *Sorel Journal*, Nelson records meeting Ducharme on the steamboat wharf near Sorel in 1836. He describes him at that time as "Kings interpretor to the Algonquin & Nipisingue tribes. I last saw him at Bas de la riviere Winnipick, in the spring of 1806 ... Poor old fellow, he is now in his 73^{d} year as active & vigorous as most men at 50. - A small man ... I am not sufficiently acquainted with all the circumstances of his entrance & leaving of the North West C^{os} Service, but I well remember there was a secret enmity to his National origin & his merits as a Trader, the only trait worth looking into in a Company of merchants was complete, his character as a man unimpeachable. Yet he was left out, struggled for a while a lone, & I believe, by the influence of the N.W. C^{o} got his present situation. Fine, worthy old fellow" (*Sorel Journal*, 21–2). Leighton (1985) describes Ducharme's activities as an independent trader at Green Bay, Lake Michigan, in the 1790s, as a militia officer in the war of 1812, and as a storekeeper at the time of the 1837 rebellion in Lower Canada. Leighton's statement that Ducharme employed William McKay as a clerk on the Menominee River in 1793 must be wrong (McKay was in northern Manitoba at the time), but how the error arose is unclear.

DUCHARME, ETIENNE: Freeman; *see* Collish Ducharme.

ERMATINGER, CHARLES OAKES: XYC and NWC clerk; born 1780, youngest child of Lawrence Ermatinger, one of the smaller Montreal traders interested in the Northwest fur trade in the 1760s and 1770s (Momryk 1979). He must be the "Ermintinger" who was assisting the independent trader Dominique Brunet

Letang on the lower Saskatchewan in the fall of 1798. Ermatinger and a companion became lost on a hunting expedition early in December, and Ermatinger got back to his fort after sixteen days, but the other was never heard of again. Letang was part of the trading group, in opposition to the NWC, that coalesced into the XYC, so Ermatinger's first loyalties were to that firm (Lamb 1970, 478, 495). His abilities must have been recognized quickly, for at the NWC partners' meeting in 1805 he was one of three clerks offered a future partnership, to commence with Outfit 1808 (Wallace 1934, 205). He was in charge at Fort Alexander in 1805–06, and continued at the Post of Lac Ouinipique in 1806–07 (Wallace 1934, 438); Nelson states that he wintered near Drunken Lake, in the eastern hinterland of Lake Winnipeg, in that season. Nelson spoke of him with affection, and was grateful to him for introducing him to serious reading and lending him his own books.

Ermatinger left the Northwest in 1807, a year before his partnership was to have commenced, apparently in an amicable manner, though Nelson believed that he had been undeservedly laid off. The minutes of the 1808 NWC partners' meeting, in recording the admission of Kenneth McKenzie and Archibald McLellan as partners, added "Mr McKenzies Share, by Agreement with him to be burdened with the Consideration allowed to Mr Ermatinger by the Concern last Year"; this was perhaps a termination bonus (Wallace 1934, 254). Ermatinger established himself as an independent trader at Sault Ste Marie, on the American side; sold out to the American Fur Company in 1827, and retired to Longue-Pointe, near Montreal, where he died in 1833 (Momryk 1987).

Ermatinger's Indigenous wife was known as Charlotte; her surname or Indigenous name is given as "Mannanowe" in the baptismal records for their four eldest children, and as "Cattoonalutté" or "Cawoonalutté" in the records of her own baptism and marriage in 1832 at Christ Church, Montreal. Her baptismal record calls her "of the Indian country," and gives her birthdate as 3 December 1792, which is far too late, as her eldest child was born in 1800. The first four Ermatinger children were baptized by George Jenkins, chaplain to the Montreal garrison, in July and August 1815. One of them, George, born in 1806, was given a name that does not occur elsewhere in the Ermatinger family; perhaps it was in honour of George Nelson himself.

FARQUHARSON OR FERGUSON, ALEXANDER: NWC clerk; Alexander Ferguson was apprenticed to the NWC for 7 years, 16 April 1798 (Beek Repertoire, ANQ-M, No. 1206). Alexander Ferguson, clerk, is in the 1798 NWC roster, with eight years to serve from 1797 (PAC Report 1939, 54), and in 1799 he was in Fort Dauphin department, wages 120 livres (Masson 1960, 1:62). These small wages are those of an apprentice clerk. Daniel Williams Harmon, who met him at

Grand Portage in 1800 and was also stationed at Fort Dauphin, says of him "Mr Ferguson is of Irish extraction, but was born in Canada, and he like most of his countrymen is always laying what he thinks deep plans or in other words builds castles in the air ... he has a tolerable good education & blessed with good natural parts. However he is too volitile to listen to sound reason" (Lamb 1957, 23, 28–9, 31, 68, 83; see also Gates 1965, index). "Farquharson" was still in Fort Dauphin department in 1804–05 (Lamb 1957, 85–6), but is not in the 1805 list. In summer 1806 he was at Bas de la Rivière (Coues 1965, 277), and for the ensuing season he was assigned to Lake Winnipeg (Wallace 1934, 220). Nelson says that he wintered at Tête-au-Brochet in 1805–06 and 1806–07. His wife gave birth to a baby boy at Fort Alexander on 21 June 1808; and Ferguson, who may have been going to winter in the upper part of Winnipeg River that year, sent for his wife and two children on 9 September (*Nelson Journals*). No trace of him has been found in the fur trade literature after this, and he probably soon retired.

FRASER, MR —: NWC clerk; Mr Fraser was apparently in charge at Cumberland House in summer 1819, until George Nelson arrived to take over on September 9. Fraser then proceeded to his winter assignment, which is unspecified (*Nelson Journals*). Nelson does not give his first name, but he must be Simon Fraser, junior, a clerk, who joined the NWC in 1817, at a salary of 480 livres, and was charged for "sundries" at English River in 1819 and 1820 (HBCA, F.4/32, 378).

FROBISHER, BENJAMIN: NWC clerk and partner; two men named Benjamin Frobisher were associated with the NWC at about the same time. One, Benjamin Joseph Frobisher (1782–1821), was a son of Joseph Frobisher, one of the founders of the company; he worked briefly in the NWC's Montreal office, but was never in the Northwest, and died in Lower Canada. The other, the fur trader, was a native of York, England, probably a son of Joseph's brother Nathaniel, who was a bookseller there. The *Dictionary of Canadian Biography* account of Benjamin Frobisher unfortunately combined information about the two men (the conflation error was first made by Wallace 1934, 446), and its author, Fernand Ouellet, was driven to the conclusion that the whole account of the fur trader's capture, escape, and death was a hoax. In fact, the story is perfectly true (for a brief summary see p. 297). The account of it by Samuel H. Wilcocke, printed in Masson 1960, 2:179–226, makes liberal use of original documents, including the evidently tattered journal that Frobisher kept during his escape.

   The following facts are known about the career of Benjamin Frobisher, the fur trader. He was engaged by the NWC as a clerk on 10 May 1799, for six years (Beek Repertoire, ANQ-M, Document No. 1315). He was listed in the Lake

Winnipeg department, wages 120 livres (an apprentice clerk's salary), in the 1799 roster of NWC clerks and partners (Masson 1960, 1:64). In the *1805 list*, he appears as B. Frobisher, *commis* [clerk], Rivière au Rat department, and in 1806 he was a clerk in the Fort Dauphin department (Wallace 1934, 220). On 6 June 1807, Peter Fidler, en route from Cumberland House to Reindeer Lake, met "Mr Frobisher & Cartie the Guide [Joseph Cartier, the long-time English River guide] with 5 Canoes in the Woody Lake, just south of Frog Portage" (HBCA, E.3/3). *1811–21 Accounts*: charged for sundries at Athabasca, 1812–13, and at English River, 1817–20. Wages 1200 livres in each year 1813–16, but not in 1817 or later, suggesting that his partnership in the NWC began with the Fort William meeting of 1816.

GRANT, FRANCIS: NWC clerk; Nelson met Grant on the route between Rainy Lake and Fort William, 6 July 1822. Grant was in charge of four canoes of provisions, heading for Norway House. *1811–21 Accounts*: credit balance of 67 livres 15 sous, 1811; charged for "sundries" at Lac la Pluie, 1812–16, 1818–19, in the Petty Ledger, 1817–20, and at Michipicoten, 1817; salary 350 livres (1812–16), 600 livres (1818), 720 livres (1818); 840 livres (1819); 960 livres (1820–21) (HBCA, F.4/32, 426).

HALCRO, JOSHUA: NWC clerk; Joshua Halcro, son of William Halcro and Jannet Flett, was baptized at Orphir, Orkney, on 8 August 1787. Normally an Orkneyman would have entered the fur trade with the HBC (the Montreal companies did not recruit in the Orkneys), but he is first heard of as an XYC clerk, who was sent from Cumberland House on 22 June 1805 as a passenger in a canoe for Kaministiquia (Coues 1965, 280, 569, citing David Thompson journals). As with others sent out in 1805, Halcro's contract had probably ended, but he must have been rehired at Fort William, as David Thompson saw him at Bas de la Rivière with the Fort Dauphin outward canoes on 21 June 1806, too early in the year to have come in from Montreal (Coues 1965, 280). In 1806 he was assigned to Fort Dauphin (Wallace 1934, 220). *1811–21 Accounts*: Joshua Halcro, credit balance of 751 livres 3 sous in 1811; charges in Petty Ledger 1811–13, 1818, 1820; at Fort Dauphin, 1812–13, and at English River, 1813–18; also 2,000 livres "to Cash in London" (probably a payment for his family in Orkney); salary 1,200 livres (1812–13), 1800 livres (1821) (HBCA F.4/32, 460). Some details of Halcro's 1811–21 account are puzzling, as they seem to show that he was in English River during several years when he was not receiving a salary from the NWC. From the *Nelson Journals* we know that Halcro was in charge of a post at Falle-au-Perdrix (Partridge Crop), just west of Lake St Martin, for the Fort Dauphin department, in 1808–09, 1809–10 and 1810–11.

While Nelson was at Dauphin River, he tried to stay in communication with Halcro regarding the Indigenous people who had taken debt from him, to prevent debt being taken at both posts. Halcro married his country wife, Françoise Laurain, in a church ceremony at Red River in 1823. She must have been a daughter of the Lake Winnipeg clerk and interpreter, Joseph Lorrain; this would explain why Baptiste Richard, brother of the younger François Richard (who at one point was married to another of Lorrain's daughters), was going to visit "Halcro's wife, his sister" in the winter of 1810. Thus, Halcro's relationship with Françoise had lasted for at least thirteen years before they had the opportunity to marry in a church. Following the ceremony, Halcro went home to Orkney, intending to send for his wife, but he died there before he could do so. Françoise, now left without support, was pressed to marry the former NWC partner John Stuart (now a chief factor in the HBC), and she reluctantly agreed, but regretted it at once, and the arrangement quickly came to an end (Van Kirk 1980, 122).

HENRY, ROBERT: NWC clerk and partner; see Ennals 1985 for a biography, which however is in error about Henry's parentage, and dates his entry into the NWC in 1806, twelve years too late. He was actually a brother of Alexander Henry the younger, NWC partner, and a nephew of the Montreal fur trader Alexander Henry the elder (Gough 1988, xix–xx). The engagement of "Robert Henry aged 16 years pr Alexr Henry his Uncle to Northwest Company," on 1 May 1794, is in the Beek Repertoire, ANQ-M. In 1810 Henry's country wife was a daughter of the Lake Winnipeg freeman Charles Racette, who went to visit him in English River. She was presumably the mother of three children of Robert Henry, born "in the Indian country," who were baptized at St Gabriel Street Church, Montreal: Charles (age 10, on 13 October 1806; perhaps named for his grandfather Charles Racette); Alexander (age 6, on 11 November 1811); and William (age 6, on 17 October 1815). This woman probably did not accompany her husband when he left the fur country, as Henry married a widow, Christine Farrand (sister of the NWC partner Angus Bethune), in 1817. Robert Henry, clerk, is listed in English River in the NWC Arrangements for 1799 (Masson 1960, 1:62) and 1806 (Wallace 1934, 219). He was considered for a partnership in 1807, when another clerk was chosen by a vote of the partners; but he had become a partner by 1810 (Wallace 1934, 249, 264). All the references to the NWC clerk "Mr Henry" in HBC sources for the Churchill district probably refer to Robert Henry, who spent most of his career, from 1794 to 1810, in the English River department (HBCA, B.166/a/2, 9 August 1794; E.3/3, 21 July 1807; Johnson 1967, 44 n1, 228 n 1).

HESSE, CHARLES: NWC clerk; Charles Hesse was stationed at Grand Portage in 1799, wages 600 livres (Masson 1960, 1:66). Chs. Hess, contract 28 May 1801 as "clerk in the North-West" (Beek Repertoire, ANQ-M, Document No. 1557). He was with Alexander Henry at Pembina, Lower Red River department, in 1803–04, and in 1804–05 he was placed at Turtle or Salt River to oppose the XYC there. He had a wife of whom he was jealous, and on 26 November 1803 he cut her badly on the head with a cutlass (Coues 1965, 228–9, 251, 259). *1805 list*: Charles Hesse, Lower Red River department, debt 953 livres 12 sous, wages 100 livres as clerk & summer man, 1 yr left on contract. *1811–21 account*: opens 1816 with "Balance from B[ad] & D[oubtful] Debts," 956 livres 9 sous; charged for sundries at Red River, 1816–20, and in Petty Ledger, 1817–20; wages 600 livres, 1816–17; 1,200 livres for "18 months," 1818; 600 livres, 1819–21 (HBCA, F.4/32, 446). This account shows that Hesse had not been engaged by the NWC for several years prior to 1815–16, probably remaining in the Northwest as a freeman. Peter Fidler, in his census of "Free Canadians ... at present residing in the River February 1814," lists "C. Hess" and his wife, but no children (HBCA, B.235/a/3, fo. 29d). In the fall of 1815, Charles Hesse was threatening Indigenous men who had dealings with the Red River colony (Halkett 1817, Appendix p. lx).

In March 1816 Hesse was one of the NWC men present at Pembina when it was captured by the Lord Selkirk's mercenaries (Coues 1965, 961). In October 1818, after the death of Duncan McDougall, John McBean, the NWC partner in charge at Lower Red River, sent Hesse to take over command at Fort Alexander. George Nelson, at Tête-au-Brochet, was offended not to hear from Hesse immediately, and when he did eventually receive a letter, it was written in such courtly style that Nelson scoffed at it as "in the true Spanish Stile, i.e. of lovers" (*Nelson Journals*, 22 January 1819). In Nelson's *Reminiscences* is a long anecdote involving Charles Hesse, whom he described as wintering at "one of the outposts in Swan River" in 1811–12, "a tall, handsome, well made man & as active as a Squirrel. – He was also a good trader." Nelson calls him a "Creole," that is, a man of mixed race. Hesse refused to give an Indigenous man called The Lodge some ammunition, which The Lodge resented, and sometime later, in February, The Lodge decoyed two of Hesse's men, Lamoureux and Gauselin, to his tent, and murdered them (*Nelson Reminiscences*, 282). Nelson also states that he saw an account of the adventures of Charles Hesse in "The Boston Pearl, about 1833 or 34," in which Hesse laid claim to a brave fight with a bear, which was actually the deed of an Indigenous man named Bourassa (*Reminiscences*, 283). *The Boston Pearl and Literary Gazette* was a weekly periodical; issues available at the ProQuest database of American Periodicals begin with vol. 4 no. 9, 8 November 1834. The issue that Nelson saw was probably earlier than this; I have not located it. Charles Hesse died in St Louis, Missouri, aged about 54, and was buried by Catholic rites on 20 April 1837 (burial register of St Louis Cathedral; images at ancestry.com).

KENNEDY, ALEXANDER: NWC clerk; Alexander Kennedy contracted as an inden-
tured servant with John Ogilvie, "to Serve in the upper or Indian Countries
for the term of five years," 11 April 1791 (Beek Repertoire, ANQ-M, Document
No. 22 of 1791). Since John Ogilvy was one of the founders of the XYC, this
is probably the Mr Kennedy of the "New Company" who was in Athabasca
in 1802–05, according to Peter Fidler's Nottingham House journals (HBCA,
B.39/a/2, B.39/a/5ᵇ). He is not in the *1805 list*, which does not include the Athabasca department; and he is not mentioned in the NWC's arrangements for 1806
(Wallace 1934, 219–21). *1811–21 Accounts*: Alexander Kennedy, credit balance
of 1,102 livres 19 sous in 1811; charged for sundries at Lake Winnipeg, 1812–
14; at Red River, 1814–16; and at Sault Ste Marie, 1816–18; salary, 960 livres
(1812–16), 1,200 livres (1817), 720 livres (1819). He left the company in 1818,
with a credit balance of 4,313 livres 15 sous, equivalent to about £360 Halifax
currency (HBCA, F.4/32, 485). Nelson says that Mr. Kennedy was in charge of
a post at Drunken Lake "near River Blanche," i.e. the upper Winnipeg River, in
1809–10 (*Nelson Journals*; this Drunken Lake is unidentified). He was at Portage de l'Île in 1813–14, whence he wrote a badly spelled letter to John Dougald
Cameron, the partner in charge of the department, on 28 March 1814 (Selkirk
Papers, 8,825–8). Another Alexander Kennedy, a contemporary of this man,
had a long and distinguished career with the HBC's York Factory establishment,
starting in 1798; see HBCA Biographical Sheets. This man came into contact
with the NWC's Lake Winnipeg operations when he brought an outfit to another
Drunken (Brandy) Lake (now Wrong Lake on the Poplar River), in 1807–08.

LA CROIX, PAUL: NWC clerk; Paul La Croix, of Lachine, contract 5 March 1793
with Myer Michaels & Co, to go to the Mississippi; and contract 23 December
1801, "engagement" with McTavish, Frobisher & Co. (ANQ *Rapport* 1942–43,
322; 1943–4, 444). Not in 1805 list, but Nelson mentions him on 7 March 1806
as visiting Mr. Ducharme's house on upper Winnipeg River, from "his house at
six days journey from here" (*Nelson Journals*). A clerk in the 1806 arrangements
for Lake Winnipeg (Wallace 1934, 220). In a letter to Duncan Cameron, dated
Scabitchewine (near the present Ear Falls, Ontario), 9 October 1808, the NWC
clerk Æneas McDonell, who was assigned to Monontagué, the next department
to the east, pointed out difficulties with La Croix advancing credits to natives
who were also trading with McDonell (Selkirk Papers, 9004–5). La Croix is not
mentioned in the *1811–21 Accounts*, and had probably retired. He may reason-
ably be identified with Paul-Joseph Lacroix (1778–1858), son of an independent
trader, Paul Lacroix (1740–1823), who had licences to take goods to Michilimackinac in the 1770s, but disappears from the lists after 1780 (LAC, RG4, B28,
vol. 113: 1219–26; vol. 115: 2244, 2269, 2273).

LAMAR, SÉRAPHIN: NWC clerk; Séraphin François Lamarre, son of Seraphim, was born 15 December 1765, and baptized the same day at Longueuil, Canada (church register). Séraphin Lamare, of Montreal, contract 21 June 1791 with Levy Solomon to go to Michilimackinac; contract 2 April 1800, "engagement" with McTavish, Frobisher & Co. (ANQ *Rapport* 1942–43, 297; 1943–4, 407). "Seriphin," a clerk, was in the same canoe brigade as Daniel Williams Harmon, from Montreal to Grand Portage in May–June 1800 (Lamb 1957, 19). He was first posted to the Fond du Lac district, where he is often mentioned in John Sayer's Snake River (Wisconsin) journal, 1804–05, sometimes as "Mr La Mar" and sometimes as "Seraphin" (Birk 1987). *1805 list*: Seraphin Lamare, clerk, Fond du Lac; no wages or balance given. He appears as "Su: L Mar," clerk, Folle Avoine department, in the NWC arrangements for 1806–07 (Wallace 1934, 221). Séraphin Lamar came to the Lake Winnipeg department in 1808, and on 3 September he married a woman of the country, apparently a daughter of the interpreter Joseph Lorrain. Lamar was in charge of a post at Rivière-aux-Morts in 1808–09 and 1809–10 (*Nelson Journals*). *1811–21 Accounts*: Seraphin La Mar, credit balance of 1002 livres 13 sous in 1811; charged with "sundries" at Lake Winnipeg, 1812–13, and at Red River, 1814–16, 1818. He retired in 1817, with a credit balance of 2648 livres 7 sous (about £221 Halifax). The account says that he "Died in Montreal 1818" (HBCA, F.4/32, 583). Séraphin Lamar was heavily involved in the NWC's campaign to destroy the Red River colony in 1815–16, and is frequently mentioned in the accounts of what happened, though he was not one of the most belligerent. He was one of the NWC people tried for the murder of Robert Semple, at York in October 1818, as an accessory before and after the fact (Amos 1820, 31). There are a number of letters to and from him in the Selkirk Papers.

LEMIRE: A freeman, whom Nelson met at Grand Rapids on 1 September 1819, accompanying an HBC interpreter named Turner to Swan River; this man gave Nelson a misleading account (though he may have thought it was true) about what had been done with the NWC partners captured by Governor Williams the previous June. Nelson's party took Lemire as far as Lac Bourbon, where his friend Montreuil was waiting.

LORRIN, JOSEPH: Also Laurent, Lorain, Lorin, Lorrain. NWC trader and interpreter, Lake Winnipeg; Lorrin is interesting, not so much for his own achievements, as for how his family connections illustrate a group in fur trade society that lived in the "middle ground" between the Company proprietors and the First Nations traders. By their connections with both groups, they created some security and prosperity for themselves and their families.

Nelson states that Lorrin was in the Northwest at the time of the smallpox epidemic (1779–82), and was one of those who told Nelson stories of the suffering among the Indigenous people (*Sorel Journal*, 61). Joseph Laurent or Lorin, interpreter, is in the 1798 NWC roster, in Lac Ouinipique department, with one year to serve from 1797, and Joseph Laurent is in the 1799 NWC roster for the same department, wages 1,000 livres, a large amount consistent with the status of interpreter. Jos: Lorin, Lake Winnipeg department, is in the 1805 post-fusion NWC list, wages 600 livres, credit 76 livres 15 sous; and he is listed as interpreter, Lac Ouinipique, in the NWC arrangements for 1806 (PAC *Report* 1939, 54; Masson 1960, 1:64; MS 472, MASS 2357.31, p. 23 [Masson Collection], McGill University Libraries, Rare Books and Special Collections Division; Wallace 1934, 220). William McKay's Cross Lake journal, 1805–06, shows that Lorrain was wintering with Venables, an unsatisfactory clerk whose career was short, at Pike River in that year (LAC, MG 19 C1 vol. 9, 13 September 1805; 3 February, 21 March 1806). Lorrin and Nelson were together at Fort Alexander in the summer of 1808, and Lorrain was assigned to go with Alexander Campbell to Grand Rapid in 1808–09. In the fall of 1818, "Old Lorrin" was sent to take charge of a post called "the Grd Equisitte," on the upper part of Winnipeg River (*Nelson Journals*). *1811–21 Accounts*: Joseph "Laurent," opening credit balance, 291 livres 14 sous by his last year, 1820–21, this had swollen to 4,304 livres 16 sous (almost £360 currency). He was regularly charged for sundries at Lake Winnipeg, confirming that he remained in the department, and was paid wages of 600 livres per annum for the years ending July 1812 to 1818; 900 livres in 1818–19; 1,000 livres in 1819–20; and "half wages" of 500 livres in 1820–21. Unusual items in his account are a charge for repairing his watch – very few in the Northwest would have owned such a thing – and a contribution of 60 livres towards the cost of building a church in Glengarry, presumably St Raphael's, the first Catholic church in Upper Canada. (HBCA, F.4/32, 586). The large credit balance that built up in his account is surely a sign that his bourgeois treated him favourably in this period, and that he could save most of his wages.

See the entry for Charles Racette, below, for Nelson's account of a practical joke played on Lorrin and Racette, with the connivance of the bourgeois, William McKay.

The most interesting thing about Joseph Lorrin was his daughters and the marriages they made. One of the Mashkiegon trading men on the lake, known to Nelson as Le Gendre or Son-in-Law, was called this because he was Lorrin's son-in-law; thus, one of Lorrin's daughters was the wife of one of the most prominent hunters in the department. Another daughter was married to François Richard, junior, by 1807, but in the spring of 1810 Lorrin took her from Richard, and "donnée'd" her to Duncan Cameron himself, the bourgeois for the district. This woman's name was apparently Susan, as appears from a letter that Duncan Cameron wrote in 1814 to John Dougald Cameron, his fellow clansman and protégé, now in charge at Fort Alexander: "Thousands of Compliments and Kisses from me & Susan to the Belle Soeure, Children & all the old mans family" (Selkirk Papers, 8852). The "old man" was probably Joseph Lorrin. A third daughter, apparently, was the woman who married the NWC clerk Séraphin Lamar on 18 September 1808; for in a letter to Dougald Cameron in 1815, Lamar sent love to "Pere Laurain." In another letter of the same date to Duncan Cameron at Fort Gibraltar, Lamar included greetings to Susanne and the two little girls (Selkirk Papers, 8811–12, 8813–15). Françoise Laurent, wife of the NWC clerk Joshua Halcro, was probably a fourth daughter. With these marriages, Lorrin ensured that he and his family had friends at all useful levels of the fur trade hierarchy.

Even such elaborate family connections were not enough to protect Lorrin from harm. Nelson's Canoe Journal of 1822 states that "Poor old Lorain" had been killed about two years previously, at "Mr McMurrays house at Grande Equierre," a minor trading establishment on Winnipeg River. This incident must have happened midway through the season of 1820–21, and explains why Lorrin's account for that year was credited with only half wages (see above). Lorrin's son confronted his father's murderer at Bas de la Rivière the following spring, and stabbed him to death.

The son was probably Joseph Laurent Jr, whose account also appears in the *1811–21 Accounts* (HBCA, F.4/32, 595). It begins in the year 1815–16, when he was credited with 9 months' wages at Red River, 262 livres 10 sous, plus 100 livres for "services rendered." He was charged for sundries in the Red River Book, 1817, and had wages of 350 livres in 1817 and 1818. In 1819 his wages were raised to 450 livres, and in 1820–21 to 500 livres. In 1818 he was charged for "Sundries p Montreal Book," and in 1819 sundries p Fort William Book and St Maries Book, besides "Cash paid him in Montreal"; and sundries at Lake Winnipeg in 1819–21. The items showing travel to Montreal and back in 1818–19 must reflect the younger Lorrin's appearance at the trial of Semple's accused murderers at York, Upper Canada in October 1818. He testified, in French, that he had been in charge of a cart with pemmican that had got past the site of the Seven Oaks confrontation, on 19 June 1816, before the shooting started; he took refuge under his cart (Amos 1820, 154–5). The extra payment of 100 livres for "services rendered" in this year may have been a reward from the NWC for his presence at Seven Oaks, where he may have been more involved in the fighting than he admitted. His killing of the Indigenous man on Winnipeg River, though not unusual as retaliation for his father's murder, would have left him vulnerable to a further round of revenge, and he may not have survived long. There is no evidence that he left descendants in the Northwest.

MCBEAN, JOHN: NWC partner; John McBean engaged with Forsyth, Richardson & Co (the Montreal agents of the XYC) on 10 October 1800, to serve as a clerk in the Northwest for five years (Beek Repertoire, ANQ-M, Document No. 1489). Wallace 1934, 461, has a brief biography, which states that he entered the fur trade by 1804; became an NWC partner about 1816; was made a chief factor in the HBC after the union of the two companies in 1821; and retired to Canada in 1836. Nelson's 1818–19 journal tells us that McBean had been in charge at The Pic on Lake Superior when Nelson was there in 1813–15. He was in charge of Lower Red River department in 1818–19, when he sent Charles Hesse to replace the deceased Duncan McDougall at Fort Alexander.

MACDONELL OR MCDONALD, ALEXANDER: NWC clerk and partner; known as Alexander Macdonell "Greenfield," he was a member of a large Roman Catholic family from the Glengarry estate in the Scottish Highlands. Many of the Glengarry Macdonells had emigrated to the Mohawk valley of the colony of New York in the early 1770s, and, at the outbreak of the American Revolution, they chose the British side and made their way to Canada as Loyalists. The Greenfield branch did not come to Canada until 1792, direct from Scotland, to join the so-called Glengarry Settlement, in the easternmost part of what shortly became Upper Canada. The family was deeply involved in affairs in the Northwest. Members included John Macdonell "Le Prêtre," the NWC partner; his brother Miles Macdonell, who became the first Governor of Assiniboia, Lord Selkirk's Red River Settlement; and Æneas Macdonell, the NWC clerk who was killed at Eagle Lake in 1809. A distant cousin of John Macdonell was the XYC and NWC partner John McDonald "le Borgne."

Alexander Macdonell, contract with McTavish, Frobisher & Co, 12 March 1803, as apprentice clerk in the North West trade for seven years (Beek Repertoire, ANQ-M, Document No. 1711). His brother Æneas McDonell had signed a similar contract four days earlier. *1805 list*: Alexandre McDonald, Lac Ouinipique, summer man; no debt, no wages. *1811–21 Accounts*: credit balance of 172 livres 2 sous in 1811; sundries per Petty Ledger, 1811–20; in Red River book, 1812–18; English River Book 1818–19, 1821; Fort des Prairies Book, 1819; Fort William Book, 1820; Lake Winnipeg Book, 1820; wages 1,200 livres 1812–14; then credits paid by McTavish & Co., showing that he became a partner in the NWC in 1814. Other charges: 1812, "cash paid his Father," 300 livres; 1813, "cash paid his Brother Duncan," 360 livres; 1814, "2 Buff[alo] Robes sent his father," 48 livres; and 1815, "To McTavish McGillivray's & Co," 1,581 livres – probably a payment towards the purchase of his share in the NWC (HBCA, F.4/32, 715). Nelson states that Alexander Macdonell, clerk, wintered at Pigeon River in 1807–08 and 1808–09 (*Nelson Journals*). According to Nelson's

Reminiscences, p. 227, Macdonell was sent to Red River for the season of 1809–10, and the Grand Ledger accounts show that he remained there until 1818. He visited Duncan Cameron at Fort Alexander for Christmas in 1811, and George Nelson accompanied him back to Red River for a visit (*Nelson Letters*, 9/17 February 1812). In the spring of 1816, Alexander Macdonell was responsible for organizing the Métis force intended to attack the Red River colony, one section of which took part in the incident at Seven Oaks in which 22 HBC men and colonists were killed. He published his own account of the events at Red River, but did not continue in the fur trade following the coalition in 1821. He was twice elected to the Legislative Assembly of Upper Canada, served as sheriff of the Ottawa District, and died in 1835 (Wallace 1934, 465).

MCDONALD, JOHN: XYC and NWC partner; known as "le Borgne" (the one-eyed); see Brown 1987b, for a biography. Nelson's account of his season of 1804–05 shows that McDonald was in charge of the XYC's operations in Upper Red River (now, the upper Assiniboine, where most of the fur companies' pemmican came from). Nelson also states that McDonald was a relation of John Macdonell, known as "le Prêtre," a NWC partner who spent much of his career in charge of his Company's activities in Upper Red River (for him see Mays 1987). John McDonald "le Borgne" was a source of anxiety for Nelson during his years at Dauphin River, for McDonald, then in charge of the Fort Dauphin department, regarded Nelson's Dauphin River post as an encroachment on McDonald's own territory. In January 1808, McDonald met the HBC's Peter Fidler, and provided him with a sketch of the lakes and rivers in the Fort Dauphin department, probably the first time that any information about that part of the fur country had reached the HBC's hands (HBCA, E.3/3, fo. 48).

MCKAY, WILLIAM: NWC partner; published information about William McKay, the NWC partner who was in charge of the Lake Winnipeg department from 1796 to 1807, consists of a short biographical note in Wallace 1934, 474, and a biography by Robert S. Allen 1987. The latter account concentrates mainly on McKay's life after he retired from the fur trade in 1807, and in particular his activities during the War of 1812–14. Much more has been discovered, however. This account supplements the published information with fuller details about his fur trade career.

William McKay was the eldest son of Donald McKay and Elspeth Kennedy, from Achness in Sutherlandshire, Scotland, who came to Canada with their six children (Wallace 1934, 474; McKay 1892), and settled in Charlottenburgh township, part of the Glengarry settlement. William is said to have been born in 1772. He and his next brother, Alexander, both entered the fur trade. Two surviving letters of William's, and his Cross Lake journal of 1805–06, are full of misspellings, consistent with the fact that he grew up in a frontier settlement, where schooling was not yet on a firm basis. In one of these letters, written to Simon McTavish in 1794, William McKay gives some information about his early career. He had first traded in the Mississippi River valley, until McTavish recruited him for the Northwest, and he was assigned to the English River department as a clerk (HBCA, F.3/1, 142). Thus he was the "Mr McKay" or "Mr Mackie" who is mentioned in a number of HBC records referring to the Churchill River trade at this time (Tyrrell 1934, 482–3; and HBC's Chatham House journal, HBCA, B.32/a/1, for McKay's activities in 1791–92). In the fall of 1794, McKay was transferred to the Red River department, to reinforce the NWC as it struggled to cope with an unexpected influx of opposition traders in that region. He superseded another less aggressive trader at Portage la Prairie, and was reported to have done pretty well against his opponents (HBCA, B.22/a/2).

In the spring of 1795 McKay's old bourgeois in Rat River, Robert Thomson, was shot and killed by an Indigenous man at his post,[1] and McKay was sent back to the district to take charge. No partner of the NWC had been murdered before, and when the news reached the partners' meeting at Grand Portage, they determined not to let the deed go unpunished. The supposed murderers usually traded directly with the HBC posts on the Bay, and so letters were sent to Joseph Colen and Thomas Stayner, the HBC's chiefs at York Factory and Churchill Fort, respectively, asking for their assistance in arresting them.[2] Colen had not received his copy of the letter as late as February 1796, when Stayner told him of it; and he hesitated to act. On 16 June 1796, a canoe from inland brought to York a Canadian, Joseph Le Rocher, who said that he wished to be hired by the HBC. Colen suspected that he was trying to escape a large debt with the NWC, which so many voyageurs had, but hired him conditionally. Three days later, Le Rocher attempted to kill an Indigenous man on the plantation, but was prevented; and Colen realized that the intended victim was one of those whom the NWC letter had accused of Thomson's murder. Le Rocher was sent to an inland post after this, but a few weeks later was back at York, and succeeded in stabbing an Indigenous man, though not fatally. Colen and his officers now realized that Le Rocher was in fact an assassin, sent by the NWC to kill Robert Thomson's murderers. He was again sent inland, this time carefully supervised,

1 HBCA, B.83/a/1, 4 June 1795; B.178/a/1, 2 June 1795. The copy of David Thompson's map in the National Archives, Kew, labels the narrows of Lake Ooskootim (now Wuskwatim Lake) "Here Mr Robt Thompson was killed." I am grateful to Andreas Korsos and David Malaher for this information.

2 Colen's copy of the letter from the NWC proprietors, dated at Grand Portage, 27 July 1795, was copied into his correspondence book (HBCA, B.239/b/57, fos. 12d–13).

and was handed over to the NWC's William McKay when he arrived at Jack River to take up his winter station in September 1796 (HBCA, B.239/a/99, 16, 19 June; 7, 17 July; and fo. 19d; and Johnson 1967, 64 n).

It is not clear that Thomson's murderers were pursued further, or ever punished, but when some Indigenous men committed another murder in the English River department in the winter of 1795–96, William McKay was determined not to let that pass. He and his fellow NWC officers happened to be at Cumberland House on 1 June 1796, when the two murderers arrived, soon realizing their mistake. McKay himself shot one of them dead as he tried to flee in his canoe, while the other was caught and summarily hanged from the nearest tree.[3] This deed of McKay's became well known in the Northwest, and in later years he could easily stir fear in other Indigenous people by referring to it. Thus, in the fall of 1797, McKay threatened to hang anyone who dared to trade with his HBC rival at Pike River, directing them to go to the NWC post at Poplar River instead (McKay to John Cameron, Pike River 3 January 1798: Selkirk Papers, 8527–8). Three years later, Thomas Vincent, the HBC trader at Bas de la Rivière, heard that McKay had sent word to all the natives round about that he would shoot or hang any who attempted to enter the HBC post there (Lytwyn 1986, 100, citing HBCA, B.4/a/1, fo. 4d). While telling the tale of a native called The Lodge, who had murdered two voyageurs in the Fort Dauphin department about 1810, Nelson describes his capture, and notes that the bourgeois of the department "instead of hanging him immediately as did Mr. McKay, decided upon taking him to Montreal" (*Reminiscences*, 282–4).

William McKay became a partner in the NWC for a one forty-sixth share in July 1796.[4] The Lake Winnipeg district, following the end of the Company's agreement with Lesieur and Fraser, had just been reorganized into a regular department, and McKay was placed in charge of it.[5] At first he located himself at the northern end of the department, near where he had traded in the early 1790s, and would know his former customers and his HBC rivals. Thus, he wintered at Jack or Pike River in 1796–97 and 1797–98, and in 1798–99 moved to Cross Lake; in the first season he was opposed by the HBC's Henry Hallett, and in the next two by Charles Isham (Johnson 1967, 96 n 2; 123 n 1; 171 n 1). In 1799–1800 and 1800–01, he moved to the south end of his department, to Bas de la Rivière, probably in

---

3 Johnson (1967, 40 fn), citing HBCA, B.49/a/27[b], Peter Fidler's rough copy journal at Cumberland House. The victim of the murder was "a Canadian," but he is not otherwise identified. Fidler gives a chilling account of the episode and its effect on the Indigenous people who witnessed it.

4 On 13 July (HBCA, E.4½6, fo. 1d, 7d) or 5 July 1796 (HBCA, Copy No. 75)].

5 He was in charge of the Lake Winnipeg department in 1798 and 1799 (PAC *Report* 1939, 55; Masson 1960, 1:64).

response to the HBC traders who had settled there (HBCA, B.4/a/3, 10 June, 23 &
25 August 1799; B.4/a/4, 21 & 25 August 1800). There is no specific information
about where McKay wintered in the next few seasons, but he probably remained
in charge of the district. He was scheduled to go on furlough in 1801, but did not
do so, and was persuaded in 1802 and again in 1803 to delay further, probably
because of increased pressure by the XYC opposition. He finally went down to
Montreal in 1804–05, Alexander Fraser taking over the Lake Winnipeg department for that year (Wallace 1934, 208–9; *Sorel Journal*, see p. 6 of this book).
McKay then returned to the department for two more seasons. In 1805–06 he was
again at Cross Lake; various writers have pointed out that the unsigned journal
for this season, in the Masson collection at LAC, must have been kept by him (LAC,
MG 19 C1 vol. 9). He wintered at Bas de la Rivière in 1806–07, and at the end of
that season he retired to Canada (Lamb 1957, 104; Nelson, *Reminiscences*).

William McKay had at least four children, born from relationships with
Indigenous or mixed-race women. Two daughters, aged seven and five, were
baptized at Williamstown, Upper Canada, in 1800. Their mother's name is
unknown, but their births had occurred while McKay was in the Rat River
district, so she was probably an Indigenous woman of that country. Later, he
made a country marriage with Josette Latour, probably the daughter of an old
Winnipeg River trader, Charles Latour; two children of theirs were Alexander
William McKay, born about 1802, and Mary McKay, who married the NWC
clerk, Charles McKenzie.[6]

Following his retirement to Montreal in 1807, McKay married Eliza David-
son, a member of a prominent Montreal family. He served as one of the "Agents"
or operating officers for the NWC at Montreal, and threw himself into militia
affairs. During the War of 1812 he assisted with the transportation of messages
and provisions for the military on the Great Lakes, using NWC resources, and led
a successful recapture of the fur trade village of Prairie du Chien on the Mississippi. He became superintendent of the Indian Department in 1830, and died in
the cholera epidemic of 1832.

MCKENZIE, RODERICK: NWC apprentice clerk; He began his service in 1815
(HBCA, F.4/32, 745). He was a mixed-race son of Daniel McKenzie, the NWC

6 See John Bethune's register at Williamstown, 21 October 1800, for baptisms of Jenny
McKay (aged 7) and Cecilia Isabella McKay (aged 5), children of William McKay Esq. N.W.
Company, born in the "Indian Country" [the Northwest] (LAC, MG. 9/D7/14, vol. 1; micro-
film C-3030); St Gabriel Street (Montreal) Presbyterian register, 18 July 1809, for baptism of
Alexander William McKay, son of William McKay of Montreal, Esq., and a woman of the
"Indian country"; Arthur (1978) for Charles McKenzie's wife. After McKay retired, Josette
Latour married another NWC partner, John Haldane.

partner who was induced to sell Fort William and its stock to Lord Selkirk, under duress, in 1816. A letter from Roderick to his brother George McKenzie shows him as formally educated but with the enthusiasms of a plainsman (Selkirk Papers, 8571–3). George Nelson was exercised when, after the death of Duncan McDougall at Fort Alexander in October 1818, Roderick McKenzie was not allowed to take over the post, but was instead assigned to spend the rest of the season at either Nelson's or John Crebassa's post. Nelson believed that he had been superseded because he was "a brulée" (a Métis), but it later emerged that he had been having an affair with the wife of a voyageur who was absent giving testimony in Canada. This man was probably either Roderick McKenzie (A) or (B), both mixed-race clerks who were taken over by the HBC in 1821; for notes on them see Wallace 1934, 479.

MCPHAIL, JOHN: NWC clerk; John McPhall, contract with McTavish, Frobisher & Co., 13 January 1802, as apprentice clerk for six years in the North West trade (ANQ-M, CN601, S29, 1795–1821, p. 77). *1805 list*: John McPhale, Lake Winnipeg, clerk, debit of 68 livres 12 sous; no salary listed. *1811–21 Accounts*: credit balance 1769 livres 17 sous in 1811; charged with sundries per Petty Ledger, 1811–19; Nipigon Book, 1813, 1815–16; Lac des Isles Book, 1819; Michipicoten Book, 1820; Also small payments to individuals, 1815 and 1817. Salary 840 livres, 1812; 960 livres + 120 short for last year, 1813; 960 livres, 1814–17; 1,200 livres 1818–19. In 1820 his salary payments end, and are replaced by credits from McTavish & Co. (HBCA, F.4/32, 724). This change in accounting apparently indicates that McPhall was made a partner in the NWC in 1819; this partnership, taken up in the last year before the NWC amalgamated with the HBC, is otherwise unknown. There is no indication that McPhail continued in the fur trade after the amalgamation. He may have been the John McPhale, son of the late James McPhale and Geeny McDonell, who married Margaret McDonell, daughter of Donald McDonell and Catharine Grant, at the Catholic church of St Andrew's, Upper Canada, 26 May 1821 (St Andrew's West [Catholic; co. Stormont] register 1802–35, copy in Drouin Collection, at ancestry.com). Nelson refers to him as "another poor friendless & brow-beaten creature" (*Reminiscences*, 211), perhaps regarding him as a clerk who, like Nelson, had no particular sponsor among the NWC partnership.

MARTIN, —: A "free Canadian, but much interested for the NW," whom Nelson met at Lac Bourbon on 4 September 1819, finding him old, sick, and starving; With him was one Montreuil, apparently another freeman.

MAURICETTE, —: Apparently a freeman; He was wintering near the mouth of Red River in 1804–05, when Nelson's voyageur Jolie went to visit him.

Mauricette's River, one of the rivers falling into the south basin of Lake Winnipeg, on the east side, was perhaps named for him.

MÉNÉCLIER, LOUIS: NWC clerk; Louis, son of Nicolas Ménéclier de Montrochaud, a former officer in the French army, and Marie-Charlotte Trudel, was baptized on 23 March 1764, at Pointe-aux-Trembles Quebec. Louis Ménéclier, of Sorel, contracted with McTavish, Frobisher & Co. on 5 April 1788, to go where they should direct (ANQ *Rapport* 1942–43, 266). J Bte Perrault found him at Lac des Sables (Sandy Lake, Minnesota) in the fall of 1791, outfitted by Mr. Nolin at Sault Ste. Marie (Cormier 1978, 85–6). He was part of John Sayer's Fond du Lac operation in 1795, wintering with Charles Gauthier at Rivière des Sauteux (HBCA, F.4/1, 42–56). He is not in the NWC rosters of 1798 or 1799 (*PAC Report* 1939; Masson 1960, 1:65–6). *1805 list*: Louis Ménéclier, clerk, debt 1,493 livres 4 sous, wages 100 livres, 3 yrs left on contract; noted as "In Land." Ls Minecker [*sic*], clerk, Lac Ouinipique, in the NWC arrangements for 1806 (Wallace 1934, 220). In 1805–06, he had been left in Winnipeg River with Dominique Ducharme to establish one or more posts there; midway through the season, Ducharme did not know where Ménéclier's post was (*Nelson Journals*). Ménéclier probably retired from the fur trade at the end of his contract in 1808. Jeane, daughter of Louis Manechier [*sic*], voyageur, and his wife Marianne Piquet, was baptized 24 July 1804 at Oka, the Catholic mission on Lake of Two Mountains near Montreal, and their son Nicolas was baptized there on 30 August 1816, the father being called "Louis Meneclier de Morachon cultivateur de la paroisse de Vaudreuil." Meneclier went up to Sault Ste Marie with his family in the spring of 1818 (Cormier 1978, 149), and settled on the American side. Members of the family were still living at Sault Ste Marie, Michigan, well into the twentieth century.

MONTREUIL, —: Apparently a freeman, whom Nelson's party met on Lac Bourbon (Cedar Lake) on 4 September 1819; he had some fish, but would not let them have any "unless we laid cash down," which in the fur country would have meant a credit note to be used for goods at one of the NWC posts.

NELSON, GEORGE: XYC and NWC clerk; the author of the journals *Sorel Journal* and *Reminiscences* included in this volume. For biographical details see Van Kirk and Brown 1985; Brown and Brightman 2008, 4–20; Peers and Schenck 2002, 3–10. George Nelson's baptism was recorded in the register of the Protestant congregation at Trois-Rivières, under the year 1786: "Le quatre de Juin est né George et a été baptisé le dix huit du dit mois fils de William Nelson et de Jeanne Nelson les pere et mere" (copy dated 1885; images at www.ancestry.com). The birthdate given in this entry agrees with Nelson's own statement. His father was an English schoolteacher, and his mother, Jane Dies, was the daughter of a New York Loyalist (Thompson 1987). Nelson's summary account with the NWC for the years 1811–21 is in HBCA, F.4/32, 758. In 1811, when the ledger opens, he had a credit balance of 1,513 livres 8 sous. His salary was 960 livres in 1812, and 1,200 livres in 1813–16. These were typical salaries for an experienced clerk, and he could save most of the money if he was not extravagant. Nelson spent little while he was in the Northwest, and he retired in 1816 with a credit balance of 3,638 livres 5 sous (perhaps equal to the purchasing power of roughly £6,000 sterling, or $10,000 CAD today). Returning to the Northwest in 1818, he had a salary of 1,500 livres in each of the next three years. The debit side of the account shows small charges in the Petty Ledger in every year up to 1816–17; in the Lake Winnipeg book, 1812–13 and 1819–20; the Pic book, 1814–16; in the Montreal book, 1818; and in the Cumberland House book, 1820–21. These charges confirm his movements between departments, and to and from Montreal, in this period. The account also shows that he had 600 livres paid to his father in 1811–12 and 1812–13, and in 1819–20; 663 livres paid to "B Gibb" (probably the Montreal merchant Benaiah Gibb, acting as an agent for Nelson) in 1819–20; and 720 livres paid "in Montreal" in 1821. Nelson was evidently saving as much as he could, and was transferring cash to Lower Canada to further future plans, or, after 1818, to support his family at Sorel.

PERIGNY, LOUIS: NWC clerk; Louis, son of François-Marie Paplau dit Périgny and Marie-Elizabeth Brisson, baptized 25 March 1764, Batiscan (Tanguay 1871–90, 6:207). He was perhaps the "Perrence" who was employed by the HBC's Charles Isham at Swan River in 1791–93, but left for "the Canadian Service," 28 November 1793 (HBCA, B.213/a/2, 11 November 1791, 28 February 1792; B.213/a/3, 6 April, 28 November 1793). David Thompson found "Perrinnu" at Swan River for the NWC, 21 September 1797 (Coues 1965, 299). Perigny, still with the NWC, was in charge at Swan River in summer 1800, and he and Daniel Williams Harmon were sent to build a new post at Bird Mountain in the fall (Lamb 1957, 34–5; Gates 1965, see index). *1805 list*: Louis Perigny, Lake Winnipeg, clerk & summer man, credit balance 780 livres, wages 750 livres, 1 yr left on contract. Perigny operated a small post for the NWC at the Barrier Portage in Winnipeg River in 1804–05, and in 1805–06 he was in charge of a post at Lac du Bonnet, with Nelson as his writer (*Nelson Journals*). Perigny is not in the 1806 NWC arrangements (Wallace 1934, 219–21), and probably retired from NWC after the season of 1805–06. André Poitras, Pierre Falcon, and Louis Perignie had a contract with the NWC, dated 19 March 1807, to hunt for the NWC (ANQ *Rapport* 1945–46, 263); like Périgny, the other two were former NWC clerks or interpreters. Perigny met Harmon at Grand Rapids, 6 August 1808, and told Harmon that he had been to Canada and had returned to the Northwest as a free trader (Lamb 1957, 111). Another agreement between Louis Perigny and the NWC, dated 19 June 1811 at "O'pas" (The Pas) and witnessed by "four partners of the North West Company," is mentioned by Bell (1928), but the present whereabouts of this document are unknown. *1811–21 Accounts*: credits for beaver & foxes, 1812–14; no wages [confirming that he was a freeman]; died during 1814–15, leaving a credit balance of almost 900 livres, paid "his Heirs in Montreal." Three small debts due to him, from fellow clerks William Connolly, Edward Harrison, and Jacques Chastellain, were settled later; the total, 60 livres 5 sous, was "transferred to Voyag: fund" (HBCA, F.4/32, 1054). Les Fonds des Voyageurs was a kind of welfare or insurance scheme, established by the late 1780s, to which the fur traders and voyageurs were supposed to contribute; for annual statements of its receipts and outgoings, see printed notices in the *Montreal Gazette*.

PERONNE, PIERRE PHILIP DIT: NWC and XYC clerk; Pierre Philippe dit Péronne, son of Pierre Philippe dit Peronne and Catherine Gendreau, was baptized 26 June 1761 at St-Laurent-de-Montreal. His parents, Pierre Philippe dit Peronne, a soldier, and Marie Catherine Gendreau, had been married at Notre-Dame-de-Québec in 1749 (Tanguay 1871–90, 6:341). Pierre Philippe dit Perronne, contract 23 March 1778 with William Grant, to go to Nipigon; Philippe Perronne, contract 28 April 1783 with Francis Winter (an agent who hired many men for the NWC), to go to Michilimackinac (ANQ *Rapport* 1946–47, 305, 321). "Mr. Peron" was in charge of the Canadian post at Bas de la Rivière in 1796–97 (HBCA, B.236/a/1). Pierre Philip Peronne, clerk & interpreter, Lac Ouinᵃ, 1 yr to serve from 1797, in 1798 NWC list (PAC *Report* 1939, 55).

Charles Chaboillez met Peronne, along with Messrs. Cameron, La Violette, and Reaumes, and the Portage Neuf en route inwards from Grand Portage, 11 August 1797 (Hickerson 1959); Laviolette, at least, had been assigned to the Lake Winnipeg department (HBCA, B.4/a/2, 13 September 1797, 11 September 1798), and the others likely were as well, apart from Peronne, who was leaving the NWC. On 24 November 1798, at Montreal, he was hired by Forsyth, Richardson & Co., Montreal agents for the XYC coalition, to serve three years in the North West (Beek Repertoire, ANQ-M, No. 1247). Alexander Mackenzie, in noting this hiring, observed that Pierre Philippe dit Peronne one of only two of their clerks "that ever wintered above St. Maries" (Lamb 1970, 489).

In 1799, Thomas Miller, the HBC's summer master at Bas de la Rivière, recorded that "Mr Peron Arrived from the Grand Portage with a canoe lightly loaded he belongs to a New Company formed this Year" (HBCA, B.4/a/3, 22 July

1799). Peronne must have been heading for the North Saskatchewan, to organize and lead an expedition into Athabasca by way of Lac la Biche and the Athabasca River, avoiding the usual English River route that the NWC was trying to prevent the XYC from using. Peronne succeeded, and he arrived at Fort Chipewyan with three loaded canoes on 22 May 1800, to the NWC's surprise and dismay (Masson 1960, 2:389). From this point onward, the XYC maintained a vigorous trade in Athabasca, the heart of the NWC's prosperity, until the companies joined in 1804–05. Peronne himself is not heard of after this season, and must soon have retired after this key achievement.

RACETTE, CHARLES: Freeman, Lake Winnipeg; Charles Racette (also spelled Rasette, etc.) was probably a member of a family living at St Augustin-de-Demaures, on the north shore of the St Lawrence a little above Quebec City. He may be the Charles Racette who was baptized there in 1765. His career in the fur trade was underway by the late 1780s, when he is found working for Duncan Cameron in the Nipigon country. James Sutherland, one of the leading HBC traders in the area, visited a Canadian settlement on Lake Seul in 1791, where he found "Mr Cameron recipting The Trade of Mr Rucit, his Clerk who winter'd near Lake Sturgeon and who I finde has been on his own account and has received 6765 Livres for the whole which is only 7 Packs and which will put him in Debt to Mr Cameron as not being equal to the value of his outfit" (HBCA, B.177/a/1, 3 June 1791). This was an old-fashioned arrangement, in which the wintering clerks, though completely dependent on their local suppliers, were treated as if they were independent entrepreneurs. Sometimes, perhaps often, they ended up as Racette did, worse off at the end of the trading season than at the start.

In 1797 the HBC trader John McKay, who had been in the Nipigon country since 1791, said of him, "Mr. Charles Ricette ... I knew him to be a good Trader in my time ... he is well acquainted all over Lake Wenipeg and was formerly there on his own particular account as a Trader" (HBCA, B.105/a/4, 1 June 1797). In the meantime, Racette had been down to Montreal, over the winter of 1795–96, where he brought a lawsuit against the estate of Gabriel Cotté, the Montreal trader who had employed Cameron for many years, for breach of contract (documents in private archive, information courtesy of Warren Baker). Racette spent part of the winter at Oka, the Huron mission on Lac des Deux Montagnes, where his three daughters, aged six, five, and two, were baptized. Their mother, Okekeninan or Marie Josette, "sauvagesse du Pic agée de vingt et une ans," was also baptized, and she and Charles Racette were married by the priest there (Oka register, entries of 29 November, 27 & 28 December 1795).

Racette must have returned to the Upper Country in 1796, for in the following spring, John McKay met him on Lake of the Woods, and Racette asked to be hired by the HBC. Knowing his reputation, McKay hesitated only because his demand for wages was too high, but a few days later he agreed with Racette for five years at £50 per annum (HBCA, B.105/a/4, 1 & 4 June 1797). McKay took Racette with him when he was sent to Brandon House in the fall of 1797. Racette was to take charge of a new post up Red River, but the HBC servants refused to go with him, "they said that, they did not know him, neither did they understand French." Racette thereupon resigned, and another man, John Richards, took the command instead. Supplied with a gun, powder and shot, Racette was left on his own, telling McKay that "he thinks of passing the winter up the Red River somewhere nigh Jno Richards as his opponent" (HBCA, B.22/a/5, 27 August & 2 September 1797). He may have wintered with the Métis community at Pembina, if that community was already in existence.

After this, there is no mention of Racette for about ten years, until he appears in George Nelson's journals. By now, Racette was well settled into the life of a freeman. When Nelson arrived to establish the Dauphin River post in the fall of 1807, Racette and his family were there, with a cabin already built, where they would live for the winter. Racette and his family spent the summer of 1808 at Blood River on the east side of Lake Winnipeg, and for the ensuing winter they were at Tête-au-Brochet. In 1809, they summered at Black River in the south basin of Lake Winnipeg, then wintered in Rivière Blanche, the middle stretch of Winnipeg River. In the summer of 1810, according to Nelson, Racette was en route to English River to visit his son-in-law, the NWC proprietor Robert Henry. As noted under Robert Henry (above), Henry had a ten-year-old son baptized at Montreal in 1806, and if the mother was Racette's daughter, she cannot have been born later than about 1782. This would date Racette's arrival in the Upper Country, and in a country relationship, at least as early as that.

In the *Sorel Journal*, 82–3, Nelson gives the following anecdote about Charles Racette:

> We also found here one Chs: Rassette a free man, with his family a very
> eccentric character. He came to this country a common Servant, but having
> some abilities for trade, he procured an outfit of several hundred pounds
> from the NW. Co. at Grant [Grand] Portage, & finished by ruining him-
> self. He was well aware of the "all little streams run into the great" but
> he thought to be able to gather enough yet for a thirsty day, but he was
> deceived!
>
> I will here relate a story of this man which made me laugh so much
> that I had stiches in my sides for a day & a half. He had his amour propre
> too (Self love) & did not chuse to associate with the Common labourers.
> Being a free man, he was almost always invited to our table. Another very

humorsome man of the name of Lorrain, an interpreter & enemy of Rassette's was with us, the preceding year. These two would often have strong arguments together, Lorrain would turn the pride of Rass. into the utmost ridicule. The latter would retort & abuse the other for being a slave (i.e. hired) and a notorious drunkard. I have heard the most laughable colloquies between these two, & altho' sometimes rise so high as one would think them going to fight, yet would they always separate & meet the best of friends. One day, Ras. as usual was invited to dinner & as usual he hesitated, to be the more pressed "why do you press that fellow, Mr McKay? Don't you see he sneaks about here at meal hours to be invited; for, altho' he thinks & stiles himself Lord of Lake Winnipick, yet the wretch starves" said Lorrain. Ras. stammered a great deal, & at long last he brought out a reply in accordance. By this time we had entered, Mr. McKay gave a large dose Jallop & Epicacuanta to Lorrain to put in Rassettes plate [Jalap or jollop is a purgative, and ipecacuanha, or ipecac, is an emetic]. This was too good an opportunity for fun to be lost, & Lorrain returned, made Suitable apologies & bent [?] in his old cronie, Mr McKay wanted to do the thing still, & sent Lor. to the store for some Liquor and while he was gone gave a Similar dose to Ras. to put in Lor. Plate. Ras. hesitated, saying it was ungenrous & might hurt him, we at last persuaded him. Lor. was soon back again, & set his batteries again to work on R. telling & urging him to stir well up his rise, "because you /83/ know the best always lays in the bottom," insuring this with a leer which called a momentary suspicion in R. "aye! aye! replies he, stir you yours, you will also find some good stuff in the bottom of y^r plate." Here they went on all the while joking each other. The bottle was handed round. Rass. was a very sober man & satisfied with little, but L. prevailed him to take a little more still. We remained about 2 hours at table, & certainly half an hour after the medicine began to work. R. he made wretched faces poor fellow & wanted to retire, but Lorrains course & home jokes (for he wanted R. to do in his breeches) induced him to remain longer than he wished. Rass. at last seeing Lor. punching his belly, "it would become indeed you to criticise my want of manners, in wishing to leave the table what are you punching at?" "Why, you eat so voraciously, so much like a hog", replied Lor. "that I feel a <u>nausea</u>." But he (Lor) could not finish his sentence, so rising from table he tells McKay "do let that poor hog go for you see how he suffers, & upon my word I am almost as bad by <u>looking</u> at him" so saying he pushed off R. who moved very well 'till he got to the door & off he scampered as hard as his legs could bear him. McKay called on L. "There not time now Sir – I am too much pressed" said he running off, by the back door Mckay & I went out for a walk through the bushes. When

we got by the corner of the garden, which was picketed, we saw Lorrain
busy both ends: he heard something round the corner, he moved thither as
well as he could, & saw his friend Rassette "Ah! my dear friend!" says Lor.
"I see you are very busily engaged too" (& indeed I never saw medicine
operate better than this did on both of them) & drawing, rather crawling up
to Rass. he put his hands on the others shoulders "at my d^r friend – we are
both in the same plight – let us support each other, for I cant stand alone! R.
was much the weaker man, & besides already worse, since he could dis-
engage from L. put his hands too on L. shoulders, & there they were both
of them locked as it were in each other's embraces & spueing all over each
other. R. was in a terrible fury, which made him worse, as well he might be
for Lor. threw up, not only upon him, but over his back & on his (R.) shirt.
I never have laughed so much in my life before or since, Let any one suppose
two such persons, and one doing his worst to besmear the other, himself
indifferent. They beg to go to the River to wash, & then would not wash
their clothes for some days after! I have seen many tricks of this kind there."

Racette was living at Grand Rapids, at the mouth of the Saskatchewan, in
June 1819 when Governor Williams captured the NWC partners, and he saw
what happened. The NWC took him down to Canada to give evidence when
a lawsuit was brought over this incident later that year. George Nelson's last
Lake Winnipeg journal mentions Racette twice. In February 1819, Nelson heard
that Racette had killed an Indigenous man who had eloped with his daughter,
and Nelson's own men were threatened by the dead man's friends, who wanted
revenge. In August, when Nelson had just set off on a trip from Fort Alexander to Cumberland House, he met "old Raçette's family" heading south along
the east shore of Lake Winnipeg, "all very ill & Complaining much." Nelson
gave them a note for the clerk in charge at Fort Alexander, "as they are now at
the Company's Charge, the father being taken down as witness to what passed
at Grand Rapids between the two Concerns." Some of Racette's testimony is
quoted, apparently in the original, in Wilcocke's account of "The Death of Mr.
Benjamin Frobisher 1819" (Masson 1960, 2:183).

The end of Racette's life is unrecorded, but it is probable that all the Métis
persons with this surname in western Canada are his descendants. At least two
of Charles's children, George Racette and Margaret Racette (wife of James
Swain), were still alive in the 1870s, when they claimed land as Métis resi-
dents of Rupert's Land; and several other Racettes of the next generations also
made successful claims. The affidavits of George Racette, who said that he was
born about 1800 at Fort Pelly, and James Swain (on behalf of his wife Margaret, daughter of Charles Racette, born about 1809 at Lake Winnipeg) are LAC,

RG 15, v. 1323 & 1324. These affidavits name their parents as Charles Racette, French Canadian, and "an Indian woman"; George's affidavit names his mother as Josephte. As pointed out in the Introduction, George Racette, whose given name is unusual among Quebeckers of the time, may have been named in honour of George Nelson.

RICHARD, FRANÇOIS, SENIOR: NWC clerk and interpreter; Nelson named François Richard as one of his sources for stories about the smallpox epidemic of 1781–82 (Sorel Journal, 61), so presumably he was already in the west at that time. 1805 list: Frans Richard Senr, interpreter, wages 600 livres, 1 yr left on contract. Richard was in charge of the Pigeon River post in 1805–06. He was to be Nelson's interpreter at Dauphin River in 1807–08, but was badly burned in the powder keg explosion on the way in, and after weeks of suffering died in the night of 18 October 1807. His supposed age was sixty-two years. Nelson said that he left a wife; his eldest son François junior [see next]; other sons Michel and Baptiste; and one more son whose name is not given, only eight years old in 1807. Of the sons, Baptiste Richard worked for Nelson in 1809–10, probably on a casual basis, living in a house on the other side of Dauphin River. In January 1810, Baptiste Richard went with Auger, Nelson's courier, to visit Joshua Halcro at the Falle-au-Perdrix post; Richard "has a mind to go & see his sister Halcro's wife" (probably a daughter of Joseph Lorrain, and thus the sister of the wife of Baptiste Richard's brother François: see entry for Joshua Halcro in this Appendix). "Little Michel Richard" did some hunting for Nelson in 1807–08 and summer 1810 (Nelson Journals).

RICHARD, FRANÇOIS, JUNIOR: NWC interpreter; son of François Richard, Senior. 1805 list: Frans Richard Junr, interpreter, wages 400 livres, 1 yr left on contract. Nelson sometimes calls him "young Richard." He was with Nelson at Dauphin River in 1807–08 and 1808–09, a useful man, who could interpret Ojibwe and build canoes, besides the usual hunting, fishing, and winter travelling. After his father's death in 1807, young François, probably just out of his teens, was left the head of a large family, including his mother, his wife (a daughter of Joseph Lorrin), three brothers, and some further relations: see Nelson's entry at 11 July 1809, "His Canoe consist of twelve people (with their lumber) mostly women!" Richard was planning to build a house for all his relations at Dauphin River, but he himself wintered with Seraphin Lamar, his brother-in-law, at Rivière-aux-Morts in 1809–10. On 18 June 1810, young Richard arrived at Dauphin River with his family, but brought news that Joseph Lorrin had taken his daughter from Richard, for alleged "ill treatment and jealousy." Later, it was learned that she had been "donnée'd" to Duncan Cameron, but François got his own son back, and spent the summer with Nelson, taking charge of the Dauphin River during Nelson's absence at Fort Alexander.

Richard was assigned to Fort Dauphin department for 1810–11 (*Nelson Journals*), and this ended his connection with Lake Winnipeg. *1811–21 Accounts*: François Richard, "Int" [interpreter], credit balance of 823 livres 15 sous in 1811; charged for sundries in Petty Ledger 1811–13, 1815–21, and in Fort Dauphin Book, 1812–14, 1816–18; wages 500 livres 1812–20, 600 livres 1821 (HBCA, F.4/32, 825, 1005). In 1818, Nelson heard that Richard was in charge of the Fort Dauphin post at Falle-au-Perdrix. Following the coalition with the HBC, Richard continued in the Swan River district (the HBC's equivalent of the NWC's Fort Dauphin department), and can be traced there until 1848, sometimes as a freeman, but in many years as a trader and interpreter at Manitobah House. He eventually settled at Red River (HBCA Biographical Sheet, "Francois H. Richard"). Marguerite, wife of François Richard, died 24 August 1858, aged about seventy, and was buried at St François Xavier, the mission to the Métis community there.

SAYER, JOHN CHARLES: Assistant or interpreter for the NWC clerk Louis Dorion, who opposed Nelson at Rivière-aux-Morts in 1804–05; Sayer, whom Nelson describes as a "half-breed," was a son of the NWC partner John Sayer and his Ojibwe wife, Obemau-unoqua; for the father and his family see Birk 1983. There is a letter from John Charles Sayer to his father, dated Lac la Pluie 12 August 1816 and "honour'd by Mr. William Henry," a NWC clerk. John Charles had wanted to visit his father, but his employers had engaged him for a further year for £100. His brother (not named) was "engaged again for his old Quarters at £100 a year" (Selkirk Papers, 8672–3). John Charles Sayer's brother, Pierre-Guillaume Sayer, was the free trader whom the HBC prosecuted for infringing on its monopoly in 1849. The trial is generally recognized as an early step in the recognition of Métis hunting rights in Rupert's Land (Morton 1988).

SUTHERLAND, DONALD: HBC servant, based at York Factory, from which he conducted a successful trade in the difficulty country east of Lake Winnipeg, for many years (Lytwyn 1986, 147–57); Nelson met Sutherland in March 1819, during a visit to John Crebassa's post at Little Grand Rapids; he concluded that Sutherland was completely in control of the fur trade in the district, to the point where the Indigenous people would threaten NWC men who tried to trade with them. Sutherland was not an Englishman, as Nelson calls him, but a Scotsman, from Clyne in Sutherlandshire, about forty-six years old in 1819. He had been hired by the HBC as a tailor in 1795, and apart from occasional trips home he had served in the fur country since then. From 1814 onwards he was the master of trading posts, and in 1815 he established the first permanent HBC post on Lake Manitoba (his journal of this season is HBCA, B.121/a/1). Sutherland had at least four children with an Indigenous woman. He finally retired to Scotland in 1824, and lived until 1872. See HBCA Biographical Sheet.

VENABLES, GEORGE: NWC clerk; George Venables, of Stansted, Hertfordshire, age 20, hired with the HBC as a writer, in London on 26 May 1802, for 5 years at a salary of £15 per annum (HBCA, A.32/17, fo. 110). He was immediately dispatched to Churchill Factory on Hudson Bay, where he spent the winter, and in July 1803 he went inland with the HBC trader John Charles (HBCA, B.42/a/128). No further mention of him has been found in the relevant journals, and he was probably soon hired away by the NWC. He must be the same as Venables, now a NWC clerk in the Lake Winnipeg department, who is mentioned in William McKay's Cross Lake Journal for 1805–06 (LAC, MG 19 C1 vol. 9) as in charge of the NWC post at Pike or Jack River. According to that journal, Venables and his interpreter, an Indigenous man, and two of their wives, had drunk up all the rum at their post, six kegs of high wines, in four months, and Venables was guilty of other "Scandless doings" (Cross Lake journal, 3 February 1806). Venables is not found in the NWC arrangements for 1806 (Wallace 1934, 219–21), and presumably had left the fur trade.

Place Names Mentioned by Nelson

Most of the place names in Nelson's writings are mentioned in connection with his journeys on the lake, in summer and winter, and their general locations can be inferred from the order in which they appear during the different journeys. Very few of these names appear on the modern map. The best maps of Lake Winnipeg in the NWC period are David Thompson's well known map of 1812, in the Archives of Ontario (excellent facsimiles of several portions in Coues 1965), and the lesser known map that he drew for the Colonial Office in 1825, and now in the National Archives at Kew. Few Lake Winnipeg place names appear on either of these maps. Thompson's geography soon appeared on printed maps, but after him, there were no new surveys until the Hind and Dawson explorations of Rupert's Land in 1857 and 1858, under the auspices of the Canadian Legislative Assembly. These expeditions produced high quality maps, based on the new surveys, which were included in the Reports to the Legislative Assembly, published in 1859. Two of the maps show Lake Winnipeg in detail, and many places names are marked on them, but very few of those names were in use in Nelson's time. The voyageurs' nomenclature, most of it in French, seems largely to have disappeared during the forty years after Nelson left Lake Winnipeg. A number of old names, now anglicized, have roots in Cree or Ojibwe place names that the fur traders heard about from their Indigenous associates.

Modern names are given as they appear on the Topographical Maps, 1:250,000 series.

L'ANSE DU BONNET: A bay in the northwest corner of Lac du Bonnet, which gave its name to a portage.

LA BARRIÈRE: One of the portages in the Rivière Blanche section of Winnipeg River. Périgny had a post here in 1804–05.

BAS DE LA RIVIÈRE (Bottom of the River): The fort or depot near the bottom of Winnipeg River, established by Toussaint Lesieur in 1792. It soon became the principal post in the NWC's Lake Winnipeg department. In 1808 and later it was usually known as Fort Alexander, which see.

BEAVER RIVER: Now Bradbury River (Lytwyn 1986, 138).

BIRCH LAKE: Unidentified place near Dauphin River post, mentioned in journal entry of 1 February 1810.

BLACK RIVER (Riviére-Noire): Still so called, river on the east side of Lake Winnipeg, south basin. At the mouth is the present Black River First Nation.

BLOOD RIVER (Rivière-du-Sangue): Now Bloodvein River.

BROKEN RIVER (Rivière-Cassée): Now Rice River. One of Peter Fidler's sketch maps, from his survey of Lake Winnipeg in 1809, places a small house (his usual symbol for a trading post) at the mouth of the river, on the south side. He notes that the "Bungee [Ojibwe] name" for Broken River was Burnt Wood River, and mentions that by ascending the river 6 miles, "full of rapids," one could reach a lake 4½ miles long (now Shallow Lake), "Rice plenty in this Lake or Zizania aquatica" (HBCA, E.3/3, fo. 60). The NWC maintained a post at Broken River in several seasons. By a careful comparison of Fidler's series of sketch maps with the modern map, Lytwyn (1986), Fig. 24, shows that Broken River is the modern Rice River.

CHEMIN DU GUERRIER (warrior's road): The warpath or war road, mentioned frequently in Nelson's Dauphin River journals. The term refers to the Warpath River, and the portage into it from Dauphin River. A war road was an inland route, well concealed in forest if possible, which was used by war parties wishing to penetrate into enemy territory without being detected.

LA CHUTE BLANCHE: A high fall on Pigeon River, Nelson says about 150 feet high. Perhaps the present Grant Falls.

CROSS LAKE: Still so called. William McKay wintered there in 1805–06, and kept an unsigned journal; see Lindsay and Brown 2010, Appendix D.

DALLES, THE (French: tiles or slabs): A section of Winnipeg River, presumably so-called because of the appearance of the rocky banks.

DAUPHIN RIVER: George Nelson's post in the seasons of 1807, 1808, and 1809, located near the month of the present Dauphin River, within the present land reserve of the Dauphin River First Nation. In Nelson's first season, the post was built on the south side. The location is clear from Nelson's *Reminiscences*, where he describes the site as "on the left (S.E.) bank 2, or 300 yards from the lake." He is speaking about his left as he approached the site from Lake Winnipeg, and "S.E." makes it clear that the south bank was meant. This location rationalizes Nelson's remarks in his journal at 26 May 1809, explaining why he had moved the post to the north side of the river. The earlier site was exposed to all winds except the south, which would be the case if it faced north, with the forest at the back, while at the new site "We have the Sun in our doors & are shelter'd from all winds except the S. & S.E. which Comes from the Lake." The new location was about 400 yards from the old site, near the point where the Dauphin River makes a sharp bend from north to east, before entering the Lake.

DÉTROIT DE DUC (Le Duc's Strait): Now Loon Straits, on the east side of the south basin of Lake Winnipeg. This is one of the few place names in this part of the lake that most travellers mentioned, so it was an important landmark, but most references are too vague to place it. David Thompson's 1825 map marks it clearly, as does one of the sketch maps from Peter Fidler's 1809 survey, where he has the note "La ducs straight a Canadian of this name was drownded here in 1773" (HBCA, E.3/3, fo. 61). Canoes coming up the east shore from the south, by passing through Loon Straits, could stay close to the east shore, and travel for a few miles in the lee of the present Monkman Island. This avoided an exposed six-mile traverse to the west shore near Bull Head, followed by traverses across four more bays before reaching The Narrows.

DÉTOUR, THE: Now Long Point, on the west shore of the north basin of Lake Winnipeg. This feature, on the main canoe route through the lake, added about 60 miles to the trip.

DRUNKEN LAKE (Lac de l'Ivrogne): A post up Poplar River, on the east side of Lake Winnipeg. Lytwyn 1986, 116, identifies it with the present Wrong Lake.

DRUNKEN RIVER: Unidentified, but near the Rivière Blanche of Winnipeg River. Alexander Kennedy had a post there for the NWC in 1809–10, with an HBC man as a neighbour.

FALLE-AU-PERDRIX (Partridge Crop): A gathering place on the west side of Lake St Martin, where the Fort Dauphin department usually had a post, occupied during the trading season only. An Anglican mission was established here in 1842, to which the name Fairford was given.

FESTIN, ÎLE-AU (Feasting Island): An island in Lac Vaseu, the western part of Lac Bourbon (Cedar Lake). Alexander Henry calls it "Isle aux Festion" (Coues 1965, 468 and note). This lake, like most of the Saskatchewan River delta, was completely inundated by the hydroelectric power dam at Grand Rapids, built in the 1960s.

FISHER RIVER: On the west side of Lake Winnipeg, falling into the present Fisher Bay. Also known by the French equivalent, Riviére-au-Peccant.*

FOIN, RIVIÈRE-AU- (Hay River): One of the rivers falling into the south basin of Lake Winnipeg from the east, but unidentified.

FOLLE AVOINE, LAC LA (Rice Lake): East of Lake Winnipeg, approached by way of Poplar River. Lytwyn (1986, 114) identifies Rice Lake with Harrop Lake, using the HBC trader Donald Sutherland's 1819 map of the Berens River District (HBCA, B.16/e/2, fos. 3d–4). See Lytwyn (1986), Figure 26 for a comparison of the details of Sutherland's map with the modern map.

FORT ALEXANDER: The Bas de la Rivière post and provision depot, near the mouth of Winnipeg River. It was established in 1792, as the place where pemmican would be brought from the upper Assiniboine, where it was made, for the use of the other NWC canoe brigades. This name was first used in 1808. According to Nelson, the name was chosen by Alexander McKay, the NWC partner who completed the rebuilding of the fort in 1807–08, because, he said, so many of the Lake Winnipeg clerks were named Alexander. It may also have been a subtle reference to the explorer Alexander Mackenzie, Alexander McKay's old mentor, who still commanded the respect of many Nor'westers, though he had been excluded from the management of the NWC because of his role in the XYC opposition. Naming posts after individuals was probably a reaction to the NWC's decision, in 1807, to confer the name Fort William upon the depot at Kaministiquia on Lake Superior, in honour of William McGillivray. In some NWC partners' letters in the Selkirk Papers, we find the Lake Nipigon post being called Fort Duncan (evidently after Duncan Cameron, who had done the most to develop the Nipigon trade), while Fort L'Ésperance or Qu'Appelle, the principal post of the Upper Red River department, was sometimes called Fort John, probably after one of the most vigorous of the partners in charge of the Upper Red River district, John Macdonell. These names may have been used ironically,

to express disapproval of the exaltation of William McGillivray. The name of
Fort Alexander was not immediately accepted by everyone: letters in the Selkirk
Papers are dated from "Bas de la Rivière" as late as 1816, and Nelson himself
did not always use the new name.

FORT DAUPHIN: Not to be confused with Dauphin River. A department of the
NWC, centred around the present Lake Dauphin, and including Lake Winnipegosis, the northern part of Lake Manitoba, Swan Lake, and Red Deer River.
The eastern boundary was the post at Falle-au-Perdrix and the western bound-
ary was the upper Assiniboine River, in the present Saskatchewan. The original
Fort Dauphin, on Dauphin Lake, was established in the French period. During
Nelson's time on Lake Winnipeg, the NWC partner in charge of Fort Dauphin
was John McDonald "le Borgne." The traders faced constant difficulties trying
to avoid Indigenous people taking credit in both the Fort Dauphin and Lake
Winnipeg departments.

GRAND EQUIERRE: Or Grand Equisette ("Big Pine"), a place on the Winnipeg
River, not located exactly, where the NWC had a post in 1818 and 1822. On his
way up Winnipeg River in June 1822, Nelson passed the Grand Equierre about
one hour and forty minutes before he reached Portage de l'île. The interpreter
Joseph Lorrin managed the post in 1818, and was killed there by an Indigenous
man two years later.

GRAND MARET (south basin of Lake Winnipeg): Still called Grand Marais, a
prominent point on the east shore, on the way from Fort Alexander to Red
River.

GRAND MARET (north basin of Lake Winnipeg): Probably the swamp at and
around Morass Point, on the west shore of the lake about 25 miles north of
Dauphin River.

GRANDE POINTE: Now Saskatchewan Point, the south end of the long traverse
across the mouth of Sturgeon Bay, by way of the Îles-de-St-Martin.

GRANDE POINTE (another): Landmark on the canoe route along the west shore
of Lake Winnipeg, between Sturgeon Bay and Long Point. The two landmarks
that Nelson names along this part of the west shore, Grande Pointe and Pointe-
aux-Renards (*Journals*, entries of 27 and 29 August 1819), no longer go by these
names. The other detailed itinerary through this part of the route, in Alexander
Henry's journal, also names two landmarks, Pointe du Canot Cassé (Broken

Canoe point) and Pointe Maligne. Henry's first editor, Elliott Coues, annotated this route heavily (Coues 1965, 458–60), and concluded that Pointe du Canot Cassé is the present Dancing Point, while Pointe Maligne must be Wicked Point. Nelson's Grand Point and Pointe-aux-Renards may have been alternative names for those two features.

GRAND RAPID: A trading post near the present Little Grand Rapids First Nation in eastern Manitoba. The HBC from Albany Fort, which called it Great Fall after the native name, had been there since 1801 (Lytwyn 1986, 100). According to Peter Fidler's survey of Lake Winnipeg in 1809, the NWC canoes reached Grand Rapids by way of Berens River (HBCA, E.3/3, fo. 61).

GRAND RAPID (another – not a trading post): Cree, *Misepawistik*, great fall, the long system of rapids through which the Saskatchewan River system reaches Lake Winnipeg. Its natural condition has been completely tamed by the hydroelectric dam at this place. Nelson mentioned this Grand Rapid as the northern limit of Old Muffle d'Orignal's hunting ground in 1809–10 (*Journals*, 6 October 1809).

ÎLE-À-BERIAU: One of the islands just NW of the Narrows of Lake Winnipeg, probably either the present Matheson or Black Bear Island. The camp where Nelson was badly burned in the explosion of the powder keg, in September 1807, was on the south side of this island (*Journals*, 26 September 1818).

ÎLE-À-LA-BICHE: Now Elk Island, at the mouth of Traverse Bay, where the Winnipeg River reaches Lake Winnipeg.

ÎLE-DU-CAMPEMENT (Camping Island): An island at the mouth of Sturgeon Bay, on the south side, the usual camp ground for canoe brigades passing through Lake Winnipeg, at the south end of the long traverse across the mouth of the bay. It may have been the small unnamed island 2½ miles due west of Saskatchewan Point, at 52°10' N, 97° 46' W, where there is a very well sheltered harbour.

ÎLE-AUX-CHEVAUX: A small island on the north shore of Long Point, Lake Winnipeg. Alexander Henry mentions the "Horse islands," the English equivalent (Coues 1965, 461). Just beyond this is Nelson's "last point," now called Scots Point, where the canoe route turns north toward the mouth of the Saskatchewan River.

ÎLE-À-LA-FRAMBOISE (Raspberry Island): Landmark on the journey from Dauphin River to Fort Alexander; probably the present Kinwow Bay Island.

ÎLES-DU-MASQUIEGE: *See* Swamp Islands.

ÎLE-AUX-MOUFFLES: Island off the north shore of Long Point, Lake Winnipeg, now called Horseshoe Island. Alexander Henry uses the English equivalent, Moose Nose Island (Coues 1965, 461). On 31 August 1819 Nelson camped opposite this island on a "rascally point," now Nistwawneyapiskaw Point.

ÎLE-RONDE (Round Island): Said to be opposite Tête-au-Brochet; probably the present Jackhead Island.

ÎLES-DE-ST-MARTIN: A group of islands scattered across the wide mouth of Sturgeon Bay. On the modern map, St Martin Islands is used for the islands on the north side, but Nelson and others extended the term to include those on the south side, now called the Sturgeon Islands. As Nelson himself states, the Îles-de-St-Martin were generally considered the halfway point for canoes passing through Lake Winnipeg. Duncan Macgillivray, in his journal of his first canoe voyage to the Saskatchewan in the fall of 1794, also says that the St Martin Islands were "supposed to be the Centre of the Lake" (Morton 1929, 11).

ÎLETS-VERTES (Green Islets): The islands just NW of the Narrows of Lake Winnipeg, at the end of the long traverse across the mouth of Fisher Bay.

ÎLE-AU-WINDIGO: In Lac du Bonnet, probably the small island offshore from the present Wendigo Beach.

KAKINOWACHAGUE: Alexander Campbell's fort in 1807–08. While passing north along the east shore of Lake Winnipeg on 30 May 1808, Peter Fidler encountered a flotilla of twenty-three canoes of "Bungee Indians" [HBC name for Ojibwe people] "going to River Winnepeg – They have traded with a Mr. Campbell, in a Deep Bay beyond Broken river on S side the Lake." The next day they "stopped at mouth of Broken river from 6½ to 9½ AM – where was Mr Campbell & 5 Canadians, who had wintered in a deep bay on SW side of the Lake near here – he had made 14 Packs from 23 Bungee Hunters – 18 Canoes of them" (HBCA, E.3/3, fo. 58d). The deep bay must be Washaw or Humbug Bay, the only deep bay on the W side of Lake Winnipeg (to Fidler, the SW side), and Campbell's fort was likely at the bottom of the bay. The modern name "Washaw" is probably a truncation of the name that Nelson gives.

KAMINISTIQUIA: The new NWC depot, built in 1803 when the company abandoned Grand Portage because it was on the wrong side of the US border. The depot was named Fort William in 1807.

LAC DU BOIS: Lake of the Woods.

LAC DU BONNET: Still so called. A large widening of Winnipeg River, below the many falls and rapids of the Rivière Blanche and above the last series of portages before the bottom of the river. Périgny and Nelson occupied a post here in the season of 1805–06, in a bay on the south side of the lake, close to the modern community of Wendigo Beach.

LAC BOURBON: Now Cedar Lake, on the main canoe route to the Saskatchewan River and beyond. The old name goes back to the La Vérendrye era. Since the 1960s, it has been much altered by flooding due to the Grand Rapids hydroelectric dam.

LAC CARRIBOEUF: On Pigeon River, where McDonell and Nelson camped on 15 March 1809, en route to the NWC post at Little Grand Rapids.

LAC DES GRAINES (Seed Lake): Site of a NWC post dependent on Cumberland House, not identified. Mr Cardin was to winter here in 1819–20.

LAC DU GRAND RAPID: Now called Family Lake.

LAC DU LIMON: Somewhere in the Winnipeg River region, apparently near the Rivière-Blanche section, but unidentified. In 1805–06, the people at the Lac du Bonnet post believed that Méneclier was wintering at Lac du Limon.

LAC DE LA POULE D'EAU: Waterhen Lake, on the drainage river between Lake Winnipegosis and Manitoba Lake.

LAC-DE-LA-ROCHE: Unidentified; a lake near Cumberland House, where the HBC had a post in 1819–20.

LAC ROND: Still called Round Lake, on Pigeon River, where McDonell and Nelson camped on 12 March 1809, en route to the NWC post at Little Grand Rapids.

LAC ST MARTIN: Still called Lake St Martin, in the Interlake district of Manitoba. The Détroit of Lac St Martin is the Narrows of the Lake, both sides of which are now parcels of the Lake St Martin First Nation reserve lands.

LAC TRAVERSE: Now Cross Bay in Cedar Lake.

LAC VASEU (Muddy Lake): Now Pineimuta Lake (Cree word for partridge crop), on the Fairford River between Lake Manitoba and Lake St Martin.

LAC VASEU (another): With Île-du-Festin (Feasting Island) in it. Somewhere on the lower Saskatchewan River or its delta into Cedar Lake. Probably a well known landmark, as Alexander Henry also mentions it, but much of the area has been inundated by the hydroelectric dam at Grand Rapids, and Lac Vaseu has probably disappeared.

LITTLE WHITE RIVER: *See* Petite Rivière-Blanche.

LOON LAKE (Lac du Huard): Unidentified, but a dependency of the NWC's Nipigon department, and far enough west for John Dougald Cameron, who was stationed at Loon Lake, to pay a visit to Fort Alexander at Christmas 1810.

MANITOBANE, THE: Lake Manitoba, or the Narrows of that Lake, a well-known landmark.

MAURICETTE'S RIVER: Named presumably for the voyageur or clerk of that name, whom Nelson mentions. The name has been lost, but it was on the east side of the south basin, between Broken River (present Rice River) and Black River. Wanipigow River (which Fidler names as Swan's Thropple River), Manigotogan River and Sandy River are all possibilities. Nelson once refers to a Pointe aux Sables in this general area, which presumably was close to the present Sandy River; and Mauricette's River may be the present Manigotogan River [see note to Pointe-à-Mauricette]. By elimination, Rivière-au-Gavion may be the present Wanipigow or Hollow Water River. Fidler's 1808 survey gives the name Mainwaring River to Manigotogan River, evidently honouring a member of the HBC's Committee (HBCA, E.3/3, fo. 60).

MONATAGUÉ RIVER: Now Montagao River. Montaguée Point must be one of the points near the mouth, at the bottom of Sturgeon Bay. There was said to be a lake called Monatàguée Lake "on the upper part of Monotâguee River," where Nez Corbin and Ayagon were hunting in winter 1811, but no likely candidate appears on the modern map.

MOOSE LAKE: Still so called, the large lake to the north of Cedar Lake. George Nelson was in charge of a post here in 1819-20.

OUINIPIQUE: *See* Winnipeg.

PARCHES: *See* Porches.

PEMBINA RIVER: Still so called, a major tributary of the Red River.

PETIT CHENAIL ("little channel"): Apparently an alternative channel of the Saskatchewan River, between The Pas and Cumberland House.

PETITE RIVIÈRE-BLANCHE (Little White River): Now Whitemouth River, which falls into Winnipeg River just south of Lac du Bonnet.

PIGEON RIVER: A river on the east side of Lake Winnipeg, still so called, and also the name of one of the NWC posts in the department, occupied in 1807–08 and 1808–09, and also in 1812–13 (when Nelson was in charge), but closed in 1809–10 and probably in 1810–11. Nelson's account of a visit to the post indicates that the post was about two leagues (6 miles) up the river (*Journals*, 6 March 1809). The first falls in Pigeon River are about 6½ miles from the mouth, so the post was probably just below this point. One of Peter Fidler's sketch maps, from his survey of Lake Winnipeg in 1809, places a small house (his usual symbol for a trading post) at the mouth of "Pidgeon River," on the south side, but as he crossed the mouth of Pigeon Bay, without going to the bottom, the location of the house must have been approximate (HBCA, E.3/3, fo. 61).

There is sometimes confusion about this river, as the Ojibwe name for the river now called the Berens, Omiimiisiipi, also means Pigeon River. Fidler used the name "Berens's River" in his 1809 survey, and probably chose it himself to honour the gGovernor of the HBC. His notes show that he introduced his own names to some other features on the lake, but these did not survive.

PIKE HEAD: See Tête-au-Brochet.

PIKE RIVER: Now Gunisao River (from Cree word for pike or jackfish), which falls into the Nelson River opposite Norway House.

PINAWA RIVER: A "back road" that could be used by small canoes to avoid the Rivière Blanche section of Winnipeg River, with its many portages, if the water was unusually high. The name is said to come from an Ojibwe word meaning calm or sheltered.

POINTE-AU-BATEAU: A point on the east side of Lake Winnipeg, 8 leagues from

Fort Alexander. Using the best estimate of the length of Nelson's league (3 miles) would take us to the present Mink Point, or less probably Poplar Point or Little Birch Point.

POINTE-BRÛLÉ (Burnt Point): On Lac du Bonnet, near Nelson's post of 1805–06, but unidentified.

POINTE-À-LA-FRAMBOISE (Raspberry Point): A point reached just before taking the traverse across Kinwow Bay; probably either the present Willow Point or Pages Point.

POINTE-AUX-LIÈVRES (Hare Point): "Near Tête-au-Chien and Bloody River." Probably one of the points in Bloodvein Bay. According to Hallowell's informant Adam Bigmouth, "Rabbit Point" was 45 miles from Berens River (Brown 2018, 16).

POINTE-À-MAURICETTE: On east side of Lake Winnipeg, 11 leagues, according to Nelson, from Fort Alexander on the way to Tête-au-Brochet. From this distance, it could be the present Observation Point. Presumably close to Rivière-à-Mauricette, which thus could be the present Manigotogan River.

POINTE-À-LA-MITASSE: Now Point Mitas, the north side of the entrance to Traverse Bay, near the entrance of Winnipeg River into Lake Winnipeg. *Mitasses* is Canadian French for leather leggings. Fidler labels this as Stocking Point on his sketch map of what is now Traverse Bay (HBCA, E.3/3, fo. 59). The island of the Pointe-de-la-Mitasse may be what is now called Devil's Island; Fidler's map calls it Kirkness Island, probably a name he chose to honour one of the HBC's Orkney servants.

POINTE-AUX-RAGOMINAIRES: On Lake Winnipeg north of Tête-au-Brochet, within a day's walking distance of the Tête-au-Brochet post. Alexander Henry describes rounding "Pointe aux Ragominoire" just before camping at the foot of the traverse across the mouth of Kinwow Bay, on his route through Lake Winnipeg in August 1808 (Coues 1965, 457). From its position, it must be the present Wicked Point or Willow Point. *Ragominaire* or *ragouminère* is an obsolete word for a native cherry tree, formerly used in Quebec and believed to be a loan from an indigenous language. The word is preserved in the name of the Île-aux-Ragominaires, a small island in the St Lawrence River opposite Répentigny (Vézina 2009, 23).

POINTE-AUX-RENARDS (Point of Foxes): Landmark on the canoe route along the west shore of Lake Winnipeg, noted by Nelson as he passed in 1819. He camped here on his way out in 1822, after getting round the Detour, describing it as "in the bottom of ye bay." Perhaps the present Wicked Point. *See also* Grande Pointe (another trading post).

POINTE DE ROCHE (Rock Point): Now Stony Point, about 3½ miles north of Jackhead, Lake Winnipeg.

POINTE-AU-SABLE (Sandy Point): On the east side of Lake Winnipeg; probably the point nearest the mouth of the present Sandy River.

POPLAR RIVER: Still so-called, a river on the east side of Lake Winnipeg, North Basin; known in French as Rivière-du-Tremble.

PORCHES, THE (or Parches): A place at the south end of Lac du Bonnet, where the Winnipeg River flows in. Nelson's journal entry of 2 February 1806 seems to show that the name covered the last 3 leagues of the Rivière Blanche; but other descriptions of this major canoe route do not use the name. The word could be English or French, and the reason for the name is unknown.

PORTAGE DE CAJIN (perhaps the Acadian's Portage): A place on Pigeon River, where McDonell and Nelson camped on 13 March 1809, en route to the NWC post at Little Grand Rapids.

PORTAGE-DU-GUERRIER (Warrior's Portage): The place, close to the sharp bend of Dauphin River from northern to southeastern flow, where there is a short portage into the headwaters of the present Warpath River.

PORTAGE DE L'ÎLE: A place on Winnipeg River, near where the English River comes in from the east. There was a fur post here from early times, as an earlier description of the Lake Winnipeg department was "the post of Riviere des Trembles and Portage de l'Ile." The site of the post was probably within the boundary of the present White Dog (Islington) reserve, Ontario.

PORTAGE DU LAC DU BOIS: Now called French Portage Narrows, near the middle of a channel that cuts through the Aulneau Peninsula, in Lake of the Woods. The length of the portage was quite variable, depending on the height of the water. In some years it was possible to paddle all the way through, but when the water was low, as in the summer of 1804, Alexander Henry "made a very long, ugly portage in Lac des Bois, in mud and mire up to the knees" (Coues 1965, 248).

PORTAGE LA PRAIRIE: The eighteen-mile portage from the south end of Lake Manitoba to the Assiniboine River. The modern city of Portage la Prairie is located at or near the south end of this portage. A fur trade post had been located at the Assiniboine end of the portage, off and on, since La Vérendrye's time, when it was known as Fort la Reine. The NWC operated a post here in 1805–06 and 1806–07, with Louis Dorion in charge, as part of the Lower Red River department. Alexander Henry, the partner in charge, stated that in the latter season the trade there was unsuccessful, mainly because of "an unfortunate quarrel which took place last spring, when some were killed and others wounded, among them one of our principal men, whose skull was split open with an ax ... The loss of this man may be said to have given the death-blow to Portage la Prairie" (Coues 1965, 423). The "strange Indians" with whom Nelson traded in December 1807, near Fisher River, had previously been at the Portage la Prairie post, so that post must have been continued in spite of Henry's pessimism.

PORTAGE DU RAT (Rat Portage): The portage between Lake of the Woods and the Winnipeg River. There is surprisingly little detailed information about the portage itself, most travellers mentioning it without description. David Thompson's large map of Lake of the Woods, drawn from his surveys for the Boundary Commission in 1823 and 1824, clearly shows that the portage was across the neck of land at the head of Keewatin Bay. I am grateful to David Malaher for this information.

PORTAGE SAUVAGE (Indian Portage): A portage across the narrow neck of land that connects the peninsula on which the modern communities of Wanising Beach and Victoria Beach are built. Saving only a few miles of paddling, it would hardly be useful for fully laden canoes, which would have to be unloaded and reloaded; but for a small canoe with little freight it was worth taking. Nelson, who was travelling light in August 1808, used the Portage Sauvage on his trip from Bas de la Rivière to Rivière des Mort, and again on his return. On 27 May 1794, en route from the mouth of Red River to Bas de la Rivière, John Macdonell recorded "Left the Grand Marais at noon. Mr Grant's canoe turn'd into the Bay of the Indian Portage but I went straight for the usual one of Isle a la Biche – And arrived at the Sieur's Fort with a fair wind an hour before sun set" (McGill University, John Macdonell's Assiniboine and Fort Qu'Appelle journal).

RIVIÈRE-AU-BARBEU (Beard River?): Somewhere near Fort Alexander, but unidentified.

RIVIÈRE-BLANCHE (White River): The turbulent lower part of the Winnipeg River between Slave Falls and Lac du Bonnet. The character of the river has been changed completely by the building of the Seven Sisters Dam, turning it into a chain of placid lakes.

RIVIÈRE-CASSÉE: *See* Broken River.

RIVIÈRE-CHEBANAGEN: Unidentified river on the east side of Lake Winnipeg, flowing into the south basin, where the Mashkiegon Petites Couilles had a cache of wild rice in April 1810. In this area there are many wild rice lakes.

RIVIÈRE-DU-CHEMIN-DE-GUERRIER: Warpath River.

RIVIÈRE-AU-DIABLE (Devil's River). On 26 August 1808, Nelson was returning from Rivière-des-Morts to Fort Alexander, and camped at Rivière-au-Diable; it was evidently to the west of Rivière la Tête-ouverte (now Brokenhead River), which was reached the next day. According to John Macdonell, the mouth of the Red River had three branches, of which the centre one was the best for canoes, "the others being 'choaked up by Sand at thier entrance into the Lake.'" The east branch might well have been known to the voyageurs as the Rivière-au-Diable.

RIVIÈRE-AU-GAVION: Not identified, and the meaning is unknown; but it was one of the rivers that falls into Lake Winnipeg from the east, and south of Broken River (Rice River), perhaps most likely the present Wanipigow River. See note to Mauricette's River.

RIVIÈRE-MALIGNE: The upper part of the Sturgeon-Weir River, part of the route that the canoe brigades took into the Churchill River and beyond.

RIVIÈRE-DU-MILIEU (Middle River): A place on the inward journey for the Fort Dauphin brigade. Little information is available about the fur traders' names for places in the Fort Dauphin department. John McDonald "le Borgne," the NWC partner in charge of the district in Nelson's time, made a sketch map of his department for Peter Fidler of the HBC in 1808, which Fidler copied into his private journal (HBCA, E.3/3, fo. 48), but the names given are in English. The Rivière du Milieu may have been a name for the Rivière-du-Poule-d'Eau or Waterhen River (the English name is used on McDonald's map), which links Lakes Manitoba and Winnipegosis, and would have been a natural place of rendezvous.

RIVIÈRE-AUX-MORTS (River of the Dead): Now Netley Creek, which falls into the Red River from the west, close to where the Red River Delta begins. According to Nelson's *Sorel Journal*, the river was named "from a terrible slaughter of the Sauteuxs, by a large party of Siouxs, perhaps some sixty years or so before my time." Alexander Henry gives a longer account. According to him, the Crees, in preparation for their annual trip to the HBC's York Factory on Hudson Bay, were accustomed to leave their children and old people to pass the summer at this place, where there was a good supply of fish and game. One year, a Sioux war party fell upon the camp, and slaughtered many (Coues 1965, 41).

RIVIÈRE-DE-L'OURS (Bear River): Now Masqua River (*makwa* is the Ojibwe word for bear), which falls into the Winnipeg River a little above the modern town of Powerview.

RIVIÈRE DU-PAS: Nelson uses this name for the lowest part of the Saskatchewan River, between the Grand Rapid and Lake Winnipeg.

RIVIÈRE-AU-PECCANT: *See* Fisher River.

RIVIÈRE-AUX-SABLES (Sandy River): South of the Detour (Long Point). The name is no longer in use. The principal streams falling into this part of Lake Winnipeg are now called Twin Creeks (North and South) and the Two Rivers (North and South). Coues 1965, 460 n, had found reference to a Sand River and an Ebb and Flow River here, but his source has not been identified.

RIVIÈRE-DU-SANGUE: *See* Blood River.

RIVIÈRE-DE-LA-TÊTE-OUVERTE (Open Head River): Now Brokenhead River, the English equivalent. Alexander Henry called this the Catfish River (Coues 1965, 40).

SMALL GOOSE LAKE: A place on Pigeon River, near where McDonell and Nelson camped on 14 March 1809, en route to the NWC post at Little Grand Rapids.

SWAMP ISLANDS (Îles-du-Maskquiege): Ojibwe *mashkig*, swamp or marsh. The group of islands about halfway along the traverse across the southern end of the north basin of Lake Winnipeg, between the Pigeon River and Dauphin River posts. Nelson and his fellow traders used the islands as landmarks, and sometimes shelter, when they made this traverse in winter. The islands are indeed low and swampy; the largest is now called Commissioner Island.

TÊTE-DU-BOEUF: David Thompson's 1825 map shows the "Tête de Boef" at the E end of the present Black Island (which his map shows as much smaller than it really is); the present name of the place on the topographical map is Drumming Point. The Détroit de la Tête-du-Boeuf is therefore the narrow strait between Black Island and the east shore of Lake Winnipeg. One of Peter Fidler's sketch maps marks Buffalo head here, with the little house symbol he used for a trading post (HBCA, E.3/3, fo. 60). Nelson's and Thompson's Tête-du-Boeuf should not be confused with the modern Big Bullhead Point and Little Bullhead Point; the bullhead is a type of catfish.

TÊTE-AU-BROCHET (Pike Head): Now Jackhead. George Nelson's post in the seasons of 1810, 1811, and 1818. The post was near where Jackhead River falls into Lake Winnipeg, within the present Kinonjeoshtegon First Nation reserve lands. The Détroit of Tête-au-Brochet was apparently the name given to the strait between the present Matheson Island and Big Bear Island, at the east end of the long traverse across Fisher Bay to Tête-au-Brochet. Nelson also mentions small (or *petite*) Tête-au-Brochet, a short distance south of Tête-au-Brochet proper, where his brigade stopped to wash and tidy themselves before arriving at the post in 1818; it may be the present Passage Point.

TÊTE-AU-CHIEN: The Narrows of Lake Winnipeg, a place that Nelson was to pass repeatedly during the next few years. The points on either side, now called East and West Doghead Point, preserve the old name.

TÊTE-AU-PISHEW: Now Lynx Point, the English equivalent. Ojibwe: *bizhiw*, lynx.

THUNDER LAKE: Located in the upper part of the Poplar River basin, east of Lake Winnipeg; unidentified.

WARPATH RIVER: *See* Chemin du Guerrier.

WINNIPEG: In various place names: from a Cree word, variously spelled, meaning dirty water. The Cree applied the term to Hudson Bay with its salty, undrinkable water. Its application to Lake Winnipeg was established in written sources by the late 1700s, displacing other names proposed by European visitors. See discussion in *Geographical Names of Manitoba* (Winnipeg: Manitoba Geographical Names Program, n.d.), 299–300. The Northwest Company spelled the name Ouinipique.

References

MANUSCRIPTS

Library and Archives Canada (LAC), Ottawa:
    MG 19 C1 vol. 5 (William McGillivray's journal kept around Île-à-la-Crosse (Saskatchewan), winter & spring 1793).
    MG 19 C1 vol. 9 (unsigned journal kept at Cross Lake (Manitoba), 1805–06; author now identified as William McKay).
    RG 4, B28, Vols. 113, 115 (records of licences issued for the fur trade, ca.1765–90).
Archives Nationales du Québec, Montreal (ANQ-M):
    Repertoire of the Montreal *notaire*, John Gerbrand Beek, CN1-29. Cited in the text as Beek Repertoire, ANQ-M.
Archives of Manitoba, Winnipeg:
    Hudson's Bay Company Archives (HBCA):
        Fort Alexander Journals, B.4/a/1–4.
        Brandon House Journals, B.22/a/1–13.
        Chatham House Journal, B.32/a/1.
        Nottingham House Journals, B.39/a/2, B.39/a/5ᵇ.
        Fort Dauphin River Journal, B.51/a/1.
        Fort Dauphin District Report, B.51/e/1.
        Granville House Journal, B.83/a/1.
        Lac du Bonnet Journal, B.103/a/1.
        Manitoba Lake Journal, B.121/a/1.
        Red Lake Journal, B.177/a/1.
        Reed Lake Journal, B.178/a/1.
        Sturgeon Lake Journal, B.211/a/1.
        Swan River Journals, B.213/a/2, –3.

Winnipeg Journal, B.235/a/3.

Winnipeg Lake Journal, B.236/a/1.

York Factory Journal, B.239/a/99.

York Correspondence Book, B.239/b/57.

Peter Fidler's private journal, E.3/3.

North West Company "Grand Ledger" of men's accounts, 1811–1821, F.4/32. Cited in the text as *1811–21 Accounts.*

Biographical sheets. HBCA staff have prepared biographical notes on many people mentioned in their records. These are available on the HBCA website, www.gov.mb.ca/chc/archives/hbca/biographical/index.html.

McGill University Libraries, Rare Books and Special Collections Division (consulted on website, http://digital.library.mcgill.ca/nwc/.

List of NWC clerks and men following the amalgamation with the XYC, 1805. MS 472, MSS 2357.31. The catalogue entry for this manuscript, "North West Company. Men's Names at the Athabasca River Department (etc.). 1805," is misleading, as this is actually a list of almost all the men on the rosters of the NWC and XYC following their amalgamation in 1804–05. Cited in the text as *1805 list.*

Toronto Reference Library, Baldwin Collection of Canadiana:

George Nelson Fonds, Accession No. S 13. One box containing nineteen titled but unnumbered folders of papers, plus an envelope of typed copies of some of the papers. The titles of the folders, and their contents, are as follows. For convenience, numbers (in square brackets) have been assigned to the folders here; the order is arbitrary:

[1] Folder "S 13 Nelson, George, Journal, 13 July 1803–25 June 1804." Nelson's journal at Folle Avoine (printed by Peers and Schenck 2002).

[2] Folder "S 13 Nelson, George, Journal, 29 Aug 1805–08 Mar 1806." Nelson's journal at Lac du Bonnet (printed in this volume).

[3] Folder "S 13 Nelson, George, Journal, 3 Nov 1807–31 Aug. 1808." Nelson's first Dauphin River journal, printed in this volume.

[4] Folder "S 13 Nelson, George, Journal, 1 Sep 1808–31 Mar 1810." Nelson's second Dauphin River journal, printed in this volume.

[5] Folder "S13 Nelson, George, Journal 1 April 1810–11 May 1811." Nelson's third Dauphin River journal, carrying over to the new post at Tête-au-Brochet; printed in this volume.

[6] Folder "S 13 Nelson, George, Journal, 2 August–16 Nov 1813; 30 Nov. 1815–13 Jan. 1816." Portions of Nelson's journals kept in Pic department, Lake Superior. The first journal, and the second as far as the entry of 30 December, are entered at opposite ends of the same book or

gathering; entries from 31 December 1815 to 13 January 1816 are in a second small book or gathering. Not printed.

[7] Folder, "S 13 Nelson, George, Journal, 29. Jan. 1815–23 June 1815." Nelson's journal kept at Manitonamengon Lake, Pic department, continuing the last. Not printed.

[8] Folder, "S 13 Nelson, George, "Journal B," 1 May–8 June 1819; 16 Aug–15 Sept. 1819." Nelson's journal of the end of the 1818–19 season at Tête-au-Brochet, and his journal of a voyage from Fort Alexander to Cumberland House. Both printed in this volume.

[9] "S 13 Nelson, George, Notebook, 1820–1828 (Journal 3 June–29 Sep 1822)." Various items, as follows: a page written in Nelson's code; a list of arrivals and departures at Cumberland House, 13 June–17 September 1820 and 6 June–4 August 1821; diary of Nelson's return voyage from Fort William, starting 21 June 1822 (printed in this volume as part of the *Canoe Journal*); list of distances from Hudson's Bay to the Saskatchewan; list of latitudes of various places in the North West; summary of Nelson's return voyage from Fort William in 1822, duplicating information in the journal; list of people, perhaps letters sent to or from Nelson; another page written in code.

[10] "S 13 Nelson, George, Journal, 19 April–8 June 1821; 3 June–6 July 1822." The first is Nelson's journal of the end of his trading season 1820–21 at Moose Lake, followed by his voyage to Cumberland House (much of this is in Nelson's code). The second is the first part of Nelson's journal of his voyage from Cumberland House to Fort William, printed in this volume as part of the *Canoe Journal*.

[11] "S 13 Nelson, George, Journal, 6 July–22 Aug 1822." The second part of Nelson's *Canoe Journal*. Printed in this volume.

[12] "S 13 Nelson, George, Description with many anecdotes … 29 Mar–6 June 1823." Printed by Brown and Brightman 1988.

[13] Folder, "S 13 Nelson, George, 1 Dec. 1825–13 Sept. 1836." The *Sorel Journal*, extracts from which are printed in this volume; others are printed by Peers and Schenck 2002.

[14] Folder, "S 13 Nelson, George, "A short account…" " Nelson's account of some events in the Rebellion in Lower Canada ain 1837, particularly those involving his brother Dr Wolfred Nelson.

[15] Folder "S 13 Nelson, George, No. 1, Journal." Part 1 of Nelson's *Reminiscences*.

[16] Folder "S 13 Nelson, George, No. 5 Journal, June 1807–Oct 1809 (dated 7 February 1851) pp. 185–209." Part 5 of Nelson's *Reminiscences*.

[17] Folder "Journal #7 (pp. 278–92) 1819." Part 7 of Nelson's *Reminiscences*.

Extracts from Part 5 and Part 7 of the *Reminiscences* are printed in this volume.

[18] Folder "S 13 Nelson, George. Letters to parents etc. 1811–1812." Briefly described in this volume.

[19] Folder "Miscellaneous recipes, vocabularies, etc. 7 pieces." Contents: one sheet, "Statement of Peltries at River Dauphine 16 March 1810"; small slip with some details of Nelson's first voyage to the fur country, 1802; three sheets with various household recipes, etc.; small sheet with three drafts (all very similar) of a paragraph about the beginnings of the Canadian fur trade; draft of a letter to an unidentified estranged family member; large sheet folded to make four pages, headed "Clavis Calendaria: or a Compendious Analysis of the Calendar..." (apparently extracts from John Brady's book of this title (London, for the author, 1st edition 1812), dated "Geo. Nelson Jany 17ᵗʰ 1823"; one page with a typescript copy of entries for 25 December 1808 to 1 January 1809, from Nelson's Dauphin River journal for that season.

[20] Envelope containing typewritten copies of some of the Nelson manuscripts, those in Folders numbered [8] (second journal only), [12], [14], [15], and [17].

North West Company Papers, 1 volume. A bound volume, containing a number of items, of which one has been used here: a book of men's accounts (92 men, mostly voyageurs) for purchases made at Fort William in July and August 1803.

PRINTED PRIMARY SOURCES

Armour, David A., ed. 1972. *Treason? At Michilimackinac: The proceedings of a general court martial held at Montreal in Quebec 1768 for the Trial of Major Robert Rogers*. Mackinac Island State Park Commission, rev. ed.

Bardon, R., and G.L. Nute. 1947. "A Winter in the St. Croix Valley." *Minnesota History* 28:1–14, 142–59, 225–40.

Belyea, Barbara. 1994. *Columbia Journals [of] David Thompson*. Montreal & Kingston: McGill-Queen's University Press.

Birk, Douglas A. 1989. *John Sayer's Snake River Journal, 1804–05*. Minneapolis: Institute for Minnesota Archaeology.

Brown, Jennifer S.H., and Robert Brightman. 1988. *"The Orders of the Dreamed": George Nelson on Cree and Northern Ojibwa Religion and Myth, 1823*. Winnipeg: University of Manitoba Press.

Cormier, Louis-P. 1978. *Jean-Baptiste Perrault marchand voyageur parti de Montréal le 28e de mai 1783*. Montreal: Boréal Express.

Coues, Elliott, ed. 1965. *New Light on the Early History of the Greater Northwest: The Manuscript Journals of Alexander Henry and of David Thompson*. 2 vols. Minneapolis MN: Ross & Haines, Inc.

Douglas, R., ed. 1929. *Nipigon to Winnipeg: A Canoe Voyage through Western Ontario by Edward Umfreville in 1784*. Ottawa: Thoburn & Abbot.

Duckworth, Harry W., ed. 1990. *The English River Book: A North West Company Journal and Account Book of 1786*. Montreal & Kingston: McGill-Queen's University Press.

– ed. 1999. *The Yellowknife Journal*. Winnipeg: Nuage Editions.

Gates, Charles M., ed. 1965. *Five Fur Traders of the Northwest*. St Paul: Minnesota Historical Society.

Glazebrook, G.P. de T., ed. 1938. *The Hargrave Correspondence 1821–1843*. Toronto: the Champlain Society.

Gough, Barry M., ed. 1988. *The Journal of Alexander the Henry 1799–1814*, vol. 1. Toronto: The Champlain Society.

– ed. 1992. *The Journal of Alexander Henry 1799–1814*, vol. 2. Toronto: the Champlain Society.

Hall, Roger, & S.W. Shelton, eds. 2002. *"The Rising Country": The Hale-Amherst Correspondence, 1799–1825*. Toronto: the Champlain Society.

Hickerson, Harold, ed. 1959. "Journal of Charles Jean Baptiste Chaboillez, 1797–1798." *Ethnohistory* 6, no. 3 (Summer, 1959), 265–316; and no. 4 (Fall, 1959), 352–427.

James, Edwin, ed. 1956. *A Narrative of the Captivity and Adventures of John Tanner … during Thirty Years Residence among the Indians in the Interior of North America*. Minneapolis: Ross & Haines, Inc.

Johnson, Alice M. 1967. *Saskatchewan Journals and Correspondence*. London: Hudson's Bay Record Society.

Keith, Lloyd, ed. 2001. *North of Athabasca: Slave Lake and Mackenzie River Documents of the North West Company 1800–1821*. Montreal & Kingston: McGill-Queen's University Press.

Lamb, W. Kaye, ed. 1957. *Sixteen Years in the Indian Country: The Journal of Daniel Williams Harmon 1800–1816*. Toronto: Macmillan Company of Canada.

– ed. 1960. *Simon Fraser. Letters & Journals, 1806–1808*. Toronto: Macmillan Company of Canada.

– ed. 1970. *The Journals and Letters of Sir Alexander Mackenzie*. Toronto: Macmillan Company of Canada.

Mackenzie, Alexander. 1801. *Voyages from Montreal on the River St. Laurence through the Continent of North America to the Frozen and Pacific Oceans in the Years 1789 and 1793*. London: Thomas Cadell.

Masson, L.R. 1960. *Les Bourgeois de la Compagnie du Nord-Ouest*. 2 Vols. New York: Antiquarian Press.

Moreau, William E., ed. 2009. *The Writings of David Thompson: The Travels, 1850 Version*. Toronto: The Champlain Society.

Morton, Arthur S., ed. 1929. *The Journal of Duncan McGillivray of the North West Company*. Toronto: MacMillan Company of Canada.

Peers, Laura, and Theresa Schenck, eds. 2002. *My First Years in the Fur Trade: The Journals of 1802–1804 George Nelson*. Montreal & Kingston: McGill-Queen's University Press.

Provost, Honorius. 1983. *Les premieres anglo-canadiens à Québec. Essai de recensement 1759–1775*. Quebec: Institute québecois de recherché sur la culture.

Quaife, Milo M. 1931. *The John Askin Papers. Vol. II: 1796–1820*. Detroit: Detroit Library Commission.

Rich, E.E., and R. Harvey Fleming, eds. 1939. *Colin Robertson's Correspondence Book, September 1817 to September 1822*. London: Hudson's Bay Record Society.

Rich, E.E., and A.M. Johnson, eds. 1951. *Cumberland House Journals and Inland Journal 1775–82. First Series 1775–79*. London: Hudson's Bay Record Society.

– 1952. *Cumberland House Journals and Inland Journal 1775–82. Second Series 1779–82*. London: Hudson's Bay Record Society.

– 1955. *A Journey of a Voyage From Rocky Mountain Portage in Peace River To the Sources of Finlays Branch And North West Ward In Summer 1824*. London: Hudson's Bay Record Society.

Tyrrell, J.B., ed. 1916. *David Thompson's Narrative of his Explorations in Western America 1784–1812*. Toronto: The Champlain Society.

– ed. 1934. *Journals of Hearne and Turnor*. Toronto: The Champlain Society.

Wallace, W.S. 1934. *Documents Relating to the North West Company*. Toronto: The Champlain Society.

Williams, Glyndwr, ed. 1975. *Hudson's Bay Miscellany 1670–1870*. Winnipeg: Hudson's Bay Record Society.

SECONDARY SOURCES

Entries in the *Dictionary of Canadian Biography* (Francess G. Halpenny & Jean Hamelin, eds., Toronto & Quebec: University of Toronto Press & Les Presses de l'Université Laval, 1966–) are listed under the authors' names, with the abbreviation DCB. The articles are now available online at www.biographi.ca/en/index.php.

Adney, E.T., and H.I. Chapelle. 1983. *The Bark Canoes and Skin Boats of North America*. Washington: Smithsonian Institution.

Allen, Robert S. 1987. "William McKay," DCB, 6:464–6.

Amos, Andrew. 1820. *Report of trials in the courts of Canada, relative to the destruction of the Earl of Selkirk's settlement on the Red River, with observations*. London: John Murray.

Angel, Michael. 2002. *Historical Perspectives on the Ojibwa Midewiwin: Preserving the Sacred*. Winnipeg: University of Manitoba Press.

Anonymous. n.d. *Geographical Names of Manitoba*. Winnipeg: Manitoba Geographical Names Program.

Baraga, Frederick. 1992. *A Dictionary of the Otchipwe Language Explained in English*. Minneapolis: Ross & Haines, Inc.

Bell, C.N. 1928. "The Journal of Henry Kelsey, 1691–1692." *Manitoba Historical Society Transactions*, Ser. 2, no. 4.

Berens, William, and A. Irving Hallowell. 2009. *Memories, Myths, and Dreams of an Ojibwe Leader*, edited by Jennifer S.H. Brown and Susan Elaine Gray. Montreal & Kingston: McGill-Queen's University Press.

Bigsby, John J. 1969. *The Shoe and Canoe or Pictures of Travel in the Canadas*. 2 vols. New York: Paladin Press.

Birk, Douglas A. 1983. "John Sayer," DCB, 5:741–2.

Bishop, Charles A. 1985. "Charles McKenzie," DCB, 8:557–8.

Bond Head, Sir Francis. 1852. *A Fortnight in Ireland*. London: John Murray.

Britton, Nathaniel L., and Addison Brown. 1970. *An Illustrated Flora of the Northern United States and Canada*. Dover Books, Mineola, New York.

Brown, Jennifer S.H. 1980. *Strangers in Blood: Fur Trade Company Families in Indian Country*. Vancouver & London: University of British Columbia Press.

– 1983. "Duncan McDougall," DCB, 5:525–7.

– 1984. "'Man in His Natural State': The Indian Worlds of George Nelson." In *Rendezvous: Selected Papers of the Fourth North American Fur Trade Conference, 1981*, edited by Thomas C. Buckley. St Paul, MN: North American Fur Trade Conference.

– 1985a. "Central Manitoba Saulteaux in the 19th Century." In *Papers of the Sixteenth Algonquian Conference*, edited by W. Cowan. Ottawa: Carleton University.

– 1985b. "John Clarke," DCB, 8:158–9.

– 1987a. "John Hodgson," DCB, 6:320–1.

– 1987b. "John McDonald," DCB, 6:436–7.

– 1988. "Duncan Cameron," DCB, 7:137–9.

– 2017a. "Partial Truths. A Closer Look at Fur Trade Marriage," in *An*

Ethnohistorian in Rupert's Land: Unfinished Conversations, 103–22. Edmonton: Athabasca University Press.

– 2017b. "Kinship Shock for Fur Traders and Missionaries. The Cross-Cousin Challenge," Ibid., 137–44.

– 2017c. "'I Wish to Be as I See You': An Ojibwe-Methodist Encounter in Fur Trade Country, 1854–5," Ibid., 237–54.

– 2017d, "Fair Wind: Medicine and Consolation on the Berens River," Ibid., 299–320.

– ed. 2018. *Ojibwe Stories from the Upper Berens River: A. Irving Hallowell and Adam Bigmouth in Conversation*. Lincoln: University of Nebraska Press.

Bumsted, J.M. 2003. *Fur Trade Wars: The Founding of Western Canada*. Winnipeg: Great Plains Publications.

– 2008. *Lord Selkirk: A Life*. Winnipeg: University of Manitoba Press.

Campbell, Marjorie Wilkins. 1983. "John Ogilvy," DCB, 5:635–7.

Carver, Jonathan. 1778. *Travels through the Interior Pars of North-America in the Years 1766, 1767, and 1768*. London: for the author, 1778 [facsimile edition by Coles Publishing Co., Toronto, 1974].

Chapin, David. 2014. *Freshwater Passages: The Trade and Travels of Peter Pond*. Lincoln and London: University of Nebraska Press.

Dickason, Olive. 1997. *Canada's First Nations: A History of Founding Peoples from Earliest Times*. 2nd ed. Oxford: Oxford University Press.

Douglas, William. 1954. "New Light on the Old Forts of Winnipeg." *Manitoba Historical Society Transactions*, Ser. 3 (1954–55).

Duckworth, Harry W. 1983. "The Last Coureurs du Bois." *The Beaver*, Spring 1983.

Edmunds, R. David. 1983. *The Shawnee Prophet*. Lincoln & London: University of Nebraska Press.

Ennals, Peter. 1985. "Robert Henry," DCB, 8:390–1.

Hackett, Paul. 2002. *A Very Remarkable Sickness: Epidemics in the Petit Nord, 1670 to 1846*. Winnipeg: University of Manitoba Press.

Halkett, John. 1817. *Statement respecting the Earl of Selkirk's settlement of Kildonan, upon the Red River, in North America; its destruction in the years 1815 and 1816, and the massacre of Governor Semple and his party*. London: J. Brettell.

Hallowell, A. Irving. 1992. *The Ojibwa of Berens River, Manitoba: Ethnography into History*. Case Studies in Cultural Anthropology. Edited by Jennifer S.H. Brown. New York: Harcourt Brace Jovanovitch.

– 2011. *Contributions to Ojibwe Studies. Essays, 1934–1972*. Edited by Jennifer S.H. Brown and Susan Elaine Gray. Lincoln & London: University of Nebraska Press.

Holzkamm, Tim, and Leo Waisberg. 2000. *Agency Indian Reserve 1: Selection, Use and Administration*. Draft report prepared for Grand Council Treaty #3; formerly online at www.treaty3.ca/pdfs/grandchief/gct3/draft_report. pdf, accessed 5 June 2006.

Houston, Stuart, Tim Ball, and Mary Houston. 2003. *Eighteenth Century Naturalists of Hudson Bay*. Montreal & Kingston: McGill-Queen's University Press.

Innis, Harold A. 1930. *The Fur Trade in Canada*. 2nd ed. Toronto: University of Toronto Press (reprinted 1970).

Judd, Carol M. 1985. "John Pritchard," DCB, 8:713–15.

Kaye, Barry. 1981. "Flour Milling at Red River: Wind, Water and Steam." *Manitoba History*, 1981, no. 2.

LaBrèque, Marie-Paule. 1983. "James Caldwell," DCB, 5:133–4.

Lamb, W. Kaye. 1976. "Simon Fraser," DCB, 9:282–6.

Leighton, Anna L. 1985. *Wild Plant Use by the Woods Cree (Nihithawak) of East-Central Saskatchewan*. Ottawa: National Museums of Canada.

Leighton, Douglas. 1985. "Dominique Ducharme," DCB, 8:244–6.

Lemieux, Lucien. 1985. "Joseph-Norbert Provencher," DCB, 8:718–24.

Lindsay, Anne, and Jennifer S.H. Brown. 2010. *The History of the Pimicikamic People to the Treaty Five Period, from Documentary Sources*. Winnipeg: Centre for Rupert's Land Studies. Available online at www. uwinnipeg.ca/ rupertsland/pimdigitalopt.pdf. This contains (Appendix D) a full copy and transcript of William McKay's journal kept at Cross Lake in 1805–06; the original is LAC, MG 19, C1, vol. 9.

Livermore, C.N., and N. Anick. 1976. "John McDonald," DCB, 9:481–3.

Lovisick, Joan A. 1993. "The Political Evolution of the Boundary Waters Ojibwa." In *Papers of the Twenty-fourth Algonquian Conference*, edited by W. Cowan, 280–305. Ottawa: Carleton University.

Lytwyn, Victor P. 1986. *The Fur Trade of the Little North: Indians, Pedlars, and Englishmen East of Lake Winnipeg, 1760–1821*. Winnipeg: Rupert's Land Research Centre.

McCloy, T.R. 1983. "John McKay," DCB, 5:534–5.

Mackenzie, Alexander. 1801. *Voyages from Montreal on the River St. Laurence through the Continent of North America to the Frozen and Pacific Oceans in the Years 1789 and 1793*. London: Thomas Cadell. A facsimile edition was published by M.G. Hurtig Ltd (Edmonton) in 1971.

Macmillan, Hugh P. 2009. *Adventures of a Paper Sleuth*. Newcastle, ON: Penumbra Press.

McLean, Marianne. 1985. "John McGillivray (Dalcrombie)," DCB, 8:546–7.

McKay, John "Ben Reay." 1892. *John O'Groats Journal*, 6 September 1892

(Wick, Sutherlandshire, Scotland). Clipping in McKay papers, McCord Museum, Montreal; copy in HBCA.

Malalney, Mary E. 2005. "The Gros Ventre/Fall Indians in historical and archaeological interpretation." *Canadian Journal of Native Studies,* 25:155–83.

Mays, Herbert J. 1988. "John McDonell," DCB, 7:552–4.

Momryk, Myron. 1979. "Lawrence Ermatinger," DCB, 4:262–3.

– 1987. "Charles Oakes Ermatinger," DCB, 6:236–7.

Morice, A.G. 1905. *The History of the Northern Interior of British Columbia.* Toronto: William Briggs.

Morrison, Jean. 1983a. "Alexander MacKay," DCB, 5:532–4.

– 1983b. "Donald McTavish," DCB, 5:559–60.

– 1988. "Peter Grant," DCB, 7:356–7.

– 2003. *Lake Superior to Rainy Lake: Three Centuries of Fur Trade History.* Thunder Bay: Thunder Bay Historical Museum Society.

Morse, Eric W. 1979. *Fur Trade Canoe Routes / Then and Now.* Toronto: University of Toronto Press.

Morton, Arthur Silver. 1973. *A History of the Canadian West to 1870–71.* 2nd. ed. Toronto: University of Toronto Press.

Morton, W.L. 1988. "Pierre-Guillaume Sayer," DCB, 7:776–7.

Ouellet, Fernand. 1987. "Benjamin Joseph Frobisher," DCB, 6:267–8.

Peel, Bruce. 1988. "William Connolly," DCB, 7:204–6.

Peers, Laura. 1994. *The Ojibwa of Western Canada 1780 to 1870.* Winnipeg: University of Manitoba Press.

Peers, Laura, and Jennifer S.H. Brown. 2000. " 'There is no End to Relationship among the Indians': Ojibwa Families and Kinship in Historical Perspective." *The History of the Family* 4, no. 4, 529–55.

Peterson, Jacqueline. 1985. "Many Roads to Red River: Métis Genesis in the Great Lakes Region, 1680–1815." In *The New Peoples: Being and Becoming Métis in North America,* edited by Jacqueline Peterson and Jennifer S.H. Brown, 38–71. Winnipeg: University of Manitoba Press.

Podruchny, Carolyn. 2006. *Making the Voyageur World: Travelers and Traders in the North American Fur Trade.* Lincoln: University of Nebraska Press.

Rich, E.E. 1959. *The History of the Hudson's Bay Company 1670–1870. Vol. II: 1763–1870.* London: Hudson's Bay Record Society.

Ruggles, Richard I. 1991. *A Country So Interesting: The Hudson's Bay Company and Two Centuries of Mapping, 1670–1870.* Montreal & Kingston: McGill-Queen's University Press.

Russell, Hilary. 1980. "Angus Bethune," in *Old Trails and New Direction: Papers of the Third North American Fur Trade Conference,* edited by Carol

M. Judd & Arthur J. Ray, 177–90. Toronto: University of Toronto Press.

– 1985. "Angus Bethune," DCB, 8:85–6.

Scott, W.B., and E.J. Crossman 1973. *Freshwater Fishes of Canada*. Ottawa: Fisheries Research Board of Canada.

Smith, Shirlee Ann. 1985. "William Williams," DCB, 7:912–14.

Stewart, Kenneth, and Douglas Watkinson. 2004. *The Freshwater Fishes of Manitoba*. Winnipeg: University of Manitoba Press.

Tanguay, Cyprien. 1871–1890. *Dictionnaire généalogique des familles canadiennes*. 7 Vols. Montreal: Eusèbe Senécal et Fils.

Thie, J. 1974. "Distribution and Thawing of Permafrost in the Southern Part of the Discontinuous Permafrost Zone in Manitoba." *Arctic* 27, no. 3, 189–200.

Thompson, John Beswarick. 1987. "William Nelson," DCB, 6:536–7.

Van Kirk, Sylvia. 1980. *Many Tender Ties: Women in Fur-Trade Society, 1670–1870*. Winnipeg: Watson & Dwyer.

– 1984. "George Nelson's 'Wretched Career,' 1802–1823." In *Rendezvous: Selected Papers of the Fourth North American Fur Trade Conference, 1981*. St Paul, MN: Minnesota Historical Society.

– 1985. "John Dougald Cameron," in DCB, 8:121–2.

– 1988. "'This rascally and ungrateful country': George Nelson's response to Rupert's Land." In *Rupert's Land: A Cultural Tapestry*, edited by Richard C. Davis, 113. Waterloo, ON: Wilfrid Laurier University Press.

Van Kirk, Sylvia, in collaboration with Jennifer S.H. Brown. 1985. "George Nelson," DCB, 8:652–3.

Vézina, Robert. 2009. "Amérindiens et franco-canadiens: une rencontre inscrite dans la langue." *Cap-aux-Diamants: la revue d'histoire du Québec*, no. 96.

Waisberg, Leo, & Holzkamm, Tim. 2001. *"We have one mind and one mouth. It is the decision of all of us." Traditional Anishinaabe Governance of Treaty #3*. Report prepared for Grand Council Treaty #3, October 2001.

Wallace, J.N. 1929. *The Wintering Partners on Peace River*. Ottawa: Thorburn & Abbott.

Wallace, W. Stewart. 1954. *The Pedlars from Quebec and Other Papers on the Nor-Westers*. Toronto: The Ryerson Press.

Warkentin, Germaine. 2012. *The Collected Writings of Pierre-Esprit Radisson*, vol. 1, *The Voyages*. Toronto and Montreal: The Champlain Society and McGill-Queen's University Press.

– 2014. *The Collected Writings of Pierre-Esprit Radisson*, vol. 2, *The Port Nelson Relations, Miscellaneous Writings, and Related Documents*. Toronto and Montreal: The Champlain Society and McGill-Queen's University Press.

Warren, William W. 1974. *History of the Ojibway Nation*. Minneapolis: Ross & Haines, Inc.

White, Bruce M. 1987. "Montreal Canoes and Their Cargoes." In *Le Castor Fait Tout: Selected Papers of the Fifth North American Fur Trade Conference, 1985*, edited by Bruce G. Trigger, Toby Morantz, and Louise Dechène, 164–92. Montreal: St Louis Historical Society.

– 2005. "Grand Portage as a Trading Post: Patterns of Trade at 'The Great Carrying Place.'" St Paul, MN: Turnstone Historical Research.

Williams, Glyndwr. 1985. "Peter Skene Ogden," DCB, 8:660–3.

– 1988. "Alexander Roderick McLeod," DCB, 7:569–70.

Willmott, Cory. 2005. "From Stroud to Strouds: The Hidden History of a British Fur Trade Textile." *Textile History* 36:196–234.

Willmott, Cory, and Kevin Brownlee. 2010. "Dressing for the Homeward Journey: Western Anishinaabe Leadership Roles Viewed through Two Nineteenth-Century Burials." In *Gathering Places: Aboriginal and Fur Trade Histories*, edited by Carolyn Podruchny and Laura Peers, 48–89. Vancouver: University of British Columbia Press.

Winterburn, Joseph D. 2003. "Lac la Pluie Bills Lading, 1806–09." In *Lake Superior to Rainy Lake. Three Centuries of Fur Trade History*, edited by Jean Morrison. Thunder Bay, ON: Thunder Bay Historical Museum Society. Article revised and reprinted from Thunder Bay Historical Museum Society *Papers & Records*, IX (1981), 7–12.

Woodcock, George. 1985. "Cuthbert Grant," DCB, 8:341–4.

– 1988a. "Samuel Black," DCB, 7:78–9.

– 1988b. "Colin Robertson," DCB, 7:748–50.

Index